Maori and the State:
Crown–Maori Relations in New Zealand/Aotearoa, 1950–2000

Maori and the State:

Crown–Maori Relations in New Zealand/Aotearoa, 1950–2000

Richard S. Hill

Victoria University Press
2009

VICTORIA UNIVERSITY PRESS
Victoria University of Wellington
PO Box 600 Wellington
vuw.ac.nz/vup

First published 2009

National Library of New Zealand Cataloguing-in-Publication Data

Hill, Richard S.
Māori and the State : Crown-Māori relations in NewZealand/Aotearoa, 1950-2000 / Richard S. Hill.
Includes bibliographical references and index.
ISBN 978-0-86473-611-6
1. Maori (New Zealand people)—Government relations—History.
2. Maori (New Zealand people)—Politics and government—20th century.
[1. Kāwanatanga. reo 2. Tino rangatiratanga.] I. Title.
323.1199442—dc 22

Printed by Astra Print, Wellington
Typeset by Ahi Text Solutions, Wellington

To my parents, Jean and Herbert

Contents

Preface *ix*

Introduction *1*

Chapter 1. Challenges for Crown and Maori *11*

Chapter 2. Adjustments by Crown and Maori *25*

Chapter 3. Autonomy and Official Institutions *47*

Chapter 4. Autonomy and Voluntarism *65*

Chapter 5. Rangatiratanga Challenged *85*

Chapter 6. Rangatiratanga under the Maori Welfare Act *111*

Chapter 7. Protest and Response *149*

Chapter 8. Towards Rangatiratanga? *187*

Chapter 9. Principles and Partnership *221*

Chapter 10. Rangatiratanga: the Continuing Quest *247*

Conclusion and Prospects *275*

Endnotes *295*

Bibliography *329*

Preface

This book examines the principal interrelationships between the Crown and Maori in New Zealand/Aotearoa over the second half of the twentieth century. It complements my earlier examination, in *State Authority, Indigenous Autonomy*, of Crown–Maori relations in the first half of the century. Ever since the British Crown annexed the islands of Aotearoa in 1840, Maori have continuously asserted their distinctive politico-cultural identity, despite the relentless pressures of colonial and post-colonial policies – especially those aiming at the eventual assimilation of Maori into western ways of 'seeing and doing'. Assimilationist policies intensified in the 1950s and 1960s. Under the pressure of the 'Maori Renaissance', however, from the 1970s policies and goals based upon biculturalism began to replace assimilationist measures and aims (although Crown motivations were and remain problematic). For this reason, some of the book's subject matter, while examining the relationship between the same parties, differs greatly from that of its predecessor.

There is another key difference, too. Until the middle of the twentieth century, Maori were mostly rural dwellers leading lives quite different and separate from the majority of those New Zealanders of European descent who are now generally called pakeha. Then came mass migration to the large towns and cities, a phenomenon which had major implications for the modes of interaction between the state and Maori institutions and leaders. But even during the height of urbanisation and government assimilation policies, and despite considerable intermarriage with pakeha, Maori continued to organise their lives collectively. They maintained old ways, and created new ones, in an ongoing struggle to preserve and enhance their culture. They sought Crown recognition that their status as tangata whenua, the (original) people of the land, required a special relationship with the state – one which honoured the rangatiratanga, or autonomy, accorded to Maori by the Crown in the Maori-language version of the Treaty of Waitangi.[1]

State Authority, Indigenous Autonomy was interpreted in some quarters as a work of advocacy for Maori autonomy. My purpose in canvassing the history of Crown–Maori relations, however, is to better understand the past and therefore the present. Unlike adherents of some recent schools of history, I contend that while 'the truth' as to 'what happened, and why' might be elusive or even unattainable, scholars should still do their best to seek it. I also believe that readers should be left to draw their own conclusions about, for example, what is unjust in the past or desirable in the present and future. If the historian has any role in public education or policy formation, it is to provide an explanatory and analytical context to inform and assist understanding. This is to take a different position from that of fine and influential scholars such as Paulo Freire, Frantz Fanon or Walter Rodney, who viewed scholarship as 'incomplete' if it fell short of activist engagement in 'the empowerment of the oppressed' or 'the autonomy of peoples'. But rejecting the fashioning of history as an overt tool in the politics of liberation does not of course imply anything about how scholarship might be *used* by 'liberationists' – or anyone else, for that matter.[2]

It should be noted that, as I am primarily an historian of state institutions, this book focuses on the way the Crown attempted to contain, control and assimilate Maori, and the way Maori have responded. In my assessment, Maori never accepted that Crown sovereignty precluded the possibility of running their own affairs in their own ways. At least until the 1970s, however, the Crown decreed that 'British'/pakeha culture, ways of living and modes of organising were the norms to which all citizens needed to aspire. There was a certain accommodation of Maori organisational and cultural forms by the Crown, but these were essentially seen as temporary or transitional arrangements pending an eventual full assimilation of Maori. After assimilation policies were officially abandoned, moreover, Maori leaders and scholars frequently asserted that replacement policies did not provide meaningful recognition of rangatiratanga.[3]

To contain the huge subject of Maori aspirations and Crown policies over half a century of intense discourse and activity, this book focuses on interactions between Crown and Maori at an organisational level. There were many indigenous institutions involved, from local to national, and all of them – like the state itself – experienced internal contestation. This study, however, covers internal state and Maori debates and conflicts only where they impact on the contours of the key relationships between the two broad parties to the signing of the Treaty of Waitangi – the official and the indigenous.

This is not to say that the book is based upon the Treaty of Waitangi or the great amount of scholarship focused on it (and nor was *State Authority, Indigenous Autonomy*, *pace* some of its reviewers). However central the Treaty to Maori claims and aspirations, Crown–Maori relations reflect circumstances typical of settler colonies and their successor states. Government policies aimed at suppressing, appropriating and assimilating the political economy and culture of indigenous peoples, and ongoing but adaptive struggle by indigenes for self-determination, are integral to the history of colonialism and post-colonialism. Marginalisation of political and cultural indigeneity in New Zealand would have occurred whatever the colonial regime, although the exact configurations of the Crown's policies and actions and Maori responses to them were shaped by circumstances specific to the country. While most literature on Crown–Maori relations is Treaty-related, then, the analyses in this book are not posited upon that 1840 document or its long history.

It is sufficient here to note with regard to the events of 1840 that Maori and Crown had differing perceptions of what was being signed. Since that time, Maori have generally focused on Article Two of the Treaty, the one which promised them rangatiratanga, a term generally seen as representing some sort of 'autonomy' or ability to run their own affairs, but which in the English-language version was rendered as 'the full exclusive and undisturbed possession' of land and other properties. The Crown has always, in contrast, focused on Article One, under which Maori ceded to the Queen 'absolutely and without reservation all the rights and powers of Sovereignty' – kawanatanga ('governorship') in the Maori version. In the state's eyes, Article One provided the indivisible Crown sovereignty that was considered suitable for a 'settler state'. Whatever this article implied to Maori, the Crown considered in early 1840 that it had taken unfettered constitutional control of the resources and people of New Zealand.

While the Treaty of Waitangi has remained the symbolic document of the Crown–Maori relationship, the two broad interpretations of the Treaty have never been reconciled – mirroring the tensions and conflicts integral to all colonisation projects and their post-colonial inheritances. But reconciliatory arrangements have always been sought by the parties involved, at least on an 'agreement to disagree' basis, and the Treaty has proven a useful device for both Crown and Maori in pursuit of sometimes similar and sometimes differing aims – and, in more recent times, in pursuit of constitutional or other arrangements which might possibly satisfy both.[4]

I would like to thank those scholars working in the Treaty of Waitangi reconciliation processes who first turned my mind to the neglected subject of Crown–Maori relations in the twentieth century, and the Marsden Fund, which has supported my research focus on rangatiratanga and helped make this book possible (including through a publishing grant). I owe much gratitude to many people who have discussed this and related subjects with me ever since, especially various scholars who have been based at the Stout Research Centre for New Zealand Studies from time to time. I would like to thank, in particular, two members of the Centre's Treaty of Waitangi Research Unit (TOWRU),

Maureen West and Gwyn Williams; Dr Williams offered many helpful suggestions on shaping this book, undertook its editing and prepared its bibliography and index. I am also grateful to Sonja Mitchell and Alice Miller for their research contributions, and to Lana Le Quesne and Louise Grenside, the current TOWRU and Stout Research Centre administrators. I would like to thank Fergus Barrowman, Heather McKenzie and the rest of the team at Victoria University Press for their warm support and assistance, and Sarah-Jane McCosh who typeset the book.

The Director of the Stout Research Centre, Professor Lydia Wevers, has been unfailingly supportive, as has another friend and colleague (who joined 'the Stout' in 2008), Professor James Belich. I can think of no more stimulating research environment than the Stout Research Centre. My life has also been enlivened, and my work possibly enhanced (and perhaps occasionally impaired), by Wellington's traditional Friday night gathering of scholars in convivial surroundings. I am fortunate to have a great deal of support from the various members of my family, although they are scattered far and wide, and I owe a special debt of thanks to my wonderfully patient and supportive partner Nicola Gilmour.

Richard S. Hill
Wellington,
November 2008.

Introduction

The first half of this book focuses on the New Zealand state's longstanding aim of fully assimilating Maori to 'European' modes of behaviour and ways of viewing the world.[1] In the earliest days of the colony, the Crown sought the 'amalgamation of the races'. This was so much on the state's terms that it amounted, in essence, to assimilation. Official terminology changed from time to time, but by the 1950s the state's policy of 'integration' into broader New Zealand society remained – certainly in Maori eyes – scarcely distinguishable from the goal of assimilation. Early Crown and settler propaganda about amalgamation and equality had proven to be a seemingly benevolent cloak for the alienating of indigenous resources and the disappearing of indigenous culture that typified colonisation everywhere. Despite the occasional changes in labelling, in fact, the goal of full assimilation remained in place until the 1970s. But Maori had never lost hope of retaining or restoring ways of controlling their own destiny. Tribal society, moreover, had proved inventive, dynamic and resilient in its many organised responses to colonisation and pakeha politico-cultural domination. And so the Crown had needed constantly to delay and compromise over its assimilationist policies and aspirations for Maoridom.[2]

During the Second World War, tribally-based and other Maori organisations had achieved semi-autonomy through the Maori War Effort Organisation, and their leaders struggled to continue and further develop this in peacetime. But as the war neared its end and the Maori contribution became less imperative for the state's war aims, the Labour government became increasingly alarmed at the ramifications of what was being sought by the Maori leadership – including by its own Maori MPs. Ministers and their officials attempted to control, steer, tame and utilise Maori proposals for autonomy to their own ends. This was the background to the Maori Social and Economic Advancement Act of 1945, which established a network of official Tribal Committees and Tribal Executives operating within (rather than, as Maori wanted, replacing or operating outside of) the Department of Native Affairs (from 1947, the Department of Maori Affairs). Nevertheless, the Act did concede a cautious degree of autonomy to

Maori. The election, as 1950 dawned, of a conservative National government promised Maori little, particularly given the party's strong ideological support for laissez-faire policies which seemed to threaten the welfare-statist approach to governing established by Labour. The incoming government, however, did not radically reverse official practices and policies. In Maori policy, faced with the realities of the situation, it had little choice but to continue Labour's expedient approach in its relationship with Maoridom.[3]

However, in official eyes such compromise would need only to be very short-term. Policy-makers believed that the goal of full assimilation was finally attainable as Maori migration from rural to urban areas, which had intensified during the war, regathered momentum after it. Maori were expected to become quickly detribalised in the big towns and cities, far from their traditional rural environment. Demographic change was expected, in particular, to remove what was seen as a key roadblock to assimilation, that of 'clinging' to a collective socio-organisational approach to life.

What began as 'urban drift' became a massive migration, for both 'push' and 'pull' reasons, in the third quarter of the twentieth century. By some definitions, more than 80% of Maori eventually ended up living in urban environments – as opposed to less than 10% in 1926. This remarkable, and as yet under-studied, phenomenon was seen by the Crown (and most pakeha) as the means by which the desired goal for Maoridom could be achieved. Far from their tribal homelands, Maori would give up their distinctive and collective outlook and 'settle down' to become brown-skinned pakeha. Even their 'brownness' would be modified through intermarriage. Official policy, after some initial doubts about the wisdom of Maori urbanisation, would be re-geared from time to time to speed up, organise and shape the process. The Department of Maori Affairs, for example, provided incentives for Maori to move to the cities in orderly fashion, thereby procuring labour for industry and encouraging Maori 'integration' into mainstream society.[4]

Even after mass migration had turned a predominantly rural people into an overwhelmingly urban one, Maori nevertheless continued to resist full assimilation to 'western' ways. While anxious to adapt successfully to the cities and to modern times, they 'stubbornly' (as it was often put) refused to abandon their culture, identity and aspirations. In effect, many Maori lived biculturally after moving to the urban areas, oscillating and negotiating between two worlds on a daily basis. Despite the exodus from rural marae, moreover, tribal organisational structures retained their importance, and new collective entities that were predominantly or wholly Maori were established in the new urban environments. Officials and political parties were constantly reminded by leaders from all sectors of indigenous society of their people's desire to control their own affairs. As a consequence, the Crown came to recognise that supplanting of collectivist and autonomist impulses would not occur quickly or unproblematically. Eventually, governments (and pakeha) needed to come to terms with the fact that Maoridom, in its many manifestations, was not going to go away.

For not only did Maori collectivist perspectives and tribal/sub-tribal identification survive the great urban migration, but also the Maori people found new modes of expression in the changed environment of the post-war world. The official organisations established under the 1945 Maori Social and Economic Advancement Act themselves provided significant means through which Maori could resist the Crown's agenda of rapid 'integration' and, ultimately, full assimilation. From the beginning of colonisation, the state had sought to appropriate Maori organisational modes and energies for its own purposes. In turn, however, Maori were always adept at seeking to reappropriate the state's appropriations, while simultaneously engaging in other traditional and non-traditional forms of resistance and adaptation. These patterns were repeated in the decades after the Second World War.

The official tribal committee system, in particular, was increasingly used by Maori as a vehicle for transferring their collective ethos and organising capacity to the large towns and cities. An appreciation of Maori assertions of rangatiratanga in the quarter-century after the war, with their constant and complex negotiations and manoeuvrings at all levels from local to national, provides a basis for understanding the dramatic resurgence of Maori as a powerful politico-cultural force from the early 1970s – the period of the Maori Renaissance. The post-war adaptation of rangatiratanga to an increasingly urbanised world had therefore not only preserved Maori agency but – despite a degree of temporary cultural loss at the time of the migration – actually made Maori cultural forms more resilient. The Crown had to come to terms with this from the early 1970s; faced with the size of the renaissance and ever more determined assertions of rangatiratanga, the state soon abandoned assimilation as its overarching policy towards Maori.

Continuing the broad themes of its predecessor, this book explores a continuous and complex series of Crown–Maori interactions whose essential patterns – despite the emergence of very different Maori lifestyles and demographic environments – were similar to those of the pre-war period. Neither Crown assimilation policies nor mass urban migration, then, were able to extinguish expressions of Maori autonomy, of rangatiratanga. Rangatiratanga continued to be exercised in traditional ways, and it emerged in new forms, ultimately strengthening Maoridom in general. Maori cultural and other adaptations often flourished in what has been called a 'dance with the state', with the Crown, in turn, adapting its policies to meet the challenges posed by an increasingly assertive Maori leadership. The task of this book is to explore the changing ways by which the state sought to assimilate Maori, Maori expressed their autonomy in relation to the state, and the Crown responded by attempting to control the Maori organisational forms of the second half of the twentieth century.[5]

The concepts of both the Crown and the state have been much contested in recent historiography. I use the expression 'the Crown' to refer to the lego-constitutional institution generally called 'the state'. The Crown is the official name for the entity with which Maori had continually to deal, ever since annexation by Britain in 1840, when interacting with state institutions and those in positions of legally-constituted authority and power. I thus use the terms 'Crown' and 'state' interchangeably, and I also use subsets of these, such as 'government', when appropriate. Scholars such as myself who appeal to the notion of state or Crown authority have been taken to task by others for presenting the Crown/state as a 'disembodied entity'. We are asked to disaggregate this entity and explore it as a 'non-monolithic' body that incorporates 'ambiguity and inconsistency between agencies'. As an historian of state institutions, one moreover who has worked on policy and operational matters within the state machinery, I am fully aware that official policies are frequently internally contestable. The state is multi-layered and complex, citizens have different relations with different aspects of it, and the configuration of personnel and lines of responsibility within it change through time. I cover some of these contestations and varying relationships in both this book and its predecessor, and also in other works.

However, I place myself in the company of those who believe that it is a scholarly duty to identify broad-based patterns within and between peoples and institutions, leaving it to others to present a fragmented history or a history of fragments, to deplore 'meta-narratives', or to 'unpick' tapestries woven by 'conventional historians'. I am untroubled by drawing generalisations about state policy or operations (or anything else) at any given time, or through time (quite apart from the impracticality of 'disaggregating' decades of intra-state attitudes to Maori in a single volume). It is, for example, of central significance for Maori that the Crown retained its policy goal of full assimilation for more than quarter of a century after the Second World War; whatever the niceties of internal debate between public servants and ministers or the occasional official decision that gave them some relief or hope, *that* is what Maori had constantly to contend with.

Indigenous people are, of course, not alone in having no choice but to deal with an entity – variously called state, government, Crown or other things – which, despite its internal deliberations, controls the parameters of their lives through broad policies which are not generally negotiable, at least in the short term. Those unhappy with the way the state and its representatives interact with them need organisation and leadership to challenge official policy. Even where there is something akin to an appeals process or the right to take judicial action, it is 'the Crown' which, in the final analysis, is in charge of compliance to rules and decisions or allows for change. As the lego-constitutional expression of the state, the Crown overarches 'the core functions of government'. As one senior politician has noted, these involve matters such as 'internal order' and the establishment and maintenance of markets. The conditions of 'peace and good order', to use an official term, are defined by those in charge.[6]

Where it counts for the purposes of this book, then, at the interface between rulers and ruled, the state presents a monolithic front, 'the Crown'. This monolith, through time, has been destructive towards Maori political and social organisation and culture, however much indigenes exercise agency in resisting or accommodating 'the juggernaut of the state' or the pressures of the settlers and their descendants. As a lego-historian has written recently of both New Zealand and international literature, 'new tendencies in historical writing can be pushed too far in the interests of creating a self-consciously new historiography which fails to adequately address the extent to which there really *were* "impacts" … which undoubtedly left the indigenous communities reeling'. This refers to colonial times, but effects and policies did not stop when a settler colony cut loose from its 'Mother Country'.

Insisting on the power of the continuous entity called the state does not deny the struggles of those who are subjected to it and who resist its dominance. Such exercise of agency is central to this book. By dealing with the state (either in its central or some devolved form), individuals and community leaders may be able to negotiate accommodations on behalf of themselves or their constituencies. These arrangements, while they may suit both sides, will not however damage the central interest of the state and its agents, who will act in accord with what they consider to be 'the public good'. However much one deconstructs the modes by which the Crown, political executives, legislators or bureaucrats reach the laws and policies they require citizens to obey, those laws and policies constitute an ongoing reality of life for those subject to them. In Crown–Maori relations, continuities are more common than discontinuities, the latter usually being the result of accumulated pressure for change.

Scholars who contend, explicitly or implicitly, that people are free to negotiate their own terms with the state, by picking and choosing which agencies to deal with, might do well to examine the history of people, indigenous or otherwise, who have long confronted states' negative responses towards their culture, beliefs and aspirations. A Canadian labour leader, having been charged in 1919 with seditious conspiracy during a strike, observed that it 'was a mystery during the whole of that period as to who constituted the Crown. We could not find out'. But this did not stop he and his fellow workers from feeling the wrath of a state which, consistent with its previous attitude towards militant organised labour, aimed to ensure continuing peace and good order as defined by itself.

Sometimes the state will violate its own legal rules to ensure its long-term survival as sovereign. As the possessor of full sovereignty, the state is distinguished from all other entities by its capacity to decide what the *exceptions* to the normal legal order will be. This has not happened often in countries such as New Zealand. But the point is that all citizens are subject to state intervention in their lives, and the fact that this is usually by legal means is not necessarily of comfort – at least for those who are subject to laws or practices which discriminate on race, class, gender or other grounds. Most people are not particularly exercised by the precise routes by which such interventions reach them, interesting as these might be for specialist historians and their readers.[7]

While some people experience the might of the state exercised coercively against them (particularly when state agents decide that exceptions to the 'rule of law' are necessary), more commonly individuals experience state power hegemonically. They are often unaware of the forces acting upon them, or are aware of them only vaguely. In Raymond Williams' words, endorsing Antonio Gramsci's analyses, hegemony 'constitutes the substance and limit of common sense for most people under its sway ... deeply saturating the consciousness of a society'. It comprises 'the central, effective and dominant system of meanings and values, which are not merely abstract but which are organized and lived', making up 'our ordinary understanding of the nature of man and of his world'. This world is complex and does, it is true, admit a certain amount of contestation; the 'effective and dominant culture' can accommodate 'alternative meanings and values ... [and] even some alternative senses of the world'. This book explores, with reference to Maori, how hegemonic requirements are 'continually challenged and in certain respects modified'. But it also examines the 'modes of incorporation' developed by the state, including those pertaining to belief structures which operate to ensure that any modification does not fundamentally challenge the interests of those who wield effective power.[8]

Just as state/Crown is a contested concept, so too are 'Maori' or 'Maoridom', terms which have been challenged by pakeha and non-pakeha scholars and commentators alike for a number of reasons. They are used in this book in the familiar way to refer to those who have Maori descent and define themselves as Maori in whole or in part. These terms are, for present purposes, also a short-hand means of referring to the many and varied collective organisations (often, but not always, tribally focused) which have had a relationship with, and exercised rangatiratanga towards, the Crown.

Ever since 1840, and perhaps before that, many meanings have been given to rangatiratanga, and its translations into English have been varied, though

with such patterning, and a related appreciation of the interconnectedness of often seemingly disparate phenomena, can complexities (and departures from the rule) be understood. This work, in attempting to uncover the essence of what happened and why it happened, contributes to what is increasingly being seen as 'the specialised genre of non-specialised history'.

In doing so, the book builds upon a great deal of my own and others' New Zealand-based research, but it also has theoretical and universalist bases and aspirations. It does not view the Maori pursuit of autonomy as a peculiarly New Zealand phenomenon. Many scholars have noted that, through time, all submerged and dominated ethno-cultural groupings have sought (and often fought) to reassert their autonomist presence in various ways – seeking to achieve 'ever new possibilities of fuller and richer life individually and collectively' in the face of attempts to assimilate or dehumanise them. Others have analysed the many and often subtle ways in which resistance to coercion and hegemony is countered by dominant cultures and ruling authorities. Indigenous and other peoples, in asserting their agency, have to face overwhelming odds, confronted by a 'technology of occupation' which includes both overtly coercive tools and those less obviously so, such as private and public law. Those sectors which exercise power, moreover, shape social patterns and exercise social control not just through the threat or use of force, but also through control of the means of knowledge. In this respect, indigenous groups have been doubly disadvantaged, having to grapple with a world dominated by concepts different from those inherited from their ancestors. In view of all such factors, any struggle by indigenous peoples against assimilation and for autonomy is necessarily fraught with difficulty.[11]

In the first half of the period covered by this book, the odds against Maori achieving substantial Crown recognition of rangatiratanga seemed overwhelming, because of a combination of an ethnocentric pakeha worldview and the rapid urbanisation of the Maori people. But the struggle continued, even in the new and seemingly unpropitious urban environments. This, and international influences, set the scene for significant developments in the exercise of Maori agency in the last quarter of the twentieth century. By the 1980s, Maori demands for recognition of rangatiratanga were beginning to be addressed, and the 1990s saw the emergence of significant Treaty settlements to redress past injustices. Despite these achievements, however, by the dawning of the new millennium, autonomy had not been realised. The Crown showed little sign of conceding any significant form of it, and Maori continued their struggle for state recognition of rangatiratanga. But there was much dialogue between the parties, Maori were in a far more powerful position than they had been half a century before, and many were optimistic about the possibility of continuing progress on the issue.

Chapter 1

Challenges for Crown and Maori

Urbanisation

During the Second World War, many Maori served overseas or migrated to the cities and big towns to contribute to the war effort, intensifying an 'urban drift' which had begun before the war and which partly reflected a thriving Maori population growth. This was the demographic backdrop to the fundamental socio-racial developments of the post-war years. In 1946, a traveller on the East Coast could still write of Maori children 'watching the strange pakeha' arrive. But the two separate peoples of Aotearoa/New Zealand were already coming closer together, mostly as a result of the movement of tangata whenua, the people of the land, to the urban spaces in search of better opportunities. With increasing numbers of young Maori workers joining those enjoying the perceived benefits of new lifestyles in urban centres, the withdrawal of the 'other New Zealand' into rural isolation – much observed in the first decades of the century – was being reversed. In 1926, 8.7% of Maori lived in urban areas. By 1951, the figure had risen to around 30%, and had reached 46% ten years later. By 1966, the proportion of urban dwelling Maori had escalated to 62%, and it was continuing to rise rapidly.

While urban migration was often prompted by 'pull' factors, such as work and excitement in the cities, it was also driven by an overarching 'push' factor. By the beginning of the war, the Maori birth rate was already double that of the pakeha, and colonisation and its aftermath had left little Maori-owned land to provide sustenance in the countryside. The land, then, was increasingly unable to sustain the rising Maori population. Rural-based land development projects could not provide sufficient jobs for the growing numbers of young Maori workers, and Maori needed to seek employment in the cities as the indigenous birth rate continued to burgeon. By 1961, the Maori population of some 200,000 was more than double that of a quarter-century earlier. In the first half of the 1960s, three quarters of Maori in their mid to late teens migrated to urban areas. By the mid-1960s, over half of Maori children were being born in the big towns and cities, and a decade later only a quarter of Maori lived in rural areas. In one (typical) assessment, 'the rate of urbanisation, in the decades after the war was … arguably the most accelerated shift for a national population anywhere'.

The state had encouraged the move of Maori to towns and cities in wartime to fill chronic labour shortages. This migration had been expected to be temporary, with officials and politicians generally thinking that after the war most Maori would return permanently to their home communities, frequently based at pa/villages centred upon marae/meeting place complexes. After some immediate post-war worry about negative implications of the 'urban drift', however, politicians and officials began to welcome Maori urban migration. Maori provided much-needed labour for post-war reconstruction and industrialisation. From 1948, the government began to encourage the migration.[1]

Wartime urbanisation had already reinforced the Labour government's pre-existing focus on Maori social and economic development. New city dwellers lived, as various reports noted, in unsatisfactory conditions, and this could potentially lead to stresses or tears in the fabric of society. Labour's 'full equality' policies for eradicating, or at least minimising, class disparities became all the more urgent with respect to Maori. But these policies were essentially assimilationist in conception, socio-economic rather than 'socio-racial'. The government and its officials downplayed the repeatedly expressed Maori desire not only for affirmative action to offset the marginalisation which had come about through colonisation, but also for politico-cultural autonomy. A 1943 election pamphlet on Maori policy listed five 'Milestones of Progress Under the Labour Government'. While charting issues related to socio-economic equality, which Maori voters undoubtedly appreciated, the pamphlet avoided discussion of autonomy in outlining policy on 'future security and future welfare'.

The Maori Social and Economic Advancement Act

Yet during the Second World War, autonomy had been much discussed in the context of the Maori contribution to the war effort. Some 300 tribal committees had been established nationwide as part of the Maori War Effort Organisation (MWEO). Coordinated by several dozen tribal executives, the committees operated independently of government, rallying support, recruiting Maori into wartime employment, fundraising, and engaging in activities which exceeded their official brief, such as community-based welfare work or cultural revival. Towards the end of the war, Maori leaders had attempted to get the government to recognise the 'self administration and discipline' their people had demonstrated in contributing to the war effort. In arguing that the committee system should supersede the official state agency for Maori, they envisaged vibrant tribally-based committees operating at community or marae level and reporting to superior, but equally autonomous, bodies. At very least, Maori leaders (including the Maori MPs, all four of whom were Labour after Sir Apirana Ngata lost his seat in 1943) argued, the department in charge of Maori affairs should be reorganised along similarly decentralised lines to those of the MWEO. Maori, in other words, could run their own affairs autonomously, albeit within the parameters of Crown sovereignty.

The Maori Social and Economic Advancement Act (MSEA Act) of 1945 has usually been portrayed as 'a compromise' between those who advocated a certain autonomy for Maori and those who wanted Crown–Maori relations to revert, essentially, to pre-war modes. In reality, the Act gave Maori only a small degree of what their leadership had sought. Government authorities had been frightened off by the very successes of the Maori War Effort Organisation: its demonstration that Maori could run their affairs autonomously – a concept most pakeha of the time found difficult to accept – and its fostering of kotahitanga or Maori unity. While community-building activity was better provided for in the MSEA Act than in previous legislation, then, the blueprints proposed by Maori leaders proved too problematic for the legislators. The government's policy focus for Maori would remain socio-economic 'uplift'. This would be superintended by what was generally seen by Maori as a paternalistic bureaucracy: the old Department of Native Affairs was retained and placed in charge of all operations under the Act. To great Maori disappointment, tribes were thus denied control and decision-making functions. If communities wanted official recognition for their tribal committees, they had to opt into the new system. Such committees would be incorporated into departmental structures as constituent *parts of* Native/Maori Affairs, their activities overseen by departmental officers.

The new committee structure became operative from 1 April 1946, part of the department's new Maori Social and Economic Welfare Organisation (soon generally called the Maori Welfare Organisation, and from 1952, the Welfare Division). The key people in the hierarchy were to be the department's district officers, in full charge of all issues and structures in their regions. The committees were to be bound by strict procedural rules and operating parameters. All bodies, from marae-based komiti/committees to hapu- or iwi-based executives, had to 'follow European administration and meeting procedure'. Decisions were to be 'taken by a majority vote, minute books to be kept, and audited annual balance sheets to be submitted. For many communities this was the first time such procedures had been introduced'.

The Board of Native/Maori Affairs retained ultimate bureaucratic control, and the committee system was denied regional ('district') or national levels, which would have enabled Maori to place stronger pressure on the state. The committees did not get the comprehensive economic, social and political power that Maori had asked for; in fact, the system disempowered them relative to the position they had attained in the political economy during the war.

Rather than representing any sort of compromise, then, the system put in place by the MSEA Act was in many ways a victory for powerful forces in governing circles (and, more broadly, in 'mainstream society') which opposed the prospect of the MWEO being transformed into a peacetime embodiment of rangatiratanga. The 1945 legislation did, however, provide the basis for broadening the work of the department in such a way that it had little choice but to take some account of Maori views. A now ailing government was particularly conscious that it could not afford to alienate Maori. To assist its chance of surviving in office, it needed to retain the four Maori seats in Parliament, which it held in alliance with the Ratana movement. While the two principal peoples of New Zealand were eventually supposed to become one, the MSEA Act and its system of tribal committees would meanwhile permit a coexistence of cultures along lines long urged by Ngata and other Maori leaders. In the words of the Acting Prime Minister, Walter Nash, it was 'not for you to be as we are, but for you to be as you could and would be', enhanced by 'all the advantages' possessed by pakeha.[2]

At the very beginning, Maori were slow to join the new system, and a number of the wartime tribal committees disappeared. Many Maori soon realised, however, that the official structure did provide some advantages, and allowed them, generally, to run their own affairs at the local level. It could, for example, be utilised to gain subsidies for community development initiatives. Before long, tribal committees constituted under the Act, 'located in and representative of their respective communities', were revived or created, and tribal executives followed later. By 1949, the Department of Maori Affairs (DMA) was describing the workings of the system thus: 'The tribal executives and committees work in the closest possible contact with the communities they serve. The ancient Maori custom of full public discussion on the marae of all the problems of the tribe ensures close integration between the executives and committees and their people.'

That Maori continued to opt into the official committee system indicated that a certain degree of truth underlay this idealised depiction. By mid-century, Maori leaders all over the country had signed up their people to the Maori Welfare Organisation. There were 72 tribal executives and 430 tribal committees by 1950, and by then the new institutions technically covered all Maori in New Zealand. The system was already producing some discernible results in terms of improvements to meeting houses, marae complexes, sports facilities and the like, usually carried out by voluntary labour using subsidised materials. Committees entered into numerous and often involved interactions with the Department of Maori Affairs, and numbers of them began to go beyond their official briefs. Some would 'take an interest in anything at all' which helped advance the aspirations of their communities. The Crown generally tolerated this, given that the whole set of arrangements was perceived to be temporary – pending the advent of an assimilationist world of supposedly race-free communities, something that would be hurried along by urbanisation. 'The departmental goal', therefore, 'may have been to harness Maori wartime energy and apply it to post-war concerns, but that did not ... preclude Maori from applying that same energy to their own concerns'. In official eyes, this could be accommodated if those concerns assisted state goals, such as preventing social discontent through instilling (as the permanent head of Maori Affairs noted) pride in 'Maoritanga'.[3]

The Maori Welfare Organisation

Crown policies had once contained strong 'divide and rule' resonances for tribes. Policy developments from the mid-1930s had increasingly emphasised Crown responsibilities to 'the Maori people' as a whole, as opposed to tribes. These privileged 'equality for all citizens' above rangatiratanga. But there were gains as far as the pursuit of Maori autonomy was concerned. While Maori urbanisation encouraged the official mind to conceptualise 'Maoridom' as an alternative to 'tribalism', the emerging paradigm also provided more leverage for Maori as a national force. The increasing importance of Maori as a people with political power was epitomised by the removal of the word 'Native' from official discourse in 1947, and the appointment in the following year of the first Maori to head the department, Tipi Ropiha. Partly as a result of their contribution to the war effort, Maori were now seen as a people not only to be engaged with, but also to be shown respect as integral members of a country which had finally proclaimed its nominal independence from the imperial power. Policy-makers in Wellington could no longer see Maori as a series of tribes hidden in the countryside, to be patronised from time to time. The government also remained aware, however, of the ongoing importance to Maori of their tribal links, as the word 'tribal' in the institutions established by the MSEA Act indicated. It recognised, for example, that the Maori contribution in wartime was in many ways successful *because* it was based upon tribal structures. The best way of harnessing Maori energies in the post-war world, the Crown believed, was to utilise tribal structures in the short-term, in the interests of their long-term disappearance beneath the dominant culture.

There were precedents for the concept underpinning the new structure. Both the new institutions and their powers were resonant of those of the Maori councils established in 1900 and whose last remnants were abolished under the 1945 Maori Social and Economic Advancement Act. The Maori Councils Act had granted 'powers comparable to [those of] local government'. The councils had been permitted to pass approved by-laws, which the village committees that operated under them, and their own policemen, enforced. The committees had ensured the observance of sanitary regulations, controlled undesirable drinking and gambling practices, and fulfilled other functions under the watchful eye of the state (such as collecting taxes, on which Maori councils depended). The system had allowed, in principle, for the exercise of a certain degree of Maori autonomy, for the state had appreciated that unless the councils were 'designed to draw their energies from the rhythms of everyday tribal life', they would not get the support of their communities. But denied 'meaningful rangatiratanga', and insufficiently resourced, the system had languished. While it had remained useful in some circumstances and areas, only six councils were still operating when it was superseded in 1945.

At first Maori were cautious about using the institutions of the Maori Welfare Organisation (MWO). Scant advantage was taken, for example, of the potential of tribal executives (and, from 1947, of tribal committees) to pass and enforce by-laws. Nonetheless, increasing numbers of communities were prepared to accept that the new structures might be used for their own purposes as well as for the Crown's – that the benefits could be mutual. Working through the only system proffered by the Crown, for example, could help to preserve some of the collective gains made during the war. It might also be used as a vehicle to re-establish and secure a certain degree of autonomy, although here there were many frustrations. The old departmental bureaucrats generally ran things much as before, and with niggardly resources available for Maori communities. While committees were able to get state funding for specific, approved projects in fields such as welfare, most projects needed to be resourced from local efforts. The type and extent of committee activities thus often reflected their fund-raising capacity.[4]

The post-war Prime Minister/Minister of Maori Affairs, Peter Fraser, had a higher degree of empathy with Maori autonomist aspirations than many others within the state apparatus. In 1948, he declared that the welfare organisation over which he presided should be 'practically ... autonomous' and 'to a very large extent independent and self-reliant'. The organisation was not merely to be just another branch of Maori Affairs but one that 'should be looked upon by the Maori people as their organisation which they control locally as a form of local expression, direction, and control, and up to a point [it would provide] even a measure of local government in matters affecting the living conditions, housing, health, and the general welfare of the Maori people'.

There was, in fact, a considerable degree of official acceptance that, so far as the foreseeable future was concerned, some significant degree of Maori culture as well as organisation would, even should, survive. One of the stated aims of the new structure which proved to be enduring, for example, was to ensure the 'preservation of Maori culture', or at least (in the words of the department) to help 'develop in the Maori an appreciation of the modern content of his own culture'. The idea was based on an acknowledgement that the 'history of other races has shown that a culture will not really die out even without intense cultivation. There is in every individual an instinctive compulsion towards and an inherent attraction for his own indigenous culture'. This culture might be fragmented, but remnants were not unimportant – both per se and for touristic reasons.[5]

Sympathies for the survival of some degree of indigeneity were contained, however, within a broad welfarist perspective that was essentially rigorously assimilationist. It was no accident that the organisation under which tribal committees worked had 'welfare' in its title, and its legislation's purpose was to promote 'social and economic advancement'. In addition to maintaining Maori culture, and far more importantly in the eyes of the legislators, 'committees were charged with producing responsible and fully participating citizens' and ensuring their adaptation to modern conditions. In 1949, in one of its publications, the department summed up the main thrust of the Maori Social and Economic Advancement Act as being 'to facilitate the full integration of the Maori race into the social and economic structure of the country'. It cast the 1945 legislation as the 'most important single step ever taken in the progress of the Maori people towards complete integration with the pakeha way of life'.

In particular, it was the DMA's welfare officers who were to play key roles in ensuring the 'progress' of the Maori people. Welfare officers, as the department would put it, were there to 'assist the Maori, particularly of the younger generation, in adapting himself to the new culture'. From the beginning, they were tasked with promoting 'race uplift' of a social and economic nature within a policy environment that focused on 'equality' and European beliefs and standards of behaviour. Welfare officers formed part of a broader grouping of officials who 'grappled with how to assist their clients to be successful members of the larger Pakeha (European) society that they were increasingly a part of'. This task included acting – in departmental words – as 'friend, counsellor and guide', especially to Maori migrating to the cities.[6]

Such functions were coordinated in seven administrative MWO districts. DMA officials ran the bureaucracies at this level, and at the sub-regional level of organisation. Only in the layers beneath these – in tribal executives and tribal committees at marae or community level – were Maori people themselves given a representational voice. The original intention was to have some provision for Maori views to quickly reach the highest levels of the Crown. The executives and committees would, in conjunction with the welfare officers, 'think out proposals and plans for the advancement of the Maori people in all directions'. The welfare officers could then represent their views directly to government through the Controller of Maori Welfare at head office, rather than through the district officers.

Committees

But the reality was that the official committees, as an integral part of the Department of Maori Affairs, struggled to make their voices heard. One assessment that the committees were 'only a shell of the effective organisations' that had operated under the Maori War Effort Organisation indicates the magnitude of the task faced by those determined to make the best of the opportunities the new system afforded. The Prime Minister's strictures that bureaucrats should not 'nullify the purpose of the legislation' by turning the MWO and its committees into 'merely another branch' of the department had brought little as mid-century approached. The independence of committees was, in effect, negated by structural provisions in the Maori Social and Economic Advancement legislation itself. Senior Maori in the Labour Party, along with other Maori leaders, frequently expressed their disappointment at the departmental straitjacketing of Maori efforts to control their own affairs. Despite Labour having promised a degree of autonomy to the Maori constituency at the 1946 elections, a levelling and Europeanising policy of 'equality' dominated the rest of its term in office. In the final analysis, the MWO existed to do the Crown's bidding within a dominant assimilationist paradigm that was being reinforced by the trend towards Maori urban migration.[7]

On the other hand, the official committee system could be used to a certain extent to challenge that paradigm. Before long, for example, some Maori were using it to help recreate rangatiratanga in the detribalised environment of the large towns and cities. Although their work was officially sanctioned by the DMA, both here and in rural environments the committees did not necessarily become 'obedient servants of the state. [They] worked out for themselves what activities they would undertake, responding largely to the concerns and circumstances of their respective communities and not just departmental policy'. Those in official committees made deliberate choices as to the best strategy for their people at a given time and place.

In the rural areas, for example, these committees could be of considerable benefit to Maori by providing farming advice and assistance. Some worked towards developing lands hitherto 'locked up' due to problems relating to multiple ownership and a lack of access to capital. In 1949, the Crown and Maori leaders working within the official committee structure finalised new ways of helping tangata whenua farm their own lands rather than lease them to pakeha. In urban areas, official committees were often place-based rather than marae-based, welcoming individual Maori from many different tribes. Sometimes they alone gave Maori urban migrants voice, a point of contact and advice to assist them in making the often painful adjustment to new ways of life. They also offered channels for migrants to seek government financial and welfare assistance: 'everybody went to the Maori Affairs', as the DMA was colloquially known.

Unofficial komiti/committees also flourished throughout the period covered in this book. Operating largely beyond the scrutiny and control of the DMA, such structures were freer than official committees to respond to local need rather than to the demands of bureaucrats, although they went without the support and resourcing that the DMA could provide. Sometimes, however, such komiti were able to use the official system for their own ends. Some would even come to seek the official franchise, proving their worthiness by adopting the formal minute-taking practices and other requirements of the MWO system. When official status was granted, they might well continue to operate much as before, but now with access to, for example, subsidies to carry out projects of which the Crown approved.

Some of the wartime Maori structures which continued independently after 1945 (as well as some new ones) operated as rivals to the official committees. Non-official bodies included the Maori Women's Health Leagues, which sometimes considered it necessary to interact with the authorities for the benefit of their members. But because of this, they were deemed by some Maori to be state-contaminated. In fact, because of the stigma attached to getting too close to the government, even some of the official MWO committees resisted direction from head office from time to time, reporting this back to their communities and gaining kudos accordingly. However, numbers of non-official committees continued to seek integration into the MWO, including some of the War Effort committees which had previously opted for independence from the Crown after 1945. Many people cooperated with, or worked within, both official and unofficial systems, and new leadership strata began to develop. When around mid-century a number of key leaders died, including Ngata, Princess Te Puea, Bishop Frederick Bennett and Peter Buck/Te Rangihiroa, the way was clear for new leaders to flourish – including, increasingly, those in the urban spaces.[8]

Policing and Social Control

Under the MSEA Act, volunteer Maori Wardens were authorised to provide the valuable (and cheap) service of enforcing 'order and regularity' within the MWO/Welfare Division's official committee system. Some Maori committees were quick to see the advantages of this, and began operating a warden system even before the first wardens were formally designated under the Act in 1949 – a delay partly caused by the need for New Zealand Police Force vetting of appointees. As well as their formal role in community policing, Maori wardens began assuming various leadership duties at flaxroots level early in the scheme's operation. Numbers quickly escalated. In 1950, there were 32 official wardens, a figure which increased to 134 in 1951. By 1954, there were 205 and, as their uses in controlling Maori who had migrated to the towns and cities became manifest, their numbers continued to grow. There were over 500 in 1962, and by 1975 the number of wardens had reached a thousand.

The Department of Maori Affairs saw wardens as the 'police force' of the tribal executives and their committees, although their only identification at first was a metallic badge, and they were not remunerated for their work. In a dispatch to welfare officers, the department described a warden's principal job as being to 'stamp out mischief before it becomes a crime' – in other words, to act mainly as preventive police. Wardens were said to be the 'eyes and ears of the Executives ... They are virtually policemen without the powers of policemen'. There were substantial penalties, applicable to pakeha as well as Maori, for obstructing their work. Because wardens were responsible to elected institutions, they could be – and were – seen as a community resource. But they were also part of the coercive wing of the MWO, a state-franchised institution.

Despite such an uneasy mix, there were few demands for their disbandment. In particular, both Crown and Maori communities wanted wardens to help regulate alcohol consumption, with excessive Maori drinking increasingly seen as detrimental to both the Maori community and the 'public good'. Wardens could order Maori off licensed premises, or prevent publicans serving them liquor. In 1951, wardens gained increased liquor-related powers, such as the ability to enter Maori gatherings on marae without a warrant in order to seize liquor. On such matters involving order within Maori communities, both they and tribal committees could act even if no relevant by-laws had been passed.

In addition to wardens' formal duties, committees frequently used them for their own, informal social control purposes. The mana of being Crown-franchised officers sometimes gave wardens a better capacity to deal with 'recalcitrance' than had they been non-official tribal or other authorities. Moreover, given that they were voluntary and unpaid members of the community operating under a principle that has been described as 'aroha ki te tangata' (love for the people), the wardens often assumed the status of community social workers. Although integrated into the state system, they came to epitomise the determination of Maori to run their own affairs and resolve their own problems. The official committee system's responsibility for wardens assisted its capacity to survive and, in many areas and arenas, to thrive.[9]

Responding to Challenge

As mid-century approached, tribal organisation was coming under strain, with 'drift' to the large towns and cities starting to become a huge and rapid migration. From 1948, the Crown assisted rural Maori to gains skills necessary for urban life, and the government began to implement (in the words of the Secretary of Labour) 'practical measures for ensuring the ultimate absorption of the Maori Race into full employment', providing, for example, temporary accommodation in the cities. The disciplined and ethnically-situated modes of behaviour required in collectively-orientated rural communities began to yield to the atomised lifestyles of the urban spaces. The new challenges to tribally-based organisation and discipline would soon escalate as the Maori population increased: up from 134,097 in 1951 to nearly four times that number half a century later. The Crown considered the problems engendered by urbanisation were best addressed by securing jobs and better living conditions: Maori would benefit primarily from socio-economic improvement strategies posited on full assimilation to the ways and mores of the dominant culture. The Crown's refusal at the time of the MSEA Act to countenance official regional and national Maori representation, because this had the potential to promote Maori autonomy, meant that (apart from unofficial movements such as Kingitanga and Ratana) there was no cross-tribal organisation to fight urban threats to 'Maoritanga'. The DMA and its Maori Welfare Organisation handled matters at a central official level, and tribal committees and executives sometimes became involved in pursuing transitional measures through departmental channels, seeing these contributions to adjustment procedures as a case of Maori helping control Maori issues.[10]

However, such collectivity-based collaboration, while welcomed, did not form a major part of the strategy of the post-war government. In Labour's social-democratic philosophy, Maori were individuals who tended to be disadvantaged by their class location and needed welfare or other state assistance to participate in socio-economic uplift. Past welfare efforts would be consolidated and extended as Maori moved to the towns, a migration that would encourage industrial expansion and diversification in the interests of all

New Zealanders. As Minister of Maori Affairs, Fraser emphasised in his 1949 annual report to Parliament that he believed socio-economic development to be the key to the Maori future. This would not only benefit the tangata whenua but also contribute to 'national wealth'. A raised income and standard of living for Maori was thus of 'great importance not only to the Maori people themselves, but also to the economy of the country'.

Such sentiments, which were expressed twice in the report, were typical of state pronouncements of the time, and they were always underpinned by an assumption that Maori should be helped to become as close as possible in all respects to Europeans. However, these goals of social and economic assimilation could meanwhile accommodate (again, in Fraser's words) some form of 'independent, self-reliant, and satisfied Maori race working side by side with the pakeha'. Such rhetoric may have damaged Labour in the eyes of the European electorate at the 1949 election, given a vigorous National attack upon Labour's alleged pandering to Maori and the Prime Minister's apparent concessions to Maori self-determination. But in reality, the Labour government had remained reluctant to offer Maori anything but a cautious and constrained degree of control over their own affairs.

In the election campaign, Labour essentially stood on its previous assimilationist and equality-focused policies, while the National Party ostentatiously offered Maori less than Labour. National won, reflecting a mood swing within sectors of pakeha New Zealand which, when combined with urbanisation and other trends, did not seem to bode well for the future of rangatiratanga and of Maoridom in general. Already there was a racial backlash against the growing and visible Maori presence in urban spaces. Race relations could be deemed to be 'the best in the world' when most pakeha knew Maori only at a distance, but such official discourse could come under challenge when individuals and, later, families moved into urban areas and brought with them customs unfamiliar to surrounding pakeha.

While pakeha attitudes reflected a general European ethnocentrism, racist incidents were on the rise, especially as a reaction to increased Maori involvement in urban-based disorder or crime. The National politicians had taken heed of popular pakeha sentiment in their campaign, and afterwards. Once in office, however, they did not attempt to turn the clock back on urban migration. And, despite some urban pakeha resistance to mingling with newly-arrived Maori, the National government continued the assimilationist policies of its predecessor – policies so deep-seated in both officialdom and civil society that they formed part of accepted wisdom, whatever the difficulties posed by Maori adjustment. Significant voices within Maoridom, too, saw assimilation as the most desirable goal. In 1949, the Maori Purposes Fund Board published Peter Buck's *The Coming of the Maori*, which treated official policies as though rooted in fact. The book argued that a blending of the two races was occurring, and that 'in nationality', the Maori were 'as British as anything which ever came out of Britain'.[11]

Almost all Maori leaders, however, including the most conservative, aspired to some degree of autonomy for their people. Although the outlook may have seemed bleak in 1950, prospects for self-determination were not unpromising if long-term developments were taken into account. The first half of the century had seen considerable social, economic, demographic, cultural and political advances for Maoridom. Many marae-centred communities continued to thrive, or were reconstructing themselves within a vigorous tribal environment. Since the 1930s, Labour policies had led to significant increases in Maori health and material well-being. From this considerably improved socio-economic base, which would eventually find further enhancement as people found jobs in the cities, Maori leaders could work to pursue politico-cultural autonomy. To be sure, urban migration, essentially the province of the young, implied intermarriage, and the state welcomed this as an agent of assimilation. But increasing intermarriage, and general Maori adoption of city ways, did not necessarily (or even usually) mean complete abandonment of tribal affiliation.

Urban life, moreover, could actually help to promote identification with 'Maoridom', as newly arrived individuals naturally sought out 'their own kind', including through the official committees and their activities. The various types of Maori development in both urban and rural environments did not, of course, come to a halt under National. Just as pre-1950 gains were made in the absence of any great understanding by Labour of Maori desires for autonomy, or indeed of tikanga Maori (Maori custom), further accomplishments – socio-economic, cultural, political, even autonomist – were possible under the new government, however unsympathetic or uncomprehending it might be on Maori issues. Obviously, many achievements would need to come from the people themselves, but Crown intervention could assist Maori aspirations – especially if government officials and politicians could be persuaded that intervention was in 'the national interest'. The process benefited from the emergence of new leaders within Maoridom, often people able to work within both pakeha and Maori worlds, and from the inputs of the small number of Maori associated with the National party – some of them of very high rank in tribal Maoridom.

Observers, even within some National circles, were soon noting a general feeling within society that a new era of Maori development was about to begin, one that would build upon the gains of the previous half century, the potentialities of urbanisation, and the post-war economic boom. Development, as Maori saw it, would draw much on Maori culture, and its maximisation would depend upon Maori being able run their own affairs unimpededly while engaging with urbanisation and modernity. Maori aspirations for recognition of rangatiratanga, then, did not sink beneath the weight of urbanisation, assimilation policies and growing wealth for individuals who had adjusted to work and life in the cities. In some ways, hopes were reinforced in the decades which followed. This was partly a result of pakeha and Maori New Zealanders becoming increasingly aware of national issues of 'race relations' and Maori aspirations. International developments – decolonisation, self-determinationist discourse and anti-racist movements – were also widely discussed. Debates and politico-cultural trends which would eventually lead to momentous changes throughout the world were already present, sometimes in more than incipient form, in mid-century New Zealand.[12]

Chapter 2

Adjustments by Crown and Maori

The Committee System under the National Government

Following National's victory at the polls in late 1949, the new Cabinet lacked both expertise in matters Maori and any great sympathy with many Maori aspirations. For the first time since the provincial period of the third quarter of the nineteenth century, New Zealand had a government with no Maori support in Parliament. National, moreover, made no arrangements to appoint any Maori to the political executive, ending six decades of political tradition, and declined to place any of the Maori MPs on the Board of Maori Affairs, which oversaw the principal activities of the Department of Maori Affairs. An historian has noted of National's leader, Sidney Holland: 'No Prime Minister since William Massey had come to office with so little contact with Maoris and so little interest in Maori affairs'.

Many Maori were understandably dismayed. Before long, the new government's attitudes were to have serious repercussions for Crown–Maori relations. Labour had nourished ambitions of building state housing on ancestral land of Ngati Whatua in the Orakei/Bastion Point area of Auckland, but this had been stymied as a result of strenuous tribal opposition. National, however, now began plans to develop the area and compulsorily acquire land. Rather than assist the improvement of the 'unsightly' and unhealthy Ngati Whatua settlement and meeting house at the Okahu Bay marae, where tribal visitors to Auckland had traditionally been hosted, the government destroyed them and relocated the inhabitants. Such actions created new, and eventually high-profile, grievances.[1]

But the committee system kept operating, whatever the new tensions induced by harsher Crown policies and practices. Some Maori had predicted that the system would be run down or even discontinued, given that National's assimilationist messages were even stronger than those from within the Labour camp. Certainly, the MWO system had to prove itself to a government which initially viewed it as too accommodating to the tangata whenua. However, the country's new political leadership quickly came to appreciate that there was a wide gap between theory and reality, and that it was in fact beneficial to keep the committee system going for the foreseeable future. It heeded advice from its district welfare officers that the MWO's marae projects provided for 'healthy group life' – social health among a significant sector of society could only contribute to the public good. More broadly, while the government shared its predecessor's belief that Maori discontent was best addressed by socio-economic improvements, it was increasingly forced to come to grips with Maori priorities – as, indeed, was 'the Maori Affairs'. Officials, for example, might report on poor quality housing and assume this was the primary concern of local Maori, but then find that people were more concerned with securing a tribal community centre. Only with this built, thereby enhancing their collective identity, would Maori leaders seek improved housing.

In some ways the official tribal institutions actually strengthened in power and activity under National, partly because they were seen by increasing numbers of Maori as potential tools to help counteract the government's brashly stated policies of assimilation. Often the system worked well for Maori to this effect, in spite of the unpromising political environment. A Maori anthropologist doing field work with Huria Tribal Committee, in the area covered by the Ranginui Tribal Executive, reported that its leaders were 'recognized members of the community ... including a few kaumatua [elders] and a majority of young men'. The committee focused on matters within its official brief, such as regulating alcohol, eliminating gambling from within village confines, working on by-laws, presiding over the local peace and calling up offenders for 'admonition'. It also took responsibility for rebuilding the meeting house. All of this benefited some of the tribe's aspirations as well as several state objectives.

Problems were rife, however. There was, for example, a heightening of paternalism within the Department of Maori Affairs, despite an increasing number of Maori staff. Maori widely perceived a 'department knows best' attitude, and resented the way in which officials went about their tasks. Staff paternalism was encouraged by assimilationist attitudes that found reinforcement in a context of welfarist politics, urbanisation and economic boom. At a large intertribal meeting of leaders at Raukawa Marae in March 1950, Ngata was selected as spokesperson. He questioned whether Maori Affairs, 'with its complicated organisation and the inquisitorial attitude of some of its officials', was 'best fitted' to oversee the Maori Social and Economic Advancement Act. Too many in the DMA were 'doubtful of the ability of representative Maori committees to administer the functions vested in them by the Act'. There was much 'deliberate obstruction and the appropriateness of Maori projects [was] questioned at every term' by officials. When would officials 'let Maori people have a say in their own affairs?' The marae, it seemed to the Maori leadership, was 'the only place the Maori could rule'. Leaders were 'most emphatic' that they did not want all things Maori to be governed by Maori Affairs.[2]

Te Rangiataahua (Rangi) Royal, Controller of Maori Social and Economic Advancement, had similar concerns. It was anticipated in 1950 that before long 'some of the more advanced Executives and Committees [would] be self-reliant bodies able to solve their problems on the spot as they arise'. But even Royal felt constrained in his ability to assist committees in their quests for autonomy. He believed that he was 'being reduced to a figurehead' within the department. In 1951, he declared that his welfare officers had experienced 'hostility manifested in various ways and forms' in the public service. The 'present set-up', he concluded, was 'a failure'. While various Maori working within the welfare system did not fully agree, joining or staying precisely because it offered possibilities for progress for their people, the bleakness of Royal's assessment was understandable.

'Good Government'

On 1 June 1951, top DMA bureaucrats decided that it was opportune to 'strangle the autonomy and freedom' which some of the Maori welfare officers had established for themselves and, by extension, for the committees they liaised with. The officers were told, as a body, that they had been over-emphasising matters such as marae and cultural development. All were now placed fully under the control of the (pakeha) district officers. In the words of a Maori historian, the changes instituted by the DMA signalled 'the end for another potentially exciting and positive policy aimed at providing Maoridom with a measure of self-determination'. Subsequent attempts by Maori welfare officers (such as at a meeting late in 1952 with departmental officials) to seize back at least some degree of their operational independence made little headway – even when assisted by forceful leadership within their ranks, including former 28th (Maori) Battalion veterans such as Lieutenant-Colonel Arapeta Awatere and Norman Perry.[3]

By the time the new arrangements were imposed, many tribal committees were already carrying out state functions which, on the surface, had little to do with 'Maori welfare': acting, for example, as enforcement agencies or official revenue gatherers, including collecting rates levied on Maori land by local bodies. The Huria Tribal Committee was frequently 'used by the Tauranga County Council as an agency for the encouragement of rates payment, or by the police in periodic endeavours to discipline the adolescents from the village'. Such cooperation with various authorities was perceived to have downstream benefits. Committees also often focussed on doing things which were, strictly speaking, state responsibilities, but which had not been officially prioritised: improving the lot of their people by installing running water for houses in the pa, for example, or securing better sanitation. Tribal executives might build recreation grounds for the whole community, or promote education and employment opportunities for their own people. Urban Maori committees, in particular, were also involved in addressing complaints and requests from schools, government departments and 'pakeha' institutions and individuals. While such activities served a useful purpose in assisting good relations with state and pakeha, they also ate into the capacity of the committees to support the political and cultural aspirations of their people.

A number of Maori and pakeha sought to counteract the possibility of the committee members becoming little more than functionaries of the Crown. Sectors and individuals within the Maori welfare system urged that committees focus on matters important to their communities. In particular, they encouraged the committees to operate as autonomously as possible, beginning with rejecting all efforts at Crown co-option. They believed that the government would attempt to minimise confrontation over a wide series of fronts (as opposed to making symbolic statements through such acts as dismantling the pa at Okahu Bay) so as to preserve the community-based strength of the MWO organisation. The trade-offs that committees needed to make in order to further their own agendas might be some degree of work on behalf of the Crown. This could be a problem, but not an insuperable one. In such circumstances, boundaries were always blurred, 'making it difficult to assign labels of collaboration or resistance, conservatism or activism'. The evidence indicates that '[e]ven the most co-operative relationships were tempered with resistance when required.' Thus many flaxroots committees, performing functions that were crucial to local Maori well-being, pressed ahead in giving priority to pursuit of their own aims, while at the same time assisting the DMA and other local, regional and central state agencies. Such assistance might, in turn, lead to financial and other support for 'their own' projects.[4]

Even the most autonomous committees, however, gained little in the way of meaningful political independence. This was a reflection at micro level of the systemic official constraints preventing the development of Maori autonomy at a macro level within the state, with Holland's Cabinet asserting assimilationist policies even more vigorously than its predecessor. The tribal executives and committees were not mentioned in the National government's first annual report on Maori matters to Parliament. While the government appreciated the need to come to a temporary accommodation with Maori institutions, there was a prevalent feeling within state circles that the time when Maoridom would begin to dissipate was nigh.

National's interest in the official committees was principally in their contribution to 'good government': the MWO should assist with rapid Maori assimilation, avoiding significant spending along the way, rather than help Maori determine their own destiny. This might seem ironic given National's ideological emphasis on self-reliance, but its focus was always on individual self-reliance rather than collective self-determination. National's Minister of Maori Affairs, Ernest Corbett, who farmed confiscated Taranaki land, was principally interested in inducing Maori, as individuals, 'to accept the responsibility of citizenship'. In the terminology of later times, he stressed Article Three of the Treaty, which spoke to the equality of rights and obligations for all citizens, as opposed to Article Two's emphasis on rangatiratanga. When Dick Scott's *The Parihaka Story* was published in 1954, Corbett set DMA head office staff 'combing through the book ... to find errors of fact' that would discredit what was essentially a pioneering, rangatiratanga-based perspective on a grim chapter in New Zealand's race-relations history. Corbett and others assumed that sympathy from pakeha for the struggles of Maori might help prolong Maori organisation rather than work towards its disappearance. The National government sought, even more than its predecessor, to control and appropriate Maori energies in the cause of marginalising Maori as political players. By the late 1950s, anthropological fieldwork was revealing an accumulated build-up of flaxroots distrust of the Crown and its attempted impositions upon, and plans for, Maoridom.[5]

The Land

Even with respect to development of Maori-owned land, the Holland government restricted the opportunities for the owners to exercise autonomy. Large tracts of Maori-owned lands were controlled by the Maori Trustee and other official or officially franchised bodies. Much was on long-term lease to pakeha farmers. With many leases nearing expiry in the post-war years, severe problems began to surface. Under the 1909 Native Land Act, for example, leases on the bulk of the lands had been vested in Maori Land Boards (MLBs). Maori had often put their trust in them, but MLBs proved essentially to be creatures of the Crown, operating primarily in the interests of the perceived 'public good' rather than on behalf of the Maori owners. As leases were due to run out, hopes of re-establishing collective control of communally-owned property were high. But the leases contained provisions for compensation to lessees for any permanent improvements they had made, and complexities of title, lack of collective access to loan capital and other problems meant that the Maori lessors faced significant difficulties in regaining control.

Moreover, Maori owners had long hoped to take back thriving 'going concerns', but many lessees – expecting non-renewal – neglected the properties in the final years of their leases. Owners thus faced the prospect of farming lands that were, say, weed infested or bereft of recent fertilisation. The potential problems had been recognised after the war, and a royal commission into 'vested lands', established in 1949, recommended that committees of beneficial owners be established so they could be consulted on the future of their land. But a 1951 official enquiry into the MLB-vested leases found that the boards were neither adequately consulting owners about the use of the lands, nor planning for the future of the land in the event of non-renewal of leases.

The Crown's 'basic policy' from the end of the 1940s, when significant post-war land development recommenced, continued in fact to be that of 'public good' productivity. In this pursuit, even the Board of Maori Affairs paid scant regard to the desire of many Maori, collectively and individually, to retrieve or enhance whatever connection they could with the land. In 1949, Prime Minister Fraser wrote that 'the full utilization of all available Maori land is of national importance'. That year, the Crown authorised the improvement of more than a quarter of 'unproductive' Maori land. The concern with productivity, however, meant that before Maori-owned and Maori-controlled land could be accepted for developmental aid, owners would have to agree in advance to DMA control of operations. This meant essentially that they would have to sign up to an arrangement that was antithetical to many collective tribal aspirations: subdivision into 'economic farm units', on which lessees (who might or might not be Maori) would be placed and granted long-term tenure. In this way, it was expected that more Maori-owned rural property would be brought to its full potential production. There would be the added advantage, in the words of a Maori historian, that such policies would help bring Maori people 'into the mainstream, thus silencing public criticisms of the perceived idleness of Maori land'.

The Crown's renewed attempts to develop long-term leasing arrangements under official auspices in effect invited many owners to shed any vestiges of control over their land far into the future. For many iwi, this would mean yet another protracted delay in the very long struggle to exercise rangatiratanga over their land in a meaningful way, even if they retained ultimate ownership. Holland's Cabinet endorsed its Labour predecessor's productivity-based policies by adding extra incentives to produce. But the various official plans for Maori-owned land already faced difficulties of both implementation and resistance.

The National government early adopted more coercive techniques to promote developmental and 'national interest' imperatives. These included using the concept of trusteeship to acquire a tighter degree of control. The Maori Purposes Act of 1950 allowed the Maori Land Court to authorise the Maori Trustee to lease out any Maori lands deemed to be 'unproductive', a measure not matched with respect to state powers over pakeha-owned land. In

1952, the Maori Trustee gained greater power over Maori-owned land. The Maori Land Boards – which, for all the difficulties associated with them, had helped ensure the retention of Maori land – were abolished, and their assets and administrative functions assigned to the Trustee. After 1954, the Maori Trustee's powers were enhanced even further regarding the management of vested lands.[6]

Despite the combination of such developments and urbanisation, the Crown was well aware that land remained 'an important part of the Maori social structure'. For purposes of social harmony, therefore, it conceded that Maori should be enabled to 'retain the bulk of their remaining lands'. But a reluctance on grounds of the 'national good' to trust Maori to farm had become rooted in bureaucratic culture. Officials would typically suggest that it was premature to hand back a finished Maori development scheme to its owners. If transfer were insisted upon, they would contend that the farm should be placed with an incorporation rather than returned directly to those with interests in the land. Maori frustrations at such attitudes were intensified by bureaucratic inertia, and there were long delays in returning developed land to any form of non-departmental control. All the same, as a Maori scholar pointed out later, returning control to incorporations not only allowed retention of ownership but also frequently enabled shareholding control to go to tribal, sub-tribal or whanau groupings. By the early 1970s, three quarters of shareholding entities defined themselves by use of tribal-based terminology.

Meanwhile, officials had long recommended that the escalation of individual titles on blocks of Maori-owned land needed addressing. This system, imposed on Maori by the Crown in the first place, did have seriously adverse ramifications for Maori owners as well as for 'national productivity'. In 1952, when the Maori Land Court's progress on consolidating land titles was reviewed, public attention was drawn to the problem of multiple ownership of land. 'Chaotic' title fragmentation made it difficult to use land economically and efficiently at a time when the 'national interest' required greater outputs for the international market. Multiple title also made it hard for owners to fulfil their responsibilities to the state in such matters as paying rates or clearing noxious weeds. Because of the large numbers of very tiny shares, retaining the land in Maori hands often brought costs rather than productivity benefits. Reform was widely said to be urgent in the interests not just of Maori but of all New Zealanders.[7]

And so officials set to work on solutions. The DMA claimed to have 'discussed the question [of title fragmentation] with Maori leaders and organisations'. In reality the consultation was selective, and in any case the recommendations made to government 'disregarded traditional Maori values'. Without significant consultation, then, a 'revolutionary' (as a later official report put it) new approach to Maori land title was developed and adopted in the 1953 Maori Affairs Act. The legislation's measures to 'halt, or at least slow down, fragmentation' focussed on 'conversion'. The Department of Maori Affairs later explained it thus: if 'a satisfactory arrangement' between successors as to land use could not be found, 'interests may be vested in the Maori Trustee and due compensation paid to the successors from whom the land has been acquired'. In other words, the Maori Trustee gained powers, under certain circumstances, to buy up interests in land which the state deemed to be 'uneconomic' (those under £25 in value) and on-sell them.

There were supposedly safeguards for Maori: 'The intention is that the Maori Trustee will dispose of the interests in such a way that they are kept in useful Maori occupation or ownership.' But the state's rationale was really to create 'economic farms from uneconomic holdings'. While the minister argued that this would improve race relations by removing pakeha criticism of Maori landowners, the main goal remained that of increasing national production. The Maori Land Court, too, was given wider powers under the 1953 Act to effect new arrangements among successors to interests in title, a development of pre-war consolidation policies. The new measures were aimed at preventing the splitting-up of interests to such a degree that the land could not be farmed or otherwise profitably used. Officials were tasked, for example, with 'encouraging successors to agree to one of them succeeding to the whole interest of the deceased owner, buying out, if necessary, the interests of his co-successors'. That way, it was argued, all parties would benefit. Owners could control and manage their land more effectively, especially by consolidating or creating farmable units; state agencies would be able to disengage gradually from the management of Maori land and revenues; and the public would benefit from greater employment, taxes and productivity.[8]

Because the Maori Affairs Act attempted to address the very real problems arising from the multiplication of fragmented interests in Maori-owned land, there was less opposition to bureaucrats gaining coercive rights than might have been expected. But even before passage of the legislation, there was recognition among Maori leaders that it held the potential to finally sever many tangata whenua links with their ancestral lands. Strong opposition to conversion came from the Maori MPs and other leaders. Opponents often appealed to ancestral bonds to the land. The smallest link to the earth, Eastern Maori MP Tiaki Omana argued, even if only a few shares in its ownership, enabled a person to retain both interest and speaking rights in the tribe. Whatever the practical arguments presented by the Crown, the provision in the Act for the Maori Trustee to convert 'uneconomic interests' was 'a horrifying breach of the Maori principle of turangawaewae [the tribal 'place to stand'] because it ignored the need for every Maori to retain ownership of some ancestral piece of land'. Many Maori regarded conversion as akin to confiscation. The Crown's power to compulsorily remove land-based property rights certainly meant the undermining of mana and, ultimately, rangatiratanga.[9]

Some government land reforms, however, insofar as they allowed for voluntary rationalisation, could lead to a significant exercise of rangatiratanga at local level. Whatever the Crown's intentions and the political environment, tangata whenua were not deterred from continuing to fight to have their aspirations met. As in the past, that included making use of state-provided institutions, however marginal the opportunities. In 1949, following Maori representations, the Board of Maori Affairs had recommended that committees of 'practical men' be set up to advise on land development. Officials could see that this would benefit national productivity, and the new government agreed. As a result, District Maori Land Committees (DMLCs), holding delegated powers from the board, were established in 1950.

The Crown's main aim was essentially to facilitate enterprise and development schemes, and when DMLCs had first met in 1951, Maori found themselves in a distinct minority. The standard DMLC composition was to be three officials and 'one reputable Maori farmer well-known in the area'. A government publication noted in 1964 that '[v]isits to schemes by these committees, with a Maori of proved competence in their midst, makes for smooth relations between the owners and farmers and the administration'. Rural and tribal Maori communities, although dismayed at their lack of greater representation, were often able to get their views heard through the committees. It is clear that Maori gained a number of practical and empowering benefits from the new system, especially after 1952 when the committees gained greater powers.

There were other modes of land-based collectivised empowerment at local level. When the Maori Trustee acquired accumulations of 'uneconomic interests', Maori incorporations and other groupings were able to purchase them, enhancing the economic base – and therefore the influence – of indigenous rural communities. Bureaucratic inefficiency, together with the sheer complexity of the title system, also helped preserve landed rangatiratanga. The policy of partitioning out Crown interests and then selling these to people (often not Maori) who would develop farms and promote settlement often took many years to effect. Meanwhile, Maori shareholders continued to have a stake in their ancestral land, and some could use the opportunity to plan for a future in which their rangatiratanga might be acknowledged. Both unavoidable delays and bureaucratic inertia gave Maori trusts, incorporations and other entities time to prove that they could effectively manage multiply-owned land through committees appointed by the owners. The DMA itself also often helped the collectivities to manage and develop properties. Such developments increased over time, with 'Section 438 trusts' under the 1953 legislation, for example, becoming popular in the 1970s and 1980s. The trusts were able to manage blocks as if they were single owners but on behalf of many Maori landowners. Thus, while Maori had to work within relentlessly assimilationist official parameters, sectors of officialdom provided them leeway in pursuing their aspirations to control their own destinies.[10]

Modernisation and Discrimination

While official state structures were still seen by many Maori as offering a viable means of assisting them handle their own affairs in a variety of fields, government policies remained geared to opposing the emergence of any significant degree of Maori autonomy. The decollectivisation of Maori social organisation, the withering away of most Maori culture and the assimilation of a tribally-based people to European ways all remained the official goal. The 1953 Maori Affairs Act was part of a raft of legislative measures passed that year and shortly afterwards that focused on moving Maori on from (in the words of the historians of the DMA) the 'communal way of life'. Making Maori individuals and families 'self-reliant' was the stated aim of welfare officers. By the mid-1950s, this meant that the officers were 'primarily concerned to introduce modern ideas' and assist adaptation to the urban spaces: willingness of Maori to undertake the tasks of an urban manufacturing and service workforce, it was believed, would benefit the economy as a whole, as well as their own future.

Officials sought to counter the persistence of customs which did not fit well with city-based and pakeha-dominated life, such as informal adoption and fostering (matua whangai), large families, customary (extra-legal) marriages, and open and lavish ('wasteful') hospitality. Maori customary marriage was 'invalidated' in 1953, and an official committee investigated indigenous adoption practices. While its report sought to remove 'racial discrimination' by allowing Maori to adopt non-Maori children, the committee was also 'anxious to encourage the gradual disappearance of the practice of adoption by custom' within Maoridom. The resultant Adoption Act in 1955 sought to diminish non-legal adoption by enabling Maori to legally adopt children through the relatively informal Maori Land Court, assisted by Maori welfare officers (redesignated child welfare officers for such purposes). Such measures signified much more than the attitudes and policies of the politicians in charge of the nation: they reflected pakeha opinion, now that demographic change had thrust Maori issues before the majority culture.[11]

The 'problems' of Maoridom stemmed, according to the official mindset, from a people finding it difficult to adapt to modern, especially urban, life. Immediately following World War II, many officials and politicians had continued to believe that 'the Maori problem' could best be addressed (and contained) in ancestral homelands, an inadvertent compliment to the efficacy of customary and collectivised Maori social control devices. During the war there had been many observations of the negative effects on individuals thrown abruptly into the individualised environment of urban areas. Their 'loneliness and the feeling of not belonging' could lead to both personal difficulties and public disorder. But now the increasing visibility of Maori in towns and cities had negative consequences of a different kind. As Maori migrated into the urban landscapes, differences in behaviour and lifestyle from those of pakeha became manifest. They were often frowned upon by 'mainstream society', for it was not just official policy which demanded conformity; in an assimilationist society, all minority ethno-cultural groupings were expected to adhere to 'British ways'. As the migration increased, with official encouragement, tensions grew.

Ways were sought to assist the adjustment, to ease the 'sense of diffidence in European company' which was seen to delay assimilation and sometimes promote inter-racial misunderstandings. From 1950 the government pursued a policy of what came to be called 'pepper-potting' in the cities. This involved 'dispersing', as a later Maori Affairs head would describe it, 'Maori houses amongst European houses for better integration', a policy which eventually aimed at one Maori family per street. The practice faced opposition from Maori who wished to live in proximity to other Maori, in an effort to recreate indigenous community in what was a new and difficult environment for them. Conversely, with Maori and pakeha coming into ever greater contact in the suburbs, there were many complaints by pakeha neighbours of 'unseemly' Maori behaviour. Welfare officers were often called upon to mediate, with the aim of bringing urban Maori 'up to scratch'. The transplanting of traditional hospitality to visitors into an urban environment was quickly identified as a key problem. This, combined with overcrowding and poor housing (especially in inner-city areas), led to numerous tensions over such matters as – reportedly – noise at 'unseemly' hours, 'incessant beer drinking, foul language, and generally bad behaviour'. As the most senior DMA bureaucrat put it in the mid 1960s, 'Maori and island migrants are apt to become unpopular with their pakeha neighbours because of their high-spirited way of enjoying themselves'. Resulting inter-racial tension would drive some Maori, especially those in 'pepper-potted' households, to seek out other Maori for socialising and other purposes, sometimes through the medium of the official committees.[12]

The problems surrounding transference of indigenous cultural and behavioural traits to alien environments were compounded by 'anti-social' and extra-legal behaviour by individuals, especially youths, suddenly freed from the relatively ordered and disciplined life of the marae. In official words, the 'abrupt change from country to city life ... was for the majority of young people the first release from the restraining influence of the family and communal life. The pattern of their upbringing and education has its roots in traditional customs and in the simple rural life of the community', which 'poorly equipped' them to overcome the difficulties of transition to 'a highly individualistic urban life'. A newspaper writer argued, typically, that the 'constant drift of Maoris to the towns' was accompanied by a 'disquieting amount of delinquency' and a disturbing decline of moral standards. Whatever the truth of the many pakeha observations, urbanisation clearly involved ongoing disruption in the social structure of Maori life which had ramifications for how Maori were viewed in mainstream society. This latter, in turn, had implications for how Maori could best reconstruct rangatiratanga in the cities.[13]

It was as a consequence of very many factors that Maori were systemically 'looked down upon' as urbanisation grew. Such prejudice existed at the beginning of the urban migration, when there was 'almost automatic segregation in city slums', something which assisted the development of the pepper-potting policy. '[A]s the white man is confronted with increasing numbers of depressed Maoris, the soil is ripe for the sowing of seeds of racial animosity and strife', wrote the author of a newspaper article in 1952. The increasing interaction of Maori and pakeha in the cities heightened public discourse on race. 'Race relations' in New Zealand had been widely viewed by officials and the public as the best in the world, and even a visiting liberal American academic could write in 1954 of 'little racial discrimination in New Zealand'. Increasingly, however, relationships between pakeha and Maori were taking 'a turn for the worse'.

When interracial contact had been 'virtually non-existent', as one commentator put it, the 'pakeha congratulated himself profusely on his tolerance and humanity, proudly proclaimed to the world that no colour bar existed in New Zealand, and scathingly condemned racial bigots in America and South Africa for their treatment of the Negro'. But with pakeha and Maori now increasingly mixing and living together, racist and ethnocentric attitudes escalated, and incidents of 'racial discrimination' began coming under public scrutiny. Talk of a 'colour bar' being imposed by pakeha upon Maori increased, as did the reporting of discriminatory and racist incidents. There were reports of impediments to Maori people acquiring rented accommodation, securing jobs, drinking in pubs or entering premises of different types, including shops. In 1959, a prominent Maori physician was refused a drink in a hotel, and the publicity and agitation resulting from this and other such incidents led the Prime Minister to make a statement on the 'legal impropriety of such discrimination'.[14]

The legality of exclusions upon Maori was in fact a grey area. In any case, existing or new legislation provided little solution to problems of discrimination in the absence of changes in societal attitudes. The fact was that Maori were often branded as uncivilised and as perpetrators of disorder and crime. This latter attitude could find some support in reports and observations, and Maori leaders were the first to acknowledge the existence of a growing problem. In Manu Bennett's words, the 'equilibrium of Maori youth [became] upset' when they arrived in the city, with consequences that were not atypical in an international context. Observed difficulties of adjustment by young people, however, merely reinforced the prejudice which permeated official and civil society as contact with a people with different customs and lifestyles increased. Indeed, indigenous migrants were frequently perceived as having many negative characteristics. Not only were they felt to be 'happy-go-lucky', they were also seen as work-shy, feckless, dangerous or to be 'taking over' (especially through intermarriage).

One writer to the minister in 1952 put an inchoate pakeha set of perceptions in their extreme form: 'allowing the Maoris to associate and work freely amongst the European population is a disgrace. I do not despise any race, but racial purity is a necessity'. With 'the Maori absorbing the Pakeha through inter marriage to an alarming degree ... [t]he colour bar should be put in operation at once to save the white race'. The writer implored the government to stop 'paying for the Maoris to be lazy, dress up, and procreate' through the welfare state's system of pensions and benefits. Some observers argued that urban-dwelling Maori often seemed to internalise the stereotypes they had encountered, and either took on stereotypical characteristics or tried to obliterate their own culture in their daily lives. This was resonant of an international phenomenon of subsumed peoples seemingly 'accepting' the inferiority and self-loathing ascribed to them by the colonisers. As a study from the 1960s put it, 'to the extent that the Maori subscribes to the "bad" prototypal image of himself, he becomes his own oppressor'. One Maori migrant recalled how, on moving to Wellington, she 'pretended to be a Pākehā because [she] was ashamed'. But even when she desperately tried to conform in the required ways, she remained 'Maori' in the eyes of the city folk. 'We felt like intruders in our own country'.

Racial stereotypes also held sway in official circles. When the Commissioner of Police proposed recruiting Maori to the regular police in 1950, his senior officers were 'almost unanimously opposed' for fear that the recruits would be lazy or susceptible to tribal influence. The fact that the police did begin to recruit Maori from late 1952 (following a similar development in the defence forces) indicates that, even inside the official world, attitudes were changing in line with new ideas spreading through society. But as yet, such voices were in a distinct minority, and the alteration in police policy also reflected another circumstance – that the perceived threat to order from urban

Maori was considered too great for the Maori warden system alone to handle. The Minister of Maori Affairs chose to emphasise the incipient changes in public and official thinking: 'Not only can Maori constables be of great assistance working among the Maori people in straightening out some of the present social difficulties, but more important, we would be doing away with discrimination.' But with urban disorder among migrants increasing, the social control argument became stronger. From 1955, there were greater efforts to attract Maori into the police, with the permanent head of Maori Affairs, Tipi Ropiha, asking his district officers to seek out recruits: success in this would assist 'in relation to our drinking problems and our own warden system'.[15]

Urban Adjustment

Whatever the prejudices within officialdom, there were no thoughts of attempting to discourage Maori urban migration. Urbanisation was seen as a way by which all citizens could benefit from the flourishing economy, with Maori contributing mostly to the unskilled and semi-skilled industries. It was a better investment, the Crown believed, than bringing in assisted immigrants from overseas. The welfarist policies which the National government had taken over from Labour remained available to assist. While 'social problems' among Maori were better able to be contained in a rural, marae-based environment, the short-term social costs of adjustment to urban life would be considerably outweighed by the public good benefits. Not only would Maori join the growing work sites of an industrialising New Zealand, they would internalise the rhythms of industrial and social discipline as a result of living and working in the city environment. A number of Maori themselves saw a need for 'adaptation' to the western values of 'order and regularity' in the interests of urban adjustment. An article in the *New Zealand Listener* in 1950 presented the views of a 'Maori Housewife': 'A young girl who goes to work in town has to adapt or her way will be much harder. She must conform within narrow limits of dress, neither beyond nor beneath pakeha fashion, she must learn the industrial meaning of time, learn to do a job she probably isn't trained for, and conform with the custom of saving money so that it lasts from pay day to pay day.'

From the late 1940s, officials began to manage urban migration in ways designed to ease the pain of adjustment – for the sake not only of the individuals concerned but also for that of the wider society itself. Many urban migrants were temporarily housed in workers' camps in the two main North Island cities and their suburbs. Blocks of flats were built, schemes to build houses for rental or purchase were put in place, and loans were offered to migrant Maori to purchase or renovate houses. Officials had earlier developed an apprenticeship training scheme for migrants with appropriate aptitudes, and in 1949 Cabinet approved the construction of hostels for this purpose. In 1951, the Maori Affairs and Labour Departments established hostels in Wellington and Auckland, and Rotorua and Christchurch followed in mid-decade.

The hostels were to provide 'equal opportunities' for Maori to become tradespeople. They aimed to create an 'atmosphere that makes for that social stability and security' especially needed by newly-arrived Maori youths. The government often subsidised church and welfare organisations in large towns like Hamilton and Gisborne to assist migrating youth. But there was a growing concentration of migration to a handful of urban destinations from the mid-1950s, especially Auckland and Wellington. By the end of the decade, the Crown had systematised its assistance to Maori urban migrants into a coordinated adjustment policy involving temporary or permanent accommodation, employment and general 'guidance'. By 1961, well over half of the DMA's houses were being built in urban areas, and by the middle of the 1960s, three-quarters of state dwellings built for Maori were in urban spaces.[16]

Migrants did not stop 'being tribal' in the new environment, whatever the pressures and temptations to fully assimilate. However far they were living from their home marae, whanau, hapu or iwi, most kept up contact with friends and relatives back in their tribal homelands. Urban households would act as the anchor points for those from rural marae who visited or migrated to the city, and the hospitality would be reciprocated. Urban families would 'return home' for marriages, christenings, twenty-firsts and funerals/tangi, sometimes establishing whanau funds to be able to afford such contingencies. As the chair of the Waitangi Tribunal would later put it, speaking of his people, keeping up such connections reaffirmed 'our meaning for life'. The concept of 'home', then, was not constrained by geography, and many at first were not necessarily wedded to staying in town once assets had been accumulated. Many newly-arrived Maori were too preoccupied with coping with difficult adjustments to their daily lives to do very much, at least initially, by way of reorganising collectively. But even if they seldom or never returned to the rural pa, few completely abandoned all vestiges of Maori culture or identification, despite the myth peddled by many pakeha (including officials and scholars) that 'detribalisation' was rampant. More broadly, Maori did not cease to 'be Maori'. They sought out fellow Maori in social and other circumstances, such as at playcentres, in church congregations and sports clubs, and outside school gates. Established households became centres of Maori life, whether or not people were of the same tribe. Such environments were microcosms of Maoridom in a pakeha landscape to a degree that most non-Maori never realised.

Lifestyles and interactions in such microcosms often segued into participation in the larger, voluntarist organisations covered in Chapter Four. Suffice to say here, in the immediate post-war years and early 1950s, Maori-run institutions strengthened or emerged to cater for the needs of urban-dwelling Maori, assisted by urban-based tribal groupings and marae. The most significant of the new associations were Wellington's Ngati Poneke complex (which arose in 1937 out of earlier religious and welfarist formations) and Auckland's Akarana Maori Association (which included liberal pakeha). These reflected an appreciation that one way of establishing ethno-cultural collectivity among the individuals from various tribes who had come to the urban spaces was to establish independent Maori structures with pan-tribal membership. They would be run along non-tribal lines, while typically exhibiting a whanau-like atmosphere. Such initiatives gradually came about in larger towns as well as cities. They would eventually culminate in the establishment of pan-tribal urban marae and service institutions. Various cooperative efforts in West Auckland, for example, would lead first to the founding of Hoani Waititi Marae and then to an urban authority, Te Whanau o Waipareira Trust, in 1984.

Such developments did tend to redirect Maori attention away from the homeland marae and their tikanga, especially for those generations brought up or born in the cities. Other factors contributed to this process. The most obvious was intermarriage, which generally led to the pakeha culture predominating in the urban household. Some factors were more subtle. Although Maori tended to have the lowest paid jobs, constituting a 'race-based' sub-sector of a proletarianising workforce, there were 'trickle down' benefits from a 1950s economy whose health had been boosted by the effects of the Korean War. It was a time of boundless socio-economic optimism in most sectors of society, with continuing economic expansion and very low unemployment rates. In public perception at least, there was nothing to stop individuals or families (Maori or pakeha) thriving. Economic opportunities for Maori workers, even though the urban jobs available to them were among the least appealing, did help many gain confidence in their capacities *as individuals*. This, in turn, fed into the individualistic ideology so pronounced within the ruling National Party and the dominant interests it overtly represented. It might be said that whereas Maoridom attempted to transfer collective autonomy to the cities, the pakeha ethos was to proclaim the sanctity of individual autonomy. Insofar as the pressures of assimilation worked, many Maori lost some (but very seldom all) of their tribal or even Maori identity. As elders increasingly noted, the harsh facts of being a displaced minority within dominant cultural and socio-political structures meant that assimilationist pressures were intense and, to a degree, successful.[17]

Many urbanising Maori, better off materially than ever before, pinned future hopes not on their iwi, hapu or whanau, but on the employment, cultural and educational opportunities of the city. The DMA journal endorsed such views, and argued that European attributes assisted all Maori. 'Education and the possession of European skills are the highest qualifications for leadership in Auckland', it stated. Their acquisition was 'necessary because of the close association of Maori and European'. Possessing pakeha skills and knowledge did not mean leaving Maoridom behind: 'While the educated leader is given prestige by virtue of his education, he maintains his position through concretely expressed interests in the welfare of the Maori community.' At a time when government and white society were increasingly unsympathetic to any aspirations that would lead to the constitution of 'a race apart', however, the integrationist pressures of the pakeha lifestyle and education were intense: 'Maori welfare' could mean any one of a number of things. Many new urban dwellers, while uneasy at some of the consequences of migration, saw their welfare improved through enhancements to their previously restricted lifestyles. Rural marae-based leaderships instead often saw a decline in traditional morality and sense of tribal pride amongst their people who had gone to the towns and cities.[18]

State and pakeha opposition to Maori socio-political autonomy, and the realities of life in a pepper-potted urban landscape, meant that large numbers of migrants mostly just got on quietly with adjusting to the urban environment on a day-to-day level. It was observing this phenomenon on the surface which made many pakeha conclude that urban-based Maori were drifting away from a collective quest for control over their destiny, substituting instead the ethos of individualised endeavour; officials and scholars saw their evolutionist-based preconceptions vindicated. Some pakeha who were invited (sometimes due to intermarriage) to take up leadership roles within the Maori population in the cities, however, saw that Maori perspectives remained, and sought to combine these with pakeha worldviews in new ways. In such endeavours, they worked alongside very many Maori, including Maori scholars.

While encouraging education as a 'training ground for effective future Maori leadership' and a prerequisite for doing well in the 'pakeha economy', observers noted that the emerging Maori leaders who were at home in the pakeha world still had cause to frequently interact with 'the kaumatua, the kuia and the rangatahi leader'. These more traditional leaders were required within urban Maoridom for 'specific occasions', especially when 'Maori deals with Maori'. An occasional return (if that) to the rural marae for a tangi was not, whatever most pakeha or officials might think, going to represent the future of urbanised Maoridom. Few believed it possible to turn back the clock, but many felt that aspects of Maori community could and should be reconstructed or reconfigured in the cities. Urban Maori leaders (supported by some pakeha) took many steps to ensure that 'while western education was highly valued, the Maori community still prospered, as a separate cultural and social entity'. It would develop in its own ways, defying the official rules if necessary. One urban 'tribal committee' had five more members than the statutory limit, seeing itself as an elected, pan-tribal community group rather than as an official body, and causing the DMA to sigh that 'reducing the number was almost impossible'. The author Bill Pearson put matters thus: Maori were seeking 'to be Maoris among Maoris when they want to be', doing it their own way wherever this was possible.

Crown Policies and Social Attitudes

Increasingly, as bureaucrats and politicians realised that Maoridom was not about to disappear entirely into the 'urban jungle', Maori leaders were consulted on public issues. In such transactions, they managed to an extent to have Maori culture and aspirations taken seriously. In the early 1950s, for example, they resisted pressure to abolish Maori schools which was exerted under the rubric of removing 'race discrimination'. In 1955, the Minister of Education established a committee with strong Maori representation to consider such issues. This was the first time Maori had taken part in national-level policy formulation on education. The committee appreciated that Maori schools, while they had begun as assimilationist devices, had become assets to many Maori communities. It concluded that such schools should eventually become absorbed into mainstream education run by the Education Boards, but that this should only be done under persuasion. Meanwhile, all schools requiring it should get special assistance for 'more recognition for Maori culture, including the Maori language', building on what Labour had introduced in the 1930s. And all New Zealand's schools should pay greater attention to matters such as Maori history and Maori arts and crafts. Such approaches were integrated into government policy, and the committee – eventually called the National Committee on Maori Education – was reconvened on an annual basis.[19]

There was also some assistance from government departments to aid communal adaptation to the cities in Maori-friendly ways, with Maori Affairs pronouncing that it did 'not seek to impose standards from without'. It interpreted 'Maori welfare' in such a way that it 'concern[ed] itself with almost every phase of life', and its policies did often accommodate a collectivist ethos. There was, for example, some effort at building 'group housing ... where Maori communal spirit is strong' on gifted or purchased land in towns such as Opotiki or Rotorua. Some Crown support went to the informal initiatives of Maori in the cities, including those developed within the official committee structure. The formation of youth clubs and other social groups to 'cushion the effect of migration from one way of life to another' gained Welfare Division backing, and financial and other assistance was made available.[20]

But the fact remained that, in general, Crown policies remained posited upon an expected disappearance of Maoridom beneath western values and lifestyles and through intermarriage. The state's overarching policies continued to promote the hastening of what were seen to be natural evolutionary processes – accelerating what urban migration and the arrival of modernity among Maori were believed to be already effecting. In this environment, the reconstruction of Maori organisational values and communal ways would always be difficult. Conformist pressures were led by a strong and paternalist state, which played a key role in such matters as economic management, wealth creation, the direction of labour and the construction of housing. At the same time as assisting Maori initiatives, officials and ministers believed that once Maori had cast off their 'tribal shackles', they should preferably join (if anything) groups that were non-racially based, such as school committees.

Even pakeha sympathetic to the idea of retaining some aspects of Maoritanga tended to be hard-line on the need for thorough westernisation, as expressed in a 1952 article in the *New Zealand Herald*: 'The aim should be, in education or whatever else, to weld into one nation ... The Maori can with equal pride preserve the best of his culture and recall traditions and history, as do the English, Scots, Irish, and Welsh. But it will be well if, like them, he becomes first and fundamentally a New Zealander, whose culture is and will remain basically European.' Another newspaper article expressed an even more typical stance: the 'Maori is now becoming a useful worker ... More and more he casts off the old tribal shackles. He can best be helped and encouraged by treating him simply as a New Zealander'. Even conservative pakeha could foresee, approvingly, a society of legal and social equals, some of whom happened to be brown-skinned – although skin colour would preferably lighten through continuing intermarriage.

The theoretical vision of rapid assimilation, however, was complicated by the practical ethnocentric and racist barriers that became apparent when pakeha and Maori began living and mixing together in an urban setting. It was because of such difficulties, as well as the evolutionist assumptions embedded deeply into pakeha culture, that liberal and left-wing pakeha generally failed to support the Maori quest for rangatiratanga (although usually being more sympathetic than most to retention of some aspects of Maoritanga). In other words, it was partly as a result of the discrimination, indignities and socio-economic inequalities encountered by Maori in the towns and cities that 'progressive thought' tended to stress *removal* of legal and other distinctions between Maori and pakeha. When Labour opposition leader Walter Nash mounted a campaign to make discrimination against Maori illegal, there were many public calls to overturn *all* official recognition of differences between ethnicities, even where these operated in ways which helped overcome social inequalities. Broader principles reflecting humanist, class-conflict, social-democratic, Christian-socialist and other philosophies also had a role to play in promoting such 'egalitarian' ideals.

Thus, while official New Zealand tolerated differences between Maori and pakeha, including some legalised differentiation generally supported by Maori (such as tribal committees and wardens), most left-of-centre people continued to stress that which the pre-war Labour Party had stood for: sameness of treatment; 'equality'. One commentator, in arguing that assimilation was 'inevitable', suggested that it was 'a logical result of the "equality" for which the Maori so persistently strives'. Indeed, some writers of the time equated assimilation with equality and contrasted it to the 'distinction' or 'segregation' which in other parts of the world kept the races apart. More broadly, for those concerned with social and economic equality (including a number of Maori), assimilation was an unquestionable good. 'Assimilation of the two races', in the words of a Maori adult education tutor, was 'an ideal'. Even the Ngati Poneke association reportedly considered assimilation a goal worth striving for, while Maori university and training college students were similarly recorded as agreeing that a form of 'integration' with Europeans was necessary.[21]

Of course, notions such as difference, sameness, equality, integration and assimilation, to which Maori and pakeha commentators, decision-makers and others appealed, could mean different things to different people, and their meaning could change in different circumstances. There was a particular lack of clarity in the 1950s over what such concepts ultimately meant, and where Maori urbanisation might or should take both Maori and the nation. Sympathetic officials and others tried to differentiate between integration and full, or near-full, assimilation. An anthropologist employed by the DMA, John Booth, argued that Maori could be 'integrated with not assimilated by Europeans'. His department declared its intention to help 'perpetuate Maori culture', while simultaneously facilitating 'full integration into the social and economic structure of the country'. But a very strong current of public and official opinion clearly favoured Maori adopting European ways and abandoning their culture almost entirely. This was seen to be the price of progress in a Social-Darwinist world. Maori should behave, in the ironic words of Auckland anthropology professor Ralph Piddington, like 'good little Pakehas'.

But for most Maori, living in the urban, modern and 'pakeha' world implied nothing of the sort, and they had some allies within that world. Anthropologists, for example, often publicly defended the Maori right to difference within a westernised New Zealand. Raymond Firth suggested that Maori sought 'full participation and they want, at the same time, to retain ... elements of Maori culture'. Piddington, in particular, strongly rebuked pakeha New Zealand for its 'cultural arrogance'. He was accused by some of leaning towards the defence of 'racial separatists', but continued openly to condemn the idea of 'racial and cultural absorption' – the scenario in which Maori were to 'solve their social problems by rapidly becoming like pakehas' – as a 'demographic pipe-dream and a very dangerous one'. He warned that there was a need to avoid Maori in the cities becoming little more than a 'brown proletariat' in a white world. In the struggle to ensure that urban Maori did not form a permanent 'under-privileged and despised community', he argued, the preservation of Maori culture was essential – as was a move away from 'absorption or assimilation towards encouraging Maori to solve their own problems in their own way'.[22]

In 1957, however, the Minister of Maori Affairs was having none of this kind of approach. 'The policy of the government is that Maori and European form one people. Everything that is done in legislation ... stems from that basic assumption', he wrote. 'With Maoris and Europeans living together, side by side in towns and villages, the idea of Maori political autonomy would be quite impracticable. The ... only type of autonomy that exists is in the form of ... Tribal Committees which ... have the task of promoting social and economic progress.' In view of all the obstacles, from racist popular sentiment to official policy, it is scarcely surprising that the decade was not one where rangatiratanga aspirations could be *significantly* progressed. One historian has even suggested that the 1950s 'saw basically a hiatus in Maori political life'.

Nevertheless, politico-cultural aspirations among Maori could be and were progressed when they were placed firmly within 'official' structures and hegemonic discourses. That way they had chances of state and/or pakeha support – if 'Maoriness' were redefined to fit modern life and the urban setting, it could be tolerated until intermarriage and supposed western superiority led to its long expected demise. Such official and mainstream cultural recognition (however reluctant) of 'the Maori Other' became, in fact, a significant weapon in the arsenal available to promote Maori self-identification from the 1950s. It assisted a countervailing tendency to those powerful forces in politics and society which viewed the urbanisation process as little more than a medium for rapid assimilation. The vague post-war concept of 'Maori' held by the state and many pakeha varied enormously from its expression by various movements within Maoridom, but at least it existed and remained a force to be reckoned with.[23]

Chapter 3

Autonomy and Official Institutions

Trust Boards

The Maori struggle for control of their own affairs continued through the 1950s within a variety of state sanctioned forums, as well as in other ways. While official committees often attempted to provide a delicate balance between Crown control and Maori autonomy, so too did trust boards. The trust board model had been pioneered by the Crown in the 1920s to allow tribes to manage compensation payments which had been negotiated. The model was later developed to provide tribal representation for more general purposes. But trust boards also provided the Crown with a considerable degree of control.

The boards were constrained by official accountability procedures under both general trust and dedicated legislation. Officials scrutinised board activities and spending, and the Crown held ultimate power over the boards and their personnel. Though tribally elected, board members were appointed by the Governor-General, and the endorsement of the Minister of Maori Affairs was required for the chairs and secretaries boards selected. The minister was not only in final control of both budgets and the purchase and disposal of land and resources, but could also 'direct that board administration be investigated'. Such interventions could lead to 'adjustments' in operations, as bureaucrats put it. In short, trust boards were scarcely regarded by the Crown as agents of Maori autonomy except in a very attenuated sense. Even conservative pakeha, seeing the usefulness of boards as tools for accommodating and containing Maori counter-discourse, could approve of them.

For tribes, however, boards were foci for communal reinvigoration and sites for working towards controlling their own affairs. They offered opportunities for retaining or regaining a degree of autonomy in a generally unsympathetic socio-political environment. In the view of many board and tribal members, too, trust boards embodied a certain degree of state recognition of tribal authority. When controversy arose around systematising and consolidating boards under the Maori Trust Boards Act in 1955, the desirability of the boards went unquestioned by tribal leaders.

Both parties, Crown and Maori, thus saw benefits in trust boards, although neither considered the arrangement perfect. So entrenched did the trust board model become that the acting head of the Department of Maori Affairs noted with great confidence in 1960 that any future resolutions of historical claims would 'result in the setting up of additional trust boards'. The mere fact that he was in effect predicting future reparations regimes placed him firmly among the 'progressive' pakeha of that time. But his view that trust boards were appropriate vehicles for compensation was held partly because they offered a means for the Crown to further its welfarist and assimilationist agendas.

Government and officials had hoped that settlements between 1944 and 1946 with the three groupings which had traditionally and persistently presented the largest claims (Ngai Tahu, Taranaki and Waikato–Maniapoto) would, by providing annual payments, help remove impediments to 'progress' among Maori. The settlements, coupled with drift to the cities and towns, were supposed primarily to smooth the way for assimilating Maori into the welfare state. Although the payments were later seen as less than generous, at the time they underpinned the administration of trust boards established by compensation legislation. They also allowed some small beginnings to be made on closing the large gaps in living standards between Maori and pakeha. But not only did the Crown soon realise that there were significant difficulties in implementing such plans, it was also quickly reminded that there were many other tribes seeking compensation for their historical losses.

Negotiations between officials and various non-compensated tribes had begun after the 1946 Waikato–Maniapoto settlement, and the late 1940s and the 1950s saw further compensation agreements reached and new boards established accordingly. One was provided with £22,500 compensation for matters relating to the purchase of the Aorangi Block; a Wairoa board received £20,000 on account of forced cession of the Kauhouroa Block to the Crown; and its Taitokerau equivalent was founded on a £47,000 payment in compensation for the Crown's taking of 'surplus land' (land deemed early in the life of the colony not to have been validly purchased from Maori before annexation). In 1957, a Tuhoe delegation saw Minister of Maori Affairs Corbett about broken promises over roading in the Urewera. The minister, suggesting that any compensation would need to be monetary, typically advised that this should be channelled through a trust board. When the negotiations were completed, the Tuhoe Maori Trust Board was established with a lump sum of £100,000 to use for the 'betterment of the people'.[1]

The settlement sums, especially when income could be guaranteed by annual payments, not only provided funding to run basic tribal affairs, but also enabled boards to expand their scope of activity for the benefit of their members. Funds could be used to assist with education or farming, for example. In this sense, the (still small number of) tribal trust boards were in a better position than the official committees, which were required to earn their own funds and to supplement these by applications for subsidies. The Maori Trust Boards Act of 1955 endorsed aspects of the social and economic role which had gradually been developed by the boards.

Over time, in fact, the concept of the trust board came to have considerable flexibility for the Crown as well as the tribes. The Aupouri Trust Board was established to 'control income from certain land and capital funds from a communal enterprise at Te Kao', but received no payment from the Crown. The Tuhoe-Waikaremoana Maori Trust Board, in which the Waikaremoana reserves and lake bed had been vested, had 'taken on a broader role than just the administration of "compensation" funds' under provisions in the new legislation. Widely seen to act 'as a tribal voice', it established 'young people's committees' to encourage continuity in tribal management, and it controlled significant areas of land vested in it by the Maori Land Court. In time, trust boards would come to boost their income by investing portions of their annuities or lump-sum compensation payments in, for example, local-body stock or rental housing. Each board developed its own priorities, many of them aiming to balance the needs of the present with those of the future. Ngai Tahu's board provided assistance to needy tribal members, giving out around 500 grants per annum by the late 1960s, and making educational grants which approached similar numbers. It also involved itself in hospital, harbour and power boards in the 1960s, and purchased blocks of flats in Wellington. While it had been spending a third of its income on administration in 1953, this had been reduced to less than an eighth within two decades.[2]

The concept of trust boards became very significant for the post-war aspirations of many Maori, especially after the Crown saw the benefits in expanding the system to include different types of trusts. Trust boards were viewed by various Maori groupings as providing a means for pursuing economic development, as forums that could reflect Maori cultural and other values, and as leaders in the fight for recognition of rangatiratanga. A number of the politico-cultural roles that they took on reflected a propensity by their members and beneficiaries to subvert their official raison d'etre. Some boards developed a momentum that took them well beyond the Crown's comfort zone. On the other hand, the state, too, could capitalise on the multiple uses to which boards could be put. It could encourage them, for example, to become adjuncts of the Crown in providing a variety of services for their people which the state would otherwise have to organise (at least in theory).

Moreover, the Trust Boards Act, in addition to expanding board responsibilities, 'clarified' their role after a series of tribal actions and assertions through the boards had troubled the Crown. After pondering the appropriate degree of latitude that should be allowed on issues relating to land, for example, the politicians secured restrictions on boards' abilities to regain a landed base for their tribes. Funding extensive, collectively-orientated land development within tribal rohe was seen as turning the clock back at a time when Maori urbanisation and assimilation, rather than rurality and tribalism, were to be encouraged above all else. This aspect of the legislation, Maori argued, breached the original agreements with some of the boards, quite apart from more generally hindering tribal aspirations relating to turangawaewae. But Parliament's decision on the issue was a clear reminder that the boards were established by the Crown and accountable to it, their powers conferred by its grace. As with the 1900 Maori councils, boards remained heavily constrained in the degree of autonomy they were allowed to exercise.

In fact, despite (and because of) their efforts to expand their activities, the trust boards were increasingly pressured to concentrate on functions reflecting the Crown's original intentions under the trust board model. The 1955 Act thus specified that Maori trust boards needed to focus on matters which were essentially within the Crown's area of responsibility: health, social and economic welfare, education, vocational training and the like. Board attempts to redirect predetermined uses of Crown funding were not well received by the monitoring bureaucrats. 'The Maori Affairs' provided continual 'guidance' as to how state-provided monies might best be spent, within a restricted range of permissible activities. Crown spokesmen openly remonstrated that 'education is not assisted more liberally' by the boards, which were ideally expected to devote at least half of their income to educational matters.

The trust boards, however, continued to attempt not only to determine their own priorities within official parameters, but also to operate outside them. When defending such activities to the Maori Affairs bureaucracy, they drew upon their terms of reference, which included the words: 'Such other purposes as the boards determine'. When heading Maori Affairs in 1960, Jack Hunn noted the discrepancies between the formal (and, he might have added, often bureaucratically imposed) limitations on the trust boards and the 'seemingly wide power' in their briefs. He declared that, in actual fact, their powers had been 'probably exercised without limitation'. While this was an exaggeration, a later analysis concluded that until new legislation was passed in 1988, it was 'notorious that Trust Boards were engaged in activity beyond and with only a casual regard for the limitations of their statutory authorization'. While the Crown never stopped intervening in board activities which it considered a challenge to its authority (or to financial propriety), it clearly turned a blind eye for a very long time to many small (and a few not-so-small) usurpations. In the final analysis, trust boards remained, in the eyes of both state and judicial bodies, convenient repositories of funding for state-required tasks. For many Maori, too, the advantages presented by boards overrode their disadvantages.[3]

The Official Committees

Along with many other indigenous people globally, Maori were becoming experienced at utilising for their own ends the laws, practices and modes of representation imposed upon them. By 1952 the number of committees had increased under the new government, up from 381 tribal committees to 440 and from 65 tribal executives to 75, a reflection partly of their expansion to towns and cities. The expansion had been encouraged by National, once it had seen early on in its administration that the MWO's Maori institutions could offer (among other things) useful mechanisms for urban adjustment. Committees could become vehicles for social as well as economic 'progress', 'fitting the Maori fully and usefully into the community'. This could contribute to an emerging 'National Blend' that would 'weld all in one nation'. From the beginning, the system had been provided with model by-laws which reflected Crown ambitions. The committees faced sanctions if they deviated too far from these blueprints or from other administrative 'suggestions'. Officials attended committee meetings ex officio 'for the purpose of guiding and leading as far as possible the activities of the Executives and Tribal Committees'.

While the committees gradually became key vehicles for rangatiratanga, albeit stronger in some areas than others, the struggle was always uphill. In 1956, Maori Affairs reminded Maori bluntly that the committees came under departmental direction. In face of such attitudes and associated difficulties, resignations were many. A number of committees (especially those in depopulating areas) were scarcely functioning by mid-decade, although state assessments of inactivity sometimes reflected disinclination by committees to submit paperwork and/or inclination to do things other than those outlined in their official terms of reference.

Some committees proved 'more successful in carrying out administration directives than in formulating the plans and activities and hopes of the people'. These and others tended to take heart from the concessionary tone of state pronouncements; the system was said to constitute 'the true nature of Maori self-government', supposedly giving Maori greater local government powers than those possessed by the general population. While this was hardly the case in reality, committees were able frequently to pressure local government agencies on behalf of their people, with considerable success. A tribal committee in Onehunga, for example, persuaded the borough council to provide Maori with a community centre at very low rent, and established sporting, social and cultural subcommittees which themselves worked with local authorities. Committees sometimes dealt confidently with central authority too. To combat racism in its area, the Pukekohe tribal committee secured support for the establishment of a Maori-dominated school, an institution which in turn became 'a rallying point' for the retention and revival of local Maori power, culture and 'philosophy'. Through such efforts, the committee gradually increased its ability to act locally, with the authority born of successful ventures. Such activities, as one observer put it in 1952, were at the forefront of a 'social revolution on a small scale'.[4]

Insofar as Maori were successful in the MWO/Welfare Division at carving out their own autonomistic spaces, however, this generally needed to be in association with performing functions required by the Crown. The Onehunga committee, for all its autonomist impulses, carried out many a function or activity approved by state officials as fitting into their adjustment and assimilation agendas. In the rural areas, many concentrated on procuring state assistance to raise the living standards of those who remained in the rohe. They hoped that, in the process, a viable tribal core would stay on rather than migrate. In the early 1950s, Maharaia Winiata found in a semi-rural locality that both the tribal committee's official franchise and its links with the Welfare Division gave mana and prestige to its leaders, providing a base from which to pursue development for the people. With success in obtaining subsidies and other funding, the committee gained greater influence. But, echoing leaders who feared 'governmental invasion into Maori affairs', the tribe was acutely aware that cooperation with the Crown came at a price that could, if they were not careful, undermine the development of rangatiratanga. In short, trade-offs had to be negotiated very carefully, with Maori in each local area having to assess how far they would accept state help, and in what fashion.

Broadly speaking, urban committees in the 1950s developed in different ways from their rural counterparts. Both Joan Metge and Winiata, observing the committee system in an Auckland urban context, noted that members were selected on a wide range of criteria that included modern as well as customary factors. While traditional leaders tended to dominate committee proceedings in rural environments, the 'educated person [was] very much in evidence' in the urban committee. It was in this context that a kind of division of labour arose, with better educated Maori brought 'to the fore' and traditional leaders (especially elders – kaumatua and kuia) called upon mostly for ceremonial and similar purposes. The search for leaders able to operate in a pakeha environment could be a slow one. Development of the necessary expertise was not helped by deliberate educational policies which stereotyped

Maori in ways which restricted their potential; in 1956, less than 3.5% of the Maori workforce lay within the 'professional, technical, and related fields'.

Auckland city's tribal executive, representing the combined weight of its half dozen committees, was (in contrast to many of the rural areas) the 'most important body' in the local official system. Its leadership frequently negotiated with and lobbied non-Maori organisations, both official and non-official. But the problems of representing a newly-arrived and hence relatively atomised population were manifold. Many young Maori did not know of the existence of the committee system, partly because of their mobility. Those who did know, were often not inclined to attend meetings or other activities sponsored by the committees: partly because of problems of transport, timing and the like, but also due to a much reported disrespect for authority among those 'liberated' from the constraints of the marae. All this was in contrast to many marae-based committees, where attendance was relatively easy to obtain from those in the surrounding pa, for reasons which included proximity, tribal social control mechanisms and lack of alternative activities.

In Auckland, as in other urban areas, there were tensions within the system between old and young, and many difficulties inherent in a situation in which leaders dealt with constituents from a multiplicity of tribes. Their limited access, in a non-tribal operating environment, to both coercive power and tribal sanctions was just one of many problems they identified. The urban leaders, in short, had to struggle hard to bring the community together, and at one point, only two of Auckland's six committees were functioning well. Despite all the problems, however, the results of the work of these two committees – as well as that of the executive – indicated that the rewards could be great. Committees frequently came to focus their attention on specific tasks, reflecting a combination of what they were good at and what their communities most needed. Many of the urban ones sought mostly to alleviate difficulties surrounding drinking and other causes of social disruption, often using the services of their wardens extensively in doing so. Over and above holding such negative social control roles, successful committees were significant and proactive players in carving out viable Maori communities in pakeha cities and suburbs.[5]

Anthropological studies have provided good insights into the workings of the MWO/Welfare Division's committees. Ranginui Walker's Auckland-based study of a tribal committee found, like other studies, that its members focused their work on a community centre and its attendant activities. Such foci of committee attention often had a degree of pakeha involvement – sometimes, but by no means always, as a result of intermarriage. In the new suburbs, committees would often engage in infrastructural development that would assist all people living in the community regardless of ethnicity. This reflected a reality that pakeha who did not come into any great contact with Maori did not fully appreciate (if at all): Maori aspirations were not separatist, but were geared to establishing Maori control and exercising rangatiratanga in its many forms *within* the dominant political economy.

Maori-run institutions opening the doors to pakeha might also be seen in some circumstances as a reflection of the overwhelmingly assimilationist paradigm in mainstream society. In urban settings, in particular, pressures to conform to pakeha ways were intense and sustained. The MWO's institutions had been established by the Crown partly with such goals in mind, and even initially resistant Maori could be inexorably drawn into such an agenda – taking on western beliefs and behavioural patterns and helping impose them on other members of the Maori community. Official committees, in fact, often became agencies for 'policing the mind' as well as 'policing the body' – often with the help of their wardens for these two (interrelated) purposes. In a typical case, a welfare officer warned a tribal committee in 1950 that if it did not bring a family 'up to scratch' in its attitudes and activities, the family's house would be placed under official observation until matters improved. In such circumstances, committees had little choice but to work with the family or risk even greater state intervention. In assisting their own people, committees often had to accept hegemonic 'received wisdom' as their guiding norm. At best, the committees constituted 'separate but parallel strategies of adaptation ... on terms that respect[ed] Maori cultural values', but in which the forces of 'socio-cultural separation and self-determination' were necessarily in problematic 'interplay [with] the forces of assimilation and adaptation'.

By the later 1950s, committees operating under the MSEA Act which did not engage in 'approved' activities were receiving little official support, or none at all if they were carrying out activities of which the Crown strongly disapproved. Many were struggling financially and in other ways. A number of those which did meet with official approval had become limited in their foci, and some of them had reportedly become compromised in their search for effective rangatiratanga by the nature (and sometimes sheer load) of Crown requirements. Nevertheless, many committees achieved some kind of equilibrium between the demands of the Crown and their own autonomist aspirations, and this was sufficient to ensure that the state did not abolish the institution. The flaxroots components of the Welfare Division could no longer be seen, even by the most conservative of bureaucrats and politicians, as a potential rival to state power. An American observer at the time concluded that the very best Maori could hope for was no more than 'a certain measure' of cultural, rather than political, 'autonomy and separateness'.[6]

Regional Organising

The tribal committees and tribal executives served as vehicles for communication for both the Crown and Maori. They were used by officials for sending messages and instructions into the heartland of Maoridom. And as conduits for Maori concerns in a way that 'fully official' bodies could not match, they could provide early warnings for officials and politicians of problems ahead. This often led, however, to the Crown sidestepping rather than addressing Maori concerns. If their aspirations to run their own affairs were to be even partly met, many Maori believed, devolved authority to a higher level than that embodied in the 1945 legislation was needed. There was increasing appreciation within the Crown, too, that such a development might prove to be of national benefit. Politicians and bureaucrats debated how, and how far, to further place authority in the hands of Maori institutions. In 1945, the government had refused not just national but also regional representation for the MWO's committee system, wary of the power this might give Maoridom to pursue separatist designs. But before long, officials were noting that, however independently they operated, the tribal committees and executives did not pose any real threat to state authority. With Maori aspirations being expressed mainly within Crown sovereigntist parameters, the official committee system's usefulness to the state outweighed its disadvantages. Thus, when tribal executives began liaising and engaging in informal, regional-level organising activities, there was little alarm within official circles.

Spearheaded by Waiariki tribal executives, Maori leaders took steps to institutionalise such initiatives in the early 1950s. Some began first to plan and then to form unofficial 'district councils' of tribal executives on a regional basis. The new levels of representation were established, reportedly, 'with an enthusiasm that brought new life' to the committee system. Once more the Crown accepted the logic of and the uses for this development. Before long, the new regional bodies were suggesting that the Crown should authorise a national Maori organisation comprised of district council representatives. This idea of a national body which could provide a central channel of communication with the minister was strongly mooted at a conference of tribal executives in 1952.

Initially, the Department of Maori Affairs 'wholeheartedly' endorsed these various developments, partly because of the model provided by the Maori Women's Welfare League, which operated successfully at regional and national as well as flaxroots levels. Whatever his preconceptions before taking up the Maori Affairs portfolio, Ernest Corbett had to address the realities of the issues in front of him. He was persuaded by his officials that a national Maori body, given that it would be constrained by its relationship with the DMA and the functions established in the 1945 statute, could assist him in his tasks. In 1953, the minister gave executive approval not only for officials to cooperate with the district councils but also for a national-level organisation to be established to operate in liaison with the Welfare Division.

Almost at once, however, the inherent struggle between Crown authority and indigenous autonomy threatened the viability of such promising developments for Maoridom. The district councils quickly joined forces to oppose new items on the government's flourishing assimilationist agenda. They protested at aspects of planned new legislation, and deplored the exclusion of Maori representation from key public events. District councils were especially critical of proposals for further land alienation which Corbett had circulated through the Welfare Division's systems for comment. The minister had not expected responses that were fundamentally opposed to governmental plans, an indication of the Crown's inability to fully understand the strength of rangatiratanga within the committee structure it had nurtured.

Some of the critical feedback came in letters signed by departmental officers acting as secretaries for the newly recognised district councils, a development which caused politicians to fear that some of their Maori Affairs officials had been 'captured'. Corbett told departmental head Tipi Ropiha that 'the terminology in some of the correspondence is of such a nature as to be inappropriate as between a departmental officer and his Minister'. He suggested that should things 'develop further, it may be necessary to issue prohibitions'. Prohibitions indeed came quickly when Maori assertion of rangatiratanga continued. A planned national conference to be hosted by the Crown was postponed and then abandoned, and the district councils were now essentially without channels of formal communication to government. Although it had been approved in principle by government, there seemed little point in setting up a national body that would be ignored, and none eventuated. District councils, while mostly continuing on and retaining a certain degree of official recognition, lacked Crown empathy or support.[7]

Labour and the Committee System

The reasons for the government's disinclination to recognise and more fully work with Maori representation above tribal executive level was summed up in a Department of Maori Affairs response to continued submissions in favour of a national organisation: 'It is not considered desirable or necessary that Government should assist in promoting a national body that would tend to formulate policies of its own and press these upon Government'. The district councils, unable to exercise the power they sought through a central body, waned, and a number of committees and executives lost heart.

Labour's election to the treasury benches again in 1957, however, offered renewed hope. The party's election manifesto incorporated a 'new outlook' that involved giving Maori 'a greater say on events of importance to them'. Two principal modes of ensuring this were mooted. The first involved injecting new energy into the tribal committee/executive system, which was especially languishing in the rural areas where, partly because of the land issue, many Maori people were opting to engage in collective endeavours untainted by the Crown. The second mode focused on the urban spaces: a better adaptation of the functions of the committees and provisions of the MSEA Act to the increasingly urbanised realities of Maori life was proposed. While there would be no bold structural initiatives, Labour's commitment to boosting the existing system was widely seen to constitute a policy of improving the Crown's responsiveness to Maori.

But when Labour entered office, such improvement failed to manifest itself, and Maori frustration led to a further fall-off in the activities of both tribal and executive committees. This downturn in committee activity was accompanied by a great deal of active withdrawal of support for the government, and some leaders were even recommending that their people abandon the longstanding electoral support for the Ratana/Labour MPs – however hard these had worked to secure better policies and representation within the Labour movement. But a significant number of elders, together with younger leaders, believed that it might be possible to persuade Labour, through both a revived committee/executive system and higher-level pressure, to fulfil its explicit and implicit commitments to Maoridom. If kotahitanga/unity could be achieved within the Welfare Division system at regional and especially national levels, this could reinforce that degree of influence still exercised by the Maori MPs.

The government, alarmed at both the decline in committee activity and with much very vocal evidence of the disappointment of its Maori electorate, sought to retrieve the situation. On the issue of regional representation, it held out the possibility of significant concessions. In view of this and other encouraging official noises, the informal district councils began to revitalise or re-form. In 1959, by mutual agreement between Crown (under strong pressure from advisers such as Erik Schwimmer) and Maori, seven district councils were formally established (although they were not designated part of the Welfare Division, there being no legislative provision for this). In October that year, moreover, a non-official national body, the Dominion Council of Tribal Executives, was established at Rotorua, the Waiariki committees having again taken the initiative. The renewed and new regional and supra-district groupings gave a fillip to Maori politico-cultural activity, prompting in turn some revival in flaxroots activity. But official endorsement of the national organisation was still wanting. In early 1960, the Secretary for Maori Affairs told his minister, Walter Nash, that continued refusal to recognise the new national body as an integral part of the new system 'could quite conceivably result in the people becoming antagonistic to the Department, and we could well find a militant private association that could retard our already difficult task in Maori Affairs'.

Through such logic, Nash came to see the need for a national organisation that could cooperate with government. But he was concerned – among other things – at both the potential power of an officialised representative national body and its potential capacity to undermine the authority of the Maori MPs. One scholar has suggested that in 'spontaneously resolving to form a national council', the committee system's leadership had acted prematurely: such a body would be accepted only if it were the government which decided to initiate, 'convene and sponsor' it. Nash's reaction probably reflected such a view. But soon, however, under renewed pressure from various quarters, politicians and officials were exploring ways of making the national organisation a statutory body (albeit along lines that would suit the Crown's needs). Hunn noted in August 1960 that a 'Council is about to be set up by statute to speak for the tribal organisation on a national plane [and to] provide a two-way channel of communication'. But some elements of the Crown dragged their heels, concerned that a national council might become a 'policy forming body' that would present 'its own views and recommendations to government'. By the time Labour lost the election later that year, no legislation had been presented to establish a statutory official national organisation.[8]

The second Labour government's relationship with Maori, then, had proved to be far less harmonious than its election promises had suggested. Maori could see that whichever of the two main parties attained office, the Crown remained firmly committed to its long-term assimilationist policies. Yet many Maori leaders also saw clearly that the Crown and political parties could not avoid addressing, at some level, both Maori organisational energies and the culture and causes dear to the tangata whenua. National's post-war electioneering had trumpeted 'One Race – One People'. But as early as the beginning of the 1930s, even the Governor-General had presaged the notion of 'two peoples, one nation'. This was now slowly appearing as a modifying theme within the official assimilationist discourse, although even the most 'progressive' corners of the state machinery envisaged that the pakeha culture would remain overwhelmingly dominant. Inside officialdom, this incipient idea of 'two peoples' dovetailed with a stronger line of thought: that special measures were needed to bring Maori up to the pakeha level of socio-economic development. 'Equality', at least of opportunity, between pakeha and Maori would supposedly eventuate. Neither the 'two peoples' nor the 'special measures' position generally embodied an enthusiastic acceptance of difference. Rather, they represented a preparedness to tolerate those aspects of Maoridom which were not able to be suppressed. And even such tolerance was qualified by the assimilationist assumption that ultimately most, if not all, Maori culture would disappear under the weight of the 'superior civilisation'.

While the official willingness to appropriate organisational expressions of rangatiratanga and accommodate aspects of Maori culture needs to be viewed in this context, the very existence of such policies often enabled Maori to further their own causes. The issues surrounding ideas of 'two peoples, one nation' were discussed, argued and debated extensively in public and private, including among pakeha. Debates within the labour movement in the lead-up to the 1957 election helped focus the Labour Party on Maori questions. Labour's Maori Advisory Council changed its name to the Maori Policy Committee (MPC), embodying a hope that it would soon gain a more significant role inside the party. In the year of the election, Labour's annual conference unanimously adopted the MPC's report, and key policies of its 'new outlook' were incorporated into the election platform.[9]

The National government's toleration of difference had mostly focused on what could be appropriated through the existing official committee system, its Labour predecessor's alleged 'generosity' to Maori having been characterised as a 'folly' with consequences that needed containing or minimising. The Holland ministry's brief flirtation with adding higher levels to the official committee system had led to little result for a number of reasons besides the propensity for such bodies to turn upon it. These included the broad ideological context. After several settlements with Maori over historical grievances had been reached and trust boards established, for example, influential commentators of the right had opposed enhancing the official committee system. They argued that trust boards were more acceptable, being both accountable to the state and able to attend to the needs of Maori pending their (rapid) assimilation in all respects except skin colour and residual 'culture'. Such views were strongly held within the National government, and this increased the resolve of many Maori to place increased pressure within the labour movement as the 1957 election approached. The Labour Party's reinvigorated Maori policy platform reflected the strength of such mobilisation.

Labour in Office

When Labour won, Maori received an early sign of the policy difficulties ahead when the veteran Labour/Ratana MP Eruera Tirikatene, chair of the Maori Policy Committee, was passed over for the Maori Affairs portfolio. That Prime Minister Nash took it up himself, as Peter Fraser had done in the previous Labour government, could be depicted as an acknowledgement of the importance of Maori issues in the body politic. But this move, many Maori believed, was essentially a reflection of the perceived need to constrain the Maori aspirations that had been heightened by Labour's electoral success. Maori had long been uneasy about Nash: when Arnold Nordmeyer had challenged him for the party's leadership in 1954, the Maori MPs had abstained (to Nash's hurt and surprise). Tirikatene was to be on the Board of Maori Affairs, through membership of the Executive Council, and a new position was created for him of 'Associate to the Minister of Maori Affairs'. But his allocation to the lowly forestry ministerial portfolio in Cabinet was widely seen as an insult to Maoridom, some commentators presciently viewing it as a prelude to the government's ignoring of election promises. Shouldering a sense of betrayal, the Maori MPs, members of the Maori Policy Committee and other prominent Maori and Ratana leaders within the Labour Party nonetheless set about trying to persuade the government to engage in meaningful dialogue on its Maori policies and actions.

Nash and his inner core, however, were soon positively rejecting, rather than just ignoring, such pressure, sometimes against officials' advice. When the DMA, having listened to representations from Maori leaders, had recommended recognising a national Maori representative body, the idea was dismissed out of hand by the politicians. Before long, the Maori Policy Committee felt it had no choice but express no confidence in the Prime Minister. Its secretary, who was on the Labour Party National Executive, noted that while 'plenty' was happening in government on indigenous issues, this was 'in a totally different direction to that expected by the Committee'. In other words, Labour had essentially reverted to treating Maori issues as little more than class issues to be resolved by socio-economic uplift, without consultation with Maori and ignoring key requirements of rangatiratanga.

While seeing socio-economic development as necessary but very far from sufficient, Labour's Maori activists pressed their demands vigorously upon the government. One strand of pressure stressed the many land claims and other historical grievances that remained unaddressed, all of them revolving around breaches of the 1840 promise to respect rangatiratanga. In the absence of a sympathetic holder of the Maori Affairs portfolio, Labour's Maori membership called for re-establishing something akin to Tirikatene's former position of Minister Representing the Maori Race, with the incumbent to be advised by not only the Maori Caucus in Parliament but also by the Maori Policy Committee. This, of course, cut across Westminster parliamentary conventions, and when Tirikatene put the proposals before Nash, the response was one of angry rejection.

In the summer of 1958, race issues were to come to public prominence through New Zealand's rugby connections with South Africa. When an All Black tour of the apartheid country was announced, many predicted that the team would be a totally pakeha one, and opposition gathered. When, in mid-1959, the predictions were confirmed, Maori (including Kingitanga) took a prominent role in the mass and biracial 'No Maoris, No Tour' protest campaign. The Maori Women's Welfare League secretary, who was also secretary of the Citizens' All Black Tour Association (CABTA), stated that 'our battle is a domestic one against an act of racial discrimination committed by a New Zealand sports organisation'. Nash refused to intervene even to put pressure on the rugby authorities, to Maori and liberal pakeha anger. Though the tour proceeded, the denial of 'equality of opportunity' to Maori raised consciousness of issues of both national and (especially after the South African police massacre of civilians at Sharpeville) international indigeneity.

Meanwhile, at the 1958 Labour Party annual conference, the Maori Policy Committee had severely criticised the government for non-implementation of the party's Maori policies. Conference delegates unanimously pressed for action on conference policy resolutions, and in the following months the Maori MPs and the MPC kept up the pressure. But to little effect. In 1959, there was essentially a rerun of the same events (and non-events), and in such disappointing circumstances a number of new Maori voluntarist organisations began forming – especially among urban-dwelling and educated Maori. Pan-tribal or non-tribal gatherings of various types were held, and interest in non-official ways of organising kotahitanga revived – 25,000 signatures to a petition on the issue were reportedly collected. In this general context of feelings of both betrayal and revival, a second Young Maori Leaders' Conference was convened, following on from that held in 1939.

The Maori Policy Committee's report to the 1960 Labour Party conference was later described as the 'most pointed criticism levelled at the Government regarding lack of recognition and action on Maori policies'. It stated that 'mere words cannot even describe the void that is obvious in [Labour's] activities'. It declared that the government's contempt for policy adopted unanimously at the previous conference meant that the 'practicable effectiveness of this Committee is completely nullified'. For an election year this was extraordinary wording, a revelation of the depth of Maori yearning for the honouring of election pledges and, more broadly, for political recognition of Maori authority. Party officials tried in advance to get the report withdrawn. Eventually, a compromise was reached that it would be published only in part – and for the sake of election-year unity, strong words at the conference were averted. But the discontent continued. The Maori MPs were not consulted in drafting that year's Maori Purposes Bill, and when they deemed the wording to be unsatisfactory, their protests went unheeded.

In theory, the Maori MPs held the balance of power and could threaten, in a two-party system, to bring down the government. They were often vocal, and

Tirikatene was particularly critical of the South African rugby tour going ahead without government intervention or even protest. But they found themselves in a painful dilemma. The Labour Party, for all its faults, continued to provide sites for debate and action relevant to furthering Maori aspirations in a way that National did not. Tirikatene noted that he had 'not lost sight of the Treaty of Waitangi' since entering the House: progressing rangatiratanga seemed still to be possible under the Labour banner. Because of its stronger welfarist history and orientation, too, the Labour government was seen to offer the bulk of the Maori population considerably more by way of socio-economic advancement than the opposition. Certainly, judging by consistent voting patterns, most Maori deemed it better to be with Labour than to switch to the only real electoral alternative.

Hence the Maori MPs were trapped rather than liberated by their strategic positioning. They, the Maori Policy Committee and other Maori leaders knew that Nash was fully aware that Maori, however frustrated, would not (in the foreseeable future, at least) desert 'their own' party. Members of the MPC had themselves noted that the consistency with which its 'requests have been ignored' by ministers was not unrelated to the fact that the government 'publicly states that the Maori adherence will remain loyal to it'. Labour lost office in 1960.

After the Labour Government

At the party's 1961 annual conference, the Maori Policy Committee scathingly indicted the Nash government's record: the Labour leadership's acceptance over several years of the MPC's annual report had been but 'empty gestures'. The actual policies put in place, the committee stated (with more than a hint of irony), were 'forced on the Maori by pakeha experts as a patronising measure because the Maori was too improvident to know what is good for himself'. Some 'higher power' in the Labour Party had apparently decreed that 'the Maori would never be given the opportunity to analyse himself'. But for all that, Maori *had* been able to work inside Labour en masse and in a structured way, and had even been able to make some policy headway – occasionally more than merely in theory. Some of their leaders noted, for example, that towards the end of its period in office, the government had begun to succumb to membership pressure. Its concessions that district councils at regional level needed to be properly authorised and that a national body with appropriate resources should be formally established were manifestations of this.

The fact remained that the words of condemnation of the Nash government by the MPC and other Maori leaders were harsh – essentially because of the sense of betrayal after the 1957 election, which, after years of National rule, had raised hopes enormously. During the three years of the Nash government, some Maori Labour Party members decided in despair or disgust to work outside parliamentary politics – or to abandon politics altogether. But while the results to date were disappointing for the MPC and those it represented, the possibility of influencing a future Labour political executive remained. Maori wanting to work to effect change through the parliamentary system had little choice but to stay with Labour, especially since the new government of Keith Holyoake seemed to embody National's old aversion to Maori input into decision-making. Support for National continued, in fact, to decline among Maori (except for a brief surge in 1963), as it had done ever since the positive effects of Labour's welfarism began to become evident after 1938. By 1969, National was winning only an eighth of the Maori vote.

While often dispirited, then, many Maori activists decided to continue working within the Labour party, focusing on securing progress through changing their own party's stances. As a corollary to this, many opted to work on boosting the potential of the committee structures established under the 1945 Act, especially given the recent concessions on higher level organisation. Moreover, a cautious practice of building on what already existed seemed a prudent course to take in countering the new government's rapid assimilationist agenda: there was a discernibly reinforced attitude within 'official New Zealand' under National that the absorption of all things Maori into the western political economy and culture was not just inevitable but should be vigorously encouraged and hastened.

Despite this, Holyoake's government did not reject the recent developments in, and plans for, the official committee system. In the past, the state under National had viewed any devolution to Maori as the most temporary of expedients within the grand assimilationist strategy – or, alternatively, as a minor departure from the norm, one involving the antiquarian preservation of 'outmoded' but emblematic and touristic customs and practices. While the Maori migration to urban areas was seen as speeding up the goal of full assimilation, the 'spectacular' growth in the Maori population (considerably more than a tripling over four decades) presented National with a problem of critical mass pending that desired goal. It had no choice but to consider the needs and wishes of Maori, especially those newly arrived in the towns and cities.

There were very practical matters to address. With increasing numbers of low-paid (relative to the pakeha norm) Maori youth accumulating in urban areas, some of them fuelling the problems of disorder and crime that punctured the official/liberal paradigm of the times, few officials believed the situation could any longer be downplayed. Finding ways of dealing systematically with the difficulties posed by Maori urbanisation, and seeking the best means of phasing out rural tribalism, remained pressing issues for various agencies within the Crown. With any institutional assistance for these tasks appreciated, the post-election focus of a number of Maori leaders on expanding and enhancing the existing official committee structure held some attraction for the Holyoake government and its advisers. They were aware, too, that a number of Maori leaders inside the official system had always been conservative or, if not, had become profoundly disillusioned with the Labour leadership. All this helped National politicians and their officials make up their minds. Significant developments, albeit based upon ideas and plans emerging in the last days of the Labour government, were quickly to occur.[10]

Chapter 4

Autonomy and Voluntarism

Voluntary Associations

Through the 1950s, many Maori were vocal in stating their belief that their mana and organisational capacities were being demeaned or undermined by Crown attitudes and actions. Maori leaders argued, for example, that various pieces of legislation, such as the Maori Affairs and Town and Country Planning Acts of 1953, opposed or ignored Maori interests. The latter legislation, for example, had the capacity to displace entire Maori communities on grounds of 'public good'. If communities were deemed to be in 'economically retarded areas', their inhabitants could be denied departmental loans for repairing houses or building new ones. People would, instead, be encouraged to move to the large towns and cities which needed their labour. Other formal rules of state similarly reinforced a general social and bureaucratic climate of hostility to manifestations of autonomy. Many of those who saw decreasing prospects of official assistance for ways of meeting their aspirations for rangatiratanga looked to alternative means of organisational expression.

Maori in the cities and large towns adjusted to the loss of everyday tribal-based kinship bonds in various informal ways. New communities of interest were constructed from ties based not just on kinship but also on friendship and the sharing of new experiences; networks and activities based on 'affiliatory ties' and 'belonging by association' developed. At first, churches played an important role. In 1950s Auckland, the Ratana Church, followed by Catholic and Anglican communities, featured most prominently. Associational linkages around these and other institutions – schools, playcentres, childcare facilities, sports clubs, community centres and the like – would assist urbanised parents to bring up their children surrounded by 'new' whanau as well as, or in place of, kin-based whanau. Local associations might help to establish or revive yet other institutions – a branch of the Maori Women's Welfare League, a tribal committee's community hall or, eventually, an urban marae.

Even in the most adverse of urban circumstances, a 'strong residuum of traditional values' continued to inform Maori life. This was partly as a result of the very abruptness of the 'resumption of contact' between the two peoples after the war. Urbanising Maori could clearly see that their collective ethos was under threat from the dominating social and other forces of the cities. In response, many continued to organise their daily lives along associational principles. Large numbers participated in developing broader Maori-based associations to complement their interactions with pakeha and western institutions. Such collectivist adaptations suited both the Crown (in terms of its short- and medium-term policies) and Maori. By allowing individuals to adjust to their new way of life without losing all aspects of the old, associations helped minimise or contain the social turmoil inevitable in the context of mass urban migration, benefiting both parties. Ultimately, a collective approach helped 'Maoridom' survive and (in some aspects) thrive in apparently unpromising times. It also progressed aspects of the Crown's assimilationist agenda. In 1964, the Department of Maori Affairs noted the apparent paradox of both individualist and collectivist agendas working in tandem: 'religious, family, and tribal ties are still strong, and these have given [Maori] a moral and spiritual stability', assisting their 'transfer to a highly individualistic urban life'.

New and renewed ties of associational adjustment, extending into many non-official (as well as official) institutions, happened outside of the cities and towns as well. Some Maori who stayed on in the rural areas sought to adapt to the challenges of modernity (as well as to local or regional depopulation) by forming new organisations and linkages which supplemented traditional tribal institutions. Such community reorganisation formed part of Maoridom's 'resistive acculturation' to the post-war world. There were many ways in which this occurred, ranging from a new 'racial nationalism' (as it was once perceived) based on Maoritanga, to whanau retaining a few of the old ways in the midst of countervailing pulls in the city. In the spaces between, many Maori groups and individuals founded or joined 'voluntary associations', which tended to transcend tribal divisions. Some observers have seen these as 'the key to the successful adjustment of the Māori to urban life'. Top bureaucrats in the DMA approved: 'Many [Maori] will want to continue mixing mostly with their own kind and it has often been found that in such associations they learn about their new community from people like themselves far more readily than they would if cut off completely from their familiar Maori world.'[1]

Cultural clubs had been established during the first manifestations of urbanisation and these now flourished, particularly Wellington's Ngati Poneke and Auckland's Ngati Akarana organisations. That these two major clubs had transliterated and non-traditional names symbolised both the reconstitution of Maoridom in the urban spaces and an emerging 'consciousness of pan-tribalism'.

They, and before long others in cities and towns, not only kept alive traditional songs, dances, customs and crafts, but also assisted with adjustment to the cities. Such cultural organisations generally focused upon youth displaced from the countryside, and broader cultural groups often established youth sectors. The Crown soon recognised that many voluntary associations were doing useful work in urban adjustment and was willing to help.

In 1956, the DMA, noting the importance of clubs in the cities, described the 'formation of Maori youth clubs or organisations [as] a stated function of [officially-assisted] welfare'. Such clubs 'cushion the effect of migration from one way of life to another'. Officials would later note that Ngati Poneke 'gathers into its fold the young Maori boys and girls who come to the city in search of work [and] is also a social and cultural centre that has a unifying influence'. By the early 1960s, in 'every town where there are any number of Maoris there are youth clubs [providing the migrant with] a moral support that helps him to find his feet in the course of adapting himself'. The clubs' role in both adjustment and retaining Maoritanga was therefore important for Maori per se, while also helping to foster the 'new relationship that is growing between Maori and pakeha'. It was not surprising that the state was increasingly interested in appropriating, or at least 'guiding', such Maori-inspired initiatives. In addition to involvement by the DMA, many clubs were supported by tribal committees or executives, or the Maori Women's Welfare League.

Such state and quasi-state interest did not guarantee that things would proceed as the Crown or Maori elders working with or within the state wished. Some youth clubs were 'mainly run by young people themselves' and were not necessarily amenable to intervention. Sometimes young people 'adjusted' to city life in ways that did not please their elders. Although youth clubs often provided entertainment based on Maori cultural forms, by the late 1950s the 'age of "Rock-n-Roll" ha[d] infiltrated'. In 1958, Auckland's senior Maori welfare officer spoke of 'Maori songs being sung to rock'n'roll tempo, tight pants, gaudy clothes – these are some of the signs of the new breed of Maori race growing up in Auckland ... The young Maoris in the city have lost their respect for their elders and their pride in their race ... Somehow the influence of the marae has to be replaced'. Many elders, and some of the new leaders in the city, agreed.[2]

The community centres and halls which served the needs of youth and cultural clubs were clearly 'incomplete substitute[s] for ... marae' and unable to host many customary activities. They were, for example, inappropriate for holding tangi, 'one of the bastions of cultural conservatism in the alien environment of the city'. Soon, urban-based whanau, tribal, pan-tribal and religious groups formed associations to plan for 'urban marae' (as opposed to the marae of tribes whose rohe had been urbanised). This could be done in conjunction with the official committee system. The work of the committees of South Auckland, operating under the Waitemata Tribal Executive, was instrumental in establishing the city's first urban marae, Te Puea, at Mangere in 1965. This was run in traditional kin-based mode: in some built-up areas where large numbers of people from specific tribes (usually from nearby rohe) concentrated, urban associations could take on a quasi-tribal hue. Other urban marae (church-based or secular) were pan- or multi-tribal, linking migrants 'who had nothing in common except residence in the same suburb'. This clustering together was partly made possible by the State Advances Corporation's lending policies, which dealt with Maori applicants as individuals and did not take into account other departments' policies of 'pepper-potting' Maori within pakeha communities. Through a natural desire to resettle near people of similar cultural background, Maori using corporation assistance came to concentrate in 'their own' suburban areas. This made it easier to form the cultural, political and social organisations (both voluntary and officially franchised) that were the prerequisites for the development of the urban marae.

In rural areas, where kaumatua and kuia continued to predominate in decision-making, adaptation to the post-war world often took different routes. All the same, many adjustments did occur. These included improving community living standards through collectivised methods that took advantage of a booming economy. 'Community development' was supported, at least in principle, by sectors of the state. Following a state-franchised experiment at Panguru from 1954, for example, investment groups providing credit facilities in isolated districts began to spread through Northland and into parts of the Bay of Plenty. Participants pooled their savings, and loans were made out of the common fund to members who had, as the DMA put it, 'worthwhile use for the money'. Such 'investment society' resources were to be used either for individual purposes or, more importantly, to 'revitalise Maori communities … and encourage members to turn their energies towards building a better future'.

It once used to be argued from the evidence then available that the rapid development of voluntary associations and community development schemes was not necessarily a significant factor in, or even a reflection of, the pursuit of autonomy or the preservation of Maoridom. Instead these were seen as adjustment mechanisms to urbanisation and modernity which had little to do with tikanga Maori. This was a stance taken both by observers who were approving and disapproving of assimilative trends. Such a perspective was situated within a discourse which saw rangatiratanga only in traditional terms, and therefore interpreted urban initiatives and modernity as disconnected from, or alien to, its exercise. In the 1960s, anthropologist James Ritchie argued that the new Maori 'proto-communities' in the cities needed to strengthen, but in order to further the process of 'integration'. In the mid-1970s, Ranginui Walker saw the 'integrative function of voluntary associations in the multi-tribal situation' as primarily assisting the mass adaptation of Maori to the foreign urban environment of the pakeha, a New Zealand version of an international phenomenon.

But, as Walker later noted, voluntary associations were essential in 'transplanting [Maori] culture into the urban milieu'. Most succeeded at this by dint of operating in Maori ways and engaging in Maori cultural activities: in keeping alive an aura of Maoriness, in giving individuals and families who were far from their tribal headquarters a sense of 'being Maori'. Even when voluntary Maori associations emerged from, or were assisted by, the state or its approved agencies, they quite often separated themselves from it and went in their own directions. There seems little doubt that, as a result of voluntary associations, rangatiratanga was assisted not only to re-establish but also to flourish in the large towns and cities.[3]

Establishing the Maori Women's Welfare League

One remarkable development in rangatiratanga which was in essence voluntarist, but which had strong official encouragement before, during and after its inception, was the establishment of a pan-tribal movement of Maori women. Maori Women's Institutes had been established in rural areas from 1929, and health committees among Maori women from the mid-1930s (these later coalesced into branches of the Women's Health League, or WHL, often called the Maori Women's Health League in reflection of the great bulk of its membership). Such groupings had done much to improve daily living in tribal areas, but tended initially to operate in close association with pakeha individuals and organisations and to work in conjunction with male-dominated groups. The voluntarist efforts of Maori women during the Second World War paralleled and supplemented the essentially male thrust of the Maori War Effort Organisation. In particular, women stepped in to take over many tasks from men who were serving abroad or assigned to essential industries, and some of their groups were officially recognised and assisted.

After the war, the tribal committees operating under the MSEA Act remained mostly male-dominated, although some wartime women's committees/komiti wahine continued, either within the official structure or outside it. These, together with WHL branches, were often powerful embodiments of Maori women's conceptions of rangatiratanga – in ways which at times complemented the male-dominated institutions of traditional Maoridom but challenged them at others. While there were increasing numbers of women welfare officers in the MWO, they sometimes had difficulty liaising with the tribal committees because of the official structure's focus on 'men's work', with the tribal committees and executives tending at first to orientate their activities around such concerns as retention and use of land or the rehabilitation of returned servicemen. In the late 1940s, the welfare officers undertook a stocktake of the work of the women's committees and concluded that they were contributing proactively to many post-war developments of benefit to Maoridom. Noting that they often operated in separate spheres from (and sometimes performed better than) the tribal committees and executives, the MWO encouraged their continuance and the creation of new ones. Seeking to systematise their operations throughout the country, Rangi Royal's staff began to assist Maori women in forming a nationwide network of komiti wahine, by then called Women's Welfare Committees (WWCs). These would focus on issues on which activist women had been concentrating, such as family, health and housing. The Crown ideal was that eventually they would merge with the branches of the Women's Health League, and come under greater state guidance and direction.

Some of the WWCs modelled themselves on WHL local branches or other 'approved' models, encouraged to do so by Royal and his welfare officers. The fact that a number of them had emerged from within the Maori War Effort Organisation, or various komiti wahine working alongside it, helped good relationships between the MWO organisations and the women's committees to develop. The MWO's aim was that there would be a kind of division of labour, with the WWCs focussing on 'aspects of welfare which are the prerogative of women' and the tribal committees on the rest. But the women's committees would also draw strength from liaising and cooperating with other groups, such as the Maori women's committees of the Country Women's Institute.

Maori women who had gone to the cities and subsequently felt a degree of freedom from the male orientation of rural-based tribes formed, joined or developed relationships with WWCs. Despite their official franchising, these committees were often able to operate quite autonomously. The broad-ranging nature of their 'welfare' brief generally allowed them to work under the auspices of the 1945 Act without compromising their independence. They could concentrate on their own agendas, rather than on those of the Crown's agents, to a degree that the more deeply entrenched official committees of the MWO could not. As a consequence, the number of WWCs grew quickly.

However, a feeling soon arose among the WWCs that they would be more effective if they acquired a united voice. Their aim was, in effect, a national body of the type denied to Maoridom in general, and key elements of the Crown were not averse to such a development. In fact as early as 1948, the Controller of Welfare had suggested that the WHL and the various komiti wahine should, under departmental guidance, form a national committee. Its aims would be so specific that it would not constitute a danger to the sovereign unity of the state – a perception which no doubt in part reflected prevailing mores about the place of women in society. Bureaucrats and politicians, moreover, could see that not only would a national women's organisation better help to improve the socio-economic lot of Maori and help migrants adjust to city life, it could also serve as a useful conduit for information flow both upwards and downwards. Some circles within the machinery of state were already regretting the action of the legislators in 1945 in denying Maori a national voice. A unified voice for Maori women might be some kind of substitute, and even if it were not, it held much promise of benefiting the Crown as well as Maori. While a national organisation would lead to better networking among women and an improved capacity to pressure the government, then, it would also assist the state in its various aims – including, in the final analysis, fully assimilationist ones.

There were, however, tensions between the fiercely independent Women's Health League and the MWO. The WHL was acknowledged as 'a significant force in the delivery of Maori health', but its range of work tended to be relatively restricted, despite a broad definition of 'health'. The DMA's women welfare officers and others within the official system did not want the WHL's focus and stance to interfere with the emergence of flaxroots expressions of the voice of Maori women – which, they believed, would at the same time assist official goals. The WHL's leaders reportedly attempted to secure agreement that their organisation would dominate the central secretariat of a united body. When this failed they withdrew from discussions, without much regret from the WWCs. The women's committees forged ahead with what they saw, in essence, as ways of expressing their own rangatiratanga, whatever the degree of assistance and encouragement they received from the welfare officers and the rest of the MWO machinery. Few in the WWCs were worried about the fact that, after many discussions on unification at official and non-official levels, the draft constitution for a nationwide body that was adopted at a conference in Rotorua in 1950 had largely emanated from official sources. Nor that it was based on that of the Returned Services' Association, a model chosen because it provided for district and central representation as well as local branches.[4]

With such strong backing from Maori women, the MWO's women welfare and other officers went about setting the groundwork for the yet-to-be-established national organisation, and WWCs in effect transformed into branches. The officers encouraged the formation of new branches and helped set up district councils at regional level. By March 1951, there were 160 committees/branches and 14 district councils coordinating their activities. In September 1951, a general conference of the WWCs was convened in Wellington by Maori Affairs Minister Corbett to discuss 'the formation of a national organisation to unite Maori women in the common objective of homecraft and mothercraft and the general welfare of the Maori mother and child'. There had been a last effort to persuade the WHL to attend, but that organisation remained sceptical that it could retain its independence and decentralised structure in the face of governmental/MWO overview. The conference was well organised (and, some suggested, orchestrated) by Royal's staff. The draft constitution was endorsed and the Maori Women's Welfare League (MWWL; or Te Ropu Wahine Maori Toko i Te Ora) thereby founded with a three-tiered organisation of local branches, district councils and a Dominion Council. The Crown agreed to pay for a central secretariat. This was accepted by the delegates as a practical matter of administration rather than one involving state interference in policy, although it did heighten the suspicions of groups like the WHL.

At this inaugural conference, there were delegates from 187 branches (reporting to 22 district councils) and 27 'isolated branches' (which were independent, but would in future report directly to the central executive), with a total membership of 2503. Committees on housing, child welfare, health, employment and other matters were set up. The activist Whina Cooper became the MWWL's first president and Kingitanga's Princess Te Puea its founding 'patroness'. The appointment of both indicated that this would be an organisation intending to make its voice heard fully. Indeed, these two became the first Maori women to have truly national profiles. Cooper had 'begun her public career in the manner of a traditional rural and tribal rangatira' and moved to the city in 1949. She came to epitomise the new 'urban and national Maori figure whose position was based to some extent on the consent of Maori electors, to some extent on acceptance by Pakeha leaders and institutions, as well as on her own capacity and mana'. As MWWL president, she travelled the country with departmental welfare officers, setting up or consolidating branches and working for 'the general uplift of our people'.

The Work of the Maori Women's Welfare League

By 1954, there were 303 branches and 3842 members in the MWWL. The league's influence went well beyond formal membership, with many Maori (and numbers of pakeha) women working informally with its branches. The branches, too, had a great deal of interaction with other groups and individuals, Maori and pakeha. There was also much networking between the branches and district councils (whose numbers had quickly increased), whereas other Maori women's organisations generally remained locally or area orientated. Taken together, it was clear that Maori women, especially those who were educated and/or making proactive efforts to adapt to modernity, were increasingly prominent in running the affairs of their people – whether in tribes, sub-tribes or whanau, or in newer collectivities. This trend became more pronounced as educational opportunities improved for women in urban environments. Maori women leaders often brought new perspectives on ways of progressing Maoridom, and Maharaia Winiata noted that a number of Maori women leaders were 'assuming the role of mediators and representatives *vis-a-vis* the Europeans'.

The MWWL constitution worked well, despite the misgivings of some about state financial and 'moral' support. Based on flaxroots activity but with ongoing coordination from higher representative levels, the central secretariat and annual conferences, the MWWL quickly became a highly influential body both within Maoridom and in representing it. With the absence of regional and national layers in the MWO's committee machinery, the league became the main arena of discussion for issues of regional or nationwide significance – such as education, health and housing – for the rest of the decade. Although its constitution declared it to be non-partisan and non-political, it did what it needed to do to represent Maori women and their concerns to officialdom and politicians. As these concerns often had strong resonances with those held by Maori men as well, the MWWL became a powerful voice for Maori causes in general. Government and officials treated its annual conferences and their resolutions seriously. Throughout each year, its headquarters acted as a vibrant clearing-house for ideas, a number of them provoking or embarrassing the Crown.

But the MWWL did need to operate within parameters that generally reflected, or did not fundamentally challenge, the dominant culture and the interest and worldview of the state. Its main emphasis, for example, was on improving Maori family life and upholding values which were also generally those of pakeha leaders and society. Cooper urged Maori women to 'take their rightful place as leaders in the homes of our people. Take care of your children, see to their education, make the home the centre of your family life, be real helpmates to your husbands and assist them in their efforts to provide happy and contented homes'. The league, in short, assisted Maori to adjust to modern conditions, with similar goals (and sometimes methods) as the Crown; it acted as a welfarist (and, from the Crown's perspective, cheap) complement to 'the welfare state'.

Families not coping well with the adjustment to urban living or modernity were often helped by the MWWL in a variety of practical ways. Its members assisted poor families by providing basic necessities, raised money to educate and clothe needy children, and gave budgeting advice. Over the years, the MWWL promoted (among other things) good parenting, immunisation, mental well-being, training programmes for the unemployed, increased electoral enrolment, the playcentre movement and housing improvements. It took an 'active interest in all matters pertaining to the health and general well-being of women and children of the Mäori race'. In essence, the principal thrust of the league's activities gelled with state assimilationist values and goals. The Crown was particularly interested in how the MWWL could assist adaptation to the post-war world, especially in the cities.

Here the league helped both to tackle problems arising from the visibility of Maori in the cities and towns, and to address social difficulties arising from urban adjustment. An important part of its early work dealt with racial discrimination. The Maori women of the MWWL were often aided by pakeha women members and associates, a reflection of their constitution's aim of promoting 'understanding between Maori and European women' as well as of a growing liberal trend in non-Maori society. The league also worked closely with Maori Affairs officials, particularly the welfare officers, both male and female. And while the ultimate Crown goal remained assimilation, the league promoted Maoritanga and teaching te reo Maori/the Maori language in schools.

A particularly pressing issue for the MWWL was that of improving housing in both urban and rural spaces. Welfare officers increasingly concentrated their work on the provision of modern housing, while MWWL members gave instruction in the 'care and maintenance of home and garden'. In 1947, Prime Minister Fraser had acknowledged that despite a Maori housing drive at least half of all Maori housing was of insufficient quality, and the problem continued despite the subsequent economic boom. In 1951, Auckland's school medical officer investigated 'dirty and neglected' children in the large urban Maori community in Freeman's Bay and concluded that the most significant causes related to overcrowded living. In its early days, the league made the difficulty of finding affordable, decent urban accommodation a central campaigning issue. Cooper lobbied Corbett and secured resources for a broad survey of Maori housing in Auckland, and this confirmed widespread substandard housing and squalor. The results gave the MWWL a firm platform for many representations in governmental and bureaucratic circles. Improvements of various types gradually eventuated, with slums demolished and quotas of state and council housing for Maori increased. The Crown was among those parties which acknowledged the beneficial results of the efforts it had been pressured into making. Housing crusades assisted not only individuals or families, but also helped further the government's promotion among Maoridom of what an official called (in 1957) 'civic responsibilities [to] live up to normal European standards'.[5]

Because of the MWWL's successes, especially with aiding the needy and working with those attempting to adjust to city life, the state came to give it a great deal of supervisory and welfare work that had formerly been mostly within the province of the tribal committees. Indeed, DMA officials eventually considered the MWWL to be, in effect, the female counterpart to the tribal committees and executives – and some believed that it had been established by the department for this very purpose, albeit with a subordinate role to that of the official structure. The league was said to have been 'created to assist tribal committees on aspects of welfare which are the prerogative of women', namely activities which 'are centred on the house and all its aspects'. The MWWL had only been 'born as a voluntary body with a constitution of its own', wrote the Assistant Secretary of Maori Affairs in 1955, because it was 'beyond the normal exercise of prudence to have two distinct organisations function separately under the same Act'.

The Maori Women's Welfare League has been variously interpreted as an agency of autonomous operation, as a quasi-Crown body, or as some kind of combination of the two. It was voluntarist and genuinely flaxroots in terms of its everyday operations, and its constitution ostensibly gave it independence from the Crown. Winiata concluded that the league could 'be seen as an illustration of the general urge to self-determination which had also produced the Ratana movement', Kingitanga, 'cultural revivals in various districts' and other expressions of Maori autonomy and assertions of rangatiratanga. But as observers have frequently noted, the MWWL came into existence with extensive state assistance and, indeed, under its patronage. The Crown provided its administrative support, and the league worked closely with the (especially female) welfare officers of the MWO/Welfare Division. Among the leading Maori who advised the MWWL and attended its conferences were long-time bureaucrats such as Michael Rotohiko Jones. In 1952, the league invited DMA and Health Department representatives to join its executive, ex officio.

The MWWL's increasing capacity to access project-based government funding brought danger that its activities might be skewed to suit state needs. The state, seeing great usefulness in the league and its work, was careful to avoid appearing too overbearing. The DMA denied, for example, 'any thought whatever of attempting to say, in any way, how the League should do its work'. But, with the MWWL's Secretary-Treasurer an employee of the DMA, it had to insist that the league's funds qualified as 'public moneys' and that standard 'western' accounting procedures be followed. Clearly the league was not fully independent of 'the Maori Affairs' and its intensive monitoring and 'guidance'. An authorised chronicler of its activities has said that the MWWL was a 'quasi-voluntary organisation ... more or less formed by government officials, and it constituted an integral part of the department's welfare organisation'. A Maori scholar later wrote that while the league was 'born out of Māori enthusiasm and initiative, it was often perceived as a vehicle for the aims of the Māori Social and Economic Advancement Act 1945 and too closely linked with the Department of Māori Affairs'.[6]

On the other hand, the league's work would have been much diminished without governmental support. Cooper found in Corbett a source of 'much help and encouragement'. In 1953, she thanked him for the 'personal interest' he had shown in the MWWL: 'We know that without your sanction and deep understanding of our basic problems and the help of your Department, our organisation would not have flourished as it has done in the past two years.' In the DMA's assessment, the costs and difficulties involved in supporting the league sometimes outweighed the advantages of its addressing significant socio-racial issues. At times, indeed, officials appeared keen to abandon support for the MWWL. In June 1953, the Secretary for Maori Affairs enquired as to whether the league would be 'in the happy position' of assuming 'complete autonomy': the 'Department is happy to continue its assistance to the League, but the thought is that the League should work toward its fulfilment in handling fully its own affairs'. Cooper responded hotly: 'It would appear from your letter that the department is somewhat anxious to get rid of this organisation', but the league 'cannot be considered anything other than an auxiliary organisation to the Department and to the Welfare Division'.

Cooper argued that her league's work assisted both parties equally. The league was 'entitled to whatever the department is able to give us since our work is basic and fundamental to all phases of Maori life'. While the objective was that the league should eventually achieve full independence from state assistance, this should only be when it decided that was possible: 'financially the league is not yet ready'. The MWWL would continue in the following years to insist on Crown assistance and argue that it was premature to disassociate itself from government. At the 1955 annual conference, Cooper invited Corbett to 'just say *yes* to our wants', prompting a lecture from the minister about the difference between wants and needs.

The Maori Women's Welfare League and Autonomy

While the MWWL proved reluctant to leave the embrace of the state, ministers and officials were equally reluctant to lose the influence they could wield within it. Their stated wish to cast it adrift from the Crown often amounted to little more than attempts at cost-cutting and/or to a feeling that its usefulness might be impeded if Maori saw it as a lackey of the state. The MWWL's leaders were well aware, from their own perspectives, of the dangers of such a perception among their people. At the annual conference of the league in 1957, as she departed from the presidency, Whina Cooper affirmed that she was 'worried about the independence of our organisation'. She saw that it was inevitably a 'temptation ... for government departments with all the good intentions in the world to use voluntary organisations almost unconsciously' for their own purposes. 'I know we are dependent on the Maori Department. Without its help we would not have functioned as effectively as we have done ... In a way that is the price we pay for the assistance given us'.

But, she added, this price was neither ideal nor necessarily long lasting: 'most of us would like to see our own organisation stand absolutely on its own feet. Quite independent ... Let us remember as a voluntary body we spring from the hearts, minds and needs of the Maori people ... We have a standing in the world no other Maori organisation has ever achieved. In view of all these things', she asked, 'should we not try to establish our real independence ... as an autonomous body'? Cooper noted that conference remits had 'a strong tendency to stress the principle of independence, and also the call for greater freedom for the leagues and also the Maori people ... All these remits can be seen as an expression from the Maori side for freedom to express his own soul as a Maori – his Maoritanga'.

As the first Maori organisation to speak with a truly national voice, the MWWL contributed hugely to the growing feeling of 'Maori' interconnectedness in post-war New Zealand, to Maoritanga, and to the desire for both modernity and autonomy. Cooper herself, despite her insistence on Crown help for the league, embodied the spirit of the independence from the Crown which she sought for her people. During her six years heading the league, Royal and other officials often had to remind her of the terms of reference of the organisation – as, indeed, did the MWWL's secretary, Mira Szaszy. However much the functions of the MWWL reflected state aims, both the mere fact of its existence and the work it did inside and (particularly) outside the comfort zone of the Crown helped promote a Maori autonomist vision.

By the creation, endorsement and use of the league, the state had in effect attempted to replicate its wartime appropriation of spontaneous and voluntarist collective energies among the indigenous people of New Zealand. It was generally satisfied with the MWWL's performance in this light – its work in helping Maori adjust to post-war urban life, for example, or its role alongside the WHL in improving Maori health. Corbett himself believed that 'the greatest social advancement' for Maori in the 1950s was 'due to the Maori women themselves, under the Welfare League's inspiration'. Such social progress was achieved at little cost to the state. The small amount of state investment, however, was of considerable assistance to the league, which was thereby able to run a year-round operation at national and devolved levels. Maori women working in the league at the flaxroots had the structural framework within which to advance their various tasks, sometimes with the help of the welfare officers and the official committees, but often with only a minimal degree of state intervention or none at all.[7]

In this partnership between Crown and Maori on 'women's issues', both parties had constantly to manoeuvre to assert themselves and/or to create a workable compromise. MWO/Welfare Division officials, for example, would show periodic concern that the MWWL was acting too independently from the tribal committees, while the league was wont to place considerable pressure on government for reform on matters such as education, child welfare and employment. It ranged far and wide on other topics as the need arose, often stepping in where the DMA's committees would not venture because of their structure and terms of reference.

The league's focus on assisting urban migrants and their families both to adjust to modernity *and* preserve their Maoriness did create some difficulties. As migration sped up, the organisation needed increasingly to rely on the activities of urbanised women for its smooth running. But, with the demands of both the new environment and their own families, their time was at a premium. From the mid-1950s, both MWWL membership and activity were beginning to fall (although monitoring of its personnel and productivity tended to overlook the many informal networks and activities associated with it). Such developments were not just of concern to the MWWL. In 1958, the Minister of Maori Affairs was worrying about the 'disturbing' decrease in membership and an apparently 'waning' enthusiasm. In view of the fact 'that the Leagues have contributed greatly to the spectacular surge forward made by the Maori people within the last 10 years', he wrote to the Secretary, the 'possibility of disinterest creeping into the work of the Leagues must be guarded against. The organisation is too important to be allowed to drift towards ineffectiveness'. The MWWL must 'be encouraged and the Movement strengthened'.

In the event, the league was to remain powerful and significant for its own, autonomist reasons. At an MWWL conference in 1957, while members were 'not yet ready to take over the responsibilities of running the organisation without Departmental assistance', there was resistance to constraints on the use of the government's administrative funding: members were determined to utilise their resources in ways they thought best for promoting Maori aspirations. Increasing numbers, moreover, did not believe in accepting *any* funding because of the actual or perceived dangers of creating a dependency relationship. When those who argued for full league independence gained ground, especially given disappointment with the Nash government, renewed enthusiasm ensued. As part of efforts to claw back credibility within Maoridom, in 1960 Nash changed the funding and accountability arrangements. The league became an incorporated society, no longer tied directly to administrative support from the DMA – which itself felt that it might not need to rely on the league so much in the future in view of the prospective changes to the Welfare Division's system of official committees. Many in the MWWL rejoiced at the new independence, although some viewed with 'trepidation' the fact that officials had 'severed their connections with us'. In the event, 'the Maori Affairs' would continue to loom large in the affairs of the MWWL, which needed state support for general funding and project-specific grants.

That same year, the acting Secretary for Maori Affairs, on the basis of officials' investigations, made an assessment of the league's 358 branches and 3200 members as part of his stocktake of the state of Maoridom. He concluded that the MWWL was 'generally more alive than the tribal organisation', and saw its independent status as a boon. It was now time for the Crown, he argued, to entrust the MWWL to take on extra, specified tasks for Maoridom in the fields of 'welfare and culture'. This high-level public approval of its importance for both Maori and government was couched in language which also endorsed the accelerating sense of a national 'Maori' identity. In Maori eyes, this latter development had helped counteract the harmful ethnic consequences of the detribalising forces of urbanisation, and meetings of the MWWL and other pan-tribal organisations served to promote Maori identity. For its part, the Crown too was positively encouraging 'shared ethnicity' or 'Maoriness', appreciating the need for some form of transitional indigenous substitute for the tribalism it was working to displace.

But in the Crown's eyes, as the history of relations with the MWWL indicates, non-tribal embodiments of rangatiratanga, as much as their tribal counterparts, needed to be carefully controlled. In some ways, this would now be more difficult to achieve with the MWWL, given its independence of the Crown for administrative support. But it would be easier in other ways, since the grants the MWWL now relied upon could be made conditional. They could even dry up in the event of extreme difficulties in the relationship between league and state, although a modus vivendi would generally be worked out: officially-sourced grants and subsidies would be made available to the MWWL to further the interests of Maori in ways which, at the very least, the state could live with. Such a system persisted in the decades which followed. In the early 1990s, indications that the MWWL's 'ability to apply to the Government for assistance [was] in effect being withdrawn' raised concerns among both rank and file and leadership. In the end, government funding continued, and the league both continued to maintain its distance and represent Maori women on many state and other committees.

Ever since its inception, the MWWL had repeatedly raised issues for debate, and pressured government (and sometimes tribes) for change. It helped very many individuals and whanau, and other elements of Maoridom, adjust to 'the modern world' in ways that would both preserve Maoritanga and allow for gendered expressions of self-determination. Many Maori women, especially radical activists from the 1970s, came to see its structures and policies as passé or even to view it as helping perpetuate gender differentiation. In Maoridom, it was often argued (although not without much contestation, including from Maori women), women continued to be subordinated in decision-making processes, paralleling the position traditionally allocated women in the patriarchal society of the pakeha. Such critical scrutiny reflected a number of trends – demographic, feminist, socio-economic, educational, ideological and ethno-cultural. These were all to have profound implications for many aspects of Maori being and being Maori.[8]

Leadership and Kinship

The reforms dating from the 1930s which resulted from Labour's 'equalising' policies had led to an increase in the quality of life among Maori. The years following World War II saw the emergence of a new generation of Maori leaders who benefited from these and other factors, such as wartime experiences (including service in the Maori Battalion), post-war urbanisation and rising educational standards. Many new leaders were not of traditional chiefly/rangatira status, and sizeable numbers rose through the ranks of the institutions of the Maori War Effort Organisation or the 1945 MSEA legislation. Others came to prominence working either directly for the Crown, especially at DMA head or district offices. A number of non-rangatira gained leadership experience through using their education or workplace experience to advance their tribes' interests during the adaptation to modernity. Others attained positions of influence or authority through quasi-official organisations such as the MWWL, or through voluntary associations with no links at all to the state. In the early 1960s, the Department of Maori Affairs declared that since the Second World War, the various Maori leaders – in the Welfare Division, tribal committees, the Maori Women's Welfare League and elsewhere – had experienced 'striking success': 'there is as never before an abundance of leaders on a local level throughout the country'. Maori numbers also began rising in professional, craft and trade employment. There were benefits in terms of race relations from such developments: the increasing power and profile of the post-war leadership strata demonstrated to pakeha New Zealand that a commitment to Maoriness did not preclude willingness and ability to take responsible, 'respectable' and leading positions in the broader society.

The new Maori urban and tribal leaders were often 'impatient with anything less than full equality'. Those emerging from the labour movement, in particular, focused their attention on working towards achieving social and economic parity with pakeha in all quarters of Maori life. At the same time, most sought to preserve those aspects of Maoridom which had survived colonisation and were seen to be capable and worthy of preservation, revival or adaptation. In this sense, they had taken on board the ideas of 'Ngataism', that strand of Maoridom which had emerged from the Young Maori Party of half a century before. Adherents of this school of thought, in Ngata's words, had long been developing a vision of 'a truly united Maori people ... conscious in all its parts of a distinct and separate existence, but nonetheless subject to law and government [and] loyal to the flag that protects it'. Such views had become mainstream within Maoridom, accommodating rangatiratanga within Crown sovereignty but insisting on maintaining a distinctive identity, whatever the assimilative wishes of the government. Various aspects of traditional culture, and the Maori language in particular, needed proactive protection and state assistance in the process. Above all, arrangements needed to be worked out between Maori and Crown in terms of the appropriate modes of interaction between their respective authorities, including those of the tribes which underpinned the evolving concept of 'the Maori race'.[9]

Despite their brief to work in – and sometimes their belief in – the tribal committee system, a number of its leading members came to form Ngataist views on making progress through the unified actions of Maoridom. This was consonant with the perspectives of many who had gained practical experience in the MWWL and other voluntary and pan-tribal organisations: there was a need to lobby *as Maori* rather than, or as well as, tribal representatives. In the modern urbanising world, Maori everywhere were seen to share a common interest. Pressures from Crown and private institutions, and from pakeha in general, to *fully* integrate into the political economy and adopt its behavioural norms were great, and effective resistance required united action. Such a front to the Crown was urgent, with traditional values, practices and knowledge coming under enormous strain in the urban spaces, far from the customs and controls of the marae.

Anthropologists were already finding that even whanau were evolving into groups whose 'members cooperated not on a daily basis but from time to time and on special occasions ... Members had to work individually for money incomes, had limited opportunities for cooperative activity, and often had to leave their home communities in search of work'. But these changing circumstances saw 'new variations [of the whanau] arise as migrants settle[d] and put down roots outside their ancestral communities'. Joan Metge identified a new category of whanau that was not descent/whakapapa-based, but 'kaupapa-based'. Primarily an outcome of urbanisation, this involved Maori from different iwi, hapu and whanau coming together for a common purpose (kaupapa). The new kaupapa-based whanau complemented other pan- and non-tribal formations in the cities and big towns.

Urbanisation was also having an effect on marae throughout New Zealand, and in the rural areas in general. In 1950s Northland, Maori anthropologist Pat Hohepa noted that while '[t]raditional cultural ways and cultural values' had continued, this was in 'modified form'. Those who had left to experience urban life made periodic returns, but they had primarily become permanent city dwellers with developing attitudes to match. These attitudes, brought back on visits, made big impacts on (especially) younger people. The combined processes of 'abandonment and change' had such significant local consequences that Hohepa coined the word 'whaamere' (family) to describe what was now, in his observations, the 'most effective socio-economic group'. Unlike the whanau of the past, whaamere kin did not cooperate on a daily basis in securing their livelihoods. Single households within the kinship grouping were now the units of day-to-day existence. Even here, households were so integrated into the broader money economy that their members often left for work in nearby towns or more distant cities. Members of the whaamere did, however, offer mutual assistance to individuals and households in times of need, and they came together on special occasions and for community events. In both city and country, modernity led not to full but to selective adoption of non-Maori ways, and often also to adaptation of tikanga and custom – eventually, too, to processes of 'retraditionalisation'.[10]

Kinship, then, continued to provide an important source of identity within Maoridom, but the role of iwi, hapu and whanau in the lives of many Maori was slowly being transformed. With Maori from different tribal backgrounds increasingly coming to share experiences in the urban spaces, and given the high degree of social interaction between town and marae, many 'new leaders' believed that activity focused on the common interests of all Maoridom was all the more necessary. One important area of concern was combating the ongoing problem of discrimination and racism; another was the need for socio-economic improvement. Overarching everything was the question of affirming rangatiratanga.

Addressing Rangatiratanga

All Maori leaders, however, had to confront various and varied dilemmas and frustrations. Pakeha officials were averse to publicly recognising the existence of racism or discrimination, for example, making the task of fighting them harder. More significantly, for the long run, promoting socio-economic advance entailed encouragement of many essentially assimilationist policies. Urban Maori leaders, even those working within the Welfare Division, sometimes had to operate in the face of official disinclination to utilise their services fully – a corollary to Tirikatene being denied the Maori Affairs portfolio.

That the Crown was very slow to appoint Maori to positions of authority stemmed partly from concerns which paralleled those it held about regional and national Maori bodies: too much influence and status for (especially urban) leaders might increase the power of pan-tribal and other 'new' movements. This was seen as having the potential to do harm to unitary state sovereignty.

In the 1950s, Maori matters were therefore often addressed as if the rural tribal past, sanctioned in the nomenclature of the tribal committee/executive structure, was the Maori reality. This resonated with a general assessment that tribal units were easier to deal with (and perhaps to 'deal to') than urban, pan-tribal groupings. It also possibly played to a subliminal image, whatever the official policy on assimilation, of Maori as a pre-modern tribal people finding it difficult to adjust to modernity.

Official attempts to address problems arising from socio-racial displacement in the big towns and cities were thus more intermittent and half-hearted in the 1950s than some sectors of the state wished. Some advisers, moreover, believed that special assistance to Maori through the Crown encouraged an undesirable degree of recollectivisation, and this led to some ultra-cautious policies. But increasing numbers considered that interventions brought clear advantages for the state and the citizenry as well as for Maori – such as a decrease in social distress and disorder. The solution to the dilemma of reconciling assistance with self-reliance was seen to lay in a deliberate speeding up of assimilation, bypassing or downplaying both formal and informal Maori channels which emphasised rangatiratanga and related aspirations.

One arena of official activity which eventually picked up momentum involved moving Maori away from urban areas of high indigenous population density – addressing the problem first prominently highlighted by the MWWL survey in Auckland. At first there was widespread approbation from Maori that the state was making efforts to eliminate 'slum' conditions. However, officials increasingly developed assimilative solutions to housing problems, such as escalating pepper-potting of Maori families among pakeha in the suburbs, and in many Maori quarters this was not appreciated. The promotion of 'racial mixing' in such coercive (if well meaning) ways made the creation of new organisations which were Maori in nature even more of a necessity – and a challenge – to Maori urban leaders, official and unofficial.

As Maori were becoming an established presence in the suburbs, a future generation of their young people, including significant numbers of those who would become 'new leaders', was growing up in the urban spaces. While there were many assimilationist pressures, family links with home marae and the existence of Maori religious cultural, sporting and other organisations meant that most did not lose their core sense of tribal and/or Maori identity. They grew up in environments in which, however bleak the future for Maoridom might seem on the surface, discussions of ways of containing or resisting assimilation were continuous – if not always (or often) couched in such terms. Their tactics and strategies included, in a reversal of dominant processes, a partial 'colonising' by Maori and their pakeha sympathisers of structures provided by the state. The journal *Te Ao Hou*, for example, established by the DMA in 1952 and edited by

Erik Schwimmer, was touted as 'a marae on paper, where all questions of Maori can be discussed'. In its initial hosting of debates 'on the issue of assimilation versus the retention of Maoritanga', it promoted assimilative 'social progress'. But it eventually became a means for increasing numbers of Maori to share ideas on methods and goals of self-determination. It became, in effect, a site of resistance to the assimilative processes which it had been set up to promote.[11]

Maori political and intellectual leaders, then, continued to further the claims and demands of rangatiratanga in many ways and by various means. In the mid-1950s, Winiata gained great publicity (and in some quarters, notoriety) when he joined pakeha scholars such as Piddington in reminding the 'one nation' of New Zealand that it contained 'two peoples' whose relationships had yet to be worked through satisfactorily. Rather than bridging the gap between the two groups, he argued, state agencies had more often sought 'to retain power in the hands of the dominant European'. It is 'an illusion', he continued, that Maori 'rights are being preserved' and their culture 'held intact'. A sign that the many debates on these kinds of issues might lead to concrete developments came in 1959 with the second Young Maori Leaders' Conference. While spearheaded by University of Auckland staff who had attended the first conference twenty years earlier, the discussions emphasised how very far the problems and potentialities had moved in the intervening years. Kaumatua and young delegates alike agreed that education was the key to Maoridom's development in the modernising and urbanising world. They were also of one mind in their caveat to this: it was crucial that 'education for Maori', formal and informal, should also preserve what was best and most appropriate in Maori culture. As a result of the conference, yet another Maori pan-tribal organisation was born.

A number of the 'young leaders' at the 1959 conference, moreover, moved on to pioneer some of the radical forms of activism which were to take root from the late 1960s. The political and career trajectories of this new generation were based on the increased educational and vocational opportunities which had opened up to Maori youth following urbanisation and the general prosperity of the 1950s. These leaders, ironically the products of assimilationist strategies in the official education system, caused chagrin for the authorities, especially when their struggles for rangatiratanga took new and sometimes alarming forms. The radicalism of many of them – which increasingly amounted to promoting the fully-fledged implementation of Maori autonomy – was partly based on new, 'liberationist' ideas in the pakeha world. But it was also rooted in the struggle of, and took heart from the momentum built up by, the Maori post-war leadership and the continuous assertions of rangatiratanga by the Maori people – who refused to countenance that adaptation to urban New Zealand meant subsuming their Maori identity.[12]

Chapter 5

Rangatiratanga Challenged

Urban Adjustment and 'Race'

The Maori population more than doubled in the twenty years after World War II, at the same time as urban migration gathered great pace; the ten years or so after 1956 saw the most intensive population movement. Almost half of all Maori were living in built-up environments at the beginning of the 1960s, many of them mixing with pakeha on a regular basis. By the mid-1970s, some three-quarters of Maori were urban dwellers. Adjustment problems of some magnitude within the migrant population were inevitable with such a speedy relocation, and with these came an upsurge of ethnocentric incidents and racist attitudes towards Maori. Official pronouncements, however, still tended to promote the idea that New Zealand had as near to perfect an understanding and tolerance between the races as was possible, and this seemed to be generally believed throughout pakeha society. K C McDonald's 1963 textbook *Our Country's Story* stated that 'there is no country in the world where two races of different colour live together with more goodwill towards each other', echoing the generally rosy perspective of the two general histories of New Zealand written in the late 1950s.

Such views partly reflected a long-held idea which had been nourished when Maori were out of sight of most pakeha, something amounting to a national (or pakeha) myth. This took the Treaty of Waitangi as its 'enlightened' founding statement. In 1960, Parliament declared that the date of the initial signing of the Treaty in 1840, February 6th, would be known each year as 'Waitangi Day'. This would provide an opportunity for thanksgiving that New Zealand's racial and other fortunes had been enabled to flourish under the protection of such a supposedly progressive iconic document.

There was some element of truth in the perception that race relations were healthier than in other western jurisdictions. This would often surface in the empirical and anecdotal evidence mustered in public comment (including from Maori) favourably comparing New Zealand's race relations with those of Australia and other former settler colonies. There was little overt opposition to the notion of interracial dating among young people, and rates of intermarriage were increasing as urbanisation proceeded. By 1960, a full half of Maori marriages were reported to be to non-Maori. Authorities noted this approvingly, stressing that it indicated assimilation in action as well as racial harmony – intermarriage, as a key figure of the time put it, 'is a powerful solvent'. On the left and liberal end of the political spectrum, pakeha marched together with Maori in protest against the All Black rugby tour of apartheid South Africa in 1960, demanding 'No Maoris, No Tour'. On the moderate political right, there was an increasing realisation that race incomprehension and hate could lead to widespread civic strife.[1]

'No impartial observer could deny', however, 'that racial discrimination exists in New Zealand'. Government officials 'generally agreed that a widespread problem of discrimination did exist', and that 'the problem was probably growing more acute' (although they remained reluctant to draw public attention to these issues). The marginalisation of Maori in most facets of New Zealand life, too, remained obvious, despite better prospects in the urban-based workplaces and spaces. Even McDonald tempered his populist vision with the caveat of 'disturbing evidence that in some districts at least complete social equality has still to be achieved'. Although many pakeha refused to concede that there were any, let alone fundamental, flaws in New Zealand's much vaunted race-relations environment, the evidence to the contrary was becoming hard to ignore.

In 1960, American scholar David Ausubel published *The Fern and the Tiki*. The book described in detail the pervasive race prejudice and discrimination against Maori which Ausubel had encountered in New Zealand. He had been sponsored as a Fulbright research scholar by anthropologist and psychologist Ernest Beaglehole, who had hoped that a liberal outsider's perspective would stimulate a rational race-relations debate. Instead the book provoked much fury, even among pakeha liberals, for the way it challenged the paradigm of excellent race relations. However, meaningful debate did emerge before long, even if initially defensive in tone. For the year 1963 alone, one scholar identified 151 books and articles produced on race in New Zealand, a reflection of the large amount of time and space devoted to the subject in newspapers, on the radio and in public and private forums.[2]

Even the Department of Maori Affairs was soon to have public doubts about the state of race relations in New Zealand. The department conceded that Lieutenant-Governor William Hobson's foundational statement upon the signing of the Treaty in 1840 that there was 'now one people' in New Zealand had proved to be 'not strictly so'. But despite this and other waverings, it continued to laud the 'happy circumstance' of an alleged 'fusion of the two races'. Maori and pakeha were said to be 'remarkably uniform, economically, socially, and culturally'. And it still saw the 'one people' route as the appropriate way forward: 'the future of the Maori is bound up with the pakeha social and economic structure'.

That did 'not mean the death of Maori culture', however, at least not fully and not yet. As the Secretary for Maori Affairs had said in 1957, the journey to 'full integration' needed to incorporate some Maori ways of thinking and seeing if it were to succeed. 'A large number of Maori people still find the old community structure intensely meaningful and beneficial and while working for those people's individual material advancement, we must respond to their frequently expressed aspirations for a good and progressive community life with balanced material, social and cultural features.' Another commentator put it a different way: on a daily basis, 'consciously or unconsciously every Maori is engaged in a personal debate whether to assert or abandon some particular attitude or habit or whether to adopt or reject some new one'. If racism or discrimination intensified, members of the Crown believed, non-assimilationist choices might be made more often, and the appropriate 'balance' between the past and the present would not be attained.[3]

There was increasing appreciation that the pre-war rhetoric about 'perfect race relations' had more accurately pertained to a situation of 'non-relations', with Maori living a largely separate existence from pakeha at that time. Many observers, officials and politicians took from this realisation a belief that progress on removing discrimination and racism depended on encouraging mutual understanding between pakeha and Maori through fully integrated living and working environments. The senior DMA official who would lead the call for racial enlightenment opined that cross-ethnic living and mixing would 'prevent a "colour" problem from arising in New Zealand'. People 'understand and appreciate one another better and mutually adjust themselves easier if living together as neighbours than if living apart in separate communities'. Once neighbours got to know each other, Maori could 'feel that [they had] a rightful place in [the] community.' The very fact of urban migration, despite initial race tension, would – it was believed or hoped – assist not only the development of race harmony but also its supposed corollary, assimilation.[4]

But by 1960, there was an increasing official conviction that to get such results in the context of rapid and comprehensive urban migration, two key things were needed: greater state regulation and new measures to 'smooth the process of integration'. A 'calculated' paternalism in areas such as education, health and housing would assist both urban adjustment and long-term assimilation. It was still believed, for example, that even greater dispersal of Maori homes throughout suburban streets would ultimately prove to be one of the most effective ways of both countering racism and integrating Maori into the pakeha world. '[T]he home', Peter Fraser had said, 'is the place where character is moulded and lasting impressions made', and the home was influenced heavily by its immediate social and spatial environment. Many thought that as new generations of Maori were brought up within the physical and hegemonic landscapes of the pakeha, actual and perceived separateness would gradually disappear: Maori 'will grow up with a set of values very different from their own', as top DMA officials put it. And so, the argument went, any need for special measures and separate organisations for Maori would eventually, to a large degree, disappear.[5]

The Hunn Report

By the beginning of 1960, publicity about social maladjustment in the cities had focused the Labour government's attention on Maori issues. Crown monitoring put figures to popular perceptions: 'Maoris appear in disproportionate numbers in the Court records and their educational achievements (but not their capacity) are below par.' Under sustained fire for ignoring their own party's policies, Labour ministers were attempting to find more efficient ways and mechanisms for interacting with Maori and solving the problems arising from urban resettlement. Prime Minister Nash, in particular, had become increasingly aware of a general Maori disquiet about, or even hostility to, the Department of Maori Affairs. Relating essentially to perceptions of departmental paternalism and inefficiency, such widespread attitudes were seen as a major impediment to progress.

One significant line of advice on addressing the difficulty was posited on reports that committees and welfare agencies were still held in high regard. A full 10% of Maori, in fact, were estimated to have some kind of connection with an official committee. It was argued that progress on Crown–Maori relations could best occur through building on the concepts which had originally underpinned the committee system. If committees were to be given greater powers and range, they could become anchors for better integrating the department with Maoridom and attuning its bureaucrats to the needs of the people. It was in the context of such advice that the government was prepared to accede to several significant demands made by individuals and groups supporting and operating through the institutions of the 1945 Maori Social and Economic Advancement Act. At the very least, addressing some of their wishes was increasingly seen as better than ignoring them and thereby handing ammunition to elements within Maoridom which advocated a more confrontational stance.

Not only were concessions made over representation in the official system, moreover, but also on issues such as coordinating arrangements between departments dealing with urban adjustment – a response to criticisms from delegates at the Young Maori Leaders' Conference, among others, of 'piecemeal' bureaucratic procedures. It was just as a number of new arrangements were being put in place that the Labour government lost office in late 1960. The incoming National administration, despite its formal commitment to laissez-faire policies, was not averse to planning and social intervention. Moreover, it appreciated that it would need to rely a great deal for its success in Maori policy on the staff of the public service, especially those in Maori Affairs who mediated between the official committee system and the government. Given its small Maori base, in fact, the government would need to lean particularly heavily on its officials for policy and operational advice. Fortunately for Prime Minister Holyoake and his ministers, the DMA officials had already undertaken a complete re-examination of Crown–Maori relations.

At the beginning of the 1960s, in the middle of the most intensive period of urban migration in New Zealand history, few observers would have disagreed that it was timely to revisit the premises and implementation of the 1945 legislation under which Maori Affairs operated. Its structures had been worked out at an early stage of urban migration, before it was clear that this migration would become both huge and permanent. In his capacity as Minister of Maori Affairs, Nash had eventually been forced to give more serious attention to Maori aspirations. In early 1960, he tasked his department with investigating the state of Maoridom. This initiation of a comprehensive 'stocktaking' of Maori policies, management and 'assets', both human and material, was designed to provide a factual basis for more coherent and coordinated forward planning. In addition to providing a better knowledge basis for addressing the many problems relating to urban relocation, Nash had other outcomes in mind as well. He had, for example, become convinced of the need for the state to finally redress the problems arising from the relentless fragmentation of ownership of interests in Maori land – particularly the consequent locking-up of would-be productive farmland. More generally, he and his ministry believed that the pace of urban migration meant that it was now timely 'to prevent further dissipation of [Maori] material resources'; Maori should be able to build upon, rather than lose, those assets they still retained. In doing so, they would both better integrate into pakeha society and contribute to the general prosperity of the nation.[6]

Maori welcomed the proposed review as being, among other things, one way by which they might be able to further pursue both rangatiratanga and socio-economic betterment. On the surface, the prospects of the Crown acceding to autonomist aspirations at this time were far from likely. Elements within the bureaucracy and polity, for example, had even expressed disquiet at the government's endorsement of the regional groupings coordinating the tribal committee system. In the eyes of many left-leaning or liberal-minded pakeha, moreover, use of any remotely 'separatist' terminology was anathema, resonant of South Africa or the southern United States. Even those who empathised with the Maori aspiration for self-determination generally placed it well behind the goal of socio-economic advancement. For them, the material benefits brought by urban migration and the loosening of tribal identities considerably outweighed, in the final analysis, any cultural or governance difficulties Maori might face – let alone any aspirations they might harbour to effect rangatiratanga. Few pakeha observers, in fact, believed that greater political autonomy was compatible with significant socio-economic progress, given the extent to which (in their eyes) the latter implied integration into the world of the pakeha. The best that could be achieved was for 'remnants of Maori culture to be perpetuated' in the process of Maori procurement of full equality before the law and socio-economic parity with white New Zealand.

In the context of this pakeha-led discourse, on 18 January 1960 Nash appointed a senior public servant (Deputy Chairman of the Public Service Commission), Jack Kent Hunn, to head the DMA as Acting Secretary and Maori Trustee for a fixed period. He was tasked with both carrying out the stocktake and injecting an increased vigour and sensitivity into the DMA. On the basis of his findings on the state of Maoridom, Hunn's review was to recommend any structural and policy changes which might assist both departmental operations and the state's immediate, medium-term and ultimate goals for Maori. In other words, what was publicly billed as essentially a stocktaking exercise was designed to have an instrumental result – not just better use of 'Maori assets' but, relatedly, better policies to rapidly implement the socio-economic advancement of the Maori people. As with most liberally minded pakeha of their era, Labour politicians and the top DMA and other officials saw these improvements as coming about principally through implementation of the assimilationist vision.

Hunn's formal terms of reference, then, essentially relating to 'an accounting of Maori assets', masked the broad-based nature of the review of the position of Maori in society which he set at once in place, and from which he aimed to formulate recommendations for future policy. Nine interdepartmental research teams conducted the enquiry, travelling and consulting widely. In an exhausting and remarkable few months, the investigators examined, collated and probed a huge range of statistical, policy and operational matters relevant to Maori. Hunn coordinated the findings and developed the recommendations. 'The Hunn Report', completed in August 1960, would become one of the most famous documents of Crown–Maori interaction in New Zealand history.

Surveying trends in population, land settlement and titles, housing, education, employment, health, legal differentiation, crime and other matters, its findings, commentaries and conclusions were thoughtful and comprehensive. They made clear that Maori continued to lag far behind pakeha in all socio-economic indicators, and remained an essentially marginalised people.

The report was, implicitly, an indictment of post-war governments' implementation of the Maori policies originally set in place by Labour in the 1930s. More positively, it constituted a manifesto of proactive measures for assisting Maori to acquire parity with pakeha, something seen to be a matter of urgency if New Zealand's much vaunted race harmony was not to be jeopardised – and if Maori were to contribute their full potential to the national good. With an election looming in November, the Prime Minister 'sat on' the report. His official reason for delaying its release was that he did not have sufficient time to study it. If that were true, given that he was a man of prodigious report-reading capacity, it would say a great deal about the Labour leadership's priorities. But the major reason for non-release of the Hunn report in election year was to avoid publicly highlighting (in pakeha eyes) 'the Maori problem' and (in Maori eyes) the government's inability or unwillingness to seriously address indigenous marginalisation. In his delaying tactics, Nash may have been motivated by more than just electioneering. Labour knew that it was in trouble with the electorate, and Nash later said that he suppressed the report in order to deny National the chance to use its statistics as anti-Maori ammunition in the heat of an election campaign – thereby possibly preventing an incoming conservative government inheriting unfortunate policies conceived in haste.

The Hunn report has been demonised in recent years, but generally for anachronistic reasons. Critics have tended to condemn its lack of interest in Maori autonomy. It is unrealistic, however, to expect official analyses and recommendations made in 1960 to have encompassed rangatiratanga. Any such review would naturally fall within the constrained parameters of the received wisdom of officials and politicians concerned, for whatever reasons, to improve the socio-economic lot of Maori. Hunn told his working parties that the stocktake should not question the thrust of the Crown's socio-economic intentions with regard to Maori: 'The main purpose is not to examine *what* we are doing for the Maori people but to ascertain the *rate* or *tempo* at which it is being done in relation to the dynamic growth of the Maori population.' Social, educational and economic advancement was the urgent and overriding priority expressed within the report.

Maori, of course, did aspire to parity with pakeha social, educational and (especially) economic standards. But the Hunn report, a product of Crown assumptions and priorities, did not reflect their oft expressed aspirations for

Crown recognition of rangatiratanga. In urging, instead, a speeding up of official programmes, it sought to provide both the solution to Maori social and economic problems and to 'the Maori problem' perceived by the state. Its recommendations aimed to hasten the assumed natural evolutionary path towards the 'integrationist' version of assimilation and (ultimately) the 'distant end-result' of 'final blending'. Efforts to accommodate ways of 'seeing and doing' that were different from those of Anglocentric culture were not on any state agenda.[7]

On 17 January 1961, soon after Labour lost the election, the Hunn report was released to the public by the new Minister of Maori Affairs, J R Hanan, the third-ranking minister in Cabinet. There was, no doubt, a political element to its publication. The National government could extract mileage from the fact that an official enquiry had implicitly indicted Labour ministers for failing to adequately address the needs of one of their own most stalwart sectors of support. National held out hope that it could use this as a lever to gain some increase in the scant backing it received from Maori rank and file. However, the views of Hanan and like-minded colleagues on Maori policy differed little from those of Labour politicians and 'progressive' officials. All reflected, to a greater or lesser degree, the broad post-war consensus which had been emerging on the need for both Maori socio-economic progress as a fast-track towards assimilation. Moreover, such beliefs formed part of a liberal package on issues such as race-based discrimination and the virtues of equality of opportunity. When Hanan and other liberal minded pakeha read the Hunn report, they saw their own views presented in a forthright and systematic fashion. When he took on ministerial responsibility for Maori Affairs, the new minister (in Hunn's testimony) 'soon became devoted to the Maori cause'.

For the first time, then, an official analysis had comprehensively taken into account the various post-1945 developments both among Maori and in society in general, and drawn policy conclusions within a broad context of 'enlightened' national and international thought. Hanan depicted the Hunn report as having 'a fundamental bearing on the well-being of the Maori people, the well-being of New Zealanders as a whole, and on race relations in New Zealand'. He viewed the report's recommendations as a general blueprint for indigenous policy in New Zealand, and told Hunn even before its public release that it 'was to be Government policy in its entirety'. On 2 February 1961, Hunn was confirmed as permanent head of the Department of Maori Affairs and placed in charge of overseeing the new policy directions.

In one sense, both Hunn's recommendations and the government's decision to adopt the main thrust of these as policy were bold steps. In addition to proposing measures which could be effected fairly rapidly, such as removing legal differentiation between Maori and pakeha, the Hunn report 'called for recognition that special assistance to the Maori people was needed if living standards, occupational distribution, educational and health levels of the Maori were to be brought to approximate equality with general non-Maori standards'. The report overtly called for targeted measures and a policy of short-term or medium-term positive discrimination in the interests of long-term equality. Despite the post-war consensus on fundamental issues and goals, a policy of 'special measures' was not an obvious path for a conservative government to take, with its philosophical ethos of hands-off policies and its aversion to race-based funding and programmes. But Hanan, some other ministers and key advisers saw little choice than pragmatic policies to effect public-good outcomes with regard to 'the Maori problem': the Crown was the guardian of the nation's racial harmony, which was under threat by rapid Maori population increase and urban migration. The situation demanded temporary departures from the ideal, in the pursuit of ultimate goals.[8]

The Meaning of 'Integration'

The Hunn report's assimilative parameters were obfuscated by definitional issues. In line with official nomenclature, Hunn differentiated between 'assimilation' and 'integration', declaring the latter to be already 'a fact of life': 'Evolution is clearly integrating Maori and pakeha. Consequently "integration" is said to be the official policy whenever the question is asked.' Building upon the pre-existing processes of integration provided the best prospects for the immediate and medium-term future. Assimilation was taken to mean that Maori would 'become absorbed, blended, amalgamated, with complete loss of Maori culture'. Integration was seen to be a more realistic option, defined as a policy that aimed to 'combine (not fuse) the Maori and pakeha elements to form one nation wherein Maori culture remains distinct'. Integrating processes would inevitably build in momentum, but could speed up greatly with Crown assistance. The reality of integration, brought about by developments such as urbanisation and modernisation, needed to be fully embraced and enhanced by the state. Urbanisation should be especially 'welcomed as the quickest and surest way of integrating the two species of New Zealander'. 'Full integration of the Maori people into the main stream of New Zealand life is coming to be recognised as just about the most important objective ahead of the country today.' The report, Hunn later said, merely codified the policy of integration which was already in place but which had 'never been articulated by any Government' – at least not in so dramatic or explicit a way.[9]

Although Hunn distinguished integration from assimilation, the goal of official policy remained assimilative in all but name. Both integration and assimilation were seen to be part of the 'successive stages of evolution, wherein different races in the same environment pass from their original segregation to integration and ultimately to assimilation'. The report was thus informed by Social-Darwinist assumptions. With 'only the fittest elements' of Maori culture able to survive the 'onset of civilisation', the 'object of policy' was to 'raise' Maori who were still 'complacently living a backward life in primitive conditions' to the level where they became 'integrated', retaining marginal elements of their culture while feeling totally 'at home' in pakeha society – or, if they so chose, completely 'assimilated'. Any prospect of 'two dissimilar peoples living together but as separate entities', called 'symbiosis' by Hunn, was roundly rejected. Liberal minded officials, politicians and advisers were confident that in two generations, Maori would be 'well nigh fully integrated', an outcome supposedly different from that entailed by nineteenth-century 'amalgamationist' or 'absorptionist' programmes of assimilation. For those Maori resentful of the 'pressure brought to bear on them to conform to what they regard as the pakeha way of life', the report offered the advice that they could adapt not to 'a *pakeha* but [to] a *modern* way of life, common to advanced people ... Full realisation of this fact might induce the hesitant or reluctant Maoris to fall into line more readily'.[10]

The spelling-out of integration as a policy can be (and was) seen as a way of minimally taking into account Maori aspirations for self-determination. For Hunn and others the term did imply 'some continuation of the separate cultures', although this seemed to mean little more than survival of 'the [Maori] language, arts and crafts and the institutions of the marae'. Only 'the Maoris themselves could keep alive these features of their ancient way of life', something that was 'entirely a matter of individual choice'. There was, therefore, a realm of permitted (though inexorably declining) Maori culture, but the possibility of a 'distant future' in which a full assimilation of minorities might occur was held out – as was believed to have happened in England.

A balance was needed, officials and liberals argued, if New Zealand were to continue to be 'in the vanguard of [nations] that are building multi-racial societies'. This involved a way forward that would 'give equal opportunities ... without imposing unnecessary uniformity' upon Maori: in 'closing the gap' between the two 'cultural groups' of New Zealand, state and pakeha needed to be ever mindful of being 'tolerant of diversity'. The result would be a country in which 'no citizen differs from any other citizen, because of his ethnic origin, in his economic and social rights, opportunities and responsibilities'. Thus, integration had, in the liberal pakeha political milieu, been developing as a policy option which made a virtue of temporary or limited accommodations to Maori culture and organisation. It claimed that even the 'whole new culture' which would emerge from intermarriage and other assimilative tendencies would not involve 'a submergence' of Maoridom.

Hunn insisted, then, that while integration meant bringing two distinct cultures together in order 'to form one nation', it allowed both to remain distinct. But the reality was, as he and others knew, that the intermix of cultures in post-colonial New Zealand was very much a one-sided affair. At best the dominant political economy and culture would tolerate selective aspects of the Maori organisational ethos and worldview. Hunn, Hanan and many others believed that ultimately Maori would be assimilated within a 'blended new species' in which, essentially, they would be brown-skinned pakeha. The 'fundamental tenets' of 'communal' Maori culture and of 'individualistic and self-centred' European culture were, Hunn eventually concluded, 'incompatible', and it was for Maori to adapt to the European world. Such views lay towards the progressive, left-liberal end of the political spectrum. In the final analysis, the report, embodying the worldview of white liberals and state alike (whatever their varying motivations), had no place for the exercise of rangatiratanga – and nor should anyone be particularly surprised at this, in view of the dominant discourses of the times.[11]

The concessions the National government was prepared to make to Maori aspirations for an ongoing separate presence in state and society, then, were severely limited and temporary. They could be nothing else in view of the Crown's aims for, and prevailing social attitudes to, Maoridom at that time. The future for rural Maori, for example, was said to be best served by continued urban migration, which would remove the problems of 'backwardness' which were said to flow from the collectivist outlook and activities of the home marae. The many urban migrants who had 'adopted the 1960 pattern of living in every way' were seen to need assistance into socio-economic parity with pakeha to strengthen that new pattern. This was believed to be the best that could be done for Maori, given a prevalent view that (in the words of an anthropological assessment) 'the economics and social consequences of their history of acculturation have made many of the elements of maoritanga functionless'.

In the early 1960s, the state's plans to incorporate Maori fully into mainstream pakeha life became more fully articulated. While Hunn's report eschewed the concept of full assimilation except for those (relatively few) Maori who were willing, its implementers were not so squeamish in enunciating the processes they were engaged in as ending in 'social, economic and cultural fusion'. Politicians were guided by many other official statements and reports as well as Hunn's. In 1959, Nash, noting that '[g]overnment policy is to integrate Maoris with the European community', declared that the most important way of doing so was 'by arranging for Maori and European children to attend school together'. The 'school is the nursery of integration', Hunn agreed, sharing the widespread frustration within officialdom that Maori schools were slow in transferring to the mainstream system: over a quarter of Maori children remained in Maori schools. On the question of culture and language, the 1962 report of the Royal Commission on Education (appointed in 1960, with no Maori members) was resonant of the Hunn report: essentially, any responsibility for preserving Maori culture lay with Maori themselves (although assistance could be given to schools with significant numbers of Maori pupils).[12]

To continue its predecessors' policies of integration on western terms was a safe policy for the new Holyoake government, one unlikely to meet with much organised opposition in the pakeha world except from relatively small numbers on the right. Even the far left generally supported the assimilationist policies which had been a key feature of 'progressive thought' in New Zealand. Ron Meek's left-wing wartime publication *Maori Problems Today* had argued that both the Maori and the pakeha working classes shared the same struggles and goals. Even such posing of the issue as involving *two sets* of class interests, rather than a single working class in and for itself, was queried in some quarters. A diary entry by youthful Dick Scott, who would later champion Maori causes, saw a dual-class analysis as 'only a good liberal effort' that was not reflective of historical laws of inevitability. One of his comrades in the communist milieu argued that it was 'nonsense to worry about [Maori] tribal survival, to restore their arts and crafts etc.', particularly given the inexorability of urban migration: the thing to do was to provide sufficient resources to eradicate the 'gross maladjustments of [Maori] existence'. Under socialism, he argued, the 'Maori problem [would] "wither away" and so [would] probably the Maoris themselves'.

While a few members of the far left applied Marxist-Leninist analyses which accommodated self-determination as the means of removing a 'roadblock' to socialism, Scott summed up the views of most 'progressive' thinkers in the first post-war decades: there was 'no value in artificially attempting to preserve a race which is being assimilated'. The mainstream centre- and far-left vision among pakeha essentially reflected the views of most non-Maori sectors of society, especially those concerned about the much publicised difficulties of urban adjustment: if the state needed to do anything for people of Maori descent, it should help hasten the inevitable disappearance of 'Maoridom', for their own good and that of everyone else. Enabling their full participation in all that the 'highest civilisation in history' had to offer would also help alleviate socio-racial difficulties and assist the growth of a unified nation working together for the class or common good. There was little appreciation that the tangata whenua had any special Treaty-based or other place in New Zealand society, only that Maori 'cannot be expected to give up their entire Maoritanga in the process of adopting the ways of the pakeha'. Within the 'one nation' Hunn and Booth allowed, 'Maoris will make a considerable contribution to the common culture in areas where their numerical proportion is high'.[13]

The Hunn report led to general public awareness of the adverse socio-economic situation of both urban and rural Maori, and also generated a great deal of debate over proposed efforts to overcome their problems (and problems of society at large). Many pakeha still opposed spending state resources on Maori. In the publicity surrounding the report's release, and in the extended discussions which followed, the government sought to persuade the pakeha constituency that 'special measures' to assist Maori *as individuals* were legitimate so long as they were geared to assimilative, 'public good' ends. Many were seemingly won over to the view that significant socio-economic improvements should and could be achieved within Maoridom, building upon (in Hunn's assessment) the 'quite remarkable strides' taken by Maori in recent decades. There had undoubtedly been many positive developments in matters such as housing, social security, state-assisted relocation and employment in the cities, and insofar as the Crown had been involved in these, precedents had been created for state intervention to narrow the socio-economic gulf between Maori and pakeha. The Crown, and seemingly most pakeha, thought that goal was sufficient. Implementation of a number of Hunn's recommendations was fast tracked, aiding those Maori aspirations which lay within the parameters defined by officially sanctioned discourses.[14]

Responses to the Hunn Report

Maori continued to have little influence in formulating official Maori policy, although the situation did improve after the release of the Hunn report. An historian of Maori policy would later conclude that the 'main problem' with the report was 'its failure to consult adequately with the Maori community and to include a proper Maori perspective'. Despite the relative lack of Maori engagement in the Hunn recommendations, however, in the early 1960s Maori reaction was generally positive. This reflected a number of factors: the Hunn report's identification of the large socio-economic disparities between Maori and pakeha; its call for action to achieve 'equality' between the races by closing these gaps; Hunn's endorsement of special state measures to assist this aim, and politicians' willingness to address the matter seriously; the consideration the report gave to at least some Maori views; and Crown willingness to engage in some degree of Maori consultation at the implementation stage of the report.

In general, immediate Maori response to the Hunn report coincided with that of pakeha who identified themselves as progressive on race and other issues. James Ritchie, who had conducted fieldwork among people who 'feel themselves to be Maori, call themselves Maori, and speak Maori at least some of the time', summed up the report as being 'wise, balanced and fair'. Along with many Maori and pakeha, he endorsed the report's emphasis on affirmative action to bring about Maori socio-economic uplift at a time of demographic upheaval and transition, and applauded a seemingly new willingness to listen to Maori views (if not to bring Maori into decision-making processes).[15]

The report's rapid endorsement 'in principle' by the Minister of Maori Affairs on behalf of the Crown gave hope that a bright social and economic future for Maoridom might finally be achievable. This ambition was summed up in a newspaper headline (in an inadvertent indication of pakeha stereotyping): 'Minister wants to put motor behind Maori canoe'. Officials believed Maori were poised to take up fully not only the tools of the pakeha but the attributes that were seen to accompany their proper use. In 1963, Hanan declared that the country was giving 'the world a lead in showing how two ways of life can become one, each enriching the other. Maori and pakeha, though having two different pasts, have one common future'. The permanent head of Maori Affairs applauded Maori-run youth and other clubs in cities welcoming pakeha particiaption, rejoiced that Maori and Europeans worked, travelled and danced together, and saw a rosy future based on the propensity for interracial marriage in the towns and cities. While these harmonious prospects were seen to rest on urban-based socio-economic uplift for Maori, the emergence of 'one New Zealand' was often presented as a logical continuation of the golden race relations that were supposedly characteristic of New Zealand's past.[16]

By the middle of 1961, however, second thoughts about official aims were emerging in some quarters as the import of Hunn's message began to sink home. A number of Maori who had benefited from the new educational opportunities in the cities, for example, while welcoming the Hunn report's thrust regarding socio-economic equality for Maori, also saw that it embodied (albeit relatively benignly) the politics of assimilation. Ritchie noted in 1966 that there had been 'deep suspicion' that its endorsement of 'integration' was a cover for full assimilation. The report's concessions to Maoriness were increasingly seen to be tokenistic – even, in the eyes of some, to be touristic. Maori analysts such as Bruce Biggs came to criticise it for lacking any interest in Maori culture and for failing to recognise Maori aspirations for rangatiratanga. A number of pakeha public intellectuals, such as Richard Thompson, argued that the report was 'representative of an essentially European point of view'.

The Maori Synod of the Presbyterian Church was particularly critical of aspects of the Hunn report soon after its publication. This grouping was all in favour of socio-economic advance, and applauded the report's commitment to this. But it saw Hunn's lauding of integration to be based on the dangerous ethnocentric assumption that Maori, not pakeha, needed to do all the adjusting. 'A race cannot be forced into taking steps towards its own elimination', the authors wrote. In any case, if the policy of integration really did allow for a meaningful Maori identity and presence, it was the tangata whenua who should decide the pace and degree of their adoption of European ways. Conversely, pakeha needed to adjust to Maori ways of seeing and doing. Some Maori, imbued with the experience of being seen as 'queer' neighbours in the city, were already looking sceptically upon the desirability of joining the more materialistic and individualistic way of life of the pakeha. One wrote to the editor of the *Listener* that 'the biggest problem for the Maori is not how he can master the European way of life, but trying to decide whether or not it is a way of life worth mastering. And a lot of us are convinced that it isn't'.[17]

Increasingly, commentators added caveats to their general approval of Hunn's acknowledgement of the need for accelerating government intervention on socio-economic, educational and other issues concerning Maori. Many felt that the Hunn report ignored the 'elementary rules of community development' among tangata whenua. In a 1967 textbook, an historian noted that while Maori had never wanted total physical segregation, neither did they want assimilation. People would continue to make their own choices as to whether they identified as Maori. 'So long as this separatism of spirit persists, assimilation will never come about.' Criticisms of the integrationist thrust of the Hunn report and government policy, and of their ultimate assimilationist goals, slowly became mainstream in Maori interpretation and, eventually, in liberal pakeha thought. The report's essential premise of rapid Maori socio-economic and educational progress in the cities, together with its rejection of 'rural segregation', were seen to stem from a deep-seated desire by the Crown to detribalise and de-maorify. Maori were to constitute little more than ever-whitening individuals of the urban proletariat.[18]

A decade after the Hunn report, dissenting voices were becoming increasingly loud and insistent. Hugh Kawharu would bluntly state, with regard to the Hunn prescription to work through 'individualised aid' rather than 'tribal organisation', that 'when the Pakeha says "integration" he really means "assimilation"'. In the 1970s, Hirini Mead criticised the Crown for continuing the 'one people, one nation' policy, which he believed to have largely been successful in 'alienating us from our own culture' ever since 1840. In 1978, Pat Hohepa firmly rejected all policies posited upon assimilation or integration. We are, he stated, 'one nation of two peoples', arguing that colonisation had not 'really affected Maori attitudes – the things of the heart, the mind and the spirit'. An anthropologist declared in 1985: 'To Maori leaders the conclusion was inescapable: both assimilation and integration shared a common political objective, that is, the creation of a uniform society, united under a conformist set of political and social values, and shorn of cultural distinctiveness except in the most trivial sense of the term.'[19]

Quickening the Pace of Change

The Crown had, indeed, never been at ease with indigeneity. The weakening of tribal links that accompanied the move to the cities was therefore welcomed and encouraged by it, despite all the problems of social order which eventuated as a consequence. These were expected to be gradually overcome by good management, prosperity and the passage of time. In the decade after the Hunn report, the voices of those who used the language of self-determination, autonomy, rangatiratanga and the like were scarcely heeded, and state franchised urbanisation proceeded apace alongside other integrationist measures. In 1965, official commissioners noted that the way Maori had been 'compelled to move to the towns ... is so pronounced that [the Crown] already has a word which describes it. That word is relocation'.

Coordinated interdepartmental arrangements to assist urban migration had been evolving over the years, with a flurry of activity in the last months of the Nash government. The idea behind this, as Hunn expressed it in 1960, was to 'guide [the urbanisation process] along proper channels', given that 're-location from under-developed areas was already taking place on a fairly large scale'. '[I]nstead of standing passively aside and watching the Maoris drift aimlessly into town in a stream, we should be there to meet them ... with accommodation and jobs'. Earlier efforts were now to be built upon, coordinated and supplemented. 'Planned relocation' was discussed by a joint departmental committee on Maori employment, a pilot scheme was established to find jobs and accommodation for single workers, and plans were developed to place families in homes and work in Auckland, Hamilton, Wellington and Rotorua. Welfare officers gained resources to help those newly arrived from the country to make 'helpful associations' in the urban environment. In 1961, the DMA established a comprehensive relocation programme to further propel Maori people from 'retarded areas' in the countryside to the towns and cities. Maori were seen more than ever to constitute a 'reserve army of labour' (as it has been described in other contexts), ready to be called in to assist urban-based industrialisation. 'We think', said one official prior to the commencement of the DMA programme, 'that this re-location of families from rural to urban areas should be continued as much as possible. There is a growing demand for labour of a permanent nature'.[20]

Whatever the Crown's motivations for its Maori migration agenda, it cannot be doubted that urban relocation packages and similar bureaucratic policies assisted many Maori, both individuals and families, to greatly improve their living standards. The policies foreshadowed comprehensively in Hunn's report also led to other positive developments for many Maori people. There was 'tremendous improvement', in one assessment, 'in the standard of Maori housing' and, for a few years, a steady betterment in indicators of health, mortality rates and education. These occurred alongside increasing efforts 'to take advantage of the Maori viewpoint' in various spheres of official activity. An interdepartmental advisory Maori Health Committee, for example, channelled Maori opinion to officials in a coordinated way, and other such structures followed. While far from meeting the increasingly vocal Maori demand for Maori control of things Maori, such developments were widely seen by Maori as steps in the right direction.

In a few cases, the steps seemed considerable. In 1961, the government launched the Maori Education Foundation 'to provide specialised assistance and information to help the Maori people improve their level of educational attainment'. It noted that the 'economic, environmental, and cultural' factors hindering Maori educational advancement needed to be overcome. The foundation aimed to 'raise Maori educational standards to equal those of the pakeha'. With seeding funding and subsidies from the state, it was organised as if it were a partnership between Maori and pakeha, albeit a Crown-established one.

The foundation was described as an 'independent statutory authority jointly managed by four Maori and four pakeha trustees [and] financed by Government and private enterprise, Maori and pakeha'. But despite its initial promise as a prototypal bicultural model, the foundation proved to be another example of short- to medium-term targeting aimed at producing the necessary conditions for integration in the longer run. As the Department of Maori Affairs reminded, 'Maori welfare authorities consider education of primary importance in Maori adjustment to modern civilisation'. In the post-Hunn report atmosphere, the pace needed to be forced. The chair of the foundation's Board of Trustees, D G Ball, referred to high stakes (at a time of growing race tension in the United Kingdom): 'We are determined to avert any possibility of a racial problem in New Zealand through the Maori people having lower educational standards than the remainder of the community.'[21]

In the Crown's view, Maori adjustment to modernity could not be anything but integrationist in nature. Despite some increased attention being paid to Maori opinions, the main concern of politicians and officials was to create a willing workforce of healthy, educated and westernised individuals. The state had not abandoned its longstanding policies of appropriating tribal structures, imperatives and organisational culture to assist with the process of integration. It was now, however, increasingly focussing on utilising collective indigenous organisations in the cities. Certainly the pan-tribal nature of most of the official (and other) urban committees, and their voluntary memberships, meant that urban-based appropriation could be less efficient for the Crown than its equivalent in rural areas, with their strong kin-based forms of social control.

But putting resources and time into urban Maori institutions was often seen by officials and politicians as preferable – given that tribal energies were generally regarded, even in their appropriated form, as potentially undermining that which the Crown wanted ultimately to achieve.

On the other hand, the Crown's unwillingness to regard Maori mores, customs and social organisation as integral to urban-based life was of increasing concern to many among the Maori leadership. Such worries became more acute as the movement to the cities accelerated. The Presbyterian Maori manifesto had been unequivocal at the very beginning of feedback on the Hunn report: 'Let it be understood that ... we have no desire whatever to become Pakehas.' Strategies for avoiding cultural submergence in the face of overwhelming government, demographic and other pressure were fraught with difficulty. But while the Crown worked towards the demise of Maoritanga, the organisations whose energies it appropriated often became sites of both political and cultural resistance to full assimilation. Even the urban committees, while assisting adjustment to capitalist and pakeha ways of doing things, were determined 'to steer a course between two cultures, the literate and the oral', and to affirm rangatiratanga in the process. There were many weapons in the fight to recover what the Presbyterian declaration called the 'lost soul' of Maoridom.[22]

The state could draw on the help of some Maori groups which endorsed an integrationist perspective, but even they did not share any consensus with officialdom on what integration meant. More broadly, 'Maori attitudes towards the costs and benefits of achieving integration are clearly different from those of the non-Maori', Kawharu would write. This was due to 'a difference in assumptions about the nature and significance of the evolutionary trends in Maori social organisation and cultural values'. Opinions may 'have shifted on both sides from time to time, [but] they have failed to coalesce'. Maori of various stances, and organised in discrete ways, were not about to relinquish the possibility of meaningful control over their collective destiny, whether or not they were prepared to work within the parameters of debate and policy established by the Crown.[23]

Reaction to Crown Policy

In 1961, however, the Crown believed that Maori weapons of rangatiratanga lacked significant power, given both urban migration and its own hegemonic strength: things distinctively Maori could soon be relegated to a cultural and touristic marginalia. But it would quickly encounter determined resistance to the most overt of its assimilationist policies. In particular, there was profound Maori resistance to the government's efforts to implement Hunn's 'solutions' to the problems of Maori land title development. The Hunn report noted that land title consolidation processes had become, because of the exponential laws of succession, 'a treadmill effort, endless and hopeless' – although it did acknowledge that the land title system was 'a European invention imposed on [Maori] in the first place'. Maori welcomed Hunn's criticism of the inadequacy of state policy on Maori land, but many saw his recommendations to be posited on 'public good' paternalism. His views, and those of the officials and politicians working with him, were considered to be those of an analyst looking to the state's 'natural interest' rather than to Maori-generated, let alone Maori-controlled, solutions.

This state-led perspective can be seen in the Hunn report's handling of the question of developing Maori rural land, including that leased out to owner-nominated Maori farmers. The productivity of many such lease-hold farms was assessed as falling far short of that which the country needed. Under-utilised or idle land, Hunn wrote, was not in the 'national interest', which included 'of course[,] the Maori interest'. A key problem was that many Maori farmers were deemed inadequate. In cases where more than one Maori lessee farmer had been nominated by owners, District Maori Land Committees had made the selection, but even this had not guaranteed 'aptitude or experience'. The remedy Hunn proposed was to take, when necessary, selection of the lessee of Maori-owned land out of the owners' hands: 'In future, Maori owners will be asked to agree in advance that, failing a satisfactory nomination by them, the Board of Maori Affairs will have the right to select the settler. They may not take kindly to that suggestion.' They did not, and they remarked that there were no equivalent restrictions applied to pakeha owners.

But it was Hunn's solution to the very real problem of fragmented land tenure which created real anger within Maoridom. He argued that national production suffered as a result of multiple ownership because it 'obstructs utilisation'. His report proposed that the Crown acquire multiple or 'uneconomic' interests and hold these 'in trust for the Maori people' while the land was developed or utilised in the name of the public good. Bureaucrats began, at the behest of the minister, to work on detailed solutions along the broad lines established by the report. As in many past policies related to land, state interventionist impulses took scant heed of Maori concerns and wishes – which often centred on overcoming impediments faced by collectivities in acquiring development capital. Soon, officials were recommending that, since it was in the national interest to dramatically raise ewe numbers, 'unoccupied and undeveloped Maori land' would have to be 'both occupied and developed' by the state. Collective ownership and management were seen as both anachronistic in terms of 'evolution' and wrong in terms of ethical/ideological values. The two came together in Hunn's words: 'Everybody's land is nobody's land'. Solutions to the combined problems of land tenure and development involved, in short, the state deciding on the best course of action to take based on pakeha assumptions about appropriate ownership modes and economic uses for the land.[24]

While land was of central concern to Maori, for cultural as well as productive reasons, it was just one domain in which the Crown's assimilationist policies posed difficulties. Even where post-Hunn policies did bring improvement – such as in housing, health and education – and therefore Maori approval, this was generally seen to constitute 'assistance' from a top-down government. This minimised Maori involvement in policy formation, let alone allowing for ethnic duality in political or bureaucratic decision-making. Those in charge of the capitalist democracy of New Zealand operated with an individualistic vision with little tolerance for collective, plural or tribal involvement in social, economic or political matters. State development programmes and initiatives were aimed squarely at an assimilative 'New Zealand', one which excluded 'Aotearoa' except where the Crown was forced to do otherwise – and such cases were viewed, conceptually, as largely temporary or (at most) medium-term accommodations to Maoriness.

Such an analysis does not imply that finding ways of meeting Maori aspirations within the New Zealand state was (or is) easy. Maori often appreciated the difficulties, and expressed a multitude of views as to viable ways forward. Following the Hunn report, for example, consultation on the fate of the Maori schools confirmed that many Maori supported their proposed abolition. They were seen as out-dated impediments to acquiring the western education Maori needed if they were to hold their own, individually or collectively, in modern New Zealand. Such views lay behind 22 Maori schools abandoning their special status or closing down in the ten years after the mid-1950s. Many other Maori, however, viewed the ongoing disappearance of the schools as signifying the triumph of assimilation in education, and they fought the trend. They had come to see the Maori school institution, originally set up as a state device to fast-track assimilation among Maori, as 'their own'. Maori schools were useful, both practically and symbolically, for the promotion of Maoritanga and in the general interests of Maoridom.

Even on the land issue, reactions could be mixed and complex. While many opposed the paternalist and potentially coercive recommendations in the Hunn report, not all opposed Crown purchase of small interests in land, especially those who needed the wherewithal to migrate to the cities in search of better economic opportunities. Some had already pointed out that the increasing propensity for the Maori Land Court to protect Maori collective rights in land could disadvantage individuals who wanted to sell their interests to acquire a 'house site in town'. In the words of a 1965 official enquiry, there was 'nothing in the Treaty which forced Maoris to retain their land'. Rangatiratanga could be expressed, in some perspectives, through the freedom to sell – an attitude which went back to the previous century.[25]

Assimilation and International Protocols

For all the welfarist and economic advantages for Maori that emerged from the Hunn report and consultation over its implementation, assimilation – under whatever name and in its varied and various forms – remained the official policy towards tangata whenua. DMA and other departmental schemes were all directed towards Maori making (in the words of Booth and Hunn) 'the necessary adjustments to their changed and changing environment'. In 1962, for example, the Adoption Act was amended to remove the Maori Land Court's jurisdiction in adoptions; now, in the name of removing discrimination, applicants were forced to go to the less congenial surroundings of the Magistrates' Court. In this arena, as in many others, Maori resisted in whatever way they could; in this case, 'customary adoptions' rose again.

In summary, Maori knew that in the final analysis 'equality' meant mainstreaming and assimilation. In 1970, Booth, a key bureaucrat in developing the Crown's integration policies, acknowledged that there had been a strong assimilationist trend in their implementation. His argument that this need not have been the case revolved around the distinctions embodied in the Hunn report. But the fact remained that the great majority of the liberal minded politicians and officials who had carried out the implementing were in essence assimilators, as were many of their counterparts elsewhere: assimilationist goals focussing on socio-economic equality reflected 'progressive' thinking in other post-colonial settler countries. Such views were shared by many 'enlightened' and well-meaning individuals and organisations worldwide. The first United Nations body to attempt a written definition of indigenous people's rights, for example, was the International Labour Organisation (ILO), whose 1957 Convention on International Indigenous and Tribal Populations (ILO Convention 107) is widely seen today as having promoted policies of assimilation. It was declared to apply to populations which were 'less advanced' (Article 1), and it aimed to ensure their 'progressive integration' into mainstream societies (Article 2).

The fact remains that at the time Convention 107 was seen among progressive forces as an advanced and enlightened document. Indeed, it was initially greeted with suspicion in conservative sectors of the New Zealand state for allegedly taking indigenous rights too far, even though it generally accorded with Crown policy on 'integration'. It was related content in the convention, particularly its call for governmental anti-discrimination measures, which made some politicians and their advisers uneasy. One official wrote in late 1959 that the convention could cause difficulty for the country 'on the grounds that there is racial discrimination in New Zealand and the Government is not actively taking steps to improve matters'. He recommended that '[a]ny possible danger of publicity must be avoided' and suggested the need for a 'thoroughly confidential' report to help find a way forward. Another official advised similarly: since the ILO's protocols implied doing 'everything possible' to prevent discrimination, 'the Government could be embarrassed if it ratified the Convention'.[26]

Following the Hunn report and the beginnings of its implementation, however, official reservations over the issue of discrimination had begun to fade. But Maori were increasingly concerned about the ramifications for rangatiratanga of the international conventions being heavily assimilative, giving the Crown potential ammunition in its discouraging of separate customs in modern society. Indigenous representations on the issue were partly met by the United Nations' International Convention on the Elimination of All Forms of Racial Discrimination of 1965. This allowed for 'special and concrete measures' to achieve the 'adequate advancement of certain racial or ethnic groups' where these were deemed to be warranted. In 1966 the Assistant Secretary for Maori Affairs received advice that, while 'international scrutiny' of New Zealand's racial situation could still result in 'embarrassment', any delay in signing the convention could cause even greater difficulty by attracting domestic and international criticism. Eventually the Race Relations Act of 1971 removed difficulties in international perception that New Zealand was remiss over its lack of legal sanctions against discrimination.

There was another potential line of international criticism, however, which related to assimilationist assumptions in the convention: some Acts, institutions and measures pertaining to Maori could be interpreted as falling foul of these, even though Maori supported (and had negotiated for) them. There were worries, for example, that 'legislation governing Maori Wardens was a clear breach of the convention'. Delays occurred, but despite continuing concerns about existing legal differentiations between Maori and pakeha, New Zealand eventually ratified the convention in 1972. Maori felt encouraged in their struggle for rangatiratanga by this development, which highlighted their sharing of indigenous aspirations with peoples elsewhere in the world. Such voices were increasingly being heard, and their demands sometimes incorporated into the pronouncements of international bodies and the texts of an emergent international law. With processes of decolonisation now in full swing, the general Maori rejection of total assimilation to 'the west' could be clearly seen as part of a worldwide indigenous phenomenon – however much international organisations had initially attempted to assist indigenes by promoting their assimilation. By the early 1970s, evolving international human rights conventions were giving campaigners on indigenous issues in New Zealand considerable domestic leverage.[27]

Regional and National Representation

Few would have predicted such rapid international developments – or the extent to which they would be taken up in New Zealand – in the immediate aftermath of the Hunn report. This had implicitly dismissed rangatiratanga in favour of assimilationist socio-economic progress, in an official climate in which advancement and tribalism were seen as incompatible. There was little initial opposition from any quarter, with Maori grateful for its major thrust of state-assisted 'uplift'. The most the Crown would concede in response to that degree of criticism which did arise in the early 1960s was to take into account the insistent Maori call for better consultation. This occurred partly through ad hoc procedures implemented in specific policy arenas. But with increasing Maori disillusionment at the lack of systemic ways of getting Maori needs, requests and suggestions attended to, there was clearly room for a more structured approach. Given that there was already enormous pressure to endorse fully the recent informal developments at regional and national level in the official committee system, Crown proposals for reform centred on finessing the plans already developed under Labour. There was little internal opposition within the state, as most advisers had come to the position that the proposals were in the Crown's interest as well as those of Maori. Since the case for reform had been made by the Hunn report, a mandate could be argued to exist.

Legalising representation at regional and national levels of Maoridom would, it was hoped, inject new vigour into an official committee system discernibly flagging in enthusiasm after the failure of the flaxroots Ratana/Labour organisations to get 'their own' government to deliver anything much by way of recognising rangatiratanga. A quarter of the 80 tribal executives and 440 tribal committees were officially deemed 'inactive' before the fall of Nash's Labour government. Entire areas had no functioning committees, nor were cities and large towns comprehensively covered. Moreover, the National government believed that reviving the work of the official committee structure would also provide it with an opportunity to increase its own influence among Maori.

With the election in 1960 having put paid to the structural plans Labour had been formulating, Hunn took the lead in pushing for swift statutory recognition for regional and national groupings above the tribal committees and executives. On his advice, the new Minister of Maori Affairs consulted the unofficial Dominion Council of Tribal Executives and was quickly convinced on grounds of both merit and politics. The Maori seats remained impregnably Labour, however disappointed its Maori followers at their party's failure to recognise rangatiratanga when it held office. National was therefore disposed to seek political capital within Maoridom by other means. A national body representing Maoridom, certainly if the reassuringly non-militant unofficial council was anything to go by, was likely to provide 'an alternative leadership system at the centre with which the Government could have more sympathy than with the 4 Labour Maori MPs'. Moreover, such an organisation could be established in ways which might contain, even harness, rangatiratanga. Officials' advice, then, gelled with political expediency. Henare Ngata would later put the matter bluntly: 'In 1961 there was an urge to set up an organisation to give voice to the National Party interests'.[28]

Ministers were quickly persuaded that a national statutory body based on representation from regional councils could not be seen, as it had been in the 1940s and early 1950s, as potentially threatening to indivisible sovereignty. It would constitute no more than the sum of its parts: the now-weakened traditional tribal system, often led by conservative elders, and the increasing amount of organised Maori representation in the cities and towns, generally of pan- or non-tribal nature. A national body might usefully provide Maori viewpoints which differed from those of the Maori MPs, whose positions were underpinned by the mass, non-tribal Ratana movement. It would also, no doubt, be useful in more efficiently relaying governmental intentions and requirements back to Maori. It might be of particular assistance in implementing the Hunn recommendations, and could act as an early warning device if Maoridom was finding difficulties with aspects of policy.

The new government accepted officials' advice that the plans for a national structure not be taken before Parliament until consultation with Maori had occurred. A major hui of leading Maori was convened by Hanan in June 1961, a number of delegates chosen for their political conservatism – indeed some key rangatira present were prominent National Party members or supporters. Attendees emphasised that if those aspects of the Hunn report which Maori supported were to be properly implemented, improved modes of communication between Maori and the Crown at all levels needed to be cemented in place. Since this gelled with the views of the official representatives, there was ready agreement over the type of enabling legislation required to legitimate regional-level Maori councils and a national body. The now four-tiered organisation would be deemed to represent legally all of Maoridom. Government intentions to establish it were foreshadowed in Parliament that same month. The various moves 'to complete the committee structure' for Maoridom were declared to have been carried out 'on the initiative of the Maori people themselves' and to constitute a true reflection of their wishes.

In October 1961, Hanan introduced legislation to amend the 1945 legislation governing the official committee structure, and support by Labour and its MPs reflected bipartisan consultation. The Maori Social and Economic Advancement Act Amendment Act passed that same month. It authorised a New Zealand Maori Council of Tribal Executives and regional District Maori Councils of Tribal Executives. Each of the three higher levels of the revised structure was elected from the layer below, extending the democratic ethos of the 1945 system. There was no attempt to remove the language of tribalism, despite the many urban organisations which had arisen since the original legislation and however much the Maori future was seen by the Crown to be urban and detribalised. This decision was ostensibly an indication of respect for the traditional Maori structures from which the official national leadership would be drawn, including men with public links to the National Party. Retention of tribal terminology, then, arose from the consultation processes. But the thrust of government policy did not change. The amending legislation was, in the words of the chronicler of the DMA, 'far from a charter of Rangatiratanga', and assimilation remained at the forefront of policy. 'The Minister and Secretary still loomed large' in the new structure, moreover, 'retaining considerable powers of initiation and, in the case of District Councils, dissolution.' Essentially, the government saw the restructured official committee system as a vehicle to effect its post-Hunn report policies. Within a few years, its intransigence over issues of assimilation and rangatiratanga were to meet much criticism from within Maoridom, and not just from those who depicted the concept of a statutory national body as yet another attempt at appropriation. Opposition would, in fact, arise from within the new national organisation itself.[29]

Chapter 6

Rangatiratanga under the Maori Welfare Act

Establishing the New Zealand Maori Council System

It was not long before the apparent respect for traditional tribalism by the government was revealed to be chimerical. On the advice of Hunn and other key officials, the National leadership quickly decided to fully overhaul the 1945 official committee structure. This was particularly aimed at both addressing the reality of the urbanising process and providing greater transparency about the Crown's policy intentions with regard to 'modernising' Maoridom and further reducing tribal influence. The new ministry had given tribal chiefs the higher levels of representation they and other traditionalists had sought, and undertook some consultation about the future. But it took pains to stress that 'conservative' attitudes about protecting tribalism would not be endorsed by the Crown. On the contrary, the government symbolised its intentions to accelerate detribalisation by declaring that it would remove tribal nomenclature from the official committee system. The old titles were depicted as both anachronistic for a population dominated by the experiences of urban migration and out of kilter with the government's 'one people' vision. The state, encouraged by its relationship with the leaders forming the new Maori Council of Tribal Executives, intended to intensify its focus on 'Maoridom' as a way of encouraging the assimilation processes. It would view Maori as an entity with which it could deal at a national level, rather than as a congeries of tribal and post-tribal communities.

Traditional tribal leaders did gain quid pro quos during discussions with state representatives over this strategy. First, the new national body would be allowed to remain the legal representative of Maoridom even though it was dominated by the tribally-rooted rural regions. While their leaders' policies had often differed markedly from those of the MPs selected by both urban and rural voters, then, those leaders were to be deemed officially representative of the entire Maori people. Secondly, it was tribal leaders who would benefit most from the degree of rangatiratanga accorded Maori under the new proposals.

While the revised system would still be a statutory one and hence inexorably linked with the Crown, the committees underpinning its structures, the majority of them rural, were finally to be freed from the ex officio presence of DMA officials. The central official voice of Maoridom, however constrained by its official parameters, could therefore be said by its supporters to embody an untainted expression of flaxroots opinion; whatever the degree of truth of this, the perspectives of traditional tribalism and rangatira would continue to loom large in the official structures for Maoridom.

However, the fact remained that any national Maori council would be tasked with overseeing on behalf of the Crown the continuing evolution of Maoridom, and providing a kind of state-approved version of kotahitanga/unity. The Crown expected that separate and autonomous Maori strands of New Zealand society, whatever the new organisational concessions to rangatiratanga, would disappear – certainly faster than would be the case if tribal identity were encouraged (although few observers or advisers thought that Maori would abandon all of their cultural characteristics, at least not in the foreseeable future).

With the renaming of the various levels of the official system, the central and regional bodies became the New Zealand Maori Council (NZMC) and District Maori Councils respectively. The Tribal Committees and Tribal Executives became Maori Committees and Maori Executive Committees. Together, the various parts were to be called 'Maori Associations', although the system became widely known under the title of the central body, the NZMC. The revamped structure was to be even more closely modelled on that of the national Maori organisation which the government regarded as a success, the Maori Women's Welfare League, despite (and, in some ways, because of) the league's capacity to represent widely-held Maori views which could be challenging for the Crown. Understanding oppositional views was a prerequisite for containing them.[1]

Before long, Maori commentators saw the removal of tribal-based terminology as reflective of a new phenomenon: while the Crown had seemingly abandoned its fear of Maori unity, it had done so on the basis of a new assimilationist strategy of (in John Rangihau's words) 'unite … and rule'. Ritchie, who would become a key adviser to Waikato–Tainui tribes, saw the move as a government attempt to utilise a widely held belief among Maori people of the existence of 'a resurgent *Maoritanga*, of a cultural renaissance, of a national Maori identity'. It had suited the Crown, he believed, to act 'as though Maori nationalism were, if not an accomplished fact, at least a potential reality'. It could do so with some hope of success, he believed, because its detection of an increasing Maori identification as a resurgent people did have some basis in observable events and trends.

The Crown's aim was to find 'ways in which this mythical nation might represent its views to the Government and yet have in fact no power'. Writing not long after the revamped system was inaugurated, Ritchie suggested that 'so-called Maori national politics [had] become a shadow theatre whose substance is thin and whose representativeness is more symbolic than real'. He predicted that 'the genuine political life of the Maori community', rural or urban, would not be properly represented by any such official national structure. Early in Hanan's ministry, the non-official Dominion Council of Tribal Executives had told him that while Maori elders were appreciative of an apparent new official willingness to consult, they were 'sensitive to the difference between a policy which works *for* them and one which aims at working *with* them.'[2]

Despite such an important caveat, at the time of its formation in 1962, the NZMC was widely welcomed throughout Maoridom as embodying a Crown determination to forge ahead with implementing the recommendations of the Hunn report, many of which Maori supported. It could provide a workable way of consulting an increasingly diverse and dispersed people. Many Maori commentators spoke of the benefits for 'Maoridom' that the NZMC would bring, and a pakeha sympathetic to Maori causes could describe the council, in 1968, as the 'crowning achievement in unifying the Maori people' around their own causes. In 1963, in the early days of the Maori associations, National even came close to winning the Northern Maori parliamentary seat in a by-election.

The Maori associations operating under the NZMC umbrella were embedded in the 1962 Maori Welfare Act (MWA), which replaced the (amended) Maori Social and Economic Advancement Act of 1945. Central to the long-term structural and conceptual developments in Crown–Maori relations which the new legislation cemented into place was a concern to boost official Maori organisation in the cities and towns. The mostly rural district council regions which elected the NZMC would help the Crown ensure that conservatism (of method, if not of aspiration, at least as far as mainstream New Zealand was concerned) prevailed at top levels. The base of the new welfare system, the Maori committee, was defined non-tribally, being 'elected by the Maori public of a given area to administer matters of Maori interest'. In rural areas, however, its boundaries generally reflected marae-based organisation. In turn, the Maori committees elected two to three delegates to Maori executive committees (MECs), 'which deal with matters of common interest to a group of Maori Committees'. In 1963, there were 477 flaxroots committees and 84 executive committees.

The community or neighbourhood committees at the base of the structural pyramid were, at first, generally just the old committees under a new name. They continued to do what they had always done, which might not necessarily accord with what officials wanted. The same applied to the MECs they reported to. But these also now had an expanded role, in that they could officially feed ideas to regional level – to the eight district Maori councils (DMCs) to which they elected representatives. Along the way, tribal-aligned influence could be diluted by various means. Seven of the district councils, for example, were based on the Maori Land Court's boundaries, and these did not always coincide with perceived areas of common tribal interest. There was an additional DMC for the Auckland urban area, giving the migrant people in New Zealand's largest city considerable voice. The whole structure culminated at national level with the NZMC, where tribe-specific concerns could quite easily be swamped. However, although all levels held elections only at three yearly intervals, many tribal leaders saw the system as both more democratic and responsive to tribal pressures than triennial voting for MPs in the 'pakeha parliament', particularly because the various levels could formally liaise with each other and undertake combined action if necessary.[3]

Yet the revamping of the system was aimed, in the final analysis, at putting an end to 'separate status' for Maori: the Maori associations would work towards their own quick demise, which would come about when Maori had achieved equality with the dominant ethnicity in modern New Zealand. The words 'social and economic advancement' had embodied this 'egalitarian' goal in the 1945 legislation, but mass urbanisation and perceived progress in assimilation had altered the conceptual landscape: the ideological urge for rapid removal of difference and discrimination of any type between the races (with the planned disappearance of the positive alongside the negative, after some temporary tolerance) called for a new terminology. It was far from accidental, then, that in the title of the new legislation the term 'social and economic advancement' was replaced by 'Maori welfare'.

Because of the underlying implications of this for rangatiratanga, Tirikatene and the other Maori MPs had been among those Maori leaders fighting for retention of the former term and what it stood for – essentially, a form of modernisation which had a place for tribal and other Maori customs. Proponents of the new ethos argued that while intervention to assist socio-economic advancement remained a significant part of the government's plans for Maoridom, this was best carried out in conjunction with all other aspects of planning and policy. The term 'Maori welfare' was seen to be more attuned to the times: the future welfare of all components of Maoridom lay in moving quickly towards institutions and policies which were solidly integrationist. The government's reorientation of Maori policy would aim to force the pace of integration in every aspect of Maori life.

State intervention would now be targeted in terms of a totalised conception of the welfare of Maori, rather than being tribally or economically focused.

The 'general aim of the Act is to promote and maintain the health and general well-being of the Maori community', as the DMA put it. But the 'general well-being' of Maori meant, in essence, faster assimilation in all aspects of life than before, speeding up even further what was supposedly already happening as a result of urban migration. For Labour, too, 'Maori welfare' had meant, ultimately, Maori disappearance. But that party's dependence on the Maori vote had made it more receptive (or, as many would see it, less unreceptive) than National to the Maori determination to promote rangatiratanga as well as socio-economic and other types of uplift.

While the Department of Maori Affairs, then, depicted the NZMC system as 'a form of local government for the Maori people on matters of particular Maori interest', the intended end result was far different. Aspects of the legislation, indeed, pointed to the government's long-term anti-autonomist agenda. For example, although 'appointment to the Maori Council was derived from the flax roots (the Maori committees) authority was dispensed from the top down' by men subjected to considerable official pressure. While the committees had been unshackled from the DMA, their independence was formally curtailed within their own system, with the NZMC assuming responsibility for functions assigned directly to the committees under the 1945 Act. The new legislation also abolished some local government functions which had been present in the previous system: those relating to such matters as sanitation, water and control of liquor in villages. Hanan considered that with each such specialist function removed from the purview of the Maori institutions franchised by the Crown, 'we are further along the road to becoming one people'. While the Act would help 'to perpetuate Maori culture', in the words of the DMA, this stated aim embodied a rather narrow vision of culture.

Both the MWA and its predecessor had been 'designed to facilitate the full integration of the Maori race into the social and economic structure of the country', but there were now faster ways of doing so in the changed demographic climate. The New Zealand Maori Council, legally entitled to act on behalf of all Maoridom, was ('by its own request', the Crown was wont to note, referring to discussions with Maori leaders leading up to the legislation) 'charged with the duty of maintaining and promoting harmony between Maori and pakeha'. A number of Maori wondered at the priorities this implied.[4]

From the beginning, there was a degree of Maori disapproval of aspects of the 1961–62 restructurings. Some did not like the 'western' system of geography-based selection, which, among other things, gave all Maori living within the requisite boundaries a vote whether or not they were from local tribes. Others did not welcome boundaries decreed by the state, and/or the fact that these sometimes cut across tribal boundaries. Tirikatene claimed that the NZMC was not truly representative, suggesting that the DMA had 'engineered' its membership, and he called for secret postal elections. His views were publicly backed up by his former private secretary, and long-time Labour Party member, Te Atiawa leader Ralph Love, who described the council as a total 'jack up'. Love considered that the NZMC's 'representivity was diluted by the extent of departmental involvement'. Concerns over the question of representation were widespread, even among some members of the NZMC itself – including those who worried that such a central body would soon lose touch with the flaxroots.

Soon there were claims about lack of consultation with the people and decisions made 'without reference even to District Councils'. Increasing numbers of Maori saw the system as 'an artificial construct of the bureaucratic mind'. They and others emphasised that the NZMC received annual funding from the government, and argued that, even if it felt able to criticise the government from time to time, it still needed to operate within constraints which excluded any possibility of fully-fledged opposition should that be needed. The NZMC system represented, at best, an 'accommodationist' approach to self-determination, one which 'effectively shackled the councils and committees to the government's integration agenda'. By the mid-1970s, an anthropologist was suggesting that 'the system has not captured the imagination or the support of the people' and that it was seen as a 'Government plan'.[5]

Certainly, with the founding membership of the New Zealand Maori Council dominated by members or supporters of the National Party, Maori who saw the new system as part of a government attempt to bypass the Labour Maori MPs were averse to participation. Since the urban committees were swamped by the rural associations, moreover, the odds seemed stacked against urban-based delegates attaining the highest positions of the organisation. But the remodelled system was also seen by many Maori (including critics) as having potential for contributing to at least some of their aspirations. Indeed, the NZMC soon concerned itself with topics that exercised the minds of Maori around the country, urban and rural. It focussed especially on the Treaty of Waitangi, education, land and 'Maori advancement', and it opened the doors to greater and more systemic consultation and influence with government. Founding president Sir Turi Carroll urged unity as a way forward for all Maori, and 'exhorted members to ensure that the Council did not become involved in party politics or religious differences'.

Moreover, the 'integrationist' spirit which pervaded the legislative initiative of 1962 allowed, in some respects, considerable leeway for the Maori associations, whatever the ultimate Crown goal. A corollary of the governmental stress on removal of all forms of discrimination was an attempt to downplay traditional state paternalism towards Maori. One thing which the tangata whenua had stressed ever since their disappointment over the 1945 legislation had been distrust of the DMA as the institution governing their affairs (although they frequently acknowledged its assistance to individuals and communities on many levels). The National government, while seeing the need to place some official constraints upon the NZMC system, was predisposed by its founding ideological and philosophical principles to put 'self-reliance' structures in place as far as possible and to minimise formal Crown control. It was in this context that the Maori associations had been technically freed from control by the Department of Maori Affairs, whose Welfare Division was now assigned to do no more than offer advice or assistance to them. Now more than ever, the DMA's officers concentrated on 'special measures' assisting individuals and their families to adapt to cities and modernity, leaving conceptual space for the NZMC system to address concerns of relevance to 'Maori as Maori'.

Under several interpretations, the government had taken some degree of cognisance of Maori representations about autonomy of operation in the consultation leading up to the Maori Welfare Act. The minister was seen to have shown respect for rangatiratanga in actively divesting himself and his officials of the function of actively managing the associations. While such interpretations can be taken too far, the fact remained that the DMA officers assigned to work with Maori (such as the welfare officers) would no longer be an integral part of the official committee structure. The department, moreover, now had a lesser role in overseeing, and considerably fewer opportunities to intervene in, the workings of the official system. Committees at various levels in the structure consequently gained a new authority. 'The degree of decision-making power placed in the hands of each Maori association was', it could be argued, 'notably increased.'

The whole NZMC structure embodied greater independence of the state than had its predecessor. The reasons for this concession were not necessarily altruistic. It had been argued, for example, that with Maori organising their own affairs, some of the burden of the welfare state would be taken from governmental shoulders. All the same, things *had* changed and the revised official ethos can be glimpsed in Hanan's words: Maori would now 'not have to go cap in hand to anyone for attention, nor need they be influenced by any fear of offending anybody'. On some levels, whatever the ultimate government aims for the Maori associations, this statement can be seen as embodying a degree of Crown recognition of rangatiratanga.[6]

The Maori Associations in Operation

When Hanan launched the revised structure for the centralised official committee system at a hui on 28 June 1962, he did so with a Maori proverb:

'The old net is cast aside – the new net goes a' fishing'. But the New Zealand Maori Council's beginnings were not auspicious. The minister emphasised that the system had been established by the Crown, and made it clear that he expected Carroll to be elected the founding president. In his turn, Carroll stated that 'the councillors must not offend the government'. Despite this, many Maori looked forward to making use of the system to promote causes of their own at all levels, from flaxroots initiatives to developing a united Maori perspective on issues of national significance. There was considerable optimism that what might be seen as a 'rather toothless' legislative mandate to discuss with, advise and assist the government could be turned into something proactively Maori. There was some appreciation that, in various ways, the NZMC structure was built on the accomplishments of the 1945 system in improving 'bicultural political relations', ensuring 'greater collaboration between Maori leadership and Pakeha administration', and (whatever the political and bureaucratic decision-makers would have preferred) preserving and enhancing Maori socio-cultural distinctiveness.

Although they often had few resources, the Maori associations developed lobbying expertise and worked hard on issues in which the government was not necessarily much interested, such as preserving Maori language and customs. At central level, efficiency was boosted by the appointment of the DMA's anthropologist, John Booth, as a fulltime secretary for the NZMC. While some believed that this move was symptomatic of the Crown's controlling agenda, Booth became an essential conduit in faithfully passing on Maori wishes to the government. Within a short period, the NZMC came 'to be viewed as a significant and thoroughly "Maori" institution'. When, in mid-decade, the New Zealand Broadcasting Corporation established a policy on pronunciation of Maori place names that was deemed to be unacceptably compromised, Booth helped bring 'organisation to the spontaneous resistance' which occurred within Maoridom. Given the strength of flaxroots feeling on a number of issues, the conservative leadership was sometimes compelled to take over leadership of spontaneous protest campaigns to calm things down and forge a compromise acceptable by both sides; the NZMC secretary was generally in the foreground of such efforts.[7]

To be sure, at first much of the council's work was done on the government's terms, seemingly vindicating state impulses to appropriate Maori organisational energies. Many of the initial activities carried out within the system in fact amounted to administrative assistance to the government. The district councils, for example, prioritised the applications for state subsidies for marae-building programmes. When difficult questions were raised by the associations, or they gave 'wrong' answers to questions posed by the state, the government and officials might well ignore or marginalise them. When the NZMC was consulted on the role the Treaty of Waitangi might play in a proposed Bill of Rights, ministers baulked at the council's views (expressed on behalf of its constituents) as to how the 'the spirit of the Treaty' should be applied to modern circumstances, seeing these as advocating discrimination in legislation rather than removing it.

But the official associations system also proved to offer much to Maori. A number of committees in the cities throve, providing an enhanced level of representation and advocacy for urban Maori – some of the 13 committees in greater Wellington, technically representing more than 50,000 Maori, were forthright in their work on behalf of the migrant population of the area. For many contemporary Maori (and later scholars), the organisational legislation of the early 1960s, which gave 'birth to the first statutory, government supported, national Maori organisation', amounted to 'a major breakthrough for the Maori people'. At its regional and national levels, the NZMC system acquired considerable status among both Maori and pakeha publics, as well as with the Crown, as an articulator of Maori interests. It assumed responsibility for some issues over which the Maori Women's Welfare League had once had the main franchise, such as land and housing. Observers were soon claiming that 'the League assumed a secondary leadership role and somehow lost its momentum' as the NZMC gained in influence. Certainly, the Crown was soon routinely consulting with the Maori associations on matters of relevance to their constituents, and flaxroots committee members often took steps to ensure that their voices were heard inside the whole structure. In one assessment, the Maori associations represented a 'hybrid of both European and Maori traditional forms'. Their key figures acquired 'specialised skills in brokerage and negotiation' with various state and other organisations, while remaining 'true to tribal principles'.[8]

Whatever the official role of the institutions established under the Maori Welfare Act, moreover, Maori began to take them in new and informal directions – just as they had with predecessor committees of various types. Many of their members believed that now 'the power was really in the hands of the people'. Some set out to subvert assimilationist aims by using the facilities on offer through the system. As in the past, then, a structure which suited the government also provided sites of autonomist opportunity. The Tauranga area executive, for example, headed a regional struggle for reparations from the Crown for nineteenth-century land confiscations. Ultimately this led (in 1981) to a lump-sum 'full and final' settlement and the establishment of the Tauranga Moana Maori Trust Board to control the monies. This settlement was a precursor to later negotiated settlements with iwi elsewhere.

Generally the government tolerated members taking the committees in directions more or less as they wished, so long as their activities were not too 'extreme' and the required functions were also carried out. Departures from the rules included unauthorised organisational forms as well as operational matters (as had happened in the 1945 system), such as having a larger membership than permitted by law. In some sub-districts, Maori committees decided not to elect Maori executive committees, instead choosing to have a direct relationship with the district councils. Even the latter developed operating parameters of their own, often quite independently of the NZMC to which they both contributed representatives and were formally accountable. One scholar has argued that, in fact, each DMC 'was a politically discrete and autonomous unit'. It is certainly clear that local committees and their executives 'maintained a remarkable degree of autonomy'. In all, the NZMC represented a 'segmented democracy of ... various units', with 'greater coherence' within local segments than between them. The central council did not have 'the power to command', but remained 'essentially a mechanism for co-ordination ... and a channel for influence' to government, public service and other agencies. It was also a 'symbol of a will towards unity'.[9]

Some aspects of both the 1962 legislation and its implementation held out considerable potential for both Maori development and the retention or reconfiguration of Maori identity. Official committees in the cities and towns were building Maori community groupings across tribal barriers. This in itself did not derogate from tribal links. But increasing numbers of individuals and families had been urbanised for so long that their ties with their home marae were fading. As tribal bonds loosened, people began identifying ever more closely with the community in which they lived and with pan-tribal groupings within it. The official and quasi-official pan-tribal associations, in conjunction with voluntary associations, helped keep 'being Maori' a 'going concern' even for those who were subjected to 'detribalising' influences.

Adjustment processes were particularly aided by a new aspect of the official system. While the MWA removed departmental welfare officers from the NZMC structure, it sanctioned the establishment of voluntary Maori Welfare Committees within it. Those set up by urban-based Maori began to complement other Maori support mechanisms, and in some cases provided the sort of support to new arrivals previously afforded by kinship networks. In conjunction with the official Maori committees and other organisations, welfare committees were soon instrumental in helping expand a pan-Maori collective consciousness in urban, or more specifically suburban, spaces. Increasingly, experience in the cities produced an emergent sense of 'Maori' identity that was superimposing itself upon tribal affiliation.

The quasi-official welfare committees, along with the informal voluntary associations, assisted the Maori associations to fulfil both official roles and unofficial functions. Urban dwellers, especially, would often contact them to help cope with difficult circumstances, and significant numbers participated in their activities. With increasing legitimation in the eyes of the people, the committees became a vital part of community life. By the 1970s, it was being argued that the MWA's granting of statutory authority to voluntary committees 'provides for a form of self-government and makes legitimate leadership in a multi-tribal situation'. While Maori associations were still seen by many to be integrally part of the official machinery, however independently they operated, the close working relationships between the informal and official committees helped make the latter more acceptable. Although the welfare committees were authorised to operate by the Act, for example, they inhabited the same quasi-official spaces as the MWWL, and few saw them as being completely 'official'.

The Maori associations' work was most needed by those who struggled to adjust to the cities, and by the 1970s there were over three dozen official Maori committees operating under the umbrella of the Auckland District Maori Council. In the pepper-potted environment of a new housing estate, they would assist with the creation of Maori welfare committees, which in turn helped consolidate the base of the NZMC structure. Such modes of ethno-social adjustment to urban living became a means of forging or enhancing collective or cultural relationships with and between displaced Maori families. The welfare committees, comprising seven to eleven people elected triennially, were in fact tasked with functions that were more broad-based than their titles might suggest. Their brief amounted, in effect, to improving the social, economic and cultural situation of Maori. Among other things, they sought to 'promote harmonious race relations', assist in 'physical, economic, social, educational, moral and spiritual well-being', and 'help the Maori enjoy the full rights, privileges and responsibilities of New Zealand citizenship'.[10]

More specifically, welfare committees engaged in activities such as promoting health and sanitation and preventing excessive drinking, functions which were once the province of the Welfare Division's tribal committees. They could nominate Maori wardens to take on complementary 'additional duties' such as 'patrolling streets, hotels and places of public assembly'. They could also appoint Honorary Welfare Officers (HWOs) to assist them in their role, and by 1968 there were 30 of these. The HWOs were, along with the wardens, among the most visible of the voluntary workers associated with the official system. In one contemporary assessment, '[m]ost of the department's welfare work ... relies heavily on voluntary assistance'. The honorary welfare officers had the same powers as salaried DMA welfare officers – whose numbers had reached 81 by 1970. An increase in demand for HWOs can be seen by the fact that their numbers had by that time reached 46. Government departments and other official institutions were authorised, even encouraged, to cooperate with Maori welfare committees and their volunteer staff, and the committees in turn were expected to cooperate with state agencies.

Some of the functions of welfare committees formally overlapped with those of the DMA. Maori would reportedly compare favourably the work of the HWOs with the activities of departmental staff, who (especially those who were pakeha) could be seen as 'outsiders and representatives of officialdom'. For example, after sundry officials had failed to gain entry to the house of a 'problem family', an honorary welfare officer knocked on the door and said in te reo Maori: 'Greetings, I am a Maori'. This was sufficient to gain her entrance, and when she 'spoke kindly and gently and in a spirit of goodwill', the way was opened for the suburb's welfare committee to help the family. This case, concerning a family whose children were reportedly 'dirty, poorly clothed and hungry', was just one of very many recorded in the literature and archives. Such assistance to migrants making the difficult, even traumatic, adjustment to urban life was welcomed by most to whom it was offered, partly because the official powers of the volunteer staff and committee members were exercised lightly. The committees were effective, in short, because they were an integral part of their communities.

However, urban adjustment assistance on a large scale, so clearly necessary for the physical well being of very many families and individuals, was provided within a general context of 'appropriate' (westernised) ways of behaving and viewing the world. These might include, for example, wearing particular kinds of clothes and the abandoning of customary hospitality practices. In other words, the social control functions assigned by Parliament to the whole system of Maori committees, honorary welfare officers, welfare committees, wardens and the MWWL (together with some of the less formal and entirely non-official organisations which liaised with them) was posited upon the demands of the assimilating processes. While they had undoubtedly quickly gained community support, Maori associations can be seen on one level of analysis as operating on behalf of a state whose overarching priority was to ensure its own, culturally specific definitions of 'peace and good order' and private as well as public behaviour.

As formal, semi-formal or informal assistants of the Crown in this task, the committees and volunteer workers linked with them helped impose hegemonic mores, codes of behaviour and modes of thought upon their own people. An honorary welfare officer's statement is indicative of the types of values she upheld on behalf of the state: 'a man's duty is to go out and earn money. A woman's duty is to cook the food and clean the house'. Under such guidance, social organisation and rhythms of life of the dominant culture, including a mode of family organisation as near as possible to that of the 'ideal' pakeha nuclear family, were seen as integral to the future development of the Maori people. The

Maori Welfare Act's purpose, from the legislators' perspective, was to fast-track Maori migrants to become 'irrevocably integrated into the economic system of mainstream society' – to become assimilated as far and as fast as possible.[11]

The Functions of Maori Wardens

The Crown, then, was much exercised to ensure that Maori observed appropriate forms of (essentially western) behaviour. The MWA confirmed Maori wardens, in particular, as 'agents of social control and law enforcement', to cite the words of Augie Fleras, an anthropologist who would conduct pioneering research into their work. Although nominated from within official associations, wardens were appointed by the Minister of Maori Affairs for a period of three years. They carried out their various tasks with minimal state assistance and provided their services for little or no remuneration (or even reimbursement for expenses). From an official point of view, wardens were of most value in exercising their interventionist powers in the monitoring, supervision and sometimes disciplining of 'troublesome elements'. Although their formal constraining powers were severely restricted, they often undertook informal coercive actions to get their work done. As multi-purposed agents of the state (like regular police personnel but with far fewer formal coercive powers) wardens enjoyed a stronger interventionist presence in Maori communities under the MWA than before it. But their role was of considerable benefit to the communities they served. Sometimes, when the committees which technically deployed them went into operational abeyance, individual wardens would continue their services on behalf of the community, and with widespread support and assistance.

Broadly speaking, wardens were expected to help guide the adjustment to modernity and urban resettlement of Maori, and their tasks included providing 'material and spiritual assistance for those unable to stand on their own feet'. By the end of the 1970s, on the basis of his fieldwork, Fleras would conclude that wardens had proved to be of considerable assistance 'in facilitating a Maori adaptation to an urban milieu'. Since their work often reflected community wishes and priorities as much as or more than those of the Crown, they were often more responsive to people and leaders at local level than to those within officialdom – including those exercising official powers within the official system's lines of command. In 1963, such trends were officially recognised to have boosted both social efficiency and general Maori morale, and the local Maori committees gained control of the more than 500 wardens. The NZMC declared in 1967 that the system of wardens represented 'acceptance by Maoris of a form of self discipline based on pride in being Maori and on the ties of aroha that bind Maori to Maori'.

Working with the local Maori leadership, wardens could apply disciplinary sanctions against members of their own people for matters such as 'riotous, offensive, threatening, insulting or disorderly' behaviour. They could retain the car keys of any Maori they considered unfit to drive, and order those who were 'intoxicated, quarrelsome or violent' to leave licensed premises. Along with other members of Maori committees, wardens could 'take out a prohibition order against a Maori who has a problem with alcoholism or neglects his family by spending his wages on liquor'. They could expel people at Maori gatherings who were behaving in disorderly fashion, and confiscate liquor distributed without a permit from the local Maori committee. The wardens would clean up after acts of vandalism or neglect by Maori, accompany honorary welfare officers to problem homes, and have committees direct Maori offenders to come under their 'close supervision and surveillance'. Obviously, such activities generally suited the Maori community and the state alike, and the warden system flourished in many areas.[12]

In particular, the wardens were seen as a crucial component of their communities' fight against crime and disorder. By the later 1950s, Maori offending in the cities and large towns had increasingly come to public attention, and the Hunn report had confirmed, through collation and propagation of statistics, a significant upwards trend in Maori-generated crime and disorder. The Maori male offending rate had reached three and a half times that of pakeha men, for example. As the report's recommendations were gradually implemented, the wardens forged closer bonds with the regular police in a joint effort to prevent or suppress social disorder. Their levels of cooperation were boosted from time to time, and an amendment to the MWA in 1963 made provision for formal cooperation by wardens with regular and traffic police. In the following year, the authority of wardens was further enhanced when they secured – after many years of submissions – permission to wear uniforms.

As crime rates among Maori continued to rise due to a combination of causes, including social dislocation, cultural alienation and absolute and relative poverty, a greater focus on 'enforcement and sanction-type roles' came into play. By 1968, Maori were over-represented in the summary convictions figures by a factor of three and in the prison population statistics by a factor of four. Two years later, Maori had a four to one arrest rate relative to pakeha, and a conviction rate of eight to one. Whatever the causes of such statistics (and ethnocentrism and racism among coercive authorities played their part), wardens had increasingly to take on the 'connotations of a Maori police force', as an official review of their role noted at the end of the century. This ongoing enhancement of the policing functions wardens had performed since their establishment in the 1940s hooked them increasingly into state social control imperatives. Individuals from lower socio-economic strata tended to volunteer for the position of warden, especially in the cities, replicating the ancient policing practice of 'like policing like'. At an urban meeting in 1969, the 15 wardens recorded as present had occupations such as railway worker, machine operator, driver, postal assistant, linesman, factory worker and housemaid. They represented communal self-discipline, a specialist complement to, and (especially in the cities and towns) a replacement for, the tribal-based discipline of the home marae.

In rural communities, the tribal mana of wardens afforded a considerable amount of the backing needed to cope with the demands of their role. The authority of wardens did not, however, always go without challenge, especially in the multi-tribal setting of the cities. Here an offender from a tribe other than that of the warden might well fail to respond to initial attempts at persuasion or mediation, possibly causing the police to be called in (especially if the offender had assaulted the warden, who might or might not have attempted informal physical coercion). Nor did the wardens' uniform or official warrant necessarily accord them respect even of people from their own tribe.

Periodically, Maori youths in the cities and large towns resented and resisted their authority. Young men asked to leave pubs by uniformed semi-policemen of 'their own race' were not concerned about such niceties as whose ultimate interests the wardens were protecting. The quasi-police powers of wardens were regarded by many as yet another indignity to be borne as a result of their generally low status in society and/or as another attempt by a communal Maori control system to discipline them in a fashion that pakeha were not subjected to – despite their having opted for the attractions of individualised life in the urban spaces. In the final analysis, they were right to see things in such ways, for the raison d'etre of the committee system's policing powers was that they were exercised exclusively for socio-racial control within Maoridom. In the eyes of a number of Maori, including some urban intellectuals, this differential exercise of coercion was a derogation from, rather than an endorsement of, rangatiratanga.

The New Zealand Police, too, were sometimes ambivalent about the wardens, whose semi-professional 'assistance' could prove to be more trouble than it was worth. At times, wardens might even provoke rather than contain disorder – when, say, they were resisted by youths resentful of the differential attention paid to them, because of their colour, in a mixed-race situation. But although not all police welcomed at all times the intervention of Maori whose badge and warrant came from the Minister of Maori Affairs, the holders of the office of constable generally appreciated their back-up presence and were sometimes very grateful indeed for their assistance. Wardens acted in conjunction with them, for example, to ensure public order at large gatherings involving Maori, especially in circumstances in which the regular police (with few Maori members at that time) might well feel uncomfortable. Maori wardens not only complemented preventive or reactive official policing, they also served as social workers with at-risk youth in the justice and education systems, as private ancillaries on state-funded order tasks, and eventually (when the contracting out of public services gained strength) as state-sanctioned private security operators for local bodies, hospitals, businesses and the like.[13]

Organising and Scrutinising the Warden System

Maori wardens responded to the difficulties inherent in their tasks, and the desire to improve and professionalise their work, by forming local and district-level associations. In 1966, a number of these began to moot a national organisation. The NZMC supported the concept in principle, while seeking to ensure that any such organisation would fully respect the needs and wishes of the official system of which it would form part. That May, the Maori Council established a Subcommittee on Maori Wardens, and after a great deal of groundwork a draft constitution for a national association was prepared. Its functions would include overseeing selection, supervision and training of the wardens, and liaising and coordinating activities with the Maori committees. After much further deliberation, the New Zealand Maori Wardens' Association was founded in 1968.

By then, however, wardens had become so responsive to local committees in some areas that both the Crown and the upper echelons of the NZMC were attempting to regain fuller control over them. Moreover, the increasing propensity for wardens to coordinate their activities had led in some places to a collective assertion of a level of independence from the NZMC machinery that was unacceptable to both state and council. At a meeting in Wanganui, for example, wardens agreed that surveillance-patrolling should be downgraded in favour of activities communities had asked for, which were more in the line of social work – helping families in distress at a time of economic downturn, for example, or rescuing young people in danger.

The state and the NZMC had been supportive of the concept of a national wardens' association partly in the hope that it could help combat local or regional 'separatist' tendencies among the wardens. But now, perceptions among both of a unified separatist tendency among wardens caused just as much, if not more, alarm. The national association should be able to help contain any propensities of separatism rather than reflect or coordinate them. After many pressures, discussions and negotiations, in 1969 a compromise between the interested major parties was hammered out, holding the promise of more cooperative relationships at all levels. A legislative relocation of supervision and control of wardens followed. Responsibility for their management reverted to the district

Maori councils (which of course reported directly to the NZMC). Where the district councils were satisfied that Maori committees were acting appropriately in supervising their people, control of wardens could be devolved back to the flaxroots committees.[14]

Over and above issues of 'control of the controllers', however, from the beginning there had been controversy as to whether the institution of wardens should continue to exist in a supposedly integrating society. With the increasing numbers and visibility of wardens, officials and ministers were among those who had become uneasy at the implications of a 'separate police' based along racial lines. The increasing presence of uniformed wardens on city streets highlighted matters that the Crown preferred not to expose to public scrutiny and debate – the expedient existence of race-based institutions which clearly sat uneasily, at least on the surface, with its assimilationist goals for Maoridom. As the years went by, moreover, the expansion of the Maori warden system drew attention not only to the existence of race-based official organisations, but also to the fact that 'Maori had not achieved the full measure of equality' officials had aimed for in implementing the Hunn report. Maori continued to require a 'special attention' – in the urban case, one focused on crime and disorder – that ran counter to the paradigmatic aspirations and the primary discourses of government and officialdom.

High-profile separate official organisations within Maoridom, in short, symbolised the difficulties inherent in the Crown's ability to persuade the public that it was properly and fully pursuing its own policy of 'integration'. The truth was that the wardens and other such institutions embodied attempts to appropriate Maori communal energies to assist the Crown impose certain standardised ways of behaving, ways which assisted the assimilationist strategies of state at the same time as helping Maori communities in many positive ways. But the apparent discrepancies involved in this scenario became the more obvious when assimilationist policies aimed at formal equality before the law, and sameness of treatment for all citizens, were legislated into effect from time to time to remove special treatment for Maori. In 1962, for example, provisions for Maori juries in circumstances where the parties were Maori had been abolished, and concomitantly tangata whenua were made eligible for general jury service.

As Minister of Justice as well as Maori Affairs, Hanan was increasingly concerned that the legislation governing Maori wardens was manifestly 'discriminatory, in that it was a policing mechanism that applied to only one race'. The warden system was coming under greater scrutiny from both other ministers and officials, too, for its implications of separatism in a country boasting of its 'one New Zealand' and 'equality' policies. By the late 1960s, the propensity of the wardens to think of themselves as a fully-fledged 'auxiliary police force with attendant powers of arrest and physical force, uniforms, patrol cars, interrogation headquarters, private filing systems, rubber truncheons and badges of rank', as an official memo put it, added to the disquiet in a number of quarters.

Their cause was not helped by an excessive zeal among some wardens, a few of whom were prone to use force, or to equip themselves with items such as two-way radios which were widely perceived to reflect a vigilantist approach to their duties. Such over-enthusiasm led such unlikely bedfellows as civil libertarians and regular police to similar misgivings. Moreover, in 1970 another Young Maori Leaders' Conference, reflecting among others the views of radicalising urban Maori, demanded abolition of the wardens. By the start of the new decade, governmental and official agencies were responding to many such pressures and beginning to rethink not just the nature and role, but also the desirability, of the Maori warden scheme.[15]

Wardens, Communities and State

With the very existence of wardens under intensifying critical scrutiny, Maori communities generally responded protectively. As with the Maori schools, in effect Maori had appropriated a Crown-initiated and accredited institution as 'their own'. Maori committees affirmed that wardens were their much needed 'eyes and ears' as well as their strong arm. Responding to considerable pressure from the Maori associations and elsewhere within Maoridom, elements in both the DMA and other government institutions endorsed Maori communities' calls for continuance of the warden system. Faced with the potential disappearance of wardens, the New Zealand Police also came out strongly in their support, despite their misgivings about how aspects of the system had developed. When the NZMC's subcommittee on wardens met in Wellington in 1970, it endorsed continuance of the wardens: while they were established by legislative and ministerial fiat, they constituted a Maori 'cultural right'. They gave much needed organisational strong-arm assistance to communities which were 'helping themselves', and could assist mediation between their leaders and those members who were actually or potentially in difficulty of various kinds. In 1971, after much internal deliberation, the Crown agreed that, for the time being, wardens were integral to the work of the NZMC system.

Nevertheless, debate over their role and function continued, and changes in approach occurred as a consequence. There was, in particular, a deliberate lowering of the official profile of the warden system. Relatedly, both DMA and NZMC publicity now tended to de-emphasise the policing role of wardens and instead to highlight their community work, almost a reversal of previous stances. By the mid-1970s, in any case, controversy over the wisdom of separate institutions for Maori was dying. A significant degree of positive pakeha response to the recent 'renaissance' within Maoridom had helped legitimate the possibility of things being done in different ways in Maori communities if these were genuine reflections of Maori desires. Difficulties with regard to the warden system now centred on a lack of systematisation of wardens' activities, as communities developed 'their own' ways of managing social control. The wardens' association, accordingly, became moribund, causing the DMA, the Maori Council and elements within the wardens movement to work on ways of reconstructing a national body.

Eventually, a government-financed meeting at Ngaruawahia in November 1979 made such progress that a new association was established in 1980. This technically constituted a subcommittee of the NZMC, and so although the wardens system became more streamlined and regularised, it also became more fully officialised. There were now to be tighter controls on appointments, for example: after nomination by Maori committees, names of candidates needed to be approved first by district Maori councils and then at the highest level. Recruits, furthermore, would now be professionally trained, and they would have a warrant to act anywhere in the country rather than just in their localities. These professionalising tendencies mirrored trends in both state and society.

On one plane, such developments were welcomed by most Maori committees. But there remained some concern that an officially supported, centralised body to superintend the wardens system could jeopardise flaxroots control. There was also a worry that certain of the new developments seemed to be moving back towards emphasising the auxiliary policing role of wardens rather than stressing service to the community, and that in any case their community work was becoming too heavily state-prescribed. Certainly, wardens were increasingly expected to conform to standardised rules and procedures, and act as exemplars and enforcers of 'western standards'. It seemed to some observers that, inexorably, those volunteering to be wardens were being drawn into the state's plans for management of its Maori citizenry. It was a familiar problem: while wardens were 'in the vanguard of a drive to achieve Maori goals', as Maori communities saw it, the Crown had a different underlying motivation. This was, in the words of a 'participant observer' among the wardens, writing in 1980, to 'provide assistance to the Maori public but for the ultimate benefit and within the framework of pakeha power structures'.

By the end of the 1970s, however, government policies had moved far from the rampant assimilationism of the immediate post-Hunn years, and so the convergence of benefits for both Crown and Maori ensured that the wardens system would survive. For the state, wardens were valuable agents of order imposition, order maintenance and social control. Despite the tightening of state controls on wardens, community-based Maori, both in city and rural spaces, still tended to see them as agents of localised autonomy. Certainly, wardens generally operated in accord with the wishes of those who worked in or with the Maori committees. In turn, the committees often had allies within kinship-based networks, other local or marae committees and official agencies, as well as liaising with local police personnel and welfare officials among others – and so the wardens system penetrated and interacted with a great many social and bureaucratic arenas.

While wardens were agents of the state, then, they were also – and, in some areas, increasingly – operatives on behalf of community aspirations, especially insofar as such goals were channelled through officially sanctioned leadership structures. Through their work with emerging new leadership strata in the urban areas in particular, wardens were important in the reconstruction of Maori communities in pan- or non-tribal environments. Some of the wardens carved out semi-autonomous spaces in those communities, and the most successful were often those who interacted well with Maori and pakeha alike. Generally, the evidence suggests that the Maori wardens' endeavours were appreciated by Maori from most walks of life, their authority often respected even by the alienated young people of the cities. Whatever their objective location in the corpus of the state disciplinary apparatus, therefore, they could also be seen as embodiments of Maori agency – of rangatiratanga. Although in one way 'symbolic of a paternalistic and indirect strategy of State control', then, wardens also worked for 'the benefit of the entire Maori community'. 'Their objective', as outlined in the constitution of the original Maori Wardens' Association in 1968, was 'Maori self-determination'.[16]

'Maori Courts'

The Maori associations were tasked with overseeing, upkeeping and improving Maori welfare in general, and this brief included addressing crime, disorder and disfunctionalism through means other than policing. The state authorities were so concerned about levels of offending and disruption within Maoridom, especially in the urban spaces, that the Maori Welfare legislation had departed from the ideology of legal sameness in more ways than just that of confirming the usefulness of wardens for indigenous social control purposes. It also enabled the Maori committees to constitute themselves as Maori Tribunal Committees (commonly called 'Maori courts' or tribunals) with power to adjudicate on low-level offences. The tribunals needed to comprise at least three Maori committee members, and operated under judicial principles different from those of the criminal justice system. They could, for example, make decisions on the basis of *prima facie* evidence.

One intention behind this was preventive. To deflect potential or actual offenders (especially 'errant youth') from entering the mainstream justice system, tribunals sought to bring community pressure to bear upon them in the early days of their 'misbehaviour' or offending. The principles of the scheme emphasised reform and restitution rather than punishment. The aim was 'reintegration' (or, in the case of people new to the city, integration) into the local Maori community, avoiding a 'slippery slope' that might end with incarceration and its consequences – such as young men learning criminal techniques from 'old lags'. 'Saved' youth would eventually, through their communities and their support mechanisms, be helped to integrate into wider society.

In pursuit of pre-emptive or actual rehabilitation, the Maori courts tended to operate by such means as 'social criticism, group therapy and conciliation'. They were often concerned with what the regular judicial and other authorities regarded as 'domestic issues', as well as with matters such as petty theft or drinking and brawling in public. They were responsive to matters referred to them by schools, regular police, government departments, pakeha-dominated organisations and pakeha individuals, as well as by wardens and other members of the Maori community. Frequently, they would adjudicate upon behaviour that they felt would reflect adversely on Maori in the eyes of wider society, even if it were not actually illegal. They formed part of the apparatus attempting to replace the influence of kaumatua that had been lost in the post-war years, especially among those in the cities. The Secretary for Maori Affairs in 1966, Jock McEwen, noted to his counterpart in Justice that the urban Maori courts were struggling because the traditional authority exercised by elders had 'largely disappeared', making their social control functions all the more important.[17]

Despite operating difficulties, many tribunal committees managed to perform satisfactorily as far as their communities were concerned. They could confirm traditional patterns of social organisation and behaviour in both old and new environments, and provide opportunities for new leadership strata to emerge. Wardens often played key roles in the Maori courts system, offering (among other things) an intermediary presence between accused individuals and tribunal members. Such success as the Maori courts experienced in making communities safer by monitoring and punishing untoward conduct also lay to a considerable degree in the fact that the accused could choose whether or not to subject themselves to the coercive authority of the tribunals. When a case of a minor breach of the law was brought to a Maori committee's attention, for example, the alleged offender could have it either adjudicated by tribunal or heard in the Magistrates' Court. Accused persons would often seek guidance from within the Maori community over their options, including from the wardens, and a sizeable proportion decided on hearing and judgment by the Maori court.

This did not mean that the tribunal committees were a 'soft touch'. They frequently exercised their power to impose fines (up to a hefty maximum of £10). And similarly to other official systems which harnessed Maori organisation, many exceeded their formal authority, including when imposing sanctions. Despite this, many offenders agreed to make an appearance before a tribunal committee even if their behaviour would not have seen them hauled before a 'pakeha court'. They appreciated (or had been made to appreciate) that they had violated the mores of the Maori community, even where this might be composed of families scattered throughout pakeha populations in suburban housing estates. Over and above their low-level judicial powers, then, the tribunal committees possessed a communal standing and authority that was highly significant in Maoridom.[18]

The 'physical setting' of Maori courts often 'emphasised the official nature of [their] proceedings', and sittings frequently incorporated the imposing attendance of wardens. Their 'presence in uniform symbolised the authority of the court'. In various ways, in fact, Maori courts involved a meld of pakeha and Maori systems. In one tribunal studied by Ranginui Walker in a new Auckland suburb in the 1960s, proceedings began with a whaikorero in both English and Maori, as if to symbolise the partnership between Crown and Maori that many Maori believed the system was, or should be, moving towards. The charges against the accused were often brought by the wardens and generally fell within the parameters of those decreed by 'pakeha' law. But after they were announced, the secretary, in 'explain[ing] the nature of the court', would declare that 'it was a people's court to deal with the problems of the Maori people'.

Punishments imposed in this court were not necessarily those available to the mainstream judiciary. In a case regarding the harbouring of state wards, the offender was severely reprimanded and 'sentenced to prohibition for twelve months'. It was also ordered that her affairs 'be put on a businesslike basis', and she was be placed 'under a budget officer [to] ensure the cupboards are filled and the children well-fed'. The verdict, in effect, made the harbourer of state wards a temporary state ward herself, but one overseen by a Maori network to which general supervisory powers had been devolved by the Crown. Such an outcome was seen by both the local Maori leadership and the state authorities to be to the benefit of all parties: the offender (who may have thus escaped a more severe sanction by a pakeha court), her whanau, the community and 'the nation' itself.[19]

Most Maori committees that took on judicial functions were acutely conscious of racism and discrimination in mainstream New Zealand society. They believed that rising levels of 'misconduct' and crime by Maori youth were not only tragic per se but also encouraged unfavourable pakeha reactions to

Maori in general. This impeded progress for Maori on many fronts, including the search for autonomy. Greater recognition of rangatiratanga needed widespread support among pakeha as a prerequisite, and gaining this required enhancing the public image of Maoridom. Behaviour which involved harassing pakeha was treated particularly harshly by the tribunals. One individual who had troubled his pakeha neighbour was fined a maximum sum and placed under the scrutiny of wardens for three months. The elders who dominated the tribunal admonished him because, as a result of his noise and abuse, 'Maori people lost face'. The committee secretary added: 'The loss of face is felt by us, the Maori people. We feel that if Peter goes down we all go down. Therefore Peter heed carefully the cry of your people.' Many statements made in the court were of similar ilk: 'When you fall we fall'; 'When you succeed we succeed'. One tribunal committee put it thus: 'This Court empowers us to see to the welfare of our children, to see that we live cleanly so that we can't be called "Dirty Maoris".'

Those who fell foul of 'the law' or breached expected standards of behaviour were seen by Maori courts (and more generally by those who supported the committee system) to be contributing to the stigmatisation of all Maori – thereby jeopardising official and public acceptance of a strong Maori influence within state and society. Tribunals attempted to reinforce the offending individuals' sense of communal identity and responsibility. Modes of behaviour that were seen by the various authorities, Maori and pakeha, to be universally desirable were stressed. In Walker's words, 'when an offence is committed, the Maori community closes its ranks, reaffirms its solidarity and reintegrates into itself the deviant member. A Maori offender is reminded that, despite the anonymity of urban life, his every action for good or ill reflects on the Maori people ... The courts provide an opportunity to reassert and promulgate what are considered to be the norms of good conduct.'[20]

A collective solidarity, then, pervaded those who operated and related to the Maori court system: 'When you die who will mourn you? We your Maori people will.' It was even possible for offenders to be rehabilitated by being given official positions in Maori associations, including as wardens and honorary welfare officers. In a significant number of areas, the local people took a very keen interest in 'their' court's transactions. In one Auckland suburb in the 1960s and 1970s, attendances at the tribunal, convened once a week, averaged fifty. Such community support for the system was particularly important in state housing areas which were Maori-dominated. Suburban ethnicisation was increasing, especially in the outer suburbs to which, by the 1970s, the majority of migrants were heading to rent houses from the state. This process of spatial ethnicisation was a consequence of the phasing out of pepper-potting, together with a small amount of what would be later dubbed 'white flight'.

These new communities were by definition poor, given that the allocation criteria for renting 'state houses' focused on low income and family need. They confronted many problems, such as planning decisions which left them devoid of adequate community amenities. Social difficulties were further compounded from time to time by recessions, starting from 1967. Various demographic changes exacerbated social disorder. Sectors of Maori youth born or brought up in the cities or towns, far from their tribal marae, were increasingly dismissive of social control efforts by kin or committees. Their growing disinclination to place themselves under the jurisdiction of the Maori courts was one of the reasons for the eventual decline of the institution.[21]

Abandoning 'Judicial Separateness'

Most observers felt that, despite such problems, the tribunal system provided a good service for both the Maori communities which embraced it and the state. Later, in fact, it came to be seen as a model for general youth justice initiatives. But in the 1970s, the Maori courts were coming to be viewed increasingly sceptically in non-Maori as well as in some Maori circles. For a number of pakeha (including officials), their existence seemed even more problematic than that of the warden system. Maori courts were seen to embody a 'discriminatory' system of justice which might favour (or sometimes disfavour) some offenders on grounds of ethnicity. They ostensibly cut across the concept of 'equality' in one of its most hallowed ideological locations, the criminal justice system. As early as 1970, even the minister in charge of them described tribunals as 'kangaroo courts'. Under increasing attack thereafter, their supporters fought back, some of them claiming that efficiency would be enhanced if the Maori courts and the official committees within which they were located were given even greater powers. But in 1978, the tribunal committees were criticised by the Royal Commission on the Courts for reasons which reflected their very raison d'etre and their past success in dealing with many potential or actual offenders – their separateness and their non-professionalism. Moreover, the many areas in which tribunals were now proving ineffective, especially among the ever increasing migrant population in the big cities, allowed the commissioners to declare that the system had come to lack moral authority among the Maori people.

Their report disagreed with a reportedly 'strong feeling that Maori attitudes were not fully appreciated or catered for within the existing judicial system and that Maori Committees should be given greater involvement in dealing with minor offences'. The commission had been 'informed that local Maori committees are anxious to play their full part in helping their own young people', but believed that any development that might be construed as moving in a separatist direction should be rejected in order to avoid 'a divided society'. It 'did not consider that the Maori people should be singled out as a class requiring special treatment under our system of justice'. The report suggested that Maori committees might mediate relations between offenders and the justice authorities, but it opposed 'special courts for minority groups'.[22]

While critics of the report noted that its language and perspectives harked back to policy that was prevalent in the aftermath of the Hunn report, the days of the Maori judicial authorities were numbered. A comment by an expert on the historico-judicial interface between Crown and Maori provides an indication of official thought on such issues by the mid-1990s: 'the devolution of minor judicial authority to *marae* or the recognition of a form of *runanga* in Maori-populated suburbs to take cognisance of disputes and delinquency, appear, in recent decades, still to be frowned upon by responsible ministers and officials as divisive of Maori and Pakeha, rather than received optimistically as a means of helping young Maori to develop a sense of belonging and confidence and of enabling older Maori both to develop improved social control and to enjoy a larger sense of responsibility in New Zealand society'.

The Maori court system had also been overtaken, however, because of developments within Maori as well as broader society, the voices of Maori detractors having grown ever louder in the 1970s. Urban-based radicals of the Maori Renaissance had tended to see the tribunals as part of the NZMC system's complicity with the hegemonic aims and institutions of the dominant culture – as, in effect, Maori consenting to their own oppression. Increasing numbers of Maori of varied opinions and backgrounds came to see the court system as part of a state-dominated attempt to contain Maoridom and its autonomist aspirations by imposing western standards of behaviour and beliefs upon their people. At best, they regarded the tribunal committees as irrelevant to their lives. Even the NZMC itself decided, by the end of the 1970s, that the courts were increasingly anachronistic, emerging as they did from the imperatives and opportunities of the pre-renaissance period.

The council had come to believe, moreover, that the tribunals were impeding acceptance among pakeha of Maoridom and its aspirations, that they helped to further prevalent notions that Maori needed special measures because they were in many respects socially 'backward'. As early as 1964, leaders from various sectors of Maoridom had formed a united front to portray their people as modern and adaptive. An Education Department booklet for schools, Ans Westra's *Washday at the Pa*, had documented through text and photographs 'the happy life of a rural Maori family with nine children'. The MWWL declared that the primitive conditions depicted might be seen by pakeha to typify Maoridom and demanded withdrawal of the publication. Other Maori leadership strata supported their stance that the booklet (in the NZMC's words) 'strengthens the out-of-date stereotype of the Maori'. Under such unified pressure, the Minister of Education withdrew the publication on grounds that it could be seen to have 'degraded' Maoridom and might hinder 'trying to draw the Maori and Pakeha together'. Officials attempted to destroy all copies, although it was quickly republished privately with the support of those who noted that it presented an empathetic account of the life of a Maori family.

Another strand of criticism of the booklet, including from some pakeha, had been that since the family were portrayed as having been allocated an urban state house, *Washday at the Pa* was actively (and officially) promoting urbanisation and assimilation. After this controversy, debates on subjects relating to the place of Maori in wider society were even more intensive than in the past. Changing attitudes to Maori courts among Maori need to be seen in the context of such discourse. Influenced by and under pressure from the Maori Renaissance, Maori leaders were increasingly concerned that the tribunals served to promote an unfavourable impression of a separatist and enclosed Maori way of life, one in which Maori were seen to have rights and privileges denied to pakeha – a stigma less attached to the work of wardens, which was more visibly of benefit to pakeha as well as Maori. For some Maori, too, the rangatiratanga the tribunals may have once embodied had been compromised by the very officialness of their proceedings and functions. All in all, many Maori leaders came to see them as anachronisms. According to anthropologist-observer Fleras, the NZMC set out to 'suppress [the Maori courts] in all but a few rural areas'. While some Maori communities persisted with 'their' courts, the institution was rapidly fading away among the plethora of new ways of asserting rangatiratanga which arose in the 1970s.[23]

Modernity and Tikanga Maori

Although the official committee system and its offshoots constituted a state-sanctioned mode of socio-racial control, it also became a site for efforts to reforge Maori politico-cultural solidarity in both traditional and urban environments. While welcoming the benefits that 'the west' and modernity offered, the committees represented a rejection of full assimilation (in the guise of 'integration') and an affirmation of autonomy. Just as western ideas and technologies added value to Maori lifestyles, moreover, so too could Maori, by retaining and developing indigenous attributes, add value to the pakeha world. 'Official New Zealand' gradually came to see this.

If very generously interpreted, official acceptance of a degree of tikanga Maori/Maori custom during the days of integrationist policy could be viewed as embodying support for a significant presence of rangatiratanga in New Zealand life; in such a view, the early evolution of the MWA system could even be seen as exemplifying integration in action. The committees affirmed that while there was a strong Maori desire to 'succeed' in a pakeha- and urban-dominated New Zealand, doing so required, as a matter of both practice and principle, culturally-based and collective forms of organisation and mutual assistance. In their adaptation to modernity, Maori did not want to become the same as pakeha: 'Maori want[ed] to be Maori in a Pakeha world', and for the pakeha world to take up Maori perceptions and ways of doing things.

However wanting the Hunn report's motivations and some of its conclusions were for increasing numbers of Maori, it had renewed general discussion on ways in which the state could and should take a lead regarding the appropriate place of Maori in New Zealand society and governance. Its cautious endorsement of the need to retain some degree of Maoritanga, even within an integrated society, held out hope to many Maori leaders that progress could be made on preserving or even enhancing Maori language and culture. Among promising developments was the formation of the Maori Graduates' Association, which became active on a number of fronts, both integrationist and autonomist.

The continued strength of tikanga Maori even in non-tribal milieus became increasingly apparent to officials and their advisers, and Maori values and customs gradually began to be taken into greater account in Crown policies. Some degree of tikanga Maori could be accommodated partly because of a widespread belief within state circles that other aspects of Maori culture inappropriate to modernity were being obliterated, and that Maori were gradually moving towards western hegemonic norms. Such accommodation does not mean, therefore, that ethnocentric policies had entirely disappeared, as a 1971 bureaucratic utterance indicates: 'The Maori is not sufficiently removed from his past to be well adapted for commerce with its demand for strongly individualistic traits, which are in sharp contrast to his ancient mode of living.' But an increasingly common view within officialdom was that the retention of some traditional Maori ways could help with adaptation to modern life. The Department of Maori Affairs believed that the 'complex and perplexing' transition from a rural to an urban people would be eased by the Maori 'capacity to identify himself with one culture whilst striving to master another'. Thus, 'Maori culture or "Maoritanga" in its modern form is ... more than an end in itself, for it is also a stepping stone to adjustment to the new world'. While retaining aspects of indigeneity and collectivity, Maori would supposedly come to see, for example, that 'free enterprise' and an 'individualistic spirit' were both good and natural.[24]

As a result of relentless state influences and pressures upon the committee system, a number of members of rural or small-town Maori committees believed that its social control functions were so tied to the state's desires as to make it a threat to local, especially tribal, values. Some went so far as to attempt to operate completely independently of the requirements of the legislation. There was much internal discussion or dissent within the NZMC system, with vigorous debates among candidates standing for election and complex configurations of beliefs and proposals. Sometimes hereditary rangatira would assert traditional tribal custom, in opposition to the values of younger, modernising tribal members who wanted to work with or alongside the Crown. At other times or in different places, older traditional leaders saw adaptation to the changing order and cooperation with the state as the key to survival for Maori customs and organisational forms. Some of these supported collective reorganising in the cities to try, in the words of John Rangihau, 'to take into the urban situation aspects of tribal living ... that would ... stand the test of urban pressures'.

Some tribes had been making adjustments to modernity and urbanisation over a long period, including those conventionally seen as the most resistant to the Crown's assimilation policies. Tuhoe, for example, had seen many of its people leave for Rotorua, and had moved to procure an urban base, Mataatua Marae, in that city. In the 1960s, its tribal leadership began to address the fact that large numbers of the people were now moving to Auckland. In 1971, Te Tira Hou Marae was established there, and on this urban marae the tribe acted 'as tangata whenua, the host people. In a very real sense these marae are part of Tuhoe tribal organisation', an observer noted.

Tuhoe continued to establish institutions, both formal and informal, outside of its traditional rohe. This did not mean any diminution in the iwi's focus on its role as tangata whenua of its Urewera rohe, where its major political and cultural events were held. These events included an annual whare wananga, established at a hui at Ruatahuna in 1969–70, for teaching tribal customs to the young. The work of tribal institutions was complemented by a flourishing network which included the Crown-franchised institutions of trust board and official committee. By the mid-1980s, the region in which Tuhoe was located hosted six Maori executive committees and 33 Maori committees, most of them based at marae. All Tuhoe organisations, including those which were officially franchised, were said to be 'based on the continuing concept of tribal identity and sense of belonging, turangawaewae, in Te Urewera'.[25]

In urban settings, migrants from rural areas carried with them '[t]raditional knowledge, marae etiquette, songs and chants', and many other varieties of tikanga Maori, all of which were fortified and replenished by trips 'home'. Assisted by frequent interaction with those remaining in the tribal rohe, many rangatira and kaumatua continued to exercise leadership after they had moved to the cities. Such leaders often forged alliances with state and other organisations, and cooperated with non-traditional Maori leaders, some of whom had gained their power bases by being respected and selected by Maori who had become 'isolated' from their tribes. Maori urban leaders of all types, but especially those representing mixed-iwi areas in the cities, sought to make use of official committees whether they liked the concept or not, because committees could help them in their many and difficult tasks. 'The close scrutiny and supervision of the lives of Maori people by a Maori committee and its officers fills the vacuum in the lives of those who migrate from the face-to-face tribal community to urban society and anonymity', an observer noted in the 1970s. 'The work of a Maori committee is clearly a response to the problems of a minority adjusting to urban life.'

Anthropologists at the time, trained in participant-observation methodology, generally agreed that the committees represented a significant means of securing state support for organising along collective lines in the interests of both adjusting and 'staying Maori'. Prominent among them was Joan Metge, who analysed the post-war situation of Maori as follows: 'Maori have resisted cultural and political domination by developing management strategies of their own, putting up barriers behind which they organise their lives their own way, unknown to most Pakeha, adapting borrowed practices to Maori ends, editing and re-interpreting traditional tikanga ("right ways") to meet contemporary needs.' The Maori committees were but one domain in which indigenous culture displayed a dynamism which belied the simplistic belief among many pakeha that Maori society was generally one of a static traditionalism which would (and should) soon disappear.

In the process of reappropriating Crown appropriations, Maori both affirmed tikanga Maori and made adjustments to meet the times and circumstances. A number of social, organisational and cultural forms which had remained virtually intact in the pre-war period of 'resistive acculturation' were being reasserted through official bodies intended, ultimately, to usurp them. All the while, Maori themselves were subtly altering their perspectives and strategies as a result of the complex and developing mix of negotiations with, and adaptations to, pakeha society and its institutions. The 'norms of good conduct' in the Maori world, then, were adapting to post-war modernity, urbanisation and other circumstances. The degree of balance struck between the old and the new in any given situation was among the factors which both dictated which parties benefited most fundamentally and shaped the patterns of the fast evolving New Zealand society.[26]

Official Committees and Rangatiratanga

Within the paradigm of the hegemonic state, many Maori argued, a successfully operating official committee could further, or even embody, a community's wishes to assert and control that which was important to its members: 'real power lay with the people who were prepared to support it, participate in its affairs and accept its authority and leadership'. Whatever the formal duties it was tasked with, a committee could be the focal point in the lives of local Maori people. It could support individuals and families who were finding it hard to transfer to the urban political economy, and provide such services as budgetary advice for maladjusted households. Its secretary might guarantee creditors that accounts would be paid, contact local authorities to have cut-off water and power restored, negotiate with court staff and other officials, and fight to avert repossessions, summonses or eviction orders. Maori associations, then, could become powerful embodiments of collective hopes and aspirations when people put their trust in them. Official committees were vehicles of one-way social control generally only in specific circumstances, such as when individuals were reported to the 'pakeha authorities' for transgressing the law (although even with transgressors, the system could formally handle the cases of minor offenders who chose to be sanctioned under committee auspices).

Communities or their representatives would replace committee officeholders if they proved unable to properly represent and assist the people, although in a number of rural areas the entrenched power of customary rangatira precluded much possibility of significant leadership change. In the towns, however, the committees provided 'an adaptive mechanism to urban life' that might well owe little to traditional kin inheritances. 'New' leaders who arose within the urban committee structure often used techniques better suited to the dominant political economy than those traditionally used by iwi, hapu, whanau or marae leaders in the countryside. City-based elections led to a greater turnover than at rural marae, and to a much higher percentage of non-rangatira members and officeholders.

That urban committees were adaptive, however, does not mean the system was without problems, some of these caused by the sheer number of constituents compared with rural areas. City or suburban committee members were often personally unknown to those who voted for them, and many they supposedly represented might not even have heard of them or been aware that the committees formed part of the wider NZMC structure. Even many Maori working at local committee level would fail to take advantage of the 'opportunity for input into the upper levels', often because of the pressures of urban life and work.

On the committees themselves, as in organisations everywhere, quarrels and personality conflicts were not uncommon. Members often reportedly lacked the skills and resources required of their office, were 'uncertain of their duties and powers', or allowed personal or tribal relationships to unduly influence their public roles. Officeholders were sometimes accused of authoritarianism or of 'stacking' majority-vote meetings with kin, or those who owed them favours, or those who were in 'official relationships' with committee members such as 'budgetees' or wardens. Such actions generated dissent within committees and/or their communities, and led to tensions, counter-stacking and resignations. The emergence of consensus, the preferred Maori way of reaching decisions on issues, could be a very lengthy process, although it could also be highly effective, with observers noting that customary modes of decision-making often seemed to provide the best way of proceeding.

While there was disquiet in many quarters about the quid pro quos necessary to receive Crown help, those who operated and supported official committees were often more concerned about insufficient state support or such matters as the shortcomings of committee memberships. The problem for many Maori was not that the committee system was embedded in the state, but that the state provided inadequate resources to enable committees to develop their services in ways that fitted local community circumstances. Whether flaxroots committees developed their own trajectories – often independently from the higher echelons in the system – or fully pursued Crown guidelines, all needed resources to do so. But state funding was limited, with the government reluctant to fund committees even to the level needed to carry out their statutory responsibilities. Traditional Crown parsimony towards Maori had been exacerbated when, early on, opposition to state policies had come from Maori leadership quarters which the government had expected to be quiescent.

Committees were required to compete with other bodies for 'welfare'-based funding, a burden which often diverted their attention away from other activities. Since only officially approved activities would be financially supported by the state, moreover, those wanting to branch out into other domains had to spend inordinate amounts of time fundraising. Poor resourcing especially affected those in urban areas who were assisting in the establishment of 'new communities'. As networks of mutual support developed, both official and non-official committees worked together to put pressure on the Crown for adequate infrastructural, project-based and other assistance. There was a consciousness that the stakes were high. A National Conference of Maori Committees held in August 1978 declared the common objective of the committees to be nothing less than 'the welfare of our people'.

While more resources were frequently sought from the state, there remained a deep awareness that such support held dangers of further state appropriations of Maori organisational energies, forms and culture. Communities engaged in many discussions on ways of ensuring that assistance was provided without too great a degree of state prescription. Requests for Crown support often involved attempts to ensure jurisdictional autonomy for use of resources. Such approaches tended to bring scant results, given both the Crown's need for public accountability for state monies and broader issues of control. It was much easier, both within the NZMC structure and outside of it, to receive state funding if projects and their implementation were amenable to the Crown's agenda and the applicants showed preparedness to cooperate with the appropriate state authorities over concepts and details. Organisations or leaders critical of state policy, or seeking projects which did not meet Crown requirements, were likely to meet with delay or rejection.[27]

There were ongoing reservations in many quarters of Maoridom, including from 'insiders', about the very existence of the official structures of representation. During the process of establishing what became the NZMC system, some critics had declared that, along with the Maori Women's Welfare League, the official committees were designed essentially to transmit state policies 'downward', whatever Hunn's insistence that national and district councils were to be vehicles for 'two-way' communication. The Maori associations were seen to be resonant of the institutions of 1900 in this respect, and some critics depicted them as acting as creatures of government, noting that the state hosted the NZMC at its pleasure and on its terms – including designating it to be the legal representative of all Maori.

The national body's secretariat, in particular, was seen to be under Crown influence by dint of the fact that it was both relatively heavily state-subsidised and hosted by the Department of Maori Affairs. Observers were soon noting that the New Zealand Maori Council leadership 'seems to talk only for the more conservative elements within Maori society'. This perception was strengthened because the more radical individuals among the NZMC's central and regional leadership had little choice but to move cautiously until the political climate was more auspicious. Another strand of criticism related to the NZMC's 'hierarchy of structure', which was said to entrench a culture of central- or regional-level decision-making within the official system. The 'most serious criticism of the Maori Council', a scholar reported in 1971, was that it 'tends to have strangled communication from the local level'.

As noted above, a discernible tendency towards criticism of aspects of government policy by the NZMC had developed even in the early years of the council. But despite this, many tangata whenua (and sympathisers in the pakeha world) continued to perceive it to be both too top-heavy and too heavily state-influenced. With rural-based district councils dominating the national body's membership selection procedures, the 'elderly males' in charge of the Maori Council were often regarded by younger and urban Maori as dupes of government. For some, indeed, the NZMC was akin to a 'puppet organization'.[28]

Overlooking the system remained the paternalistic Department of Maori Affairs. Hunn's assimilationist policies had envisaged that the department would gradually wind down as integration proceeded. The institution would increasingly contract out its programmes to mainstream departments on the way to, ultimately, disappearing altogether. But with 'Maoriness' continuing to be affirmed, organisationally and culturally, the government saw value in the DMA surviving, at least in the meanwhile, for monitoring and control purposes. Under a strong head between 1963 and 1975, Jock McEwen, it continued much as before, including hands-on intervention in all Maori Welfare Act processes and policies.

Appreciation within many Maori circles of the autonomist potential offered by the NZMC system, however, meant that criticism of the official infrastructure for Maori affairs was often tempered. The DMA and the NZMC, for all their faults, presided over a system that could work well for Maori on a number of matters at both high level and low. Verdicts in urban Maori courts, for example, would be accepted as 'just and proper' not because of Crown authorisation but because the whanau of the accused welcomed reconstituted disciplinary channels within an environment which had enabled (especially young) people to break free of tribal ties and constraints. Family and tribal members were able to participate in the committee proceedings, and tribunal strictures and punishments often reflected traditional sanctions. In effect, the Maori committees and their adjuncts operated as expressions of 'a collective moral force' within local Maori communities, and often served to reinforce the importance in Maori life of 'personal contact, a life-giving component of Maori politics'. The committee system, therefore, could be – and frequently was – the formal and/or informal point of reference for Maori life at a local level. It provided for something akin to communal self-governing mechanisms, and offered a training ground for leadership at flaxroots and higher levels.[29]

Revitalisation and the Maori Community Development Act

Questions of leadership and self-governance were of increasing significance within Maoridom, including at its interface with the official and pakeha world. Maori had gained better educational opportunities in the urban centres and had been rapidly intermarrying with pakeha, and from 1971 the Race Relations Act outlawed discrimination on race grounds. But many Maori still lacked (in Robert Mahuta's words) the 'experience, education and sophistication required to act as effective political participants' within dominant power structures. The committees helped many to gain confidence and experience in a world dominated by pakeha socio-economic constructs and culture. A commentator noted in the later 1970s that tangata whenua were seeking to become 'legitimate participants in the decision-making processes and in the social institutions of society', while at the same time retaining their own 'cultural forms'. The NZMC system allowed for political participation for sizeable numbers at flaxroots level, and for new leaders to emerge at its higher levels.

By the 1970s, a growing number of young, articulate and well educated Maori had begun to gain a voice, and even elected positions and kudos, in some of the flaxroots committees. Before long, a few individuals among them were taking up regional and national positions, replacing some of the conservative leaders of the NZMC structure. They were, in some senses, better placed by their education and (urban) experience to liaise with state agencies and pakeha sympathetic to Maori causes. The most successful leaders, it was widely noted, tended to be those 'comfortable with the values and customs of both the Maori and the Pakeha'.

Many contemporary observers and participants, moreover, saw the Maori associations system as a means of revitalising Maori unity in a way that was reminiscent of the Maori Parliament of the late nineteenth century or of Ngataism in the first half of the twentieth. Official committees and councils interconnected with other organised sectors of Maoridom, tribally-based or otherwise, from the local level to the national. The Tuhoe Trust Board, for example, complemented the work of marae-based official committees, their executives and the Waiariki District Maori Council. Its tribal urban outposts in Rotorua, Auckland and later Wellington acted as conduits for the involvement of its members outside the rohe, and a number of Tuhoe also participated in pan-tribal voluntary organisations in the cities.[30]

Experience of leadership and general community service through the official committee structure was especially important among newly urbanised Maori seeking to recollectivise aspects of their lives in a different and often difficult environment. Within a year of the founding (in 1964) of one suburban Auckland committee, a marae project was under way 'as a focal point for community sentiment'. Many of the committee members had already been members of other Maori organisations, and now wished to further develop their 'Maoriness' within structures that partially replicated the social collectivism inherent in tribal-based life. At the committee's triennial elections in 1967, fuller community representation ensued, after people involved in a wide range of occupations, and tribal, church, school and other organisations, stood for office.

Five pakeha were invited to join the committee as well, in order both to introduce a 'multiracial' dimension and to provide additional expertise. The European associates were professionals (especially in the education sphere) whose attributes complemented those of the members who were Maori. Their skills were especially needed for the marae project. Reflecting the general class position of the tangata whenua, many of the Maori members of official committees were drawn from the lower socio-economic ranks. In the case of the suburban committee under scrutiny, at one point there were four drivers, two clerical workers and a freezing worker, as well as a pastor. Its Maori members acquired new skills and attributes from intermingling with the co-opted members and with other contacts in the course of the various committee activities. The 'committee grew in stature in the eyes of the community', especially because of its welfare work. It was one of the many official committees which gained 'a sense of control and mastery' over local Maori affairs.

The official system, in short, continued to offer a great deal to very many Maori people. There had been a number of administrative changes over the years, such as the 1969 alteration to allow direct Maori committee representation upon district councils, giving flaxroots organisations greater potential influence. But the changes had been piecemeal, the government was increasingly predisposed (for its own ideological and fiscal reasons) to hand Maori issues (and problems) to Maori, and self-determinationist voices from voluntary sectors and radical groups within Maoridom were becoming louder and more insistent. Because of its propensity to develop in non-approved directions, moreover, and because ways of responding to the Maori Renaissance needed to be addressed, in the late 1970s the Crown decided to carry out a reappraisal of the whole system. The government review considered a variety of structural and other issues, from local empowerment initiatives (within and outside the NZMC structure) to recent social and cultural developments. The reviewers addressed both the Maori Renaissance and the increasing pakeha acceptance of Maori culture and organisation. As a result, the Maori Welfare Act was overhauled in 1979 and renamed the Maori Community Development Act (MCDA). Replacement of the word 'welfare' by 'community development' was intended to be a powerful signal that the paternalism which had once dominated the Crown and its official committee system was now deemed to be anachronistic. The theme of the changes was greater autonomy: there would be a move from welfare-statism towards community empowerment and self-reliance.

One analysis has concluded that the new Act 'would seem to empower' the various levels of the official system 'to take an interest in any activity they wish'. Maori committees were renamed Marae committees, reflecting an appreciation of the continuing importance in Maori life of an institution once thought doomed to ultimate disappearance under the impact of modernity and urbanisation. Instead, marae were being reinvigorated in the rural areas and continued to be established in new forms (formally or otherwise) in the urban spaces. Marae of disparate types, in effect, combined functions of 'local self-government' with those of cultural perpetuation, renovation and development. Subsidies to Maori committees had already generally become known as 'marae subsidies'.[31]

Radicalisation

The MCDA, then, was an attempt to adjust to new social and political developments in both Maori and wider New Zealand society. Its broadening of the functions allocated to the Maori associations reflected, among other things, pressures stemming from the increasing radicalisation of (especially young) Maori. Over the previous decade, many members and associates of the associations had become increasingly frustrated that their participation had led to neither fundamental control of their own affairs nor other types of change (even if some communities had experienced an increasing feeling or degree of empowerment through working in or with the NZMC system).

Such thinking partly reflected the growing influence within Maoridom of international 'alternative discourses' and the rise of a new generation of urban-based Maori activists. Seeking to utilise lessons learned from political movements overseas in the struggle for rangatiratanga, many activists judged the state's record and intentions harshly. Whatever it might have said and done, whatever concessions it had apparently made to Maori autonomist and other wishes, the Crown was still seen to be assimilationist in its aims. It was seen to have exploited the fact that many Maori living in the cities had drifted away from a traditional or collective base, some of them as a result of lumpenisation but many because of a belief that the only way of 'getting on' was to adopt a pakeha worldview and its accompanying set of behavioural characteristics. Urbanisation, then, provided the backdrop for what many saw as new and disguised Crown ways of implementing old policies which essentially incorporated the vision expressed by an official inquiry in 1965. Seeking to characterise the Maori who had entered the 'new world' of urban life, the inquiry members had approvingly commented: 'He believes in integration and wishes to fit in and not be a man apart.'

However much they were products of a city upbringing (and sometimes because of it), many of the new Maori generation rejected the underlying premises of this integrationist vision. Some of the most alienated, especially those 'at the bottom of the social heap' and who had failed to acquire educational qualifications, had begun to form or join Maori gangs. A 'form of inarticulate protest', the gangs were nevertheless collectivist in orientation, the Stormtroopers being the first (in 1970) to gain a high profile. As the years progressed and the gangs proved to be both durable and increasingly intractable and even criminal in their activities, they attracted much adverse public attention from pakeha and Maori alike.

Meanwhile, growing numbers of radical young political activists were concerned with reclaiming and reconstituting rangatiratanga. They, too, would have little truck with constituted authority, including with established Maori institutions of either official or non-official ilk. They considered the official committee structure, and quasi-official and other 'respectable' organisations, to have produced little for their people, and even to have led Maori people into 'collaboration'. One member of a Maori committee inadvertently expressed what many radicals thought about the underlying nature of the system: when a committee secretary 'rings you up or comes around and sees you and tells you you're a great white chief it makes you feel good inside'.

With Maori generally becoming more forthright in their methods of seeking Crown recognition of rangatiratanga, and the rise of a Maori Renaissance spearheaded by younger activists, increasing numbers of individuals in both city and country tended to ignore or bypass the committee system. The local committees – with their policing powers, their punishment regimes and their expectations as to proper ways of living – were coming to be seen as agencies of the state rather than as organisations which might utilise and even appropriate state-provided resources for Maori purposes. An historian writing in the late 1960s and influenced by international radicalising tendencies, interpreted Maori politics as an interplay between cooperation and protest; he speculated that past government structures which had encouraged cooperation between Crown and Maori had been a key reason behind the quiescence of Maori over many decades and the relative absence of overt protest.

By the 1970s, confrontational protest was very much on the agenda again. While considerable numbers stayed with the Maori associations, many others decided that the structures established in the early 1960s had failed to restore 'the dignity that has been lost to us' or to constitute a sufficient force in the 'struggle ... against the forces of colonisation'. The Maori Welfare Act's structures had sometimes provided a platform to advance Maori aspirations for self-determination, but they were also seen to have served to co-opt Maori into 'the pakeha system'. This implied, for many within the protest movement and in other sectors of Maoridom too, that mere structural reform of the official system would achieve little by way of advancing autonomy. While it survived, and remained an important player in the fight for rangatiratanga, including (and increasingly) at its upper levels, the NZMC system was viewed as overly timid or compromised in its methods by the more radical sectors of the Maori world. One response from the Crown was to incorporate flaxroots initiatives into new 'self-reliance' policies, providing for this within the structure of the MCDA, but this was generally appreciated mostly by those already working with or within the official system. Another response, from within Maoridom, was to seek innovative ways of asserting rangatiratanga and, in some cases, to pursue radical, sweeping and even extreme goals, aims and aspirations.[32]

Chapter 7

Protest and Response

The Maori Renaissance

By the 1970s, the old 'politics of stability and consensus' in New Zealand was rapidly being superseded by a 'politics of volatility and increasing political polarization'. While this reflected an international western phenomenon, it was given an antipodean edge by a growing propensity among pakeha citizens to see themselves as New Zealanders rather than 'British'. This trend would escalate after Britain joined the European Economic Community in 1973, foreshadowing the ultimate demise of its protective economic relationship with New Zealand –and hence of New Zealand's 'colonial' relationship with its Mother Country, except in terms of residual sentiment. Such was the socio-political context in which Maori matters came to have much greater prominence in New Zealand than any time since the wars of the nineteenth century. In fact, Maori voices had been heard in the many and various protest movements arising in New Zealand in the late 1960s.

Increasing Maori demands for recognition of rangatiratanga gelled with strong challenges to the status quo from many quarters, with the 'founding myths' of New Zealand (including those of paradisal race relations) placed under especially wide-ranging critical scrutiny. It was an exciting intellectual and social time for many (particularly young) people, including Maori youth growing up in the cities with access to educational opportunities denied their forebears. The mood of strengthening Maori assertion was reflected in a commentator's words in the Maori Council's newspaper in 1968: vocal Maori demands were based on countering 'denial of [their] separate identity' and 'establishing their identities *as Maoris*'. As an activist said in 1971, ever greater numbers of people of Maori descent were beginning 'to review the validity, the justice of this present system, and question it'. A growing 'renaissance in Maori awareness' meant that '[c]onsciousness of being Maori is reviving'. Auckland-based radical activist group Nga Tamatoa declared in 1973 that assimilation had 'failed' and detected instead 'a feeling of Maoriness in the air'. By then, campaigns for 'Maori rights' had gathered great momentum.[1]

Ironically, the offerings of urban life, rather than leading to full assimilation, had (in Tipene O'Regan's words) 'dramatically fuelled' Maori political consciousness. This was intensified when the economy began to falter: now, even Maori who had been drawn into the 'equality' myth could see that their people constituted, in general, a subset of the New Zealand working class and suffered disproportionately within the capitalist political economy. Much public attention was drawn to both class and social-racial discrepancies, and Maori workers with trade union or similar organisational and ideological backgrounds gained experience which helped bring them to the fore of the 'new ethnic activism'. So too did Maori tertiary students, many of whom were members of the New Zealand Federation of Maori Students, founded in 1959.

Among the various groupings which younger Maori contributed to, founded or joined were both pan-tribal or detribalised voluntary activist associations and a host of new cultural clubs and societies. Such organisations constituted a key part of the outer geographical limits of a worldwide 'ethnic revival'. As indigenous politics were increasingly globalised, young Maori activists gained ideological and organisational insights into ways of furthering their causes. Models ranged from the 'black power' and American Indian movements in the United States to Marxist, unionist, feminist, anti-racist, gay rights and environmental movements there and elsewhere. This international upsurge of ethnicity and of the 'New Left' and other movements had precursors in New Zealand among both Maori and pakeha. Dick Scott's *The Parihaka Story*, and later publications, were to help inspire new generations of radicals such as Syd Jackson, a founder of the Tamatoa Council/Nga Tamatoa in 1970.[2]

In the rural-based past, and during their post-war displacement to the cities, many Maori had not seen themselves as part of 'a separate national community'. Cultural and linguistic identification as Maori had gradually been joined by the realisation that the more united their activity, the more likely they were able to advance the struggle for rangatiratanga – at whatever level and however this might be manifested. With the advent of the Maori Renaissance, in the early 1970s united action intensified, and new political demands and renewed cultural vigour complemented the ever-present fight for better housing, pay, working conditions, health services and so forth.

It can be argued that the word 'renaissance' is, in some senses, a misnomer. As we have seen, 'the spirit of ethnicity ha[d] never died' within Maoridom. But while its roots were embedded in tribal-based custom, polity and struggle, significant portions of the renewed consciousness were urban based and focussed on 'Maoriness' rather than on tribal identity. Young Maori activists, in particular, would often combine their tikanga knowledge and their in-depth experience of the 'alienating culture' with the application of protest methods influenced by borrowings from overseas. These methods, often founded in urban indigenous experiences, made the 'Maori protest movement' a new phenomenon, even if many of the customs it sought to revive or procure respect for were 'traditional'. Activists brought new tools for, and modes of, expressing Maoriness. They joined and reinvigorated the ongoing Maori struggle for autonomy in its varied configurations, tribal and non-tribal, rural and urban, cultural and political. Given this vigorous politico-cultural renewal among Maori, complemented by a rapidly increasing pakeha interest in Maori arts, craft and literature, it is legitimate to speak – as people did at the time – of a 'renaissance' within Maoridom. This renaissance needs to be seen in the context of a broader social, political, cultural and intellectual regeneration, with 'intersectional' links being made nationally and internationally on issues of race, gender and class.[3]

The Maori campaign to 'reconcile Aotearoa with New Zealand' accompanied, informed and stimulated post-colonial nationalist debate and 'nation-building' discourse and terminology. Increasing numbers of non-Maori were coming to see themselves as 'pakeha' rather than 'European' or 'British'. In the 1970s, observers were noting a sense of unease, dislocation or 'homelessness' among sizeable sectors of non-Maori New Zealand. In response to the Maori assertion of indigeneity, many native-born pakeha stressed *their* strong identity with the land of their birth. Significant numbers began, consciously or otherwise, to seek a new pakeha *identity*, one which drew both on critiques of the assimilationism and racism of 'monocultural' white New Zealand and on a willingness to concede that Maori society, culture and organisation would and should survive and thrive. But large numbers of other New Zealanders were antagonistic to Maori activists and their increasingly vocal demands. In this environment, anti-racist and indigenous support organisations were revived or established.

The self-imposed challenge for white liberals was first to 'examine critically their own attitudes and institutions' and to develop 'a new consciousness'. Then they could set out to undermine the old ethnocentric pakeha beliefs and to combat 'institutional racism'. As a joint paper by the Citizens Association for Racial Equality (CARE) and the Auckland Committee on Racism and Discrimination (ACORD) stated, the aim was 'to build a truly multi-cultural society' and to stop the authorities and white citizens attempting 'to enforce mono-cultural uniformity'. In fighting for a multicultural world – talk of 'biculturalism' often occurred within a broader discourse on 'multiculturalism' in the 1970s, and often the terms were used interchangeably – pakeha activists sought, then, to situate themselves at a 'progressive' location within mainstream culture. They worked alongside and with Maori co-thinkers and organisations, and were to have an important role to play in complementing or assisting the new Maori activist movements.[4]

While some Maori protest groups tended to eschew pakeha membership, many Maori activists quickly recognised that their struggles resonated with other progressive causes and that immediate goals needed contextualising within a broader politico-economic framework. Work with and within different types of pakeha-dominated bodies could well be fruitful. There was, in particular, a close working relationship in the 1970s between Maori activists and pakeha-led anti-racist organisations such as CARE, ACORD and HART (Halt All Racist Tours, which arose out of the campaign to stop sporting contact with apartheid South Africa). Maori women participated in the broader women's liberation movement, adopting feminist theoretical analyses which saw them struggling on several fronts, both for 'Maori liberation' and against the oppression of women within Maori and pakeha society. Activists from groups such as the Maori Organisation on Human Rights (MOOHR) were also working within the trade union movement, and 'advocated an alliance between Maori and progressive elements of the working class'. The aim was to unite the various races, 'Maori and Pakeha and all', but 'especially all working people'. Linking the 'struggle for Maori rights with the class struggle' was particularly pertinent at a time of recessionary trends which hit Maori disproportionately.[5]

MOOHR sought pan-racial workers' unity in combating racism, exploitation and oppression. The organisation emerged in tandem with a Wellington-based underground newspaper called *Te Hokioi*, which was 'written for Maoris along with their Pakeha class brothers'. Reviving the name of a Maori resistance newspaper from the previous century, *Te Hokioi* first appeared in August 1968, that momentous year of socio-intellectual upheaval in many parts of the world. The newspaper saw racism as the inevitable outcome of class inequality, and conceived of Maori as particularly oppressed members of the working class. Like *Te Hokioi*, Nga Tamatoa and later others, MOOHR's focus was on raising Maori consciousness. In addition to its class analysis, it declared that Maori were oppressed as an ethnicity as well – through contemporary happenings such as pollution of seafood beds as well as due to historical actions by Crown and settlers. It was very much concerned with the way Maori rights, identity and culture had been denied by decades of 'assimilationist' policy and 'monocultural attitudes'. Language, which was seen as underpinning culture, was a major issue. MOOHR 'accused the education system of "cultural murder" of the Māori language', and campaigned for the revival of te reo Maori.

The Tamatoa movement arose out of discussion at the 1970 Young Maori Leaders' Conference in Auckland, whose attendees were especially concerned about the alienation of urban youth from their roots. Tamatoa membership was dominated by university students who tended to elevate race above class.

Initially they focused on advocating the teaching of the Maori language in schools, but other demands made at the founding of Nga Tamatoa (as well as its name, meaning Young Warriors) pointed towards the more 'political' package of goals which soon emerged. As it declared in 1972, Nga Tamatoa wanted Maori 'control over those things which are particularly Maori, including Maori monies and their distribution, Maori lands [and] the integration of Maori language and culture in the New Zealand education system'. A year later, it proposed that 'the education of Maori people ... be in complete and autonomous control of the Maori people'. It would call for equal Maori representation in Parliament, the return of confiscated land, and Crown ratification of the Treaty of Waitangi.[6]

The various protest groups, Maori and pakeha, had linkages in ideas and personnel. At the 1968 conference of the Federation of Maori Students, Syd Jackson initiated protest action over the scheduled All Black rugby tour of South Africa, regardless of whether Maori players were allowed to be included in the team. The resulting multiracial campaign was both internationalist, in solidarity with oppressed indigenes elsewhere, and New Zealandist in orientation. The voice of Maori, campaigners stressed, needed to be heard by national institutions, private and state. Other Maori organisations and sectors joined the cause, including trade unionists, churches, the Ratana Youth Movement and the Maori MPs. Even relatively conservative organisations took up the call, such as the Maori Graduates' Association and the MWWL (although the NZMC felt that South African acceptance of non-white players would be adequate).

The Treaty of Waitangi

The Treaty of Waitangi tended to be iconically central to the political claims of many of the new single- and multi-issue radical movements, with activists rarely separating out Treaty rights from more general issues of race, class and capitalist exploitation. The Treaty had always been, in Ngata's words in the 1920s, 'on the lips of the humble and the great, of the ignorant and of the thoughtful'. There had been many and varied proposals to have the Treaty 'ratified' or adhered to by the Crown. Hunn commented in 1963 that '[p]ressure from the Maori people to ratify the Treaty of Waitangi has been sustained over the years and will presently be exerted again in a Petition to Parliament'. In a speech before the Queen on Waitangi Day of that year, NZMC president Turi Carroll hoped that Her Majesty would 'fully understand and sympathise with the desire of the Maori people to press for the embodiment of the Treaty in our country's statutes'. But such requests posed the Crown something of a 'dilemma', as Hunn put it, and the many vigorous calls for ratification were never heeded.

Those seeking ratification generally focused on rights to land and resources claimed under Article Two and, more broadly, on that article's Maori-language promise of Crown recognition of rangatiratanga. Campaigns tended to highlight the issue of the ongoing alienation of what little Maori-owned land was left, and the Maori bond with turangawaewae, their tribal 'place to stand', underpinned such claims. Ratification of the Treaty, especially entailing its incorporation in legislation, it was argued, would serve to better guarantee Maori rights and prevent continued alienation of their resources.

It was hoped, too, that ratification would also ensure Maori had equal rights as citizens, as promised under Article Three of the Treaty. The 1966 petition of Rangi Makawe Rangitaura of Waitara and others, for example, called for ratification of the Treaty, repeal of discriminatory Maori land legislation, review of land claims and other grievances, and winding up the paternalistic DMA. It referred to 'two vital matters in the Treaty': 'ALL the rights and privileges of British subjects', and the preservation of Maori land ownership. In matters of land and citizenship there was, the petitioners claimed, 'one law for pakeha and another for the Maori'. In the towns and cities, discrimination and racism made equal citizenship a particularly pressing issue.[7]

While Maori leaders had often sought its ratification in the past, the Treaty was put to new ends in the 1970s, providing as it did a solid foundation and point of focus for protest. The emphasis went increasingly on compensating for the violated guarantees of Article Two and securing proactive Crown recognition of the rangatiratanga it had promised. Given the government's stated intention following the Hunn report to continue alienating Maori land, activists saw land retention as an achievable target of great importance – one symbolic of many others, as well as being highly important per se. Nga Tamatoa cast Waitangi Day as a 'day of mourning' in 1971, and protested against Maori land loss at the official celebrations at Waitangi. When it called for a Maori boycott of the 1972 Waitangi Day celebrations, a new era of Maori pressure on government could be said to have fully begun. The group was, recalled one of its leaders, 'seeking nothing less than the restoration of what we once had'; the stakes were seen to be very high indeed.

Waitangi Day-centred protest activities now occurred annually, and there were continuing actions of various nature in between. Activist tactics often alienated the very many elders who believed that the key to the future lay in dialogue rather than confrontation. Young protestors frequently used 'direct action' and other methods borrowed from socialist and liberation movements overseas (although armed or otherwise violent resistance remained confined to the realm of small-group rhetoric). The confrontational approach of activists sometimes led to tense encounters with traditional and conservative Maori leaders and people. Tribal elder Eruera Stirling believed that Maori youth were 'trampling on the mana of their elders and degrading the customs of their own people ... The men of chiefly line are the right ones to talk about these things'. And in the official, quasi-official and other committees up and down the land, too, the work of rangatiratanga proceeded along relatively conciliatory lines.

Nevertheless, there was a general acknowledgement in Maoridom that, as one activist later recalled, 'we were driven by the old people. We were driven by their pain more than ours'. Indeed, activists often deliberately engaged in 'an attempt to create an ethnic identity that would unite bearers of traditional grievance with alienated urban youth, working families, and the unemployed'. It was not their cause that was queried by many tribal and other leaders, but their methods. Some traditional chiefs and other established community leaders displayed a 'shrewd appreciation that Maori causes could well be served by the frisson of apprehension which unruly dissident youth could provoke among complacent Pakeha', and elders often stood by radical activists who were arrested and charged.

The annual protests on 6 February drew public attention to the many issues revolving around the loss of indigenous resources and of 'Maori identity in the face of the forces of acculturation'. While activists' confrontational methods remained inimical to most elders, their autonomy-based goals were increasingly approved by Maori leaders in many arenas, tribal and otherwise – including some working within the NZMC structure. With many liberal pakeha also lending their support to Maori causes and beginning to look outside the monocultural, assimilationist paradigm, the Crown had little choice but to begin to address the various intellectual, ethnic, cultural and other challenges it was presented with. It felt particularly obliged to listen when activists and traditionalists confirmed that they shared aims and goals, if not methods.[8]

Land and Struggle

The 'ferment of political activism' of the early 1970s 'coalesced into a Maori land rights movement' towards mid-decade. But the scene for confrontation over land issues had already been set by developments in the 1960s. The longstanding Maori desire – including among Maori who had settled in the urban areas – to preserve and restore tribal turangawaewae, the traditional underpinning of Maori communal life, had suffered much in the aftermath of the Hunn report. Hunn had detailed the problems associated with the administration and utilisation of Maori-owned land. He recommended moving *away* from what was left of communal ownership, on grounds that multiple title impeded efficient use. His report recommended empowering the Maori Trustee to compulsorily alienate land deemed uneconomic because of fragmented ownership interests. Not only would this make economic sense, Hunn and others thought, but urban migration indicated that Maori had become both less attached to their land and positively welcoming of detribalisation. If they wished to continue aspects of a collective approach to life, the many official and unofficial committees and other associations in the cities ensured that this was possible in an environment far from ancestral soil.

Some went further than Hunn and like-minded officials in their reasoning. The problems of Maori land stemmed, as Hanan saw it, not from the land title system imposed on Maori in the nineteenth century, but from the 'evils of turangawaewae'. This concept 'can prevent good land from being used or even looked after, and poorer land from being improved; it can cause Maori children to be brought up in areas where there is no employment for them or their parents; it can perpetuate inter-family and inter-tribal rivalries; and it can represent a formidable barrier to the advancement of the race. Perhaps it will sooner or later change its character, as other Maori customs have done, to fit in with the changing times.' The Crown would help it to do so.[9]

The policies advocated in the Hunn report and enunciated by its implementers blatantly violated the continuing and deep-seated Maori nexus with the land, and so were greeted by increasingly intense opposition. Any attempt by the state to trample on this strongest of bonds in pursuit of economic rationalisation was to ignore, as the Presbyterian Maori Synod put it, 'the cardinal principle of the need for tribal ownership, and the importance to us of *turangawaewae*'. Hunn had reinterpreted turangawaewae as 'home ownership'. His assimilationist assumption that it could be understood in terms of a section owned by a Maori family in the city reflected a vast gulf in worldview between Maori people and official New Zealand. Despite the urban reorientation of much Maori life, Maori generally agreed that 'well-being as a people' involved collective ownership of land. This did not mean that they were not concerned about the difficulties inherent in fragmented title. They had long, in fact, been trying to get solutions which did not involve alienation. The Synod, for example, regarded 'incorporation' of farmland under state auspices – with land vested in a body corporate – as an acceptable compromise that enabled both production and a collective controlling voice over land use.[10]

The official committee system provided one of many forums in which widespread opposition to land alienation was discussed. When the NZMC was established, Carroll and his vice-president, Pei Te Hurinui Jones, were particularly interested in the issue of land. Both came from rural backgrounds, and as leaders who saw themselves as having a special responsibility for kaitiakitanga/guardianship of the land, they and their colleagues drew a line in the sand for the government. Despite their traditionalist conservatism, and indeed because of it, they felt compelled to join the Maori MPs and many other Maori leaders in taking a strong stance against the government's land policies. Crown proposals to alienate 'uneconomic interests' and to utilise the funds for the Maori good (as well as to free up lands for development in the national interest) were seen as both paternalistic and confiscatory. The plans included, for example, extending leaseholds in a way that would deny future generation full returns from lands they nominally owned. In 1964, the NZMC established a committee to investigate the land issue and formulate solutions for government consideration.

Faced by pressure from many quarters of Maoridom, the government appointed a commission of enquiry. The appointees, Judge Ivor Prichard and DMA official Hemi Waetford, were asked to find ways of improving Maori-owned title and better utilising the land. They consulted widely and recorded general Maori dissatisfaction with the system of fragmented ownership which had been imposed upon the tribes. They noted that this system remained a major problem despite the various strategies of incorporation, amalgamation and other options proffered to and imposed upon Maori since the late nineteenth century. Fragmentation continued to stymie development in rural areas, and it offered little benefit to Maori making the difficult adjustment to city life. Maori observers were grateful that such longstanding criticisms had been recognised.

But while the 'great majority' of Maori agreed on the need for substantial change, the Prichard–Waetford recommendations merely endorsed the general thrust of the Hunn report. The authors dismissed some of the concerns raised during consultations as insignificant, an indication to many Maori that a Maori presence on official bodies did not necessarily provide results acceptable to the majority of Maori. The report remarked on the 'many unjustified complaints of a trivial nature', and believed that 'objectors were resisting the removal of differences between the law relating to Maoris and ... that relating to non-Maoris for the reason that those very differences gave them something to raise at meetings and that without such talking point they would not have the same claim to prominence'. It seemed that the commission's purpose had been to find ways to justify the targeting of communally held title, thereby striking at the heart of the tangata's special relationship with the whenua, rather than to seek a Maori solution to a Maori problem.

In stating that 'after 100 years change is inevitable', Prichard and Waetford seemed to miss the point that it was the *type* of change that mattered to Maori. In one analysis, their general 'aim was simply to allow individual Maori owners to do what they wanted with their land and to end ... the whole Maori land title system'. Certainly they believed that if Maori-held land was to be used for the good of all, individual farmers of ability needed to be placed on it – many of them, by implication, pakeha. In pursuit of public-good efficiency, many of the Prichard–Waetford proposals were 'coercive in nature' and 'advocated, in essence, a major expansion of compulsory conversion'; that is, the compulsory acquisition and pooling by the Crown of uneconomic interests.

There was widespread Maori dismay in 1965 at the report's recommendations – 'something approaching panic', in Hugh Kawharu's words. Meetings were held throughout the country. Maori from many walks of life feared that the commission's advice would embolden the government to step up its efforts to phase out multiple ownership of Maori land, rather than to find ways of making collective ownership and turangawaewae more viable in the modern world. The government made no secret that it was indeed determined to act coercively, now that it had before it a rationale for a drastic restructuring of titles in the interests of both 'the national good' and Maori – whether Maori agreed or not.

The New Zealand Maori Council, in association with the Extension Department of the University of Auckland, was at the fore of opposition to the new report. The two organisations hosted a conference in 1966 to discuss the Prichard–Waetford recommendations, and this well-attended gathering rejected most of them. In doing so, the attendees reflected an escalating feeling, widespread in both rural and urban Maoridom, that the report foreshadowed an imminent and comprehensive 'last land-grab' by the Crown. The conference produced ten pages of recommendations in response. These were moderate in tone, a reflection of the steadying influence of the NZMC. The alternatives proposed included Indigenous Land Utilisation Committees to work out title and other improvements, following a precedent among Whanau-a-Apanui; officials could work in partnership with these and the Maori associations 'to increase production from Maori land'. Despite such practical suggestions for avoiding state coercion, and in the face of vocal and ongoing Maori opposition, Hanan and his fellow ministers rejected the various criticisms of the report. Calls for the Crown to investigate, with Maori leaders, solutions to what all parties acknowledged were very real problems were dismissed. Keith Holyoake's National government believed it knew what was best and merely tinkered with the details of the Prichard–Waetford proposals, incorporating their essence into a Maori Affairs Amendment Bill.[11]

The Maori Affairs Amendment Act

In line with the Crown's desire to remove all kinds of legal differentiation between the races, the entire separate Maori land title system was, ultimately, to disappear. The proposed legislation was designed to hasten, therefore, something that many officials and politicians believed to be already underway: the 'two races rapidly becoming one'. Specifically, the Amendment Bill incorporated a Hunn recommendation to double the value of compulsorily acquirable 'uneconomic shares', a policy said to recognise a need by urban migrants to access relocation capital. The state would use its increased powers of 'conversion' to develop land in the 'national interest', regardless of the wishes of Maori. The Maori Land Court, moreover, would be able to declare any 'Maori land' owned by four or fewer owners to be 'European land', and such property thereby lost all protection against alienation. There were also provisions making Maori land subject to the same constraints as European land, one typical consequence being that 'village communities grouped about a *marae* [could no longer] be set up on Maori rural land'.

From now on, the Crown could never rely automatically upon the support of its own creature, the NZMC, having underestimated Maori anger at what seemed, from a pakeha perspective, to be logical proposals. Working from a submission drafted by its Tairawhiti Council, the NZMC joined with the Maori MPs (headed by Matiu Rata) and very many other prominent Maori in leading the opposition to the Maori Affairs Amendment Bill. Rata, in particular, campaigned on the basis that multiplicity of ownership still reflected, however perversely this had been embodied in law, the 'Maori tradition of tribal ownership and association with a specific area of land'. But the enormous amount of protest led to little more than amelioration of the Bill's worst aspects, and Maori leaders continued to oppose it to the end. Finally, the much reviled 1967 Maori Affairs Amendment Act – the 'land grab Act' – was passed, embodying and expanding the state's right to alienate Maori-owned land even against the wishes of the interested parties. The Maori Council declared, on behalf of the entire range of official committees, that it would be placing the government under great scrutiny.

While the NZMC helped lead the campaigns against the new legislation, many other Maori organised to voice their opposition. Some were willing to engage in dialogue within parameters set by the state, but others were not. The high degree of intransigence on the land issue was partly influenced by Maori disillusionment at being hit disproportionately during the first post-war recession. The legislation generated a campaign that proved to be a turning point in the Maori struggle for rangatiratanga. In focusing Maori attention on finding solutions to enormously complex issues, solutions which demanded recognition of rangatiratanga, the fight against the legislation helped stimulate both the formulation of more concretised positions and the unification of struggle across all significant sectors of Maoridom – radical and conservative, tribal and non tribal, young and old. The struggle thus produced a basis for future cross-sector action within Maoridom to protest against social injustice and further the cause of autonomy in its many actual and potential manifestations. Such united action began almost at once, in fact, focused around a campaign for repeal of the legislation. Activists like Tom Poata of the

Wellington Drivers' Union secured considerable pakeha support – in Poata's case, that of the New Zealand Federation of Labour in 1968.[12]

The government was much concerned that the NZMC had found common cause with the Maori MPs and with liberal pakeha. When, in 1968, the Maori Council made a bid to become a fully autonomous organisation, officials advised keeping it within the Crown's sphere of influence so that pressure could be more easily applied (from 1972, it received an annual Crown grant, making it more accountable). There were, however, overtures towards Maori perspectives on land from within the state. The head of Maori Affairs stated that there would be a cautious approach to implementation of the Act, and this was confirmed by Hanan's successor, Duncan MacIntyre, when he took office in 1969. Such concessions were, however, insufficient to prevent land from remaining the iconic rallying point for all Maori struggles for rangatiratanga. Nor could they prevent a loose Maori alliance from coalescing around another cause that very year: the ending of the institution of Maori schools. The implementation of this Hunn recommendation was also vigorously opposed, given that the schools – whatever their founding role as assimilation devices – had become an integral part of 'the Maori world'.

As the new Minister of Maori Affairs, MacIntyre soon took stock of the damage that had been done in recent years to Crown–Maori relations by the government's relentless pursuit of assimilation. He and officials, reacting to the incipient Maori Renaissance, sought to repair the Crown's relationship with Maoridom through discussion and reform aimed at heading off autonomist activism. He placed more Maori (including an NZMC nominee) on the Board of Maori Affairs; he established committees which included Maori owners to manage land development programmes in each Maori Affairs district; and he encouraged community development in various ways. But a momentum had already built up, and the pursuit of rangatiratanga would not be deflected. Ratana leaders, for example, resuscitated the idea of a separate Maori Parliament in late 1969, and called for the pledges contained in the Treaty of Waitangi to be 'revived'.[13]

The Changing Role of the New Zealand Maori Council

Initially, the Maori Council had been slow to adjust to the perspectives of urban Maori leaders. The divisions between rural and urban leaders within the NZMC (and, relatedly, between the system's conservative and liberal factions) reflected real differences in their respective tasks. Urban leaders had to deal with poverty, discrimination, crime, disorder, growing unrest and (eventually) protest groups and gangs. Solutions to urban problems faced by Maori were often discussed and addressed in pan- or non-tribal ways that rural-based district

Maori councils and some other sectors of the official system found difficult to comprehend. After becoming secretary of the Auckland District Maori Council in 1969, Ranginui Walker had been radicalised into a commitment to struggle on behalf of all of his people, wherever they were. Along with other activists who opted to work within the NZMC system, such as fellow academics like Hohepa, he was in the 'vanguard of a new elite' of educated leaders whose radical roots lay in the huge social and cultural changes stirring in the later 1960s. Such leaders became increasingly visible, a number of them aiming to fight 'the establishment' from within the official system, while at the same time trying to push it in more radical directions.

By the early 1970s, Pei Jones (who had succeeded to the NZMC presidency) and others had come to the conclusion that a younger leader who could relate to urban as well as rural Maori was needed to head the whole Maori associations edifice – one who could modernise the NZMC, strengthen its hand and contain its more radical urban elements. Their deliberations led to Graham Latimer, a man with first-hand experience of life in both city and countryside, taking up the presidency from 1973. Although he was a National Party member, Latimer's succession nevertheless led to greater NZMC independence from the party and to new elements entering into the higher reaches of the system. He was a strategic operator who could accommodate more radical concerns when the cause of Maori agency required. By the beginning of the 1980s (founding NZMC member Henare Ngata later recalled), the NZMC had 'a far different type of leadership' than in the 'earlier days': an educated grouping reflecting 'the change in the Maori community itself'. Of the two dozen founding delegates, only two still sat on the Maori Council in 1981.[14]

As the 1970s and the Maori Renaissance progressed, the NZMC's agenda increasingly came to reflect several of the key concerns of Maori activists, despite official and internal attempts at containment. Taking cognisance of the growing prominence of urban radicals, the council continued, albeit cautiously, to establish its independence from the government despite its role as the legal embodiment of the Maori voice. It would come to use a number of routes, including the courts, to challenge the government on matters that disadvantaged Maori, eventually with notable successes. It preferred dialogue to confrontation, however, arguing that the spirit of the Treaty of Waitangi underpinned its methods. It raised many issues with ministers, officials and public alike, especially the need to repair historical injustices as well as to prevent further land alienation. It also promoted the urgent task of protecting language and culture. Except on keynote issues such as the struggle against the 1967 legislation, however, it was tardy in translating its various concerns into detailed and proactive policy demands, and so remained heavily criticised by younger activists.

But the NZMC had influence with the Crown in a way the radicals did not, and so the unofficial and official pressures were in a sense complementary. After the annual Waitangi Day protests began, for example, the government sought NZMC advice on which Acts, in its view, contravened the Treaty. It was surprised to be presented with a long list of key statutes, including those which it had not expected, such as town and county planning legislation. More broadly, the Maori Council and its subordinate bodies contributed to a discourse in which the state was increasingly forced to assess the progress and, ultimately, viability of its polices of integration/assimilation. The NZMC system has been characterised as providing, over its first two decades, 'a forum within which a variety of conflicting impulses in the Maori world could be articulated and tested'. It 'contributed to the growth of a pan-Maori consciousness and habits of consultation and cooperation that laid solid foundations for future autonomy'. The fact that it was a statutory and apparently conservative body that was being pushed inexorably by circumstances in such directions made governmental and official circles more ready to listen to the causes it espoused – even if they were not yet conceding them.[15]

The Third Labour Government and Rangatiratanga

In 1972, Norman Kirk's Labour government entered office under the slogan 'Time for a Change'. Expectations were high, and Maori noted with approval some early statements about biculturalism. They applauded Kirk's elevation of the Treaty to 'the foundation stone of our nation'. With Matiu Rata appointed as Minister of Maori Affairs, there was much appreciation of the new Prime Minister's insistence on having a Maori presence in his Cabinet. Widespread public confidence over the possibility of improved relations between Crown and Maori was epitomised in an iconic photograph of Kirk walking hand in hand with a Maori boy across the Treaty grounds at Waitangi in 1973. He announced that Waitangi Day would henceforth become a public holiday, renamed 'New Zealand Day' to symbolise 'bi-cultural togetherness'. Developments in Maori policy gelled with a rapidly growing pakeha awareness of Maori culture, history and customs, a period when a scholarly work of history, Alan Ward's *A Show of Justice*, published in 1974, could become an 'historical landmark in its own right' and 'a guide to mediating future race relations'. A general history of New Zealand dates the full beginning of the 'Treaty revival' from that year.[16]

In three crowded years, the government did a great deal on many fronts. This included – after years of campaigning and much consultation with, and pressure from, the NZMC and the Maori MPs – a major reconstitution of the detested Maori Affairs Amendment Act in 1974. The new legislation rescinded such highly unpopular processes as 'conversion' and the enforced recategorisation of Maori land as 'European', and consolidation schemes for regrouping uneconomic interests in land would no longer be forced on Maori. It was now realised, in any case, that such practices had not only 'disenfranchised' many Maori landowners but could also never have provided more than temporary solutions to the problems of title fragmentation and land use. The changes the legislators introduced were not piecemeal, but occurred within a new policy framework: remaining Maori land could be, and indeed should be, retained and used for its owners' benefit and in accord with their wishes. Key Maori demands had been interpreted as consonant with 'the public good'.

Greater involvement of Maori owners in the use and development of their land was applauded by conservative and radical Maori alike. A Maori Land Board would delegate functions to Maori Land Advisory Committees in each district, and all such institutions were to have Maori majorities, appointed by the minister after seeking Maori advice. Official dominance over Maori lands held for consolidation or development was now a thing of the past. The reforms were hailed as a major breakthrough in Crown recognition of rangatiratanga. At the same time, the Maori Land Court was beginning a journey that would eventually end with its chief registrar declaring it 'the vehicle that re-establishes the link between te iwi Māori and their whenua'.

There were many other developments introduced by the Minister of Maori Affairs, often prompted by advisers in the Maori communities, that were much appreciated by Maori. Electoral legislation, for example, was reformed. The 1956 Electoral Act had been heavily prescriptive as to who qualified for the Maori electoral roll, with those of less than half 'Maori blood' obliged to register on the general roll. Under the Electoral Amendment Act of 1975, a 'Maori' was defined permissively as 'a person of the Maori race of New Zealand; and includes any descendant of such a person who elects to be considered as a Maori'. All adult people with any Maori heritage were given a five-yearly option of registering on the roll of their choice, Maori or general. In other reforms, there would be large subsidy increases for marae development and, given its 'principal obligation' to assist Maori, Rata determined that the Department of Maori Affairs should actively promote Maori culture and language. Along with some like-minded ministers and their advisers, he did a great deal to update the Labour/Ratana legacy to suit modern times and address the concerns of the Maori Renaissance.

The legislative package on Maori issues during the Labour government of 1972–75 (headed by Prime Minister Bill Rowling after Kirk's death in 1974) took its cue from an anti-paternalistic official 'White Paper' which has been seen as 'represent[ing] a major philosophical shift in the administration of Maori affairs in New Zealand'. The thrust of the policies clearly reflected longstanding

Maori wishes, and there was greater and more meaningful consultation than in the past. The legislative and official activity of this period 'corrected, to a considerable extent, earlier legislation which had disadvantaged Maori' and 'inaugurated a more tolerant attitude towards Maori social and cultural integrity in Maori affairs policy'. Direct Maori community participation in planning and management of departmental programmes began. The official message was that *full* assimilation was at last no longer on the Crown agenda. Instead, the government was willing to listen to Maori aspirations and to implement at least some of their goals.[17]

Treaty, Tribunal and Notions of Partnership

Mindful of a discernible pakeha backlash, however, Labour was not by any means prepared to address the more radical of Maori demands. This is understandable in the sense that the autonomist and other platforms were varied and often inchoate. But one aspirational strand did stand out so much that the Crown had no choice but to try to come to terms with it: the demand made by urban radicals and NZMC conservatives alike for the Crown to honour the Treaty. Maori acknowledged, of course, that circumstances had changed much since 1840, but the 'spirit'/wairua of the Treaty needed to be confirmed and respected. The words increasingly used by various parties to encapsulate this concept were 'the principles of the Treaty'. While the term 'principles' had been used by Prime Minister George Forbes in 1932, and not long after, Labour leader Michael Joseph Savage had pledged 'to give effect to the spirit as well as the letter of the treaty', extensive debate on 'the principles' had not occurred until the Maori Renaissance. In 1975, the last year of the short-lived Labour government, the Waitangi Tribunal was established to investigate contemporary Maori grievances. The Treaty of Waitangi Act, by which the Tribunal was bound, made reference to the 'principles of the Treaty' and their 'practical application'. While the principles were not defined in the legislation, and needed to be determined by the Tribunal, the focus on the Treaty and what it meant would prove to be of great significance for the legal and political advancement of Maori causes.[18]

Getting the Tribunal established had been far from easy. Rata had quickly gathered influential Maori advisers such as Pat Hohepa around him. Among other things, he had begun, early on in the life of the government, to listen to Maori claims for compensation for past wrongs. The new ministerial and official ethos gave Maori hope. So, too, did increasing pakeha awareness of the Maori past and the Crown's coercive involvement in it. Information came in a variety of forms. In 1974, Michael King and Barry Barclay produced a highly successful television documentary with the self-explanatory title

Tangata Whenua, The People of the Land. Books on Maori subjects were increasing, and Witi Ihimaera spearheaded a Maori literary renaissance that complemented the political one. Dick Scott's account of Parihaka was expanded and rewritten. The 'new book', Scott later reminisced, 'came out in a different country, Parihaka photos and headlines capturing all the newspapers, the *Herald* reporting that 2800 copies of a 3600 print run had sold within nine days of publication'.[19]

But despite such relatively favourable political circumstances, even a determined Rata could not get his ministerial colleagues to agree to the possibility of reparations for historical breaches of the Treaty. He attempted to persuade Cabinet that the proposed Waitangi Tribunal ought to have jurisdiction back to 1900, a compromise (based on spurious advice that historical material was lacking) from the ideal of retrospective jurisdiction back to1840. But even such a limited historical mandate – covering the years after the major resource and autonomy losses had occurred – was seen as being too threatening for the general pakeha constituency to accept. The Waitangi Tribunal, therefore, was given the authority to investigate only those grievances against the Crown which dated from the passing of the Treaty of Waitangi Act. Even then, as a standing commission of enquiry, it could only produce findings and make *recommendations* to the government. In line with Labour's 'equality' principles, it was intended that the Tribunal focus on what later came to be called Article Three-based grievances, those relating to Maori being denied the rights that all citizens were supposed to enjoy. With no mandate to examine the past, let alone to assist the quest for Article Two-based rangatiratanga, the Tribunal was seen by many Maori as a gesture that did little either to compensate for past devastation or to institute a 'partnership' between Maori and the state.

Some notion of partnership between Maori authorities and the Crown – a concept arguably held by the chiefs in 1840 – had been evoked within Crown circles in earlier times. Lord Bledisloe, in gifting the Treaty house and grounds at Waitangi to the nation in 1934, for example, had hoped the site would come to symbolise the 'unique relationship between the indigenous and colonising peoples'. In the early 1970s, the Maori Organisation on Human Rights criticised the government's policies of 'absorption rather than partnership'. It was not until the mid-1970s, however, that the concept of partnership acquired any great currency; from then, gradually, the notion evolved, eventually informing the emergence of modern Treaty principles. In 1976 Rata posited that from the 'spirit embraced in the Treaty of Waitangi ... a unique partnership was founded upon mutual respect and understanding'.[20]

The idea of reviving the concept of partnership gained increasing momentum as a potentially achievable goal that might satisfy both the state and Maori. The groundwork needed for this, the abandonment of the official policy of assimilation, had been laid by Labour in its brief period in office. That government, in responding to the Maori Renaissance, had often sought specialist Maori advice in its policy formation and implementation. Robert Mahuta, for example, had chaired a group which fed ideas into the education arena on how the country could become 'truly *bicultural* and *bilingual*'. In 1973, Rata rejected 'negative integration', and the following year, Kirk declared New Zealand to be 'one nation in which all have equal rights, but we are two peoples'. By the time of Labour's exit from office in 1975, assimilation had, in effect, disappeared as Crown policy. The strength displayed by Maoridom, bolstered by a growing number of pakeha who saw value in biculturalism and partnership, was such that no successor government envisaged returning even to a policy of 'integration'.

But a great many questions and difficulties remained. What, for example, did 'partnership' imply, and what bodies should constitute the Maori partners? A number of influential Maori were supplying answers which envisaged partnerships between the Crown and iwi institutions. To facilitate this, various tribes sought to build up stronger politico-economic bases, some operating independently of the Crown in doing so. From the mid-1970s, for example, Ngati Raukawa, Te Atiawa and Ngati Toa in the southern North Island implemented Whakatupuranga Rua Mano, a tribal development plan which looked towards a rebuilding of rangatiratanga in the twenty-first century, based on hapu-led development. Others utilised official channels; after being approached by Frank Winter and other tribal leaders, Tipene O'Regan agreed to join Ngai Tahu's trust board with the aim of helping regenerate the major South Island iwi.

Some developments were not tribally based, including officially sanctioned projects with commercial foci such as Paraninihi ki Waitotara, established in 1976 to better administer, on behalf of multiple shareholders, Maori-owned leasehold lands on the western seaboard of the North Island. In urban areas, official and voluntary associations which were 'groping towards the idea of a community' set about boosting their resources with the assistance of a Crown now more willing to help. Ultimately, large 'Maori urban authorities' also emerged, independently of the state but often providing contractual services to it. There was widespread resistance from iwi- or hapu-based groups to Crown assistance for, or even dealing with, such urban organisations – assistance or contracts which, they believed, should best go to tribal authorities embodying continuity with the past. But the Waitangi Tribunal would eventually declare urban authorities to have a status similar to that of iwi. Maori socio-political reorganisation was, in short, continually flexible in seeking maximal results from collective endeavours and in negotiating arrangements of many and varied kinds with the state.[21]

In time, Maori were encouraged in their pursuit of rangatiratanga by the Waitangi Tribunal's strictures regarding the past behaviour of the Crown and its guidelines on how state authorities should behave henceforth. With hindsight, the creation of the Waitangi Tribunal has sometimes been viewed (in the words of a right-wing analyst) 'merely as a response to the threat of disorder posed by longstanding Maori agitation. Essentially political responses are often cast in the moral idiom of a rectification of injustices'. Such a vision of the Tribunal, as a 'touchstone for defusing' protest, was (and is) shared in a number of Maori quarters and in some left-leaning pakeha circles. Even Matiu Rata is said to have 'intended the Tribunal to be a social and cultural safety valve'. In the words of a later Tribunal head, the Tribunal represented a 'shift from protest to process'. But, whatever Parliament's motivations in establishing it, and despite the limitations of its mandate, the setting up of the Waitangi Tribunal was widely interpreted as a crucial step toward the Crown's honouring of the Treaty. Rata had called the Treaty 'an instrument of mutuality', and after a lacklustre start, the Tribunal became given to exploring the appropriate configurations of the Crown–Maori relationship.

In 1975, however, the Labour government faced enormous challenge from Maori, a consequence of the exceedingly high hopes they (and liberal pakeha) had held at the prospects of what 'their party' might effect in addressing rangatiratanga. In the event, the government had not been prepared to push the parameters of its Maori policies too far beyond the views of its (mostly pakeha) support base. Disappointment at the pace and extent of reform was palpable, and many Maori perceived continuity with previous governments in Labour's deflection of key demands. A political scientist noted that so great were Maori expectations, and so mixed the responses of a government cautiously feeling its way into post-assimilation policies, that 'the result was bound to be confusion and disappointment'. In such a climate, Nga Tamatoa and other groupings gained increasing support for their protests, and conservative Maori too began to mobilise.[22]

The Maori Land March

In early 1975, the idea of a 'Maori Land March' from Te Hapua in the far north to Parliament was discussed. The aim would be to dramatise the entire package of Maori demands and aspirations which had yet to be addressed. The march would focus on the most iconic element of Maori losses and hopes: the land. Plans began to come together at a meeting of tribal representatives convened at Mangere Marae by the founding MWWL president (and National Party stalwart) Whina Cooper. In her address to the hui, Cooper implied that she was operating under the mantle of great Maori leaders such as James Carroll,

Apirana Ngata and Peter Buck, all of whom she had known. She asserted customary Maori protocol through a 'Memorial of Right', thereby linking the march to a long tradition of earlier petitions to the Crown, especially those by Kings Tawhiao and Te Rata in 1886 and 1914. But she now viewed the 'respectable' tactics of older times, to which the NZMC and MWWL still generally adhered, as somewhat anachronistic. A 'more dynamic approach' was needed, she argued, and this struck a chord with listeners of many backgrounds and beliefs.

The planned land march would combine the forces of Nga Tamatoa-type radicalism with the wishes and protocols of traditionalist elders, attracting the support of Maori from both urban areas and rural marae throughout the country. All elements of the incipient movement loosely grouped themselves under a new organisation, Te Roopu Ote Matakite, a title designating 'those with foresight'. The momentum swept up the NZMC and MWWL, as well as other official and quasi-official organisations. Latimer and MWWL president Mira Szaszy came onto the organising committee, sitting alongside comparatively radical members of the official system such as Ranginui Walker and even more radical activists such as Nga Tamatoa's Syd Jackson and Titewhai Harawira. The march was to be focused on the 'twin themes of landlessness and cultural loss'.

When the march first set off from Te Hapua on September 14, there were few on the road, but before long numbers swelled. Marchers sought respect for communal ownership of tribal lands, believing that Labour's reforms had fallen short. They demanded, in the words of a key slogan, that 'not one more acre of Maori land' be alienated. As a leaflet entitled 'Why We Protest' explained: 'Land is the very soul of a tribal people'. The leaflet linked the land with broader autonomist aspirations: '[We want] a just society allowing Maoris to preserve our own social and cultural identity in the last remnants of our tribal estate ... The alternative is the creation of a landless brown proletariat with no dignity, no mana and no stake in society.' While the focus was on Maori land and identity, some marchers also emphasised their solidarity with all working people: 'We see no difference between the aspirations of Maori people and the desire of workers and their struggles.' By the time the march converged on Parliament on 13 October, publicity was enormous. It had dramatically (in Mason Durie's words) 'demonstrated the extent of Maori dissatisfaction'. In a short time, the iconic photograph of Kirk guiding a Maori boy had been overtaken by one of Cooper holding her grand-daughter's hand, leaving rural Te Hapua to take Maori protest to the heart of government.[23]

Ministers, especially Minister of Maori Affairs Rata, felt chagrined that the government's extensive consultation procedures and 'progressive' Maori policies and legislation had been 'rewarded' in such a way. In the middle of the year, Rata had stated that there was no need for such a protest: the points outlined in the 'Memorial of Rights' focussing on land control and retention had already been addressed by his government's legislation on Maori land. As well as implementation of Labour policy, he noted, there had been other initiatives relating to land. Rata and his officials had been working, for example, on the concept of returning to Maori ownership Crown land which was not being used for the purposes for which it had been taken. But, in a sense, the march was not so much about specific land policies or, necessarily, even about land at all. It was a reassertion of autonomist Maori demands and aspirations at a time when the political and social climate was becoming more receptive to them. As one historian later noted, the march represented Maori, at an auspicious moment, 'symbolically reclaiming the tino Rangatiratanga promised by the Treaty of Waitangi'.

There was an underlying Maori awareness that the government, true to its social democratic roots, continued essentially to believe in 'equal treatment for all' rather than in measures that envisaged any kind of 'separateness'. When ministers talked of replacing Maori integration, with its implication of subsuming Maori within the dominant culture, with policies of 'full participation', these seemed seldom to venture far beyond stressing that there was a place for some degree of Maoriness within a predominantly pakeha 'one nation'. Anything more would risk superseding the social democratic 'equality' paradigm, something seen as neither possible (given pakeha opinion) nor desirable (on philosophical grounds). Maori had now taken up the challenge of forcing the Labour government to pay greater respect to rangatiratanga.

Activism during the Third National Government

The many different ideas on both goals and methods in the struggle for rangatiratanga remained a major problem for Maori. Even the land march organisation broke up into new groupings with varying tactics when it reached Wellington. One of these, Matakite o Aotearoa, would take up (among other things) the cause of the Tainui Awhiro people at Raglan for the return of ancestral land. The Te Kopua Block had been compulsorily taken for public works in the Second World War and later leased to a golf club. In 1976, demonstrations focused on a burial site in the block. Eventually, following help from the NZMC, the land was revested in the tangata whenua. Many Maori watched this and other direct actions closely, and took heed of their lessons.[24]

When the general elections were held soon after the land march and the setting up of the Waitangi Tribunal, many Maori voters registered protest at dashed hopes (and, perhaps, at being disproportionately hit by economic recession from 1974) by abstaining from voting. With Labour leaving office, however, Maori now faced a government with policies rather less sympathetic (or, in many eyes, even more unsympathetic) to Maori aspirations. With dissatisfaction widespread, protest escalated, along with intense public debate on the past, present and future position of Maori in New Zealand. The Treaty of Waitangi was generally the symbolic and convenient focus of public discourse. Although one radical Maori stance had, since the early 1970s, been to argue that the Treaty was 'a fraud' and should be rejected altogether, most called for the Crown to 'Honour the Treaty' – something which seemed potentially within grasp as pakeha consciousness of past Treaty violations grew.

Maori interpretations of ways of implementing the Treaty tended to revolve around an autonomist perspective which called for arrangements that accommodated 'two peoples in one nation'. As in other post-settler countries, New Zealand's indigenous population sought not just to question and de-centre dominant western notions, but also to '*re-recognize* the authority of particular colonial discourses'. States had long appropriated and redeployed things indigenous, in the process forging 'cross-cultural and cross-national agreements'; in turn, indigenous peoples attempted to force governments to ratify and/or renegotiate such agreements. In New Zealand, the Treaty of Waitangi was the powerfully symbolic focus of such struggle. Maori utilised the discourse inscribed in 'treaty language' as part of their weaponry for regaining the rangatiratanga they had lost.[25]

Many pakeha in the 1970s, including those with legal and other types of professional expertise, were beginning to complement Maori action by becoming interested in or committed to the Treaty. By the end of the decade, the Waitangi Tribunal's investigations were drawing public attention to matters that most pakeha had scarcely known about or considered. And although it could only hear contemporary claims, the Tribunal was increasingly to realise that it needed to explore their historical context in order to come to appropriate findings and recommendations.

At Waitangi Day in 1981, Governor-General Sir David Beattie reflected a growing public consciousness that the 'one New Zealand' paradigm was anachronistic: 'we are not one people ... nor should we try to be. We do not need to be'. This contrasted with the attitude of his predecessor, Sir Keith Holyoake, who had wanted to eliminate 'any form of distinction' between the races. Two years later, the Waitangi Tribunal declared, in the context of landmark findings and recommendations that received great publicity, that the Treaty 'made us one country but acknowledged that we were two people'. Forms of partnership between cultures, peoples, institutions and structures seemed both attainable and desirable, especially in a society in which the two peoples increasingly inhabited the same spaces and intermarried freely. By the time of the official 1990 sesquicentennial commemoration of the founding of the nation, the 'two peoples, one nation' rhetoric had been widely taken up within the state. Ways in which this idea could be better reflected in arrangements between Crown and Maori were being actively explored.[26]

To get to this point of engagement, a lot had happened both politically and socially in New Zealand. Fewer than twenty five years had passed since the Crown had forced through land legislation that was universally rejected by Maori leaders. Maori had generally retained allegiance to Labour, and their experiences of the reforms of the Kirk–Rowling government confirmed their loyalty while also inducing dismay and anger that 'their party' still fell far short of meeting their autonomist goals. Under the successor National government (1975–1984), headed by the domineering Robert Muldoon, a populist leader who had sympathies neither with white liberal nor Maori aspirations, the Maori struggle seemed set to be a difficult one. The new government was as anti-liberal on race relations issues as on much else, symbolised early on when it not only allowed the All Blacks to tour South Africa in 1976, but also gave them (in Muldoon's words) 'the Government's blessing and goodwill'. When National talked of the Treaty in a positive sense, though it did so rarely, it was to use it as a unifying symbol for the 'one nation' of New Zealand.[27]

One of Muldoon's first moves was to clear Parliament grounds of a 'tent embassy' set up by some protesters after the land march, setting the scene for a propensity to use coercion in relation to issues deemed to concern public order. In the later 1970s, radical action to dramatise Maori aspirations prompted an especially harsh reaction by the state, particularly towards movements or activities seen to be undermining Crown sovereignty or (in what more or less amounted to the same thing in the eyes of the Muldoon government) challenging 'the majesty of the law'. The biggest confrontation occurred in urban Auckland over the troubled and contested Orakei Block, which hosted the only significant area remaining to the city's Ngati Whatua iwi after 1869.

The saga recommenced in late 1976 when the government proposed to subdivide and develop 24 hectares of Crown land at Takaparawha/Bastion Point for high-income housing and parks. This land had been (as the Crown later conceded, following Waitangi Tribunal findings) unjustly alienated from the iwi, and Ngati Whatua had signalled that they wanted it returned. After the Crown proposals were announced, young Maori activists and radical leaders argued that the cautious advocacy exercised by traditional kaumatua had been, and remained, ineffective. They decided to take direct action when tribal leaders came to the conclusion, after negotiations with the Crown, that accepting a 'compromise' offer was the best that could be achieved.

Joe Hawke and others formed the Orakei Maori Committee Action Group, and on 5 January 1977 its members and supporters occupied Bastion Point. They demanded its return, and that of surrounding land, to the tangata whenua. Many Maori from other tribes, pakeha activists from socialist and other groups, and Pacific Islanders joined the protest. It also found support from a wider network which included even traditionalist Maori. When the Crown offered to discuss a further compromise in February 1978, the protesters rejected suggestions by moderate leaders that this be explored.

After 506 days of tense but non-violent occupation, a 600-strong police and military operation broke up the protest camp and demolished its buildings on 25 May 1978. Police arrested 222 protesters, although they were in effect later exonerated after continued campaigning. A government olive branch, an offer to return some property to a trust board, was accepted by the tribe by year's end. But Maori (along with many pakeha) had been shocked at the government's tactics, and the eviction served to reinforce activist sentiment, especially among the young. Images of the state's strong-arm procedures produced many evocations of previous coercive state operations against Maori defiance of 'the law', including the bloody invasion of Maungapohatu in 1916. While traditional leaders were seen to have the luxury of 'tribal time', which meant that it would 'take as long as it took' to rectify historical injustice, younger, often urban-educated, Maori were the more determined to force the honouring of Treaty promises. At very least, they sought to dramatise autonomist issues in the face of the unyielding attitudes of the Muldoon government. There was further activity at Takaparawha in 1982, and radical voices were heard ever more vociferously on Waitangi Day and at various protests and occupations until the mid-1980s.[28]

Treaty-based Discourses

The growing stridency of demands reflected an international trend among marginalised peoples. At first, Maori demands had been centred around equal rights within New Zealand's dominant structures and hegemonic culture. Some sections of Maoridom continued to make this their focus, with conservative leaders concerned that public protest constituted a threat to their congenial relations with the pakeha establishment – through which deals could be struck in the interests of greater equality. Other Maori noted the emergence of bicultural ways of seeing and doing, and argued that the Maori cultural renaissance provided an adequate basis for progress without constitutional upheaval. Increasingly, however, Maori began to conclude that such stances downplayed crucial matters of power and class. As with members of indigenous movements worldwide, they started to reject aspects of the dominant culture and its worldviews, and to opt, to a greater or lesser degree, for alternatives to the established 'pakeha order'.

A number of radicals claimed that neither at Waitangi in 1840 nor ever since had Maori been willing to surrender their sovereignty. Since this had been 'seized' from Maori, they demanded that it be restored, with the return of Maori land to provide an economic and ancestral underpinning of a Maori sovereign order. Such views were not new. Even the Labour/Ratana MP Whetu Tirikatene-Sullivan had noted in 1976 that the Maori-language version of the Treaty 'does not forfeit the right of sovereignty as it is understood in the English version'. But voices in favour of Maori sovereignty were now increasing in number and loudness. Some radicals even insisted, as Donna Awatere would put it, that 'Maoris should have control of New Zealand because it is *our* country'. In such an interpretation, 'Maori must no longer seek a bicultural sovereignty with the white nation': the Treaty, in effect, promised full independence and control for Maori.[29]

While this was a minority position, discrepancies between the English and Maori texts of the Treaty had been the subject of much debate since a scholarly article on the subject was published in 1972. The English version of Article Two confirmed Maori rights to 'full exclusive and undisturbed possession of their Lands ... and other properties' until Maori chose to dispose of them. In Crown eyes, this signified no more than confirmation of pre-existing rights of property ownership. Such a view was reinforced by what became called called 'Article One readings' of the Treaty, which dominated New Zealand's race relations paradigm up until the mid-1970s. In the first article, 'all the rights and powers of Sovereignty' – kawanatanga, in the Maori text – were said to have been passed by Maori to the Crown in 1840.

But following the establishment of the Waitangi Tribunal, in particular, 'Article Two readings' began to assume an ever more prominent place in the national Treaty discourses. These came to focus on the meaning of the 'rangatiratanga' guaranteed in the Maori version of Article Two. Rangatiratanga, it was increasingly accepted, implied much more than ownership rights; it was akin to sovereignty or, at very least, to certain forms of sub-sovereignty arrangements between the Crown and Maori authorities. The historical, contemporary and potential meanings of the Treaty of Waitangi were thus being reinterpreted in the light of the differences between the 'two Treaties', te reo Maori and English. In the 1980s, especially, the implications of the term 'tino rangatiratanga' (often translated along the lines of 'full autonomy') became of prominent public concern.[30]

Such an *explicit* focus on the word 'rangatiratanga' was a new factor in Treaty and indigenous discourse in twentieth-century New Zealand. Maori leaders had long sought greater tribal and other forms of autonomy, and the terminology used for this had altered through time. In the decades of urbanisation and adaptation to modernity following the Second World War, they had seldom characterised their authority as 'rangatiratanga' or publicly voiced demands for the Crown to respect it. Ngata's 1922 published 'explanation' of the Treaty, long afterwards cited as authoritative, had been influential in shaping Maori attitudes on both terminology and meaning in the Treaty. He had asserted that the 'English expressions in the Treaty were not adequately rendered into Maori', but sought to dispel the confusion that surrounded the Treaty by privileging the English text.

Ngata had pronounced that, under Article One, Maori transmitted 'absolute ['chiefly'] authority ... into the hands of the Queen', and he urged his people to accept all laws made by the Parliament she had later established. While Article Two guaranteed Maori a certain 'authority' and 'sovereignty', indeed 'rangatiratanga', this (he had argued) was merely the 'right of a Maori to his land, to his property'. He dismissed as 'wishful thinking' the various schemes for a Maori parliament or for different types of absolute Maori authorities 'as the authority of the Maori was set aside for ever by the first article of the Treaty'. Influenced by Ngataism, Maori tended to eschew the word rangatiratanga. But just as Ngata never stopped urging greater Maori control over their own affairs, Maori continued to fight for what was essentially rangatiratanga both during his lifetime and in the decades after his death in 1950.

To the extent that demands for autonomy were raised in the official committees, voluntary associations and other Maori organisations that emerged and flourished in the period of mass post-war urbanisation, these fitted within Ngata's parameters of indivisible Crown sovereignty. During this period, alternative Maori words or English expressions came into vogue within Maori society to replace those considered outmoded by modernity – words such as mana for rangatiratanga, or tribe for iwi. Others, such as runanga, remained almost as quiet in the context of Crown–Maori relations, and in pakeha consciousness, as rangatiratanga. But a number of these traditional terms sprung back into public discourse during the ferment of ideas and activities of the Maori Renaissance.

One key element in that regrowth of words and the concepts underpinning them was to be found in the energies of the new activist generation of the later 1960s and the 1970s. For many activists, the past Maori tendency for accommodation to European words and ways, including through the operations of the urban committees, associations and clubs, needed confronting and overturning. The 'various Maori Committees seem to have done very little', declared an early Nga Tamatoa pamphlet, the protest group which most emphasised language revival. Initially, the new movements focused on cultural renaissance, and did not systematically challenge indivisible Crown sovereignty and Article One readings of the Treaty. But such challenge was implicit, with the Maori Organisation on Human Rights claiming, for example, that Ngata had written his explanation of the Treaty partly as an 'apologist for the Pakeha government'. The cultural and the political were inextricably intertwined, and Nga Tamatoa's (and others') work on reviving te reo focussed minds on, among other things, connections between politico-cultural suppression and linguistic trends.[31]

From the very beginning of the new wave of Maori radicalism, moreover, *Te Hokioi* and MOOHR newsletters were concerned with matters of autonomy, self-determination and Maori 'control over those things which are particularly Maori'. This was in the context of claimed rights to equality, culture and land within the existing constitutional framework. The early renaissance activists wanted Maori to assume 'that which is rightfully theirs', particularly 'the right to determine their own destiny in our multi-racial society'. Like Ngata, however, they tended to accept that, with the Treaty, 'sovereignty over New Zealand was transferred from the Maori Chiefs to Queen Victoria' in indivisible form. Thus, in 1970 MOOHR declared that the signing of the Treaty 'marked the birth of our bi-cultural New Zealand, when by consent of most Maori Chiefs all rights and powers of sovereignty were ceded to the British Queen, who thereby secured to the Chiefs and Tribes..."the full, exclusive and undisturbed possession of their Lands".'

In other words, the English language text of the Treaty still dominated discussion, so much so that when *Te Hokioi* presented 'The Differing Versions' of the Treaty, the Maori version was given in an English translation (with Article Two granting Maori 'complete dominion over all their lands, houses, customs and goods'). The aim was to emphasise state violations of the Treaty, contextualising protest by pointing out that the Crown had fallen far short on its promise to guarantee 'complete dominion' and 'exclusive and undisturbed possession' for Maori. In 1974, Ranginui Walker argued in terms of the English version, declaring that the 'chiefs yielded their sovereignty' because of the 'undisturbed possession' that the Treaty guaranteed them. Even a booklet called *Te Tiriti o Waitangi*, published in the early 1980s by the radical Waitangi Action Committee (WAC), referred only to the English text of the Treaty.[32]

But as the 1970s turned into the 1980s, the significance of the differences between the English and Maori versions was slowly coming to be realised. Walker compared the different versions in one of his influential *Listener* columns in 1980, and increasing attention was now generally being paid within Maoridom to issues which touched on sovereignty. 'Maori people are a sovereign people', declared the Waitangi Action Committee in 1981, while the Maori Peoples Liberation Movement of Aotearoa claimed a couple of years later that 'the majority of young Maori activists' were taking up Awatere's call for Maori sovereignty 'as a basic thrust'. As Maori terms increasingly entered the English language, talk of indigenous autonomy, self-determination or sovereignty gradually became talk of rangatiratanga. Activists made the tino rangatiratanga guaranteed under the Treaty – a notion which was generally applied to the rights of all Maori, not just to the governance roles of chiefly rangatira – a central political focus. They were ever more vocal and proactive in their quest for its recognition by the Crown. By the mid-1980s, sizeable numbers of liberal pakeha, together with the Waitangi Tribunal, had firmly entered the public discourse on the Treaty and the meaning of its different versions. Rangatiratanga viewpoints, including claims relating to equal or greater authority for the Maori-language version of the Treaty, were firmly entrenched in those debates.[33]

Direct Action

By the early 1980s, the Waitangi Action Committee had taken over from Nga Tamatoa at the 'radical cutting edge of Maori politics', both in its methods and its demands. Formed in 1979, it headed Waitangi Day protests and called for a boycott of official celebrations of the national day. In 1981, some of its protesters were arrested for 'rioting' at Waitangi. WAC's rhetoric was 'couched in terms of revolutionary struggle', condemning colonisation and the exploitation and oppression of indigenous peoples. It sought to 'expose the nature of the Capitalist state', to free Maori from the 'yoke of Capitalism' and to defend the '[r]ight of all indigenous peoples to self-determination' as part of the ongoing 'struggle against imperialism'. While it took a broad 'international perspective', central to its New Zealand agenda was the belief that the Treaty was 'a fraud'. WAC aimed to educate people about the nature of that fraud, and the actual rather than mythical history of New Zealand. It circulated newsletters, networked with other activist groups, and organised many protests and demonstrations. Increasingly, WAC activists 'carried their activism to the edge of the law'.[34]

The Bastion Point, Raglan and other direct-action protesters, and organisations such as Nga Tamatoa and WAC, with their actual or implicit criticism of the cautiousness of much of the traditional Maori leadership, aroused the ire of many elders and those working inside the official and quasi-official committee systems. But as an increasingly-embattled Muldoon government chased the 'redneck' vote with its Maori policies and stances, protesters were able to draw upon the support of more conservative figures within Maoridom. There were also increasing numbers of pakeha who identified with, or participated in, Maori activist causes. The combining of discourses of class and exploitation with those of ethnicity assisted the building of solidarities between Maori and pakeha.

Sometimes, however, rifts developed, especially when Maori placed aspects of 'traditional culture' in a position of primacy over matters dear to the hearts of 'progressive' pakeha. On 1 May 1979, pakeha engineering students in Auckland were doing a rehearsal for their usual mock haka in capping week, despite escalating opposition over recent years by the Maori Club and others. They were attacked by a group of young Maori, spearheaded by activists from WAC, this 'raiding party' subsequently adopting the name of He Taua, the avengers. The physical nature of the attack shocked many pakeha liberals who believed in dialogue or peaceful protest rather than violence. There was further consternation when established Maori leaders, including those from conservative organisations such as the NZMC and the MWWL, refused to condemn He Taua's actions and spoke up in defence of the accused in the legal processes that followed. Vocal Maori commentators such as Ranginui Walker placed the kaupapa of the 'haka party incident' in the same category as causes many pakeha had supported, such as the land march and reclaiming the Raglan Golf Course. Walker spoke for many activist and other Maori in seeing all such phenomena, along with the activities of Maori gangs, as 'manifestations of the stifled desire of the Maori people for self-determination in the suffocating atmosphere of political domination and pakeha paternalism'.[35]

Alliances between pakeha and Maori became even more troubled when pakeha in general, rather than simply 'the pakeha capitalist class', were seen as the oppressors. The emphasis on the commonalities between Maori and working-class pakeha that had once marked much radical discourse declined in the 1980s. One Maori radical organisation castigated 'Pakeha people, who ... try to tell us what the Maori struggle should be about' for their 'shamelessness'. 'They tell us to fight for a change in our material conditions [and] that our struggle is the struggle of the working class', whereas 'Pakehas are racist, regardless of class'. Maori activists rebelling against monocultural pakeha institutions, and nearly a century and a half of pakeha domination, saw their struggle as rooted in a Maori past and considered their present (and future) as lying in Maori culture and polity: 'Contemporary Maori Activism is a product of generations of Maori struggle, fuelled by the continued injustice against Maori people and sustained by the Wairua of our Tipuna.'[36]

Activists were increasingly affirming, in particular, that a vibrant Maori culture was an essential part of any political expression of autonomy. In the late 1970s, it was widely agreed, the immediate task was to 'retain our cultural identity as Maori' as a prerequisite for a New Zealand in which 'our future was our business and our responsibility'. Many people who had subsumed their Maoriness, or who had only a small amount of 'Maori blood', were rediscovering and identifying with that part of their heritage, encouraged by the sanctioning, from 1975, of self-identification for electoral purposes. By 1980, with Crown–Maori relations remaining tense, no New Zealanders could ignore the fact that Maoridom was resurgent. Maori were affirming, ever more vehemently, that their culture would not disappear as officials and pakeha had once believed (and often hoped). 'What we did in the past was to go underground and to hibernate until the moment was right to re-emerge', one commentator later wrote. Indigenous peoples elsewhere in the world (the Ainu of Japan, for example) were similarly reasserting themselves by the 1980s. After such long histories of coercive and hegemonic subjugation, however, it was not surprising that the pathways towards autonomy would be contested internally as well as externally, and take many and varied courses.

It is clear, nonetheless, that those who chose to identify themselves as Maori were increasingly inclined to lend active or passive support to protest organisations. By late 1983, with its focus on the Treaty of Waitangi and its action-orientation, WAC had gained such support within Maoridom that it could convene a national hui at Tainui's key Waahi Pa and bring the Kotahitanga and Kingitanga movements together in the course of planning a hikoi/march to Waitangi. Eventually, a wide range of people set off for Waitangi, proclaiming Maori unity and pakeha/Maori solidarity, in an attempt to stop the 1984 Waitangi celebrations. Along with Maori rights activists and pakeha from ACORD, CARE and HART were representatives of the NZMC and MWWL, members of the Labour Party, and even some National supporters. The police forcibly stopped the main section of the protest, which had swollen to 4000 people, from crossing the bridge to the Waitangi Treaty grounds to meet the Governor General, adding extra layers of symbolism to the events.[37]

Mana Motuhake

The Hikoi ki Waitangi was, in part, a response to years of intransigent conservative rule under National and an accompanying reluctance by the Labour opposition to 'rock the boat' too greatly on indigenous issues. But direct-action or confrontational protest tactics had not been to the taste of very many Maori who preferred to pursue their cultural and political agendas through more conventional channels. After the Labour defeat of 1975, however, Maori working inside the party had been quickly disappointed by the leadership's fear of engendering a 'racial' backlash among constituents. This was primarily a consequence of widespread pakeha support for the Muldoon government's populist, ethnocentric and sometimes racist messages. Although integration had been officially abandoned and 'Maori self-reliance' was being encouraged in its stead, National's policies remained infused with the assimilationist attitudes and assumptions of the past.

In the eyes of many Maori, even those of traditionalist ilk, Labour's caution seemed to indicate that integrationism lived on within its ranks, too, especially inside its parliamentary wing. Matiu Rata was particularly frustrated with the situation. National had created, for its own reasons, a programme for Maori self-reliance along directions that he and his advisers had been proposing during the third Labour government. Instead of regarding both his reforms and National's new policies as a beginning, the Labour leadership was now tending to back away from further progress towards rangatiratanga. Rata gradually came to consider that his own 'party had become "insensitive" to and "neglectful" of the interests of the Maori people'. While protest-focused movements were getting great publicity for Maori causes, however, Rata and his followers saw that their methods and demands were alienating many Maori (and pakeha). Towards the end of the decade, he felt that it was time to offer a political movement less conservative than Labour and less frightening than 'direct action' protest.

On 6 November 1979, he announced his intention to resign from the Labour Party. This dramatic step by 'the most influential Maori politician of his generation' epitomised the frustration of many Maori inside the party who agreed that 'we must command our own destiny'. Rata argued, on the basis of his own experience, that Maori would always be marginalised if they remained inside the big political parties. Pursuit of self-determination required an independent nationwide campaign. At a meeting attended by a wide cross-section of Maoridom, Rata announced that he would promote a new 'movement' based on a vision of 'mana Maori motuhake'. It would work for social and political autonomy, and he hoped that it would gain the support of Kingite and Ratana followers. He stopped short as yet of forming a new party, as it would be vulnerable to attack from 'enemies' until the appropriate foundations had been laid. His movement, 'more than a political party', was endorsed by the Auckland District Maori Council, which technically represented almost a quarter of Maori in New Zealand. Its secretary and chair, Hohepa and Walker respectively, became the key theorists and philosophers of mana motuhake. Given the speed of the movement's growth, a party soon appeared to be viable, and Rata announced that he would resign from Parliament. He launched the Mana Motuhake Party at an Easter hui in 1980 at Tira Hou Marae in Auckland.[38]

Walker was instrumental in developing the new party's policy framework, arguing that what was required was a 'total institutional transformation of New Zealand society from monocultural dominance to bicultural sharing'. This was an autonomist vision of Maori partnership with, not separation from, the Crown and pakeha culture. Mana Motuhake, then, did not reflect the most radical voices in Maoridom. There was no proposal for a Maori parliament or an exclusively Maori sphere of decision-making. Rather, national institutions and public authorities needed to be reshaped to reflect the bicultural direction of New Zealand society. Maori institutions should be allowed to get on with things mostly or wholly pertaining to Maori, while interacting with the state in partnership arrangements. The emphasis would be on local and regional self-determination, with authority devolved to revitalised traditional institutions such as runanga, albeit within the framework of Parliament-based governance and structures. The basic policy, Rata announced, was to establish 'communal authority by restoring to the people the power of decision-making on all matters affecting their affairs'. The party sought 'the beginning of a co-operative society' rather than one dominated by a competitive ethos.

On a philosophical level, Mana Motuhake should not have alarmed those who valued social democracy. But with its dominance of the Maori electoral constituency under threat, Labour fought back vigorously. Rata was defeated at the by-election for the Northern Maori seat on 7 June 1980. Labour was, however, rattled at the level of public assistance he had received from Maori leaders, and by the fact that he took a very respectable 37.9% of the vote (to Labour's 52.4%); the party was on notice that the reforms of 1972–75 were insufficient and that its alliance with Ratana seemed shaky. In the period after the by-election, New Zealand was convulsed by political turbulence which provided fertile ground for Mana Motuhake's campaigning. In particular, massive protest centring on race issues was beginning, particularly around the planned 1981 tour by the South African national rugby team. Matters such as the oppression of indigenous people worldwide and ways of rectifying this were under discussion in many quarters. The objectives adopted by the Mana Motuhake Party in November 1980 brought together many strands of thought relating both to the past, especially the demand for reparations for breaches of the Treaty by the Crown, and to a future based on 'self-reliance and advancement of the Maori'.[39]

Mana Motuhake positioned itself as a recent manifestation of historical movements for Maori unity and self-determination, including Ratana and Kotahitanga. It had chosen one of the terms analogous to rangatiratanga to encapsulate its cause. It aimed to build political solidarity between the diverse strands of Maoridom and to minimise competition with traditional tribal or religious organisations. 'We are all fighting for reform in our different ways', its leaders said. Many radical activists believed the party's emphasis on common struggle, necessary to ensure the inclusion of conservative Maori, meant a compromised stance – one that might weaken its commitment to meaningful exercise of rangatiratanga, or even divert detribalised Maori from truly autonomist goals. But Rata and key advisers were determined to unite radicals and traditionalists under a party of Maori unity. Mana Motuhake's proposals for organised Maoridom superimposed regional representation upon tribal, and during the 1981 general election campaign it presented a platform emphasising both self-determination and biculturalism in the social and political life and institutions of New Zealand. It came second in each of the four Maori seats.

Although many Maori declined to follow Rata out of the Labour orbit, the advent of Mana Motuhake was undoubtedly of great significance within Maoridom. A new party of considerable credibility was attempting to lead an essentially pan-Maori pursuit of rangatiratanga within the parliamentary system. Its election result has been described as 'the most spectacular launching of a political party since the appearance of the Ratana Movement'. Its policies and support levels constituted an affirmation that the 'fraud' and 'honour' positions on the Treaty of Waitangi were not incompatible. Whatever the original motivation behind the British drawing up of the Treaty, and whether people believed it had embodied fraudulent intent or not, Maori had always pushed for the promises made by the Crown in 1840 to be honoured. Mana Motuhake was another in a long line of organisations that had ideas on how that 'honouring' should be observed and how best to organise to secure it.[40]

The new party's aim of uniting diverse groups of Maori across the country in pursuit of a common political goal was based on a vision of cultural unity. As a Maori academic had put it in 1975, Maori people, rural and urban, tribal and detribalised, all shared 'a common cultural identity and a strong desire to retain this identity on their own initiative'. Political and socio-economic forces may have seemed about to overwhelm them at points in the twentieth century, but a determined 'desire to pursue common interests together on the basis of a shared cultural heritage irrespective of tribal origin' had ensured powerful and ongoing resistance within Maoridom to assimilation to 'the west'.[41]

People, Land and Politics

In the past, many Maori, even those within the Young Maori Party and Ngata's 'modernising' sphere of influence, had assumed that land was integral to 'being Maori', that the tangata was inseparable from the whenua, that without rohe-based turangawaewae the future of 'the race' was one of inexorable assimilation into the pakeha political economy and culture. But throughout the century, the very many efforts to retain and restore tribal landed bases had not experienced much success until Rata's legislation, and even with this the impact had been limited. By then, not even the most fundamentalist rural kaumatua believed that Maori would, as a people, generally de-urbanise. The reality was that, however tribal/indigenous they remained in tikanga, worldview, whakapapa- and marae-identification and the like, Maori people had become predominantly an urban-situated ethnic group. If indigenous autonomy could only be based upon an intimate nexus with customary land in the tribal rohe, as some traditionalists still argued, the chances of restoring and enhancing rangatiratanga for most Maori would appear to be bleak.

As the very fact of the Maori Renaissance indicated, however, after some third of a century of widespread urbanisation, rangatiratanga was far more resilient than might have been suggested by literal interpretations of 'conventional wisdom' about the inexorable, physical nexus between land and people. In the final analysis, indigenous societies, cultures and polities centre upon collectivities of *people*. An ancient tribal proverb asks the listener about the 'most important thing … in the world' and answers: 'He tangata! He tangata! He tangata! ... People! People! People!' Communities continued to assert their rights to and aspirations for autonomy, even if links to the land had been largely or fully severed by loss of ownership or access (or, in the case of pre-1840 migrational or displaced tribes, the people had re-established themselves in new homelands). Certainly, the possibility of land recovery was never lost sight of, however distant or unlikely it may have been, and this often remained a focus for tribal vitality. Alienation of ownership did not necessarily – or, even, often – denote loss of ancestral connection, either. On the contrary, the tangata and the whenua shared whakapapa, in that the land and the ancestors were seen as one and the same thing. This was one key reason why land remained, along with the Treaty, the iconic symbol of the Maori struggle for autonomy. But the principle of collective identity, the pursuit of the present and future well-being of the tangata in its various configurations, was – many Maori confirmed, actually or implicitly – *the* crucial element in the struggle for autonomy/rangatiratanga.

Tracing this struggle through the twentieth century involves an attempt to unravel a myriad of configurations whose commonality is their ethos of collectivity. In their pursuit of autonomist goals, Maori would alter and adapt their organisation (tribal, sub-tribal, pan-tribal, non-tribal, anti-tribal) and policies to meet the challenges of changing social, economic, cultural and political circumstances. But the bottom line was always that of people working together for goals which involved a future based on group identification and endeavour. Tribally significant sites (even if they had been alienated) and the quest for the return of land loomed large both in the weaponry Maori used and in their goals. The strongest cement of indigeneity, however, was variably said to be found in whakapapa, or the tribe or its subset(s), or shared culture or worldview, or community or institution, or Maoridom – all of these, alone or in combination, in their multiple and changing manifestations and their varying relationships with land or place. Soon, tribes and other groupings would put new life into the traditional institution of runanga, and the pakeha public would hear much more about Maori offices such as that of tohunga, institutions such as the marae and wharenui/meeting house, concepts such as kaitiakitanga and matauranga Maori/indigenous knowledge systems, and emergent collectivities in areas such as literary culture (the first Maori Writers' Conference had been held, for example, in 1975).

Despite its formal and symbolic focus on land, the developing Treaty-based discourse had also (and increasingly) concentrated on Maori culture and on enshrining rangatiratanga in 'constitutional' or political arrangements. In the later 1970s, for instance, Hirini Mead weighed up the Maori quest for 'a better reflection of the agreement in the Treaty of Waitangi' and posed four alternative futures, all of them options at national level. First, further mainstreaming of Maori into a pakeha-dominated society. This, in line with almost all Maori commentators, he dismissed out of hand: the days of Hunn-type policies were definitively over. Second, he cited the *full* autonomy of a totally independent state such as Tonga. However desirable this might be in theory to many Maori, Mead believed it was unachievable in New Zealand. His third option was a 'soft version' of autonomy by which Maori would gain increasing, but always highly circumscribed, power through reasoned debate, infiltration of the system and gradual influencing of government decision-making. This, he argued, is in essence what had been tried so far, without success.

Mead advocated (at a Labour Party conference, among other places) a fourth nationwide solution, a 'hard version' of autonomy, albeit one that fell considerably short of requiring the formal constitution of a fully independent state. This embodiment of rangatiratanga would come about through a 'political deal' under which a council with parliament-type functions would be authorised to both represent Maori and exercise authority over institutions and resources pertaining to Maori alone, such as marae, Maori land and Maori-owned businesses. Such an arrangement would also see a parallel court system and police service run by and for Maori. Areas of government traditionally reserved to the overarching sovereign power, he reassured his audiences, such as defence and foreign policy, would remain the province of the New Zealand Parliament and its political executive.[42]

While many did not agree with the viability or concept of establishing what would be, in effect, an autonomous Maori Parliament, there was a growing consensus among those advocating significant change which broadly aligned with Mead's position. There were many variations on the theme. On the 1984 hikoi, for example, Mahuta called for the incorporation of the Treaty of Waitangi into new constitutional and governance arrangements, and that same year Whatarangi Winiata released a paper arguing for a Maori Senate/Upper House in the existing Parliament. Maori proposals often referred to overseas models, with Mead citing Israeli–Palestinian negotiations in his 'hard' version of autonomy and later seeking inspiration from the Hawaiian quest for self-determination.

In the early 1980s, arguments for new political or governance arrangements were being taken considerably more seriously by Crown and pakeha than during even the recent past. Naturally, the government was prepared only to engage with the less radical solutions proffered, and it was still inclined to look to the NZMC for guidance. Not that this proved to be an easy ride for it or its officials. The Maori Council lobbied industriously during and between its quarterly meetings, and there was much activity within the committees under its umbrella – of which there were some 450 in 1982. That year, an NZMC paper on 'Kaupapa' had offered the government a solution to addressing rangatiratanga that eschewed Mead's hard version of autonomy, but which sought to balance Crown sovereignty by Treaty-based fiduciary duties. Such ideas were explored within officialdom, and preparation of a Maori Affairs Bill that attempted to meet some of them was in train by the time of the 1984 election.[43]

The Labour Party, too, shaken by Mana Motuhake's campaigning, was by now taking much greater cognisance of Maori issues, and Maori were encouraged when it committed itself to the longstanding demand to make the Waitangi Tribunal's jurisdiction retrospective to 1840. In July 1984, Labour won the general election, and both liberal pakeha and Maori put great pressure on the new government to address indigenous aspirations. That September, a thousand-strong hui was convened at Kingitanga's Turangawaewae Marae, after preparatory work by the Maori Ecumenical Council of Churches and other organisations. It had grown out of the hikoi to Waitangi earlier in the year, and was an attempt to produce consensus on the way forward for Maori under the Treaty. After reiterating the need for legislation to implement Labour's policy of extending the Tribunal's jurisdiction, the hui went much further, calling for mana motuhake and constitutional change to recognise rangatiratanga. There were signs the new Labour government was starting to listen, and its officials began to investigate possibilities that went far beyond the local 'self-reliance' institutions which National had been establishing. When in 1985 the Treaty of Waitangi Tribunal was authorised to consider claims dating back to 1840, this was seen as a good omen.

Three years earlier, Race Relations Commissioner Hiwi Tauroa's *Race Against Time*, based on a public survey, had noted two commonly held views within New Zealand society. One indicated that the old assimilationist position – that 'all New Zealanders are one people' – was still strong, while the other stressed national 'unity through diversity'. The work concluded that New Zealand was 'a multicultural nation' that was still 'operating on a largely mono-cultural level', thereby 'failing to take advantage of the rich diversity of cultural heritage of too many other fellow New Zealanders', especially tangata whenua. Official institutions, it argued, needed to be in the vanguard of change, something reiterated by the New Zealand Planning Council the following year. In the contest between the old integrationism and the new desire to embrace diversity, Maori were now being given signals by the new Labour government which suggested that they might finally have a chance of seeing their 'cultural heritage' and rangatiratanga respected under the Treaty of Waitangi.[44]

Chapter 8

Towards Rangatiratanga?

Reports and Consultations

By 1984, Maori and Treaty matters that had previously seemed esoteric for 'mainstream New Zealand' were increasingly common topics of national debate, and the Waitangi Tribunal was becoming a significant factor in counter-hegemonic processes. The Tribunal had been disposed to take greater account of indigenous aspirations following the 1980 appointment of a Maori chairperson, E T J Durie, who was also made the Chief Judge of the Maori Land Court. Durie's double appointment both reflected and heralded social and political changes. He had joined the Maori Land Court in 1974, helping propel its development away from being an institution which protected individuals' interests in land towards a body assisting the retention of land within the various tribal and other collectivities of Maoridom.

The Waitangi Tribunal's future discursive significance was signalled with its *Motunui Outfall Report* of 1983. This took seriously claims that traditional fishing grounds had been contaminated. The Tribunal had used tribal protocols in the course of proceedings, and made recommendations which clashed with government policies. From that time onwards, its hearings and reports gained enormous publicity. In 1985, the Tribunal's new direction was firmed up with the *Manukau Report*, which presented a strong message relating to the interconnections between present circumstances and past happenings. Manukau iwi, having found the Planning Tribunal ineffective in countering pollution of their harbour, had turned instead to the Waitangi Tribunal.

The Tribunal's report went into history in some detail, and expanded on its *Motunui* findings about the Crown's obligation to protect Maori cultural values. It discussed the meaning of the Treaty and found that the kawanatanga ceded in Article One was 'something less than' the western concept of absolute sovereignty, but rather 'the authority to make laws for the good order and security of the country but subject to an undertaking to protect particular Māori interests'. The Crown needed to 'restore the mana of the tribes' which had rights to the harbour by consulting and working with their authorities. In their general thrust, these and other reports affirmed the rangatiratanga or self-determination assured Maori in the Second Article of the Treaty and 'tested the boundaries' on Treaty principles. One academic commentator has gone so far as to argue that the Waitangi Tribunal's reports of this period 'played a crucial role in liberating the treaty from the colonial mentality, and irrevocably affirmed the right to tino rangatiratanga and the challenge to British legal sovereignty'.[1]

The government rejected the Tribunal's key *Motunui* recommendation, which called for preventing waste disposal from a synthetic fuels plant from polluting Te Atiawa's traditional sea fisheries. The recommendation was seen to threaten National's 'think big' economic development strategies and, more generally, to pose a challenge to the state's longstanding adherence to 'indivisible Crown sovereignty'. But the Muldoonite dismissal of the report generated heated public debate at a time when pollution was of increasing concern throughout all sectors of New Zealand society. Both Te Atiawa and other coastal tribes gained a great deal of pakeha support for their cause. Eventually, after much negotiation, Te Atiawa won considerable protection for its mahinga kai/food gathering areas near the plant. In the context of the grand struggle for autonomy, this might have seemed a small step. But Maori were cognisant of the fact that the importance of rangatiratanga had been endorsed by an independent commission within the state. By this step alone, the cause of rangatiratanga had been advanced.[2]

Moreover, the relatively successful outcome showed that pressure on the government within a Treaty context could produce satisfactory results, however reluctant the Crown in the first instance. The Muldoon government, indeed, had already succumbed to Maori pressures in other areas. New legislation, for example, required the state to take into account issues of significance to Maori in such matters as town and country planning. After the 1978 elections, the Prime Minister appointed Ben Couch as the first Maori National Party Minister of Maori Affairs. He and other ministers frequently utilised the channels provided by the New Zealand Maori Council, whose increasing radicalism was symbolised in its president's public opposition to a proposed 1977 All Black tour of South Africa (which never eventuated). The council was being taken ever more seriously by the government on matters of relevance to Maoridom, and provided input into a number of reforms.

In 1978, the NZMC made extensive submissions to Parliament's select committee on the consolidatory Maori Affairs Bill. As a result, the draft legislation was rewritten and went out for nationwide deliberation under the council's auspices. The episode has been assessed as 'a major break-through in

Maori/government relations'. It suited the state to be able to negotiate with Maori institutions, coordinated at a national level, which eschewed extreme demands and tactics. But the council and its bodies were less inclined than in the past to compromise on fundamental issues. It was mounting pressure from below that led the NZMC to convene the Conference of Maori Committees in 1978. This sought to reconcile the conflicting pressures of activism, cooperation and containment. One of the themes to emerge was the particular efficacy of the Maori associations in pursuing collectivist aspirations in areas, especially the urban spaces, where traditional tribal structures had been weakened or fragmented. Another was the need for better coordination within the official sector, and between it and the quasi- and non-official sectors, if full Crown recognition of rangatiratanga was to be achieved.

The ensuing years saw an increasing propensity within Maoridom to appreciate that although tactics and strategies might differ, aspirational goals were often similar. In 1983, the NZMC was again asked by the Crown to examine legislative matters relating to land, and its feedback stressed the continuing significance of whenua for the various and varied Maori communities. However bastardised the collective land tenure system, and however urbanised the population, land continued to provide Maori 'with a sense of identity, belonging and continuity' – expressed through concepts such as turangawaewae and kaitiakitanga. The NZMC submission essentially constituted a warning to Muldoon and his ministers to avoid any residual thoughts they might have to revert to legislative proposals resembling any of the coercive measures of the hated Maori Affairs Amendment Act of 1967. The Crown, already well apprised of the universal Maori wish to retain or regain both their land and their collective responsibility for it, now conducted its ongoing discussions with Maori on the issue within a retentionist and non-prescriptive framework.[3]

Meanwhile, within the Department of Maori Affairs itself, changes had been occurring as the Maori Renaissance grew in strength and conservative leaders joined radicals in rejecting the many residual assimilationist elements left in departmental policies, guidelines, practices and attitudes. Under such pressures, in 1977 Duncan MacIntyre had commissioned the State Services Commission (SSC) to conduct a survey of the DMA. On the surface, its policies had seemed relatively sound from a rangatiratanga perspective even during the period of intensified assimilation following the Hunn report. Its quest to engender integration had encompassed efficiency and pride in 'Maoriness' as necessary ingredients of ultimate assimilationist goals. Soon after the passage of the Maori Welfare Act in 1962, for example, the DMA had put its own interpretation to the legislation. The Act encouraged, it stated, 'the Maori people to exercise control and direction of their own communities in the essentials of good citizenship and civic responsibility', placing 'responsibility for the advancement of the race on the Maori people themselves'.

But the fact remained that in the wake of the Hunn report, the DMA had been obliged to pursue 'integrationist' measures as a matter of urgent and overarching policy. While these imperatives were now seen as unrealistic, if not as undesirable, many of their systemic and functional resonances remained within the bureaucracy. The DMA, too, was still widely seen as paternalistic, despite its employment of the language of self-reliance. Its increasing advocacy of Maori agency, for example, was tempered by its stress on 'the State providing trained officers to guide and help'. The State Services Commission's report found that the DMA's Welfare Division embodied a 'paternalistic, centralised bureaucracy' removed from its clients' cultural and developmental needs. Reflecting longstanding Maori criticisms that the DMA failed to meet Maori needs and wants, the report declared that reform was essential. What was particularly needed was the development of policies promoting 'greater community participation and autonomy'.

The Muldoon government was not averse to such messages. These, indeed, reflected National's philosophical emphasis on 'self-reliance', an ideological stance which focussed on individuals' independence from state tutelage and assistance, but which could be expediently extended to cover self-reliance by collectivities. From its beginning in 1975, in fact, the third National government had worked with both traditional Maori leaders and Maori urban leaders who were not radical in orientation to develop ways of promoting greater self-reliance. Its continuance of marae subsidies, for example, was designed to help build stronger communities which could then 'liberate' themselves from the need for further assistance.

Its approach to the NZMC on land issues in 1983 had been preceded by considerable discussion over the years. It had soon abandoned thoughts of trying to repeal Labour's land legislation, instead opting to enquire into specific difficulties while also commencing a process to eventually consolidate Maori land legislation. In 1979, the government had authorised officials to begin working on ideas which would incorporate Maori aspirations, and it was this process which had led to the significant consultations of the new decade. Essentially, the days of coercive rationalisation of Maori land holding and use were over. The processes that were set in place in the 1970s and strengthened in the 1980s were eventually to lead to the retentionist Te Ture Whenua Maori Act of 1993. Despite a shaky beginning with a Prime Minister versed at 'playing the race card' among his many populist tactics, discussion and consultation with Maori did improve under National, even if in fits and starts. Prospects of greater Maori control over Maori affairs were improving.[4]

Establishing Tu Tangata

One of the SSC report's authors, Assistant State Services Commissioner Kara Puketapu, was appointed in 1977 to head Maori Affairs. He was only the second Maori to be selected to lead the department in its history, his appointment an indication of the significance of the Maori Renaissance. Puketapu was an advocate of 'taha Maori', and had called for the DMA to be a 'people oriented, people managed agency' which would ask Maori what they wanted and try to effect it wherever possible. He initiated a series of meetings with Maori in each district to help develop new policies, which were then considered by a conference of Maori leaders held at Parliament. This Hui Whakatauira, became an annual event.

Puketapu was given considerable leeway by the government for several reasons. It especially sought to assure 'responsible Maori' that working through 'proper channels' (as opposed to protest and disruption) would yield results. Moreover, Puketapu's views had the potential to reduce the Maori 'welfare burden' on the state. They could also be seen to gell with National's self-help philosophies. Under the new departmental ethos which Puketapu insisted upon, Maori were encouraged to 'stand tall' in conducting their own affairs. Tu Tangata/Standing Tall became, in 1978, the generic title for the 'new philosophy' of the DMA. Tu Tangata programmes centred on community-based Maori development, the overall aim being that of promoting 'cultural and economic advancement' through 'encouraging self-reliance and self-determination'. 'Maori cultural values were promoted ... as a source of untapped energy' which could 'enhance the effectiveness of locally based projects'. Collective Maori energy, then, would once again be utilised by the state for the development of Maori human and natural resources for (as the DMA's annual report would put it) 'the common good of all New Zealanders'.[5]

Puketapu and likeminded staff intended Tu Tangata policy to begin to address the aspirations of traditionalists and radicals alike, and in many ways it represented a significant state move towards recognising and assisting rangatiratanga. At the same time, issues of self-determination and self-reliance were being canvassed within other sectors of the state, too. Processes being discussed and set in train were, in effect, reinterpreting the configurations of the national good. They were influenced by international as well as national developments. In 1978, New Zealand became party to the International Covenant on Civil and Political Rights, whose first article affirmed the right of peoples to self-determination. Even Maori cynical of the Crown's motivations for its policy readjustments at this time appreciated the fact that Tu Tangata took the retention and enhancement of Maori cultural values to be intrinsic to the 'advancement' of their people. There was cautious approval, too, of Tu Tangata's organisational bases. It aimed to generate activity at the most grounded of community levels, and particularly recognised the value of whanau 'for reorganising the administrative basis of government-Maori interaction'. Whanau were to be encouraged to become involved in the planning and implementation of solutions to existing problems, and to suggest and promote new developmental initiatives.

While the ethos of the revamped DMA came from agreement at senior political and governmental level, its policies aimed to be bottom-up rather than top-down in both inspiration and operating mode. This 'Wairua Maori' approach was designed to seek out and 'recognise the stance of the people' by supporting (including through funding) any 'action group involved in local improvement on a voluntary self help basis' that was prepared to work in liaison with the Crown. The new philosophy thus supplemented the existing system of project-based assistance to official committees. Moreover, Tu Tangata was not an isolated policy within the public sector. Reflecting, as it did, 'growing trends to channel welfare services from amelioration to development through local participation and responsibility', it worked with and alongside other governmental agencies and programmes. However, its implementation came to be seen as a particularly good example of bottom-up initiatives for the state sector to consider, and the State Services Commission would challenge other departments to emulate the Tu Tangata approach in such matters as decentralising aspects of their management structures.

The officially endorsed (if cautious) empowering of Maori collectivities under the 1945 and 1961–62 official structures can be seen as an extension of Ngataism's critical engagement with the Crown. In this sense, the Maori associations remained important to both state and Maori. But now the voluntary sector within Maoridom would be able to have a greater influence on official policy and operations, incarnating in different ways the policies for which Ngata had been the key initiator and spokesperson. In particular, to be self-reliant Maori would need to draw on the strengths of their own culture. These included collective responsibility and modes of working, and consensual decision-making processes, at all levels of Maoridom.

Tu Tangata represented a new way of linking the politico-cultural renaissance of Maoridom with the social, educational and economic advancement of the people that was, as many adverse statistics indicated, so clearly needed. The DMA's initial role would be to encourage and facilitate the development of ideas and initiatives from within Maoridom, and those which seemed to be both appropriate and practical would be submitted for scrutiny at the annual Hui Whakatauira. The department undertook to explore policy and implementation possibilities and ramifications for those which were endorsed. The old boundaries between official and unofficial, already blurred in practice, were becoming more so in theory as well. The DMA's journal was renamed *Tu Tangata* to symbolise the changes, and its content asserted notions of rangatiratanga.[6]

Other changes in terminology also indicated a new emphasis in policy and philosophy. In particular, the word 'community' came to replace 'welfare' in first the departmental lexicon and then in legislation. A departmental restructuring, in which social workers and other staff of the Welfare Division were transferred elsewhere or reclassified as community officers, accompanied such developments. The handling of community participation in the delivery of services to Maori would now come through 'kokiri' administration units (whose name reflected the concept of 'advance'), and community officers would be placed in the field and remain permanently accessible. There was also to be an increasing indigenisation of staff as well as of style. All such concessions to Maori desires for greater recognition of rangatiratanga were widely seen, as the relatively radical Ranginui Walker put it, to be bringing to fruition the 'devolution of power and resources [that] has long been dreamed of by the Maori people'.

Of course, Crown and Maori motivations did not always or necessarily coincide. The Tu Tangata philosophy's stress on self-reliance rather than welfarism had helped lead to its backing by Muldoon and his ministers. But for them, the self-help aspects of the ideology outweighed Tu Tangata's focus on collective Maori ways of doing things, such as the stress it placed on sharing and locality-based kotahitanga. In government eyes, self-help was preferably that of individuals and nuclear families, not the larger units which generally provided the operating bases of Maori communities. 'My government has been receptive to many of your ideas', Muldoon would tell Maori leaders in 1982, 'but has always preferred' those which were based on the self-reliance of individuals. The policy's promise of potential savings for the state, too, loomed larger with ministers than with Maori, who noted that the Crown's funding on Maori issues had always been niggardly. Still, the important thing for Maori was to ensure that Tu Tangata policy became tu tangata action. Puketapu's successor from 1983 as head of the DMA, Tamati Reedy, declared that Tu Tangata meant 'that the time had come for Maori people to be self-reliant and to manage their own affairs'. That social welfare for Maori could be relegated to something necessary only in emergencies suited Maori and Crown alike.

In the course of emphasising the self-reliance aspect of Tu Tangata for public consumption, the Muldoon government also stressed its own economic and anti-welfare policies and propensities. The National Party's statement in a 1981 'Position Paper' that 're-establishment of Maoritanga will bring about self-determination' needs to be placed in this context. The party's political leadership had increasingly considered social spending cuts to be imperative, given the lack of economic growth after 1973. With the welfare state imposing what were seen to be unacceptably high financial burdens, National strategists had been impelled 'to concur with the objectives of Tu Tangata for pragmatic reasons'. Their endorsement was 'predictable', as one scholar put it, 'given the potential of Tu Tangata to: (a) hold government spending on the Maori to within acceptable limits; (b) reduce Maori dependency on welfare services; and (c) pacify Maori demands for increased self-determination'. Transferring the responsibilities of government to sub-tribal and pan-tribal voluntary organisations and other community-based groupings made political and economic sense.

Tu Tangata, then, can be legitimately seen from one perspective as an attempt to appropriate the self-organisational impulses of the Maori Renaissance in order both to contain them and harness them for the exigencies of the (pakeha-dominated) national good – just another in a long line of official appropriations of Maori associational capacities. Many Maori leaders of all stripes were certainly suspicious of the state's intentions. They feared, among other things, that Tu Tangata's much vaunted consultation procedures were designed for rubber stamping of decisions already taken by bureaucrats and politicians behind the scenes. A number of observers, including officials, expressed concern that some of the DMA's significant welfare functions were being pushed into the voluntary sector by the policy. And while Tu Tangata programmes often shifted the burden of responsibility for welfare matters onto community organisations, there was often no matching transfer of power or resources. In fact, it was widely reported that the DMA failed to adequately support local on-the-ground initiatives, even those predicated on government funding; Tu Tangata programmes had to rely largely on the 'aroha of the community'.[7]

Whatever the degree of autonomy handed over and asserted under Tu Tangata, the Crown retained the upper hand. This was to be expected in terms of matters such as accountability for public money, but the doctrine of indivisible sovereignty had wider ramifications. Whatever the rhetoric about self-reliance, all officially backed expressions of rangatiratanga would continue to be constrained by the government's 'rules', written or otherwise. Any resources or powers conceded to Maori communities could be taken back if the actions of the recipients, in their capacity as people running institutions accountable to the Crown, displeased ministers or officials. Autonomist impulses were certainly being recognised, with the ethos and operating parameters of Tu Tangata allowing both flexible and bold initiatives, and there would now be greater degrees of consultation in devising, planning and implementing DMA programmes. But Crown-franchised and Crown-assisted rangatiratanga could only proceed in authorised and revocable ways once bottom-up initiatives had been officially endorsed. Another 'official system' had been set in place that was, in the final analysis, subject to essentially the same constraints as previous ones. That being said, Maori observers at the time perceived that Tu Tangata constituted a forward march of not inconsiderable magnitude on the long road towards rangatiratanga.

Implementing Tu Tangata

In theory, the DMA, its related systems and other government departments were encouraging and facilitating the emergence and implementation of collective, self-help schemes so that the role of the state within Maoridom could progressively diminish. This was one reason why the NZMC and its constituent bodies not only saw little threat from implementation of the new philosophy, but also participated in putting the Tu Tangata scheme into practice. The committees operating under the Maori Council umbrella, in fact, became heavily involved in various initiatives aimed at empowering Maori communities. Tu Tangata both reflected and fed into their changing roles and functions in the New Zealand of the Maori Renaissance. It was not coincidental that this was the period when the judicial functions of the official committees were rapidly declining. Not only were new generations of urban Maori ill-inclined to voluntarily submit to 'alternative' punishments in situations alien to them (and which might well be harsher than those of the 'pakeha courts'), but – in line with Tu Tangata thinking – the committees were generally moving away from Crown-franchised social control and towards encouraging flaxroots initiatives for community empowerment.

There was still a role for the institution of wardens, who had adapted to modernity in such a way that they were perceived as integral to the operations of their communities. Among other things, they were exercising greater selectivity and discretion in their coercive interventions. Moreover, the trend towards community empowerment included *informal* policing and disciplinary functions. Later, in fact, community involvement in handling actual or potential offenders meant that committees began to re-enter the coercive arena in different and often more subtle ways. More immediately, Tu Tangata's stress on community service had assisted the rejuvenation of the Maori warden system, an enhancement of particular importance in the cities. The number of wardens went up in urban Wellington from 21 (half of whom were deemed to be inactive) in mid-1978 to 38 (two-thirds of whom were categorised as active) two years later. Wardens and their associated networks were often tapped for their knowledge and help when Tu Tangata initiatives were being planned and established.[8]

The support or participation of established Maori organisations, however, was just one component of the rapid rise of Tu Tangata from a vague ideal into a meaningful policy and operational package. Central to the initial Tu Tangata approach was a network of 'kokiri centres' that were set up within each DMA district, the first of these opening in 1979. As the centres were established, departmental decision-making could be progressively placed into community hands. Although partially state funded, kokiri centres were managed independently and built upon the collective efforts of volunteers at flaxroots level. They ran activities decided on by the local community and offered, among many other things, basic skills training and counselling to the local people. Underpinning the kokiri centres were community advisory groups, whose allocated functions included keeping the DMA informed on the important issues for the district, especially those concerning 'education, employment, crime and culture'. The Maori Women's Welfare League, which remained an integral part of the lives of many people identifying as Maori, played a sizeable role in setting up and running the centres. It provided a 'community component essential to the success' of other Tu Tangata projects as well.[9]

There were also significant 'empowerment' developments in Maori education. Many people had long been pondering ways of reviving the Maori language and strengthening knowledge of indigenous culture. One idea was to offer parents a total-immersion environment for their pre-schoolers, and this was supported at the 1981 Hui Whakatauira. Iritana Tawhiwhirangi and others formed a team to develop proposals on this and other community development issues. After strong DMA backing for pilot schemes, and considerable input from the MWWL, the first kohanga reo/'language nest' was established in the outer Wellington suburb of Wainuiomata. Others very quickly followed, and although they operated under the umbrella of a national trust which had been formed, each of them was to be as self-sufficient as possible. Tawhiwhirangi had been involved in establishing playcentres during her earlier career as a Maori welfare officer, and the national playcentre scheme became a key organisational model for kohanga reo – an indication of the way many initiatives under Tu Tangata, as with previous developments, had emerged within broader conceptual and organisational contexts.

Like a number of other Tu Tangata programmes, kohanga reo were organised day-to-day along whanau-style operational principles. While technically not kinship-based, language nests often relied on the strength of kinship and similar associational links. In time, most came to be located at or associated with marae. In their 'underlying philosophical base', they could be seen as 'a form of whanau whose unifying element had extended beyond the boundaries of descent to include ... groups who unite under the aegis of a common cause'. Indeed, the term 'whanau' was used by the movement's founders to refer to the group of parents, teachers and kaumatua which ran each language nest.

The national Te Kohanga Reo Trust had been provided with a small DMA-financed secretariat, and this assisted 'whanau groups' to found and operate kohanga reo. Before long, a network of the institutions had been established throughout the country, with numbers increasing from 50 in late 1982 to over 500 by the end of 1987. Meanwhile, over a thousand people had attended the first national kohanga reo hui at Turangawaewae Marae in Ngaruawahia in January 1984. Kohanga reo became 'the most successful – and representative – of all programmes under the Tu Tangata umbrella', acquiring an international reputation for community-based educational and cultural success.

Although some state funding could be accessed to set up and operate kohanga reo, the language nests relied mostly on volunteer workers. The movement was determinedly independent. On occasions when the Crown decided to intervene to ensure its 'investment' monies were 'appropriately' spent, kohanga reo would sometimes resist and affirm their right to make their own decisions. In fact, kohanga reo became 'as much a political movement as ... a language-recovery programme and as such [was] an element in its own right of the modern Maori Renaissance'. Although the state aim had been to nourish community responsibility, it had not fully expected – or approved – this politicisation. Kohanga reo can, in one sense, be seen as yet another in a long line of Crown attempts to appropriate Maori organisational modes and energies. But, as with other initiatives in the past, the kohanga reo movement took on a life of its own; and this life did not always or necessarily meet Crown objectives.[10]

One Maori commentator has described kohanga reo as epitomising 'a number of educational initiatives that reflect the power of Maori human agency [and] generally sit within a wider iwi or pan-tribal plan [to] contribute to the attainment of the overarching goal of rangatiratanga'. With the growing success and influence of kohanga reo, other elements of the educational system strengthened their efforts to adjust to Maori-generated changes and utilise the impulses which had led to them. The Post Primary Teachers Association (PPTA, the secondary schoolteachers' union), for example, grappled with the place of biculturalism in education at a large Maori Education Conference at Waahi Marae in Huntly in 1984. As a result, the PPTA came to alter its own staffing profile, as well as to pressure government for more attention to be paid to such issues as Maori teacher levels. The primary sector also followed up ideas expressed at the 1984 hui and elsewhere. As one outcome, the language nest learning philosophy was extended into the primary school environment in 1986 with the establishment of Kura Kaupapa Maori. While this and related developments were state-franchised and/or state-assisted, a considerable vigilance against state co-option prevailed. Unlike the old Native Schools system, 'Kura Kaupapa Māori was designed by Māori for Māori'.[11]

Another area to benefit from the Tu Tangata environment was health. From the 1960s, some local Maori health initiatives had been validated by the Health Department. Now the Crown began to address in a more systematic way the strongly expressed Maori desire that the national system accommodate 'spirituality as a basis for good health' and, more broadly, that health needed to be seen as one component of a holistic approach to life. Under the Tu Tangata philosophy, Maori health programmes were expanded and new ones devised, especially those underpinned by holistic and indigenous healing philosophy and methodology. Then, in 1980, a report drew attention to the urgency of the situation. Eru Pomare's 'Maori Standards of Health: A study of the 20 Year Period 1955–1975' highlighted the large gaps between Maori and pakeha on such matters as mortality rates. The MWWL's health research unit (established in 1977) followed up on Pomare's findings between 1981 and 1983, using indigenous research techniques and cultural frameworks to conduct health surveys among Maori women. Its report, *Rapuora*, recommended setting up marae health centres that were both preventive and 'Maori' in their orientation and methods, and some of these were established.

There were other health initiatives, both urban and rural, based on the principle of Maori control of Maori issues. In line with Tu Tangata concepts, the 'Oranga Maori: Maori Health' model was introduced in 1984 by the Department of Health, aiming 'to assist Maori people to achieve their highest level of wellbeing'. That March, the department sponsored a landmark national hui, the Hui Whakaoranga, held at Hoani Waititi urban marae in Auckland, to discuss Tu Tangata health perspectives. The hui's 'holistic view of health' included 'recognising the importance of spiritual and family sustenance'. It discussed provision of healthcare programmes by Maori, and advocated greater funding of Maori-generated healthcare initiatives.

The hui concluded that Maori should be enabled to play a larger and more influential role in both determining Maori health needs and improving Maori health. To this effect, it recommended that Crown resources be transferred to Maori organisations accountable for the effectiveness of outcomes. The hui gave rise to programmes such as 'Waiora (total wellbeing)', which sought funding from non-governmental as well as governmental sources. Its aims included 'help[ing] improve the cultural and self esteem of Maori people' and encouraging Maori youth to identify positively with Maori culture. The government was increasingly willing to promote flaxroots healthcare services, and in 1985, the Director-General of Health announced that Maori could now be involved in various initiatives as 'partners'.

Mason Durie later summed up the new approach to 'Maori health development' as 'essentially about Māori defining their own priorities for health and then weaving a course to realize their own collective aspirations'.

He also put it more bluntly: 'Central to the notion of Maori health development is Maori control.' Crown assistance for health and other initiatives occurred under an umbrella 'Maori policy' whose purposes were summed up in the title of the Maori Community Development Act. Government resources would join with those of pre-existing and newly-mobilised Maori structures in communities of various types, be they tribal-based or otherwise. These institutions would promote community development, for both the Maori good and that of all New Zealanders. Greater devolution of various social services to local level would help lead to working partnerships between the Crown and Maori communities.

Some Maori commentators noted that such devolved measures still fell within the hegemonic parameters of the colonising power. Legislation provided definitions (of such things as 'good citizenship and civic responsibility') which were not necessarily those which suited their people, but which needed to be adhered to if resources and authorisation were to continue. All the same, there was 'a burst of energy and purpose at local level' in a number of arenas, not just in health and education, as a result of the new governmental approaches. Efforts were particularly strong where state schemes built upon pre-existing initiatives, numbers of which had been growing since the Maori Renaissance had got under way. Over and above mainstream departmental projects, moreover, DMA officials and others attached to or associated with its structures worked on a wide range of experimental programmes initiated and managed by local people. One major focus was on vocational and life-skills for youth, with the future well-being of Maoridom and its people seen to be at stake. In particular, the programmes targeted those facing actual or potential socio-economic marginalisation through lack of education, joblessness, problems with the authorities and the like. These and many other community development schemes involved Crown–Maori arrangements at localised levels. Communities regarded these as practical embodiments of the recognition and exercise of rangatiratanga.[12]

The Labour Government and Ideas of Devolution

When the fourth Labour government was elected in July 1984, there was renewed hope among Maori of making further autonomist gains, especially at a national political level. Since its 1975 defeat, the Labour Party had professionalised and modernised itself. Under increasing pressure from its rank and file, including from radical Maori members and supporters, the old party of social democracy had gradually proclaimed itself a vehicle for 'progressive' policies on a number of moral, ethical and ethnic issues, most of which rested easily within the now attenuated, but still existing, socialist parameters of the Labour movement. During this time, Maori activists had made common cause with pakeha liberals on many issues, and this nexus operated inside the evolving Labour Party as well as outside of it. Securing support from Labour for policies affirming rangatiratanga was seen by many as a key next step. When Labour entered office, then, landmark policies on such ethics-based issues as anti-nuclearism and women's rights sat alongside those which reflected Maori flaxroots aspirations.

In the frenetic early days of the administration, Minister of Maori Affairs Koro Wetere endorsed community empowerment and worked on new schemes to take the concept much further. There were developmental precedents within Maoridom to guide him. Leaders from Wetere's own Tainui tribal grouping, for example, had been consulting with their people over appropriate plans for the future. The *Tainui Report* of 1983 had inventoried tribal resources and set out ambitious goals to ultimately replace all 'government structures of organization' which dealt with their people with collective, tribal ones. This and similar initiatives nationwide were often headed by leaders equally at home in the worlds of Maori tradition and 'pakeha' education and institutions. The Tainui strategy would make use of its trust board's links with the state on the way to regaining tribal resources and placing them under collective control. Rejecting 'top down' procedures, at least in theory, the aim was to 'revitalize the tribal organization and utilize it as a vehicle to implement development policies'.

Tribal revitalisation was occurring all over New Zealand, the extent of which (and even its existence) had come as a surprise to many pakeha, policy-makers included. The 1962 Maori Welfare Act's move from the language of tribal identification to that of 'Maori' identity had reflected 'progressive' pakeha wisdom at the time. These ideas, as suffused throughout the Hunn report, envisaged and encouraged detribalisation. By the early-mid 1980s, however, increasing numbers of pakeha were beginning to realise that the outcome of urban migration was not necessarily, or even largely, detribalisation – at least not if that word implied loss of all interest in and knowledge of tribal heritage, as had been the assumption in the early 1960s. It was becoming clear that tribes, together with their institutions, tikanga and leadership continued to retain considerable significance in the lives of most of those who identified as Maori. This included great numbers who had settled into urban communities, with some observers noting a phenomenon of 'retribalisation' among individuals who had initially 'disappeared' into urban anonymity. Even Maori born in the cities returned to their tribal homelands for occasions such as weddings, tangi and birthdays, as well as to host and mix with visitors and migrants from their home marae.

Perceiving a Maori consensus on the ongoing significance of tribal and sub-tribal identification, Labour had seen that the National government's propensity to engage with Maori at the level of flaxroots community and cross-tribal Maori associations could be enhanced by strengthening links with established tribal authorities, including by encouraging those which had been languishing to revitalise. Devolution of authority and services would be more efficient at tribal level, and the tribes could then sub-devolve if they wished. By 1984 the party had begun to retrieve ground previously lost to Mana Motuhake, partly as a result of its increasing awareness of the significance of tribal identification throughout Maoridom. Moreover, in considering the potentialities of devolution to iwi entities, it was showing willingness to question the old doctrine of Crown indivisibility. By the time of the election, it was investigating reviving the idea of viewing the tribe as the major focus for Crown interaction with organised Maoridom – albeit in ways which accommodated the huge social, demographic, economic and other changes of the post-war decades.

Following its election victory, the fourth Labour government began to see devolution of powers and resources to tribes/iwi as a central way forward on Maori issues. This was not, of course, uncontested, especially by those Maori who operated outside organisational tribal parameters in the urban areas. Moreover, many 'tribal Maori', as in the past, were concerned that Crown dealings at iwi level would jeopardise the rights and authority of hapu, whanau and other groupings – although significant numbers of these accepted that any move towards fundamental devolution of governmental power would, at least at first, need to be to iwi as a matter of practicality. All in all, both state and Maori leaders perceived iwi, rather than the very large numbers of hapu (on whose behalf, generally, rangatira had signed the Treaty), as the Crown's potential Treaty partners on grounds of manageability as well as continuity in internal Maori governance.

In February 1984, Labour had also indicated that it was listening to Maori voices on the vexed issue of addressing historical grievances, placing on the political agenda the extension of the Waitangi's Tribunal's mandate back to 1840. By so doing, it gained enormous kudos among both Maori and liberal pakeha. The pan-tribal hui at Turangawaewae in September 1984, however, took the issue beyond that of merely listening to historical grievances. It called for reparations to tribal groupings for past breaches of the Treaty, including the 'return of large areas of land and other resources', and for recognition of tribal rights to coastal and inland waters. Government assistance was required for rebuilding an economic base, following the ravages suffered under colonisation and urbanisation. But these and other demands were couched within the framework of the quest for autonomy. Crucial, too, was for the Crown to acknowledge and apologise for the wrongs of the past.

On the surface, chances of transferring significant state resources to Maori were not auspicious, with the Labour government inheriting a major fiscal crisis from the outgoing Muldoon administration. At an early 'economic summit' held by the new government, moreover, it became clear to astute observers that the fiscal crisis was to be used as a cloak for the new ministers' intentions to renounce Labour's traditional social democratic policies and ethos. They and officials were about to introduce a 'revolutionary' package of free-market, deregulatory policies which essentially abandoned the principles of the welfare state and replaced them with those of capitalist individualism.

In an as yet inchoate way, however, ministers and their advisers viewed the Maori desire to run their own affairs as compatible with massive deregulation of the economy and an accompanying major downsizing of the state. They could see that finding concrete means of effecting some significant degree of rangatiratanga might help, moreover, to dampen Maori opposition to the new policies. Maori leaders had quickly voiced well-founded fears that deregulation and laissez-faire would inevitably worsen the already poor socio-economic position of their people, given their concentrations in the types of employment which would suffer most from the new policies. Some of those present at the summit, however, saw the potential for trade-offs if the Labour ministers remained determined to forge ahead with policies which harmed their people disproportionately. They would need to organise in order to maximise their chances, and so formed their own caucus at the conference. This group sought a Maori 'summit conference', and in October 1984, the Minister of Maori Affairs responded by convening the Hui Taumata/Maori Economic Development Conference.[13]

The Hui Taumata

On a formal level, this hui reflected the longstanding Labour concern with 'equality', and highlighted 'underdevelopment' in Maori society. Delegates noted that, for all the past government policies aimed at addressing such matters, Maori were featuring ever more prominently in negative social indicators, particularly those suggesting both widespread welfare dependency and that they continued to miss out, as a people, on the better educational and employment opportunities. The solution primarily lay not just in more or better departmental initiatives, nor only in greater or more appropriately targeted resources going to Maoridom. Instead, the delegates declared, Maori needed 'to determine their own future in their own way with the appropriate resources'. They were united in their desire to do so, believing that – for a number of converging reasons – the Crown might finally be prepared to pay fundamental respect to rangatiratanga.

To this end, the Hui Taumata issued a communiqué demanding 'better targeted support from government but delivered by Maori organisations'.

Its request for 'integrated cultural, social and economic development' went counter to the emerging thrust of government policies for the country, but its call for 'greater Maori autonomy, and Maori self-determination' indicated to government that possibilities existed for forging new arrangements with the Maori leadership which might suit both the Crown and the Maori people. In the words of a member of the organising team, delegates made 'a clear call': 'Give us the power – give us the resources'. After a decade of this, they believed, welfarist funding to assist Maori reach parity with pakeha would no longer be needed.

When a second such summit was held 21 years later, one of the original participants, Parekura Horomia, who had become Minister of Maori Affairs, recalled that the first conference's message had been unequivocal: 'Maori had to be empowered to initiate, design and deliver their own solutions'. The first Hui Taumata's underlying theme, then, was to find ways for Maori to obtain 'supreme control over their lives, their assets and resources'. But how to embody in practical policy the call for Maori control of Maori resources, and the attainment of Maori objectives on Maori terms? Delegates proposed building on recent tribal revitalisation by further 'strengthening the Maori tribal system to provide an environment for new social and economic initiatives'. This should be done in conjunction with the launch of a 'Decade of Maori Development'.

The name of the Hui Taumata's official communiqué, *He Kawenata*, embodied its high status as a covenant. It became both 'an inspiration' throughout Maoridom and a guide to officials. One of the planners of the conference, Ngatata Love, later recorded the feeling of many at the time: the Hui Taumata marked a turning point 'from being told what to do to establishing quietly a determination to take control of our destiny. There was a spirit that came out of it that energised people'. Integration policies had been so entrenched within the body politic that Tu Tangata, although an encouraging start, had not resulted in anywhere near sufficient shared power. Hui Taumata delegates were adamant that more autonomist spaces needed to be created both within the state machinery and outside of it. There was a recommendation from the hui, for example, that one of the existing teachers' training colleges be turned into a Maori community college operating under kaupapa Maori philosophy.[14]

In December 1984, the Maori Economic Development Commission was established to act on the hui's recommendations, especially to find ways of redirecting the 'negative funding' of state welfare services into channels providing more 'positive' and self-reliant outcomes. The commission decided that 'iwi could autonomously deliver economic and social benefits for their people without resources having to be state-controlled'. Tribal governance groups, in particular, could take up a great deal of the responsibility and accountability for better targeting of Crown-provided resources – re-devolving to sub-tribal entities where necessary. Maori collectivities would strengthen as their people were empowered, and this would lead to economic as well as social and political gains.

Most importantly, Maori would eventually be running their own affairs without the need for any state intervention or assistance. In these ways, the self-reliance lost as a result of both general colonisation and specific state policies would be restored in new form. This would also have the advantage for the government of exonerating it from welfarist spending, and would purportedly vindicate its de-statising policies. In the process of transferring resources to Maori organisations, the Crown expected that 'modern' (western) concepts of representative leadership and techniques of business efficiency would be needed. But these could be grafted onto traditional organisational structures, in the interests of both their acceptability and the achievement of maximal results.

From a Maori perspective, the key idea during the rapid developments of 1984 was, in the words of Tamati Reedy, to 'return to the mauri of the tribal base' by developing the strength of iwi, hapu and whanau structures. These, he noted, had long been downplayed by government and, indeed, had not long ago been expected to wither away. Now, however, they were seen as the major organisations to 'underpin any move towards self-determination'. The next two or three years saw the canvassing of many other ideas on the means of effecting a fundamental transfer of governance and resources to Maori. But the focus on iwi as the primary vehicle had been championed by the DMA in response to listening to the Hui Taumata, and significant devolution to tribal structures soon emerged as the principle most favoured by the great majority of the leaders of the interested parties. This implied an initial active promotion by the Crown of tribal identity and development.[15]

'Empowerment' Programmes

As the new devolutionary policies were being debated and worked through, tribally-based initiatives, both official and unofficial, escalated. The Maori employment caucus, which arose out of the Hui Taumata, was prominent in promoting self-reliant ideas. Its March 1985 Employment Conference strengthened the demand for tribal authorities to control both resources and delivery of services. The Crown bureaucracy held numerous discussions and negotiations with Maori leaders from many areas and backgrounds. Between 1985 and 1987, the government endorsed a variety of initiatives and schemes. One of these, the MANA Enterprise Development Programme, was established to provide business-orientated loan financing through tribal authorities. Its aim was to broaden Maoridom's economic base by encouraging new Maori businesses and enhancing existing ones, thereby creating work at a time when (as had been expected) Maori were suffering disproportionately from job losses. The 'Maori ACCESS' (MACCESS) scheme was set up in 1987 after its promotion by the Maori employment caucus. It was to provide special employment and vocational training for the long-term unemployed and others disadvantaged by a drastically shrinking labour market.

Not all the new programmes operated at tribal level. New community-based schemes were established, often modelled on the most successful of the existing projects. One 'flagship' for the DMA's policies of empowering Maori communities indicated clearly the way in which Labour's policies built upon those of the previous government. Matua Whangai, a community-based Maori 'foster parenting' scheme, had first been mooted by the 1981 Hui Whakatauira and piloted from late 1983. Taken up by the new government, it was fully established in 1985 under the auspices of the DMA and several other departments. It would provide whanau- and hapu-based (rather than state-welfare) care for 'youth at risk'. Its aim was both to deal with potential offenders and to 'deinstitutionalise' young Maori in Social Welfare homes and other carceral institutions by 'using the strengths of the Maori whanau' and tribal structures. Not only would the flow of Maori into disciplinary institutions be stemmed, but the very nature of a number of these institutions would also change: they would be gradually relocated within tribal, especially whanau, environments. Matua Whangai benefited from both state resources and those of tribal, sub-tribal and other Maori organisations. It marked a key development in the Crown's recognition of whanau, hapu and iwi as offering 'viable channels for renewal'.[16]

But future difficulties in Crown–Maori relations were foreshadowed early on in the life of Matua Whangai. Despite the efforts of many officials, DMA and other state involvement in 'empowerment' programmes sometimes proved far from compatible with community autonomy. In particular, officials tended to see whanau and other sub-tribal networks essentially as vehicles for government policy implementation rather than modes of returning power to the people through state–Maori partnerships, as they were touted to be. Matua Whangai schemes, for example, sometimes became little more than mechanisms for contracting out the delivery of state services. Such developments occurred in other operational areas too, adding to pre-existing suspicions in a number of Maori quarters as to the Crown's motivations.

To deal with governmental agencies effectively, tribal and sub-tribal groupings had been compelled to bureaucratise or to establish bureaucratic wings or mechanisms. Tainui, for example, created a Development Unit to deal with MANA and MACCESS programmes. For some Maori communities, getting a balance between culture and tradition, on the one hand, and the business and management practices required by a rapidly managerialising public service, on the other, could be highly problematic. Additionally, some programmes such as MACCESS could not have funding apportioned to them unless the relevant Maori institutions had gained legal status. Thus, significant prerequisite demands were laid upon Maori institutions wanting to take part in Crown devolution policies and processes. These were often viewed in themselves as impeding rather than assisting rangatiratanga. When in June 1987 the Minister of Maori Affairs announced a policy of major devolution to iwi authorities of service delivery and resource distribution, many Maori leaders expressed open scepticism.

All the same, a significant number of the large range of governmental empowerment schemes had incorporated degrees of Maori community or tribal management or control. Many were interpreted by those involved in them as providing forms of limited autonomy or opportunities for the communal exercise of rangatiratanga – or, at very least, as prefigurative structures for a rangatiratanga-based future. Modes of expressing rangatiratanga were changing, and were seen to need changing, to meet new circumstances. 'Common interest' whanau-like groups were constructed around kohanga reo, kura kaupapa Maori schools, kokiri centres and other such institutions of devolved funding and partnered management. These sometimes coincided with or overlapped descent-based whanau, but often operated in a pan-tribal or non-tribal working environment. The new common interest groups were characterised, however, by the 'core operational components' of the whanau system, based on collectivist notions such as obligation, reciprocity and cooperation. Overarching them was a common 'Maori identity', something Reedy had been careful to stress when endorsing the empowerment of Maori structures.[17]

Devolutionary Proposals and Treaty Principles

This, then, was the background to the 1987 announcement of the Crown's intention to hand significant power to iwi authorities. The decision was based, essentially, on a key convergence: both Maori and state leaders, having seen devolution and partnership schemes work with reasonable success on a number of planes, were now prepared to take such experiments much further. This did not necessarily mean coincidence of motives. With Maori leaders determined to explore all possible options for pursuing rangatiratanga, the government was, on one level, seeking to take advantage of Maori aspirations in order to mitigate the worst effects of its free-market policies. Both ministers and officials hoped especially that some degree of political and financial support for rangatiratanga would help persuade iwi to take on the burden of 'Maori welfare'. For Maori, in turn, major devolutionary concessions to institutions of tribal governance would at least partially meet what they had long been asking for. The scheme would address both political and economic/fiscal matters of concern to both Crown and Maori.

Major devolution to Maori was initiated, too, in the context of a broader restructuring of the public sector in the name of greater efficiency, accountability, cost-effectiveness and minimal government. 'Positive Maori development, with its focus on tribal responsibilities for health, education, welfare, economic progress, and greater autonomy, fitted quite comfortably with the free market philosophy of a minimal state, non-government provision of services, economic self-sufficiency, and privatisation.' The public service's various functions were to be made transparent, and this would be followed by delegation of delivery of 'non-core' services to quasi-state and non-state bodies, including iwi.

The grand design of Prime Minister David Lange's 1984 Labour government, taking it a very great distance from the social democratic ideals of the party's origins and membership, was generally called 'Rogernomics' (coined around the name of hard-right Finance Minister Roger Douglas). The beginnings of market-driven policies, including 'corporatisation' within the public service, had been introduced by the so-called 'interventionist' Muldoon government. But following Labour's election, these policies now became part of an urgent imperative to reorganise the way things were seen and done throughout New Zealand society. The supremacy of the individual, the removal of welfare statism, the minimalisation of the state and virtually unchecked freedom for trade and industry all began to be implemented through very many rapid, often ill-considered reforms. Precedents in the United States, Thatcherite Britain and elsewhere provided guidelines, although the New Zealand response to the international crisis of capitalism often exceeded overseas versions in zeal, scope and adverse impact upon (especially) the poor and the marginalised.

Rapid withdrawal of the state from as many areas of social life as possible was seen as a particularly pressing need by those running this 'right wing revolution'. A number of key Crown services and institutions – including postal services, telecommunications, electricity, coal, railways, air transport, forestry and state housing – were to be 'corporatised'. This meant, in essence, that they were put on a business footing to operate mostly untrammelled by 'public good' requirements. The ultimate intention was to privatise them, leaving the state with responsibility only for 'core', non-commercial public-service functions (which would also be placed into competitive and businesslike mode). Meanwhile, corporatised divisions of state, generally called State-Owned Enterprises, would be able to engage competitively with other enterprises on a 'level playing field', unfettered by state interference. Operating as private businesses, their overriding goal would be profit, and the successful ones would be ideally placed for later sale to private interests. The public good was reinterpreted in a way that both reflected international western developments in updating capitalism – including those in what had once been the Mother Country – and took them in extreme and (in the case of Maori) innovative directions.

The right-wing ideologues in control of the government and key departments, especially the Treasury, were particularly enamoured of the fact that Maori were traditionally grouped into 'private' entities. This could help override ideological difficulties posed by the collectivised nature of Maori institutions, the concept of collectivity being repugnant to those planning to atomise life in New Zealand. Moreover, expedients were needed during the huge task of overturning the broad socio-political post-war consensus (with its remnants of collective endeavour and its welfare-state commitment to sustain people 'from the cradle to the grave') and replacing it with fully fledged individualism, competition and minimal 'safety net' welfare provisions. Tribes (and by extension, sub-tribal groupings) and other Maori entities could, then, be reconfigured into 'private authorities' with which the Crown could work on a practical basis and to which it could legally and accountably devolve many state functions.

The government would begin by seeding such franchised entities with sufficient resources to allow them to provide to their own people many of the services which had previously been the prerogative of the Crown. Iwi authorities could look after the affairs of their people wherever those people were. Maori who had become so detribalised that they had lost all connections with their iwi, or those who chose to identify primarily with urban authorities, could be 'serviced' by other means, devolved or not. Ultimately, iwi (and other devolved) authorities were expected to break free of Crown financial assistance and therefore from any governmental controls beyond the minimal requirements of the downsized state. Thus it was that the rangatiratanga-based aspirations of the Hui Taumata seemed, to many elements of the Maori leadership, attainable under the very Rogernomics policies which (with the message of 'short-term pain for long-term gain') were putting large numbers of Maori out of work.[18]

The fourth Labour government had a number of reasons for its iwi-devolution proposals in addition to those outlined above. It may have ignored its rank and file on core social democratic values, but to retain any kind of significant membership base it needed to deliver on some of the 'moral and ethical' policies it had been developing in recent years. These included the notion of 'Treaty partnership' with Maori, which dovetailed with the ministers' devolutionary and de-statising agenda. The government also needed to address the fact that Mana Motuhake's serious inroads into its traditional Maori support base did reflect widespread Maori concerns to secure meaningful recognition of rangatiratanga. It was aware that Maori support could be further eroded as a result of the effects of Rogernomics on people's livelihoods unless it offered major concessions. Increasingly, then, the relationship between Crown and Maori was officially defined by references to partnership and the emerging 'Treaty principles' which would guide its development.

The government needed also to address the longstanding Maori demands for the Crown to investigate its historical breaches of the Treaty and to negotiate appropriate compensation. In line with its election promises, and under intense pressure (as evidenced by the Turangawaewae hui the previous September), in 1985 Labour secured passage of the Treaty of Waitangi Amendment Act, extending the Waitangi Tribunal's jurisdiction back to 1840. While the Tribunal had already been taking history into account in its findings, the new situation would soon mean an escalation in its work and considerable publicity about colonial injustices against Maori. Tribes held out hope for sufficient reparations to re-establish economic bases from which they could advance the autonomist cause. However much Rogernomics would devastate the most vulnerable sectors of Maoridom, rangatiratanga was undoubtedly becoming increasingly respected by Crown and pakeha alike. In late 1985, Sir Paul Reeves was appointed the first Maori Governor-General, a symbol of Crown–Maori partnership in an emergent bicultural New Zealand. On 23 June 1986, Cabinet instructed that all future legislation should take into account the principles of the Treaty and that departments needed to consult appropriately with Maori on all significant matters relating to the application of the Treaty.

The Environment and State-Owned Enterprises Acts of 1986 and the Conservation Act of the following year all formally recognised the 'principles of the Treaty of Waitangi'. The Maori Language Act 'placed Maori on an equal footing with English as an official language' in 1987. It was early that year that ministers, officials and Maori leaders held breakthrough discussions on making iwi the major Maori partners of the Crown for promoting Maori social, economic and political development. The DMA now set out a 'mission' for 'giving effect to the Government and Maoridom's aspiration to achieve Rangatiratanga'. This was the Crown's way of acknowledging that – as the NZMC and other Maori organisations, as well as the Tribunal, had been arguing – the 'spirit of the Treaty' transcended its actual (and sometimes contradictory and outdated) words. The Treaty needed working through at both conceptual and practical levels.[19]

Pending major devolution, many types of partnership arrangements and configurations were enhanced, negotiated or discussed. The Health

Department was one of the first public service agencies to respond proactively to the government's directives to consult with Maori on significant matters. The Director-General insisted on the Treaty's 'special significance', and talked of providing 'appropriate services' that took into account health perspectives 'firmly based' in Maori culture. The department responded to a resurgent interest in Maori healing techniques, for example, by quickly providing guidelines to the medical profession.

Bureaucracy under Scrutiny

But the DMA remained the key agency for Maori, and its performance fell short of the hopes which official statements had aroused. There had always been a generalised Maori disillusionment with 'the Maori Affairs', but this was now becoming even more widespread. The government, too, was frustrated at the DMA's incapacity (or unwillingness) to engage fully with the new policies and ethos. In 1985, a ministerial review of the department had found that it had not adjusted sufficiently to the new political environment. It was still seeking to 'do everything' for the tangata whenua rather than give communities the resources to forge their own futures. No one familiar with the evolving 'Maori policy' discourse would have been surprised at the report's recommendation that departmental policy should refocus to promote Maori self-development rather than state-provided welfare. This clearly required the widespread consultation which the NZMC and other organisations had long called for. Even if ministers failed to listen to Maori leaders on the need to protect their workers against the worst effects of deregulation and privatisation, consultation on many other issues did increase enormously as the fourth Labour government's term progressed.[20]

Rangatiratanga was at the fore of these. June 1986 saw the release of another significant document in the history of the long Maori struggle for autonomy. This report, *Puao-Te-Ata-Tu/Day Break*, has been depicted (despite its official status) as putting forward 'perhaps the most direct proposition to date from Maori to the government about power sharing'. It was the work of the Ministerial Advisory Committee on a Maori Perspective for the Department of Social Welfare, headed by Tuhoe kaumatua John Rangihau. The committee had been established in 1984 following accounts of institutional racism and other problems in the Auckland district office of the Department of Social Welfare. It carried out extensive consultation and travelled widely. Its report pulled no punches in its detection of a 'major crisis' if Maori socio-economic deprivation was not addressed adequately. Contextualising the department's difficulties on racial issues within the history of colonisation, the report identified monocultural institutionalisation as a major modern impediment to progress.

The report prescribed 'greater government recognition of Maori forms of social intervention and care giving'. Focusing on the welfare of children and young people, it recommended sweeping changes in departmental philosophy and practice. In calling for the use of Maori ways of resolving conflicts, it argued that the kin group was 'an ideal site for conflict resolution'. The report emphasised that the department needed to recognise both the value of kinship and the role of kaumatua, and that Maori children fared best in their customary environments. Recognising that urbanisation had weakened traditional kin linkages, the report urged government assistance for strengthening them and reconnecting young Maori with the tribal structures of iwi, hapu and whanau.

The report's conclusions also addressed wider issues which were reflective of general Maori concerns expressed during the committee's consultations. The overall theme was that Maori communities needed to be integrally involved in addressing Maori problems and issues. *Puao-Te-Ata-Tu* argued that Maori were willing and able to assume responsibility for many of the disparate programmes and policies still primarily handled by officialdom, and pressed the government to work through, empower and resource Maori networks. Under the heading 'Guiding Principles and Objectives', the report recommended the government 'attack all forms of cultural racism in New Zealand that result in the values and lifestyles of the dominant group being regarded as superior to those of other groups, especially Maori'. To this end, it was imperative that the Crown incorporate 'the values, culture and beliefs of the Maori people in all policies developed for the future of New Zealand'.

The committee's call for the incorporation of tikanga Maori into all government policies was to have considerable ramifications in the public sector. So, too, did its stress on the need for consultation with Maori groupings. But it noted that even if all its recommendations on these matters were to be followed, the results would still be inadequate. Consultation should only be seen as a prelude to meaningful negotiations. These should lead in turn to Maori collective organisations, large and small, retaking control of their own destinies in partnership with, rather than in subordination to, the state. What was particularly needed was 'tribal responsibility' for tribal affairs, as well as other forms of autonomous control by Maori of their own lives. The report, which discussed the Treaty of Waitangi at length in an appendix, essentially urged the Crown to negotiate partnerships with traditional Maori structures, '[s]haring power and authority over use of resources'. The Minister of Social Welfare, Anne Hercus, accepted the report's findings regarding her own department, initiated a programme of change within it and set in motion processes which would result in legislative reform in 1989. These developments created, in turn, a precedent for other departments and heightened Maori expectations of fundamental change.[21]

There were, however, boundaries beyond which the Crown would not go. The rhetoric of 'equality before the law' and the realities of urbanisation which had fed into the rundown of the 'Maori courts', for example, precluded any serious chances of reviving parallel judicial institutions. In 1986, an advisory committee on legal services suggested that the Maori Land Court be restructured with a view to returning decision-making to tribal groupings. In 1988, Maori Land Court judges themselves supported tribal-based courts in a submission to the Royal Commission on Social Policy. Later that year the second part of a report commissioned by the Department of Justice, Moana Jackson's *The Maori and the Criminal Justice System: A New Perspective/He Whaipaanga Hou*, proposed an autonomous parallel justice system for Maori, using both traditional tribal concepts of justice and social management techniques. These and similar proposals current at the time were all ignored or rejected.

Organising Indigeneity

Despite state resistance to autonomy in areas such as criminal or civil justice, Maori continued seeking to affirm their identities in a variety of ways, and to empower themselves accordingly. On a local level, a name change of one rural family from English to Maori epitomised flaxroots reconstructions of Maori identity. The core members of the whanau had gathered together its scattered members in 1985 'to learn about their ancestors and kinship connections' as a prerequisite for greater agency. On a macro level, Jackson's views remained influential in Maoridom, and there were many empowerment initiatives and developments at national and pan-tribal level in these years. Koro Wetere and Sir Hepi Te Heu Heu were among those engaged in setting up the Federation of Maori Authorities as a forum for Maori resource-based trusts, incorporations and other businesses; this organisation quickly became a powerful national voice. On a cultural level, it was only after enormous Maori pressure for state recognition and protection of te reo Maori that it became an official language, following Waitangi Tribunal recommendations. An official commission was established to promote te reo Maori, and in ensuing years the Crown gradually responded to continuing pressure and supported firmer entrenchment of the Maori language and culture in the country's media.[22]

All the while, the state was increasingly prepared to talk the language of power-sharing, especially at a tribal level. While they stressed their genealogical continuity with the past, hapu and iwi had, of course, adapted to circumstances over time. The advent of the Maori Renaissance and the economic challenges that intensified from the 1970s had stimulated the strengthening and transformation of tribal and sub-tribal structures. A number of tribal enhancements and reconstructions arose out of the need to organise or reorganise to resolve historical grievances; others arose in the processes of confronting the challenges posed by heightening economic hardship. The 1980s saw, in particular, a significant revival of tribal runanga, or councils, for these and other purposes. The Crown increasingly looked to dealing with runanga in its proposed partnership arrangements with iwi, especially if the runanga members were prepared to seek and gain legally-sanctioned mandates from their constituents.

The modern runanga offered the great advantage of flexibility to suit circumstances. Tribal or sub-tribal runanga and management committees of various sorts could be large or small, reconfiguring if necessary to maximise the interests of their collectivities, both discrete and overlapping. In 1986, the five iwi of Muriwhenua established the legal body Te Runanga o Muriwhenua to prepare the Treaty claims of the Far North. Some established groupings saw breakaways occurring, including the Waikato–Tainui federation in 1988. In many areas, fragmentation of tribal management occurred as sub-iwi groups sought to organise to meet the Crown's delivery requirements. All the while, numbers of iwi were initiating ambitious plans for tribal development, some of which – such as those of Ngati Raukawa and Tainui – included establishing tertiary educational facilities. The common theme in all such developments was organisational change in the struggle for rangatiratanga.[23]

The increasing emphasis on tribal identities and tribally-based self-determination can be seen from a number of different perspectives. For many Maori, the tribal renaissance addressed a longstanding rejection of centralised, state-franchised and government-influenced structures. As the realities of urbanisation struck home, moreover, 'Māori began to question the validity of a universal Māori identity': a return to tribal roots was seen as essential after several decades of assimilationist policies and integration into urban life, weakening tribal ties, and fading knowledge of language, tribal history and tradition. Some pan-tribal structures were losing support for a variety of reasons, including those relating to efficiency or perceived compromise. Although the official voice of Maoridom had long campaigned on a broad front of issues, the NZMC was seen by many Maori as an increasingly 'inappropriate structure' for embodying rangatiratanga. This was partly a function of historical memory, given its legacy of conservative positions, its National-associated leadership and its origins in the period of assimilation and detribalisation policies. But the council had also come to be seen as less relevant, the result of such factors as Tu Tangata, the new directions from 1984 and (more generally) the Maori

Renaissance. Various pan-tribal unity movements at different levels, and efforts to operate around the concept of 'Maoritanga', had not brought recognition of rangatiratanga.

Some Maori leaders argued that the way to re-empower their people, move them out of welfare dependency and achieve rangatiratanga was to restore responsibility not only to tribal communities but also to individuals within them, and/or to pan- or non-tribal collectivities such as those which had formed in the large towns and cities. Labour ministers were predisposed towards arguments based on individualism and urbanisation, but eventually conclusions premised on the 'base of the Maori world [being] tribal' achieved primacy (although non-tribal arrangements were not precluded). These seemed to offer the best means forward because they were supported by the great majority of the Maori leadership in various discussions and negotiations with the Crown. The emerging policy of direct Crown relationships with tribal groupings was, essentially, a response to the widespread Maori view that the 'only leaps we have made have been those centred on our iwi, our hapu and our whanau'.

The Crown's growing interest in forging arrangements at iwi level had a logistical basis as well: negotiating with and devolving to iwi would be manageable in a way that dealing with literally thousands of hapu and whanau would not. Customarily, there were said to be some five dozen iwi/tribes (although the matter was more complicated than that), a handleable figure for macro-devolution purposes. What mattered at the most fundamental (and ideological) level for the government was finding the best mechanism for divesting itself of many of its previous responsibilities. Transferring 'service delivery' to iwi-based authorities was a convenient method, in return for short-term transitional investment, of cutting costs and devolving responsibility to the collectivities themselves. A collective form of self-reliance was not seen as the ideal, but urgency reinforced expediency: the Maori sector used a high proportion of welfarist resources, and the need for self-reliance was clearly going to increase with state deregulatory policies impacting most heavily on a Maori population concentrated in the non- and semi-skilled workforce.[24]

A number of Maori and other commentators argued that attaining rangatiratanga by devolving service delivery was an attempt to make use of iwi organisations rather than to empower them. They noted that the Crown's rhetoric about proactively removing economic differentials between races, so trumpeted at the time of the Hui Taumata, was being quickly replaced by free-market and non-interventionist pronouncements. Many Maori leaders, however, took consolation in the parallel official rhetoric of self-determination: as in the past, they would aim to maximise their opportunities within whatever parameters the Crown had set. Because of recent Maori pressure, these parameters were (or seemed to be) more generous than ever before.

Nevertheless, there was much debate and contestation. Some argued that state divestment of responsibility would mean Maori tribal organisations became 'dumping grounds' for the welfare programmes made all the more necessary by the socio-economic consequences of the 'New Right revolution'. A few contemporary commentators who took a Maoritanga approach (and many more, later) saw government willingness to talk the language of tribal power as a modern form of the old colonial 'divide and rule' policy. Internal tribal disputes over representation and mandating seemed to confirm that this was an effect, if not an intention, of government devolutionary policies.

For others, the situation involved no more than a supreme central authority paternalistically franchising some of its functions to Maori organisations: 'With the Government ultimately retaining power and authority, devolution programmes often delivered the *perception* of rangatiratanga more than rangatiratanga itself'. Those arguing that government intentions did not amount to any genuine form of power sharing could soon cite a number of developments. When the Crown came to implement the thrust of *Puao-Te-Ata-Tu* through the 1989 legislation, for example, it was the minister who was tasked with appointing tribal nominees to district executive committees – and many Maori communities quickly came to clash with the managers of these institutions.

Tribally-based critics noted that the government seemed prepared to interpret the word 'tribal' very loosely. Conversely, many non- or pan-tribal organisations sought to legalise their status in the hope of being recognised as an 'authority' through which devolved programmes would flow. This added broader dimensions to the 'divide and rule' argument. Some Maori and pakeha went as far as to argue that while much Labour government rhetoric implied that Maori were at last being invited to enter a 'partnership' with the Crown, the two parties were really on a collision course. In the words of one academic observer, by 1984 'New Zealand was in the embryonic stage of two separate revolutions', that of right-wing 'economic rationalism' and that of Maori revivalism. 'Both sought control over the country's economic and political sovereignty. They were set to collide whichever political party was in power.'

There can be no doubt that the Crown, primarily responsive to right-wing 'solutions' to capitalism's global crisis, sought to appropriate rangatiratanga to a market-driven environment. To do so, it redefined rangatiratanga to mean 'commercial self-governance'. This reflected a neoliberal model of indigenous development which, for many Maori, merely reconfirmed their allocated subordinacy within a state still essentially 'colonial'. Those Maori who throve in the new laissez-faire environment, many noted, tended to possess western managerial and capitalist skills, experiences and mindsets. Even 'traditional' tribal organisations, it was argued, were in danger of becoming tools for neoliberal policies if they were contemplating taking on devolved functions. For these could only be, in the final analysis, antithetical to the collective tribal ethos, especially when exercised on behalf of an extreme right-wing government and responsive to its requirements.

Notwithstanding such arguments, and misgivings based upon the economic brutality of Rogernomics, sizeable portions of the renaissant tribal leadership did opt to join discussions and negotiations. Some were fully aware that the outcomes might result only in a rangatiratanga that was both sub-sovereign and required accountability based on western business and managerial ideology. While the state's response to Maori 'assertion of economic and political power – te tino rangatiratanga' was one which 'left its [own] power intact', then, the desire of the government to divest itself of the 'burden' of Maoridom meant that meaningful autonomist gains might be made regardless of the government's motives. Maori leaders were generally confident that their organisations would be able to use their 'collective strengths, in accordance with their cultural values', to operate in ways that 'reflected their needs and circumstances'.[25]

Debating Devolution and Tribalism

The discussions and debates of the later 1980s about the intersections between Rogernomics and rangatiratanga, between devolution and duping, have raged ever since. Some participants added a twist to that main strand of original opposition to devolution which saw the devolving of authority to Maori institutions as a tool for appropriating tribal energies to the service of right-wing capitalist restructuring imperatives. Rather than devolution proposals having reflected an attempt by neoliberalism to take advantage of iwi, it was contended, tribalism had been enhanced or even 'reinvented' by new-right sympathisers within the Maori world even before Labour took office.

In such a view, the politics of cultural identity ('culturalism') obscured (and continues to obscure) the real problems faced by the majority of Maori: poverty and class oppression. A new Maori leadership was said to have emerged, one which found scope for personal advancement in reviving badly ailing tribes or inventing new ones out of the ruins of the old (or even out of nowhere). These new leaders had entered the 'middle class' in the post-war period, and found in the concept of tribalism a vehicle to further their careers in the world of business and management – one with potential access, moreover, to the resources still owned by the 'old tribes'. They opted, it was argued, to create capitalistic 'neotribes' upon the ruins of a remnant tribalism rather than campaign for Maori progress on the basis of commonalities with pakeha workers, a task for which the Maori collective outlook was particularly suited.

Such arguments had some resonance with far left positions taken in the years after the war, insofar as they elevated class over race, and even more so with the once common pakeha perspective that urbanisation and modernity had detribalised Maori. Those presenting such views claimed that, along with their pakeha supporters, Maori engaging in tribal revival and 'identity politics' were establishing 'fundamentally different social structures' from those of the 'redistributive and non-accumulatory' traditional tribes. In the 1980s, these professional Maori elites were exploring (it was argued) ways of taking these processes of retribalisation, together with associated indigenous 'identity politics', onto a new plane: the role of elites in 'the accumulatory competitive environment of capitalism' would be enhanced if they could negotiate the acquisition of state power and resources for their neotribal institutions.

Similar developments were said to have occurred among indigenous peoples in North America and elsewhere. Those who 'were to become a neotribal comprador bourgeoisie' in New Zealand through exploiting their own people were depicted as the equivalents of elite collaborators with the colonial Crown and its settlers. In such a view, the ethnicised discourses of the 1980s (and ever since) have masked class inequalities and diverted a mostly working-class population away from its best interests. With 'Bi-culturalism co-opted by [the] New Right', as the title of one article put it, tribes were said to resemble increasingly corporate agents of neotribal capitalism.

Such critiques struck at the heart of the pakeha liberal alliance with Maoritanga that had been forged during the beginnings of the Maori Renaissance. They presented the Maori leaders' exploration of devolution with the fourth Labour government as setting large numbers on pathways along which cultural 'revivalism becomes subverted within the interaction with capitalism, becoming integral to capitalist hegemony by providing the ideological concealment of the imposition of exploitative class relations'. On the allegedly false basis that contemporary tribes were the legitimate inheritors of traditional tribal forms, it was argued, the new elites gained control of Maori collectivities in the name of Treaty partnership. In subsequently gaining access to both indigenous property and Crown resources, such elites were said to have dispossessed both urban Maori and the exploited 'workers-in-community within the new tribes'. This has supposedly led to a situation where '[p]roperty-owning corporate tribes are now the structures for wealth accumulation and distribution, and for class formation', and 'capital-labour political relations' have been re-sited in 'the depoliticised mode of regulation of the tribe'. All such developments are said to have been greatly boosted as a result of the Labour government's decision to open discussions with Maori on its devolution proposals: the relatively few class-based critics, during the 1980s, of these interactions are seen to have subsequently been vindicated.

Such views have been vigorously rejected on many grounds, especially from within Maoridom – including by those who are, nevertheless, uneasy about managerialist trends within their tribal authorities. Most critics of the 'neotribe argument' would, however, concede that, with prosperity collapsing in the 1970s as a result of the retraction of the global economy, some of the new Maori professionals had worked to create new collective entities in the cities and/or turned to managerialist models and laissez-faire economics. A number had even taken neoliberal messages back to their tribal bases (which clearly existed!), determined to set their people on the capitalist path. Many of the Maori professional elites had firmly embraced the new-style Labour government and sought to maximise their advantages in the discussions and negotiations it had offered. The urban education which had assisted many indigenous New Zealanders into the activism of the Maori Renaissance, then, had taken others to positions of influence from which they sought to align tribalism, however defined and constituted, with neoliberalism.[26]

As Maori commentators and various scholars have noted, however, those claiming the existence of the capitalist neotribe, and of a 'tribal fundamentalism' that disempowers and appropriates from urbanised and modernised Maori, have exhibited a shaky hold on post-war history. For it is clear that modern tribes *are* indeed contemporary manifestations of continuously existing (if reconfiguring) tribal entities, despite the complications of urban migration. It is equally apparent that most urban-dwelling Maori of migrant background know their iwi, hapu and whanau, can and do participate in their affairs, and retain linkages with home marae. More broadly, tribal members (including those who live away from their home marae or tribal rohe) are far from the passive subjects of exploitation by 'neotribal' elites, as they have been depicted. Maori observers have noted that their own people, by free choice, opted to pursue the 'politics of indigeneity'.

They observe, too, that it was Maori collectivities which made the decision, in the wake of the Maori Renaissance, to select iwi (however subdued some tribes might have been after mid-century) as the primary vehicles of discussion and negotiation with the Crown. When they had commanded sufficient resources, the Hui Taumata had declared, Maori themselves would 'provide the most appropriate and effective programmes' for their people. Pending that eventuality, many Maori collectivities chose the tribal route for dealing with the state to assist them to acquire, increase and distribute the necessary resources. This, it was noted, was far from either 'tribal fundamentalism' or 'neotribalism'; it was self-determination.

There were (and are) many variations to the debate about how modern rangatiratanga could and should be effected. Whatever the validity of claims regarding a nexus between such actual or imagined things as 'tribal fundamentalism', neoliberalism, urban Maori disenfranchisement and neotribalism, they do serve as a reminder that interpretations based upon culture and ethnicity cannot be divorced from broader socio-economic and class considerations. The 1980s processes of seeking vehicles for incorporating rangatiratanga in major and meaningfully ways into a capitalist state, especially one buffeted by political and economic efforts to meet the demands of a national and international restructuring of capitalism, provided difficult challenges to those attempting, whatever their motivations, to empower Maori people, enhance their culture and promote their worldview.

When corporatisation entered the political agenda, an anthropologist has recently noted, the 'historic aim of Maori self-determination [was] rapidly becoming the prominent issue' in New Zealand: the movements for both rangatiratanga and economic restructuring picked up great momentum almost simultaneously. Any analysis that sees in Maori developments of the time and subsequently, however, the hidden triumph of neoliberal ideology masquerading as bicultural sensitivity can only make sense in reference to the primary devolutionary mode chosen – rather than to the aims and intents of the great majority of Maoridom. One alternative mode, the hapu, once believed by many scholars to have become virtually defunct, had its supporters as the vehicle for devolution; and the localised whanau-like organisations of Tu Tangata also worked well for their own purposes. But both Crown and Maori leaders, while not discarding the worth of large numbers of localised, district-level or regionalised 'empowerments', favoured more ambitious and overarching arrangements. Many Maori, including those in the cities, appreciated the enormous gains for rangatiratanga which it might be possible to negotiate under an iwi-based model.

In summary, to see tribal (or 'retribal') leaderships as either dupes of international capitalism or in its service might be a useful exercise for analytical purposes or for establishing hypotheses to interrogate. But it disregards or downplays a great deal of counter evidence, ignoring (for example) the huge tensions and difficulties that Maori leaders experienced when dealing with the ministers and officials pursuing the right-wing economic agenda of the fourth Labour government (and its National successor from 1990); people who had little understanding of, or empathy for, Maori autonomist aspirations and goals. Such an analysis also fails to take cognisance of Maori leaders' attempts to counteract politicians' and officials' schemes to utilise indigenous institutional forms and procedures for their own ends, which, needless to say, were little to do with rangatiratanga.

A Maori Labour minister later noted that when 'iwi organisations first started dealing with government agencies, the structure of the government tended to dictate the structure of the runanga'. Numbers of officially franchised runanga soon came to resemble 'mini-governments' which were far from 'accountable to the [Maori] community', and many of their members protested at such developments. From the beginning of the devolution discussions, in fact, the Maori struggle for 'complete authority over themselves and the country's key resources of land, fisheries, waterways and minerals' did not sit easily with the politicians and officials – however much their deregulatory pronouncements held out promise of fulfilling rangatiratanga. In the final analysis, there was a clash of worldviews, of collective versus individualist ways of doing things, between Crown and Maori, and high barriers to Maori success in the pursuit of rangatiratanga remained.[27]

Chapter 9

Principles and Partnership

The Waitangi Tribunal

The fourth Labour government's primary emphasis was on pushing through its right-wing economic policies, but it had little choice but to move to fulfil a number of the promises on social, ethnic and moral issues which it had made to its liberal pakeha and Maori supporters. The Waitangi Tribunal's 1985 acquisition of the power to address historical grievances was among the most significant and enduring legacies of this process. Tribes which had not gained settlements in the past, or whose settlements had been rendered insignificant by inflation, together with sub-tribal, pan-tribal or non-tribal Maori groupings, all saw hope for a future which included Crown acknowledgement of rangatiratanga. Many believed that the Tribunal's deliberations and recommendations might assist them in re-establishing a resource base, but this was not generally the principal aim of either Crown or claimants. The Crown desired to remove Maori grievances which were believed to be diverting Maoridom (and therefore the whole country) from socio-economic progress. The thrust of what tribes wanted was a Crown apology for its past breaches of the Treaty, and reparations that would both help promote the rebuilding of the cultural, social and political (as well as economic) strength of the claimant collectivities and embody Crown acknowledgement of the seriousness of their grievances. Most were realistic on the question of compensation, and did not expect that – however hard they fought – it would ever come to represent more than a very small amount of past losses at Crown hands.[1]

All groupings placing claims before the Tribunal sought, in essence, respect for their rangatiratanga. Success in persuading the Crown of the necessity for such respect required greater public understanding of New Zealand history, as no government would forge too far ahead of 'public opinion' on 'race issues'. Publicity for the evidence presented to the Tribunal, and for Tribunal reports themselves, assisted the development of such understanding. Liberal pakeha, organised in Project Waitangi and other groupings, began proactive education campaigns on Treaty matters aimed at the general populace, complementing the efforts of Maori organisations. Claims were accompanied by direct pressure on the government. A typical submission in mid-decade urged the government to honour the Treaty and demanded that, in seeking 'principles of partnership and bi-cultural development', it focus on the Maori version and its guarantee of te tino rangatiratanga. There was also much 'Treaty education' inside many institutions, official and non-official. The first New Zealand Conference on Social Work Education incorporated a workshop on the implications of the Treaty for social work training and a role play on the events leading up to the Treaty's signing. The Public Service Association, similarly, was soon looking to 'establish a process' whereby 'Maori and non-Maori members can discuss the Treaty'.

Throughout the 1980s, official and non-official efforts, and academic outputs, increasingly attempted to address or reflect Maori perspectives. There were a great number of initiatives aimed at 'negotiating a bicultural past' in order to produce a better present and future. Historians revised their interpretations in ways which both restored agency to Maori and outlined why the country's past did not bear out the myth of racial harmony – James Belich's *The New Zealand Wars and the Victorian Interpretation of Racial Conflict*, published in 1986, being a notable example. The judiciary began to make decisions respecting Maori positions. All such developments in turn influenced the Waitangi Tribunal, and gave increased hope to Maori collectivities that achievement of Crown recognition of rangatiratanga might now be within grasp.[2]

The Tribunal's findings against the Crown on Orakei/Bastion Point in 1987 did more than simply vindicate the occupiers' arguments and lead to Crown concessions. In setting out 'relevant principles', it went some way towards accommodating longstanding Maori interpretations of the Treaty. The old 'certainty', in the pakeha world at least, was that of unconditional Maori agreement in 1840 to cede indivisible 'sovereignty' to the Crown. This could no longer be seen as unproblematic. In Article One of the Maori version of the Treaty, 'kawanatanga' (governorship) had been used as a translation for 'sovereignty'. This had meant, in Maori eyes, something less than the transfer of indivisible sovereignty to the Crown – the more so when taken alongside Article Two's guarantee of 'full authority'/te tino rangatiratanga over land and other taonga/treasures to the Maori signatories, which was seen to imply 'more than mere possession' of tangible resources.

Differing perceptions between the parties as to the meaning of the Treaty were not unusual in a bilingual colonial document. In view of this, and reflecting the emergent Treaty-based discourses, the Tribunal believed that the 'essence' of the agreement transcended its words. The Treaty provided, in fact, not just the basis for righting the wrongs of the past, crucial as these were. Even more significantly, it was said to establish the foundation for 'a developing social contract' between Crown and Maori, one in which the parties resembled partners and were 'obliged to act reasonably and in good faith towards each other'. Later reports built upon and fine-tuned such interpretations, which were in turn taken up and re-modified in the political, bureaucratic and judicial arenas as part of an evolving set of 'Treaty principles'.[3]

Judicial Developments

A major Court of Appeal decision in June 1987 in the case of the *New Zealand Maori Council v Attorney-General* was critical to principle-based perspectives being taken seriously by the Crown. In September the previous year, the government had introduced a Bill to turn nine state establishments into 'corporatised' State-Owned Enterprises (SOEs) which would operate as fully commercial entities. Maori were concerned that transfer of land and other resources to the SOEs would jeopardise fledgling moves towards processes for Treaty-based reparations. In particular, the special value of land to Maori came into great focus. On one estimate, over half of New Zealand's land area was to be transferred to the new corporations. Maori feared that the Crown would later be unwilling to claw back land and other assets from the profit-orientated SOEs to hand over to tribes in Treaty settlements. Even more significantly, SOEs would be allowed (indeed, expected) to dispose of lands surplus to their requirements on the free market, and the Crown would then be unable to utilise them as compensation to claimant groupings. Most seriously of all, many people saw (despite the official government line) that SOEs were destined for ultimate privatisation. If this occurred, all hope of reclaiming their land from the Crown would seem to have disappeared (although the possibility remained of state purchase, on behalf of tribes, of land coming onto the market). Protests from many quarters of Maoridom, and elsewhere, were vigorous.

At the Waitangi Tribunal's Muriwhenua hearings towards the end of 1986, the claimants argued that landed assets removed from direct Crown control or Crown ownership would be unavailable for settlement. An interim report of 8 December agreed that the Bill thereby breached Treaty principles. This finding increased pressure on the Crown, and induced it to insert two new clauses into the State-Owned Enterprises Bill to protect Treaty commitments. Section 9 of the legislation (passed that same month) prohibited the Crown from acting in any manner 'inconsistent with the principles of the Treaty of Waitangi' when the SOEs were established on 1 April 1987, while section 27 protected the availability of Crown land for claims lodged prior to 18 December 1986 (the date of the Governor-General's assent to the Act).

This was an improvement but not an ideal solution, and the issues continued to be much debated in a wide range of Maori forums. The clash between the raised hopes of Maori and the right-wing policies of the government was so fundamental that the 'official channels' for the Maori voice, increasingly emboldened, joined their efforts to those of the more radical groupings. While traditionalist, 'responsible' and radical methods differed enormously, Maoridom's overarching aspiration for the realisation of rangatiratanga provided a general unity of purpose. The NZMC, in particular, had been increasingly caught up in the heightening autonomist expectations which were developing during the decade of the 1980s. Like other Maori organisations, for a long time it had been moving well beyond demands for better consultation. Its members had come to believe that a significant degree of self-determination was not just desirable but achievable, and that settlements of historical Treaty-based grievances held out hope, inter alia, for providing some material bases for future development.[4]

Headed by Graham Latimer, the New Zealand Maori Council mounted its keynote legal challenge to the Crown on 30 March 1987, seeking to buy time with a last-minute prevention of the transfer of Crown assets to SOEs. Once again, the designated voice for Maoridom was showing that, although it had been created by the Crown, it would not be cowed when matters at the heart of Maori identity and resources (especially those concerning land) were at stake. The Court of Appeal responded dramatically (and, for the government, unexpectedly) at the end of June in the first judicial pronouncement on the 'principles of the Treaty' as incorporated into statute. The *New Zealand Maori Council v Attorney-General* case, also known as the *Maori Council* or *Lands* case, was depicted by the president of the Court of Appeal as 'perhaps as important for the future of our country as any that has come before a New Zealand Court'.

The five judges unanimously confirmed the Crown's duty to uphold the principles of the Treaty of Waitangi, which, they declared, overrode all other provisions in the State-Owned Enterprises Act. The court found that there were inadequate safeguards for Maori in the processes and structures intended to regulate SOEs: protection arrangements were needed over and above section 27 of the legislation. It instructed the Crown to consult with Maori to devise ways of ensuring the Treaty principles were not violated. The court saw section 9 of the Act as embodying the central principle that the Treaty was 'akin to a partnership', with each partner to the Treaty having enduring fiduciary duties with respect to the other. The obligations of the Crown included 'active protection' of Maori interests and the resolution of Treaty breaches; Maori, in turn, had a duty to be loyal to the Queen and her government. The court was endorsing, in effect, a common bicultural partnership enterprise between state and Maori leaderships to assist New Zealand to heal the wounds of the past and to honour the Treaty in the present and future.[5]

The Court of Appeal set out parameters for the future relationship between Crown and Maori: the partners needed to 'act towards each other reasonably and with the utmost good faith', with a willingness to consult, cooperate, negotiate, adjust and, if necessary, compromise. With its ruling that, within the legislation under scrutiny, the principles of the Treaty were to take precedence over all else, the Treaty of Waitangi gained a 'new life' within the realm of New Zealand jurisprudence. While the Treaty could not be enforced in the courts unless it had been incorporated into an Act of Parliament, the judges had implied that the Treaty itself possessed some kind of constitutional status.

Beyond the central principle of seeking some kind of 'partnership', however, the 'Treaty principles' were vague. One of the judges stated that 'it cannot yet be said that there is broad general agreement as to what those principles are'. Another suggested that the Treaty 'should not be approached with the austerity of tabulated legalism', but rather demanded a 'broad, unquibbling and practical interpretation'. It might well be argued that 'the principles of the Treaty' amounted only to common-sense rules for managing cooperative relationships in which one party dominated. This itself constituted a step forward, however, especially since the vagueness of the principles effectively made the Treaty a 'living instrument'. The Treaty was evolving, and its interpretation needed to take 'account of subsequent developments of international human rights norms' and adapt to 'new and changing circumstances as they arise'.[6]

The Court of Appeal's judgment became (in)famous for its implications for the concepts of principles, partnership and 'living instrument'. It contributed greatly to the 'mythologising' (and, in some quarters, demonising) of the Treaty as a 'symbol of a bicultural nation'. In a country in which biculturalism had quickly overtaken integration/assimilation as official policy, Treaty discourse provided a central contribution to the emergence of an 'indigenous constitutional identity' for New Zealand – one which incorporated rangatiratanga. Maori took great hope, especially, from judicial and other comments which implied that the Treaty had a constitutional status that should not ordinarily be negated by legislation.

The *Maori Council* judgment, in particular, was widely seen as representing a significant advance for Maori aspirations. Hiwi Tauroa emphasised this in a book with a topically optimistic title: *Healing the Breach*. Ranginui Walker, formerly a vocal critic of the 'conservatism' of much of the the NZMC leadership, felt that the case 'pitched New Zealand firmly into the post-colonial era, from which there is no retreat. It was the beginning of decolonisation of New Zealand in the sense of dismantling hegemonic domination of the Maori by the Pakeha. No government can ever again rule Maori people while at the same time dishonouring the Treaty, for the honour of the Crown itself is at stake'. The Waitangi Tribunal followed the court's general line, helping place Treaty partnership obligations firmly on the political agenda.[7]

The *Maori Council* case was subsequently subject to searching scrutiny. In one academic strand of thought, the Court of Appeal had placed the Treaty in 'common law time', a 'time without history' characterised by principles that were 'seemingly ageless'. Another critique noted that acceptance of the judgment also meant 'accepting that sovereignty was held indisputably by the Crown', the court's authority being derived from this very concept. Some assessments concluded that 'the principles' (and negotiated measures based on them) represented a reinterpretation of the Treaty which, in reinforcing 'the essential legitimacy and stability' of the Crown, was thereby engaged in the processes of 'cementing the hegemony of the state' and 'the interests of Pakeha capital'.

But the discourse was complex. The government did use the concept of the Treaty principles to counter Maori claims (and sometimes judicial and Tribunal findings) which even implicitly challenged indivisible Crown sovereignty. However, in turn, many tribes and organisations made good use of them in pursuit of their various claims and aspirations. Other groups and analyses continued to see anything emanating from the state as tainted. Some drew the Tribunal into the pool of those institutions allegedly compromised by their very location within the state. It was said to be 'inevitable' that the Tribunal, being 'an agency of the Crown', would never contemplate challenging ultimate Crown supremacy, and so it could be no more than just another co-opting institution. By the time of a 1988 report finding against Mangonui claimants on 'public good' grounds, the Waitangi Tribunal had, Jane Kelsey argued, 'become as much a vehicle to deny tino rangatiratanga and legitimate the new treaty principles as any other judicial or government agency'.[8]

'The Treaty Principles'

Whatever the critiques of the *Maori Council* judgment and Tribunal findings, however, the focus on 'the Treaty principles' helped ensure the Crown addressed ways of seeking the 'negotiated co-existence' sought by parties representing Maori. Ongoing negotiations between Crown and tribal and other groupings became an increasing and embedded feature of Crown–Maori relations. Judicial pronouncements and Tribunal recommendations on issues of Crown–Maori partnership could, many Maori felt, help them attain a meaningful degree of devolved power. The Court-ordered negotiations resulting from the *Maori Council* case provided an early example of a compromise acceptable to the major parties involved (although not all Maori believed it went far enough).

The resulting Treaty of Waitangi (State Enterprise) Act in mid-1988 gave the Waitangi Tribunal binding powers in circumstances where it found that SOE lands (or interests in them) had been originally acquired in breach of the Treaty. The Act's 'claw back' mechanisms provided for the Tribunal to direct compulsory repurchase of land by the Crown for use in Treaty settlements, even if the properties had been on-sold to third parties (who would know of the risk, because 'memorials' would be placed on the title at purchase).

The Tribunal gained further binding powers after other court-ordered negotiations, especially following the July 1988 announcement that state forests were to be privatised. Agreement reached in July 1989 between the Crown, the NZMC and the Federation of Maori Authorities paved the way for the Crown Forest Assets Act, under which only 'cutting rights' to Crown commercial forests (as opposed to the land on which the trees grew) could be sold for the time being. In the following year, the Crown Forestry Rental Trust was set up to receive licence fees paid for the use of the land. In the event that an ownership claim to state forestry land was successful, the Maori owners would be paid the accumulated rentals relating to that land. Meanwhile, interest on the trust's holdings would be made available to assist claimants to research and prepare their claims.

The Waitangi Tribunal would refer to its binding powers sparingly, especially in the face of occasional government threats to its jurisdiction (and even its existence) if it exercised them 'irresponsibly'. But the very existence of powers of compulsion boosted its capacity (whatever the suspicions about its 'independence' in some quarters) to succour Maori aspirations. So, too, did further judicially-inspired constraints on government, sometimes as a result of actions initiated by Crown-franchised bodies other than those within the NZMC system. In 1989, the Tainui Maori Trust Board was successful in having the transfer of Crown ownership of coal to the SOE Coalcorp restrained on grounds that coal constituted an 'interest in land'. In its judgment, the court reiterated concepts of partnership and good faith. The Prime Minister's response, that the decision was an exercise in judicial activism, epitomised a widespread belief that the unelected judiciary was acting untowardly in attempting to place limits on parliamentary exercise of sovereignty. But, as some politicians themselves acknowledged, pressure from legal decisions was one of the major reasons the Crown continued to grapple with ways of addressing 'principles of the Treaty' which were now pervading many areas of official life as well as occupying much public discourse.[9]

The principles were notably being applied to water-based issues as well as to matters involving land and people. In 1986, a judicial ruling in the *Te Weehi* case, to the effect that fisheries legislation gave Maori certain Treaty-based rights, had created difficulties for the government's plans to privatise commercial fisheries. The Fisheries Amendment Act of that year introduced a Quota Management System for such fisheries, based on Individual Transferable Quotas (ITQs), but this was challenged by Maori parties for overriding and appropriating Maori interests in fishing. While the Act did explicitly recognise Maori fishing rights, these were interpreted as traditional, non-commercial rights. Moreover, with ITQs allocated on the basis of catch history, part-time commercial fishers, many of whom were Maori, were effectively excluded from the system. All in all, Maori property rights under the Treaty were said to have been breached. After the Waitangi Tribunal's request for more time for the parties to talk was ignored, claimants secured an interim injunction which led in December 1987 to a government agreement to negotiate.

Further momentum was gained by Maori parties from the findings of the Waitangi Tribunal's *Muriwhenua Fishing Report*, released on 31 May 1988. This admonished the government for failing to recognise 'tribal authority, or rangatiratanga'. The Tribunal's endorsement of a role for rangatiratanga in fishing reportedly 'astonished most Pakeha' and led to dire predictions of 'an end to fishing in New Zealand'. The government was fearful of alienating mainstream public opinion by conceding 'special privileges', while Maori negotiators (selected at a national hui) were under considerable pressure from their tribes to secure up to half of all interests in fisheries (under a definition of partnership posited on an ideal scenario of equality). An interim agreement which deferred resolution of the main issues was reached in 1989, and the resulting Maori Fisheries Act allocated ten percent of commercial fishing interests and $10 million to a new Maori Fisheries Commission, as well as making provision for local Maori fisheries (taiapure) to be managed by iwi.

This was a Crown-dominated result, with an overarching trustee body to hold assets, and ultimate control over taiapure lying with the minister. But the fact remained that legal action had led to a negotiated nationwide settlement that had taken place in the context of the principles of the Treaty and Waitangi Tribunal findings. The interim settlement provided for Maori management of fishing resources at both central and local levels, respecting rangatiratanga to a certain degree; and it presaged a more generous future settlement. This and other developments seemed to make the Tribunal bolder, and eventually (in its findings on Taranaki) it would talk firmly of autonomy being 'pivotal to the Treaty and to the partnership concept it entails'.

All the same, any negotiated settlements with Maori claimants needed to be agreed within the broad parameters of Crown sovereignty, and this made the various Crown–Maori negotiations palatable (or not too unpalatable) to the mainstream pakeha public. And even as the Tribunal steered towards accepting the rangatiratanga interpretation of the Treaty, critics declared its passage to be somewhat in the nature of a zig-zag (and sometimes a retreat). When it presented its report on the Ngai Tahu claims to a new government in 1991, for example, its 'Treaty principles' had become, in the eyes of some, 'qualified a little'. While its members reiterated previous Tribunal conclusions that the Crown's right to govern was limited by Maori Treaty rights, they also concluded that rangatiratanga was not a 'form of legal sovereignty apart from that of the Crown'; if it were, how could the Crown have been able to confirm Maori in possession of their taonga and keep the peace?

While radical elements of Maoridom criticised the Tribunal for such a stance, there was a paradigmatic logic to its perspective – as well as to regarding as 'startling' a Ngai Tahu suggestion that 'the power of Parliament is subject to the terms of the Treaty'. In any case, it had been implicit in much of the rangatiratanga discourse ever since 1840 that most Maori would accept a form of autonomy that came under the Crown's sovereigntist umbrella. Even in the exhilarating debates of the later 1980s, comparatively few Maori were seriously arguing for constitutional separatism, or even expecting equal power- or resource-sharing with the Crown. The challenge for all parties had been how to establish a meaningful relationship based on Treaty principles, one that embodied a genuine partnership. Whenever the words 'partnership' or 'principles' became too imbued with implied challenges to Crown sovereignty, the state moved to 'clarify' them.[10]

Preparing for Devolutionary Partnership

Even before the systematising of 'the principles of the Treaty' in 1987, the government had reached a crucial intersection. The tension between its free-market policies and the Maori 'demand for recognition of tino rangatiratanga' had caused it to make clear that its 'economic rationalisation' and de-statising imperatives would predominate where they clashed with Maori aspirations. In some interpretations, by late 1988 governmental support for Maori initiatives had essentially dissipated except insofar as the ministers were forced to move by judicial decree or Tribunal-led opinion. This is, however, to downplay the way deregulatory and laissez-faire policies dovetailed with devolution, and also to ignore ways in which pressure from Labour's members and supporters for it to respect the Treaty contributed to some significant Crown decisions at the time. In late 1988, for example, the government decided to set up an agency in the Department of Justice to coordinate and provide strategic advice on Treaty policy across departments, the Treaty of Waitangi Policy Unit (TOWPU; later, the Office of Treaty Settlements). Before long, the unit (which came fully into operation in early 1989) gained a highly significant new function – that of pioneering negotiations to settle historical grievances.

In general terms, however, the 'juggernaut of Rogernomics' would always attempt to mow down manifestations of rangatiratanga when they got in its way. Maori launched a strong fightback against the devastating impact on their people of neoliberal economics, aided by the courts, commissions of enquiry and pakeha sympathisers (including some working within the Crown). Many tribal and other collective groupings utilised, in such campaigns, that degree of devolved power that the Crown had conceded to date. They were encouraged by a number of developments, including the proceedings of the Royal Commission on Social Policy. Appointed in 1986, this was an attempt by the Labour government to reconcile its party's traditional emphasis on equality, income-redistribution and other 'cradle to grave' welfarist policies with its devastation of the working and social lives of great numbers of the least privileged in society.

The commission's brief, to examine New Zealand society 'from a social justice rather than an economic perspective', did help prevent Labour's support base from rebelling openly against the right-wing reforms. But its deliberations also provided a rallying point for all those concerned with issues of social justice and self-determination. When the government signalled its displeasure at the commissioners' apparent empathy with such perspectives, in 1987 the endangered commission rushed out an interim 'April Report' which provided landmark findings relevant, among other things, to indigenous aspirations. It took account of Maori perceptions about their past, present and desired relationship with the Crown, generally endorsing the huge numbers of submissions which stressed the importance to Maori of controlling their own affairs in partnership with the Crown. The heavily biculturalist report concluded that state policies and actions had so far created only an 'illusion of partnership', and this was not healthy for both Maori and society as a whole. It urged meaningful consultation on how best to embed Maori rights under what it depicted as the cornerstone of the government's relationship with Maori: the Treaty of Waitangi.[11]

The 1980s saw many and varied Maori initiatives to establish bodies with which the Crown could potentially effect partnership arrangements. Primary among them was the strengthened or renewed institution of runanga and such bodies as federative tribal groupings founded to prepare (among other things) claims before the Tribunal. It was the targeted unity of purpose among the Muriwhenua cluster of iwi which had led to the breakthrough *Muriwhenua Fishing Report* and later preparation of land claims in the far north. As well as an upsurge in runanga-and federation-based organisation, there were also a number of broad pan-tribal or non-tribal initiatives, especially in the cities. Te Whanau o Waipareira Trust, established in West Auckland in 1984 to support those who had moved from their tribal areas, looked to take responsibility for delivering health and other services to Maori. It and similar urban bodies, such as the Manukau Urban Maori Authority, accepted the reality of mass urban migration and partial detribalisation as a given, and sought to effect rangatiratanga through (especially) socio-economic progress for those permanently living in the cities. Such developments marked the beginning of a trend towards Maori groupings pursuing autonomist outcomes alternative to those located within the redress-based 'Treaty rights' discourses which had predominated within Maoridom.[12]

It was under great pressure from those engaging in such discourses, however, that the Crown was increasingly compelled to move faster on the issue of devolution. Its natural inclination, particularly as the clash between Maori well-being and the demands of Rogernomics became ever more clear, was a familiar one: to appropriate Maori institutions and energies as the best way of both deflecting pressure and pursuing state goals – especially (in this case) by devolving welfarist and other responsibilities it wished to cast off. Maori leaders were aware that the government's decision to explore autonomist 'concessions' was not rooted in any altruistic desire to effect rangatiratanga. But, as in the past, many believed that if concrete progress was to be made, they needed to work with (and attempt to push the limits of) whatever the state was placing on the table. In particular, the government's desire to reduce the role of the executive within the nation state seemed to hold out the possibility of 'new configurations of political power' which could both enhance rangatiratanga and ensure economic security for the tangata whenua, the latter being so much more necessary as a result of the impact of Rogernomics.

While politicians and officials perceived 'Article Two' arrangements as little more than self-management, then, this did not dissuade Maori from varied institutions and perspectives from reading greater potential into at least some of the many proposals under scrutiny. Entrepreneurs in tribal and urban authorities, many of whom identified rangatiratanga with economic security, argued for devolutionary arrangements which both provided resources and freed Maori authorities from state managerial control. Maori of more radical ilk continued to seek at least quasi-constitutional arrangements that could be seen implicitly to challenge the supremacy of the Crown. Engaging with the Crown in devolutionary talks was a quite separate matter from endorsing the social effects of the economic reforms, and many Maori leaders vocally opposed the suffering inflicted by government policies on working people of all ethnicities.[13]

In most quarters of Maoridom in the later 1980s, there was even greater discussion than usual of breaking free from what was seen as a largely paternalistic and anachronistic Department of Maori Affairs. Sectors of the state had not been averse to listening to such messages. As early as the mid-1960s, a senior DMA official had put his name to a statement that his department had 'a long tradition of paternal attitudes', and felt it 'probable that many Maoris would prefer to be free, even if it be to make their own mistakes'. Two decades later, such views had begun to enter the bureaucratic and political mainstream. The questions were: should the department be changed (and, if so, how) or abolished (and if so, replaced by what, if anything)?

By the end of the 1980s, Secretary for Maori Affairs Tamati Reedy was conceding that within the DMA, just as with other departments, there had traditionally been 'little recognition of Maori social structure and desire for self-determination'. While the 'wairua, mana and rangatiratanga of the Maori people [had been] able to find some expression' within the department, this had been constrained – certainly until the 'revolutionary change in direction' of Tu Tangata. From that time onwards, there had been much examination of how 'the Maori people [could] take over the management of Departmental programmes': the DMA was 'heading towards its own demise'. The ultimate dissolution of the department had, indeed, generally always been official policy, at least implicitly. Hunn had advocated phasing it out so that Maori could deal directly with 'ordinary departments'. As a scholar writing in 1971 noted, the 'long-term objective to close the department' had been premised not upon devolution but upon the achievement of 'integration (or assimilation?)'. It had remained in being in the absence of that eventuality, and as a continuingly useful expedient – one into which, for example, responsibility for New Zealand's Pacific Island territories had been placed in 1968.

By the 1980s, however, the usefulness of the institution was under considerable question. Aspects of Tu Tangata, especially those relating to tribal involvement in decision-making, had raised Maori community expectations in ways with which the DMA could not fully cope. Answers to the perceived problems of a centralised, inefficient and often unresponsive department were increasingly seen (as Reedy noted in his 1986 annual report) to lie in a system of strengthened tribal structures. The mid-1987 findings of a commission of inquiry into (the very public) humiliation of the DMA over a 'Maori Loans Affair' assisted the Crown in planning its removal. The commission's recommendation of progressive transfer of community and economic development programmes to tribal authorities wielding certain devolved state powers gelled with ideas being explored within state and Maori circles. So, too, did the suggestion that a streamlined Maori development ministry replace the multi-tasked DMA: with devolved institutions conducting operations, the new entity's functions would involve little more than overarching policy advice and Crown statutory obligations. The demise of 'the Maori Affairs' was virtually inevitable when, on 24 June 1987, Cabinet agreed that 'to achieve a true partnership between the Government and the Maori people, there had to be devolution of responsibility to the Maori people themselves for the management of Government programmes'.[14]

Utilising the evolving Treaty principles, based as they were on an ultimate ideal of 'partnership', the government now set out to develop officially-sanctioned authorities which could assume roles as (junior) partners with the Crown. It was in the many discussions which ensued that Maori leaders, ministers and officials increasingly came to believe that runanga operating at iwi level would provide the best vehicles for such purposes. Some Maori voiced misgivings that runanga institutions were about to be appropriated, while others felt that the suggested modes of incorporation outweighed potential benefits for Maori. Some who were concerned that any form of devolution under Rogernomics would foster managerialist elites which would subvert the Maori collective way of life initiated the debates which would later culminate in accusations of capitalistic neotribalism. Many argued that the government's prime motive was to divest itself of responsibility to promote equality for Maori within New Zealand society, and so could not be trusted. Others were convinced that the Crown would select as its 'partners' only those tribes and/or runanga which suited its convenience.

At the fringes of Maoridom, some argued that devolution fell so short of the full 'Maori sovereignty' which, they contended, had been promised in 1840, that it could not be contemplated in any way. Many more were concerned with more practical ramifications, believing (for example) that devolution could lead to 'a dangerous version of Pakeha-style competition' among tribal and other Maori groupings at a time when Maoridom needed to be united in its struggle against the policies which so damaged its people. Certainly, many of the urban-based Maori entities rejected the way iwi were 'privileged' by the emerging policies. All such contentions were countered by many others. The urban authority perspective, for example, was met with various arguments: the migration-based decline in tribal identification was what had widened some disparities between Maori and pakeha in the first place, and restoration and revival of tribal vitality through runanga was a way of reversing these trends; the Ratana-inspired, non-tribal unity of recent decades had done little for Maoridom; urban Maori remained members of their iwi and, as such, could participate in, and would benefit from, tribal-based programmes; and primacy of 'runanga iwi' as devolved vehicles of transference of resources and power did not preclude either sub-devolving or other modes of devolution.[15]

He Tirohanga Rangapu / Partnership Perspectives

Whatever the opposition, momentum for devolution had built up to the point where the Crown could set about planning to rapidly devolve management of its services to Maori institutions. This process was headed by the Minister of Maori Affairs, assisted by a powerful, if informal, group of Maori leaders. A Maori-staffed unit within the DMA was tasked with working out detailed proposals, and in April 1988 the Crown encapsulated its ideas in a 'Green Paper' for public discussion, *He Tirohanga Rangapu/Partnership Perspectives*. This sought to do no less than 'set out the basis, and justification, for wholesale reform of the longstanding government-Maori relationship'. Management of service delivery and a great number of social intervention programmes would be devolved to iwi, and to do so, a whole new structure for iwi–government relations needed to be created. The entire edifice and adherence to the ethos underpinning it would be overseen by the kind of small ministry recommended by the 'Maori loans commission'. This would replace the DMA and superintend transfer of some of its programmes to mainstream departments, but it would not be an 'operational' division of government.

The Green Paper received huge publicity, and was considered a 'watershed' report for its restructuring proposals for Crown–Maori relations and its suggestion of a new policy framework for the relationship. Maori responses, however, were mixed. Many told a consultation team of officials headed by Rauru Kirikiri of their distrust of the Crown's motives and their concerns about the proposed tight Crown control of processes and outcomes. There was opposition from hapu and urban groups to the Crown's insistence on dealing with providers at iwi level. Some submissions expressed doubts about iwi capacity to deliver devolved services, given a suspiciously rapid timeframe allowing for little preparation or forward resourcing. Moreover, the Green Paper paid little attention to such crucial matters as how iwi were to provide for members outside their rohe (because of urbanisation, that often meant many or even most of them); the way in which iwi authorities would relate to Maori from other tribes who had migrated to their rohe; and the cross-iwi membership of so many Maori.

However, few Maori wanted the government to reverse the self-deterministic direction in which it was travelling, and the principles underpinning *Partnership Perspectives* were generally endorsed in more than 70 formal hui, many other forums and hundreds of written submissions. Respondents were almost universally critical, however, of the intention to 'mainstream' the various DMA programmes, including housing, to general government departments upon the abolition of Maori Affairs. Such plans were seen as evidence of the retention of assimilationist impulses within government, however devolutionary the new policy thrust. Many Maori felt that, despite the DMA's inadequacies, a dedicated department for all Maori affairs was far more likely than 'ordinary' departments to pay attention to the needs of tangata whenua.

The DMA's pending abolition, then, was seen as certain to compound the adverse effects of Rogernomics on the Maori people. Losing the some 350 community officers who had acted as mediators between Maori and government, for example, would be a hard blow to bear. The NZMC summed up the view of many respondents by depicting the need for an official institution acting as a buffer and facilitator between the Crown and Maori, one that could negotiate and mediate between the two parties to the Treaty in ways in which a small policy ministry could not (and was not designed to).

The DMA, or preferably a reformed version of it, seemed necessary for both continuing the fight against assimilative government impulses and helping ensure that devolution processes worked in Maori favour. Individual iwi authorities would be too under-resourced or preoccupied to be able to combat sidelining of Maori interests without the facilitational and operational help such a department could provide. Retention of the DMA or something like it would be all the more important if – as many Maori suspected – devolution represented mostly a transfer of a welfarist servicing burden 'to the clients themselves' rather than any real transfer of power. In this view, the key motivation for the Green Paper's devolving of operational responsibility to iwi was to procure cheap but accountable 'service delivery' to an ethnic grouping which 'consumed' a disproportionate amount of welfare spending. Messages coming from within government seemed to provide support to such an interpretation. When asked if the government would really 'relinquish ultimate control of the purse strings to iwi', Prime Minister Lange riposted: 'No more to the iwis than to the Rotary club'.

In presenting suggested mechanisms for incorporating rangatiratanga into the body politic, however, the Green Paper did effectively define Crown respect for rangatiratanga as enabling Maori to manage their own affairs. This, it could be argued, was already happening – all that would occur in addition was a transfer of extra resources and (especially) responsibilities to iwi-level organisations. Thus the present and proposed mechanisms of rangatiratanga arguably promised little more than a perpetuation of the uneven partnership of the past, with one party heavily dominant and the other largely subservient. Along with much approval in principle for devolution, then, came many criticisms of its suggested modes and motivations. One commentator even compared the Green Paper to the Hunn report for allegedly having similar assimilationist intent: it was 'dishonest, deceitful and dismissive of Maori rights to rangatiratanga'. Once again, many felt, the Crown was about to appropriate tribal structures and energies mostly to suit itself, interfering more deeply than ever in internal tribal affairs in the process.[16]

Widespread scepticism and opposition built upon both the collective memory of a long history of Crown appropriations and observation of the ideological impulses behind the government's new-right policies. Despite this, and bearing it in mind, many improvements to the proposals were worked on, and strategies were also developed to supplement or complement the Green Paper's devolutionary model. The NZMC, for example, supported Whatarangi Winiata's revival of the idea of a Maori parliament to handle Maori matters in Maori ways. As with demands for a separate legal system, such a stance was said by politicians and their advisers to be unworkable, in part because Maori did not live in spatial or marital isolation from pakeha. The Crown, in rejecting this as well as many other ideas, was determined to restructure along the lines of the thrust of *Partnership Perspectives*. It quickly became clear that critics of the Green Paper would be able to do little more than gain some relatively small alterations to its blueprint for partnership through 'devolution to iwi'.

Te Urupare Rangapu/Partnership Response

A post-consultation ('White Paper') policy statement, *Te Urupare Rangapu/Partnership Response*, was released in November 1988. It noted that the Green Paper submissions had endorsed the principle of horizontal partnerships between Crown and Maori bodies to replace the old vertical relationships. In meeting criticism of the Green Paper's details, it offered extra incentives for the establishment of officially franchised iwi-level runanga – greater state resourcing, for example, to strengthen the 'operational base' of iwi opting into the system. It proposed that while a policy-focussed ministry would still replace the DMA, the latter's existing operational and service provisions would pass to a new but temporary body, the Iwi Transition Agency (ITA)/Te Tira Ahu Ihu (Te TAI). Over a five year period, ITA/Te TAI would both supervise the transfer of responsibility for programmes to mainstream departments and help foster iwi independence and self-reliance.

The transitional body would help tribes to 'develop their own structures – with their own administrative procedures, negotiating skills and measures of performances – so that they can make their own decisions about what is important to them'. This allayed some fears. Even a number of those who felt that the White Paper's package had been, from a rangatiratanga perspective, a political sleight of hand now believed that it was preferable for iwi to engage with the plans rather than spurn them altogether. It seemed possible that at least a degree of meaningful rangatiratanga could be effected out of what was being proffered. A consultation exercise (albeit smaller than that for the Green Paper) found iwi generally ready to cooperate with the devolving of government funds and responsibilities along the lines suggested, and a Devolution Implementation Committee was established.

Under the Maori Affairs Restructuring Act of 1989, the new policy advice and monitoring ministry, Manatu Maori/Ministry of Maori Affairs, came into being on 1 July that year. Its mission statement tasked it with giving 'substance to the principle of partnership embodied in the Treaty of Waitangi by generating an environment which encourages Maori people to express their rangatiratanga'. But, significantly, this was qualified by the words: 'in ways that enhance New Zealand's economic, social, and cultural life'. The Crown would remain the judge of how to meet this caveat. When ITA/Te TAI came into existence on 1 October 1989 and began preparing the way for devolution, iwi wanting to opt into the new system found themselves required to comply with strict operational and policy guidelines. Funding would only be forthcoming if they adhered to reporting, accountability and audit procedures that had been approved by government. Critics argued that rangatiratanga was thus 'reduced to an "autonomy" that was granted in accordance with Government edicts', and 'partnership' seemed to imply yet further Maori subordination to the Crown. The Hui Taumata's call for fundamentally renegotiating the profoundly uneven relationship between Crown and Maori had not, in many eyes, been heeded.[17]

Principles for Crown Action on the Treaty of Waitangi

Whatever the truth about the devolution scheme, no one could gainsay that the fourth Labour government had been taking the Treaty of Waitangi far more seriously than had its predecessors. The State Services Act in 1988 instructed public servants to incorporate Treaty principles into their policies and operations. The decision late that year to appoint academic lawyer Alex Frame to establish TOWPU to coordinate, strategise and provide advice on Treaty issues within the state sector followed increasing pressure from Maori for the government to clarify and improve its Treaty policies. The government, in turn, had been particularly concerned with the potential destabilisation that land and fishing claims could cause the political economy if they were not properly managed. In July 1989, the government released the *Principles for Crown Action on the Treaty of Waitangi* with the aim of providing transparency over its operational principles for Crown–Maori relations.

The document presented five principles: kawanatanga, or government; rangatiratanga, or self management; equality; cooperation; and redress. These drew upon and elaborated current thinking within the Crown on ways of 'honouring the Treaty', a culmination of the rapid developments of the previous few years. The *Crown Action* principles confirmed explicitly for the first time the need for compensation for historical grievances, incorporated judicial and Tribunal pronouncements, stressed the need for good-faith cooperation between Crown and Maori and recognised the need to work towards Crown–Maori partnership. Taken together, they constituted a policy breakthrough, although they fell short of what many had hoped for: 'partnership' itself was not explicitly identified as a principle, for example, but as an aspiration; and while Article One's kawanatanga was said to be qualified by Article Two's rangatiratanga, the 'balance between the two' was seen as a matter for 'case by case consideration'.

Some critics noted that the new policy statement was more cautious than specific judicial and Tribunal pronouncements. Others remarked that, in effect, it reiterated interpretations coming from the Prime Minister, the DMA (for example, in *He Tirohanga Rangapu*) and other state sources that Article Two required little more than the Crown acknowledging the fait accompli of iwi self-management. This was, on the surface, consonant with fledgling ILO Convention 169's aim of promoting control by indigenous people 'over their own institutions, ways of life and economic development'. But it was seen as falling short of the aspirations of Maori people themselves, which had been better encapsulated in the words of the 1987 United Nations Indigenous People's Preparatory Meeting in Geneva. This had endorsed the right of indigenes 'to self-determination, by virtue of which they have the right to whatever degree of autonomy or self-government they choose'. What the Crown was offering in New Zealand, by contrast, appeared to critics to be a very limited autonomy, a resiling from previous commitments to respect 'a claimant group's rangatiratanga and right to organise themselves as they see fit'. Overarching such critiques was an assessment that the government understood rangatiratanga as something to be delegated rather than something that was 'inherently legitimate'.

When commentators attacked the *Principles for Crown Action* for supposedly turning court and Tribunal findings on the Treaty to state advantage, the Crown riposted that it did not seek to reinterpret the Treaty principles developed by the Waitangi Tribunal and the judiciary; rather, it addressed them respectfully, and was now indicating how it intended to apply them. Some sectors of Maoridom accepted this. Others continued to express fears that the political executive was engaging in 'a deliberate and cynical move to redefine the Treaty' or, at very least, to contain expectations aroused by judicial and other developments over the previous few years. They claimed that when Labour's Treaty policies had become an economic and political liability, its commitment to te tino rangatiratanga had waned. Indicating how it would *act* on the emerging principles was tantamount to dictating the terms of engagement. The government, it was widely alleged, had retreated from promises to provide means for Maori to fulfil their dream of autonomy. Whatever the *Principles for Crown Action* said about Article One being qualified by Article Two, the document was seen to have 'signalled the supremacy of the

Crown' in a way that amounted to 'an assertion of government control over the Treaty discourse'.[18]

Accusations of government reticence about aspects of evolving judicial-based principles seemed confirmed when, in January 1990, Lange's replacement as Prime Minister, Geoffrey Palmer, reasserted the rights of Parliament over and above those of the judiciary: 'the Government', he said, 'will make the final decisions on treaty issues'. This was not a surprising statement for the leading figure in a 'parliamentary democracy' to make, but it was uttered in a context which suggested to critics a resiling from the full ramifications of honouring the Treaty. Nonetheless, large numbers of Maori and pakeha alike continued to see in the *Principles for Crown Action* a major statement of intent to honour the Treaty that could be utilised in the services of rangatiratanga. While many felt that the policy statement itself constituted a back-off from partnership, others took comfort in the Crown declaring that it did not think that 'partnership' could be created by decree but needed to emerge organically out of cooperation. The *Principles for Crown Action* had not only tempered the previous stance of the Crown on 'indivisible sovereignty', but the five principles had given Maori significant guidelines to work within – including to develop the devolution proposals.

These principles, in fact, proved to have great durability. Although the National Party pledged to rescind them in the 1990 election campaign, this did not happen after its victory at the polls that October. When National leaders realised that they could not discard the Treaty, they and their officials used the principles as guidelines when developing a number of policy strategies which incorporated advances for Maori, such as those outlined in Social Welfare's *Te Punga O Matahorua* in 1994. Although later 'supplemented', the *Principles for Crown Action* provided longstanding guidelines for the state that could continue to be put to good use by Maori and supporters of Maori causes. When, in 2004, the Labour-led government's Coordinating Minister for Race Relations declared 'We are all New Zealanders now', he balanced his advocacy for pakeha indigeneity by stressing the continuing significance of the Crown's 1989 'action principles'. While commentators continued to declare that the *Principles for Crown Action* straitjacketed progress towards meeting Maori aspirations – even that it trapped Maori within the dominant discourse of Crown sovereignty, and so denied rangatiratanga – others noted that the guidelines in the document enabled pro-Maori policies to be endorsed even in otherwise unpropitious times.[19]

Most dramatically, the *Principles for Crown Action* furnished a context for the Crown to address seriously the case for reparations for proven historical grievances. Tribes had long sought acknowledgement of, and apology for, the colonial injustices inflicted upon them. Many now looked as well to compensation to help provide a base for rebuilding rangatiratanga, often in conjunction with resources to be conferred by devolution. The stress in the *Principles for Crown Action* on redress of historical grievances held out exciting new prospects at a time when Tribunal reports had yet to lead to significant reparational negotiations. The official 1990 sesquicentennial commemoration of the signing of the Treaty of Waitangi built on the 1989 policy statement in its celebration of the Treaty as a 'living document' that was a 'symbol of our life together as a nation'. The Treaty was officially described as a 'pact of partnership... which continues to act as a national symbol of unity and understanding between cultures'. There was extensive promotion of a distinctively bicultural 'national identity', with advertising campaigns attempting 'to capture the spirit of the two peoples, pakeha and Maori, in one nation'. In recent years, the official statements argued, 'major and irreversible adjustments had been made within New Zealand society'.

In these processes, Maori leaders and their perspectives, and judicial and other pronouncements from within the state machinery, had all enjoyed remarkably high profile. Over a decade and a half, in the words of lawyer Paul Temm, Treaty matters had come 'into the forefront of public discussion and debate'. Along the way, for him (and many others) the Waitangi Tribunal had become (as he indicated in the subtitle of a book) 'the conscience of the nation'. However much it was criticised, the *Principles for Crown Action* had encapsulated official responses to the social, cultural and ideological movement that had occurred within Maoridom. Later governments could cite its guidelines to justify resisting pressures to modify some of the concessions made in the 1970s and 1980s. Likewise, when confronted with attempts to ignore their views, Maori could always point powerfully (though not always successfully) to the Crown's very own 'action principles'.

The 1989 document, then, provided a mechanism for calling governments to account, and embodied an official statement of intent to address the circumstances which had marginalised the Maori voice. The *Principles for Crown Action* provided guidelines for ways of both compensating for that marginalisation and reversing it – a task summed up at Waitangi in 1990 by the Maori Anglican Bishop Whakahuihui Vercoe, in an address in front of the Queen that was essentially a call for official respect for rangatiratanga. The restoration of at least a significant degree of autonomy no longer seemed an impossible dream. Even Maori activists considered by many to be ultra-radical, such as Moana Jackson, had been talking the language of attainable reconciliation: 'Maori do not wish to be separatist. They want to be side by side, and be free to determine their own destiny.'[20]

The Runanga Iwi Act

In December 1989, the Runanga Iwi Bill was introduced, presenting a framework for devolution which 'acknowledged the enduring, traditional significance and importance of iwi', with legally incorporated runanga to become the administrative wings of the tribes. Responsible for devolved government services to their members, in order to gain official recognition these runanga iwi would be required to meet various criteria, such as possessing authenticated boundaries and appropriate financial structures. Of the 138 public submissions on the initial draft of the Bill, many argued that the proposals were inadequate as they sat fully within a framework of indivisible Crown sovereignty: at most, as in the *Principles for Crown Action*, the degree of autonomy to be accorded runanga seemed to be little more than that possessed by local government. Even the Iwi Transition Agency declared that iwi were 'not perceived as governmental or jurisdictional authorities in their own right – as required by the Treaty'.

More specifically, critics opposed the Bill's prescriptive definitions of how iwi were to operate, and claimed that its system 'impinged on the rights of iwi to make decisions outside the runanga structure as defined in the Bill'. Some argued that 'divide and rule' strategies underpinned the legislation, with iwi about to find themselves in competition with other tribes for scarce Crown resources – not to mention the fact that the urban Maori authorities and pan-tribal organisations were far from happy with the emphasis on iwi-based runanga. Within the non-tribal Ratana movement, reportedly, there was consternation that – yet again – Labour had taken little interest in the perspectives of its political partner. Although there was little historical analysis, some commentators implicitly suggested that the Crown was doing what it had done throughout the twentieth century, appropriating Maori organisational forms for its own purposes without any really meaningful concessions. Nine decades on from the Maori councils, and despite the now limited utility of the official committee concept introduced in 1945, for some critics little seemed to have changed. The only real difference they could see was that the Crown was now resourcing institutions deemed to offer governance at iwi level (although a very few would note that this had been the case with the official runanga of the 1860s). Whatever the details of the proposals, the central government could, in the final analysis, cancel any or all devolved powers; full rangatiratanga still seemed far away.[21]

There was, however, considerable, if guarded, optimism in many Maori quarters. This was boosted when it became clear that the Crown was at last prepared to acknowledge its past breaches of the Treaty. Even the

Queen, speaking on Waitangi Day at the Treaty Grounds during the 1990 commemoration, declared (of course, on official advice) that the Treaty had been 'imperfectly observed'. The cautious optimism of Maoridom was encapsulated in a 1990 book which, while not downplaying the problems, predicted that the two 'Treaty partners' could soon be governing New Zealand 'in ways that respect the different bases from which they draw their authority'. Meaningful changes were predicted with regard to governance and resourcing, even if they might go nowhere near far enough to meeting the requirements of full rangatiratanga.[22]

Pragmatic in their response to the likelihood of little fundamental change in the accountability provisions of the Runanga Iwi Bill, 'iwi up and down the country established runanga' or reconstructed existing ones to fit the official criteria. When the Runanga Iwi Act (RIA) was passed in 1990 (becoming operative from 28 August), it reflected some attempt to be more generous and less prescriptive, and references to the principles of the Treaty of Waitangi were now included. But many Maori commented on how restrictive it remained, noting, for example, that it made few concessions to the various submissions made to the politicians which had sought greater autonomous power for Maori organisations.

While critics were often realistic about the fact that the 'authorised voices' for iwi could possess only that power granted them by the state, many were unimpressed by the ways in which they were to be strictly monitored by it. In the first place, in order to acquire the legal mandate to deliver government-funded social, economic and cultural programmes for their people, iwi were required to meet stiff prerequisites relating to their constitution and operational systems. They were to be business entities, obliged to adopt a corporate model of management along the lines of that which the government had been implementing in the public sector. The statised runanga would embody the longstanding 'legal fiction' of 'incorporation', by which 'a body of individual persons … is regarded by law as being in itself a person', and the franchising of such 'legal personalities' would be strictly within parameters which reflected the Crown's own goals and intentions. There was one significant difference between the Bill and the Act, however. Politicians had taken into account opposition to a mono-institutional delivery system for services to Maori: the 'authorised voice' of a Maori collectivity could now be a body other than a runanga, such as a trust board or marae committee.[23]

But the government's concessions amidst its claims to have addressed self-determination issues were seen by critics as 'a convenient vehicle to sell the policy to Maori'. Many took up past criticisms of the Crown's intentions, claiming that 'a general government fixation with corporatization and a social marketplace, had animated the policy' behind the RIA. Even the limited concept of tribal self-management had come down to a set of official rules as to how Maori should be organised to 'control themselves'. On the other hand, some Maori leaders and observers appreciated the Crown's difficulties, especially since it had the pakeha public to consider, and felt that it could not have gone much further in the direction of rangatiratanga at that time. While the mandating processes could have been improved, it was difficult to conceive of any alternative to official certification when public monies and powers were involved. Moreover, given the substantial weakening of tribal bonds since the nineteenth century, it was often not at all clear which groupings or organisations were the appropriate ones to represent the Maori voice in a given area.[24]

That being said, few believed that the delivery of services to tribal organisations involved 'any fundamental change in the prevailing distribution of power'. Runanga iwi status was 'a concession by, and a creation of, the State' that was 'limited, conditional and revocable', a modern form of the old practice of appropriation by the state of Maori structures. To be sure, the proposed partnership was a less unequal one than in the 1860s, the 1900s, the 1940s or the 1960s–70s. But one party was designated a 'partner' to deliver services rather than decisions, and to operate under the other's rules and right of veto.

The Minister of State Services, while claiming that the Act reflected 'our desire for real partnership in Maori development', expressed a political truism when he noted that it was not realistic for government to do other than retain 'the responsibilities to set the basic course and to manage the overall process'. It might well be argued that no other conceivable government configuration at the time could have gone further to meet Maori aspirations for rangatiratanga; that iwi authorities needed, given the very nature of the New Zealand polity and its dominant culture and ethnicity, to be firmly accountable to Parliament and under close Crown direction. Whatever the case, as things turned out, the policies and principles of 1989–90 would be the closest Maori ever got in the twentieth century to institutions embodying some form of partnership with the Crown.[25]

Tribal Assertion and Pan-tribal Unity

Some iwi and other organisations had refused, on rangatiratanga grounds, to undergo the scrutiny required by the Labour government in order to gain official mandates for various purposes, and they were prepared to pay the price of their independence. Others had been initially franchised to provide some services, but had later refused to be named as 'agent[s] of the Crown', with the consequent lapse of the arrangements. Debate on the issues was rife within Maoridom. In the Far North, for example, a number of elders reportedly 'argued with trust boards, runanga and the Maori Council' that marae should resist being forced to produce state-required 'constitutions, even though it meant turning their back on Government dollars'. All around New Zealand, kaumatua, kuia and other tribal leaders had long felt that to accept state funding and to opt into its legal structures, values and agreements was to accept western political and cultural hegemony. In the words of one tribal leader: 'if you take their money you become their ... servants. You end up with the Government telling Maori how to run their lives'.

Tribes operating officially-franchised governance mechanisms would also at times draw a line, as with Tainui after the time in 1988 when trust boards were finally empowered to enter into contracts with the Crown. Following media-led public opposition to the way MANA, MACCESS and other programmes were being run, the government had sought tighter accountability for such contractual expenditure. The Tainui Maori Trust Board, believing that it was being required to enter a master-servant relationship, refused to sign new contracts; these, it declared, did not incorporate any real concept of partnership. Now, many critics were arguing, the master-servant situation had worsened. Given that power had remained, actually or potentially, firmly in state hands under the various proposals to devolve service delivery, the Crown was really promoting 'institutional assimilation' through its much touted partnership with runanga iwi; this, it was claimed, was a denial of rangatiratanga rather than progress towards it.[26]

The proposals for devolution of state functions to iwi-based runanga had intensified the debate and soul searching about the means to, and ends of, rangatiratanga. A number of Maori leaders, both those for and against the Crown's plans, had felt the need to counteract one potential outcome of the government's tribal focus: internal strife within Maoridom, given that its various collectivities, inside and across rohe, would be compelled to compete for government mandating and funding. Because the renaissance had been a Maori-wide one, broader than the sum of its tribal parts, there were now a number of proposals to revive some sort of pan-tribal organisation that could deal with the Crown, untrammelled by any state connections of any nature at all. Not only would a new and independent kotahitanga have to stretch beyond any of the existing unity movements, many argued, it also needed to be untainted by past tribal and other configurations: all significant tribes should be able to feel comfortable about opting in. In other words, something quite new – as opposed to, say, a widening of Kingitanga – was required. After many discussions within Maori leaderships, a representative intertribal Hui Rangatira was convened by Sir Hepi Te Heu Heu, paramount chief of Tuwharetoa, on 23 June 1989 at Taupo.

The gathering stressed that total independence from the Crown was as important as pan-tribal unity. This was 'the obvious response to a government that directed rather than listened to the people'. Hui-franchised discussions on a proposed pan-tribal body progressed over the ensuing months, at a time when the major changes in the Crown's Maori policy and structures were being planned and implemented. On 14 July 1990, the National Maori Congress (NMC; later, the Maori Congress) was founded. Regular meetings would be held in different locations, as with the late nineteenth-century Kotahitanga movement, providing opportunities for addressing cultural and political issues of concern to all Maori. Unlike the NZMC, the congress would refuse all state funding, with iwi contributing the resources necessary to sustain its administration and other expenses.

The NMC was widely seen at the time as an expression of kotahitanga which held great potential precisely *because* it was an 'autonomous Māori development'. Some even hoped that it might constitute the embryo of a Maori nation state. From the time the new pan-tribal grouping had been first mooted, the Crown saw both difficulties and opportunities in the proposal. A completely independent initiative promised a strong rangatiratanga-based challenge to the state, but it might also offer consultational and safety-valve opportunities. True to form, elements within the state noted that the new body might even hold out prospects for the Crown to co-opt or appropriate some of its expertise and energies. The Iwi Transition Agency, for example, entered into discussions with the congress on the possibility of government funding for a national Maori organisation able to assist iwi in their new service-delivery role. The NMC's insistence on financial and well as political independence, however, quite apart from its criticism of the lack of rangatiratanga embodied in the devolution system, quickly put paid to any such suggestion.

While the NZMC remained the 'official channel' for transmitting the Maori point of view, the new congress quickly came to present a united front to the Crown on a number of key issues, and soon all major tribes were participating in its deliberations to a greater or lesser degree. Meanwhile, tribal and other collectivities continued developing their own relationships with the Crown. Each of these had its own dynamic and concerns. Ngati Awa, for example, had restructured itself during its preparations for obtaining historical justice, and on the day its new runanga was established (late in 1988) the tribe secured a pardon for ancestors unjustly executed during the Anglo-Maori Wars. By 1990, Ngati Awa not only felt ready to assert 'tikanga Maori in our territory', it was also putting the Crown under pressure to provide reparations for land confiscations.

The major aim was to overcome, in the words of tribal leader Hirini Mead, the legacy of 'a pretty sullen, disorganised and very oppressed people who carried a heavy sense of being unfairly treated by the government and people of New Zealand'. The iwi's claims for reparations began to meet with a degree of success, as did those of some tribes elsewhere. In sesquicentennial year, Ngati Awa gained back a significant farming operation situated on confiscated lands, and discussions over its reparations package would eventually lead to it regaining possession of its magnificent Mataatua Wharenui in addition to land and other resources. With their radio station, investment company and other development initiatives, Mead believed, the people of Ngati Awa were 'shaking off the shackles of feeling oppressed and put down and rising up to meet the challenges of today's world'. There was 'a new mood taking over our iwi'.[27]

Chapter 10

Rangatiratanga: the Continuing Quest

The National Government's 'Middle Way'

From the turn of the decade onwards, an increasing stress in Crown–Maori relations on what seemed most achievable – compensation for past injustice – may have misled many pakeha over the ultimate aspirations of the tangata whenua. Maori observers and commentators, however, noted (and would continue to note) that 'reconciling Aotearoa with New Zealand' had required more than Treaty-based compensation. It needed to seriously address Maori aspirations for constitutional or other arrangements to embed rangatiratanga and, relatedly, partnership with the Crown. A Maori leader, soon to be Race Relations Conciliator, sought in his manifesto for the 1990 commemoration 'a majority Pakeha ... acceptance of the Treaty covenants' between the two partners. Sizeable portions of pakeha society had been influenced by the Maori Renaissance, but support for Maori had tended to focus on removing socio-economic disadvantage and supporting their cultural assertions – and for some, 'righting past wrongs' through providing compensation. In 'the pakeha world', it was mostly Crown and left-of-centre circles which were au fait with the language of autonomy, self-determination and even nationhood which permeated most Maori statements on the Treaty.

Insofar as there was any movement of opinion in 'mainstream' society in the later 1980s, moreover, it seemed to be one of intermittent backlash against Crown efforts to address Maori grievances, and the National opposition had pitched its appeal to such sentiments. Much political mileage was gained when one of its prominent MPs, Winston Peters, advocated (despite being of Maori lineage) repealing recognition of Treaty principles in legislation and scaling down the Waitangi Tribunal. Traditionally inclined to 'play the race card' and with a general election approaching, in 1990 the National Party began actively promoting a message of 'one nation, one law'. Any state assistance to Maori was to be based on 'need and not race'.

When National was elected into office that October, the prospects of retaining most of Labour's concessions to rangatiratanga looked far from promising. A number of the new ministers abhorred any form of officially-franchised 'separatism' as both socially divisive and inconsistent with the realities of everyday life. They wanted Maori to 'participate equally in the newly created competitive environment', without any kind of special relationship with the Crown. The new government sought to extend the anti-welfarism and laissez-faire political agendas of its Labour predecessor, and layered its anti-Treaty populism into such plans. There was, accordingly, soon to be a considerable degree of official resiling from 'biculturalism', and even a return to some of the assimilationist-tinged policies of the past.

In particular, the new Minister of Maori Affairs, Peters, made it a priority to repeal the Runanga Iwi Act, removing any concept that iwi were officially-franchised partners of the Crown. The sizeable degree of devolution under the RIA, in his view, was seriously flawed in theory. It was also seen to be defective in practice: runanga were said to be nowhere near to a position to manage sizeable state assets and functions. The Runanga Iwi Act Repeal Act was passed in May 1991. Even Maori who had considered the RIA to be of only limited use (or almost none at all) opposed its repeal on the grounds that the new government's agenda was so clearly anti-autonomist. It was a re-run of the abolition of the DMA – few Maori particularly liked it, but it was better than nothing and could well be improved through structural and conceptual reform. The RIA was viewed, then, as having a number of useful qualities and potentialities as well as flaws. Some of the former opponents of its mandating processes, in fact, came to believe that many later problems relating to Maori representation, which were often to delay reparational negotiations and settlements, may have been avoided had the RIA been retained or reformed.

Despite the abolition of officialised runanga, moreover, the government refused to re-establish an operational equivalent to the old DMA to ensure provision of services that were no longer to be devolved to 'runanga iwi'. National's emphasis was to be on 'mainstreaming' service delivery to Maori. Essentially, there were to be no Maori-specific operational structures responsible for Maori issues or well-being, except for those which were not able to be dispensed with for legal or political reasons – such as the Maori Land Court, the Maori Trustee and the Waitangi Tribunal. Each government department would deal with Maori just the same as if they were pakeha, although there would be monitoring and policy advice from the now small 'Maori bureaucracy' to make sure that Maori were not disadvantaged through any kind of institutional racism. In the new political climate, any moves towards Maori autonomy would seemingly have to develop both outside of Crown structures and without major assistance from the state – except insofar as the future possibility of reparations held out hope for developing tribal and other resource bases.[1]

But the new government of Jim Bolger could not avoid the fact that it was working within post-assimilation social parameters, whatever its stress on 'one nation'. It was clearly a dubious proposition that mainstreaming could, at least quickly, address the many issues faced within Maoridom, both socio-economic and those pertaining to other matters such as public order in urban spaces. Placing greater emphasis on contracting out service-delivery tasks to private organisations, already firmly on National's minimal-state agenda, might work better for both Crown and Maori interests: as with Tu Tangata and subsequent arrangements, iwi or similar organisations could become, as much as any other organisation, providers on behalf of the state. Whatever the case, it was clear that simplistic election slogans were no basis for planning the next steps in Crown–Maori relations, and Maori cooperation would be needed in their formulation and implementation. In January 1991, with all these factors in mind, Peters established a Ministerial Planning Group to make recommendations on the future of Maori policy. Its report, *Ka Awatea*, 'was designed to steer a course between devolution to iwi and complete mainstreaming of service delivery to Maori through the general government system'.

The report had mixed messages. In its interventionist mode, it proposed replacing Manatu Maori and the Iwi Transition Agency with a Ministry of Maori Development, which would play a 'significant role in the proactive development of Maori policy'. The new ministry would focus particularly on education, health, training and economic resource management, addressing the large statistical gulf between Maori and pakeha in such crucial matters. *Ka Awatea* envisaged various interventionist measures to deal with Maori socio-economic disadvantage, and recommended that the government 'retain resources and the means of delivering those resources, in order to be able to directly target areas of concern' within Maoridom.

In its hands-off mode, the report confirmed mainstreaming, but put greater emphasis on the contracting out of programme delivery. Both socio-economic development and provision of welfarist services would be organised around the private sector rather than around Crown franchising of iwi. Though iwi which chose to form legal corporate entities would be encouraged to participate in tendering processes, contracted service delivery would no longer be posited upon a systematised incorporation of tribal authorities into the state system.

The Ministerial Planning Group had given consideration to the Treaty of Waitangi, however, and its report reflected a general belief in a distinct place in New Zealand society for Maori culture. In some interpretations, at least, it recognised Maori aspirations for rangatiratanga. It equated a 'right to self development' for iwi with the 'right of self determination' guaranteed under the United Nations' Draft Declaration of Principles of Indigenous Rights. It proposed that Article Two of the Treaty be met by enabling Maori to 'retain and control their resources and manage these in whatever manner they choose'.

One of *Ka Awatea*'s authors was later to assert that the report called for state support 'to assist the Maori goal of self-determination'. It allegedly offered something better than Labour's runanga iwi 'self-management' package, given that the provisions of the RIA had fallen far short of the 'handing over of resources, with no strings attached'. Seeking a way of meeting Maori wishes that accommodated National's mainstreaming agenda, integrationist impulses, anti-welfarism and right-wing socio-economic policies, the authors had supposedly come up with a 'middle way' form of rangatiratanga. The state would continue to assign service-delivery functions, via tendering processes, to iwi and other Maori organisations, but in such a way that there would be no constitutional or even quasi-constitutional implications: Maori bodies of many varieties would tender to provide services on contract to the Crown, just as would non-Maori private providers. The special expertise of Maori organisations, however, might sometimes give them an edge in the capacity to secure the contracts.[2]

In his influence upon, and endorsement of, the report, it appeared that the new minister had been listening to Maori voices, whatever his (and his colleagues') pre-election statements. *Ka Awatea*'s concern with reducing economic disparities was generally welcomed, while its call for 'Treaty based policy to fulfil protection of te tino rangatiratanga' ensured that Maori opposition to the National government's Maori policies was more muted than predicted. However, critics argued that while the report acknowledged Maori rights to rangatiratanga, the strategies set out did 'not facilitate its achievement'. Its endorsement of mainstreaming, moreover, and its equation of iwi with private companies, did not make it popular with many advocates of rangatiratanga. But nor was it fully approved by other ministers. Its emphasis on state intervention, in particular, ill fitted their free-market and anti-welfare policies, although they did support *Ka Awatea*'s focus on private enterprise and its recommendations that iwi needed to empower themselves independently of 'hand-out' resourcing by the state.

Implementing *Ka Awatea*

Peters would quickly alienate himself from the Bolger Cabinet by publicly criticising its policies on privatisation, benefit cuts and market rentals for state house tenants, and he was soon dismissed from his ministerial position. But meanwhile the government, initially too preoccupied with developing its own form of Rogernomics to give much independent thought to Maori matters, generally took up *Ka Awatea*'s advice. The Iwi Transition Agency and Manatu Maori were abolished, and out of their ashes the Ministry of Maori Development/Te Puni Kokiri (TPK) was created on the first day of 1992. The word 'development' was significant, designed to imply a new, post-welfare ethos. Programmes inherited from the past which needed to stay within the state orbit would be mainstreamed to other departments, while 'services to Maori', especially those assisting self-reliant development, 'could be contracted from whoever provided best results' (including corporatised iwi). TPK would be orientated towards policy advice, monitoring the effectiveness of mainstreaming and contracting-out, albeit also performing some operational tasks originally intended for ITA and franchised iwi authorities. While iwi organisations were not now to be part of the state, the government saw advantages in dealing with them, and the 1991 census included questions relating to iwi membership. But under *Ka Awatea*'s philosophy, Crown relationships with iwi would be public–private ones that lasted as long as the contracts on which they were based.[3]

The whole package was generally viewed as constituting only an extremely limited recognition of rangatiratanga, certainly far less than under Labour. Moreover, even a member of the its production team later acknowledged that *Ka Awatea* lacked strategies for implementation. In practice, mainstream government agencies that assumed primary responsibility for delivering services to Maori were often bereft of significant Maori knowledge or involvement. Under Labour's public sector reforms, furthermore, departments had been tasked with operating as separate entities responsible to their ministers alone. Those which did not see much need to focus on Maori were largely unconstrained, however much TPK monitored them, for the new ministry lacked enforcement powers. Individual departments could choose whether or not to contract to iwi or other Maori agencies, and some found it easier (for cultural, accountability and practical reasons) to avoid dealing with tangata whenua. The emphasis was on the purchase of service delivery rather than on 'developing scope for Maori to exercise their own authority in choosing who should provide such services'.

Many urban-based contracts with 'Maori organisations' were not with tribal groups, for obvious reasons. But numbers of dealings were transacted with institutions more resembling companies or corporations working on Maori issues (sometimes with only token Maori membership) than organisations with any Maori kaupapa. Yet these transactions were often depicted as 'Treaty partnership' and devolution in action. Even at its best, under the new arrangements the term devolution often amounted to little more than Crown purchasing of health and other services off private Maori organisations, such as the Wanganui-based Te Oranganui Health Trust.

Essentially, there was now little state help to get iwi authorities into a position from which they could successfully compete with other providers to deliver services to their people. Meanwhile, the Maori socio-economic situation worsened in the wake of the announcement of significant fiscal cuts in December 1990. With National determined to intensify its predecessor's efforts to phase out 'welfare dependency', social services were particularly targeted in Finance Minister Ruth Richardson's 'mother of all Budgets', and Maori once again suffered disproportionately. While some Maori leaders, such as urban advocate John Tamihere, believed that a bright future for Maori did lay with public–private partnerships which could help remove them from the trap of welfare dependency, general Maori criticism of the government increased.[4]

Many individuals and organisations continued to argue for 'a measure of Maori self determination' which eschewed, in the words of a powerful Catholic group in 1990, efforts by the Crown to 'define and restrict the concept of iwi to that of financial and administrative organisations'. The Race Relations Conciliator was just one of a number of observers who stressed that the politico-cultural gains for Maoridom under the fourth Labour government, reflecting 'a recognition that Maori have as much right to exist as a separate culture as do Pakeha', were now in grave danger of erosion. Many argued that, whatever its faults, the short-lived runanga iwi devolution system had offered practical means for moving towards some form of authentic Maori autonomy in ways that the new system did not. An eminent jurist involved in Treaty claims felt that 'the most important thing in New Zealand today is to re-establish the Maori tribes ... as full legal entities' able to 'handle their own affairs in their own way'. But, whatever the intentions of the authors of the multi-faceted *Ka Awatea*, this was not on National's agenda.[5]

Labour had, however, left a legacy of a greater willingness to consult with Maori than ever before. While tangata whenua were no longer being promised devolved state functions, certainly not at iwi level or in a systematised way, TPK was tasked with facilitating Maori development. It was to do so in consultation with Maori, seeking to reduce the endemic inequalities between the two peoples of 'the one nation' of New Zealand. A significant degree of ethnically and culturally aware (or, in a phrase increasingly used, 'politically correct') rhetoric and activity had been incorporated into government departments, following socio-cultural movement in society, and the new government appreciated that it could not turn the clock back. It seemed to a number of commentators that Maori were still on the road to achieving some kind of consultative, perhaps even quasi-partner, role in matters of state.

Treaty Negotiations

Yet contracting and mainstreaming remained the desired Crown modes of interacting with Maoridom, and it was hard to see how this could result in either adequate recognition of rangatiratanga or in 'closing the socio-economic gaps'. But in one area of Crown–Maori relations there was highly significant progress: the settlement of historical grievances under the Treaty of Waitangi. Settlements would provide, many Maori believed, both a form of Crown recognition of rangatiratanga and a cultural and resource base from which autonomist developments could be enhanced. Movement towards systematised negotiations had been established under Labour's Prime Minister Palmer, with TOWPU taking the leading role among officials, but the Crown's tentative offerings in 'scoping' negotiations with Waikato–Tainui had been rejected as far too inadequate. 'It is better to have nothing than to be nothing', one kaumatua had said.

Under the incoming government, Treaty negotiations initially fell primarily on Peters' shoulders, with TOWPU and other officials attempting to keep up the momentum as the government collected its thoughts on the issue. At first, there was considerable scepticism within Cabinet as to the need for Treaty settlements, reflecting an ongoing backlash from sectors of the pakeha public. Throughout the 1990s, in fact, media coverage of Waitangi Tribunal hearings and Treaty negotiations led to considerable anti-Treaty publicity, and a corpus of racist literature by authors such as Stuart C Scott became hugely popular in some quarters. But Douglas Graham and some ministerial colleagues, and many officials and advisers, saw that Treaty-based application of healing processes was a key prerequisite for socio-cultural harmony. With Peters' fall, Minister of Justice Graham gained full ministerial control of the task of negotiating (eventually adding a separate Treaty negotiations portfolio to his ministerial positions in 1993), and the pace quickened remarkably. Under Graham's drive and commitment, and with the growing support of Bolger, together with the goodwill of the Labour opposition, negotiated settlements appeared viable.[6]

National had inherited some pioneering Treaty discussions and negotiations from Labour. It was as a by-product of Tainui's legal case over Coalcorp that the Crown had opened exploratory negotiations with the tribe in 1989. Encouraged by initial progress in these, late that year the government decided to offer the possibility of 'direct negotiations' with claimant groupings who wished to bypass the long and expensive Tribunal hearings processes. This innovation allowed ministers and officials considerable manoeuvrability. There were 'compelling reasons' of state for progressing Treaty settlements, Graham later recalled. The government could not ignore the Tribunal's moral standing, nor the embeddedness in public life of such matters as 'the principles of the Treaty', social justice impulses and international guidelines. More prosaically, the Tribunal's compulsory powers put the government in the 'perilous position [of having] unacceptable financial risk' hanging over it unless it addressed claimant grievances. On a general level, social harmony would always be impaired if a significant sector of society remained aggrieved; in the early 1990s, public order might well be threatened if Maori hopes of progressing settlements were dashed.

The lead role for developing negotiations policy had been assigned to a 'Crown Task Force' comprised of ministers and officials from TOWPU and elsewhere. This was authorised to negotiate draft settlements with tribes which could prove Crown breaches of the Treaty, whether or not they had Tribunal reports – subject to ultimate ratification by Cabinet and (for large settlements) Parliament. By the time negotiations began to escalate under Graham's leadership, however, a major problem was becoming apparent. The 1991 repeal of the Runanga Iwi Act had jettisoned, along with devolved powers to iwi authorities, systematised legal and bureaucratic mechanisms for setting up and/or mandating state-recognised tribal entities. The new government was expressing serious intentions of addressing historical grievances, and had set in place ambitious targets for doing so, but the tribal and other fragmentation accompanying colonisation and post-colonisation meant that it faced a confused and contested socio-organisational landscape (and while there were some pre-existing mandated entities such as trust boards, even their mandates were often contested within tribes). The Crown had now to grapple with the question of which Maori groupings and representatives it was to consult and negotiate with, a problem that was often to plague reparational negotiations.[7]

Fisheries, Mandating and Internationalism

The first 'closure' of an historically-based grievance was a pan-tribal one, the 1992 settlement of claims over the loss of commercial fisheries, the follow-up to Labour's interim settlement. Negotiations were held with Maori leaders endorsed by a hui convened by the Maori Fisheries Commission and deemed to be representing all Maori. The Crown offered to put up some $150 million to acquire for Maori a 50% share of Sealord Products Ltd. In addition, the commission was to receive 20% of the quota on new species entering into the quota management system. The Maori negotiators, and many others, believed that this offer, totalling around $170 million, was a one-off opportunity (given that the company had been put up for sale) that should not be passed by. The 'Sealord deal' was signed on 23 September 1992, and led on to the Treaty of Waitangi (Fisheries Claims) Settlement Act.

The settlement was, however, heavily contested, with critics (including the National Maori Congress) feeling that too much had been conceded for too little. By statute, Maori were to relinquish customary rights over commercial fisheries and to lose the ability to make further claims or pursue litigation with regard to commercial fishing. It was argued that this, and other facets of the system, eroded rather than enhanced tribal rangatiratanga. While traditional fishing areas could become mataitai reserves managed by tangata whenua, for example, the management committees and their actions were subject to ministerial approval. It could also be argued that the reserves were little different from those allowed for in the 1945 Maori Social and Economic Advancement Act. In any case, this aspect of the settlement deprived tribes of full authority over 'their own' fishing grounds.

While National took over the iwi model for quota distribution purposes (to be operated in the interests of 'all Maori'), the proceeds were not to go straight to iwi but to the fisheries commission, now reconstituted as the Treaty of Waitangi Fisheries Commission/Te Ohu Kai Moana. This would decide on all relevant matters, including mandating recipient iwi and their institutions and distributing assets secured under both the interim settlement and the new legislation. And the Sealord deal's signalled intention to subtract the cost of the settlement from 'any fund which the Crown establishes as part of the Crown's overall settlement framework' caused disquiet on broader grounds. It was ever clearer that Treaty settlements were ultimately to be governed not just by the nature of the proven breaches but, more importantly, by what politicians considered affordable. Reparations would need to reflect comparative rather than reparative justice.

The implementation stage of the Sealord deal, too, was to be marred by arguments centring on justice, in this case distributive justice. There were years of very public wrangling over such matters as the appropriate model for allocating quota to iwi – by coastline and/or population, for example. Urban Maori, moreover, considered their rights to have been neglected under the deal, and challenged the official operating definition of 'iwi' (an issue which had not been resolved as the century ended). Some groups generally regarded by others as hapu fiercely argued their status as iwi, as did some non-tribal (as well as urban) institutions. Despite all such problems, and however inadequate the final fisheries settlement may have been considered by many Maori, a pioneering transfer of major resources had been conceded. And a compensation precedent of considerable magnitude had been set.[8]

With Treaty negotiations increasingly on the agenda, problems of organisation, representation and mandating intensified. There was often no consensus on the appropriate grouping within a claims area – iwi, hapu, whanau, trust board, urban authority, incorporation or a host of others – to present and negotiate a Treaty claim. Even such fundamental issues as the number of iwi and how to define them remained contested within both state and Maori circles. There were countless debates and disputes on very many issues: tribal or sub-tribal boundaries, how leadership strata were to be selected to head various claims processes, what kind of organisation should prevail in post-settlement regimes. Apparent paradoxes arose. Some leaders who had warned that government franchising and funding of Maori organisations would (as history had shown) inevitably lead to appropriation and the debasement of rangatiratanga, now sought resources from Treaty settlements in order to help rebuild a tribal base that was free from Crown interference. Their quests were frequently hampered by the Crown's dilemma, greatly intensified by Parliament's repeal of the RIA's 'legal personality' mechanism, over what entities and leaderships to negotiate and conclude settlements with. The state now had little choice but to invoke mandating procedures on a case by case basis. What seemed, in claimants' eyes, to be already slow progress on hearing and negotiating claims was therefore often delayed even further.[9]

Divisions between and within Maori groupings opened or intensified as a result of vying for official recognition to effect settlements of historical grievances. Considerable tensions developed as leaders of various claimant groups felt their mana – both personal and tribal – was being impugned by the Crown's refusal to accept their rangatiratanga unquestioningly and/or by its decision to deal with (or consider dealing with) others. There were suspicions in many quarters that government officials selected individuals and groupings that they found amenable to deal with; that the nineteenth century strategy of divide and rule had either been revived or had never gone away. Critics accused the Crown of listening too closely to pre-existing franchised bodies, such as the trust boards or the NZMC. Ministers and officials were allegedly attempting to seduce selected tribal groups into considering low-level Treaty settlements, which would create an unfortunate precedent for the rest of Maoridom. Delays meant many claimant groups became frustrated at being unable to access Crown resources to help rebuild their economies and enhance their communities. Instead of advancing, they were having to pour scant resources into researching, preparing and presenting their claims. Even when they received a favourable Tribunal report, they then had to begin another long process, that of negotiating, which had its own very costly implications.

Despite the various difficulties, however, progress was rapid by past national, and present international, standards, and the Crown's adoption of a Canadian negotiating model expedited matters. There were interesting negotiating experiments, too, some of which had ramifications for rangatiratanga. When large amounts of railway lands were declared surplus during privatising processes, for example, the Crown participated in a 'partnership' experiment with the National Maori Congress in an attempt to balance Maori interests and government intentions. The resulting 'Crown–Congress Joint Working Party' was generously funded, although the effort produced few tangible results and differences within and between Maori components contributed to the eventual withering away of the congress itself. In other developments, aspects of local government reform, and 1991's Resource Management Act, also incorporated responses to pressure for greater partnership with Maori. Towards the mid-1990s, iwi–local government relationships were being pioneered, such as a tribal confederation's agreement in 1994 with its district authority: Te Whakaminenga o Kapiti partnership.[10]

Crown–Maori relations accompanied, reflected and were tempered by changes in the international environment, which many Maori followed keenly. In 1986, the ILO's governing body had finally agreed to revise Convention 107, following 'developments in the situation of indigenous and tribal peoples in all regions of the world'. This led to 1989's Convention 169 on Indigenous and Tribal Peoples in Independent Countries, from which many of the assimilationist and paternalist elements of the previous convention had been removed. The new declaration, operative from 1991, gave fresh hope to indigenous groupings worldwide, although many remained unsatisfied both with the sub-state category it assigned them and the reluctance of states to ratify it. In 1993, the Draft Declaration on the Rights of Indigenous Peoples, initiated by the United Nations' Working Group on Indigenous Populations, further raised expectations.

While many governments – including New Zealand's – continued (and continues) to find difficulties with terms such as 'self-determination', the establishing of 'new international standards' seemed to reinforce the feasibility of finally 'removing the assimilationist orientation' still embedded in a number of governmental policies. International legal developments had provided part of the reasoning for the Australian High Court's famous 1992 *Mabo* decision, which rejected the doctrine of terra nullius (upon which, essentially, Crown–Aborigine relations had previously rested) and recognised the existence of native title to land. The judgment also focused attention on the relatively advantaged position of Maori vis a vis the indigenous tribes across the Tasman. All such developments reinforced Maori determination to continue the struggle against remaining manifestations of previous official policies of integration/assimilation.[11]

The increasing mix of international and autochthonous developments could be seen in the New Zealand Anglican Church's adoption in 1992 of a new mode of governance. This incorporated a three-way partnership between pakeha, Maori and Pacific Islanders, and respected the tikanga of each. Supporters of the model, which had been influenced by developments in Ngati Raukawa and other tribes, would increasingly push for its adaptation and application to the governance of New Zealand. Some argued for separate Maori and pakeha debating chambers in Parliament, while others envisaged a third chamber, comprised of equal numbers of Maori and pakeha, to review all legislation to ensure that it reflected 'real partnership'. Although some private organisations adopted something akin to the Anglican model, however, the New Zealand government declined to debate such issues.

Land and Treaty Settlements

But the government was prepared to move on the question of both land retention and reparational claims based on unjust land alienation. The Treaty claimants' stress on the major ways in which their land had been lost in the nineteenth century – by unfair and pressured purchases, confiscations, and the results of individualisation of tenure through the Native Land Court – and their strong desire for ancestral land still in Crown hands to be returned, reinforced in public and official eyes the centrality of the whenua to Maori. While the quest for autonomy did not stand or fall on the issue of turangawaewae, the symbolic and practical significance of the latter for Maori cannot be underestimated. The long-awaited, painstakingly negotiated Te Ture Whenua Maori Act of 1993 aimed to promote the 'retention, use, development, and control of Maori land as taonga tuku iho by Maori owners, their whanau, their hapu, and their descendants'. It was a sea change from the assimilationist land legislation of some quarter-century earlier.

The Act prohibited the alienation of the remaining pockets of Maori customary land, and strengthened the pre-existing trend towards control of Maori-owned land returning to those who held the interests in it. In light of the inexorable political and cultural pressures of the Maori Renaissance, the Crown no longer believed that collective ownership was undesirable per se, or even that it was necessarily an impediment to full production in the public interest. The new legislation, then, addressed the wishes of the Maori owners of land. It also provided some empowerment over land at flaxroots level, to bodies such as marae committees and different types of trusts, including whenua topu trusts representing the interests of tribal collectives. Overlapping membership between these and other organisations, such as those operating under the NZMC structure, helped reinforce the intimate links between the people and the land – including for the great majority of Maori who now lived away from their tribal base.[12]

Land was at the centre of most claims before the Waitangi Tribunal. The Tribunal's *Ngai Tahu Report* was released in 1991, and as a result of preliminary negotiations with the tribe, a 'land bank' was set up to hold surplus Crown land identified for possible use in reparations. This method, preventing selling on the open market until final settlements were forged, provided a precedent for other negotiations. As claimants saw it, return of land would help create a material base for self-determination, re-establish the significance of turangawaewae in their collective identity, and see the return of sacred/wahi tapu sites of cultural significance. The Tainui federation focused its Waikato raupatu/confiscated territory negotiations on return of *all* land within its rohe that was still in Crown hands, consonant with its longstanding principle that 'as land was taken, so land should be returned'.

The Crown had confiscated 1.2 million acres of Waikato land after the wars of the 1860s in punishment for 'rebellion', and a number of subsequent hand-backs to 'loyalists' and others were not necessarily to the appropriate people. In the 1920s, a royal commission of inquiry had acknowledged that injustice had been done, and Waikato leaders had later (along with Ngai Tahu and the Taranaki tribes) negotiated annual compensation payments. But with no land returned, these had been generally seen within the tribe as constituting no more than a 'blood money' admission by the Crown of its 'sins of the past'. In 1985, the Waikato–Tainui leadership (representing 33 hapu grouped under the trust board established upon the previous settlement) had lodged a claim with the Waitangi Tribunal centring on land confiscation. The pioneering 'direct negotiations' with the Tainui Maori Trust Board in 1989–90 had resumed fully in 1992 under Graham and his negotiating officials. In 1993, the decommissioned Hopuhopu and Te Rapa military bases were handed back to the iwi (one as a gesture of goodwill, the other as a 'downpayment' on a final settlement), with title vested in the entire tribal collectivity in the name of the founding Maori King, Potatau Te Wherowhero.

December 1994 saw the parties sign a 'heads of agreement' for full and final compensation for the land-based tribal claim. The Waikato–Tainui Raupatu Treaty settlement, for land and money totalling a value of $170 million, was signed on 22 May 1995. The settlement was for some $150 million more than the government had been prepared to offer less than five years before. A mere six years before the signing, in fact, there were no state plans to supersede the 1946 agreement. Matters had, certainly in international terms, moved fast. The Crown, moreover, apologised for its past breaches of the Treaty, something which held tremendous significance for the claimants and which created both national and international precedents. A new governance structure was established by Waikato–Tainui in order to manage their settlement proceeds. An uneasy mix of ancient and modern structures and values, this created problems in the ensuing few years, but the pioneering settlement did provide funds for Tainui to invest in marae upgrades, educational grants and facilities, health services and other forms of development.[13]

Armed with its Waitangi Tribunal Report, from 1991 Ngai Tahu had also been negotiating with Graham and officials. Eventually, it gained 'recognition from the Crown' for its rangatiratanga in its own chosen fashion, by being constituted by statute as a 'legal entity'. As the chief iwi negotiator's daughter would describe it, 1996's Te Runanga O Ngai Tahu Act 'gave us back by way of the law, the Cloak they stole from us in 1865 ... The Cloak we wear now is one that we ourselves have made'. The leaders stressed that, despite the legal identity that the legislation gave, they 'would be accountable first and foremost, once more, to Kai Tahu and not the Crown'. With distinctive governance mechanisms in place to manage a settlement that also attained a value of $170 million (in 1998), the tribal leadership set about 'creating an enterprise culture within the community collective' and building future prosperity. As a member of Ngai Tahu later put it, '[b]ecause of the claim settlement we have our own autonomy ... and we can start creating and imagining what will be our future'.[14]

Asserting Rangatiratanga

Most claims, in the final analysis, were about rangatiratanga, whether they explicitly stated so or not. They tended to focus on land, but often had many other aspects, and all Maori negotiators sought more satisfactory relationships with the Crown. Durable Treaty settlements would not only recognise rangatiratanga, but also provide a package of resources to underpin its enhancement. The structures, responsibilities and powers of the collective organisations that would safeguard, enhance and distribute settlement resources were intensely debated within and between tribes. The Crown accepted the right of the post-settlement regimes to control their resources as they saw fit, under the 'self management principle' of the modern Treaty of Waitangi. But tribal autonomy could be argued to be limited, insofar as tribal governance structures receiving settlement resources required legal sanction for 'public good' (and Article Three) reasons, such as protecting the rights of potential and actual beneficiaries. Some iwi, in fact, felt strongly that the legal requirements which the Crown insisted on imposing as a precondition of settlement derogated from their rangatiratanga.[15]

A number of sub-iwi groupings which were hoping to take advantage of the new types of family and tribal trusts being offered for the administration of Maori-owned land had similar feelings about Crown requirements. The increasing judicial capacity to intervene in Maori affairs was resented in some quarters as a state intrusion, too, though it was more common for Maori to view legal processes as a way of protecting their interests. Legal challenges were launched by urban and other Maori groupings to resolve issues arising from various fisheries asset distribution proposals, and Ngai Tahu would spearhead use of the courts as a weapon during difficulties in negotiations. There were promising developments for Maori from time to time in an emerging 'Treaty jurisprudence', together with signs of a legal pluralism that could encompass aspects of Maori customary law. All the same, the heavy involvement of the judiciary in Maori issues was an ongoing reminder that in matters relating to their management of reclaimed or otherwise Crown-provided resources, in the final analysis institutions of state held the decision-making power.

In abandoning the RIA's devolutionary institutions, the government had not discarded the well entrenched notion of partnership. Given its insistence that any movement towards partnership had to remain fully and firmly within the parameters of an indivisible sovereignty, however, alternative autonomist arrangements from those now repealed continued to prove elusive. But the prospect of Treaty settlements refocused attention on the issue of what types of rangatiratanga the Crown would recognise as the bases for forging permanent relationships. A great deal of discussion within Maoridom ensued as to the regimes by which iwi, hapu and other collectivities could both deal with the Crown and best handle sizeable settlement monies, lands and other resources.

The government, stressing that Treaty settlements were by grace of the political executive and Parliament, refused any recognition of rangatiratanga arrangements that might impinge upon Crown prerogatives – let alone to consider the many radical proposals also in the air, such as variations on the quasi-sovereignty of the Native American 'domestic dependent nations'. Crown constraints upon what it would discuss reinforced within Maoridom arguments that their people needed to organise on the basis of strength through unity. Initial high hopes that the National Maori Congress might become a durable kotahitanga movement, perhaps even the nucleus of a Maori polity to sit alongside the Crown, had quickly dissipated. Now, new ideas for achieving unity of process and purpose jostled with each other. By the mid-1990s, with the Maori world remaining fractionated at its interface with the state, key leaders were reaching the conclusion that, to complement and supplement the rangatiratanga exercised by the tribes and other groupings, te tino rangatiratanga needed to be organised at national level as a matter of urgent priority.[16]

The 'Fiscal Envelope' and its Consequences

In late 1994, the government provided a catalyst for a united Maori endeavour by calling for a public debate on a raft of proposals to guide future Treaty settlements. It had already signalled in the Sealord deal that it had in mind a total sum to cover all settlements, having made clear that reparations could not be pegged to any concept of 'just' or replacement compensation for that which had been lost (even if it *were* possible to work such things out). In May 1994, it had been reported that officials and ministers were closing in on an overall settlement sum (which would include a valuation placed on land or other resources transferred). Not only were there 'fiscal constraints' on the Crown, but it was expected that a total settlements figure would be needed before any tribe would sign up to a final Treaty settlement. That was certainly the position of the claimants at the most advanced stage of negotiations, Waikato–Tainui.

In Doug Graham's formulation, a 'Treaty settlement envelope' would allow for settlements to be 'consistent and fair' relative to other settlements and to a total pool of available resources. After much internal (and highly contested) intra-state deliberation in which Treasury analyses featured large, the Crown unilaterally fixed the 'fiscal cap' at a billion dollars, to be paid out over a ten-year period. Whatever the merits of the fiscal cap, or its amount (and, to take one example, TOWPU's and TPK's recommended figures were greatly in excess of Treasury's), iwi negotiators could now consider any Crown proposals in relation to the total resources in the state's Treaty coffers. The pioneering Tainui and Ngai Tahu settlements came, in fact, to include a 'relativity clause', with the Crown agreeing to increase their settlements if the fiscal cap increased in the future; their portions of the settlement envelope would always remain at 17%.

When the Crown put its 'Treaty Settlement Proposals' out for consultation, the only non-negotiable element was the fiscal cap. Enormous Maori anger at both this unilateralism and the relatively low level of the cap greeted the release. The proposals, many of which did reflect some discussion with Maori and which the Crown was prepared to adjust, were completely overshadowed by the issue of the billion dollar imposition. Soon known as the 'fiscal envelope proposals', they were interpreted throughout all quarters of Maoridom as a 'breach of tino rangatiratanga'. Under the auspices of Sir Hepi Te Heu Heu, a thousand people from all round the country, representing a full range of tribes and Maori organisations, met in January 1995 at Hirangi marae in Turangi to discuss a unified response.

From the hui, a unanimous message went out to the Crown, definitively rejecting the imposed fiscal envelope as a massive violation of rangatiratanga. Delegates noted, in particular, that no partnership of the type supposedly embodied in the Treaty could tolerate unilateral pronouncements from one side, especially on a subject so crucial as resolving past breaches of the Treaty. The Hirangi hui demanded Crown respect for rangatiratanga, canvassed several constitutional models under which the Crown might meet its Article Two

Treaty obligations, and by unanimous decision proposed a major Crown–Maori constitutional review on the basis of the Treaty of Waitangi.

Waitangi Day was particularly tense that year, and Pakaitore/Moutoa Gardens in Wanganui were occupied by Maori activists in a confrontational stand-off that lasted until May, riveting the attention of the nation (and producing considerable pakeha backlash). Emotional and dramatic opposition to the fiscal envelope was expressed at regional consultation hui organised by the Crown during February and March 1995 – an enormous 'public relations disaster' for the Crown. The organiser of the hui, TPK's chief executive, noted that Maori 'across the political spectrum' were for the first time 'united in opposition to the government's policy proposals'. The theme of all the hui, and of protests throughout New Zealand, was reclaiming rangatiratanga.

That May, even tribes preferring to work independently of others in their dealings with the Crown agreed that issues of common concern should be handled in a kotahitanga fashion. Those working within the Maori Congress launched a national debating exercise on ways of embodying rangatiratanga in constitutional arrangements. At a hui in Taranaki it was agreed that, while diversity within the Maori world needed respecting, the 'commonalities shared by all Maori' meant that unity was possible. Indeed, unity was necessary in order to attain mana motuhake, Maori autonomy. The bottom line was that 'Maori should be able to determine their own futures, control their own resources, and develop their own political structures'.

With much frustration at the lack of progress on achieving such rangatiratanga, other high profile occupations of claimed land and property followed Moutoa Gardens. The old Takahue School, the empty Tamaki Girls' College, Kaitaia airport, Coalcorp-owned land in Huntly and the disused Taneatua railway station were among sites occupied during the course of the year. Like Bastion Point in the late 1970s, the occupations involved a 'layering of grievance upon grievance', with land and Treaty issues intertwined. The Crown's declaration of the fiscal envelope added an overarching grievance around which all protesters and occupiers could agree. Few people expected the Crown, immediately at least, to rescind or raise the fiscal cap. But many believed that the furore which greeted it might compel the government to open consultation with Maori on various issues of rangatiratanga.

Yet the chances of this seemed slim. A number of ministers and officials wrote off the various criticisms of the government's approach to Treaty settlements, as well as to occupations, as driven by radicals. They refused dialogue with anyone taking direct action, seeing this as an issue of public order and therefore for the coercive authorities to handle. And most strongly of all, they continued to reject any discussion that might imply constitutional change, ring-fencing Treaty settlement issues from any talk of constitutional or other arrangements to effect recognition of rangatiratanga. Separately or together, such refusals to engage further fuelled the mid-decade propensity for direct action. Moana Jackson spoke for many in declaring that addressing the Treaty involved not just redressing historical grievances but also 'looking at all the issues of political power, constitutional restructuring and so on, which are part of the treaty'.[17]

In a letter written to Sir Hepi Te Heu Heu a week before a second Hirangi hui in September 1995, Prime Minister Bolger reiterated the longstanding Crown view that 'the sovereignty of Parliament is not divisible'. There being 'no political will to alter fundamental constitutional arrangements of the nation', he invited the hui to 'consider the development of the Crown/Maori relationship within manageable parameters which take into account the indivisibility of Parliament'. Sir Hepi affirmed in his opening address, however, that the hui had been convened precisely to focus on 'ways Maori can assert their tino rangatiratanga' in relationship to the state. In view of the government's disinclination to debate such issues, the hui almost completely ignored the Crown's views, and it declined an invitation from Bolger for its representatives to join an officials' working group on settlement matters. Speakers emphasised the need for constitutional reform and the processes which might be used to achieve it. The head of TPK later reported that indigenous sovereignty was affirmed by many young Maori, who 'were listened to politely by the many chiefs who were present, and were certainly not dismissed out of hand. It is clear that the issue of sovereignty and tino rangatiratanga will not go away'. The prime ministerial response was to restate that the Crown 'cannot negotiate the division of sovereignty'.

The hui provided a deliberate and powerful statement by Maori that if the Crown continued to refuse to consult over appropriate ways of recognising rangatiratanga, Maori would decide matters independently and only *then* take their position to the politicians. While unilateralism was not ideal, there seemed to be little choice. The second Hirangi meeting was followed by a third in April 1996, which had double the attendance of the first, and called for the 'decolonisation' of New Zealand. This could come about through the 'establishment of protocols governing relationships between Maori and with the Crown', and these needed to be followed by 'constitutional change'. A new constitutional model could be developed incorporating Maori tikanga and a Maori worldview, with the various processes requiring 'expos[ure of] the effects of the Pakeha colonisation process' before the ultimate goal of rangatiratanga could be attained. As one commentator put it, 'sooner or later the government will have to face the issue ... because governments come and go ... but Maori will still be there with their agenda of tino rangatiratanga'.[18]

Relational Difficulties and Opportunities

After the 'fiscal envelope' fiasco, the Crown did attempt to develop a better relational working nexus with Maori, albeit one which excluded certain issues such as the fiscal cap itself and constitutional change. In practice, its efforts sometimes amounted to little more than consultation with more or less preconceived outcomes, or the incorporation of some tikanga Maori into state-sanctioned public practices. While Maori understandably saw this as very far from satisfactory, it needs to be seen in the context of huge progress in Crown–Maori relations since the 1960s, a time when it was officially believed that tribes and indigenous knowledge practices would gradually disappear, and that their disappearance should be encouraged. The Crown was now increasingly willing, for example, to draw on traditional Maori knowledge in the interests of service provision. In doing so, it was building on the many developments in the Crown–Maori health relationship since the beginning of the Maori Renaissance.

Both conservative and radical Maori voices had long joined forces to argue that western medicine needed to be complemented by traditional indigenous herbal and other healing techniques, and Maori-generated health programmes had been supported even before Tu Tangata – and more so in the years since. Early in the 1990s, especially, officials and ministers began to respond far more positively and rapidly to Maori health initiatives, such as requests from Maori healers for recognition within the public health services. From 1993, discussions were held at national level, and a pioneering contract was soon signed for traditional Maori medicinal services to be provided by a Napier healing clinic. By the end of the decade, contracts were being routinely arranged with providers whose healing methods incorporated Maori tikanga as well as medicines. Customary healing practices were often explicitly linked by their practitioners to autonomist causes. One healer who signed a contract with the Ministry of Health was later to state that it 'is very important that in all we do we retain our tino rangatiratanga, or ensure self determination, so that we never sell our souls to that which is not in our tikanga and the beliefs of our ancestors'.

The Department of Corrections was among other state agencies which also drew on Maori expertise. By 1998, it was 'working with tribes to find tohunga' to act as 'providers of Maori services to inmates', a far cry from the days of the Tohunga Suppression Act of 1907. Yet as the new millennium approached, the Crown's political and bureaucratic policy-makers, continuing to operate within fundamental (and ethnocentric) ideological, hegemonic and cultural constraints, remained seen by many Maori to be moving only glacially towards recognising rangatiratanga.[19]

There was one partial exception: the rapid progress in the 1990s, despite the fiscal envelope, in resolving historical grievances. Even though most Maori felt that the processes were too slow, there was now some considerable movement where there had been little before. Tribes had always been adamant that Crown recognition of its past breaches of the Treaty was a necessary prerequisite for significantly advancing Crown–Maori relations. That considerable movement on this issue could be made under a National government reflected a number of factors. These included a conservative leadership's propensity to better understand (if not approve) the supreme significance to Maori of rangatiratanga, as opposed to Labour's emphasis on socio-economic improvement for the Maori people. National, led by an energetic Graham, was prepared to apologise for past injustices whereas Labour had not been. Negotiations could be depicted as 'chiefs talking to chiefs'. Moreover, the National government sought to hasten the processes by which iwi could 'move out of grievance mode and into development mode'. This would, it was believed, operate for the good of all New Zealanders by adding to national productivity, helping remove Maori from welfare dependency and getting youth away from temptations to engage in crime and create disorder.

Many Maori also judged National less harshly than they otherwise might have done for reasons other than progress on Treaty settlements. At a time of electoral reform proposals, for example, it succumbed to pressure to retain the Maori seats despite much 'expert advice' to the contrary. Large numbers of Maori also retained a deep consciousness of the Lange ministry's unilateral abandonment of the longstanding Labour–Ratana pact to protect the interests of the tangata whenua. While Labour's leadership now rejected the most destructive aspects of the Rogernomics years, the party was still not seen to be addressing issues of rangatiratanga with any conviction. At the 1996 general election, the first to be fought under the 'mixed member proportional' (MMP) representation system, Ratana leaders pointedly did not endorse Labour. Many Maori voters abandoned the Labour MPs whose party they saw as having both betrayed them and expressed itself unwilling to seek redemption.

But neither did they vote for National, which had not only continued but intensified the right-wing policies that had devastated the lives of so many within Maoridom. The Maori electorate seats went to New Zealand First, a populist party founded by the minister ousted from National for his open defiance of some of their key policies, Winston Peters. The clear expectations of the Maori electorate had been that Peters' party would support Labour, forcing it to keep its election promises. Finding itself pivotal to the formation of the next government, however, New Zealand First established a governing coalition with National. Over the next few years, there would be much Maori discussion on the need to better strategise under MMP.

In addition to the Waikato–Tainui and Ngai Tahu settlements, other progress was being made on Treaty matters. There were both negotiations over middle-level claims and some small settlements, as well as landmark tribunal reports such as that on the Taranaki claims in 1996. In 1997, negotiations over longstanding problems surrounding lands reserved for Maori but administered under state trusteeship were finally completed. Grievances asserted by the nominal (and multiple) owners had focused on denial of both physical possession and market rentals. The Maori Reserved Land Amendment Act addressed such issues and provided for compensation. Owners widely saw this as recognition of their rangatiratanga – albeit as a result of compromises that many believed had given them too little and had come too late.[20]

Treaty-based negotiations and settlements, all in all, could both affirm rangatiratanga (to a greater or lesser degree) and introduce or perpetuate strains in the relationship between Maori and the Crown. Treaty-based discourses were becoming ever more complex. Some prominent Maori, such as former Labour minister Sir Peter Tapsell, condemned any 'reversion to tribalism' as a 'tragic mistake' that ignored the realities of modern life, especially its urban dimension. Others believed that with the Crown continuing to privilege iwi in negotiating settlements – rather than hapu, whanau, marae or other sub-iwi organisations – the dynamic complexities of Maori society were being ignored. Not only was a simplified or Crown-engineered view of Maori identity becoming entrenched by such means, but also (it was argued, often vociferously) the state was heaping new injustices upon sub-tribal collectivities when iwi-level Treaty settlements were signed.

There was considerable opposition, too, to the fact that the Crown preferred dealing with institutions representing what it perceived to be the 'highest natural grouping' for various of its relationships with Maori. In all such processes, the state was often depicted as commodifying certain descent groupings and practices to make its governance and development task easier, or even to appropriate collective Maori energies in new ways. In meeting such criticisms, the Crown would note that it was logistically impossible to easily or quickly negotiate or forge relationships with the many thousands of sub-iwi or non-tribal groupings, *even if* they were ready to do so and had agreed on their jurisdictional boundaries. Maori themselves, it would point out, were urging that speedy progress be made, untrammelled by the bureaucratic and jurisdictional delays which had dogged Crown–Maori relations in the past.

Reparations processes were included in the critiques of those who attacked 'tribal fundamentalism' for providing the 'structures for the materialisation of [an] indigenous identity' said to be required by international capital. Settlements with tribes were interpreted as the Crown brokering the emergence of a 'comprador bourgeoisie'. Other critical voices suggested that Treaty settlements with iwi codified 'Maori social and political relationships according to capitalist notions of property ownership', and in doing so perpetuated 'colonial practices'. While such arguments seldom impinged upon Treaty negotiations, the Crown did need, from time to time, to address concerns that its mandating of particular entities to undertake the negotiations was discouraging positive cooperation between groups within Maoridom – or encouraging divisions in a classical divide and rule sense. Undoubtedly, negotiation processes involved many tensions and conflicts, especially after the imposition of the fiscal cap, but both Crown and claimant groupings sought to find ways of minimising these in the processes of maximising their own positions, often with some success. Whatever the reconciliation processes chosen, the socio-tribal fragmentation consequent upon colonisation and urbanisation would have meant major difficulties in finding agreements to suit all parties. Most people involved knew this, and claimants generally took it into account in the processes of pursuing rangatiratanga by way of Treaty settlements.[21]

Scrutiny of the Official Maori National Voice

It would, of course, have been far easier for the Crown if it could deal with a single Maori organisation on issues affecting all of Maoridom. Many Maori felt that any such structure, if it were the bona fide voice of the people, might provide the negotiating muscle to procure a much larger Treaty settlement envelope and/or improved constitutional or other arrangements. For this and other reasons, groups and individuals continued – especially after the post-election disillusionment of 1996 – to seek a unified Maori body. Politicians and officials, together with many Maori, had concluded for quite some time that the NZMC system, useful as its ongoing work was for both tangata whenua and the state, had essentially been overtaken by history as a major vehicle for either addressing or promoting rangatiratanga. In many Maori eyes, the MWWL fell into a similar category; nor had Kingitanga, Ratana, the Maori Congress, the Hirangi hui and other kotahitanga movements produced the unity that seemed increasingly needed as the end of the century approached. Among Maori leaderships, there were numerous discussions on the next step. The government, in turn, believed that an appropriately configured national body would be useful in improving Crown–Maori relations. In 1998, it placed the Crown's current 'official' relationship with Maoridom under formal review.

That January, the Minister of Maori Affairs directed Te Puni Kokiri to scrutinise the Maori Community Development Act. Could a system dating back to the early 1960s (and beyond) 'adequately meet the development requirements of Maori communities'? The reviewers found widespread Maori desire for reform, given that the NZMC 'structure has not functioned properly for some time'. Not only had it grown remote from the people, but in some areas it scarcely operated at all, especially because tribes had been establishing their own authorities independent of the council and its subordinate Maori associations. 'The most consistent theme arising from the consultation process was that the Council at national or regional level, was not representative and as such did not have the authority to speak on behalf of Maori.'

Many of those consulted believed that an officially-recognised national body was still required. But it needed to be properly representative of the 'Maori voice' and to reflect the diversity of opinion at flaxroots level. The reviewers agreed: within a national grouping, the government should 'provide structures so that Maori communities [could] develop in a way that best suits them'. But in a reflection of rapid political, social and cultural developments, they argued that the current Crown emphasis on interacting and assisting at iwi level needed to be modified. Local communities should provide the base for state-assisted development, with due regard given to institutions such as marae (and their urban equivalents) which constituted the 'basis of Maori communities'. Rather than replacing the NZMC system, the reviewers suggested fundamental modifications to make it 'better able to meet the current and future expectations and needs of Maori communities on those issues requiring national attention'. They recommended that the national body become, in fact, 'subservient to the parent Maori communities'.

In recognition of the thrust of the submissions, moreover, the review recommended that any such revised (and renamed) structure should operate independently of the government, perhaps along the lines of the Electoral Commission. It would need only a single tier of area representatives between the flaxroots and national level; this tier would provide expertise, and coordinate and liaise with Maori wardens and other personnel 'accountable directly to their communities'. While these were relatively bold recommendations, many Maori felt they did not go far enough. The revised machinery, while possessing operational autonomy, would still be accountable to the Crown, especially in its use of funded assistance. Moreover, the reviewers had concluded that in light of its 'standing', the Crown, rather than Maori or a Crown–Maori combination, should 'monitor the relationship between the parties'. In the eyes of many critics, the new organisation would, just like the old, be an agency of the state. Pleasing few, the recommendations languished.

Sizeable numbers of Maori, in any case, were highly sceptical of the need or desirability for any national body that was sanctioned by the Crown. Some worried that any type of national organisation would invariably submerge significant tribal-based interests. In the context of earlier debates over the distribution of fisheries assets, Tipene O'Regan had expressed fears that a national fisheries commission would, through a 'tyranny of the majority', provide a vehicle for North Island iwi to gain control of South Island tribal assets and resources. He perceived in 'pan-Maori trumpets ... a real threat to ... our Treaty rights and our rangatiratanga'. Some Maori advocated regional- or interest-based federations rather than a national body. Urban leaders, in particular, sought new structures that united collectivities of Maori with similar interests in ways which transcended tribal boundaries. Such efforts were proceeding strongly as the new century began. In 2003, for example, a National Urban Maori Authority was established to lobby, among other things, for a greater share of Treaty settlement resources.[22]

Education and Autonomy

While various findings of the review of the New Zealand Maori Council system struck some chord with most interested parties, the key issues concerning an appropriate institutional relationship at national level between Maori and the Crown remained unaddressed. Questions about ways of securing Maori autonomy continued, however, and they were posed at an increasing number and range of sites of encounter. One key site was education, given its profound significance in reproducing cultural thinking and behaviour. There had, of course, been successful autonomist initiatives in the 1980s, but the momentum had slowed, and Crown assessments tended to be made in an atmosphere of pakeha concern about the ramifications of 'separatism'.

In the early 1990s, to take one example, proponents of whare wananga, or places of higher indigenous learning, had been expressing frustration at the dilemma they faced. In a reprise of many past situations in Crown–Maori relations, whare wananga needed to access state funding, at least for seeding purposes, given the marginalised socio-economic position of many of their potential constituents. Their promoters knew, however, that government funding meant in practice that their 'relative autonomy [would be] severely curbed'. Whare wananga might even, as a result of accountability agreements, find themselves in danger of serving 'as agents of the Crown [and] assist[ing] in the maintenance and enhancement of the Crown's domination'. For as 'the eels within the hinaki [trap] remind us, the hand that feeds is the hand that rules'. Remnants (or, in some arguments, the dominance) of an 'underlying agenda of assimilation' within the state complicated matters further. The challenge was to find ways of gaining assistance that would undermine the Crown's ability to control or appropriate sites of potential or actual autonomy.

A measure of the intensity of such struggles in education at large can be gauged by the Maori Education Commission's call in 1999 for autonomy for Maori in the education system. The commission had resulted from the National–New Zealand First Coalition Agreement in 1996, which included establishing a body 'to monitor progress in Maori education and design initiatives to graft on to mainstream departments'. Instead, the commission ended up not only suggesting 'more Māori control and authority', but that 'the time for a national, autonomous, separately funded Māori education entity/ies had arrived'.

It was aware that the odds were against such a development, partly because of government disinclination but also because of entrenched reluctance on the part of the bureaucrats who advised it to relinquish existing controls over the nation's educational establishments. The 'image that the Ministry of Education presents', the authors of the commission's fourth report stated, 'places itself at the centre of policy development, funding allocation and decision making while Māori educators, students and whānau remain at the periphery. Such a view is at odds with the results of our consultations and review of the literature on the topic in which Māori have expressed a strong desire for more Māori autonomy, authority and control at *all* levels of the education process including policy development and funding'. As a beginning, the commission recommended, the government should support autonomous Maori control of kura kaupapa Maori. It also explored proposals for an independent national Maori Education Authority, which many Maori supported, though it noted a clear preference of various groups in tribal areas for 'local autonomy rather than an overarching structure'. But both the concept of a national authority, and autonomist policy suggestions in other areas of Maori educational concern, continued to meet resistance from the Crown.[23]

Quite apart from the state's lack of interest in franchising or funding any body which might actually or potentially rival its monopoly of control in areas traditionally subjected to 'public good' imperatives, Crown-funded organisations which questioned state policies or directives could well find their funding drying up. When organisers of a proposed official tertiary-level whare wananga announced that they would be operating autonomously from control by the Crown, the government reacted swiftly to point out their mistake. The Waitangi Tribunal itself faced not-so-veiled threats of curtailment of its powers (or even its existence) if it made mandatory orders for the return of land which potentially violated the broad relativities consequent upon the 'Treaty settlement envelope'. There were many reminders that Crown sovereignty was supreme and indivisible – although under post-MMP coalition governments, MPs from minority parties played a greater role in official decision-making and this held out some hope of future concessions to rangatiratanga.

Millennial Debates

By the end of the twentieth century, few Maori could be under any illusion that, unless there was to be a revolutionary overthrow of the state (and very few ever seriously suggested that this was desirable, much less possible), rangatiratanga could be achieved other than by arrangements acknowledging the Crown's supreme and interventionist authority. So long as the Crown held fully to the doctrine of indivisible sovereignty, moreover, proposals for reform of the 'official' body representing Maoridom, for the establishment of unified collectivities powerful enough to be meaningful partners with the Crown, and for Maori organisations to be able to carry out significantly devolved or state-like functions would all inevitably lead to little. All that could be expected was the creation of more Crown-franchised bodies whose existence and operations would be subject to surveillance, intervention and, if they became too challenging to the Crown, abolition. The best that could be done, at least for the foreseeable future, was to negotiate as high a threshold as possible before state scrutiny and control came into play.

Stated so baldly, little had changed since 1950 – or, indeed, since the Maori councils of 1900. As Lange put it, New Zealand could have 'a democratic form of government or ... indigenous sovereignty', but not both; for the Crown, there was no contest between the former and what it perceived as an inherently 'undemocratic' latter. All the same, the situation in 2000 was a far cry from that of half a century before, as Lange also indicated when declaring that 'the exercise of degrees of Maori autonomy' had now become acceptable. In a sense, such cautious acceptance of rangatiratanga, but acceptance nevertheless, summed up the debate insofar as it impacted on actual policy development as the century neared its end. While the situation was nowhere near ideal for the proponents of rangatiratanga, it constituted a huge advance on the 130 years of assimilation policies and practices which had preceded the three decades from 1970.

The problem remained, however, of securing agreement on the extent and types of 'degrees' of autonomy. This was rendered more difficult than it might have been because of the use by many parties of terminology which obfuscated or impaired understanding and progress (and which allowed a generally ethnocentric media to indulge in sensationalist reporting from time to time, contributing to pakeha backlash). The Waitangi Tribunal's former chairperson E T J Durie has argued that demands for indigenous 'sovereignty' are counter-productive, their polarising effects drawing attention away from achievable forms of 'autonomy' in which Maori could 'determine their own policy, manage their own resources, develop their own structures of representation, and ... negotiate policy affecting them with the state'. Others were also arguing in the later 1990s that although the Crown had made no concession on the notion of full sovereign indivisibility, its continuing preparedness to envisage at least some devolution of power indicated that, if the quest for formal Maori sovereign partnership with the Crown were to be set aside, appropriate ways of embedding rangatiratanga into the body politic might be negotiated.[24]

Discussions between Crown agencies and Maori leaders at many levels increased as the approach of the new millennium concentrated minds upon the future of New Zealand society, its political economy and its ethnic relations. In 1998, TPK published a report, *Closing the Gaps*, which confirmed that some of the socio-economic disparities between Maori and pakeha had widened since the introduction of free-market economics. Its proposals, insofar as they aimed to provide Maori with a more secure social and economic base, were widely viewed as a way of enhancing rangatiratanga. The National-led government adopted their thrust on public good grounds, and when it lost office in November 1999, its Labour-led successors continued the same strategy.

Labour had long ago cast off the new-right ideologues of the Rogernomics years, and policies on closing gaps fitted neatly into the classical social democratic approach of promoting 'equality' of all types, especially socio-economic. In August 2000, in fact, the Labour government attempted to add further 'building blocks' to the 'closing the gaps' edifice. These included a new way of supporting rangatiratanga, by which Maori would 'become the managers and controllers of their own development'. A 'Capacity Building' programme would 'substantially boost ... the ability of whānau, hapū, iwi, Māori organisations and Māori communities to control their own destiny'. Through this programme, the Ministry of Maori Development was 'charged with building a partnership' between the 'state sector' and the many organisational manifestations of Maoridom. The Crown would proactively encourage independent 'bottom-up' initiatives in order to produce stronger and better resourced Maori communities; along with Maori, the whole nation would benefit.

In the event, the capacity-building policies did not come to significantly enhance rangatiratanga. Moreover, with the government promoting a 'millennial debate' on the type of nation New Zealand should become, many pakeha were thinking about a future in which 'race harmony' prevailed – and sizeable numbers of them were tending to equate this with a rejection of all or many forms of what was often depicted as 'Maori separatism'. National had once promised to resolve all Treaty grievances by 2000, and now that that goal had proven far too optimistic, many people seemed to see outstanding claims before the Waitangi Tribunal as part of a broader 'Maori problem'.

Commentators were noticing both a discernible 'Treaty fatigue', and a general lack of public understanding that appropriate Treaty-based relational arrangements had yet to be forged. Even the 'closing the gaps' programme was soon to be clawed back, following a pakeha backlash against 'special treatment for one group in the population'. It was reconceptualised as 'Reducing Inequalities' throughout all ethnicities and classes in society. On the other hand, the new Labour-led government's increasing interest in 'nation-building' did see it promote New Zealand's bicultural lifestyle and policies as integral to the identity of the nation. Biculturalism was celebrated as both a distinctive and healthy aspect of 'brand New Zealand' (along with multicultural diversity and inclusivity).[25]

For any given Maori collectivity, the quest for autonomy had always involved differential progress in securing Crown recognition of rangatiratanga according to the issues involved. As the new millennium approached, some Maori groupings had opted to explore co-management regimes with the Crown where these seemed practical, on the grounds that further gains might later follow. Some sought or achieved ways by which they could 'exercise tino rangatiratanga in cultural and spiritual terms' over taonga or resources highly significant to them, for example. In seeking a co-management partnership with the Crown over their river, the Whanganui tribes were thereby asserting new ways of exercising kaitiakitanga over waters integral to their identity, in 'a custodial exercise of rangatiratanga'.

The quest for Crown recognition of rangatiratanga continued to take many and varied forms. Around the turn of the new millennium, many leaders were now exploring partnerships with local government, leading to satisfactory results for some tribal or other Maori groupings. After wide consultation with its Maori constituents, the Taranaki District Health Board was to agree (in 2002) to work with its eight regional iwi to 'support tino rangatiratanga and Maori aspirations for self-determination', and to commit to assist them to build 'Maori capacity through a network of competent and well-resourced "by Maori for Maori" health providers'.

Along with comprehensive Treaty settlements, such developments, while falling well short of securing te tino rangatiratanga (and not always working smoothly in practice), represented socio-political progress towards embodying indigenous autonomy in practical ways. They were often viewed, in essence, as precursors for much more significant future developments – developments being canvassed in the extensive, nationwide debate about which direction(s) New Zealand should take in the new millennium. While the prospects for Crown recognition for te tino rangatiratanga were not ideal in the year 2000, they were far better than those which had prevailed half a century before.[26]

Conclusion and Prospects

Autonomy and the Crown

This book, in surveying the history of Crown–Maori relations in the second half of twentieth-century New Zealand, concludes (like its predecessor, *State Authority, Indigenous Autonomy*) that a profound desire for autonomy, for the right to run its own affairs, has been the key driving force within Maori society. This finding is consonant with the histories of indigenous peoples worldwide: the quest for independence, autonomy, self-determination, self-management, sovereignty or partnership with the state (and many other terms could be, and have been, used) underpins the history of indigeneity in colonial and post-colonial settler societies. In New Zealand, this is manifested in the search for the tino rangatiratanga promised to Maori by the Crown in the Treaty of Waitangi in 1840. As in other colonised and post-colonised nations, the quest for autonomy has waxed and waned, and means and goals have varied.

So, too, have the state's responses to indigenous pressures, around which the other major conclusions of this book centre. Defeat of autonomist aspirations was always the preferred Crown goal, especially in the long assimilationist period from the beginning of the colony until the early 1970s. But where that proved untenable, the state sought to appropriate organisational expressions of autonomy for its own purposes, often attempting to turn them into vehicles for the assimilation project. In turn, Maori attempted to reappropriate the state's appropriations. Both parties, then, resorted to compromise and subversion in pursuit of their own goals. But until the Crown abandoned the policy of full integration (as assimilation, after a long semantic journey, had ended up being called), the ultimate goals of Maori and the state seemed completely incompatible. From the 1970s, arrangements which would suit both parties to the Treaty of Waitangi (as well as pakeha and other ethnicities of New Zealand) seemed potentially achievable – that is, if they were seriously pursued through consultation and negotiation conducted in good faith.

Maori autonomist goals can be placed on a conceptual continuum. At one end lies territorial sovereignty for some or all of the Maori population over some or even all of New Zealand. Few have ever argued for this, partly because the political, demographic and tribal history of the country made it impracticable. A flavour of this perspective, however, can be seen in protest group Te Ahi Kaa's 1986 manifesto for Maori repossession of Aotearoa, or in Donna Awatere's call for 'Maoris [to] have control of New Zealand because it is *our* country'. Towards the other pole of the continuum are various arrangements whereby indigenous collectivities can pursue specified types of autonomist activity within the parameters of existing New Zealand lego-constitutional authority. Maori groupings would exercise powers devolved by a state confident in the doctrine of total indivisibility and strongly asserting its ability to intervene in Maori governance in the interests of the 'public good'. Clearly, definitions of autonomy clustered towards this pole are less threatening to the state and the majority culture than many at other points of the continuum, including those which seek an entrenched constitutional partnership between Crown and Maori authorities, perhaps involving a Maori parliament or a Maori chamber or chambers grafted onto existing parliamentary arrangements.

Internationally, indigenous groupings have not been able to acquire anything approaching full sovereignty, although some have retained or attained collective indigenous rights over and above the rights of individual citizens. Like other indigenous peoples, Maori have long been engaged in vigorous internal debate about both what is most desirable and most likely to be attainable. They have generally acknowledged that the colonial and post-colonial history of New Zealand has brought considerable benefit to them, just as they have in turn enriched New Zealand society in many ways. Many Maori perceive that the growing biculturalist nature of society in early twenty first-century New Zealand might provide an appropriate environment in which to negotiate rangatiratanga arrangements within existing or, preferably, modified political and constitutional parameters.[1]

Modes of Rangatiratanga

The interpretation of Crown–Maori relations in this book, however, has avoided prescriptive or instrumental definitions and modes of rangatiratanga and its recognition. Many Maori and pakeha have believed that iwi provide the sole or best possible basis for achieving rangatiratanga, and a number of both experiments with devolution and Treaty settlements have occurred at iwi level. The head of the Ngai Tahu negotiating team, Tipene O'Regan, defined rangatiratanga as 'iwi in control of themselves and their assets in their own rohe'. Many agree with this perspective, whether or not they accept the argument that iwi were reinvented or boosted in the 1980s in ways which suited the Crown and/or capitalism.

Others claim that the Crown's negotiating focus on iwi is artificially and destructively imposed upon a socio-cultural situation in which hapu, whanau, urban organisations and pan-tribal or non-tribal bodies individually or severally occupy an important place within the socio-political foundations of modern Maori life. Proponents of such views sometimes argue that only those institutions or collectives which they nominate can truly embody rangatiratanga. Still others suggest flexibility: either iwi or hapu can perform the function, for example, according to the protocols and history of each tribal grouping; while in certain cases, tribal federations are best placed to represent the people. Proponents of rangatiratanga residing in either 'original whanau' or reconstructed whanau often also allocate rangatiratanga to higher level structures. Urban Maori advocates generally allow for its exercise within tribal or sub-tribal milieus. Rangatiratanga, then, can be expressed multiply, according to the tasks to be performed and the groups involved.

Most iwi and other broad-based groupings, indeed, have stressed that they act as overarching bodies for their component parts. Te Runanga a Iwi o Ngapuhi was created to 'confirm the enduring tribal structure to represent its Tino Rangatiratanga', but in a way that aimed to preserve the 'independence of each Constituent Community' within it and to 'recognise the fundamental importance of whanau'. A number of scholars and others believed, when post-war urbanisation and assimilation policies were at their height, that hapu, iwi, whanau and other tribal configurations were becoming defunct (or changing into quite different types of entities). Few would now make such an assessment, but an influential sector considers that contemporary rangatiratanga resides most appropriately or predominantly in pan-tribal or non-tribal groupings – in urban authorities or some kind of regional or national organisation, for example, or in various other non-tribal manifestations of 'Maoridom'. In such views, the strong continuation of tribal organisation and 'mentality' undermines the united endeavours necessary for negotiating autonomist arrangements. Opponents of the pan- or non-tribal approach, however, argue (among other things) that any such prescription gives succour to assimilation impulses which continue to lurk within Crown circles and policies.

Any scholarly effort to define rangatiratanga precisely, or to limit it to particular organisational forms, ignores the clear evidence that different times, places and circumstances have presented different (and always contestable) definitions, configurations and opportunities. And that the Crown, in its ongoing interactions with all incarnations and manifestations of rangatiratanga, contributes to shaping the way rangatiratanga is organised and expressed. Each Maori collectivity, however, debates and selects its own path to rangatiratanga, one that emerges from the past to fit the present – and which may change in the future. Hana O'Regan notes, with regard to those descended from the base genealogical document of Ngai Tahu, that the 'tribe is the entity which is seen at the present time to be the best and most effective mechanism for Kāi Tahu to achieve the dreams and visions of the people ... [I]t is the tribal identity that the descendants of the Blue Book have opted for to lead them through the new century'. However, she continues, '[t]his may change as societal and political pressures change and impact upon the collective ... Although on the surface there is a strong primordial influence governing that identity, such as the role of the whakapapa as a determining feature, the way in which those factors manifest themselves within Kāi Tahu culture and society are continuously changing and adapting as a response to the politics of the time'.[2]

This book's focus on Maori attempts to gain Crown recognition of the rangatiratanga promised them in the Treaty and of the Crown's responses to these continuing efforts has largely omitted discussion of autonomous developments that were (to a greater or lesser extent) outside the purview of the state. Ngati Maniapoto, for example, has a long history of autonomist actions and visions that had little reference to 'external' factors such as the state and its assimilationist aims. Some tribes have tried to counter the effects of urban migration through independent means. In the 1970s, for instance, Urewera iwi set out to 'lure people out of the cities' and back into the 'self sufficient' life of the autonomous community. In 1991, Ngati Te Ata put forward a 'tino rangatiratanga charter', part of a process of establishing its 'own measures of self-determination and self-government' and asserting its 'right to govern its own affairs'. Those wishing to deal with it, including agencies of government, were told that they needed to adhere to its protocols and deal with the 'legitimate authority within its tribal territories'. Its 'Tribal Policy Statement' was seen as the iwi's first step towards 'breaking out of th[e] cycle of reacting and being controlled by others to a state of control over its own affairs'.

Ngati Te Ata and many other tribes cited the 1835 chiefly Declaration of Independence (inspired and recognised by the British) to boost – or, in some cases, to attempt to supersede – arguments based on the 'rangatiratanga clause' written into the Treaty of Waitangi some five years later. Insofar as the Treaty was relevant, many argued, it endorsed the Declaration, and so full and indivisible Crown sovereignty had never been acquired over their people and rohe. Thus, Ngati Te Ata asserted that 'all sovereign power and authority reside in the iwi' and that the tribe was a 'sovereign people and a sovereign nation'. Yet even this was not couched as an all-or-nothing separatist claim. Ngati Te Ata's policy statement put considerable weight on the views of the chair of the United Nations Working Group on Indigenous Peoples (who had visited the tribe in 1988) to the effect that Maori had the right to 'formal and substantive self-government over their own local and internal affairs'. This stance situated Ngati Te Ata's claims within the mainstream of aspirations for rangatiratanga in the twentieth century. Declarations of, and rhetoric about, independence and autonomy often amounted to tribes promoting 'their collective identities' in idealised form, while seeking autonomist outcomes which could potentially be accommodated within existing or modified constitutional and legal frameworks – at least for the time being.[3]

Autonomist movements with little direct engagement with the state were not confined to iwi, hapu or similar tribal collectivities. There was, for example, often little state–Maori interaction (apart from the relationships all citizens have with the Crown) in circumstances where Maori chose to express their collective impulses in whole or in part through religion, both mainstream or otherwise. The politico-religious Maramatanga movement on the North Island's western seaboard (which had picked up many Ratana followers when T W Ratana closed his spiritual mission in 1928) operated largely outside official (or pakeha) knowledge, even after it began making annual pilgrimages to Waitangi in the 1970s. The Te Pikinga movement in the Urewera, founded in 1929 and dominated by Tuhoe women, promoted material and cultural well-being among its people without connection with the state.

Many marae-based and community groupings aimed to operate independently not only of the state, but also of other Maori organisations. This was particularly the case with pan-tribal or non-tribal groups in the cities and large towns. A leading member of Auckland's Waipareira urban authority proclaimed, not atypically: 'We will not tolerate directives and commands from bureaucracy and government. We will not tolerate the same nonsense from a minority presently leading the tribes'. In 1998, the Waitangi Tribunal's *Whanau o Waipareira Report* found that urban groups could be deemed to possess and exercise rangatiratanga, although it also indicated the difficulties inherent in the rhetoric of total independence. In view of the realities of the state's supreme power and enormous resources, the report made a strong recommendation for much greater Crown coordination and consultation with Maori in development and delivery of social services.[4]

Relationships, Rangatiratanga and Class

What was most important for tribal and non-tribal groupings alike, however, was that rangatiratanga was – as the Tribunal put it – 'the key principle of customary social and political organisation, part of the essence of Maori identity, and a taonga in its own right'. It embodied a state of being, a non-negotiable declaration, not something to be secured with the assistance of, or requested from, the Crown. 'Its presence is detected', it has been said, 'not by what one says but rather by what one does. Thus, if you want self-determination for your iwi, do it and act as though you have it.' The problem was, then, how to secure recognition and respect for rangatiratanga from a Crown which continued to demand that Maori operate accountably within its own lego-constitutional framework, especially if they were to receive state resources (including those in compensation for past losses).[5]

There was not necessarily any need to *fully* adopt 'western values' and methods in order to gain Crown recognition, however. While some Maori groupings have believed that it was not possible to 'create management systems for one culture from within the paradigm of another', others have adopted or adapted western frameworks. Still others have sought to meld the traditional and the non-traditional, and this has not precluded (indeed, it may sometimes have assisted) the forging of mutually beneficial relationships with the state. Ngapuhi's runanga, for example, aimed to build a governance regime which had both a legal relationship with the Crown and incorporated 'traditional dispute resolution processes based in the law and tikanga of Ngapuhi'.

A number of groups have taken up the challenge of bringing rangatiratanga into the global marketplace, even if its values might be antithetical to their traditional and even contemporary worldview. Some tribal and urban organisations saw little choice after the economic rationalisation of the 1980s–90s than to participate in the international economy through such devices as joint ventures; they would be better able to engage with the Crown on their own terms once they had built up a resource base through such means. A number of groupings have attempted to extend their influence on the world stage beyond the economic, with Te Runanga a Iwi o Ngapuhi, for example, seeking to 'establish diplomatic, political, cultural and economic relations with ... Indigenous Nations', and making a number of appeals to international bodies to put pressure on the New Zealand Crown to respect rangatiratanga.[6]

Views on rangatiratanga and relationships both remain diverse and continue to diversify. Certain Maori commentators argue that rangatiratanga is, in effect, unconscionably compromised by many or most forms of its modern organisational expression, especially where these are franchised in some way by the Crown. Some declare that anything short of full kotahitanga represents surrender to a modern divide and rule strategy by the state. Others claim, for quite different reasons, that divide and rule is implicit in *any* organised mode of rangatiratanga: since Maori are disproportionately represented in lower socio-economic sectors, any form of politico-cultural separateness splits off Maori from the pakeha working-class and its struggles. This is said not only to help perpetuate the capitalist social relations which underpin Crown supremacy, but also to create downstream consequences as well. These are argued to include encouragement of racist attitudes among pakeha which further divide the white from the brown proletariat, and delaying radical socio-economic reforms which alone can bring the parity with pakeha that is implicit in Article Three of the Treaty. The quest for rangatiratanga through any exclusively Maori-orientated organisational effort, then, leaves 'intact the very social order which consigns Maori to the bottom of the heap' in the first place.

In some pakeha variants of such reasoning, the two populations are so 'thoroughly intermixed' that Maori cannot be defined as an 'oppressed nation' or anything like it. Those identifying as Maori are advised to make common cause with the white working class in a fashion which 'takes into account the double oppression of Maori workers' and utilises Maori collectivist impulses to further the class struggle. Some analysts continue to believe that the 'politicisation of ethnicity' since the 1970s, supposedly based on a process of 'retribalisation' driven by a bourgeois elite, has led many Maori to support neotribes that are 'subverting democracy'. The neotribe is defined as 'a private economic corporation in the accumulative system of global capitalism' which 'conceals its privatised character' by an appeal to 'communalism'. This ploy has allegedly seduced not just Maori but much of the pakeha left into supporting structures whose corporate operations have little to do with traditional social-democratic or socialist notions of collective endeavour and justice for all. Few Maori have subscribed publicly to such views, although some have expressed opinions that resonate with elements of the analysis – in condemning, for example, runanga flirting with Rogernomics and its successor policies under subsequent governments.

Neither this book nor its predecessor, *State Authority, Indigenous Autonomy*, is directly about class, central though this is in a capitalist society and so highly relevant as it is to the lives of the majority of Maori people, especially after 1950. Having been stripped of their resources and subjected to huge assimilationist pressures thereafter, Maori were needed in the cities from the mid-twentieth century to form an urban workforce for an industrialising nation. They continue to make up a disproportionate percentage of the working class and, more generally, of the disadvantaged in society, as a variety of statistical indicators make clear; the Maori cancer mortality rate, for example, was twice that of non-Maori at the end of the twentieth century, and Maori remain highly over-represented in court and corrections statistics. All that being said, this book examines the politico-cultural aspirations, during the second half of the twentieth century, of those who identify as Maori and the reactions of the state to their various ways of organising the quest for te tino rangatiratanga. While class forms a very necessary backdrop, indigenous aspirations, and the state's concerns (and fears) regarding them, are about much more than class.[7]

Any book analysing the *actual* organisational forms of Crown–Maori relations in the decades after 1950 is not, then, the place to examine in depth the views of those who advocate pursuing a form of rangatiratanga by subsuming it within wider class struggles – important as such perspectives were in radical Maori circles at the outset of the modern Maori Renaissance. One might note, however, that arguments centring around combining Maori and pakeha class struggle are compatible with some standard twentieth-century Marxian perspectives on ethno-cultural national minorities: self-determination is not only feasible but may be a necessary stage on the way to a socialist society, a way of removing a key 'roadblock' on the highway to socialism.

In such interpretations, moreover, the indigenous ethnic group, in its struggle against state coercion and hegemony, can (given that it is collectivist in orientation in the first place) readily establish structures and promote thinking which both assist the attainment of and 'pre-figure' a post-capitalist society. One might also reiterate, at this point, that milder versions of left-wing perspectives regarding ethnicity have been endemic within New Zealand social democratic movements – certainly since they began seeking Maori support in the 1920s. Such views live on as part of the broad debate about what kind and degree of social 'equality' should be sought, and they continue to temper Labour's attitude to Maori issues. The Labour-led governments from 1999 onwards, focusing (reasonably successfully) on 'reducing inequalities', tended to be lukewarm on issues of rangatiratanga – and even positively hostile to it at times, especially over the issue of the foreshore and seabed – and settlements.

Accommodating and Confronting Rangatiratanga

This latter would not matter under post-modernist arguments that the Treaty settlement discourse constitutes a 'mask' that 'protects the construction of Crown unitary sovereignty', 'displaces claims for recognition of *tino rangatiratanga*', and 'reinscribes the colonisation process'. Most Maori leaders and observers, however, preferring action and results to theoretical contemplation, tend to see Treaty settlements as evidence of Crown recognition of rangatiratanga to a certain, not unimportant, degree. Over and above that, many believe that some types of organisational autonomy are now within the realms of possibility. Scholars and practitioners of rangatiratanga generally concur that there are 'enough cross-ethnic common interests' for 'justice to be negotiated' between Maori and the Crown, albeit probably on the basis of new foundational principles. The Waitangi Tribunal has noted that Maori autonomy does not necessarily need to conflict with Crown sovereignty, and most historical Maori assertions of rangatiratanga have accepted the overarching sovereignty of the Crown. There is, moreover, a strong strand of international scholarship to the effect that indigenous self-determination can largely be accommodated within existing or perhaps slightly modified jurisdictional parameters.

The political exercise of Crown sovereignty, then, *can* accommodate devolution, difference and even overlapping spheres of influence and control. It is not impossible to envisage 'hybrid situations', such as negotiated partnerships or even power sharing arrangements, which combine elements of what used to be called integration (as one would expect in a demographic environment of co-mingling and intermarriage) with those of self-determination. In New Zealand, these would ideally, in the words of the United Nations Special Rapporteur after his visit in 2006, amount to constitutional (or similar) reform embodying 'positive recognition and meaningful provision for Maori as a distinct people, possessing an alternative system of knowledge, philosophy and law'.[8]

As scholars have noted, it is far from surprising that the Crown has not conceded to relinquish its full sovereign powers. But this still leaves room for many possibilities of Crown recognition of post-settlement or other governance regimes which could lay the foundations for both exercise of rangatiratanga and the establishment of a permanent autonomist nexus between Maori and Crown. With appropriate models for rangatiratanga still proving elusive by the end of the twentieth century, many Maori entities of disparate nature were engaged at that time in the quest for workable organisational forms. The fate of the Maori Congress did not dissuade some from continuing to develop ideas for federalised or centralised modes of organisation which would operate independently of the Crown and exert pressure on it as a kind of informal partner. One suggestion was for a 'ruling council of elders to act as a policy-making and policy-deciding body', so that tangata whenua could 'make our own laws and make important decisions regarding our future as Maori', advocating with the Crown where its decisions had relationship ramifications. Many groups proclaiming kotahitanga either formed or resurfaced in stronger form at this time, a few of them (such as the energetic 'Confederation of the Sovereign and Independent United Tribes of Aotearoa', which claimed a pre-colony lineage) professing not to recognise 'pakeha' law or governance in any way.[9]

But the Crown, not surprisingly, demanded that it be recognised and its rules respected. It was, moreover, prepared to talk with those self-determinationist groupings in which it perceived some kind of synergy between rhetoric and reality. A number of developments arising from such discussions had 'created genuine space for Maori initiatives', whatever the motivations from within the state might have been. At the end of the century, a meeting at Hopuhopu to discuss the possibility of alternative constitutional arrangements was just one of very many forums exploring ways of obtaining and embedding official acknowledgement for rangatiratanga. Some continued to focus on the parliamentary mode, calling for a 'unified Maori political vehicle' within the House of Representatives, or exploring the concept of a Maori House of

Parliament. Several groups asserting kotahitanga were preparing to establish their own 'parliaments'. Others preferred a localised approach, including taking up opportunities offered by programmes such as 'reducing inequalities'. Despite its needs-based orientation, this did include 'the goal of Maori and Pacific communities having the opportunity to control their own development and achieve their own objectives'.

But the next few years were to prove a disappointment to many in terms of their quest for state recognition of rangatiratanga. The needs-based discourse which underpinned Labour's resiling from the closing the gaps programme was taken much further within the National opposition, including in directions which verged on racism. Even on the question of reparations, moreover, the Labour-led government of Helen Clark (1999 to 2008) had lost momentum – that is, until its final year of office, when Deputy Prime Minister Michael Cullen took over the portfolio of Treaty negotiations and presided over many signings between Crown and claimants. Meanwhile, Crown–Maori relations had been severely strained by the government's adverse reaction to a 2003 judicial decision encompassing potential tribal ownership of portions of the foreshore and seabed. Fearful of the National politicians' potential to 'play the race card', and cognisant of broader issues of power and ownership (as well as the stance of coalition partner New Zealand First), Clark and her ministers decided to strip tribal groupings of the right to take legal action to determine whether they had ownership interests. Having made that decision very quickly, they then declined to consult in any meaningful way with Maori.

This flagrant disrespect for rangatiratanga violated some of the central tenets of the 1989 *Principles for Crown Action* and was seen by many Maori as a more serious breach of the Treaty than the foreshore and seabed issue itself, on which a negotiated position that would suit all parties was not impossible to envisage. A huge protest hikoi to Wellington in 2004 was derided by the Prime Minister, and that year the government secured legislation which overturned the judicial ruling (while enabling negotiated arrangements, against the wishes of an even harder-line National opposition). The government's refusal to even listen to the strongly voiced wishes of a united Maoridom was the catalyst for the formation of the Maori Party, a new manifestation of old strategies for seeking rangatiratanga through kotahitanga. By November 2008, the party had become so influential that it could negotiate two ministerial posts outside Cabinet (including Maori Affairs) in a support arrangement with an incoming National government.

Prior to the election, the Maori Party had indicated that, in pursuit of rangatiratanga, it would attempt to secure a governing arrangement recognising it as the Treaty partner with the Crown. Some commentators noted the extreme difficulty of such an aspiration, given the long history of the state's successes in appropriating various autonomous Maori initiatives, structures and procedures. And as in the past, the Maori desire for autonomy constituted, for many, an implicit threat to the Crown's supreme authority. In recent years, the growing number of Maori Members of Parliament under MMP had been gaining appreciation of the odds against achieving rangatiratanga, even at flaxroots level. In 1998, the Minister of Maori Affairs himself, Tau Henare, had noted that even the pioneering kohanga reo initiative was becoming a 'sanitised, bureaucratised and standardised' institution as a result of government compliance requirements.

Certainly, the hopes for partnership which had been so high in the late 1980s, and which had been dealt so major a blow by repeal of the Runanga Iwi Act, had not been met in either the following decade or the early twenty-first century. In the 1990s, the National government had tried to forge 'relational' rather than 'structural' ties with Maori, and this had seemed to have autonomist potential. Maori utilisation of post-1990 ideas of 'rights-integration', of negotiating 'rights' that were consonant with those of the broader community, also offered hope, surviving even the serious onslaught on rangatiratanga by the foreshore and seabed legislation. The enthusiasm at the turn of the millennium for 'celebrating diversity' similarly provided new opportunities, although it also brought dangers – such as attempts in some quarters to downplay the special place of Maori as tangata whenua and co-signatories to the nation's iconic 'founding document', the Treaty of Waitangi, or even to deny that tangata whenua had a different place or status in New Zealand life to that of other citizens, including the most recent migrants from diverse nations.[10]

Relational Dialogue

Whatever the difficulties, most notably over the foreshore and seabed (but also other matters, such as the state's armed raids on Urewera Maori in 2007), dialogue continued between Crown and Maori in the early years of the new century, from the highest to the lowest levels. As J G A Pocock has noted, despite a 'perpetually contested' relationship between the parties to the Treaty, conversations, negotiations, mediations and discussion remain integral to this 'history of contestation'. Ever since the final armed clash between Crown and Maori in 1916 (also in the Urewera), the indigenous quest for Crown recognition of rangatiratanga has remained remarkably peaceful, partly because of the willingness of both parties in most circumstances to keep talking, to korero. Moreover, that propensity to discuss frequently led to Crown concessions to rangatiratanga – even if these often involved a motive to ultimately appropriate Maori organisational forms, energies and policies for state purposes.

Growing pakeha awareness of the dispossession of Maori in the colonial and more recent past has underpinned the continuing dialogue since the time of the Maori Renaissance, making the prospects of realising Crown recognition of rangatiratanga to some level of Maori satisfaction rather less unlikely than during the assimilationist years. While movement in pakeha and Crown circles on issues of historical justice was slow, it was nevertheless significant. The Labour government of the later 1980s implicitly accepted responsibility for past Crown wrongdoing by mere dint of its pioneering negotiations, but it refused to admit this publicly out of concern for possible downstream effects. At the beginning of the new millennium, however, the incoming Labour minister in charge of Treaty of Waitangi negotiations openly acknowledged that she represented a Crown that 'through war, trickery and neglect deprived Maori of land, resources, cultural rights, language and, in some cases, life itself'.

Despite greater pakeha awareness of the Maori past, however, and the huge advances since 1950 in political and public appreciation of the need for reconciliation, any forging of Crown–rangatiratanga relationships acceptable to all parties seemed a long way off in 2008. When an anti-poverty 'hikoi of hope' headed for Wellington in 1998, Whatarangi Winiata (who would later become founding president of the Maori Party) reminded politicians that Maori leaders generally saw constitutional (or equivalent) change, based on Treaty partnership with the Crown, as the only way forward. In the years since, most serious observers and scholars of Crown–Maori relations, Maori and pakeha, have believed that the Crown needs to engage with the very many sustained and insistent calls for constitutionalising rangatiratanga. At the very least, there seems to be an emergent consensus in such circles on the need for the Crown to engage in a public debate on the possibilities of formalising governance arrangements which will satisfy Maori aspirations to rangatiratanga. No such 'conversations' will lead to quick-fix remedies to the many actual and perceived problems, if history is to be any guide.

But the extreme difficulties of finding adequate ways of recognising rangatiratanga can be alleviated in different ways by the various parties. The Crown might consider re-examining its weddedness to interpretations of (indivisible) sovereignty which preclude meaningful devolution of powers, for example, and some Maori parties might reconsider better dovetailing of the terminology employed with the goals sought. Furthermore, Crown and Maori cannot find in isolation that elusive solution to balancing the aspirations of the indigenous people of New Zealand against other 'public good' responsibilities of state. A pakeha population reportedly suffering from 'Treaty fatigue' will need to appreciate better the roots of the grievances underpinning the reparations system, and, even more importantly, to understand that the Treaty symbolises, in this country, the autonomist aspirations of formerly colonised peoples around he world. It is not, in other words, something that will disappear when the ast historically-based grievances of Maori are resolved (currently destined by official decree to occur in 2015). The Treaty of Waitangi, in its various forms, nterpretations and updatings, constitutes an iconic affirmation of the need for he Crown to commit to negotiating organisational modes and relationships which embody Maori aspirations that are not going to go away.

In the ongoing dialogue with Maori, and in any relational arrangements hat might be negotiated out of it, governments will do well to learn from the history of Crown–Maori relations. This might alert them, inter alia, to avoid the twin temptations of attempting to control and appropriate the organisations of Maoridom. Greater knowledge of the past history of Aotearoa/New Zealand should assist the pakeha public, too, to better appreciate that the Treaty of Waitangi is a 'living' document that embodies the Maori quest for rangatiratanga, and that its successful evolution in the new millennium depends on continued dialogue and negotiation based on good faith. New Zealand is often singled out internationally as a prime example of a nation in which 'bicultural' aspects or ways of life are successfully emerging, with both state encouragement and assistance. Bicultural Aotearoa/New Zealand, moreover, is frequently viewed as a country which accommodates a multicultural diversity based on widespread acceptance of the customs and mores of immigrant ethnicities. Its 'race relations', despite many difficulties, are seen to provide cause for cautious optimism, especially if all parties are willing and able to heed the lessons of the past.[11]

National, Regional and Local Developments and Debates

In seeking to pursue rangatiratanga in the early years of the twenty-first century, increasing numbers of Maori were looking to the past in working on various ideas for reviving kotahitanga. It was in the context of innumerable debates within Maoridom on this issue that, gradually, the main unity focus shifted towards forming a new Maori political party. In the MMP environment, many saw, such a parliamentary grouping might come to hold the balance of political power and (among other things) be able to force constitutional reform onto the political agenda. By the time of its 1999 election victory, Labour had regained the support of the Ratana movement and reclaimed the Maori seats from political opponents. But with almost universal Maori protest at its overturning of their right to access the judiciary to fight for customary rights to the foreshore and seabed, the time had come for those planning a unified party of indigeneity to put their proposals into action.

At the 2005 election, the new Maori Party presented its kaupapa, one based fully on rangatiratanga. This translated, said its co-leader (and former Labour minister) Tariana Turia, as 'self determination', and in winning four of the seven Maori seats the party made a good start to its journey towards a support role in government three years later, after it gained a fifth seat. As the end of 2008 approached, the Maori Party began preparing the groundwork – with Pita Sharples as Minister of Maori Affairs – for future discussions on Crown-Maori relations, the National leadership having agreed to set aside its proposed abolition of the Maori electorate seats.

Quite apart from this and other developments at nationwide level, many Maori – tribally-based or otherwise – had always continued to seek recognition of rangatiratanga in regional, district or local environments. As well as the ambitious devolution plans of that time, during the lead-up to local government reform in 1989 there had been discussions about including reference to the Treaty of Waitangi in the relevant legislation. When this did not happen, and the Runanga Iwi Act was repealed as well, the pursuit of rangatiratanga at regional level or below seemed to suffer a set-back. The Resource Management Act of 1991, however, in allowing for the Treaty principles to be 'taken into account' led to much greater consultation with Maori. Some local authorities went so far as to establish formal relationships with tribes in their area. Elsewhere arrangements were made in some Treaty settlements to ensure that Maori could participate more fully in local-body decision-making. When a regional council created a precedent in 1998 by establishing seats for Maori (a provision ratified legislatively in 2001), this was widely seen as a promising precedent although it proved to be controversial one.

All such measures and events provided hope for greater progress in recognition of rangatiratanga, especially in the context of a heightening national and international discourse on 'genuine *self*-rule' and much talk of tino rangatiratanga being 'the central objective' for Maori. Just before the new millennium, officials acknowledged that the 'Tribunal has shown that what is required for truly Māori development is the exercise of rangatiratanga', their definition of which clustered around 'the collective power of the group to exercise control over its resources, determine priorities and, to the extent reasonable, fix its own policies and manage its own programmes'. In 2000, Labour's Maori MPs were urging upon their own government the importance of 'Maori autonomy, self-determination or self-rule', although they were facing somewhat of an uphill struggle – partly as a result of a degree of pakeha backlash.[12]

Right-wing 'anti-Treatyist' scholars and polemicists had been worrying away for many years at the increasing weight given to rangatiratanga. One expressed the view that '[n]o matter how generous we are with land and money, [Maori] will not be satisfied, because they want power as well'. While such extreme sovereigntist stances were usually held only on the populist right, possible ramifications of rangatiratanga also concerned left-wing commentators for whom the interests of the poor and the dispossessed could only be guaranteed by an 'absolute and indivisible' sovereign state of social-democratic or socialist orientation. For some, the choice was between a 'modern, democratic and prosperous nation' based on 'equality of rights' and a 'culturally divided, economically stagnant and aristocratically misgoverned Pacific backwater'.

Responses to such binary approaches might note that states elsewhere, of many a political ilk, could readily find a place for indigenous autonomy, including through devolution of politico-cultural powers. In any case, matters within the province of sovereignty are as routinely devolved to non- or semi-state entities in New Zealand as in other western jurisdictions. A legitimated use of coercion, for example, is granted to private security firms and Maori wardens for specific purposes. Even a major exercise of devolution, of course, does present the advocates of tino rangatiratanga with the problem that whatever powers are sanctioned can later be taken away, but proponents of a devolutionist approach argue that this does not preclude the negotiation of acceptable autonomist arrangements for power sharing or partnership.[13]

Public and academic debate on such matters is often both bewildering and rapidly evolving, and history and other disciplines are frequently involved. One approach, for example, combines the insights of cultural studies with recent historical attempts to avoid interpretation of the past in terms of the present ('presentism'). It urges re-examining the 'over-simplified and essentialised' bicultural paradigm within which many debates are couched. New possibilities are posed, including a 'reconceptualisation of bicultural politics in Aotearoa/New Zealand that draws on an inclusionary and multifaceted identity politics'. Such perspectives, it is argued, could lead to concepts that move beyond the implicitly adversarial lens of bi- or multi-culturalism. The prospect of an 'interculturalism' is raised, involving a search for a hybrid New Zealandness based on 'the criss-crossing, the overlapping [and] the in-betweenness of cultures'. While the Treaty and the tangata whenua would retain their distinctive place and status, any such quest would also aim to find 'common ground within the dynamic of exchange, interchange and inclusion'.[14]

Care needs to be taken, however, at the interface of scholarship and its social or political application. The study of Crown–Maori relations, especially 'Treaty of Waitangi issues', can tempt scholars to veer towards advocacy rather than analysis. History produced for the Treaty reconciliation processes, in particular, will sometimes reflect the overt agenda of the commissioning agency, especially when the legal profession intervenes in its production. It can also have other consequences, such as a tendency 'to emphasize the particular over the general, and Maori as victim over Maori as agent' – or, indeed, Maori as agent over Maori as victim.

This book, like its predecessor, is one not of advocacy but interpretation. Given its time frame, it has focused on the general, on the essence, rather than on the specific. It has explored the endeavours of Maori institutions, first to resist the Crown's assimilation policies and, when these were abandoned through lack of success, to forge relationships with the Crown which respected Maori and their rangatiratanga. It has examined the state's attempts to contain and supersede autonomist expressions and energies, using (among other things) the tools of appropriation; and it has analysed the Crown's efforts, once it had formally abandoned assimilation, to address rangatiratanga in ways which could also contain the more ambitious aspirations within Maoridom.

Ever since 1840, Maori have faced massive armed and hegemonic conquest, loss of land and other resources, assimilationist onslaught on their culture, marginalisation, dispersal from their turangawaewae, and appropriation of indigenous organisational forms and energies. If the history of Crown–Maori relations in New Zealand – and, more broadly, the whole historical experience of ethnicity and indigeneity under imperialism and post-coloniality – is a reliable guide (and it would be remarkable were it not), the Maori quest for autonomy or self-determination, for enhancement of and respect for rangatiratanga, will not go away. Until, that is, the Crown addresses the issue of rangatiratanga in ways that satisfy Maori in their various collective modes of organisation – tribal, sub-tribal, pan-tribal and non-tribal.[15]

Past and Future

That being said, one can equally predict that what the Privy Council has called 'the continuing needs of the state' will continue to suffuse and underpin governmental attitudes towards rangatiratanga. In 2002, the Governor-General noted the Crown's stated commitment in 'fulfilling its obligations as a treaty partner to support self-determination for whanau, hapu and iwi'. But (in the words of a Te Puni Kokiri policy document) any recognition of rangatiratanga will need, in the eyes of the state decision-makers, to be 'balanced against the duty of the Crown to exercise good government (kawanatanga) for all New Zealanders'. At times, in fact, 'the demands of rangatiratanga are considered by the Government to be contrary to the national interest'. When convenor of the Maori Congress, Whanganui kaumatua Archie Taiaroa encapsulated many Maori responses on such ramifications of indivisible Crown sovereignty: 'The New Zealand Government is saying that it agrees with self-determination of indigenous people, yet it must be at the behest of the Government'.

Using the terms of the Treaty-based rubric within which most such debates are conducted, the challenge can be depicted as that of finding arrangements for reconciling Article One (and, to a lesser degree, Three) with Article Two, of negotiating accommodations between kawanatanga/Crown sovereignty and rangatiratanga/Maori autonomy. Maori who pin their hopes on 'the law' being anything more than just one tool in what is essentially a political struggle will likely continue to be as frustrated as those who have relied on the justice system in the past. Even with a judiciary as sympathetic to Maori as it can be, the political executive and Parliament (and their advisers) will still make up their own minds, within their own politico-cultural paradigms, as to what constitutes the public good and how rangatiratanga fits into it. Laws, of course, can be changed if they are inconvenient. It is not conceivable that the state would consider relinquishing ultimate power, including the authority to decide not only on laws but also the exceptions to the 'rule of law'.

All in all, any embedding of rangatiratanga into Crown–Maori relations will need (short of armed overthrow of the state, which has not been on any serious agenda) to fit the Crown's self-chosen sovereigntist parameters. This does not, however, exclude the possibility of the state's decision-makers re-examining their long-term insistence on a fully 'indivisible sovereignty' which precludes any fundamental or even significant degree of devolution, power sharing or partnership. It will not be easy to work out arrangements which satisfy the fundamental imperatives on 'both sides of the Treaty relationship', especially given the complexity within each: the state's internal contestabilities and its majority pakeha citizenry, and the multiply-based and overlapping institutions of organisation and power within Maoridom.

While Maori might have good cause to feel frustrated at the slow progress towards Crown recognition of rangatiratanga, by the approach of the new millennium, unlike in 1950, the debate on ways of finding a modus vivendi between Crown sovereignty and Maori autonomy had become intense, public and nationwide. A state agency could now declare that 'the Crown should support and enhance the exercise of rangatiratanga as far as it possibly can, limited only by its wider responsibilities to the nation'. Sociologist David Pearson has noted that by the time of the sesquicentennial commemoration of the signing of the Treaty of Waitangi, whereas the 'one people, one nation' idea had always been illusory, the replacement dream of 'two peoples, one nation' was one that seemed attainable – even if it remained a 'Dream Deferred'.[16]

For Maori to gain Crown recognition of te tino rangatiratanga, decision-makers on both sides will need to explore ways of genuinely meeting indigenous aspirations. Unless 'relative degrees of power' can be accommodated in a fashion satisfactory to all affected parties, New Zealanders remain set to reprise in new form the essential experiences of the past – in which 'solutions' accepted by Maori as the maximum achievable in the circumstances turn out to be, at very best, 'on account' ways of embedding rangatiratanga. Overall, the need to address rangatiratanga has been increasingly recognised within the state through time, even though such appreciation has developed unevenly and been subject to delays and retreats as well as to advances. Early in the twenty-first century, a paper before the Cabinet Policy Committee acknowledged that '[w]hen historical grievances are finally behind us, when Maori take their place fully alongside other New Zealanders in socio-economic terms, there will still be a distinct Maori culture, a distinct indigenous people with whom the Government will continue to have a special constitutional relationship'.

It was rare to find anything even approaching such sentiments within the state or pakeha society half a century before; in the early years of the new millennium, they were common, although often cautious about the use and meaning of the word 'constitutional'. In 2004, Parliament established a Constitutional Arrangements Committee to 'undertake a review of New Zealand's existing constitutional arrangements', and many Maori, including the co-leader of the Maori Party, projected into the ensuing debate the notion that rangatiratanga was at 'the heart of the relationship' between Crown and Maori. While this episode, as with many of its predecessors, ended inconclusively, constitutional scrutiny was one of the concessions the Maori Party received in late 2008 in return for its support role for the new National government.[17]

Autonomist issues, then, remain a central item of national political and cultural discourse, despite (and because of) the nation's growing multi-culturalism and 'celebration of diversity'. In the words of one academic commentator of Indian origin: 'The chief purpose of public policy in New Zealand in relation to Maori must be the creation of constitutional-political structures and processes which enable Pakeha and Maori (as well as the other ethnic components) to live in peace and harmony, and which facilitate the growth, in the long run, of an integrated new nation based on Western as well as on Maori ways of life and values'. There *were* ways, he believed, of 'reconciling New Zealand with Aotearoa'. Of the various suggestions in the 'national conversation' at the turn of the millennium, the concept of a 'middle way', guaranteeing both indigenous authority and the overarching authority of the Crown, was among those most frequently explored. One variation of this envisaged a post-colonial 'contract' between Crown and Maori on the basis of broad societal agreement on such issues as partnership, equity, inclusiveness, open mindedness and 'workable mutuality' at social as well as political levels.[18]

Concluding Remarks

The post-war history of Crown–Maori relations can provide information and insights of use in New Zealand's vigorous public debates about the actual and potential role of te tino rangatiratanga in state and society and the country's current and desired 'national identity'. This book does not, however, seek to apply history; instead, it provides interpretational history which can be applied if readers so choose. If it has any prescriptive contribution to make to the 'nation building' discourses of the present time, this would be to endorse the views of those who argue that if workable constitutional or other arrangements are to be developed to meet the durable Maori aspirations for state respect for rangatiratanga, informed, open-ended and prejudice-free dialogue and debate are required between all interested parties.

Solutions to the inherent difficulties of (re)incorporating Aotearoa into New Zealand under modern circumstances, of course, need to be generally acceptable to the great majority of the populace if they are to have any chance of long-term success. An anthropologist writing some three decades ago noted that '[i]f the Pakeha majority does not understand the implications of the Maori search for identity and if it reacts with hostility to the growth of Maori nationalism and remains blind to the growing necessity for cultural pluralism, then with the rise of Maori consciousness there will be a realisation of the limitations of passivity. More militant doctrines will take hold'. While no government in a democratic political system can move too far beyond the views of the majority, however, one which provided a lead that took 'mainstream society' to the edge of its comfort zone might be able to stake a claim to preside over a key turning point in the history of Crown–Maori relations in New Zealand.

Circumstances seem more propitious (or less unpropitious) for such an eventuality at the present time than at any point in the past. Before the end of the first decade of the new millennium, settlements of Maori historical grievances have become an integral part of the political and social landscape. Moreover, a finish point to this part of the Crown–Maori reconciliation processes seems substantially within reach in the foreseeable future. In many sections of state and society, there is growing acceptance that even the settling of the last of the major historical claims will not alter the need for both Crown and pakeha to recognise and respect the fundamental New Zealand truism that 'the Treaty is always speaking'. While Maori aspirations for recognition of rangatiratanga have yet to be fully addressed, Crown–Maori relations, and the social attitudes which underpin them, have moved a very long way since 1950.[19]

Endnotes

This book follows the practice of its predecessor in using references which perform several functions: to serve as general indicators of key sources used in developing the preceding paragraphs, to identify the sources of quotes, and to provide a guide to further reading. Sources are cited in full on first appearance, and abbreviated in subsequent endnotes. The book does not extensively cite general histories of New Zealand which are invaluable for placing post-war Crown–Maori relations in the broad context of the country's history, such as (and especially) James Belich's *Paradise Reforged: A History of the New Zealanders from the 1880s to the Year 2000*, Michael King's popular *Penguin History of New Zealand* and Philippa Mein Smith's *A Concise History of New Zealand*. These and other general histories are useful for providing information and analysis relevant to sizeable sectors of the text.

Preface

1. Hill, Richard S, *State Authority, Indigenous Autonomy: Crown–Maori Relations in New Zealand/Aotearoa 1900–1950*, Wellington, 2004. For some preliminary thinking on such issues, see a report for the Crown Forestry Rental Trust: Hill, Richard S, 'Autonomy and Authority: Rangatiratanga and the Crown in Twentieth Century New Zealand: An Overview', Wellington, 2000; and for a summary, see my chapter on Crown–Maori relations in *The New Oxford History of New Zealand*, forthcoming (2009), edited by Giselle Byrnes. The standard text on the Treaty is Claudia Orange's *The Treaty of Waitangi*, Wellington, 1987. See also her *An Illustrated History of the Treaty of Waitangi*, Wellington, 2004, for useful updating on 'Treaty relationships'.
2. Bhabha, Homi (interviewed by Paul Thompson), 'Between Identities', in Benmayor, Rina and Scotnes, Andor (eds), *Migration and Identity*, Oxford, 1994 (for 'empowerment' and 'autonomy' quotes); Fanon, Frantz, *The Wretched of the Earth*, London, 1967; Freire, Paulo, *Pedagogy of the Oppressed*, New York, 1970 (1986 ed, Ramos trans); Rodney, Walter, *How Europe Underdeveloped Africa*, Washington DC, 1981 (rev ed). See too Smith, Linda Tuhiwai, *Decolonizing Methodologies: Research and Indigenous Peoples*, Dunedin, 1999.
3. The name given to assimilationist policies changed over time, but, as I argue in my chapter in the *New Oxford History of New Zealand*, the goals remained essentially the same. See too Harris, Aroha, 'Dancing with the State: Maori Creative Energy and Policies of Integration, 1945–1967', PhD thesis, University of Auckland, 2007. For a comment by a leading scholar of Maori issues, Erik Schwimmer,

in 1960, see I H Kawharu, 'Introduction', in Brookes, R H and Kawharu, I H (eds), *Administration in New Zealand's Multi-racial Society*, Wellington, 1967, p9. For a different perspective, see Ward, Alan, *A Show of Justice: Racial 'Amalgamation' in Nineteenth Century New Zealand*, Auckland, 1995 (rev ed).

4. Orange, *The Treaty of Waitangi*, pp 257–9 (for Treaty text). See Ward, Alan, *An Unsettled History: Treaty Claims in New Zealand Today*, Wellington, 1999, for a modern aspect of Treaty-based relationships – reparations for past breaches by the Crown of the Treaty.

Introduction

1. Maori are seen as constituting an ethnic group, that is 'a group of persons bound together by common origin and interests': Metge, Joan, 'Alternative Policy Patterns in Multi-racial Societies', in Brookes, R H and Kawharu, I H (eds), *Administration in New Zealand's Multi-racial Society*, Wellington, 1967, p42.
2. Ward, *A Show of Justice*; Harris, 'Dancing with the State', pp 1, 5–6; O'Malley, Vincent, *Agents of Autonomy: Maori Committees in the Nineteenth Century*, Wellington, 1997 (rev ed, 1998); Mangan, J A (ed), *Making Imperial Mentalities: Socialisation and British Imperialism*, Manchester, 1990, p16.
3. On the 1945 Act, see Hill, *State Authority*, ch8; see also Lange, Raeburn, *To Promote Maori Well-Being: Tribal Committees and Executives under the Maori Social and Economic Advancement Act, 1945–1962*, Wellington, Treaty of Waitangi Research Unit, 2006.
4. Durie, Mason, *Te Mana, Te Kāwanatanga: The Politics of Māori Self-Determination*, Auckland, 1998, p54; Department of Maori Affairs, 'Report of the Board of Maori Affairs, Secretary, and the Maori Trustee', *Appendices to the Journals of the House of Representatives* (AJHR), G-9, 1960, pp 16–7; McEwen, J M, 'Urbanisation and the Multi-racial Society', in Brookes, R H and Kawharu, I H (eds), *Administration in New Zealand's Multi-racial Society*, Wellington, 1967, p77.
5. For the best general history coverage of the period of this book, see Belich, James, *Paradise Reforged: A History of the New Zealanders from the 1880s to the Year 2000*, Auckland, 2001. For the main Maori perspective on Crown–Maori relations, refer to Walker, Ranginui J, *Ka Whawhai Tonu Matou: Struggle Without End*, Auckland, 1990 (rev ed 2004); Harris, 'Dancing with the State', has in-depth coverage and an interpretation with which this book and its predecessor works generally accord. Howe, K R, *Race Relations: Australia and New Zealand: A Comparative Survey 1770's–1970's*, Wellington, 1977, has useful observations in chapter seven on relevant matters, such as Maori feeling at home in both rural marae and city community.
6. Tennant, Margaret, Review of *State Authority, Indigenous Autonomy*, in *Australian Historical Studies*, vol 37, no 127, April 2006, p232 (for 'disembodied entity' and following quotes); Cullen, Michael, 'Observations on the Role of Government', Speech Notes, 27 August 2003, http://www.beehive.govt.nz/node/17678 [accessed 17 March 2008] (re 'internal order'). State functions, Cullen states, 'create markets ... and establish and enforce the terms under which property rights transfer', whether the individual citizen likes it or not. For the concept of 'peace and good order' and related matters, refer to my multi-volumed contributions to 'The History of Policing in New Zealand' series, which were published between 1986 and 1994: *Policing the Colonial Frontier: The Theory and Practice of Coercive Social and Racial Control in New Zealand, 1767–1867*, Wellington, 1986; *The Colonial Frontier Tamed: New Zealand Policing in Transition, 1867–1886*, Wellington, 1989; *The Iron Hand in the Velvet Glove: The Modernisation of Policing in New Zealand, 1886–1917*, Palmerston North, 1995.
7. Boast, Richard, *Buying the Land, Selling the Land: Governments and Maori Land in the North Island 1865–1921*, Wellington, 2008, p17 (for 'new tendencies in historical writing' quote); Mitchell, Tom, '"Legal Gentlemen Appointed by the Federal Government": the Canadian State, the Citizens' Committee of 1000, and Winnipeg's Seditious Conspiracy Trials of 1919–1920', *Labour/Le Travail*, issue 53, Spring 2004, http://www.historycooperative.org/journals/llt/53/mitchell.html (par 3 for 'was a mystery' quote). On just how proactive the Crown can be in ensuring 'order' on its own terms, see Nolan, Melanie (ed), *Revolution: The 1913 Great Strike in New Zealand*, Christchurch, 2005. The definition of sovereignty cited here dates back to the sixteenth-century work of Jean Bodin and was most clearly elucidated in the twentieth century by Carl Schmitt: see his *Political Theology: Four Chapters on the Concept of Sovereignty*, Cambridge Mass, 1985 (1st ed, Berlin, 1922), pp 5, 8–9. Schmitt

became a fascist, something which possibly says more about the implications of wielding sovereignty than about the value or otherwise of the theory.

8. Williams, Raymond, *Culture and Materialism: Selected Essays*, London/New York, 1980 (2005 ed), pp 37–9.

9. The term 'race relations', ubiquitous in New Zealand historiography and public discourse, has been much criticised for some good (and some not so good) reasons. However, attempts by sociologists, anthropologists and others to replace it by 'ethnic relations' or other terms have not generally succeeded, partly because the alternatives are themselves contestable. More broadly, since 'race' remains the normal usage in official and general discourse in New Zealand, I have used it in this book.

10. Head, Lyndsay, 'The Pursuit of Modernity in Maori Society: The Conceptual Bases of Citizenship in the Early Colonial Period', in Sharp, Andrew and McHugh, Paul (eds), *Histories, Power and Loss: Uses of the Past – A New Zealand Commentary*, Wellington, 2001, pp 97–9, 116 (for 'law-based citizenship' quote); Hickford, Mark, *Review of State Authority, Indigenous Autonomy,* in *English Historical Review*, vol CXXI, Issue 491, April 2006, pp 639–41; Waitangi Tribunal, *Maori Electoral Option Report*, Wai 413, Wellington, 1994, ch2.1, p2 (for 'eminently adaptable' quote); Muru Raupatu Marae, 'Defining Tino Rangatiratanga', discussion paper, 13 May 1995, section 3, reproduced in Yates, Bronwyn, 'Striving for Tino Rangatiratanga', in Benseman, John, Findsen, Brian and Scott, Miriama (eds), *The Fourth Sector: Adult and Community Education in Aotearoa/New Zealand*, Palmerston North, 1996, pp 96–7 (p 97 for 'recurring theme' and 'equivalent to tino rangatiratanga' quotes); Ladley, Andrew, 'The Treaty and Democratic Government', *Policy Quarterly*, 1(1), 2005, p23 (for 'degrees of autonomy' quote); Waitangi Tribunal, *The Taranaki Report: Kaupapa Tuatahi*, Wai 143, Wellington, 1996, p5 (for 'right of indigenes' quote); O'Regan, Hana, *Ko Tahu Ko Au, Kāi Tahu Tribal Identity*, Christchurch, 2001, pp 26–7 (for 'respect the choices' quote). In declining to attempt to prescribe how Maori should and should have expressed their own concepts, I have been guided by Maori colleagues who define rangatiratanga in terms of the varied organisational forms and collective perspectives held by indigenous people in various ways, at different times and in various spatial and tribal locations (I am particularly indebted to the late Tupoutahi Tamihana Te Winitana). Some (pakeha) critiques of my previous book have argued that rangatiratanga is not a valid concept after 1900 as, very often, other terms were used by Maori to describe their mana and their aspirations; this is to ignore my caveat that the terminology often changes but concepts remain. In the second half of the period covered by this book, the word rangatiratanga comes back into vogue within Maoridom, alongside and then largely superseding words such as mana.

11. Walsh, Allen C, *More and More Maoris*, Christchurch, 1971, p44 (for 'Being Maori' quote); Hickford, in *English Historical Review*, p640 (for 'binary' critique); Bargh, Maria (ed), *Resistance: An Indigenous Response to Neoliberalism*, Wellington, 2007, pp 17–8 (for 'acts of resistance' and 'indigenous power' quotes); Shaull, Richard, 'Foreword', in Freire, Paulo, *Pedagogy of the Oppressed*, New York, 1986 ed (Ramos trans), pp 12–3 (for 'ever new possibilities' quote); Weaver, John C, *The Great Land Rush and the Making of the Modern World, 1650–1900*, Montreal, 2003, p139 (for 'technology of occupation' quote); Harding, Bruce, 'Interview with Robin Winks: The Historian as Detective', *History Now/Te Pae Tawhito o te Wā*, 7(4), November 2001.

Chapter 1

1. McCreary, J R, 'Population Growth and Urbanisation', in Schwimmer, Erik (ed), *The Maori People in the Nineteen-Sixties: A Symposium*, Auckland, 1968, pp 194–201; Wood, F L W, *This New Zealand*, Hamilton, 1946, p165; Reed, A H, *The Four Corners of New Zealand*, Wellington and Auckland, 1954, p47 (for 'watching' quote); Butterworth, G V, 'Aotearoa 1769–1988: Towards a Tribal Perspective', report for Department of Maori Affairs, Wellington, 1988, ch9, pp 6–7; King, Michael, *Maori: A Photographic and Social History*, Auckland, 1983, pp 195–6; Walker, *Ka Whawhai Tonu Matou*, pp 197–8; Ausubel, David P, *Maori Youth: A Psychoethnological Study of Cultural Deprivation*, New York, 1961, p173; Walsh, *More and More Maoris*, p12; Poulsen, M F and Johnston, R J, 'Patterns of Maori

Migration', in Johnston, R J (ed), *Urbanisation in New Zealand: Geographical Essays*, Wellington, 1973 pp 150–51; Sutch, W B, *The Maori Contribution: Yesterday, Today and Tomorrow*, Wellington, 1964 pp 26–8; Walker, Ranginui J, 'Maori People Since 1950', in Rice, Geoffrey W (ed), *The Oxfor History of New Zealand*, Auckland, 1992 (2nd ed), pp 500–501; Pool, Ian, *Te Iwi Maori: A New Zealan Population Past, Present and Projected*, Auckland, 1991, p 133 (for 'rate of urbanisation' quote); Pool, Ian Dharmalingam, Arunachalam and Sceats, Janet, *The New Zealand Family from 1840: A Demograph History*, Auckland, 2007, pp 203–5; Gilling, Bryan, *'Most Barren and Unprofitable Land': The Effectivenes of Twentieth-Century Schemes to Make Maori Land Usable and Profitable*, Wellington, Treaty of Waitang Research Unit, 2008. Maori population statistics can only be approximate, for various reasons, an those in this book are generally based on official figures; see Statistics New Zealand, 'Demographi Trends 2007', table 1.02, http://www.stats.govt.nz/tables/historical-population.htm

2. New Zealand Labour Party, 'Take No Risks – Vote Labour', Wellington 1943, p 15 (for 'future security quote); Love, R Ngatata, 'Policies of Frustration: The Growth of Maori Politics: The Ratana/Labou Era', PhD thesis, Victoria University of Wellington, 1977, pp 389–97 (p 390 for 'self administration an discipline' quote); Orange, Claudia, 'The Price of Citizenship? The Maori War Effort', in Crawford John (ed), *Kia Kaha: New Zealand in the Second World War*, Melbourne, 2000 (2002 ed), p 246; Lange *Maori Well-Being*, pp 11–14; Orange, Claudia J, 'An Exercise in Maori Autonomy: The Rise an Demise of the Maori War Effort Organisation', *New Zealand Journal of History*, 21(1), April 1987 Hazlehurst, Kayleen M, 'Maori Self-Government 1945–1981: The New Zealand Maori Council an its Antecedents', *British Review of New Zealand Studies*, no 1, July 1988, p 74 (for 'follow Europea administration' quote); Corbett, Ernest, 'Foreword by the Minister of Maori Affairs', in Departmen of Maori Affairs, 'Annual Report of the Board of Maori Affairs and of the Under-Secretary', AJHR G-9, 1952, p 1; Harris, 'Dancing with the State', pp 63–6; Butterworth, G V, 'Aotearoa 1769–1988' ch 8, pp 75–6, ch 9, p 2; Butterworth, G V and Young, H R, *Maori Affairs/Nga Take Maori*, Wellington 1990, p 92; Walsh, *More and More*, p 38; Orange, Claudia J, 'A Kind of Equality: Labour and the Maor People, 1935–1949', MA thesis, University of Auckland, 1977, pp 184–5; Orange, Claudia J, 'Frase and the Maori', in Clark, Margaret (ed), *Peter Fraser: Master Politician*, Palmerston North, 1998, p 100 Walker, Ranginui J, *He Tipua: The Life and Times of Sir Āpirana Ngata*, Auckland, 2001, p 372 (for 'no for you' quote).

3. Metge, Joan, *The Maoris of New Zealand: Rautahi* (rev ed), London, 1976, pp 207–10; Orange, 'A Kin of Equality', pp 154–6, 220–22; Harris, Aroha, 'Maori and "the Maori Affairs"', in Dalley, Bronwy and Tennant, Margaret (eds), *Past Judgement: Social Policy in New Zealand History*, Dunedin, 2004 p 205 (for 'located in' quote); Department of Maori Affairs, *The Maori Today*, Wellington, 1949, p 3 (for 'tribal executives' quote); Ormsby, M J, 'Maori Tikanga and Criminal Justice', report for th Ministry of Justice, Wellington, nd, p 14 (for 'to take an interest' quote); Department of Maori Affairs 'Annual Report of the Board of Maori Affairs and of the Under-Secretary', AJHR, G-9, 1950, p 1 (re numbers of tribal committees); Harris, 'Dancing with the State', p 67 (for 'departmental goal quote).

4. Butterworth and Young, *Maori Affairs*, p 58 (for 'powers comparable' quote), p 89; Hill, *State Authority* pp 50–64 (p 50 for 'designed to draw their energies' quote; p 62 for 'meaningful rangatiratanga quote); Lange, *Maori Well-Being*, pp 8, 10, 19.

5. Minister of Maori Affairs to the Under-Secretary, 21 Sept 1948, MA, W2490, Box 56, Part 2, 35/1 General Policy and Admin – MSEA Act 1945, 1947–50 (for 'autonomous' and 'independent' quotes) Lange, *Maori Well-Being*, p 20; Orange, 'Price of Citizenship', p 246; Harris, 'Maori and "the Maor Affairs"', p 192; Department of Maori Affairs, *The Maori Today*, 1949, p 42 (for 'preservation' quote) Department of Maori Affairs, *The Maori Today*, Wellington, 3rd ed, 1964, 'Welfare' section (for 'owr culture' and 'history of other races' quotes).

6. Harris, 'Dancing with the State', p 71 (for 'committees were charged' quote); Department of Maor Affairs, *The Maori Today*, 1949, p 38 (for 'full integration' quote), p 40 (for 'friend, counsellor anc guide' quote), p 43 (for 'most important' quote); Department of Maori Affairs, *The Maori Today*, 1964 'Welfare' section (including 'assist the Maori' quote); Labrum, Bronwyn, '"Bringing families up to scratch": The Distinctive Workings of Maori State Welfare, 1944–1970', *New Zealand Journal o History*, 36(1), October 2002, p 165 (re 'race up-lift'); Labrum, Bronwyn, 'Developing "The Essential of Good Citizenship and Responsibilities" in Maori Women: Family Life, Social Change, and th

State in New Zealand, 1944–70', *Journal of Family History*, 29(4), October 2004, p447 (for 'grappled with' quote).

7. Lange, *Maori Well-Being*, pp 14, 20 (for 'think out proposals' quote); Love, 'Policies of Frustration', p401 (for 'only a shell' quote); Orange, 'A Kind of Equality', p192 (for 'nullify the purpose' quote); Orange, 'Exercise in Maori Autonomy', p169 (for 'merely another branch' quote).
8. Harris, 'Dancing with the State', p72 (for informant quote: 'everybody went to the Maori Affairs'), p76 (for 'obedient servants of the state' quote); Harris, 'Maori and "the Maori Affairs"', pp 192–7; Gilling, *'Most Barren and Unprofitable Land'*; Metge, Joan, personal communication, 27 Nov 2006.
9. Fleras, Augie, 'A Descriptive Analysis of Maori Wardens in the Historical and Contemporary Context of New Zealand Society', PhD thesis, Victoria University of Wellington, 1980, pp 115, 119; Department of Maori Affairs, *The Maori Today*, 1949, p39; Butterworth, Graham and Susan, *Policing and the Tangata Whenua, 1935–85*, Wellington, Treaty of Waitangi Research Unit, 2008, pp 12–4; Department of Maori Affairs, Dispatch to all District Officers, all District-Welfare Officers and all Welfare Officers, 29 May 1952, AAMK, 869, Box 1050a, 35/1, General Policy and Admin – MSEA 1945, 1951–5 (for 'stamp out' quote); Corbett, E B, Memorandum for Hon W H Fortune, Minister in Charge of Police, 18 May 1954, MA, W2490, Box 81, Part 2, 36/4, Wardens, Policy and Appointments, 1954–7 (for 'eyes and ears' quote); Department of Maori Affairs, *The Maori Today*, 1964, 'Welfare' section; Hutt, Marten, *Te Iwi Maori me te Inu Waipiro: He Tuhituhinga Hitori/Maori and Alcohol: A History*, Wellington, 1999, pp 72–6; Fleras, Augie, 'Maori Wardens and the Control of Liquor Among the Maori of New Zealand', *Journal of the Polynesian Society*, 90(4), 1981; Butterworth, Graham, *'Men of Authority': The New Zealand Maori Council and the Struggle for Rangatiratanga in the 1960s–1970s*, Wellington, Treaty of Waitangi Research Unit, 2007, p18; Lange, *Maori Well-Being*, pp 38–9, 46.
10. Nightingale, Richard Beresford, 'Maori at Work: the Shaping of a Maori Workforce within the New Zealand State 1935–1975', PhD thesis, Massey University, 2007, p34 (for 'practical measures' quote); Ausubel, *Maori Youth*, pp 110–12; Poulsen and Johnston, 'Patterns of Maori Migration', p150; Butterworth and Young, *Maori Affairs* p 95; Sissons, Jeff, 'The post-assimilationist thought of Sir Apirana Ngata: towards a genealogy of New Zealand biculturalism', *New Zealand Journal of History*, 34(1), 2000, p59.
11. Fraser, Peter, 'Foreword by the Minister of Maori Affairs', in Department of Maori Affairs, 'Annual Report of the Board of Maori Affairs and of the Under-Secretary', AJHR, G-9, 1949, p2 (for 'great importance' and 'independent, self-reliant' quote); King, Michael, *The Penguin History of New Zealand*, Auckland, 2003, pp 420–21; Ausubel, *Maori Youth*, pp 114–5; Buck, Peter, *The Coming of the Maori*, Wellington, 1949, p525 (for 'as British as anything' quote).
12. Butterworth and Young, *Maori Affairs*, p93; Butterworth, 'Aotearoa 1769–1988', ch8, p70; Pearson, David, *A Dream Deferred: The Origins of Ethnic Conflict in New Zealand*, Wellington, 1990, p193; King, Michael, 'Between Two Worlds', in Oliver, W H and Williams, B S (eds), *The Oxford History of New Zealand*, Wellington, 1981, pp 299–300; Ausubel, *Maori Youth*, pp 110–18.

Chapter 2

1. King, Michael, *Te Puea: A Biography*, Auckland, 1977, p268 (for 'No Prime Minister' quote); Kawharu, I Hugh, 'Urban Immigrants and *Tangata Whenua*', in Schwimmer, Erik (ed) *The Maori People in the Nineteen-Sixties: A Symposium*, Auckland, 1968, p176; Walker, *Ka Whawhai Tonu Matou*, pp 215–7; Winiata, Maharaia, *The Changing Role of the Leader in Maori Society: A Study in Social Change and Race Relations*, Auckland, 1967, p144.
2. Winiata, *The Changing Role*, p131 (for 'recognized members' quote), p132; Notes supplied by Eric Ramsden for Major Rangi Royal from a direct statement dictated by Sir Apirana Ngata, Otaki, 17 March 1950, MA, W2490, Box 57, Part 1, 35/1/3, MSEA Act 1945 subsidies, policies, 1947–50 (for 'complicated organisation' quote); Notes from discussion at Raukawa marae, 17 March 1950, AAMK, 869, Box 1051a, 35/1/1, Maori Welfare Legislation, 1956–62 (for 'doubtful' and 'deliberate obstruction' quotes); Notes of representations made to Minister of Maori Affairs at Raukawa Marae,

Otaki on Saturday 18 March 1950 by Sir Apirana Ngata on behalf of the assembled tribes, MA W2490, Box 56, Part 2, 35/1, General Policy and Admin – MSEA Act 1945, 1947–50 (for 'le Maori people' and 'the only place' quotes); Hill, Richard S, '"Social Revolution on a Small Scale" Official Maori Committees of the 1950s', Paper Presented to the New Zealand Historical Associatio Conference, 24–27 Nov 2005, http://www.victoria.ac.nz/stout-centre/research-units/towru MaoriCommitteesJan06.pdf, p5 (for 'emphatic' quote); Lange, *Maori Well-Being*, pp 33–7, 45.

3. Department of Maori Affairs, 'Annual Report', 1950, p10 (for 'more advanced Executives' quote) Jamison, Tom and Te Ahukaramu Charles Royal, 'Royal, Te Rangiataahua Kiniwe 1896–1965' *Dictionary of New Zealand Biography*, updated 22 June 2007, http://www.dnzb.govt.nz/ (for 'reduce to a figurehead' quote); Gardiner, Wira, *Te Mura o te Ahi: The Story of the Maori Battalion*, Auckland 1992, pp 181–3 (for 'hostility manifested', 'strangle the autonomy', 'the end' and 'present set-up quotes); Awatere, Arapeta, *Awatere: A Soldier's Story* (edited by Hinemoa Ruataupare Awatere) Wellington, 2003, pp 7, 185, 214, 220.
4. Winiata, *The Changing Role*, p131 (for 'Tauranga County Council' quote); Harris, 'Maori and "the Maori Affairs"', p103 (for 'tempered with resistance' quote), pp 197–9, 202 (for 'difficult to assig labels' quote); Harris, 'Dancing with the State', p83; Lange, *Maori Well-Being*.
5. McLeay, Elizabeth, 'Representation and the Maori: Institutional Persistence and Shifting Justifications' paper presented at Annual Conference, Australasian and Political Studies Association, 2–4 Octobe 2002; Corbett, Ernest, 'Foreword by the Minister of Maori Affairs', in Department of Maori Affairs 'Annual Report of the Board of Maori Affairs and of the Under-Secretary', AJHR, G-9, 1950, p (for 'to accept the responsibility' quote); Scott, Dick, *The Parihaka Story*, Auckland, 1954; Scott, Dick *A Radical Writer's Life*, Auckland, 2004, p204 (for 'combing through the book' quote); Hazlehurst 'Maori Self-Government', p74; Metge, Joan, *A New Maori Migration: Rural and Urban Relations i Northern New Zealand*, London and Melbourne, 1964, pp 87–8.
6. Hill, *State Authority*, ch3; Butterworth, G V and Butterworth S M, *The Maori Trustee*, Wellington, nd Gilling, *'Most Barren and Unprofitable Land'*; Loveridge, Donald M, *Maori Land Councils and Maori Lan Boards: A Historical Overview, 1900 to 1952*, Wellington, Waitangi Tribunal Rangahaua Whanui Series 1996, ch14; Fraser, Peter, 'Foreword' (for 'full utilization' quote); Butterworth and Young, *Mao Affairs*, pp 2, 96; Harris, Aroha, 'Maori Land Title Improvement Since 1945: Communal Ownershi and Economic Use', *New Zealand Journal of History*, 31(1), 1997, p133 (for 'into the mainstream' quote) Prichard, Ivor and Waetford, Hemi, *Report of the Committee of Inquiry into the Laws Affecting Maori Lan and Powers of the Maori Land Court*, Wellington, 1965, p107.
7. Department of Maori Affairs, *The Maori Today*, 1964, 'Land Titles' section (for 'an important part' an 'retain the bulk' quotes); Gilling, *'Most Barren and Unprofitable Land'*, pp 43–4, 56–8 (re reluctance t hand back land); Harris, 'Maori Land Title Improvement', p138 (for 'chaotic' quote); Prichard an Waetford, *Report of the Committee of Inquiry*, pp 21–2; Parker, Wiremu, 'The Substance that Remains' in Wards, Ian (ed), *Thirteen Facets: Essays to Celebrate the Silver Jubilee of Queen Elizabeth the Secon 1952–1977*, Wellington, 1978, pp 176ff.
8. Orange, *The Treaty of Waitangi*, p242 (for 'disregarded traditional' quote); Department of Maor Affairs, *The Maori Today*, 1964, 'Land Titles' section (for 'discussed the question', 'a satisfactor arrangement' and 'encouraging successors to agree' quotes); Prichard and Waetford, *Report of th Committee of Inquiry*, p79; Harris, 'Maori Land Title Improvement, p139 (for 'economic farms' quote) Schwimmer, Erik, 'The Aspirations of the Contemporary Maori', in Schwimmer, Erik (ed), *Th Maori People in the Nineteen-Sixties: A Symposium*, Auckland, 1968, pp 22–5; Boast, Richard, 'Th Evolution of Maori Land Law 1962–1993', in Boast, Richard, Erueti, Andrew, McPhail, Doug an Smith, Norman, *Maori Land Law*, Wellington, 1999, pp 97–8; Boast, Richard, 'Maori Land and Othe Statutes', in Boast, Erueti, McPhail and Smith, *Maori Land Law*, Wellington, 1999, p256.
9. Butterworth, 'Aotearoa 1769–1988', ch9, p4 (for 'a horrifying breach' quote); Harris, 'Maori Lan Title Improvement', p141.
10. Department of Maori Affairs, 'Report of the Department of Maori Affairs and of the Secretary' AJHR, G-9, 1954, pp 22–3; Department of Maori Affairs, *The Maori Today*, 1964, 'Training Maori for Farming' section (for '[v]isits to schemes' and 'one reputable' quotes); Harris, 'Maori Land Titl Improvement Since 1945', pp 145–6, 149–50.

11. Butterworth and Young, *Maori Affairs*, p 97 (for 'communal way' quote); Labrum, 'The Essentials of Good Citizenship', p 449 (for 'primarily concerned' quote); Williams, Charlotte, *The Too-Hard Basket: Maori and Criminal Justice Since 1980*, Wellington, 2001, p 10 (for 'invalidated' quote); Anderson, L G, 'Welfare Requirements in a Multi-racial Society', in Brookes and Kawharu (eds), *Administration in New Zealand's Multi-racial Society*, Wellington, 1967, pp 98–9.
12. Hunn, Jack K, *Not Only Affairs of State*, Palmerston North, 1982, p 150 (for 'dispersing' quote); Ballara, Angela, *Proud to Be White? A Survey of Pakeha Prejudice in New Zealand*, Auckland, 1986, pp 135–6; Walsh, *More and More Maoris*, p 12; Walker, 'Maori People Since 1950', p 501; Labrum, 'Bringing families up to scratch', pp 454–6; Harris, 'Dancing with the State', pp 147–9; Pool et al, *The New Zealand Family*, p 212; McEwen, 'Urbanisation', p 82 (for 'loneliness', 'diffidence' and 'enjoying themselves' quotes); Nightingale, 'Maori at Work', pp 173–4, 177; Hill, 'Social Revolution', pp 3–4 (for 'bad behaviour' quote).
13. Department of Maori Affairs, *The Maori Today*, 1964, 'Occupations' section (for 'abrupt change' quote); 'One Race – Or Two?', *Daily Telegraph*, 26 Jan 1952, contained in MA 28, 13/13, Box 8, Racial Relationships 1952–57 (for 'constant drift' quote).
14. Grainger, J T, 'Fair and Just: Law for Both Races', *Weekly News*, 11 June 1952, p 31 (for 'almost automatic segregation' and 'depressed Maoris' quotes); Winks, Robin, *These New Zealanders*, Christchurch, 1954, p 155 (for 'little racial discrimination' quote); Ausubel, *Maori Youth*, p 115 (for 'turn for the worse', 'virtually non-existent' and following quotes); Orange, *The Treaty of Waitangi*, p 238; Ausubel, David P, *The Fern and the Tiki: An American View of New Zealand National Character, Social Attitudes and Race Relations*, 1960 (New York ed, 1965), pp 174–9; Thompson, Richard, *Race Relations in New Zealand: A Review of the Literature*, Christchurch, 1963, pp 31–5 (p 33 for 'legal impropriety' quote); Harris, Aroha, *Hīkoi: Forty Years of Māori Protest*, Wellington, 2004, pp 17–20; Harris, 'Dancing with the State', pp 135–7.
15. Hill, 'Social Revolution', p 4 (for 'equilibrium' quote); Ausubel, *The Fern and the Tiki*, p 162 (for 'happy-go-lucky' quote); Western, Marie to Corbett, Minister of Maori Affairs, 1 Sept 1952 and 10 Nov 1952, MA 28, 13/13, Box 8, Racial Relationships 1952–57 (latter has 'allowing the Maoris', 'the Maori absorbing' and 'paying for' quotes); Archer, Dave and Mary, 'Race, Identity and the Maori People', in Webb, Stephen and Collette, John (eds), *New Zealand Society: Contemporary Perspectives*, Sydney, 1973 (p 124 for 'to the extent that the Maori subscribes' quote); Ballara, *Proud to be White?* pp 143–50; Edwards, Mihi, *Mihipeka: Time of Turmoil*, Auckland, 1992, p 188 (for 'pretended to be a Pākehā' quote) and back cover (for 'We felt like intruders' quote); Smithies, Ruth, *Ten Steps Towards Bicultural Action: A Handbook on Partnership in Aotearoa–New Zealand*, Wellington, 1990, p 16; Butterworth and Butterworth, *Policing and the Tangata Whenua*, p 15 (for 'almost unanimously' quote), p 17 (for 'in relation to our drinking' quote); Nightingale, 'Maori at Work', pp 153–4.
16. 'The Maori in the City (2)', *New Zealand Listener*, vol 23, no 578, 21 July 1950, p 9 (for 'Maori Housewife' quote); Department of Maori Affairs, *The Maori Today*, 1964, 'Occupations' section (for 'atmosphere that makes for' quote); Poulsen and Johnston, 'Patterns of Maori Migration', pp 151, 162, 172; McEwen, 'Urbanisation', pp 78–9; Nightingale, 'Maori at Work', p 137ff; 'Rehua Maori Hostel', pamphlet, Eph A Maori 1955, PR-06-0005, Alexander Turnbull Library (for 'equal opportunities' quote).
17. Grace, Patricia, Ramsden, Irihapeti and Dennis, Jonathan (eds), *The Silent Migration: Ngati Poneke Young Maori Club 1937–1948*, Wellington, 2001; Walker, 'Maori People Since 1950', pp 502–6; Walker, *Ka Whawhai Tonu Matou*, pp 200–201; Kawharu, 'Urban Immigrants and *Tangata Whenua*'; Harris, 'Dancing with the State', pp 172–3; McLoughlin, David, 'John Tamihere: New Zealander of the Year', *North & South*, January 1998; Sharp, Andrew, 'Traditional Authority and the Legitimation Crisis of "Urban Tribes": The Waipareira Case', *Ethnologies comparées*, no 6, 2003 p 14.
18. Winiata, Maharaia, 'Leadership in the Auckland Maori Community', *Te Ao Hou*, no 27, June 1959, p 27 (for 'highest qualifications' and 'educated leader' quotes).
19. Hazlehurst, 'Maori Self-Government', p 72 (for 'training ground' and 'while western education' quotes); Department of Maori Affairs, *The Maori Today*, 1964, 'Education' section (for 'more recognition' quote); Winiata, 'Leadership', p 26 (for 'kaumatua' and 'specific occasions' quotes); Hill, 'Social Revolution', p 5 (for 'almost impossible' quote), p 7 (for 'want to be' quote); Bradly, R L, 'Education's Impact on the Multi-racial Society', in Brookes, R H and Kawharu, I H (eds),

Administration in New Zealand's Multi-racial Society, Wellington, 1967, pp 66–7; Butterworth, *'Men o Authority'*, p18; Kernot, B, *People of the Four Winds*, Wellington, 1972.

20. Labrum, 'The Essentials of Good Citizenship', p451 (for 'concerns itself' quote); Department o Maori Affairs, *The Maori Today*, 1964, 'Welfare' section (for 'not seek to impose' quote), 'Housing section (for 'group housing' quote); Hill, 'Social Revolution', pp 6–7.
21. 'National Blend', *New Zealand Herald*, 10 May 1952, contained in MA 28, 13/13, Box 8, Racia Relationships 1952–57 (for 'aim should be' quote); 'Racial Distinctions in New Zealand', *Weekl News*, 15 Sept 1954, contained in MA 28, 13/13, Box 8, Racial Relationships 1952–57 (for 'Maor is now becoming' quote); 'One Race – Or Two?', *Daily Telegraph*, 26 Jan 1952 (for 'logical result quote); 'Assimilation of the Maoris', *Weekly News*, 7 July 1954, contained in MA 28, 13/13, Box 8 Racial Relationships 1952–57; '"Ordinary New Zealanders"', *Taranaki Herald*, 2 July 1954, containec in MA 28, 13/13, Box 8, Racial Relationships 1952–57; *Manawatu Daily Times*, 'Address to Rotarian on Problems of Maori–Pakeha Relationships: Proposal to Form Maori Community Centre ir Palmerston North', 14 Dec 1954, contained in MA 28, 13/13, Box 8, Racial Relationships 1952–57 (for 'Assimilation of the two races' quote); 'Future of Maori Race in New Zealand Life', *Evening Star* 8 July 1957, contained in MA 28, 13/13, Box 8, Racial Relationships 1952–57.
22. Department of Maori Affairs, *The Maori Today*, 1964, 'Welfare' section (for 'perpetuate Maori culture quote); 'Rebuke for "Voice of Wellington"', *Auckland Star*, 4 Sept 1954, contained in MA 28, 13/13 Box 8, Racial Relationships 1952–57 (for 'good little Pakehas' and 'cultural arrogance' quotes); 'Future of Maori in New Zealand Life Discussed', *Christchurch Star–Sun*, 8 Sept 1952, contained in MA 28 13/13, Box 8, Racial Relationships 1952–57 (for 'full participation' quote); 'Race Discriminatior in New Zealand', *New Zealand Herald*, 21 May 1954, contained in MA 28, 13/13, Box 8, Racia Relationships 1952–57 (for 'integrated with' quote); 'Race and Crime', *Daily News*, 24 Aug 1954 contained in MA 28, 13/13, Box 8, Racial Relationships 1952–57 (for 'racial separatists' quote) 'Views of Maori Future Challenged', *New Zealand Herald*, 6 July 1954, contained in MA 28, 13/13 Box 8, Racial Relationships 1952–57 (for 'racial and cultural absorption', 'solve their social problems' 'demographic pipe-dream' and 'absorption or assimilation' quotes); 'One Race – Or Two?', *Daily Telegraph*, 26 Jan 1952 (for 'brown proletariat' quote); Ballara, *Proud to be White?* p 129.
23. Minister of Maori Affairs to Mr Craig of California, 13 June 1957, MA 28, 13/13, Box 8, Racia Relationships 1952–57 (for 'policy of the government' quote); Butterworth, 'Aotearoa 1769–1988' ch 9, p3 (for 'hiatus' quote); King, *Maori*, p250.

Chapter 3

1. Hill, *State Authority*, pp 130–39; Hunn, Jack K, *Report on Department of Maori Affairs: with Statistica Supplement*, Wellington, 1961, p62 (for 'the setting up' quote), p63 (for 'direct that board' anc 'adjustments' quotes); Marr, Cathy, *Crown Policy Towards Major Crown/Iwi Claim Agreements in the 1940 and 1950s*, Wellington, Treaty of Waitangi Policy Unit, 1990, pp 99–100; Hill, Richard S, *Settlement of Major Maori Claims in the 1940s: A Preliminary Historical Investigation*, Wellington, Department o Justice, 1989; Stokes, Evelyn, Milroy, J Wharehuia and Melbourne, Hirini, *Te Urewera: Nga Iwi te Whenua te Ngahere: People, Land and Forests of Te Urewera*, Hamilton, 1986, pp 106–10 (p 107 fo 'betterment of the people' quote).
2. Mahuta, Robert, 'Tainui, Kingitanga and Raupatu', in Wilson, Margaret A and Yeatman, Anna (eds), *Justice and Identity: Antipodean Practices*, Wellington, 1995, p26; Walsh, *More and More Maoris*, p4((includes 'control income from certain' quote); Stokes et al, *Te Urewera*, pp 87, 109–110 and p 300 (fo Tuhoe-Waikaremoana Trust Board quotes).
3. Marr, *Crown Policy*; Hill, *State Authority*, pp 50–64; Hunn, *Report on Department of Maori Affairs*, p62 (for 'seemingly wide power' quote), p63 (for 'education is not assisted' quote); McHugh, Paul, *The Maori Magna Carta: New Zealand Law and the Treaty of Waitangi*, Auckland, 1991, p202 (for 'notorious that' quote).
4. *New Zealand Herald*, 10 May 1952 (for 'Blend' and 'weld' quotes) and 2 August 1952 (for 'social revolution' and 'rallying point' quotes); for general coverage of relevant points, see Hill, 'Social

Revolution', especially p 3 (for 'usefully' quote), p6 (for 'philosophy' quote); Ritchie, James E, *The Making of a Maori: A Case Study of a Changing Community*, Wellington, 1963, p26 (for 'more successful' quote).

5. Lange, *Maori Well-Being*, pp 27–30; Winiata, *The Changing Role*, p132 (for 'governmental invasion' quote); Winiata, 'Leadership', p22 (for 'most important' quote), p26 (for 'educated person' and 'to the fore' quotes); Metge, *New Maori Migration*, pp 215–20; Walker, 'Maori People Since 1950', p500 (for 'professional, technical' quote); Hill, 'Social Revolution', pp 5–6.

6. Walker, Ranginui J, 'The Politics of Voluntary Association: A Maori Welfare Committee in a City Suburb', in Kawharu, I Hugh (ed), *Conflict and Compromise: Essays on the Maori Since Colonisation*, Wellington, 1975 (2003 ed); Labrum, 'Bringing families up to scratch', p171 (for 'up to scratch' quote); Fleras, 'Descriptive Analysis', p303 (for 'separate but parallel' and 'socio-cultural separation' quotes); Ausubel, *Maori Youth*, p174 (for 'certain measure' quote).

7. Secretary of Maori Affairs to the Minister of Maori Affairs, 16 Feb 1960, MA 1, 35/2, Part 1, Box 646, NZ Council of Tribal Executives, 1952–1962 (for 'with an enthusiasm' and 'wholeheartedly' quotes); Hunn, *Affairs of State*, pp 152–3; Fleras, 'Descriptive Analysis', p200; Minister of Maori Affairs to Secretary of Maori Affairs, 13 Aug 1953, MA 1, 35/2, Part 1, Box 646, NZ Council of Tribal Executives, 1952–1962 (for 'the terminology' and 'develop further' quotes).

8. Department of Maori Affairs, 'Dominion Council for Tribal Executives under MSEA Act', 8 Nov 1957, MA 1, 35/2, Part 1, Box 646, NZ Council of Tribal Executives, 1952–1962 (for 'not considered desirable' quote); Love, 'Policies of Frustration', p442ff; Butterworth and Young, *Maori Affairs*, p103; Hunn, *Report on Department of Maori Affairs*, p80; Secretary of Maori Affairs to the Minister of Maori Affairs, 16 Feb 1960 (for 'could quite conceivably' quote); Butterworth, *'Men of Authority'*; Harris, 'Dancing with the State', pp 152–4 (p 153 for 'riled Nash, 'convene' and 'policy forming body' quotes); Attachments to Secretary to Minister of Maori Affairs, 16 Feb 1960, MA 1, 35/2, Part 1; Hunn, *Report on Department of Maori Affairs*, p80 (for 'Council is about' quote). The word 'Dominion' continued to be used well after New Zealand became a 'Realm'.

9. King, 'Between Two Worlds', pp 296–301; Orange, *The Treaty of Waitangi*, pp 234–5; National Party, *Te Maori O Ona Ra Tuku Iho Nei/The Maori and the Future*, nd: Eph A Maori 1950s, Alexander Turnbull Library.

10. Love, 'Policies of Frustration', p442ff (p 457 for 'in a totally different' quote), p481 (for 'most pointed criticism', 'mere words', 'practicable effectiveness', 'requests have been ignored' and 'the organisation' quotes), p484 (for 'not lost' quote), p487 (for 'empty gestures' quote), p488 (for 'forced on the Maori', 'higher power' and 'Maori would never' quotes); Brown, Bruce (Private Secretary to Nash, 1954–9), personal communication (on Nordmeyer's challenge to Nash's leadership), 30 Jul 2008. The circumstances of the 1954 leadership bid by Nordmeyer remain confused: see the differing treatments in Sinclair, Keith, *Walter Nash*, Auckland, 1976, pp 293–4 and Logan, Mary, *Nordy: Arnold Nordmeyer: A Political Biography*, Wellington, 2008, pp 280–81. For the South African tour issue, see Richards, Trevor, *Dancing on our Bones: New Zealand, South Africa, Rugby and Racism*, Wellington, 1999, p20ff and Sinclair, *Nash*, pp 334–6; Butterworth, 'Aotearoa 1769–1988', ch 10, p21; McLeay, Elizabeth (ed), *New Zealand Politics and Social Patterns: Selected Works by Robert Chapman*, Wellington, 1999, pp 241, 243; Poulsen and Johnston, 'Patterns of Maori Migration', p150 (for 'spectacular' quote).

Chapter 4

1. Hazlehurst, Kayleen M, *Political Expression and Ethnicity: Statecraft and Mobilisation in the Maori World*, Westport, CT, 1993, p16 (for 'affiliatory ties' and 'belonging by association' quotes); Ausubel, David P, 'The Maori: A Study in Resistive Acculturation', in Webb, Stephen D and Collette, John (eds), *New Zealand Society: Contemporary Perspectives*, Sydney, 1973, p95 (for 'strong residuum', 'resumption' and 'racial nationalism' quotes); Department of Maori Affairs, *The Maori Today*, 1964, 'Occupations' section (for 'religious, family, and tribal' and 'transfer' quotes); Walker, 'Maori People Since 1950', p503 (for 'the key' quote); Nightingale, 'Maori at Work', p198 (for 'retarded' quote); Kawharu, 'Introduction', in Brookes and Kawharu (eds), *Administration*, pp 11–12; Winiata, 'Leadership', pp 22–3);

Booth, J M, and Hunn, J K, *Integration of Maori and Pakeha*, Wellington, 1962, p 10 (for 'their own kind' quote). The term 'voluntary associations' is used in this book in its conventional (and contemporary) sense, although most people who worked within the official committee system were also 'volunteers', usually unremunerated ones at that.

2. Grace et al, *The Silent Migration*; Walker, 'Maori People Since 1950', p 504 (for 'consciousness of pan-tribalism' quote); Ropiha to Minister, 'Revised Welfare Policy', 14 Nov 1956, AAMK, 869, Box 1051a, 35/1/1, Maori Welfare Legislation, 1956–62, para 34 (for 'formation of Maori youth clubs' quote); 'Notes on "Culture and the Rural Family" in relation to Maori', encl Secretary for Maori Affairs to Director of Education, 23 May 1956, MA, W2490, 36/10, Box 99, Part 2, Maori Club Associations and Recreation Groups, Social Organisation, 1951–56 (for 'cushion the effect' quote); Department of Maori Affairs, *The Maori Today*, 1964, 'Occupations' section (for 'gathers into its fold', 'every town where' and 'new relationship' quotes); Maori Welfare Officer in Tauranga, Report to District Officer, 2 Dec 1959, MA, W2490, Box 99, Part 3, 36/10, Maori Club Associations and Recreation Groups, Social Organisation, 1951–56 (for 'mainly run' quote); District Officer Wanganui, M G Kellar Report to the Secretary, Head Office, 3 Dec 1959, MA, W2490, Box 99, Part 3, 36/10, Maori Club Associations and Recreation Groups, Social Organisation, 1951–56 (for 'age of "Rock-n-Roll"' quote); 'Maori of today poses social welfare problems', newspaper clipping, MA 1, Box 650, Part 7, 36/1, Welfare-general, 1956–59 (for 'Maori songs being sung' quote).

3. Walker, 'Maori People Since 1950', pp 501–2, 504 (for 'incomplete substitute[s]' quotes); Walker, *Ka Whawhai Tonu Matou*, p 199 (for 'transplanting [Maori] culture' quote), p 200 (for 'one of the bastions' quote), p 201 (for 'nothing in common' quote); Williams, Melissa, 'Panguru, Te Puutu, and "The Maori Affairs": The Punguru Community Development Project, 1954–1957', MA thesis, Auckland, 2005; Kawharu, 'Urban Immigrants and *Tangata Whenua*'; Department of Maori Affairs, *The Maori Today*, 1964, 'Investment Societies' section (for 'worthwhile use for the money' and 'revitalise Maori communities' quotes); Thompson, *Race Relations in New Zealand*, p 46; Walker, 'The Politics', p 16 (for 'integrative function' quote); Ritchie, J E, 'Planning: Problems: Perspectives', in Brookes and Kawharu (eds), *Administration*, pp 119–20.

4. Hill, *State Authority*, p 247ff (p 249 for 'prerogative' quote); 'Women's Health League', *Opotiki News*, ◆ July, 1951, contained in MA, W2490, Box 131, Part 1, 36/26, Maori Women's Welfare League, 1950–56; Rei, Tania, McDonald, Geraldine and Te Awakōtuku, Ngāhuia, 'Ngā Rōpū Wāhine Māori: Māori Women's Organisations', in Else, Anne (ed), *Women Together: A History of Women's Organisations in New Zealand: Ngā Rōpū Wāhine o te Motu*, Wellington, 1993, pp 8–9; King, Michael, *Whina: A Biography of Whina Cooper*, Auckland, 1983, pp 167–8; Tautari, Marie, 'Māori Women's Institutes 1929–1950s', in Else, Anne (ed), *Women Together*, pp 25–7; Meha, Raina, 'Te Rōpū o te Ora: Women's Health League 1937–', in Else, Anne (ed), *Women Together*, pp 30–33; Department of Maori Affairs, 'Annual Report', 1950, p 11; Szaszy, Mira, *Te Timatanga a Tātau Tātau: Early Stories from Founding Members of the Māori Women's Welfare League, Te Rōpū Wāhine Māori Toko i te Ora*, Wellington, 1993, pp xiv, xvi; Durie, Mason, *Whaiora: Maori Health Development*, Melbourne, 1994 (2nd ed, 1998), pp 47–8 (p 47 for 'a significant force' quote); Walker, *Ka Whawhai Tonu Matou*, p 202; Winiata, *The Changing Role*, p 166; Byron, Isolde, *Nga Perehitini: The Presidents of the Maori Women's Welfare League 1951–2001*, Auckland, 2002, p 9; Harris, 'Dancing with the State', pp 88–92.

5. Wright, R, 'The First Conference of the Maori Women's Welfare Leagues', MA, W2490, Box 131, Part 1, 36/26, Maori Women's Welfare League, 1950–56; King, *Whina*, p 7 (for 'begun her public career' and 'urban and national' quotes), p 168 (for 'the formation' quote), p 167ff; Harris, 'Dancing with the State', pp 92–113, 169–71; Rei, Tania, 'Te Rōpū Wāhine Māori Toko i te Ora: Māori Women's Welfare League 1951–', in Else, Anne (ed), *Women Together*, pp 34–38; Szaszy, Mira, *Te Timatanga a Tātau Tātau*, pp xiv, xvi; Walker, *Ka Whawhai Tonu Matou*, p 202; Labrum, 'Bringing families up to scratch', pp 165–6; Byron, *Nga Perehitini*, pp 9–20 (p 9 for 'independent' and 'understanding between Maori' quotes, p 15 for 'the general uplift', 'care and maintenance' and 'active interest in all matters' quotes, p 16 for 'take their rightful place' quote); Winiata, *The Changing Role*, p 169 (for 'assuming the role' quote); Page, Dorothy, *The National Council of Women: A Centennial History*, Auckland, 1996, pp 98–9; King, *Maori*, p 251; Butterworth and Young, *Maori Affairs*, pp 98–9; McClure, Margaret, *A Civilised Community: A History of Social Security in New Zealand 1898–1998*, Auckland, 1998, p 124; Walker, 'Maori People Since 1950', p 507; Cox, Lindsay, *Kotahitanga: The Search for Maori Political Unity*,

Auckland, 1993, pp 127–30, 191; Labrum, 'The Essentials of Good Citizenship', p454 (for 'civic responsibilities' quote); Schrader, Ben, 'The *Other* Story: Changing Perceptions of State Housing', *New Zealand Journal of History*, Oct 2006, pp 164–5.

6. Rei et al, 'Ngā Rōpū Wāhine Māori', p9 (for 'centred on the house' quote), p10 (for 'created to assist' quote); Assistant Secretary Maori Affairs to the Secretary, Public Service Commission, Wellington, 17 Aug 1955, MA, W2490, Box 131, Part 1, 36/26, Maori Women's Welfare League, 1950–56 (for 'born as a voluntary body' quote); Winiata, *The Changing Role*, p166 (for 'may be seen' quote); Rei, 'Te Rōpū Wāhine', p34; Secretary of Maori Affairs to the President, MWWL, 6 Sept 1956, MA, W2490, Box 131, Part 2, 36/26 (for 'any thought whatever' quote); Secretary for Maori Affairs to Secretary to the Treasury, 11 June 1956, 'Public Money', MA, W2490, Box 131, Part 2, 36/26; Secretary to the Treasury to Secretary for Maori Affairs, 21 August 1956, 'Public Money', MA, W2490, Box 131, Part 2, 36/26; Under Secretary to the President, Maori Women's Welfare League, 30 Jan 1953, MA, W2490, Box 131, Part 1, 36/26, Maori Women's Welfare League, 1950–56; 'Handling of Cash in Head Office, Department of Maori Affairs', MA, W2490, Box 131, Part 1, 36/26, Maori Women's Welfare League, 1950–56; Byron, *Nga Perehitini*, p9 (for 'quasi-voluntary' quote); Durie, *Whaiora*, p49 (for 'born out of' quote).

7. Cooper, Whina to the Hon Mr Corbett, Minister of Maori Affairs, 24 April 1953, MA, W2490, Box 131, Part 1, 36/26, Maori Women's Welfare League, 1950–56 (for 'much help' and 'without your sanction' quotes); Secretary of Maori Affairs to the President, MWWL, 8 June 1953, MA, W2490, Box 131, Part 1, 36/26, Maori Women's Welfare League, 1950–56 (for 'in the happy position' quote); Cooper, Whina to the Secretary, re 'Administration of MWWL Organisation', 7 Aug 1953, MA, W2490, Box 131, Part 1, 36/26, Maori Women's Welfare League, 1950–56 (for 'It would appear' and the following Cooper quotes); Page, *The National Council of Women*, p98 (for 'just say *yes*' quote); King, *Whina*, pp 185–6 (for 'worried about' and following quotes; and for 'a strong tendency' quote), also pp 183–4; Byron, *Nga Perehitini*, p11 (for 'the greatest social advancement' quote).

8. Rei, 'Te Rōpū Wāhine', pp 34–5, 37; Minister of Maori Affairs to Secretary for Maori Affairs, 8 May 1958 (for 'Leagues have contributed' quote); Resolution MWWL Conference 1957, Policy 11, MA, W2490, Box 131, Part 1, 36/26/20 (for 'not yet ready' quote); 'Brief History of the League – its administration and financial background', MA, W2490, Box 132, Part 4, 36/26, MWWL, 1962–70; Hunn, *Report on Department of Maori Affairs* (for 'generally more alive' quote); Hazlehurst, *Political Expression*, p16 (for 'shared ethnicity' quote); Maori Women's Welfare League Archive, Nelson Provincial Museum (for 'ability to apply' quote); Maori Women's Welfare League 1951–1988, MS Papers 1396, Alexander Turnbull Library, National Library of New Zealand.

9. Department of Maori Affairs, *The Maori Today*, 1964, 'The Future' section (for 'striking success' and 'never before' quotes); King, 'Between Two Worlds', p296 (for 'impatient with anything less' quote); Butterworth, G V, 'The Health of the Body, the Health of Land: A Comparative Study of the Political Objectives and Careers of Wiremu Ratana and the Ratana Movement, and Sir Apirana Ngata', Wellington, Treaty of Waitangi Research Unit, Feb 2000, p48 (for 'a truly united Maori people' quote, taken from Ngata's 'A Plea for the Unity of the Maori People', *Papers and Addresses of the Second Conference of the Te Aute College Students Association*, Napier, 1898, p23); Sissons, 'The post-assimilationist thought', pp 49–52; Hazlehurst, 'Maori Self-Government', p72; Winiata, *The Changing Role*; Winiata, 'Leadership'.

10. Metge, Joan, *New Growth from Old: The Whanau in the Modern World*, Wellington, 1995, pp 39–40, 50, 305 (for 'centralised market economy' and following quotes); Morris, Paul, 'Community Beyond Tradition', in Heelas, Paul, Lash, Scott and Morris, Paul (eds), *Detraditionalization: Critical Reflections on Authority and Identity*, Oxford, 1996; Hohepa, Patrick, *A Maori Community in Northland*, Wellington, 1970, pp 93–103, 129–30 (p 93 for 'most effective' quote, p129 for '[t]raditional cultural ways' and 'abandonment and change' quotes).

11. Secretary of External Affairs to the Prime Minister, 24 Dec 1959, and attached draft, 'Discrimination against Maoris: The Indigenous Populations Convention 1957', Nash Papers, Series 1151, Folio 001–0165, Department Papers, 1958–60; Walsh, *More and More Maoris*, p12; Butterworth and Young, *Maori Affairs*, p99 (for 'on the issue of assimilation' quote); Nightingale, 'Maori at Work', p178.

12. Ballara, *Proud to be White?* p 30 (citing Winiata, 'Two Peoples: One Nation', *New Zealand Listener*, 25 March 1955);Walker, 'Maori People Since 1950', pp 507–9; King, 'Between Two Worlds', pp 296–7.

Chapter 5

1. Sissons, 'The post-assimilationist thought', p58; McDonald, K C, *Our Country's Story: An Illustrate History of New Zealand*, Christchurch, 1963, p148 (for 'there is no country' quote); Walker, Ranginui J 'State of the Nation', *New Zealand Listener*, 21 Feb 2004, p32; Hunn, *Affairs of State*, p147 (for 'powerfu solvent' quote); Harré, John, 'Maori–Pakeha Intermarriage', in Schwimmer, Erik (ed) *The Maori Peopl in the Nineteen-Sixties: A Symposium*, pp 121, 129; Ausubel, *The Fern and the Tiki*, pp 182–4; Orange *The Treaty of Waitangi*, p242; Booth and Hunn, *Integration*, p4; Nightingale, 'Maori at Work', pp 205, 248 Walker, Ranginui, 'The Treaty of Waitangi in the Postcolonial Era', in Belgrave, Michael, Kawharu Merata and Williams, David (eds), *Waitangi Revisited: Perspectives on the Treaty of Waitangi*, Auckland, 2005, p56
2. Hunn, *Affairs of State*, p145 (for 'No impartial observer' quote); McDonald, *Our Country's Story*, p14 (for 'disturbing evidence' quote); Secretary of External Affairs to the Prime Minister, 24 Dec 1959 attached draft, 'Discrimination against Maoris' (for 'generally agreed' quote); Ausubel, *The Fern an the Tiki*; Kersey, Harry, 'Opening a Discourse on Race Relations in New Zealand: "The Fern an the Tiki" Revisited', *Journal of New Zealand Studies*, Oct 2002; Archer and Archer, 'Race, Identity' Thompson, *Race Relations in New Zealand*, pp 31–5, 57–69.
3. Department of Maori Affairs, *The Maori Today*, 1964, 'The Future' section (for 'happy circumstance and following quotes); Harris, Aroha, 'Current Narratives of Maori and Integration in the 1950s an 60s', *Journal of New Zealand Studies*, NS 6–7, 2007–2008, p143 (for 'A large number of Maori' quote) Hill 'Social Revolution', p4 (for 'consciously or unconsciously' quote).
4. Bedggood, David, *Rich and Poor in New Zealand: A Critique of Class, Politics and Ideology*, Auckland 1980, p81 (re 'non-relations'); Sinclair, Keith, 'Why are Race Relations in New Zealand Bette than in South Africa, South Australia or South Dakota?', in Webb, Stephen and Collette, John (eds) *New Zealand Society: Contemporary Perspectives*, Sydney, 1973, p19; Ausubel, *Maori Youth*, p115; Hunn *Report on Department of Maori Affairs*, p14 (for 'prevent a "colour" problem' and 'understand an appreciate' quotes); Thompson, *Race Relations in New Zealand*, p42; Harris, 'Dancing with the State' pp 137–8; Booth and Hunn, *Integration*, p10 (for 'rightful place' quote).
5. Hunn, *Affairs of State*, p147 (for 'smooth the process' quote); Harris, 'Maori and "the Maori Affairs"' p203; Fraser, Peter, 'Foreword', p2 (for 'the home is the place' quote); Booth and Hunn, *Integration*, p9 (for 'set of values' quote).
6. Hunn, *Affairs of State*, p136 (for 'to prevent further' quote); Hunn, *Report on Department of Maori Affairs*, p13 (for 'stocktaking' and 'assets' quotes); Booth and Hunn, *Integration*, p10 (for 'disproportionate' quote); Hill, 'Social Revolution', p4; Nightingale, 'Maori at Work', pp 36–40, 181–2.
7. Hunn, *Report on Department of Maori Affairs*, p15 (for 'remnants of Maori culture' quote); Hunn, *Affairs of State*, p136 (for 'an accounting' quote), p139 (for 'sat on' quote), p137 (for 'main purpose' quote); Ballara, *Proud to Be White?* pp 133–5; Butterworth, *'Men of Authority'*, p6ff; Booth and Hunn, *Integration*, pp 1–3 (p 3 for 'distant end-result' and 'final blending' quotes).
8. Hunn, *Report on Department of Maori Affairs*, p3 (for 'a fundamental bearing' quote); Hunn, *Affairs o State*, p140 (for 'soon became devoted' quote), p141 (for 'Government policy' quote); Kenworthy, L M, Martindale, T B and Sadaraka, S M, *Some Aspects of the Hunn Report: A Measure of Progress*, Wellington, 1968, p6 (for 'called for recognition' quote); Harris, 'Dancing with the State', ch5; Booth and Hunn, *Integration*, pp 1–4.
9. Hunn, *Report on Department of Maori Affairs*, p14 (for 'welcomed as the quickest' quote), p15, (for 'Evolution is clearly' quote), p78 (for 'Full integration' quote); Hunn, *Affairs of State*, p144 (for 'a fact of life' and 'never been articulated' quotes); Harris, *Hīkoi*, pp 21, 23.
10. Hunn, *Affairs of State*, p144 (for 'successive stages' quote); Hunn, *Report on Department of Maori Affairs*, p14 (for 'well nigh' quote), p15 (for 'only the fittest', 'onset of civilisation' and 'two dissimilar peoples' quote), p16 (for 'object of policy', 'complacently living', 'pressure brought to bear' and 'a *pakeha* but' quotes); Harris, 'Dancing with the State', pp 116, 120–121, 129–30; Herzog, Christine, 'Toward a Sustainable Relationship: Pakeha and Tangata Whenua in Adult and Community Education', in Benseman, John, Findsen, Brian and Scott, Miriama (eds), *The Fourth Sector: Adult and Community Education in Aotearoa/New Zealand*, Palmerston North, 1996, pp 129, 131; Allen, Chadwick, 'Postcolonial Theory and the Discourse of Treaties', *American Quarterly*, 52(1), March 2000, pp 61–2.

The hybridisation of the colonial encounter, which leads to a whole new, negotiated culture, as argued by Homi Bhabha, is not the operative process in New Zealand; see Bhabha, Homi K, *The Location of Culture*, London, 1994.

11. Hunn, *Affairs of State*, p 144 (for 'blended new species' quote), p 145 (for 'some continuation', 'the [Maori] language', 'the Maoris themselves' and 'entirely a matter' quotes), p 150 (for 'fundamental tenets' quote); Hunn, *Report on Department of Maori Affairs*, p 15 (for 'to form one nation' quote); Butterworth, 'The Health of the Body', p 112; Ballara, *Proud to Be White?* p 134; Booth and Hunn, *Integration*, pp 1–4, (p 1 for 'vanguard' quote, p 2 for 'uniformity', 'closing the gap', 'whole new culture' and 'tolerant of diversity' quotes, and p 3 for 'submergence' quote); McEwen, 'Urbanisation', p 84 (for 'no citizen' quote); Kawharu, 'Introduction', in Brookes and Kawharu (eds), *Administration*, p 9 (for 'distant future' quote); see too Ritchie, 'Planning', p 112, and for a gendered perspective, Woods, Megan C, 'Integrating the Nation: Gendering Maori Urbanisation and Integration, 1942–1969', PhD thesis, Christchurch, 2002.
12. Hunn, *Report on Department of Maori Affairs*, p 15 (for 'adopted the 1960 pattern' quote); Ritchie, *The Making of a Maori*, p 38 (for 'the economics and social consequences' quote); McEwen, 'Urbanisation', p 84 (for 'fusion' quote); Barrington, John, *Separate but Equal? Māori Schools and the Crown 1867–1969*, Wellington, 2008, pp 268–9; Booth and Hunn, *Integration*, p 8.
13. Meek, R L, *Maori Problems Today: A Short Survey*, Wellington, 1944; Scott, *A Radical Writer's Life*, p 89 (for 'only a good liberal effort' and 'no value in artificially' quotes), p 90 (for 'nonsense to worry' and 'gross maladjustments' quotes), p 108 (for 'wither away' quote); Booth and Hunn, *Integration*, p 9 (for 'ways of the pakeha' and 'numerical proportion' quotes).
14. Hunn, *Report on Department of Maori Affairs*, p 14 (for 'remarkable strides' quote).
15. Butterworth, 'Aotearoa 1769–1988', ch 9, p 15 (for 'its failure to consult' quote); Harris, 'Dancing with the State', pp 127–8; Kenworthy et al, *Some Aspects*, pp 5–6, 60, 64, 86–90; Hunn, *Affairs of State*, p 142; Butterworth and Young, *Maori Affairs*, p 102; Ritchie, *The Making of a Maori*, p 38 (for 'feel themselves' quote); Ritchie, James E, 'The Grass Roots of Maori Politics', in Pocock, J G A (ed), *The Maori in New Zealand Politics*, Auckland and Hamilton, 1965, p 85 (for 'wise, balanced and fair' quote).
16. Butterworth, Graham, Newspaper Clippings Collection, Treaty of Waitangi Research Unit, box 2 (for 'Maori canoe' quote); Hanan, J R, 'Foreword', in Department of Maori Affairs, *The Maori Today*, 1964 (for 'the world a lead' quote); see also Fleras, Augie, 'Towards "Tu Tangata": Historical Developments and Current Trends in Maori Policy and Administration', *Political Science*, 37(1), July 1985, p 23; McEwen, 'Urbanisation', p 83.
17. Ritchie, in Brookes and Kawharu (eds), *Administration*, p 112 (for 'deep suspicion' quote); Hunn, *Affairs of State*, p 142; Walker, 'Maori People Since 1950', p 503; Biggs, Bruce, 'Maori affairs and the Hunn report', *Journal of the Polynesian Society*, 70(3), September 1961; Thompson, *Race Relations in New Zealand*, pp 38–9, 44 (p 39 for 'representative of' quote); Presbyterian Church of New Zealand, Maori Synod, *A Maori View of the 'Hunn Report'*, Christchurch, 1961, p 8 (for 'A race cannot be forced' quote); Johns, Atihana, 'What's Wrong with the Pakeha', letter to editor, *New Zealand Listener*, 4 Sept 1961, contained in MA 1, Box 655, 36/1/21, Part 4, Race Relations–Integration–Segregation, 1961–62 (for 'queer' and 'the biggest problem' quotes); Harris, 'Dancing with the State', pp 129–31.
18. Hunn, *Affairs of State*, p 142; Sorrenson, M P K, *Maori and European since 1870: A Study in Adaptation and Adjustment*, Auckland, 1967, pp 37–40 (p 37 for 'So long as' quote).
19. Ballara, *Proud to Be White?* p 138 (for 'individualised aid' quote); Kawharu, 'Introduction', in Brookes and Kawharu (eds), *Administration*, p 13 (for 'really means' quote); Mead, Sidney Moko, 'A Pathway to the Future: He Ara Ki Te Ao Marama', in *Landmarks, Bridges and Visions: Aspects of Maori Culture*, Wellington, 1997 (orig article 1979), p 124 (for 'alienating us' quote); Hohepa, Pat, 'Maori and Pakeha: The One-People Myth', in King, Michael (ed), *Tihe Mauri Ora: Aspects of Maoritanga*, Wellington, 1978, p 106 (for 'really affected Maori attitudes' quote), p 111 (for 'one nation of two peoples' quote); Fleras, 'Towards', p 24 (for 'To Maori leaders' quote).
20. Prichard and Waetford, *Report of the Committee of Inquiry*, p 76 (for 'compelled to move' quote); Harris, 'Maori and "the Maori Affairs"', pp 203–4; Butterworth and Young, *Maori Affairs*, pp 99–100 (for 'retarded areas' quote); Walker, 'Maori People Since 1950', p 501; 'Conference of District Officers', Notes of Discussions, Wellington, 22–24 Nov 1960, AAMK, 869, Box 663d, Part 2, 19/1/237, Conference of District Officers, 1960–62 (for 'guide [the process]' quote); J K Hunn to

Father P J Cleary, 25 Oct 1961, MA 1, Box 655, 36/1/21, Part 4, Race Relations–Integration–Segregation, 1961–62 (for '[I]nstead of standing' quote); Nightingale; Report from Palmerston North to Head Office, re 'Housing Target 1961/62', 28 Oct 1960, AAMK, 869, Box 663d, Part 2, 19/1/237, Conference of District Officers, 1960–62 (for 'We think' quote); Harris, 'Dancing with the State', pp 143–6.

21. Kenworthy et al, *Some Aspects*, pp 60, 64, 86–7, 89 (p 60 for 'tremendous improvement' quote, p 64 for 'to take advantage' quote); Department of Maori Affairs, *The Maori Today*, 1964, 'Education' section (for 'to provide specialised assistance' and following quotes); Butterworth, 'Aotearoa 1769–1988, ch 9, pp 15–8; Butterworth and Young, *Maori Affairs*, p 103; 'Maori Education: A New Foundation', pamphlet, Eph A MAORI 1962, Alexander Turnbull Library (for 'those of the pakeha' and 'remainder of the community' quotes).

22. Presbyterian Church, *A Maori View*, p 10 (for 'Let it be understood' and 'lost soul' quotes); Jackson, Michael D, 'Literacy, Communication and Social Change: A Study of the Meaning and Effect of Literacy in Early Nineteenth Century Society', in Kawharu, I Hugh (ed), *Conflict and Compromise: Essays on the Maori Since Colonisation*, Wellington, 1975 (2003 ed), p 48 (for 'to steer a course' quote).

23. Kawharu, I Hugh, 'Introduction', in Kawharu, I Hugh (ed), *Conflict and Compromise: Essays on the Maori Since Colonisation*, Wellington, 1975 (2003 ed), p 16 (for 'Maori attitudes' quotes).

24. Hunn, *Report on Department of Maori Affairs*, pp 46–78 (p 48 for 'national interest' quote, p 49 for 'aptitude or experience' and 'In future' quotes, p 52 for 'Everybody's land' and 'European invention' quotes, p 55 for 'treadmill effort' quote, p 68 for 'in trust' quote); Presbyterian Church, *A Maori View*, p 26; Prichard and Waetford, *Report of the Committee of Inquiry*, Wellington, 1965, p 95 (for 'unoccupied and undeveloped' quote).

25. McLeay, Elizabeth (ed), *New Zealand Politics*, p 238; Simon, Judith and Smith, Linda Tuhiwai (eds), *A Civilising Mission? Perceptions and Recommendations of the New Zealand Native Schools System*, Auckland, 2001; Prichard and Waetford, *Report of the Committee of Inquiry*, pp 67–8, 77–84, 150 (p 77 for 'house site in town' quote, p 150 for 'nothing in the Treaty' quote); Bradly, 'Education's Impact', p 67.

26. Booth and Hunn, *Integration*, p 8 (for 'changing environment' quote); Anderson, 'Welfare Requirements', pp 99–100; Nightingale, 'Maori at Work', p 226; McHugh, *The Maori Magna Carta*, p 203; Ministry of Foreign Affairs and Trade, *New Zealand Handbook on International Human Rights*, 2nd ed, Wellington, 2003, p 120; International Labour Organisation, *Convention concerning the Protection and Integration of Indigenous and Other Tribal and Semi-Tribal Populations in Independent Countries*, C107, Geneva, 1957; Secretary of External Affairs to the Prime Minister, 24 Dec 1959, and attached draft, 'Discrimination against Maoris' (for 'on the grounds' quote in letter and '[a]ny possible danger' quote in draft); B E Souter, Assistant Secretary, Instructions to District Officers, re 'Discrimination against Maoris: The Indigenous Population Convention, 1957', 23 May 1960, AAMK, 869, Box 1063c, 36/1/21A, Race Relations–Interdepartmental Report, 1964–72 (for 'everything possible' quote).

27. United Nations Office of the High Commissioner for Human Rights, 'International Convention on the Elimination of All Forms of Racial Discrimination', 1965; Bennett, R to Mr Souter, 12 Oct 1966, MA 1, Box 656, Part 9, 36/1/21, Race Relations–Integration–Segregation, 1964–68 (for 'international scrutiny' quote); McEwen (Secretary for Maori Affairs) to Secretary External Affairs, re 'International Convention on the Elimination of All Forms of Racial Discrimination', 7 Aug 1967, MA 1, Box 656, Part 9, 36/1/21, Race Relations–Integration–Segregation, 1964–68; McEwen (Secretary for Maori Affairs) to Minister Maori Affairs, report re 'Maori Wardens', 11 May 1970, MA 1, Box 657, Part 10, 36/1/21, Race Relations–Overseas Countries–Policy and Correspondence, 1964–71 (for 'legislation governing' quote); de Bres, Joris, 'Current Issues in Race Relations', Speech by Race Relations Commissioner, 16 March 2004, pp 4–5, available online: http://www.hrc.co.nz/home/hrc/newsandissues/currentissuesinracerelations2004.php [accessed June 2008]; Magallenes, Catherine J Iorns, 'International Human Rights and their Impact on Domestic Law on Indigenous Peoples' Rights in Australia, Canada, and New Zealand', in Havemann, Paul (ed), *Indigenous Peoples' Rights in Australia, Canada, and New Zealand*, Auckland, 1999.

28. Hunn, *Affairs of State*, pp 152–3; McLeay (ed), *New Zealand Politics*, p 238 (for 'alternative leadership system' quote); Hazlehurst, 'Maori Self-Government 1945'; Butterworth, *'Men of Authority'*, pp 7–9; Gustafson, Barry, *The First 50 Years: A History of the New Zealand National Party*, Auckland, 1986 pp 241–55, for Maori and the National Party.

9. Williams, John A, *Politics of the New Zealand Maori: Protest and Co-operation, 1891–1909*, Auckland, 1969, p 163; Pearce, G L, *The Story of the Maori People*, Auckland, 1968, p 148; Butterworth and Young, *Maori Affairs*, p 103; Walker, *Ka Whawhai Tonu Matou*, pp 204–5; Department of Maori Affairs, *The Maori Today*, 1964, 'Welfare' section (for 'to complete' quote); Butterworth, *'Men of Authority'*, pp 9–11 (including 'charter' and 'dissolution' quotes).

Chapter 6

1. Department of Maori Affairs, *The Maori Today*, 1964, 'Welfare' section; Fleras, 'Descriptive Analysis', p 195.
2. Rangihau, John, 'Being Maori', in King, Michael (ed), *Te Ao Hurihuri: The World Moves On*, Wellington, 1975, p 233 (for 'unite … and rule' quote); Sissons, 'The post-assimilationist thought', p. 58; Ritchie, 'The Grass Roots', pp 80, 83 (for 'a resurgent *Maoritanga*' and related quotes); D N Perry, Interim Committee, Dominion Council of Tribal Executives, to J R Hanan, 20 January 1961, MA 1, 35/2, part 1, box 646, 'New Zealand Council of Tribal Executives, 1952–1962' (for 'sensitive' quote).
3. Pearce, *The Story of the Maori People*, p 148 (for 'crowning achievement' quote); Maori Welfare Act 1962; Department of Maori Affairs, *The Maori Today*, 1964, 'Welfare' section (includes 'elected by the Maori public' and 'which deal with' quotes); Fleras, 'Descriptive Analysis', pp 200–203; Walker, *Ka Whawhai Tonu Matou*, p 204; Butterworth and Young, *Maori Affairs*, p 103; Hazlehurst, 'Maori Self-Government', pp 75–7; Ormsby, 'Maori Tikanga', pp 16–7; Butterworth, *'Men of Authority'*, p 10.
4. Department of Maori Affairs, *The Maori Today*, 1964, 'Welfare' section (for 'a form of local government', 'general aim' and following quotes); Harris, 'Dancing with the State', p 156 (for 'appointment to the Maori council' quote); Hazlehurst, *Political Expression*, p 14; Ormsby, 'Maori Tikanga', p16 (for 'we are further' quote).
5. Harris, 'Dancing with the State', p 157 (for 'jack up' and 'representativity was diluted' quotes), pp 160–61 (p 161 for 'effectively shackled' quote); 'Report of the First New Zealand Maori Council', nd, MA 1, W2490, 35/2/4, Part 1 (for 'without reference even' quote); *Evening Post*, 22 November 1962, MA 1, 35/2, vol 2; Walker, *Ka Whawhai Tonu Matou*, p 204 (for 'artificial construct' quote); Fleras, 'Descriptive Analysis', pp 198–9; Metge, *The Maoris of New Zealand*, p 208 (for 'the system has not' and 'Government plan' quotes).
6. Walker, *Ka Whawhai Tonu Matou*, p 205; Harris, 'Dancing with the State', p 160; Hazlehurst, 'Maori Self-Government', p 75 (for 'degree of decision-making' quote), pp 80–1 (p 80 for 'exhorted members' quote); Orange, 'The Price of Citizenship?', p 246; Labrum, 'Bringing families up to scratch', p 166; Labrum, 'The Essentials of Good Citizenship', p 451; Ormsby, 'Maori Tikanga', p 16 (for 'cap in hand' quote); Butterworth, *'Men of Authority'*, pp 9ff, 56.
7. Hunn, *Affairs of State*, p 153 (for 'old net' quote); Hazlehurst, 'Maori Self-Government', p 75 (for 'bicultural political relations' quote), p 79 (for 'to be viewed' quote); McHugh, *The Maori Magna Carta*, p 201 (for 'rather toothless' quote); Butterworth, *'Men of Authority'*, p 21ff (p 23 for 'offend' quote and p 27 for 'spontaneous' quote).
8. Walker, *Ka Whawhai Tonu Matou*, pp 204–5; Byron, *Nga Perehitini*, p 11 (for 'the League assumed' quote); Fleras, 'Descriptive Analysis', p 202; Hazlehurst, 'Maori Self-Government', p 75 (for 'a major breakthrough' quote), p 95 (for 'hybrid of both European and Maori' quote); Hazlehurst, *Political Expression*, pp 33–4; Butterworth, *'Men of Authority'*, p 21ff (p 29 for 'spirit' quote).
9. Hazlehurst, 'Maori Self-Government', p 76 (for 'the power was really' quote); Walker, 'The Politics', p 180; Tauranga Moana Trust Board Act 1981; Hazlehurst, *Political Expression*, p 32 (for 'was a politically discrete' and 'maintained a remarkable' quotes), p 33 (for 'greater coherence' quote), p 34 (for 'essentially a mechanism', 'symbol of a will' and 'the power' quotes).
10. Walker, 'The Politics', p 168 (for 'provides for a form of self-government' quote), p 169 (for 'promote harmonious' and following quotes); Walker, 'Maori People Since 1950', p 510.
11. Walsh, *More and More Maoris*, p 38 (for 'the department's welfare work' quote); Labrum, 'Bringing families up to scratch', p 166; Walker, 'The Politics', p 170 (for 'outsiders' and 'additional duties'

quotes), p 177 (for 'Greetings, I am a Maori', 'dirty', and 'a man's duty' quotes), pp 179–81; Walke 'Maori People Since 1950', p 502 (for 'irrevocably integrated' quote).

12. Fleras, 'Descriptive Analysis', p 28 (for 'agents of social control' quote), pp 240 and 272, p 275 (fc 'provide material and spiritual assistance' quote), p 276, p 283 (for 'acceptance by Maoris' quote abstract (for 'in facilitating' quote); Walker, 'The Politics', p 170 (for 'riotous, offensive' and 'intoxicatec quarrelsome' quotes), p 171 (for 'take out a prohibition' quote), p 178 (for 'close supervision an surveillance' quote); Hunn, *Report on Department of Maori Affairs*, pp 32–5; Fleras, Augie, 'Maor Wardens', pp 495–7.
13. Te Puni Kokiri, *Discussion Paper on the Review of the Māori Community Development Act 196* Wellington, 1999, pp 19–20, p 25 (for 'enforcement and sanction-type' and 'connotations of' quotes Fleras, 'Descriptive Analysis', pp 138–40, 275; Butterworth and Butterworth, *Policing and the Tanga Whenua*, p 33; Stenning, Philip, 'Maori, Crime and Criminal Justice: over-representation or under representation', Paper presented to the Stout Research Centre, 18 March 2005; Walker, 'Maori Peopl Since 1950', p 502; Walker, 'The Politics', pp 171, 181; Hill, Richard S, 'Maori police personn and the *rangatiratanga* discourse', in Godfrey, Barry S and Dunstall, Graeme (eds), *Crime and Empi 1840–1940: Criminal Justice in Local and Global Context*, Cullompton, 2005, pp 177, 183–4.
14. Fleras, 'Descriptive Analysis', pp 62, 64–5, 275–6, 278; Butterworth, *'Men of Authority'*, pp 26– Stenning, 'Maori, Crime'.
15. Fleras, 'Descriptive Analysis', pp 212, 214, p 278 (for 'Maori had not achieved' quote), pp 279–80 (279 for 'auxiliary police force' quote); Royal Commission on the Courts, *Report of Royal Commissio on the Courts*, Wellington, 1978, p 16; Butterworth and Butterworth, *Policing and the Tangata Whenu* pp 32–4 (p 33 for 'discriminatory, in that' quote); Walker, 'The Politics', p 171.
16. Fleras, 'Descriptive Analysis', p 206 (for 'eyes and ears' quote), pp 214–5, p 283 (for 'cultural right quote), pp 284–91, p 296 (for 'provide assistance' quote), p 303 (for 'in the vanguard' quote), pp 308– Mahuta, Robert, 'The Maori King Movement Today', in King, Michael (ed), *Tihe Mauri Ora: Aspect of Maoritanga*, Wellington, 1978, p 39; Fleras, 'Maori Wardens', p 508 (for 'symbolic of a paternalistic and 'Their objective' quotes).
17. Hazlehurst, 'Maori Self-Government', p 78; Fleras, 'Descriptive Analysis', pp 203–4 (p 204 for 'socia criticism' quote); Harris, 'Maori and "the Maori Affairs"', pp 197–201 (p 198 for 'largely disappeared quote).
18. Lange, *Maori Well-Being*, pp 47–8; Ormsby, 'Maori Tikanga', pp 17–8; Harris, 'Dancing with th State', pp 77–81; Walker, 'The Politics'.
19. Walker, 'The Politics', p 176 (for 'nature of the court' and following quotes), p 179 (for 'physica setting', 'emphasised' and 'presence in uniform' quotes); Harris, 'Dancing with the State', p 78.
20. Walker, 'The Politics', p 177 (for 'Dirty Maoris' quote), p 178 (for 'loss of face' quotes), p 180 (for 'fall' 'succeed' and 'offence is committed' quotes).
21. Poulsen and Johnston, 'Patterns of Maori Migration', pp 172–3; Walker, 'The Politics', pp 179–8 (p 180 for 'When you die' quote); Butterworth, 'Aotearoa 1769–1988', ch 9, pp 22–4.
22. Fleras, 'Descriptive Analysis', pp 204–5, p 280 (for 'kangaroo courts' quote); Lange, *Maori Well-Being* p 48 (for 'discriminatory' quote); Stokes, Evelyn (ed), *Nga Tumanako: National Conference of Mao Committees*, Hamilton, 1978, p 44 (for 'a strong feeling' quote); Royal Commission on the Courts p 122 (for 'divided society' and 'did not consider' quotes), p 176 (for 'informed that local Maori quote), p 271 (for 'special courts' quote).
23. Ward, Alan, *A Show of Justice*, p 315 (for 'the devolution of minor' quote); Labrum, 'The Essential of Good Citizenship', p 453; Harris, *Hīkoi*, pp 17, 20; Harris, 'Dancing with the State', pp 19–20 Brookes, Barbara, 'Nostalgia for "Innocent Homely Pleasures"', in Brookes, Barbara (ed), *At Hom in New Zealand: Houses, History, People*, Wellington, 2000; Westra, Ans, *Washday at the Pa* (Castl Press ed, including 'Publisher's Note'), Christchurch, 1964; Fleras, 'Descriptive Analysis', p 205 (fo 'suppress' quote).
24. Kawharu, I Hugh, 'Urban Immigrants', p 186 (for 'Maori want[ed] to be Maori' quote); Butterworth Graham, Newspaper Clippings Collection, Treaty of Waitangi Research Unit, box 4 (for 'sufficiently removed' quote), Department of Maori Affairs, *The Maori Today*, 1964, 'Welfare' section (for 'complex and perplexing' and following quotes); Butterworth, *'Men of Authority'*, p 26.

25. Stokes et al, *Te Urewera*, pp 303–7 (p 303 for 'as tangata whenua, the host people' quote, p 306 for 'the urban situation' quote, p 307 for 'based on the continuing' quote).
26. Ausubel, 'The Maori'; Hazlehurst, 'Maori Self-Government', p 67 (for '[t]raditional knowledge' quote), p 68; Walker, 'The Politics', p 180 (for 'close scrutiny', 'work of a Maori committee' and 'norms of good conduct' quotes); Metge, Joan, 'Kia Tupato! Anthropologist at Work', *Oceania*, 69(1), Sept 1998, p 1 (for 'Maori have resisted' quote).
27. Cox, *Kotahitanga*, p 76, p 107 (for 'opportunity for input' quote), pp 106–7; McRae, Jane, 'Participation: Native Committees (1883) and Papatupu Block Committees (1900) in Tai Tokerau', MA thesis, University of Auckland, 1981, p 129 (for 'uncertain of their duties' quote), p 130 (for 'welfare of our people' quote); Harrison, Noel, *Graham Latimer: A Biography*, Wellington, 2002, pp 83–4; Walker, 'The Politics', pp 172, 180–85 (p 180 for 'real power lay' quote, p 184 for 'an adaptive mechanism' quote).
28. Ritchie, 'The Grass Roots', p 85; Schwimmer, Erik, 'The Maori and the Government', in Schwimmer, Erik (ed), *The Maori People in the Nineteen-Sixties*, p 331; Hill, *State Authority*, pp 50–64; Cox, *Kotahitanga*, p 76; Hunn, *Report on Department of Maori Affairs*, p 80; Walsh, *More and More Maoris*, p 36 (for 'seems to talk', 'hierarchy of structure' and 'strangled communication' quotes); Harrison, *Graham Latimer*, pp 74–5; Ritchie, James E, *Tribal Development in a Fourth World Context: The Maori Case*, Honolulu, 1990, p13 (for 'puppet organization' quote).
29. Butterworth and Young, *Maori Affairs*, p 105 (re DMA); Walker, Ranginui J, 'The Politics', p 179 (for 'just and proper' and 'collective moral force' quotes); McRae, 'Participation', p 134 (for 'personal contact' quote).
30. Levine, Stephen, *The New Zealand Political System: Politics in a Small Society*, Sydney, 1979, p 146 (for 'legitimate participants' quote); Stokes (ed), *Nga Tumanako*, p 19 (for 'experience, education and sophistication' quote); Stokes et al, *Te Urewera*, p xviii; Hazlehurst, 'Maori Self-Government', p 79; Hazlehurst, *Political Expression*, p 18 (for 'comfortable with the values' quote).
31. Ormsby, 'Maori Tikanga', p 17 (for 'seem to empower' and 'local self-government' quotes); Butterworth, *'Men of Authority'*, pp 12–13, 20; Walker, 'The Politics', pp 172–5 (p 172 for 'focal point' quote, p 175 for 'grew in stature' quote), p 179 (for 'control and mastery' quote); Maori Community Development Act 1979 see Kernot, *People of the Four Winds* on European involvement in Maori committees.
32. Prichard and Waetford, *Report of the Committee of Inquiry*, p 111 (for 'believes in integration' quote); Walker, 'The Politics', p 180 (for 'rings you up' quote); Edwards, *Mihipeka*, p 190 (for 'the dignity' quote); Walker, *Ka Whawhai Tonu Matou*, p 205 (for 'struggle' quote); Williams, *Politics of the New Zealand Maori*, p 162; Butterworth, 'Aotearoa 1769–1988', ch 10, p 16 (for 'a form of inarticulate protest' quote).

Chapter 7

1. McRobie, Alan, 'The Politics of Volatility, 1972–1991', in Rice (ed), *Oxford History*, p 385 (for 'politics of stability' and 'volatility' quotes); Butterworth, *'Men of Authority'*, p 39 (for 'denial' and 'identity' quotes); Te Awekotuku, Ngahuia, 'He Wahine, he Whenua, e Ngaro ai te Tangata: By Women, by Land, Men are Lost', in *Mana Wahine Maori: Selected Writings on Maori Women's Art, Culture and Politics*, Auckland, 1991 (original article: 1972), p 46 (for '[c]onsciousness of being Maori' quote), pp 46–7 (for 'review the validity' quote), p 47 (for 'renaissance' quote); Nga Tamatoa, 'Submissions on the Broadcasting Bill 1973', MS Papers 1617, Folder 667, Maori organisations–Tamatoa and Nga Tamatoa Council 1971–73, Alexander Turnbull Library (p 2); Wood, Anthony, 'Holyoake and the Holyoake Years', in Clark, Margaret (ed), *Sir Keith Holyoake: Towards a Political Biography*, Palmerston North, 1997, p 44; Belich, *Paradise Reforged*, pp 425–35; for a summary version of Belich's argument concerning New Zealand's colonisation, see Belich, James, 'Colonization and History in New Zealand', in Winks, Robin W (ed), *The Oxford History of the British Empire: Volume V: Historiography*, Oxford, 1999; Bedggood, *Rich and Poor*, pp 7–8 (for 'founding myths' quote); King, Michael, *Nga Iwi o te Motu: One Thousand Years of Maori History*, Auckland, 1997, p 100; Walker, *Ka Whawhai Tonu Matou;* p 222; King, Michael, *Being Pakeha Now*, Auckland, 1999, Ch 5.

2. Sissons, 'The post-assimilationist thought', p58 (for 'new ethnic activism' quote); New Zealan Press Association, 'Maori influence growing – Sir Tipene', 3 Dec 2004 www.stuff.co.nz/stuff print/0,1478,3117011a8153,00.html [accessed 6 Dec 2004] (for 'dramatically fuelled' quote); Orange *The Treaty of Waitangi*, p245; Mulgan, Richard, *Maori, Pakeha and Democracy*, Auckland, 1989, p5 (fo 'ethnic revival' quote); Hazlehurst, *Political Expression*, p19; Pearson, David, *The Politics of Ethnicity i Settler Societies: States of Unease*, Basingstoke, 2001, p188; Coates, Ken S, 'International Perspective on Relations with Indigenous Peoples', in Coates, Ken S and McHugh, P G, *Living Relationship Kōkiri Ngatāhi: The Treaty of Waitangi in the New Millennium*, Wellington, 1998, p35; Poata-Smith, E Te Ahu, 'He Pokeke Uenuku I Tu Ai: The Evolution of Contemporary Maori Protest', in Spoonle Paul, Pearson, David and Macpherson, Cluny (eds), *Nga Patai: Racism and Ethnic Relations in Aotearoa New Zealand*, Palmerston North, 1996, pp 98–103 (p 98 for 'New Left' quote); Harris, *Hīkoi*, p1 Scott, *A Radical Writer's Life*, pp 204, 208.
3. Pearson, *A Dream Deferred*, p211 (for 'the spirit of ethnicity' quote); Vasil, Raj K, *Biculturalism Reconciling Aotearoa with New Zealand*, Wellington, 2000 (rev ed), pp 19–20 (for 'national community quote); Walker, *Ka Whawhai Tonu Matou*, p209 (for 'alienating culture' quote).
4. Vasil, *Biculturalism* (see title for 'reconcile' quote); Johnson, Miranda, '"The Land of the Wrong Whit Crowd": Anti-Racist Organizations and Pakeha Identity Politics in the 1970s', *New Zealand Journa of History*, 39(2), 2005, pp 137–8, 152–3; Auckland Committee on Racism and Discrimination information leaflet, nd [c1973], 94-106-19/07, Polynesians in New Zealand, Herbert Otto Rot Papers (MS-Group-0314), Alexander Turnbull Library (for 'examine critically' quote); Citizen Association for Racial Equality and Auckland Committee on Racism and Discrimination, 'Maor Representation – Joint Submission to the Parliamentary Select Committee established to revise th Electoral Act 1956 and Amendments thereto', nd [c1973], 95-222-1/06, Maori Struggles, Davi Wickham Papers, Alexander Turnbull Library (p 11 for 'to build a truly' quote).
5. Poata-Smith, 'He Pokeke Uenuku I Tu Ai', pp 99–101 (p 101 for 'advocated an alliance' quote Maori Organisation on Human Rights, 'Waitangi Day' Newsletter, Dec 1970, MS Papers 7888-233 Newsletters–Maori, E W G Craig Papers, Alexander Turnbull Library (p 3 for unite the variou 'races', 'Maori and Pakeha and all' quotes, p5 for 'especially all working people' quote); Harris, *Hīkoi* p35; Walker, *Ka Whawhai Tonu Matou*, p209 (for 'struggle for Maori rights' quote); Nightingale 'Maori at Work', pp 219–20.
6. *Te Hokioi: Te Reo Ote Iwi Maori*, Issue 4, vol 1, Feb/March 1969, MS Papers 7888-233, Newsletters-Maori, E W G Craig Papers, Alexander Turnbull Library (p 1 for 'written for Maoris' quote); Ng Tamatoa, 'Submissions on the Broadcasting Bill' (p 4 re 'monocultural attitudes'); Walker, *K Whawhai Tonu Matou*, pp 209–12; Walker, 'Maori People Since 1950', pp 508, 511–2 (p 512 fo 'accused the education system' quote); Nga Tamatoa, in Maori Organisation on Human Rights July Newsletter, 1972, 99-278-05/06, Papers re the Race Relations Bill, Trevor Richards Papers Alexander Turnbull Library (pp 1 and 6 for 'control over those things' quote, emphasis removed) Minutes of the Annual Conference of the Race Relations Council, Massey University, 9–11 Feb 1973, 99-278-08/09, New Zealand Race Relations Council, Polynesian Panthers, Trevor Richards Papers, Alexander Turnbull Library (p 2 for 'the education of Maori' quote); Rei et al, 'Ngā Rōpū' pp 11–2; Department of Maori Affairs, *The Maori Today*, 1964 ('The Maori Language' section); Harris *Hīkoi*, pp 26, 38, 44–8; Walker, 'The Treaty of Waitangi', pp 57–58; Nightingale, 'Maori at Work' p220.
7. Ngata, Apirana, *The Treaty of Waitangi: An Explanation*, trans Jones, M R, Wellington, 1963 (original *Te Tiriti o Waitangi: He Whakamarama*, Hastings, 1922); J K Hunn to Secretary External Affairs, Alister D McIntosh, 1 Feb 1963, MA, W2459, Box 163, Part 1, 19/1/55/1, Treaty of Waitangi – General and Policy and Submissions by New Zealand Council, 1971–1971; Carroll, Turi, Speech to Her Majesty the Queen, Waitangi Day gathering, 6 Feb 1963, MA, W2459, Box 163, Part 1, 19/1/55/1, Treaty of Waitangi – General and Policy and Submissions by New Zealand Council, 1971–1971; Orange, *The Treaty of Waitangi*, pp 228–46; Harrison, *Graham Latimer*, p107; Petition of Rangi Makawe Rangitaura of Big Jim's Hill, Waitara, and Others, 1966, in Supplement no 1 to Maori Organisation on Human Rights, September Newsletter, 1972, 99-278-05/06, Papers re the Race Relations Bill, Trevor Richards Papers, Alexander Turnbull Library (p 3 for quotes).

8. National Council of Churches Programme on Racism, 'Legislation Betrays the Treaty of Waitangi', nd, 99-266-10/1, Folder 4, Treaty of Waitangi, Alexander Turnbull Library; Ngata, H K, 'The Treaty of Waitangi and Land', Parts of the Current Law in Contravention of the Treaty seminar, Victoria University of Wellington, Feb 1972, reproduced in Maori Organisation on Human Rights, Newsletter, 6 Feb 1973, 85-002-02, Papers relating to human rights, South Pacific writers and literature, John Owen O'Conner Papers, Alexander Turnbull Library; Hohepa, P K, 'Waitangi: A Promise or a Betrayal', Papers in Race Relations no 2, 85-002-02, Papers relating to human rights, South Pacific writers and literature, John Owen O'Conner Papers, Alexander Turnbull Library (p 5 re 'day of mourning'); 'Nga Reo: Syd Jackson – The Life and Times of a Fully-Fledged Activist', Tawera Productions, Television New Zealand, 2003 (for 'seeking nothing less' quote); Butterworth, 'Aotearoa 1769–1988', ch 10, p 3; Orange, *The Treaty of Waitangi*, pp 244, 248; Harris, *Hīkoi*, pp 25–6; Stirling, Eruera (as told to Anne Salmond), *Eruera: The Teachings of a Maori Elder*, Wellington, 1980, p 225; McLoughlin, David, 'Singing Her Own Song', *Dominion Post*, 4 Feb 2003, p B5 (for 'we were driven' quote); Hazlehurst, *Political Expression*, p 19 (for 'an attempt to create' quote), p 21 (for 'shrewd appreciation' quote), p 22; Ballara, *Proud to Be White?* p 163 (for 'Maori identity' quote).

9. Walker, 'Maori People Since 1950', p 512 (for 'ferment of political activism' quote); Poata-Smith, 'He Pokeke Uenuku I Tu Ai', pp 103–5; Hunn, *Report on Department of Maori Affairs*, pp 8–9, 52–9, 66–8; Harris, 'Dancing with the State', p 145 (for '[t]urangawaewae … can prevent' and 'evils of turangawaewae' quotes).

10. Harris, 'Dancing with the State', pp 163–5; Presbyterian Church, *A Maori View*, p 28 (for 'home ownership' quote), p 33 (for 'the cardinal principle' and 'well-being' quotes), pp 41–2; Gilling, *'Most Barren and Unprofitable Land'*, p 7.

11. Harris, 'Maori Land Title, pp 147–9; Butterworth and Young, *Maori Affairs*, pp 105–6; Prichard and Waetford, *Report of the Committee of Inquiry*, p 150 (for 'that objectors were resisting' quote), p 151 (for 'many unjustified' and 'after 100 years' quotes); Harris, *Hīkoi*, pp 23–4; Butterworth, 'Aotearoa 1769–1988', ch 9, p 25 (for 'aim was simply' quote); Boast, 'The Evolution', pp 97–100 (p 99 for 'coercive in nature' quote, p 100 for 'advocated, in essence' quote); Butterworth, 'Men of Authority', p 31ff (p 31 for 'panic' quote); Walker, 'Maori People Since 1950', p 510 (for 'last land-grab' quote); Nightingale, 'Maori at Work', p 195.

12. Ballara, *Proud to Be White?* p 137 (for 'rapidly becoming' and 'village communities' quotes); Harris, 'Maori Land Title', p 148; Butterworth, 'Aotearoa 1769–1988', ch 9, pp 25–8; Butterworth and Young, *Maori Affairs*, p 106; Hazlehurst, *Political Expression*, p 46 (for 'Maori tradition of tribal ownership' quote).

13. Simon and Smith (eds), *A Civilising Mission?* p 258; Butterworth and Young, *Maori Affairs*, pp 106–7, 110; 'Maori Proposal for Separate Parliament', *The Press*, 8 Dec 1969, p 18; Butterworth, *'Men of Authority'*, pp 36–7, 40, 55.

14. Harrison, *Graham Latimer*, pp 74–7, p 81 (for 'a far different type' quote), p 82 (for 'vanguard of a new elite' quote), pp 83, 87, 89, 92; Walker, *Ka Whawhai Tonu Matou*, p 6; Ranginui Walker, interviewed by Chris Laidlaw on Radio New Zealand National, 20 Jan 2008.

15. Harrison, *Graham Latimer*, pp 89, 98, 107, 111; Alves, Dora, *The Maori and the Crown: An Indigenous People's Struggle for Self-Determination*, Westport, CT, 1999, p 65; Hazlehurst, 'Maori Self-Government, p 95 (for 'a forum within' and following quote); Walker, 'The Treaty of Waitangi', p 58.

16. Jeffries, Bill, 'Kirk's Prime-ministership 1972–1974', in Clark, Margaret (ed), *Three Labour Leaders: Nordmeyer, Kirk, Rowling*, Palmerston North, 2001, p 111 (for 'bi-cultural togetherness' quote), p 114 (for 'the foundation stone' quote); McLeay, Elizabeth, 'Roles, Rules and Leadership', in Clark (ed), *Three Labour Leaders*, p 82; Anderton, Jim, 'Kirk and Rowling: Recollections and Significance', in Clark (ed), *Three Labour Leaders*, p 51; Orange, *The Treaty of Waitangi*, p 246; Ward, *A Show of Justice*, back cover (for ETJ Durie's 'historical landmark' quote); Mein Smith, Philippa, *A Concise History of New Zealand*, Melbourne, 2005, ch 10 (p 226 for 'Treaty revival' quote).

17. McHugh, *The Maori Magna Carta*, p 357; Hazlehurst, *Political Expression*, p 35 (for 'person of the Maori race' quote), p 47 (for 'a major philosophical' quote), p 48 (for 'to a considerable extent' quote); Maori Land Court, 'Shane Gibbons – A New Direction', *Te Pouwhenua*, 8, Nov 2001, available online: http://www.justice.govt.nz/Maorilandcourt/pdf/tepouwhenua8.pdf [accessed June 2008], p 3 (for 'the

vehicle that re-establishes' quote); Butterworth and Young, *Maori Affairs*, pp 109–110; Butterworth *'Men of Authority'*, pp 42–5; Hayward, Margaret, *Diary of the Kirk Years*, Wellington, 1981, pp 39–40

18. Orange, *The Treaty of Waitangi*, p246; Forbes, George, in *New Zealand Parliamentary Debates*, vol 234 9 Nov, 1932, p223; Treaty of Waitangi Act 1975, s 6; Boast, Richard, 'The Treaty of Waitangi an the Law', *New Zealand Law Journal*, April 1999, p124.

19. Hazlehurst, *Political Expression*, p48; McLeay (ed), *New Zealand Politics*, p245; Scott, *A Radical Writer Life*, pp 286–297 (pp 288–9 for 'new book came out' quote); Scott, Dick, *Ask that Mountain: The Stor of Parihaka*, Auckland, 1975; King, *Being Pakeha Now*, p109ff. Despite the hostile reception to Scott' Parihaka book from professional historians, a number of the same people were later at the forefront c 'politically correct' history when the historical establishment's line changed.

20. Orange, *The Treaty of Waitangi*, p234, p246; New Zealand History online, 'The First Waitangi Day' Ministry for Culture and Heritage, http://www.nzhistory.net.nz/politics/treaty/waitangi-day/the first-waitangi-day, updated 25 Sept 2007 (for 'unique relationship' quote); Palmer, Matthew S R, *The Treaty of Waitangi in New Zealand's Law and Constitution*, Wellington, 2008, p187; Maori Organisation on Human Rights, Newsletter, July 1972, MS Papers 7888-233, Newsletters – Maori, E W G Craig Papers Alexander Turnbull Library (p 2 for 'absorption' quote); Rata, Matiu, in *New Zealand Parliamentar Debates*, vol 407, 1976, p3424 (for 'spirit embraced' quote); Walker, *Ka Whawhai Tonu Matou*, p212

21. Nightingale, 'Maori at Work', p229 (for 'truly *bicultural*' quote), p228 (for 'one nation' quote) p260 (for 'negative integration' quote); O'Regan, Tipene, interviewed by Paul Diamond, 'Ng Manu Taiko', National Radio, 23 February 2003; Parininihi Ki Waitotara Incorporation website http://www.pkw.co.nz/; 'Land Wrangle Leads to High Court', *Daily News*, 9 Sept 2003; Kawharu 'Introduction' in *Conflict and Compromise*, p14 (for 'groping towards' quote); van Meijl, Toon, 'Th Politics of Ethnography in New Zealand', in Jaarsma, Sjoerd R and Rohatynskyj, Marta A (eds) *Ethnographic Artifacts: Challenges to a Reflexive Anthropology*, Honolulu, 2000.

22. Rata, Matiu, in *New Zealand Parliamentary Debates*, vol 407, 1976, p3424 (for 'an instrument c mutuality' quote); Minogue, Kenneth R, *Waitangi: Morality and Reality*, Wellington, 1998, p1 (fo 'merely as a response' quote); Walker, Ranginui J, 'Hostages of History', *Metro*, Feb 2001, p86 (fo 'touchstone for defusing' quote); Rigby, Barry, 'The Waitangi Tribunal: The Significance of a 25 Yea Experiment', paper presented at 25th Anniversary of the Waitangi Tribunal conference, Wellington 10–11 Oct 2000 (for 'safety valve' quote); Williams, Chief Judge J V, speech at 25th Anniversary of the Waitangi Tribunal conference, Wellington, 11 Oct 2000 (for 'shift from protest to process' quote) McLeay (ed), *New Zealand Politics*, p245 (for 'the result was bound' quote).

23. Walker, 'Maori People Since 1950', pp 512–3 (p 513 for 'not one more acre' quote); Walker *Ka Whawhai Tonu Matou*, pp 212, 214 (for 'more dynamic' quote); Harrison, *Graham Latimer*, p99 King, *Whina*, p206ff; Butterworth, 'Aotearoa 1769–1988', ch 10, pp 5–7 (p 6 for 'twin themes' quote) Te Roopu Ote Matakite, 'Why We Protest', leaflet, nd, 2004-024-3/02, Maori Organisation on Human Rights, Peter Langdon Franks Papers, Alexander Turnbull Library (for 'Land is the very soul and following quotes); Butterworth and Young, *Maori Affairs*, pp 110–111; Legat, Nicola, 'Warrior Woman', *North & South*, April 2000, p67; Durie, *Whaiora*, p52 (for 'demonstrated the extent' quote) Harris, *Hīkoi*, pp 68–77.

24. King, *Whina*, p211; Butterworth, G V, 'Breaking the Grip: An Historical Agenda for Nga Iwi Maori' revision of a paper presented to the History Department, Massey University, 16 April 1987, p2 (for 'Maori people' quote); Walker, 'Maori People Since 1950', p513; Harris, *Hīkoi*, pp 60–62; Walker 'The Treaty of Waitangi', p59.

25. Sharp, Andrew, 'The Treaty of Waitangi: Reasoning and Social Justice in New Zealand?', in Spoonley Paul, Pearson, David and Macpherson, Cluny (eds), *Nga Take: Ethnic Relations and Racism in Aotearoa/ New Zealand*, Palmerston North, 1991, p134; Renwick, William, 'Decolonising Ourselves From Within', *British Review of New Zealand Studies*, no 6, 1993, p31; Oliver, W H, *Claims to the Waitangi Tribunal*, Wellington, 1991, p8; Kelsey, Jane, 'Legal Imperialism and the Colonization of Aotearoa', in Spoonley, Paul, Macpherson, Cluny, Pearson, David and Sedgwick, Charles (eds), *Tauiwi: Racism and Ethnicity in New Zealand*, Palmerston North, 1984, pp 41–2; Allen, 'Postcolonial Theory', p61 (for '*re-recognize*' quote), p62 (for 'disavowed' and 'cross-cultural and cross-national' quotes); McLeay (ed), *New Zealand Politics*, p245; Orange, *The Treaty of Waitangi*, pp 244–5; Poata-Smith, 'He Pokeke Uenuku I Tu Ai', p105.

26. Renwick, 'Decolonising Ourselves', p51 (for 'we are not one people' and 'made us one' quotes); Walker, *Ka Whawhai Tonu Matou*, p236; Orange, *An Illustrated History*, p147 (for 'any form of distinction' quote); Mansfield, Bill, 'Healthy Constitutional Relationships in a Culturally Diverse Society', Wellington, Ministry of Justice internal resource document, nd, p10.
27. Orange, *The Treaty of Waitangi*, p247.
28. Orange, *An Illustrated History*, pp 147, 182; Walker, 'Maori People Since 1950', p513; Harris, *Hīkoi*, pp 78–85; Poata-Smith, 'He Pokeke Uenuku I Tu Ai', pp 104–5; Walker, *Ka Whawhai Tonu Matou*, pp 183, 215–9; Tupoutahi Tamihana Te Winitana, personal communication, 28 July 2001 (for 'tribal time' and 'take as long as it took' quotes); Orange, *The Treaty of Waitangi*, pp 247–8; Renwick, 'Decolonising Ourselves'.
29. Mansfield, 'Healthy Constitutional Relationships', p10; Hazlehurst, *Political Expression*, p39; Pearson, *A Dream Deferred*, p239; Tirikatene-Sullivan, Whetu, in *New Zealand Parliamentary Debates*, vol 405, 1976, p2275 (for 'not forfeit the right' quote); Awatere, Donna, *Maori Sovereignty*, Auckland, 1984, p15 (for 'should have control' quote), p59 (for 'no longer seek' quote).
30. Ross, Ruth, 'Te Tiriti o Waitangi: Texts and Translations', *New Zealand Journal of History*, 6(2), 1972; Orange, *The Treaty of Waitangi*, pp 40–41, 246; Orange, *An Illustrated History*, p144; Cleave, Peter, *The Sovereignty Game: Power, Knowledge and Reading the Treaty*, Wellington, 1989, p59.
31. Ngata, *The Treaty of Waitangi*, p2 (for 'English expressions' quote), p5 (for 'absolute authority' quote), p6 (for 'chiefly authority' quote), p8 (for 'right of a Maori', 'wishful thinking' and 'as the authority' quotes); Orange, *The Treaty of Waitangi*, pp 228–9; King, *Nga Iwi o te Motu*, pp 101–2; 'Tamatoa Council', nd [1971], MS Papers 1617, Folder 667, Maori organisations – Tamatoa and Nga Tamatoa Council, Alexander Turnbull Library (p 1 for 'various Maori Committees' quote); Maori Organisation on Human Rights, Newsletter, 6 Feb 1973, 85-002-02, Papers relating to human rights, South Pacific writers and literature, John Owen O'Conner Papers, Alexander Turnbull Library (p 2 for 'apologist for' quote).
32. Nga Tamatoa, in Maori Organisation on Human Rights, July Newsletter, (pp 1 and 6 for 'control over those things' quote, emphasis removed); United Peoples Liberation Movement of Aotearoa, 'Attention!', information sheet, nd [c1977], MS Papers 8958-24, Papers relating to race relations in New Zealand, Andrew Dodsworth: Papers relating to left-wing activity, Alexander Turnbull Library (for 'that which is rightfully theirs' quote); Ngata, H K, 'The Treaty of Waitangi and Land', (p1 for 'sovereignty over New Zealand' quote); Maori Organisation on Human Rights, 'Waitangi Day' Newsletter, Dec 1970, (p 1 for 'marked the birth' quote); *Te Hokioi*, Issue 4, vol 1, Feb/March 1969, p10; Walker, Ranginui J, 'Keep the fires burning', in Amoamo, Jacqueline (ed), *Nga Tau Tohetohe: Years of Anger*, Auckland, 1987 (original in *New Zealand Listener*, 6 July 1974), p44 (for 'chiefs yielded' quote); Waitangi Action Committee, 'Te Tiriti o Waitangi: He Teka', nd, 95-222-1/06, Maori Struggles, David Wickham Papers, Alexander Turnbull Library.
33. Walker, Ranginui J, 'Shaky foundations', in Amoamo (ed), *Nga Tau Tohetohe* (original published in *New Zealand Listener*, 22 March 1980); Walker, Ranginui J, 'Maori sovereignty', in Amoamo (ed), *Nga Tau Tohetohe* (original published in *New Zealand Listener*, 1 March 1986); Waitangi Action Committee, 'The Treaty of Waitangi – A Broken Contract', Nov 30 1981, MS Papers 8958-24, Papers relating to race relations in New Zealand, Andrew Dodsworth: Papers relating to left-wing activity, Alexander Turnbull Library (for 'Maori people are a sovereign' quote); Awatere, *Maori Sovereignty*; Maori Peoples Liberation Movement of Aotearoa, 'Critique by Maori Peoples Liberation Movement of Aotearoa', nd, pamphlet, reprinted from MPLMA newsletter, 99-266-10/1, Folder 4, Treaty of Waitangi, Alexander Turnbull Library (p 1 for 'the majority of young Maori' quote).
34. Walker, *Ka Whawhai Tonu Matou*, p220 (for 'radical cutting edge', 'couched in terms' and 'carried their activism' quotes); Waitangi Action Committee, *Te Tiriti* (especially p 7 for '[r]ight of all indigenous peoples' quote – emphasis removed, p13 for 'expose the nature' quote, p18 for 'yoke of Capitalism' quote); Poata-Smith, 'He 'Pokeke Uenuku I Tu Ai', p105; King, *Nga Iwi*, p97; Walker, 'The Treaty of Waitangi', p60.
35. Rapson, Bevan, 'Extremist Makeover', *Metro*, Nov 2004, p58; Tauroa, Hiwi, *Race Against Time*, Wellington, 1982, p9; Harris, *Hīkoi*, pp 95–8; Walker, *Ka Whawhai Tonu Matou*, pp 221–5; Hazlehurst, Kayleen M, *Racial Conflict and Resolution in New Zealand: The Haka Party Incident and its Aftermath, 1979–1980*, Canberra, 1988; Walker, Ranginui J, 'A Maori Parliament', in Amoamo (ed), *Nga Tau*

Tohetohe (originally published in *New Zealand Listener*, 29 Sept 1979) p 104 (for 'manifestations of t stifled desire' quote). As well as being uncomfortable with Maori leaders endorsing extreme activit many sympathetic pakeha (and many Maori engaged in radical action) found (and find) equal problematic various refusals by Maori leaders to give women speaking rights on marae – including 'new' marae where protocols could be more flexible; see Philip, Matt, 'Female trouble', *Listener*, Jan 2000.

36. Maori Peoples Liberation Movement of Aotearoa, 'Critique' (p 2 for 'Pakeha people, who ... try to t us' and following quotes, emphasis removed).
37. Mead, Sidney Moko, 'The Rebirth of a Dream', in *Landmarks, Bridges and Visions: Aspects of Ma Culture*, Wellington, 1997 (original article 1980), pp 130–131 (for 'What we did in the past' quot p 145 (for 'retain our cultural identity' quote); Stewart-Harawira, Margaret, 'Maori, Who Owns t Definition? The Politics of Cultural Identity', *Te Pua*, 2(1–2), 1993; Williams, *The Too-Hard Bask* p 11; Walker, *Ka Whawhai Tonu Matou*, pp 234–5; Harris, *Hīkoi*, p 112.
38. Hazlehurst, *Political Expression*, p 49 (for 'the most influential Maori' quote), pp 51–5 (p 53 for 't party had become' quote), pp 61–3 (p 62 for 'more than a political party' quote), pp 72–3; Walke Ranginui J, 'Mana Motuhake', in Amoamo (ed), *Nga Tau Tohetohe* (original published in *New Zealar Listener*, 4 Aug 1980); Walker, *Ka Whawhai Tonu Matou*, p 228 (for 'we must command' quote); Kin Michael, *Nga Iwi*, p 96.
39. Hazlehurst, *Political Expression*, p 73 (for 'total institutional transformation' quote), pp 74–75, 94, p 1((for 'self-reliance and advancement' quote), p 127 (for 'communal authority by restoring' quote).
40. Butterworth, 'Aotearoa 1769–1988', ch 10, pp 19–22; Hazlehurst, *Political*, pp 153, 164 (for 'all fightir for reform' quote), p 165; Walker, *Ka Whawhai Tonu Matou*, p 244; McLeay (ed), *New Zealand Politi* pp 236, 248–9; King, *Maori*, p 253 (for 'the most spectacular' quote).
41. Kawharu, 'Introduction', in *Conflict and Compromise*, p 4 (for 'a common cultural identity' and 'desi to pursue' quotes).
42. Mead, Sidney Moko, 'Options for Self-Determination: Tino Rangatiratanga', in *Landmarks, Bridg and Visions: Aspects of Maori Culture*, Wellington, 1997 (orig paper: 1993), pp 147–8 (p 147 for better reflection' quote); Hazlehurst, *Political Expression*, p 57; van Meijl, Toon, 'Maori Hierarch Transformed: The Secularization of Tainui Patterns of Leadership', *History and Anthropology*, v 7, 1994, p 301 (for 'the most important thing' quote); Kidman, Fiona, *At the End of Darwin Roa A Memoir*, Auckland, 2008, p 220.
43. Hazlehurst, *Political Expression*, pp 57–8; Sharp, Andrew, *Justice and the Māori: Māori Claims New Zealand Political Argument in the 1980s*, Auckland, 1990, p 233; Winiata, Whatarangi, 'Reducir the Socio-Economic Disparities in Housing, Employment, Health and Education: A Maori Solutior paper for the Anglican Church, Wellington, 1998, available online: http://homepages.ihu co.nz/~sai/MSoln_Win.html [accessed June 2008]; Joint Methodist Presbyterian Public Questior Committee, *Tino Rangatiratanga*, TWM, July 1993, http://homepages.ihug.co.nz/~sai/Maori_tin htm#Constitutional [accessed June 2008]; Mead, 'Options', pp 148–9; Hazlehurst, 'Maori Sel Government', p 80; Walker, *Ka Whawhai Tonu Matou*, pp 246–7.
44. Levine, Hal and Henare, Manuka, 'Mana Maori Motuhake: Maori Self-Determination', *Paci Viewpoint*, 35(2), 1994, pp 196–7; Walker, 'Maori People Since 1950', p 514; Orange, *The Treaty Waitangi*, p 249; Orange, *An Illustrated History*, pp 156–7; Tauroa, *Race Against Time*, pp 22–3, p 82 (fc 'a multicultural nation' and following quotes); Nightingale, 'Maori at Work', pp 235–8.

Chapter 8

1. For the first time, the Chief Judge and the Minister and Secretary of Maori Affairs were all Maor Butterworth and Young, *Maori Affairs*, p 115; McHugh, Paul, 'Law, History and the Treaty c Waitangi', *New Zealand Journal of History*, 31(1), April 1997, p 47 (and see McHugh more recentl on principles in '"Treaty Principles": Constitutional Relations Inside a Conservative Jurisprudence *Victoria University Law Review*, 39(1), 2008, which, inter alia, discusses them in the context of th emergence of indigeneity and its relationship with 'conservatism'); Waitangi Tribunal, *Report of th*

Waitangi Tribunal on the Manukau Claim, Wai 8, Wellington, 1985, s 8.3; Walker, 'The Treaty of Waitangi', p62, p64 (for 'something less than' quote), p65 (for 'good order' and 'restore the mana' quotes); Orange, *An Illustrated History*, p153 (for 'tested the boundaries' quote); Kelsey, Jane, *A Question Of Honour? Labour and the Treaty, 1984–1989*, Wellington, 1990, p65 (for 'played a crucial role' quote). In Kelsey's view, the Tribunal was required to play a key role in mediating between Crown and Maori because, by the mid-1980s, the two were heading in opposing directions, with the key Maori demand for collectivised rangatiratanga within New Zealand sitting uncomfortably with the state's major focus on the individualistic requirements of the western globalising political-economy.

Orange, *The Treaty of Waitangi*, p250; Walker, *Ka Whawhai Tonu Matou*, pp 248–9; Oliver, *Claims*, pp 19–22; Keenan, Danny, 'Bound to the Land: Māori Retention and Assertion of Land and Identity', in Pawson, Eric and Brooking, Tom (eds), *Environmental Histories of New Zealand*, Melbourne, 2002, pp 258–9; Orange, *An Illustrated History*, pp 151–3; Walker, 'The Treaty of Waitangi', p62.

Hazlehurst, *Political Expression*, p57 (for 'major break-through' quote); New Zealand Maori Council, *Kaupapa: Te Wahanga Tuatahi*, Wellington, 1983, p10 (for 'sense of identity' quote); Richards, *Dancing*, p172; Butterworth, *'Men of Authority'*, p48ff.

Butterworth and Young, *Maori Affairs*, p111; Department of Maori Affairs, *The Maori Today*, 1964, 'Welfare' section (for 'exercise control' and 'trained officers' quotes); Fleras, 'Towards', p25 (for 'paternalistic' quote); Hazlehurst, *Political Expression*, p20 (for 'greater community participation' quote).

Fleras, 'Towards', p26 (for 'people oriented' and 'cultural and economic advancement' quotes), p27 (for 'untapped energy' quote); Walker, *Ka Whawhai Tonu Matou*, p237; Butterworth and Young, *Maori Affairs*, p113 (for 'new philosophy' quote); Fleras , 'A Descriptive Analysis', p216 (for 'encouraging self-reliance' quote); Patete, Anthony, *Devolution in the 1980s and the Quest for Rangatiratanga: a Maori Perspective*, Wellington, Treaty of Waitangi Research Unit, 2008, pp 4–5; Butterworth, *'Men of Authority'*, pp 52–3 (p 53 for 'common good' quote).

Dawson, Richard, *The Treaty of Waitangi and the Control of Language*, Wellington, 2001, p148; Butterworth, 'Aotearoa 1769–1988', ch10, pp 23, 27; Fleras, 'Towards', p27 (for 'reorganising' quote), p30 (for 'growing trends' quote); Metge, *New Growth*, pp 24–5; Butterworth and Young, *Maori Affairs*, pp 112 (for 'Wairua Maori' quote); Fleras, 'A Descriptive Analysis', p216 (for 'action group' quote), p219; Durie, *Whaiora*, p55; Walker, *Ka Whawhai Tonu Matou*, p237.

Williams, Charlotte, *More Power to Do the Work: Maori and the Health System in the Twentieth Century*, Wellington, Treaty of Waitangi Research Unit, 2007, pp 26–7 (p 26 for 'devolution of power' quote); Fleras, 'Towards', pp 27–9, p30 (for 'My government' quote), pp 31–32, p34 (for 're-establishment of Maoritanga' quote), p35 (for 'concur with the objectives' quote), p36 (for 'potential of Tu Tangata' quote); Reedy, T M, 'Foreword', in Butterworth, G V and Young, H R, *Maori Affairs/Nga Take Maori*, Wellington, 1990, p3 (for 'insistence to Maori communities' quote); Fleras, 'A Descriptive Analysis', pp 216–7; Patete, *Devolution*, p5 (for 'aroha of the community' quote).

Ormsby, 'Maori Tikanga', p18; Metge, *New Growth*, p269; Fleras, 'A Descriptive Analysis', p305.

Patete, *Devolution*, p4; Byron, *Nga Perehitini*, p12 (for 'community component' quote); Walker, *Ka Whawhai Tonu Matou*, p237; Butterworth and Young, *Maori Affairs*, pp 113–4 (p 114 for 'education, employment' quote), pp 118–9; Butterworth, 'Aotearoa 1769–1988', ch10, pp 28–9; Hunn, *Affairs of State*, p154.

0. Karetu, Timoti, 'Māori Language Rights in New Zealand', in Skutnabb-Kangas, Tove and Phillipson, Robert (eds), *Linguistic Human Rights: Overcoming Linguistic Discrimination*, Berlin/New York, 1994, pp 217–8; Rei, Tania and Hamon, Carra, 'Te Kāhanga Reo 1982–', in Else, Anne (ed), *Women Together: A History of Women's Organisations in New Zealand: Ngā Rōpū Wāhine o te Motu*, Wellington, 1993, pp 40–42; Byron, *Nga Perehitini*, p12; Boyd, Sarah, 'The Kohanga Generation', *Dominion Post*, 9 April 2005; McCarthy, Maarie, '"He Hinaki Tukutuku: The Baited Trap": Whare Wananga: Tensions and Contradictions in Relation to the State', in Benseman, John, Findsen, Brian and Scott, Miriama, *The Fourth Sector: Adult and Community Education in Aotearoa/New Zealand*, Palmerston North, 1996, p83 (for 'underlying philosophical base' and 'a form of whanau' quotes); Metge, *New Growth*, pp 24–5; Fleras, 'Towards', p29 (for 'the most successful' quote); Walker, *Ka Whawhai Tonu Matou*, pp 238–9 (p 239 for 'as much a political' quote); Walker, 'Maori People Since 1950', p515; Butterworth and Young, *Maori Affairs*, p114; May, Helen, *Politics in the Playground: The World of Early*

Childhood in Post War New Zealand, Wellington, 2001, pp 180–85; Fleras, Augie and Elliott, Jea Leonard, *The 'Nations Within': Aboriginal-State Relations in Canada, the United States, and New Zealan* Toronto, 1992, pp 211–7; Butterworth, 'Breaking the Grip', p4; Patete, *Devolution*, p5.

11. McCarthy, 'He Hinaki', pp 81–2 (for 'a number of educational initiatives' quote); Northcroft, Clair 'The Process of Establishing a Bicultural Organisation in Aotearoa New Zealand', essay for Maste of New Zealand Studies, Victoria University of Wellington, 2003, p5; Walker, 'Maori People Sinc 1950', p515; Walker, *Ka Whawhai Tonu Matou*, pp 239–40; Simon and Smith (eds), *A Civilising Missio* p 308 (for 'Kura Kaupapa Māori' quote).
12. Durie, *Whaiora*, p1 (for 'Maori health development' and 'Central to the notion' quotes), p53 (for 'spiritualit as a basis' quote), pp 56–7; Williams, *More Power*, pp 28–31; Dyall, Lorna, 'Oranga Maori: Maori Health *New Zealand Health Review*, 8(2), 1988, p14 (for 'to assist Maori' and 'holistic view of health' quotes), p1 (for 'help[ing] improve' quote); Reedy, 'Foreword', p3; Fleras, Augie, '"Tuku Rangatiratanga": Devolutio in Iwi–Government Relations', in Spoonley, Paul, Pearson, David and Macpherson, Cluny (eds), *Nga Tak Ethnic Relations and Racism in Aotearoa/New Zealand*, Palmerston North, 1991, p171; Department of Mao Affairs, *The Maori Today*, 1964, 'Welfare' section (for 'good citizenship and civic responsibility' quote); William *The Too-Hard Basket*, p12 (for 'a burst of energy' quote).
13. van Meijl, Toon, 'Community development among the New Zealand Maori: The Tainui case', i Blunt, Peter and Warren, Michael D (eds), *Indigenous Organizations and Development*, London, 199 pp 201–2; van Meijl, 'Maori Hierarchy', pp 292–3 (p 292 for 'government structures' and 'revitaliz quotes); Love, Morrie, 'Our Country, Our Choice', typescript, nd, Treaty of Waitangi Research Un collection; McLeay (ed), *New Zealand Politics*, p249; Orange, *An Illustrated History*, p155; Butterwort and Young, *Maori Affairs*, p117; Ward, *An Unsettled History*, p29 (for 'return of large' quote); Ritchi *Tribal Development*, p30; Durie, *Te Mana*, pp 6–8.
14. Williams, *The Too-Hard Basket*, pp 14–5 (p 14 for 'determine their own future' and 'better target support' quotes); Butterworth and Young, *Maori Affairs*, pp 117–8 (p 118 for 'strengthening the Mao tribal system' quote); Patete, *Devolution*, pp 7–8; Durie, *Whaiora*, p53 (for 'integrated cultural' an 'greater Māori' quotes); Keenan, Danny, 'The Treaty is Always Speaking? Government Reportin on Maori Aspirations and Treaty Meanings', in Dalley, Bronwyn and Tennant, Margaret (eds), *Pa Judgement: Social Policy in New Zealand History*, Dunedin, 2004, p210 (for 'a clear call' and 'Giv us the power' quotes); Horomia, Parekura, 'Speech notes prepared for the Hui Taumata 2005', March 2005, http://www.beehive.govt.nz/node/22330 [accessed June 2008] (for 'Maori had to b empowered' quote); Melbourne, Hineani, *Maori Sovereignty: The Maori Perspective*, Auckland, 199 p81 (for 'supreme control over their lives' quote); Venter, Nick, 'A Maori agenda', *Dominion Pos* 26 Feb 2005 (for 'being told what to do' quote); Herzog, 'Toward', p131; van Meijl, 'Communit development', p203.
15. Patete, *Devolution*, p9 (for 'iwi could autonomously' quote); Ritchie, *Tribal Development*, p1 Butterworth, 'Breaking the Grip', pp 2–3, 37; Butterworth and Young, *Maori Affairs*, pp 118–2 (including 'return to the mauri' and 'underpin' quotes); Reedy, 'Foreword', p3.
16. Booth, Pat, 'Maori Devolution: The Path to Unity or Another Tacky Affair?', *North & South*, Jun 1989, p68; Butterworth, 'Breaking the Grip', pp 4, 38–9; Patete, *Devolution*, pp 9–10; Durie, *Te Man* pp 7–8; Williams, *The Too-Hard Basket*, p52 (for 'flagship' quote); Butterworth and Young, *Mao Affairs*, p114 (for 'deinstitutionalize' and 'using the strengths' quotes); Fleras, 'Tuku Rangatiratanga p176 (for 'viable channels' quote); van Meijl, 'Community development', p203; Maaka, Roger an Fleras, Augie, *The Politics of Indigeneity: Challenging the State in Canada and Aotearoa New Zealan* Dunedin, 2005, ch4.
17. Williams, *The Too-Hard Basket*, pp 42, 52–4; Hazlehurst, *Political Expression*, pp 175–6; McCarthy, 'H Hinaki', p83 (for 'core operational components' quote), p85; Butterworth and Young, *Maori Affair* p117; van Meijl, 'Maori Hierarchy', pp 292–5; van Meijl, 'Community Development', p204.
18. Durie, *Te Mana*, pp 8, 11, 56, 224 (p 11 for 'Positive Māori development' quote); Butterworth an Young, *Maori Affairs*, p120; Patete, *Devolution*, pp 11–2; Kelsey, Jane, *The New Zealand Experiment: World Model for Structural Adjustment?* Auckland, 1997 (orig ed 1995), pp 115–49; Kelsey, *A Questio Of Honour?* A full account of the Rogernomics phenomenon has yet to be written; for a post-wa economic contextualisation, see Easton, Brian, *In Stormy Seas: The Post-War New Zealand Econom* Dunedin, 1997, ch5.

19. Harrison, *Graham Latimer*, pp 120, 126; Walker, *Ka Whawhai Tonu Matou*, pp 253–4; Butterworth and Young, *Maori Affairs*, pp 117, 120; Williams, *The Too-Hard Basket*, p 14 (for 'on an equal footing' quote); Orange, *An Illustrated History*, pp 161–2; Reedy, 'Foreword', p 3 (for 'mission' quote); Fleras, 'Tuku Rangatiratanga', p 179.
20. Durie, *Whaiora*, p 60, p 85 (for 'special significance' and following quotes); Williams, *More Power*, pp 32–7; Henare, Denese, 'The Ka Awatea Report: Reflections on its Process and Vision', in Wilson, Margaret A and Yeatman, Anna (eds), *Justice and Identity: Antipodean Practices*, Wellington, 1995, p 55 (for 'do everything' quote).
21. Williams, *The Too-Hard Basket*, p 47 (for 'perhaps the most direct proposition' quote), pp 21, 47–9; Keenan, 'The Treaty', pp 213–4 (p 213 for 'greater government recognition' and 'an ideal site' quotes); McClure, *A Civilised Community*, pp 224–5; Metge, *New Growth*, p 25; Ministerial Advisory Committee on a Maori Perspective for the Department of Social Welfare, *Puao-Te-Ata-Tu*, Wellington, 1986, p 9 (for 'attack all forms of cultural racism', 'the values' and '[s]haring power and authority' quotes); Orange, *An Illustrated History*, p 161; Nightingale, 'Maori at Work', pp 240ff.
22. Jackson, Moana, *The Maori and the Criminal Justice System: A New Perspective: He Whaipaanga Hou, Part 2*, Wellington, 1988; Harvey, Layne, 'Judge's Corner: Proposals to Reform the Māori Land Court', *Te Pouwhenua*, 16, April 2003, available online: http://justice.org.nz/maorilandcourt/pdf/Te%20 Pouwhenua16.pdf [accessed June 2008], p 8; Williams, *The Too-Hard Basket*, pp 81, 92, 95, 127–8; Metge, *New Growth*, ch 7 (p 125 for 'learn about their ancestors' quote); Durie, *Te Mana*, pp 144–5; Waitangi Tribunal, *Finding of the Waitangi Tribunal Relating to Te Reo Maori and a Claim Lodged by Huirangi Waikerepuru and Nga Kaiwhakapumau it Te Reo Incorporated Society*, Wai 11, Wellington, 1986; New Zealand History online, 'History of the Maori language – Te Wiki o Te Reo Maori', Ministry for Culture and Heritage, http://www.nzhistory.net.nz/culture/maori-language-week/history-of-the-maori-language, updated 10 July 2007.
23. Ward, *An Unsettled History*, p 161; Patete, *Devolution*, p 19; Durie, *Te Mana*, p 224; Metge, 'Kia Tupato!', p 1; van Meijl, Toon, 'Maori Tribal Organisations in New Zealand History: From Neglect to Recognition, and the Implications for the Assimilation Policy', *Ethnologies comparées*, no 6, Printemps, 2003, pp 14–16; van Meijl, 'Refining Ideology in Time: Maori Crossroads between a Timeless Past and a New Future', *Anthropos*, 90, 1995, p 11.
24. Quaintance, Lauren, 'Georgina te Heuheu', *North & South*, Nov 1998, p 84; Durie, *Te Mana*, p 55 (for 'Māori began to question' quote); Orange, 'Exercise in Maori Autonomy', p 172 (for 'inappropriate structure', 'base of the Maori world' and 'only leaps' quotes); Hazlehurst, 'Maori Self-Government', p 95; Fleras, 'Tuku Rangatiratanga', p 179; Ritchie, *Tribal Development*, pp 28–9; Patete, *Devolution*, pp 11–2; Patterson, Brad and Patterson, Kathryn (eds), *New Zealand*, Oxford, 1998, p lv.
25. Melbourne, *Maori Sovereignty*, p 81; Belich, *Paradise Reforged*, p 406ff, (p 407 for 'New Right revolution' quote); McLoughlin, David, 'Muriwhenua Muddle', *North & South*, June 1997, p 99 (citing Ann Herbert on divide and rule); Williams, *The Too-Hard Basket*, p 49; Patete, *Devolution*, p 12 (for 'ultimately retaining' quote); Kelsey, *A Question Of Honour?* p i (for 'assertion of economic' quote), p 20 (for 'in the embryonic stage' and 'Both sought' quotes); Kelsey, Jane, 'Māori, Te Tiriti, and Globalisation: The Invisible Hand of the Colonial State', in Belgrave, Michael, Kawharu, Merata and Williams, David (eds), *Waitangi Revisited: Perspectives on the Treaty of Waitangi*, Auckland, 2005, pp 82 and 98 (for 'commercial self-governance' and 'colonial state' quotes); Turia, Tariana, 'Whanau development and literacy' speech, Kaitaia, 8 Sept 2003, http://www.beehive.govt.nz/speech/ whanau+development+and+literacy [accessed June 2008] (for 'collective strengths' quote); van Meijl, 'Refining Ideology', p 12.
26. Rata, Elizabeth, 'Ethnicity, Class and the Capitulation of the Left', *Red & Green*, 4, 2004, p 19 (for 'neotribal comprador bourgeoisie' quote), p 21 (for 'fundamentally different' quote), p 23 (for 'the accumulatory competitive environment' quote); Rata, Elizabeth, *A Political Economy of Neotribal Capitalism*, Lanham, MD, 1999, p 4 (for 'revivalism becomes subverted' quote), p 226 (for 'workers-in-community' quote), p 231 (for '[p]roperty-owning' quote), p 232 (for 'capital-labour political relations' and 'depoliticised mode' quotes); van Meijl, 'Maori Tribal', pp 14, 24; Maaka and Fleras, *Politics of Indigeneity*, p 73.
27. Fleras, 'Descriptive Analysis', p 313 (for 'historic aim' quote); Turia, 'Whanau development' (for 'iwi organisations first started' and following quotes); Kelsey, *A Question Of Honour?* p 1 (for 'complete

authority' quote); Maaka and Fleras, *Politics of Indigeneity*, p73; Ballara, Angela, *Iwi. The Dynamics* *Maori Tribal Organisation from c.1769 to c.1945*, Wellington, 1998.

Chapter 9

1. The overarching requirement for the state to apologise for historical injustice as a precondition fc settlement was made very clear at the first scoping negotiations between the Crown and Waikato Tainui in 1989, which the author attended. In an international context, processes of reconciliatio and healing would later often be called procedures of 'transitional justice'. For international historica justice issues, including the concept of apology, see Berg, Manfred and Schaefer, Bernd (eds), *Historica Justice in International Perspective: How Societies Are Trying to Right the Wrongs of the Past*, Washington DC, 2009, which includes a New Zealand perspective: Hill, Richard S and Bönisch-Brednich Brigitte, 'Fitting Aotearoa into New Zealand: Politico-Cultural Change in a Modern Bicultura Nation'.
2. Orange, *An Illustrated History*, p203; Williams, David V, 'Submission to the Treaty of Waitang Commission', St Mathews-in-the-City, Church of the Diocese of Auckland, 9 Sept 1985, 99-266 10/1, Folder 4, Treaty of Waitangi, Alexander Turnbull Library (p 2 for 'principles of partnership quote); 'First New Zealand Conference on Social Work Education', nd, 99-266-10/1, Folder 4 Treaty of Waitangi, Alexander Turnbull Library; Public Service Association, 'PSA debates th Treaty', *PSA Journal*, 15 Feb 1990–14 May 1990, contained in 95-222-1/12, Papers relating to variou activist groups, David Wickham Papers, Alexander Turnbull Library; Veracini, Lorenzo, *Negotiatin A Bicultural Past: An Historiographical 'Revolution' in 1980s Aotearoa/New Zealand*, Wellington, Treat of Waitangi Research Unit, 2001; Belich, James, *The New Zealand Wars and the Victorian Interpretatio of Racial Conflict*, Auckland, 1986.
3. Walker, *Ka Whawhai Tonu Matou*, p282; Oliver, *Claims*, pp 77–9 (includes quotes).
4. Butterworth, 'Aotearoa 1769–1988', ch10, p33; Patete, p13; Ward, *An Unsettled History*, pp 34–5 Orange, *An Illustrated History*, pp 162–3; Orange, *The Treaty of Waitangi*, pp 253–4; McHugh, *Th Maori Magna Carta*, pp 248–9; Harrison, *Graham Latimer*, pp 121–2; Walker, *Ka Whawhai Tonu Matou* pp 243–4.
5. *New Zealand Maori Council v Attorney-General*, [1987] 1 NZLR, 641; Orange, *An Illustrated History* pp 164–6 (p 165 for 'akin to a partnership' quote); McHugh, Paul, 'Law, History and the Treat of Waitangi', pp 50–51; Harrison, *Graham Latimer*, p122 (for 'perhaps as important'); Walker *Ka Whawhai Tonu Matou*, pp 263–5; Ritchie, *Tribal Development*, p33; McHugh, *The Maori Magn Carta*, p249; Alves, *The Maori and the Crown*, pp 62–4; Graham, Douglas, *Trick or Treaty?* Wellington 1997, pp 20–21.
6. Orange, *An Illustrated History*, p165 (for 'act towards each other' quote), p166 (for 'new life' quote) McHugh, 'Law, History and the Treaty of Waitangi', p51; Harrison, *Graham Latimer*, p122; King *Nga Iwi*, p98; Graham, *Trick or Treaty?* p19; Boast, Richard, 'Maori Land and the Treaty of Waitangi' in Boast, Richard, Erueti, Andrew, McPhail, Doug and Smith, Norman, *Maori Land Law*, Wellington 1999, pp 272–3, 276–9 (p 278 for 'it cannot yet be said' and 'should not be approached' quotes) Callaghan, Catherine, '"Constitutionalisation" of Treaties by the Courts: The Treaty of Waitang and the Treaty of Rome Compared', *New Zealand Universities Law Review*, June 1999, pp 343–6 349 (p 344 for 'living instrument', 'account of subsequent developments' and 'new and changing circumstances' quotes); McHugh, *The Maori Magna Carta*, p249.
7. Callahan, 'Constitutionalisation', p346 (for 'mythologising', 'symbol' and 'indigenous constitutiona identity' quotes); McHugh, Paul, 'Constitutional Myths and the Treaty of Waitangi', *New Zealan Law Journal*, September 1991, pp 316–7; Tauroa, Hiwi, *Healing the Breach: One Maori's Perspective o the Treaty of Waitangi*, Auckland, 1989, pp 58–9; Walker, *Ka Whawhai Tonu Matou*, p265 (for 'pitche New Zealand' quote).
8. McHugh, 'Law, History and the Treaty of Waitangi', p49 (for 'common law time' quote); Orange *An Illustrated History*, p166 (for 'accepting that sovereignty' quote); Kelsey, *A Question Of Honour?* p 7 (for 'an agency of the Crown' quote), p237 (for 'the essential legitimacy' quote), p266 (for 'becom

as much a vehicle' quote); Kelsey, *Rolling Back the State: Privatisation of Power in Aotearoa/New Zealand*, Wellington, 1993, p234; Dawson, *The Treaty of Waitangi*, pp 163–5.

9. McHugh, 'Law, History and the Treaty of Waitangi', p51 (for 'negotiated co-existence' quote); Orange, *An Illustrated History*, pp 166–7, 185–7; McHugh, *The Maori Magna Carta*, p250; Palmer, Geoffrey, 'Treaty of Waitangi Issues Demand Clarity, Certainty', *New Zealand Herald*, 2 Jan 1990; Callahan, 'Constitutionalisation', pp 246–7.

10. Waitangi Tribunal, *Report of the Waitangi Tribunal on the Muriwhenua Fishing Claim*, Wai 22, Wellington, 1988; Dawson, *The Treaty of Waitangi*, pp 125–31, p132 (for 'tribal authority' quote), p133 (for 'special privileges' quote); Renwick, 'Decolonising', p39 (for 'astonished' quote); Te Puni Kokiri, *Nga Kai o te Moana: Kaupapa Tiakina*, Wellington, 1993, pp 22–5; Waitangi Tribunal, *The Taranaki Report*, section 1.4; Walker, *Ka Whawhai Tonu Matou*, p263; Orange, *An Illustrated History*, pp 169–75 (p 173 for 'an end to fishing' quote); Oliver, *Claims*, p79 (for 'qualified a little' quote), p80 (for 'form of legal sovereignty' quote), p81 (for 'the power of Parliament' quote); Walker, 'The Treaty of Waitangi', pp 67–8.

11. Kelsey, *A Question Of Honour?* p 77 (for 'demand for recognition' and 'juggernaut' quotes), p242; Williams, *The Too-Hard Basket*, pp 17–8 (p 17 for 'social justice' and 'illusion of partnership' quotes); Turner, Kaye, 'The *April Report* of the Royal Commission on Social Policy: Treaty Partnership as a Framework for a Politics of Difference?', in Wilson, Margaret A and Yeatman, Anna (eds), *Justice and Identity: Antipodean Practices*, Wellington, 1995, p93; Royal Commission on Social Policy, *The April Report, Volume II, Future Directions*, Wellington, 1988, pp 65–9; Royal Commission on Social Policy, *The April Report, Volume III, Part One, Future Directions*, Wellington, 1988, pp 111–127. The author joined TOWPU as its founding historian in May 1989.

12. McCarthy, Claire, 'New models of sustainability', *New Zealand Education Review*, 14 July 2000, p11; Walker, *Ka Whawhai Tonu Matou*, p289; James, Colin, 'Why we can't afford to lose the voice of Tamihere', *New Zealand Herald*, 19 Oct 2004.

13. Kelsey, Jane, *Reclaiming the Future: New Zealand and the Global Economy*, Wellington, 1999, pp 52–3 (p52 for 'new configurations' quote).

14. Prichard and Waetford, *Report of the Committee of Inquiry*, p33 (for 'a long tradition of paternal' quote), p34 (for 'It is probable' quote); Reedy, 'Foreword', p1 (for 'wairua, mana' quote), p3 (for 'little recognition' and other quotes); Hunn, *Affairs of State*, p153; Walsh, *More and More Maoris*, p36 (for 'the long-term objective' quote); Butterworth and Young, *Maori Affairs*, p12 (for 'to achieve a true partnership' quote), pp 119–20; Department of Maori Affairs, 'Annual Report of the Department of Maori Affairs and the Board of Maori Affairs and the Maori Trust Office', AJHR, E-13, 1986, pp 3–4; Walker, *Ka Whawhai Tonu Matou*, pp 284–5; Booth, 'Maori Devolution'.

15. Rata, 'Ethnicity, Class', p19; Booth, 'Maori Devolution', p71 (for 'a dangerous version' quote); Keenan, 'The Treaty'.

16. Department of Maori Affairs, *He Tirohanga Rangapu/Partnership Perspectives*, Wellington, 1988; Ritchie, *Tribal Development*, pp 30–31; Keenan, 'The Treaty', pp 214–6 (p 214 for 'set out the basis' and 'watershed' quotes); Williams, *The Too-Hard Basket*, pp 20, 22, 73; Jackson, S, 'Te Karanga o te Iwi: Devolution – The Death of a People', *Metro*, January 1988; Walker, *Ka Whawhai Tonu Matou*, pp 285–6; Orange, *An Illustrated History*, p188; Butterworth and Young, *Maori Affairs*, p120; Henare, 'The *Ka Awatea* Report', pp 55–6; Kelsey, *A Question Of Honour?* pp 248–9 (p 248 for 'relinquish ultimate control' quotes); Patete, *Devolution*, pp 13–5, 34 (p 15 for 'dishonest, deceitful' quote); Fleras, 'Tuku Rangatiratanga', pp 186–7.

17. Mulgan, *Maori, Pakeha*, pp 133–5; Department of Maori Affairs, *Te Urupare Rangapu/Partnership Response*, Wellington, 1988; Keenan, 'The Treaty', pp 216, 220; Williams, *The Too-Hard Basket*, p17; Walker, *Ka Whawhai Tonu Matou*, pp 286–8; Butterworth and Young, *Maori Affairs*, p121 (for 'develop their own structures' quote); Fleras, 'Tuku Rangatiratanga, pp 176–9, 182 (p 177, citing Manatu Maori mission statement); Patete, *Devolution*, pp 16–8 (p 17 for 'reduced to an "autonomy"' quote); Te TAI, 'Working in Partnership', brochure, nd (for 'operational base' quote).

18. New Zealand Government, *Principles for Crown Action on the Treaty of Waitangi*, Wellington, 1989; Orange, *An Illustrated History*, pp 195–6 (p 196 for 'balance between' and 'case by case' quotes); Patete, *Devolution*, p18; Williams, *The Too-Hard Basket*, pp 15–6; Waitangi Tribunal, *Muriwhenua Fishing*, p187; McHugh, *The Maori Magna Carta*, pp 50–51 (p 50 for 'tribal self-management' and 'inherently

legitimate' quotes); International Labour Organization, *Convention concerning Indigenous and Tribal Peoples in Independent Countries*, C169, Geneva, 1989 (for 'over their own institutions' quote); Tauroa, *Healing the Breach*, p 122 (for 'right to self-determination' quote); Keenan, 'The Treaty', p 219; Kelsey, *A Question Of Honour?* pp 257–61 (p 259 for 'a deliberate and cynical' quote); Maaka and Fleras, *Politics of Indigeneity*, p 141; Walker, 'The Treaty of Waitangi', p 69 (for 'supremacy of the Crown' quote). The author worked for TOWPU from 1989 to 1998.

19. Mallard, Trevor, 'We Are All New Zealanders Now', speech to Stout Research Centre for New Zealand Studies, 28 July 2004, http://www.beehive.govt.nz/node/20451 [accessed June 2008]; Palmer, 'Treaty of Waitangi Issues' (for 'final decisions' quote); Mikaere, Ani, 'Are We All New Zealanders Now? A Māori Response to the Pākehā Quest for Indigeneity', *Red & Green*, 4, 2004, p 33; Keenan, 'The Treaty', pp 219, 221–3; Durie, *Whaiora*, p 89; Kelsey, Jane, 'Māori, Te Tiriti and Globalisation', p 82; Frame, Alex, 'A State Servant Looks at the Treaty', *New Zealand Universities Law Review*, 14(1), 1990.

20. New Zealand 1990 Commission, *The Treaty of Waitangi: The symbol of our life together as a nation*, Wellington, 1989 (front cover for 'symbol of our life' quote, last page for 'living document' and 'pact of partnership' quotes); Orange, *An Illustrated History*, p 199 (for 'to capture the spirit' quotes), p 201 (citing Vercoe); King, *Nga Iwi*, p 99 (for 'major and irreversible' quote); Temm, Paul, *The Waitangi Tribunal: The Conscience of the Nation*, Auckland, 1990, p 127 (for 'into the forefront' quote); Jackson, Moana, 'A Very Quick Guide to the Treaty of Waitangi', in Anarchist Alliance of Aotearoa, *Tino Rangatiratanga: The Treaty Today*, Wellington, nd, p 21 (for 'side by side' quote).

21. Keenan, 'The Treaty', p 217 (for 'acknowledged the enduring' quote); Iwi Transition Agency, 'Report of the Iwi Transition Agency Working Group on the Runanga Iwi Bill, Local Government Amendment (No 8) Bill and the Resource Management Bill (30 January 1990)', Wellington, 1990; Patete, *Devolution*, pp 20–22 (p 21 for 'not perceived' and 'impinged on the rights' quotes); Cox, *Kotahitanga*, pp 141–2, 169–70; Mulgan, *Maori, Pakeha*, p 105; McHugh, *The Maori Magna Carta*, pp 50–51, 203.

22. Sorrenson, M P K, 'Giving Better Effect to the Treaty: Some Thoughts for 1990', *New Zealand Journal of History*, 24(2), 1990, p 142; Orange, *An Illustrated History*, p 200 (for 'imperfectly observed' quote); Renwick, William, *The Treaty Now*, Wellington, 1990, p 142 (for 'ways that respect' quote); Pearson, *A Dream Deferred*, p 241.

23. Fleras, 'Tuku Rangatiratanga', p 177; McHugh, *The Maori Magna Carta*, pp 53, 202–3; Patete, *Devolution*, pp 20, 22–3 Salmond, *Jurisprudence*, 7th ed, London, 1924, p 84 (for 'legal fiction' quote); Frame, Alex, 'Sir John Salmond 1862–1924', in O'Sullivan, Vincent (ed), *Eminent Victorians: Great Teachers and Scholars from Victoria's first 100 years*, Wellington, 2000; Walker, *Ka Whawhai Tonu Matou*, p 289 (for 'iwi up and down the country' quote).

24. McHugh, *The Maori Magna Carta*, p 52 (for 'fixation' quote); Durie, Edward T, 'A Peaceful Solution', in Young, Ramari (ed), *Mana Tiriti: The Art of Protest and Partnership*, Wellington, 1991, p 69; Orange, *An Illustrated History*, p 188; Frame, 'Fictions'; Melbourne, *Maori Sovereignty*, p 82 (for 'control themselves' quote); Patete, *Devolution*, p 22; Kelsey, *A Question Of Honour?* p 247 (for 'a convenient vehicle' quote).

25. Fleras, 'Tuku Rangatiratanga', p 184 (for 'real partnership' quotes), p 186 (for 'any fundamental change' quote); Salmond, *Jurisprudence*, p 84 (for 'a concession by' quote); Yensen, Helen, 'Some afterthoughts', in Yensen, Helen, Hague, Kevin and McCreanor, Tim, *Honouring the Treaty: An Introduction for Pakeha to the Treaty of Waitangi*, Auckland, 1989, p 147.

26. 'He Maimai Aroha: Glass Murray', *Mana*, issue 28, June–July 1999, p 9 (for 'argued with trust boards' and 'take their money' quotes); 'He Maimai Aroha: Erana Prime', *Mana*, issue 35, Aug–Sept 2000, p 9; Mahuta, 'Tainui', p 28 (for 'agent[s] of the Crown' quote); McHugh, *The Maori Magna Carta*, p 202; Sharp, *Justice and the Māori*, pp 282–3; Fleras, 'Tuku Rangatiratanga', p 189 (for 'institutional assimilation' quote).

27. Mead, Sidney Moko, 'The Significance of Being Ngati Awa', in *Landmarks, Bridges and Visions: Aspects of Maori Culture*, Wellington, 1997 (orig paper: 1990), pp 258–9 (p 258 for 'tikanga Maori' quote, p 259 for 'pretty sullen', 'shaking off the shackles' and 'new mood' quotes); Cox, *Kotahitanga*, pp 141–6, 151, 157–8, 161–3, 167, p 183 (for 'autonomous Māori development' quote); Walker, *Ka Whawhai Tonu*

Matou, p287 (for 'the obvious response' quote); Orange, *An Illustrated History*, p189; Melbourne, *Maori Sovereignty*, p31; Durie, *Te Mana*, p17; Williams, *The Too-Hard Basket*, pp 21–2.

Chapter 10

1. Vasil, *Biculturalism*, pp 1–2; Tauroa, *Healing the Breach*, p102 (for 'a majority Pakeha' quote); Orange, *An Illustrated History*, p204 (for 'one nation' quote), pp 208–9; Henare, 'The *Ka Awatea* Report, p49 (for 'need and not race' and 'participate equally' quotes); Runanga Iwi Act Repeal Act 1991; Keenan, 'The Treaty', p217; Durie, *Te Mana*, p225; Patete, *Devolution*, pp 24–5.
2. Keenan, 'The Treaty', p217; Williams, *The Too-Hard Basket*, p22 (for 'was designed to steer' quote); Ministry of Maori Affairs, *Ka Awatea: A Report of the Ministerial Planning Group*, Wellington, March 1991, p71 (for 'right to self development' and 'right of' quotes), p72 (for 'significant role' and 'retain resources' quote), p82 (for 'that Maori retain and control'); McHugh , *The Maori Magna Carta*, p53; Patete, *Devolution*, pp 25–6; Henare, 'The *Ka Awatea* Report', pp 47–59 (pp 49–50 and 57 re 'middle way', p50 for 'handing over of resources' quote and citing *Ka Awatea* 'that Maori retain', pp 58–9 for 'to assist the Maori goal' quote).
3. Patete, *Devolution*, pp 25–7; Ministry of Maori Affairs, *Ka Awatea*, p88 (for 'Treaty based policy' quote); Henare, 'The *Ka Awatea* Report', pp 50, 56–8 (p 50 for 'not facilitate' quote, pp 56–7 for 'best results' quote); Orange, *An Illustrated History*, p208; Durie, *Te Mana*, p55.
4. Henare, 'The *Ka Awatea* Report', p50; Orange, *An Illustrated History*, p208; Williams, *The Too-Hard Basket*, pp 23, 64, 73, p139 (for 'developing scope' quote); Barrett, Mark, 'Maori Health Purchasing – Some Current Issues', *Social Policy Journal of New Zealand*, 9, Nov 1997, pp 127–8; Espiner, Guyon, 'Tamihere slams Labour welfare policies', *Sunday Star Times*, 23 Feb 2003.
5. Laidlaw, Chris, *Rights of Passage*, Auckland, 1999, p137 (for 'a recognition that Maori' quote), p144 (for 'a measure of Maori' quote); Smithies, *Ten Steps*, p45 (for 'define and restrict' quote), p94 (for 'the most important thing' quote); Fleras, 'Tuku Rangatiratanga', p189.
6. Graham, *Trick or Treaty?* p 45; Graham, Douglas Sir, 'The Treaty and Treaty Negotiations', in Clark, Margaret (ed), *The Bolger Years, 1990–1997*, Wellington, 2008, p172 (for 'be nothing' quote). The 'popular' hostile writing on the Treaty remains unexplored by scholars. For samples, see Mitchell, Robin, *The Treaty and the Act: The Treaty of Waitangi, 1840 and the Treaty of Waitangi Act, 1975*, Christchurch, 1990; Scott, Stuart C, *The Travesty of Waitangi: Towards Anarchy*, Dunedin, 1995 and *Travesty After Travesty*, Christchurch, 1996; Christie, Walter, *Treaty Issues*, Christchurch, 1997, *A Race Apart: Parliament and Race Separatism, the Story*, Auckland, 1998 and *New Zealand Education and Treatyism*, Auckland, 1999; and for more sophisticated anti-Treaty critiques, see Minogue, Kenneth R, *Waitangi: Morality and Reality*, Wellington, 1998; Round, David, *Truth or Treaty? Commonsense Questions about the Treaty of Waitangi*, Christchurch, 1998; and Epstein, Richard A, *The Treaty of Waitangi: A Plain Meaning Interpretation*, Wellington, 1999. For an analysis of the anti-Treaty writers, see Hill, Richard S, *Anti-Treatyism and Anti-Scholarship: An Analysis of Anti-Treatyist Writings*, Treaty of Waitangi Research Unit, Wellington, 2002.
7. McCan, David, *Whatiwhatihoe: The Waikato Raupatu Claim*, Wellington, 2001, p264 ('scoping' negotiations); Graham, 'The Treaty and Treaty Negotiations', p166 (for 'perilous position' quote); Mahuta, 'Tainui', p29; McKinnon, Malcolm, *Treasury: The New Zealand Treasury, 1840–2000*, Auckland, 2003, p410; Walker, Ranginui J, 'The Genesis of Direct Negotiation, the Fiscal Envelope, and their Impact on Tribal land Claim Settlements', *He Pukenga Korero*, 3(1), 1997, pp 12–5; Office of Treaty Settlements, *Crown Proposals for the Settlement of Treaty of Waitangi Claims: Summary*, Wellington, nd [1994], pp 15–6; Office of Treaty Settlements, *Healing the past, building a future: a guide to Treaty of Waitangi claims and negotiations with the Crown*, Wellington, 2002; Orange, *An Illustrated History*, pp 185, 196–8; Price, Richard T, 'New Zealand's Interim Treaty Settlements and Arrangements – Building Blocks of Certainty', Presentation to the Forum on Treaty Negotiation, 'Speaking Truth to Power', 3 March 2000 (revised 26 April 2000), British Columbia Treaty Commission and Law Commission of Canada, p8; Hazlehurst, *Political Expression*, p177.

8. Price, Richard T, *Assessing Modern Treaty Settlements: New Zealand's 1992 Treaty of Waitangi (Fisheri Claims) Settlement and its Aftermath*, Christchurch, 1996, p46; Te Puni Kokiri, *Nga Kai o te Moan* pp 22–25; Walker, *Ka Whawhai Tonu Matou*, pp 295–6; Orange, *An Illustrated History*, pp 211–6 Walker, 'The Treaty of Waitangi', pp 69–72, p70 (for 'any fund' quote).
9. There are many versions of what constitutes the primary level of Maori organisation, and these ar often specific to time and place. In the 1980s, the Crown believed it to be the iwi; in the 1990s, man Maori (and some scholars) were asserting it to be the hapu; by the early twenty-first century, ther was much discussion about it being the whanau. In 2003, for example, Tariana Turia reported th the James Henare Maori Research Centre at Auckland University had found in a major study that th whanau was 'the predominant kin group among urban Maori' (see Turia, Tariana, 'Strong whana key to tangata whenua development', press release, 10 December 2003). For the principal work o these issues from an historical perspective, see Ballara, *Iwi*.
10. Young, David, *Values as Law: The History and Efficacy of the Resource Management Act*, Wellington, 2001 pp 28–9; Hayward, Janine, 'The Treaty of Waitangi, Maori and the Evolving Crown', *Political Scienc* 49(2), Jan 1998, p172; Orange, *An Illustrated History*, p192; *Whitiwhiti Korero*, Issue 13, 13 July 2008.
11. International Labour Organization, *Convention concerning Indigenous and Tribal Peoples* (for 'development in the situation' and 'new international standards' quotes); McHugh, *The Maori Magna Carta*, pp 203–4 Ministry of Foreign Affairs and Trade, *New Zealand Handbook*, pp 120, 122; Minister of Maori Affairs *Discussion Document on The International Labour Organisation Convention No 169 Concerning Indigenou and Tribal Peoples in Independent Countries 1989*, Wellington, 1999; Pearson, *The Politics of Ethnicit* pp 189–90; Magallenes, 'International Human Rights', pp 249–50. In 2007, New Zealand was one o a handful of countries to vote against a (watered down) UN Declaration on the Rights of Indigenou Peoples, because of its concerns with the national implications of its self-determinationist language Peace Movement Aotearoa, 'Support the United Nations Declaration on the Rights of Indigenou Peoples', statement, 2008. For the interface between ethnicity and nationalism, see the works o Anthony D Smith, eg *Myths and Memories of the Nation*, Oxford, 1999.
12. Anglican Church in Aotearoa, New Zealand and Polynesia, 'History', http://www.anglican.org.nz history.htm [accessed July 2008]; Diamond, Paul, 'Whatarangi Winiata', in Diamond, Paul (ed), *A Fire in Your Belly: Māori Leaders Speak*, Wellington, 2003, p61; Winiata, Whatarangi, interviewed by Paul Diamond, 'Nga Manu Taiko', National Radio, 2 March 2003; Joint Methodist Presbyteriar Public Questions Committee, *Tino Rangatiratanga*; Winiata, 'Reducing'; Te Ture Whenua Maor Act 1993/Maori Land Act 1993, section 2(2) (for 'retention' quote); Gilling, Bryan, 'The Maori Lanc Court in New Zealand: An Historical Overview', *Canadian Journal of Native Studies*, XIII(1), 1993, p26; Harris, 'Maori Land Title', p152; Durie, *Te Mana*, pp 136–8; Harvey, 'Judge's Corner: The Duties of Trustees', p3.
13. Orange, *An Illustrated History*, pp 210–211, 227, 221–3; Alves, *The Maori and the Crown*, pp 123–131 (p 129 for 'as land was taken' quote); Graham, *Trick or Treaty?* pp 71–8; Mahuta, 'Tainui', pp 30–31, Walker, *Ka Whawhai Tonu Matou*, pp 304–5; Frame, Alex, 'Compensating for Raupatu: The Situation in the late 1980s', paper presented at 'Coming to Terms? Raupatu/Confiscation and New Zealand History' conference, Victoria University of Wellington, 27–8 June 2008; Ngai Tahu, 'Economic Security', *Te Rūnanga o Ngāi Tahu* (website), http://www.ngaitahu.iwi.nz/About%20Ngai%20Tahu/The%20Settlement/The%20Crowns%20Settlement%20Offer/Economic%20Security [accessed June 2008]; Dodd, Materoa, 'Nation Building and Mäori Development: The Importance of Governance', paper for 'Contesting Development: Pathways to Better Practice', 3rd Biennial conference of the Aotearoa New Zealand International Development Studies Network, Palmerston North, 5–7 December 2002, available online: http://www.devnet.org.nz/conf2002/papers/Dodd_Materoa.pdf [accessed June 2008], p5; Walker, 'The Treaty of Waitangi', pp 73–4.
14. O'Regan, *Ko Tahu*, p153 (for 'recognition', 'accountable' and 'give us back' quotes); O'Regan, Hana, 'Legal identity of Ngāi Tahu Whānui: Ko te Ture Hou o Ngāi Tahu Whānui', *Te Karaka: The Ngāi Tahu Magazine*, 1996; Te Runanga O Ngai Tahu Act 1996; Orange, *An Illustrated History*, pp 223–6; Graham, *Trick or Treaty?* pp 79–86; Alves, *The Maori and the Crown*, pp 133–40; Dodd, *Nation Building*, p5 (for 'enterprise culture' quote); McLean, Robyn, 'Ngai Tahu shares its treasures', *Dominion Post*, 14 July 2006 (for '[b]ecause of the claim settlement' quote).

15. Sullivan, Ann, 'The Treaty of Waitangi and Social Well-being: Justice, Representation, and Participation', in Belgrave, Michael, Kawharu, Merata and Williams, David (eds), *Waitangi Revisited: Perspectives on the Treaty of Waitangi*, Auckland, 2005, pp 132–3; Ladley, 'The Treaty', pp 21–3 (re limited autonomy); McHugh, Paul, 'Aboriginal Identity and Relations in North America and Australasia', in Coates, Ken S and McHugh, P G, *Living Relationships, Kōkiri Ngatāhi: The Treaty of Waitangi in the New Millennium*, Wellington, 1998, pp 137–43; Office of Treaty Settlements, *Crown Proposals*, pp 13–4.
16. Orange, *An Illustrated History*, p216; Williams, *The Too-Hard Basket*, pp 110–11, 113–23; McHugh, 'Aboriginal Identity', pp 171–5; Durie, *Te Mana*, pp 228–31, 236–8.
17. Walker, 'The Genesis', pp 14–5; McKinnon, *Treasury*, pp 410–11 (p 411 for 'breach of tino rangatiratanga' and 'public relations disaster' quotes); Joint Methodist Presbyterian Public Questions Committee, *Politics Not Justice: The Government's Treaty Settlements Policy*, Wellington, 1999, pp 2–7 (p 6 for 'united in opposition' quote); Office of Treaty Settlements, *Crown Proposals*, pp 24–7; Orange, *An Illustrated History*, pp 217–9 (p 217 for 'consistent and fair' quote), pp 220, 222, 226, 229–32; Graham, *Trick or Treaty?* pp 58–60, 64–6; Durie, Mason, 'Tino Rangatiratanga', in Belgrave, Michael, Kawharu, Merata and Williams, David (eds), *Waitangi Revisited: Perspectives on the Treaty of Waitangi*, Auckland, 2005, pp 4–9 (p 7 for' commonalities' and p 8 for 'own resources' quotes); Harris, *Hīkoi*, pp 134–6 (p 136 for 'layering of grievance' quote); Roberts, John, *Alternative Vision, He Moemoea Ano: From Fiscal Envelope to Constitutional Change: The Significance of the Hirangi Hui*, Wellington, Joint Methodist Presbyterian Public Questions Committee, 1996, pp 3–5, 6–7 (for 'looking at all the issues' quote); Durie, *Te Mana*, pp 230–31; Walker, 'The Treaty of Waitangi', p71.
18. Joint Methodist Presbyterian Public Questions Committee, *Politics Not Justice*, p6; Roberts, *Alternative Vision*, pp 9–23, 28–30 (p 9 for 'sovereignty of Parliament' and 'no political will' quotes, p10 for 'ways' quote, p12 for 'cannot negotiate the division' quote, p17 for 'expos[ure of] the effects' quote, p23 for 'establishment of protocols' quote); Durie, *Te Mana*, p235; Gardiner, Wira, *Return to Sender: What Really Happened at the Fiscal Envelope Hui*, Auckland, 1996, pp 230–31 (p 231 for 'were listened to politely' quote); Melbourne, *Maori Sovereignty*, p31 (for 'sooner or later' quote).
19. Durie, *Whaiora*, pp 6, 59–61; Nath, Geetha, 'Healing skills not forgotten for Maori', *Daily News*, 15 May 2003 (for 'very important' quote); 'Department plans tohunga role in prisons', *Dominion*, 2 Oct 1998 (for 'working with tribes' quote); Parker, 'The Substance That Remains', pp 186–7.
20. Belgrave, Michael, Kawharu, Merata and Williams, David, 'Introduction', in Belgrave, Michael, Kawharu, Merata and Williams, David (eds), *Waitangi Revisited: Perspectives on the Treaty of Waitangi*, Auckland, 2005, p xx; Graham, *Trick or Treaty?* p 58 (for 'out of grievance mode' quote); Kay, Martin, 'Ratana's balancing act', *Dominion Post*, 24 Jan 2005; Orange, *An Illustrated History*, pp 233–5.
21. Durie, *Te Mana*, pp 56–7, 79; Orange, *An Illustrated History*, pp 216, 268; Minogue, *Waitangi*, p51 (for 'tragic mistake' quote); Levine and Henare, 'Mana Maori', p193 (for 'tribal fundamentalism' quote); Rata, 'An Overview', p4 (for 'structures for' and 'comprador bourgeoisie' quotes); Rata, 'Global Capitalism'; Poata-Smith, 'The Changing Contours', pp 182–3 (p 182 for 'Maori social and political relationships' quote); Maaka and Fleras, *The Politics of Indigeneity*, p288.
22. Te Puni Kokiri, *Discussion Paper*, p4 (for 'adequately meet', 'provide structures' and 'basis of Maori' quotes), p5 (for 'Maori voice' quote), p15 (for 'most consistent theme' quote), p16 (for 'structure has not functioned' quote), p23 (for 'better able to meet' quote), p25 (for 'accountable directly' quote), p27 (for 'subservient to the parent', 'standing' and 'monitor the relationship' quotes), pp28–31; Williams, *The Too-Hard Basket*, p59; Dawson, *The Treaty of Waitangi*, p143 (for 'tyranny of the majority' quote); O'Regan, Tipene, 'Readying the Canoe on the Beach', in Ihimaera, Witi (ed), *Vision Aotearoa: Kaupapa New Zealand*, Wellington, 1994, p47 (for 'pan-Maori trumpets' quote); Perrott, Alan, 'City-dwelling Maori get their own voice', *New Zealand Herald*, 6 May 2003.
23. McCarthy, 'He Hinaki', pp 86–7, p92 (for 'underlying agenda' quote), pp 92–3 (for 'agents of the Crown' quote), p93 (for 'relative autonomy' and 'the eels within' quote); New Zealand First and the New Zealand National Party, 'The Coalition Agreement. Policy Area: Education', 10 Dec 1996, http://executive.govt.nz/96-99/coalition/educ.htm [accessed June 2008] (for 'to monitor progress' quote); Maori Education Commission, *Report Four: To the Minister of Māori Affairs*, Wellington, 1999, p14 (for 'more Māori control', 'the time for' and 'local autonomy' quotes), p17 (for 'image that the Ministry' quote); Rivers, Janet, 'Autonomy will make kura a viable option', *New Zealand Education Review*, 18 June 1999.

24. Graham, 'The Treaty and Treaty Negotiations', in Clark, Margaret (ed), *The Bolger Years, 1990 1997*, p 166; Lange, David, 'Bruce Jesson Memorial Lecture: Inaugural Lecture', Maidment Theatre Auckland, Nov 2000, available online: http://www.brucejesson.com/JessonLecture_2000.pc [accessed June 2008], p 9 (for 'a democratic form of government' and 'the exercise of degrees' quotes Durie, Edward T, 'Maori autonomy: preventing power games', *Stimulus*, 6(2), May 1998, p 41 (fc 'determine their own policy' quote); Quirke, Michelle, 'Maori varsity to flout the rules', *Evening Pos* 23 Dec 2002.
25. Te Puni Kokiri, *Kōkiri Paetae*, issue 29, Sept 2000, p 1 (for 'boosting the ability' and 'become th managers' quotes, italics removed); Te Puni Kokiri, *Te Puni Kokiri's role in Capacity Building*, pamphle Wellington, nd (for 'charged with building' and 'bottom-up' quotes); Te Puni Kokiri, 'Capacit Building' (website) http://www.tpk.govt.nz/en/Capacity_Building/index.htm [accessed Novembe 2000] (for 'building blocks' quote); Orange, *An Illustrated History*, p 246 (for 'special treatment' quote Maaka and Fleras, *The Politics of Indigeneity*, p 135ff.
26. Young, David, *Woven by Water: Histories from the Whanganui River*, Wellington, 1998, p 261 (fo 'custodial' quote), p 264 (for 'exercise tino rangatiratanga' quote); Humphreys, Lyn, 'Board signs u to Maori health plan', *Daily News*, 20 Sept 2002 (for 'support tino rangatiratanga' and 'Maori capacity quotes).

Conclusion

1. Fleras, Augie and Spoonley, Paul, *Recalling Aotearoa: Indigenous Politics and Ethnic Relations in New Zealand*, Auckland, 1999, ch 2; Mead, 'Options', pp 148–52; Magallenes, 'International Human Rights', p 224; Legat, 'Warrior Woman', p 68; Awatere, *Maori Sovereignty*, p 15 (for 'should have control' quote). This concluding section of the book is partly based on my many conversations within Treaty policy, research and settlement environments, with both Maori leaders and advocate and public servants working on Treaty issues.
2. Melbourne, *Maori Sovereignty*, p 158 (for 'iwi in control' quote); O'Regan, Tipene, 'Old Myths and New Politics: Some Contemporary Uses of Traditional History', *New Zealand Journal of History*, 26(1) Apr 1992, pp 15–8; Te Runanga A Iwi O Ngapuhi, Constitution, nd, 6.1(e)(i) (for 'confirm the enduring' quote), 6.1(i) (for 'independence' quote), 6.1(j) (for 'recognise' quote); Webster, Steven *Patrons of Maori Culture: Power, Theory and Ideology in the Maori Renaissance*, Dunedin, 1998, p 20 O'Regan, *Ko Tahu*, pp 172–3 (for 'tribe is the entity' quote).
3. Crown, R and L, *The Rohe Potae: History and Proposals*, Te Rohe Potae Rereahu-Maniapoto Inc Te Kuiti, 1985; Crown, R, *Proposals for Rereahu-Maniapoto Autonomy*, Te Rohe Potae o Rereahu-Maniapoto Inc, Te Kuiti, 1986; Steele, R W, 'Te Marae i Roto i te Urewera', *Salient*, 29 March 197 (for 'lure people out' quote); Mead, 'Options', p 151 (for 'own tino rangatiratanga' and 'own measures quotes); Awaroa ki Manuka, 'Ngaa Tikanga O Ngati Te Ata: Tribal Policy Statement', 1991, p 2 (for 'breaking out' quote), p 3 (for 'all sovereign power' quote), p 8 (for 'sovereign people' and 'right to govern' quotes), p 9 (for 'formal and substantive' and 'their collective identities' quotes), p 60 (for 'legitimate authority' quote).
4. Sinclair, Karen, *Prophetic Histories: The People of the Māramatanga*, Wellington, 2002, pp 38, 118; Re et al, 'Ngā Rōpū', p 7; Heal, Andrew, 'The Third Way', *Metro*, Oct 1998, p 45 (for 'will not tolerate' quote); Waitangi Tribunal, *Te Whanau o Waipareira Report*, Wai 414, Wellington, 1998, pp xviii–xix, xxiv–xxv, 79; Sharp, 'Traditional Authority', p 8; Williams, *The Too-Hard Basket*, p 27.
5. Waitangi Tribunal, *Waipareira Report*, p xviii (for the key principle' quote); Mead, 'Options', p 151 (for 'presence is detected' quote); Dawson, *The Treaty of Waitangi*, p 132.
6. Royal, Te Ahukaramu Charles, 'There are Adventures to be had', *Te Pouhere Korero Journal*, 1(1), Mar 1999, p 5 (for 'management systems' quote); Te Runanga O Ngapuhi, Constitution, 6.1(n) (for 'establish diplomatic' quote), 6.1(t) (for 'dispute resolution' quote); Kelsey, *Reclaiming*, pp 20–22, 310.
7. Cox, *Kotahitanga*, p 141; Ferguson, Philip, 'Race relations and social control', *Revolution*, no 14, Xmas 2000–March 2001, p 36 (for 'the very social order'); Jarvis, Huw, 'Maori liberation versus the Treaty process', *Revolution*, May–July 2004, p 36 (for 'thoroughly intermixed', 'oppressed' and 'takes into

account' quotes); Rata, 'Ethnicity, Class', pp 14–15 (for 'economic corporation' quote), p 15 (for 'conceals' and following quotes); Wellington School of Medicine and Health Sciences, *Access to Cancer Services for Māori: A Report prepared for the Ministry of Health*, Wellington, Feb 2005, p 15; Poata-Smith, 'He Pokeke', p 112.

Rumbles, Wayne, 'Treaty of Waitangi Settlement Process: New Relationship or New Mask?', in Ratcliffe, Greg and Turcotte, Gerry (eds), *Compr(om)ising Post/colonialism(s): Challenging Narratives and Practices*, Sydney, 2001, p 235 (for 'protects the construction', 'displaces claims' and 'reinscribes' quotes); Durie, *Te Mana*, pp 238–40; Solomon, Maui, 'The Context for Maori (II)', in Quentin-Baxter, Alison (ed), *Recognising the Rights of Indigenous Peoples*, Wellington, 1998, pp 63, 64–5; Waitangi Tribunal, *The Taranaki Report*, section 2.1 (re autonomy); Sharp, *Justice and the Māori*, p 287 (for 'enough cross-ethnic' quote); Anaya, James, *Indigenous Peoples in International Law*, New York, 1996, p 76; Herzog, 'Toward', p 129 (for 'hybrid' quote); Fleras and Spoonley, *Recalling Aotearoa*, p 240.

Gilling, Bryan, *'The Most Fundamental Desire of Maori Landowners': Land Management and Governance Options for Maori from the 1950s*, Wellington, Treaty of Waitangi Research Unit, 2007; Mead, 'Options', p 151 (for 'ruling council of elders' and 'make our own laws' quotes); Quaintance, Lauren, 'Fishing Furore: Customary Rights Or Deep Sea Plunder?', *North & South*, March 1998, pp 33–4.

0. Orange, *An Illustrated History*, pp 209–210; Delamere, Tuariki, personal communication, 20 May 1999 (for 'political vehicle' quote); Hake, Ni, 'Confederation of United Tribes Affirmed', *Scoop* (website), 23 Sept 2002, http://www.scoop.co.nz/stories/PO0209/S00119.htm [accessed June 2008]; Dixon, Greg, 'Face to Face', *North & South*, 1 April 2001, p 84; Ralston, Bill, 'Godzone: the Maori kingmaker. Stubbing with Tau', *Metro*, June 1999, p 37; Williams, David V, 'Unique Treaty-Based Relationships Remain Elusive', in Belgrave, Michael, Kawharu, Merata and Williams, David (eds), *Waitangi Revisited: Perspectives on the Treaty of Waitangi*, Auckland, 2005, p 383 (for quote on 'genuine space'); Greenland, Hauraki, 'Ethnicity as Ideology: The Critique of Pakeha Society', in Spoonley, Paul, Macpherson, Cluny, Pearson, David and Sedgwick, Charles (eds), *Tauiwi: Racism and Ethnicity in New Zealand*, Palmerston North, 1984, p 88; Edwards, Brent, 'Maori not to blame for abuse – Henare', *Evening Post*, 9 Sept 1998, p 1 (for 'sanitised, bureaucratised' quote); Williams, *The Too-Hard Basket*, pp 107–8 (re 'relational' quotes); McHugh, Paul, 'Living with Rights Aboriginally: Constitutionalism and Māori in the 1990s', in Belgrave et al (eds), *Waitangi Revisited*, pp 284, 301–2 (for 'rights-integration' quote); Mitchell, Hilary Ann and Mitchell, Maui John, *Foreshore and Seabed Issues: a Te Tau Ihu Perspective on Assertions and Denials of Rangatiratanga*, Treaty of Waitangi Research Unit, Wellington, 2006.

1. Pocock, J G A, 'The Treaty Between Histories', in Sharp, Andrew and McHugh, Paul (eds), *Histories, Power and Loss: Uses of the Past – A New Zealand Commentary*, Wellington, 2001, p 80 (for 'perpetually contested' quote); Ladley, 'The Treaty', p 24; Wilson, Margaret, 'Dealing with Treaty issues', *Mana*, Issue 35, Aug–Sept 2000, p 57 (for 'through war, trickery and neglect' quote); Winiata/Diamond, 'Nga Manu Taiko'; Sharp, Andrew, 'The Treaty in the Real Life of the Constitution', in Belgrave, Michael, Kawharu, Merata and Williams, David (eds), *Waitangi Revisited: Perspectives on the Treaty of Waitangi*, Auckland, 2005; James, Colin (ed), *Building the Constitution*, Wellington, 2000; Perry, Paul and Webster, Alan, *New Zealand Politics at the Turn of the Millennium: Attitudes and Values About Politics and Government*, Auckland, 1999, pp 73–4; Fleras and Spoonley, *Recalling Aotearoa*, pp 13–18; Metge, Joan, 'Myths for New Zealand', in Bell, Adrian (ed), *One Nation, Two Partners, Many Peoples*, Porirua, 1996 (for 'Treaty fatigue' quote).

12. Turia, 'Flying the Flag'; *Dominion Post*, 17 November 2008; Orange, *An Illustrated History*, pp 190–92, pp 266–8; Dodd, *Nation Building*, p 1 (for 'genuine *self*-rule' quote); Kelsey, *Reclaiming*, p 52 (for 'central objective' quote); Te Puni Kokiri, 'Treaty Framework', draft policy document, Nov 1999, pp 4–5 (for 'Tribunal has shown' and 'the collective power' quotes); Bain, Helen, 'Maori MPs speak first in break with tradition', *Dominion*, 9 Feb 2000 (for 'Maori autonomy' quote).

13. Minogue, *Waitangi*, p 58; Round, *Truth or Treaty?* pp 102–3 (for 'how generous' quote); Trotter, Chris, 'The unanswered question', *Dominion Post*, 12 Dec 2003 (for 'modern, democratic and prosperous' quote); Vasil, *Biculturalism*, p 44; Byrnes, Giselle, *The Waitangi Tribunal and New Zealand History*, Melbourne, 2004.

14. Meredith, Paul, 'Hybridity in the Third Space: Rethinking Bi-cultural Politics in Aotearoa/New Zealand', *He Pukenga Korero*, 4(2), 1999, p 12 (for 'over-simplified' and 'reconceptualisation' quotes);

Meredith, Paul, 'Revisioning New Zealandness: A Framework for Discussion', Te Matahauariki Research Institute, http://lianz.waikato.ac.nz/PAPERS/paul/NZ.pdf [accessed June 2008], p6 (for 'criss-crossing' quote). The types of quest outlined are often influenced, consciously or otherwise, by post-structural and post-modern theories or their derivatives, such as Homi Bhabha's hybridisation theory: with the hybrid identity inhabiting more than one 'imagined community', it inherently deconstructs both binarism and ethnocentrism, and in the world of hybridity the (unattainable) concept of 'unified nation' can give way to something more in tune with the complexities of society; see Bhabha, *The Location of Culture*, pp 140–144.

15. Belich, 'Colonization and History', p187 (for 'to emphasize the particular' quote); Pearson, *The Politics of Ethnicity*, p204.
16. Privy Council Office, 'Attorney General v. Henry Michael Horton and Another, Judgment of the Lords of the Judicial Committee of the Privy Council, Delivered the 8th March 1999', 7 March 2002, http://www.privy-council.org.uk/files/pdf/JC_Judgments_1999_no_9.pdf [accessed June 2008], p4 (for 'the continuing needs' quote); Young, Audrey, 'NZ urged to give treaty certainty in law', *New Zealand Herald*, 18 Sept 2002 (for 'fulfilling its obligations' quote); Te Puni Kokiri, 'Treaty Framework', p5 (for 'balanced against' quote), p6 (for 'demands of rangatiratanga' quote), p7 (for 'Crown should support' quote); Dawson, Richard, '"Rights" and Policy', Institute of Policy Studies seminar paper, 16 Nov 2000, p5 (for 'New Zealand Government' quote); Minogue, *Waitangi*, p86; Jackson, Moana, 'Seabed deal plainly not fair to Maori', *New Zealand Herald*, 22 Dec 2003; Pearson, *A Dream Deferred*, p246.
17. Constitutional Arrangements Committee, New Zealand Parliament, 'Terms of reference', 16 Dec 2004 (for 'undertake a review' quote); Ladley, 'The Treaty', p23 (for 'relative degrees of power' quote); Cabinet Policy Committee, paper, 21 Feb 2000, para 28, (for 'historical grievances' quote); Turia, 'Flying the Flag' (for 'the heart' quote).
18. Vasil, *Biculturalism*, p1 (for 'chief purpose' quote); Maaka and Fleras, *The Politics of Indigeneity*, p255ff (p 296 re 'middle way'); Dawson, *The Treaty of Waitangi*, p240 (for 'workable mutuality' quote). On the need for constitutional change, see also the contributions to James (ed), *Building the Constitution*; Kelsey, 'Māori, Te Tiriti', p82; Brookfield, F M, *Waitangi and Indigenous Rights: Revolution, Law and Legitimation*, Auckland, 1999, pp 169–84; Dahlberg, Tina R Makereti, 'Māori Representation in Parliament and Tino Rangatiratanga', *He Pukenga Korero*, 2(1), 1996; Durie, Mason, 'A Framework for Considering Constitutional Change and the Position of Maori in Aotearoa', in *Ngā Kāhui Pou: Launching Māori Futures*, Wellington, 2003; Durie, Mason, 'Tino Rangatiratanga'; Hall, Donna, 'Maori Governance and Accountability', in Hayward, Janine and Wheen, Nicola R, *The Waitangi Tribunal: Te Roopu Whakamana i te Tiriti o Waitangi*, Wellington, 2004; Sharp, 'The Treaty in the Real Life'.
19. Webster, Peter, *Rua and the Maori Millennium*, Wellington, 1979, p279; Keenan, 'The Treaty'.

Bibliography of Cited Sources

Primary Sources

Archival sources can be found at Archives New Zealand in Wellington unless otherwise stated. The AJHR abbreviation refers to the *Appendices to the Journals of the House of Representatives.*

'Address to Rotarians on Problems of Maori–Pakeha Relationships: Proposal to Form Maori Community Centre in Palmerston North', *Manawatu Daily Times*, 14 Dec 1954, contained in MA 28, 13/13, Box 8, Racial Relationships 1952–57.

'Assimilation of the Maoris', *Weekly News*, 7 July 1954, contained in MA 28, 13/13, Box 8, Racial Relationships 1952–57.

Assistant Secretary Maori Affairs to the Secretary, Public Service Commission, Wellington, 17 Aug 1955, MA, W2490, Box 131, Part 1, 36/26, Maori Women's Welfare League, 1950–56.

Attachments to Secretary to Minister of Maori Affairs, 16 Feb 1960, MA 1, 35/2, Part 1.

Auckland Committee on Racism and Discrimination, information leaflet, nd [c1973], 94-106-19/07, Polynesians in New Zealand, Herbert Otto Roth Papers (MS-Group-0314), Alexander Turnbull Library, National Library of New Zealand.

Awaroa ki Manuka, 'Ngaa Tikanga O Ngati Te Ata: Tribal Policy Statement', 1991.

Awatere, Donna, *Maori Sovereignty*, Auckland, 1984.

Bain, Helen, 'Maori MPs speak first in break with tradition', *Dominion*, 9 Feb 2000.

Bennett, R to Mr Souter, 12 Oct 1966, MA 1, Box 656, Part 9, 36/1/21, Race Relations–Integration–Segregation, 1964–68.

Booth, J M, and Hunn, J K, *Integration of Maori and Pakeha*, Wellington, 1962.

Boyd, Sarah, 'The Kohanga Generation', *Dominion Post*, 9 April 2005.

'Brief History of the League – its administration and financial background', MA, W2490, Box 132, Part 4, 36/26, MWWL, 1962–70.

Brown, Bruce, personal communication, 30 Jul 2008.

Buck, Peter, *The Coming of the Maori*, Wellington, 1949.

Butterworth, Graham, Newspaper Clippings Collection, Treaty of Waitangi Research Unit, Box 2.

Cabinet Policy Committee, paper, 21 Feb 2000.

Carroll, Turi, Speech to Her Majesty the Queen, Waitangi Day gathering, 6 Feb 1963, MA, W2459, Box 163, Part 1, 19/1/55/1, Treaty of Waitangi – General and Policy and Submissions by New Zealand Council, 1971–1971.

Citizens Association for Racial Equality and Auckland Committee on Racism and Discriminatio 'Maori Representation – Joint Submission to the Parliamentary Select Committee established revise the Electoral Act 1956 and Amendments thereto', nd [c1973], 95-222-1/06, Maori Struggl David Wickham Papers, Alexander Turnbull Library, National Library of New Zealand.

'Conference of District Officers', Notes of Discussions, Wellington, 22–24 Nov 1960, AAMK, 86 Box 663d, Part 2, 19/1/237, Conference of District Officers, 1960–62.

Constitutional Arrangements Committee, New Zealand Parliament, 'Terms of reference', 16 De 2004.

Cooper, Whina to the Hon Mr Corbett, Minister of Maori Affairs, 24 April 1953, MA, W2490, Bo 131, Part 1, 36/26, Maori Women's Welfare League, 1950–56.

Cooper, Whina to the Secretary, re 'Administration of MWWL Organisation', 7 Aug 1953, MA W2490, Box 131, Part 1, 36/26, Maori Women's Welfare League, 1950–56.

Corbett, E B, Memorandum for Hon W H Fortune, Minister in Charge of Police, 18 May 1954, MA W2490, Box 81, Part 2, 36/4, Wardens, Policy and Appointments, 1954–7.

Corbett, Ernest, 'Foreword by the Minister of Maori Affairs', in Department of Maori Affairs, 'Annu Report of the Board of Maori Affairs and of the Under-Secretary', AJHR, G-9, 1950.

———, 'Foreword by the Minister of Maori Affairs', in Department of Maori Affairs, 'Annual Repo of the Board of Maori Affairs and of the Under-Secretary', AJHR, G-9, 1952.

Cullen, Michael, 'Observations on the Role of Government', Speech Notes, 27 August 2003, http:/ www.beehive.govt.nz/node/17678 [accessed 17 March 2008].

de Bres, Joris, 'Current Issues in Race Relations', Speech by Race Relations Commissione 16 March 2004, available online: http://www.hrc.co.nz/home/hrc/newsandissues currentissuesinracerelations2004.php [accessed June 2008].

Delamere, Tuariki, personal communication, 20 May 1999.

Department of Maori Affairs, 'Annual Report of the Board of Maori Affairs and of the Under Secretary', AJHR, G-9, 1950.

———, 'Annual Report of the Board of Maori Affairs and of the Under-Secretary', AJHR, G- 1952.

———, 'Annual Report of the Department of Maori Affairs and the Board of Maori Affairs and th Maori Trust Office', AJHR, E-13, 1986.

———, Dispatch to all District Officers, all District-Welfare Officers and all Welfare Officers, 29 Ma 1952, AAMK, 869, Box 1050a, 35/1, General Policy and Admin – MSEA 1945, 1951–5.

———, 'Dominion Council for Tribal Executives under MSEA Act', 8 Nov 1957, MA 1, 35/2, Pa 1, Box 646, NZ Council of Tribal Executives, 1952–1962.

———, *He Tirohanga Rangapu/Partnership Perspectives*, Wellington, 1988.

———, *The Maori Today*, Wellington, 1949.

———, *The Maori Today*, Wellington, 3rd ed, 1964.

———, 'Report of the Board of Maori Affairs, Secretary, and the Maori Trustee', AJHR, G-9, 1960.

———, 'Report of the Department of Maori Affairs and of the Secretary', AJHR, G-9, 1954.

———, *Te Urupare Rangapu/Partnership Response*, Wellington, 1988.

'Department plans tohunga role in prisons', *Dominion*, 2 Oct 1998.

District Officer, Wanganui, M G Kellar Report to the Secretary, Head Office, 3 Dec 1959, MA, W249(Box 99, Part 3, 36/10, Maori Club Associations and Recreation Groups, Social Organisatior 1951–56.

Dominion Post, 17 November 2008.

Edwards, Brent, 'Maori not to blame for abuse – Henare', *Evening Post*, 9 Sept 1998.

Espiner, Guyon, 'Tamihere slams Labour welfare policies', *Sunday Star Times*, 23 Feb 2003.

Evening Post, 22 November 1962, clipping contained in MA 1, 35/2, vol 2.

'First New Zealand Conference on Social Work Education', nd, 99-266-10/1, Folder 4, Treaty o Waitangi, Alexander Turnbull Library, National Library of New Zealand.

ɔrbes, George, in *New Zealand Parliamentary Debates*, vol 234, 9 Nov, 1932, p 223.

raser, Peter, 'Foreword by the Minister of Maori Affairs', in Department of Maori Affairs, 'Annual Report of the Board of Maori Affairs and of the Under-Secretary', AJHR, G-9, 1949.

'uture of Maori in New Zealand Life Discussed', *Christchurch Star–Sun*, 8 Sept 1952, contained in MA 28, 13/13, Box 8, Racial Relationships 1952–57.

'uture of Maori Race in New Zealand Life', *Evening Star*, 8 July 1957, contained in MA 28, 13/13, Box 8, Racial Relationships 1952–57.

'rainger, J T, 'Fair and Just: Law for Both Races', *Weekly News*, 11 June 1952.

ake, Ni, 'Confederation of United Tribes Affirmed', *Scoop* (website), 23 Sept 2002, http://www.scoop.co.nz/stories/PO0209/S00119.htm [accessed June 2008].

anan, J R, 'Foreword', in Department of Maori Affairs, *The Maori Today*, Wellington, 3rd ed, 1964.

Iandling of Cash in Head Office, Department of Maori Affairs', MA, W2490, Box 131, Part 1, 36/26, Maori Women's Welfare League, 1950–56.

Ie Maimai Aroha: Erana Prime', *Mana*, issue 35, Aug–Sept 2000.

Ie Maimai Aroha: Glass Murray', *Mana*, issue 28, June–July 1999.

Iohepa, P K, 'Waitangi: A Promise or a Betrayal', Papers in Race Relations no 2, 85-002-02, Papers relating to human rights, South Pacific writers and literature, John Owen O'Conner Papers, Alexander Turnbull Library, National Library of New Zealand.

Ioromia, Parekura, 'Speech notes prepared for the Hui Taumata 2005', 1 March 2005, http://www.beehive.govt.nz/node/22330 [accessed June 2008].

Iumphreys, Lyn, 'Board signs up to Maori health plan', *Daily News*, 20 Sept 2002.

Iunn, J K, to Father P J Cleary, 25 Oct 1961, MA 1, Box 655, 36/1/21, Part 4, Race Relations–Integration–Segregation, 1961–62.

Iunn, J K, to Secretary External Affairs, Alister D McIntosh, 1 Feb 1963, MA, W2459, Box 163, Part 1, 19/1/55/1, Treaty of Waitangi – General and Policy and Submissions by New Zealand Council, 1971–1971.

Iunn, Jack K, *Report on Department of Maori Affairs: with Statistical Supplement*, Wellington, 1961.

nternational Labour Organization, 'Convention concerning Indigenous and Tribal Peoples in Independent Countries', C169, Geneva, 1989.

———, 'Convention concerning the Protection and Integration of Indigenous and Other Tribal and Semi-Tribal Populations in Independent Countries', C107, Geneva, 1957.

wi Transition Agency, 'Report of the Iwi Transition Agency Working Group on the Runanga Iwi Bill, Local Government Amendment (No 8) Bill and the Resource Management Bill (30 January 1990)', Wellington, 1990.

ackson, Moana, *The Maori and the Criminal Justice System: A New Perspective: He Whaipaanga Hou, Part 2*, Wellington, 1988.

———, 'Seabed deal plainly not fair to Maori', *New Zealand Herald*, 22 Dec 2003.

———, 'A Very Quick Guide to the Treaty of Waitangi', in Anarchist Alliance of Aotearoa, *Tino Rangatiratanga: The Treaty of Waitangi Today*, Wellington, nd.

ames, Colin, 'Why we can't afford to lose the voice of Tamihere', *New Zealand Herald*, 19 Oct 2004.

ɔhns, Atihana, 'What's Wrong with the Pakeha', letter to editor, *New Zealand Listener*, 4 Sept 1961, contained in MA 1, Box 655, 36/1/21, Part 4, Race Relations–Integration–Segregation, 1961–62.

oint Methodist Presbyterian Public Questions Committee, *Politics Not Justice: The Government's Treaty Settlements Policy*, Wellington, 1999.

———, *Tino Rangatiratanga*, TWM, July 1993, http://homepages.ihug.co.nz/~sai/Maori_tino.htm#Constitutional [accessed June 2008].

Kay, Martin, 'Ratana's balancing act', *Dominion Post*, 24 Jan 2005.

aidlaw, Chris, 'Interview with Ranginui Walker', Radio New Zealand National, 20 Jan 2008.

Land Wrangle Leads to High Court', *Daily News*, 9 Sept 2003.

Lange, David, 'Bruce Jesson Memorial Lecture: Inaugural Lecture', Maidment Theatre, Auckland Nov 2000, available online: http://www.brucejesson.com/JessonLecture_2000.pdf [accessed June 2008]
Love, Morrie, 'Our Country, Our Choice', typescript, nd, Treaty of Waitangi Research Unit collection.
Mallard, Trevor, 'We Are All New Zealanders Now', speech to Stout Research Centre for New Zealand Studies, 28 July 2004, http://www.beehive.govt.nz/node/20451 [accessed June 2008].
Mansfield, Bill, 'Healthy Constitutional Relationships in a Culturally Diverse Society', Wellington Ministry of Justice internal resource document, nd.
'The Maori in the City (2)', *New Zealand Listener*, vol 23, no 578, 21 July 1950.
Maori Community Development Act 1979
Maori Education Commission, *Report Four: To the Minister of Māori Affairs*, Wellington, 1999.
'Maori Education: A New Foundation', pamphlet, Eph A MAORI 1962, Alexander Turnbull Library, National Library of New Zealand.
'Maori of today poses social welfare problems', newspaper clipping, MA 1, Box 650, Part 7, 36/1 Welfare-general, 1956–59.
Maori Organisation on Human Rights, Newsletter, July 1972, MS Papers 7888-233, Newsletters – Maori, E W G Craig Papers, Alexander Turnbull Library, National Library of New Zealand.
———, Newsletter, 6 Feb 1973, 85-002-02, Papers relating to human rights, South Pacific writers and literature, John Owen O'Conner Papers, Alexander Turnbull Library, National Library of New Zealand.
———, 'Waitangi Day' Newsletter, Dec 1970, MS Papers 7888-233, Newsletters–Maori, E W G Craig Papers, Alexander Turnbull Library, National Library of New Zealand.
Maori Peoples Liberation Movement of Aotearoa, 'Critique by Maori Peoples Liberation Movement of Aotearoa', nd, pamphlet, reprinted from MPLMA newsletter, 99-266-10/1, Folder 4, Treaty of Waitangi, Alexander Turnbull Library, National Library of New Zealand.
'Maori Proposal for Separate Parliament', *The Press*, 8 Dec 1969.
Maori Welfare Act 1962
Maori Welfare Officer in Tauranga, Report to District Officer, 2 Dec 1959, MA, W2490, Box 99, Part 3, 36/10, Maori Club Associations and Recreation Groups, Social Organisation, 1951–56.
Maori Women's Welfare League Archive, Nelson Provincial Museum.
Maori Women's Welfare League 1951–1988, MS Papers 1396, Alexander Turnbull Library, National Library of New Zealand.
McEwen (Secretary for Maori Affairs) to Minister Maori Affairs, report re 'Maori Wardens', 11 May 1970, MA 1, Box 657, Part 10, 36/1/21, Race Relations–Overseas Countries–Policy and Correspondence, 1964–71.
McEwen (Secretary for Maori Affairs) to Secretary External Affairs, re 'International Convention on the Elimination of All Forms of Racial Discrimination', 7 Aug 1967, MA 1, Box 656, Part 9 36/1/21, Race Relations–Integration–Segregation, 1964–68.
McLean, Robyn, 'Ngai Tahu shares its treasures', *Dominion Post*, 14 July 2006.
McLoughlin, David, 'Singing Her Own Song', *Dominion Post*, 4 Feb 2003.
Metge, Joan, personal communication, 27 Nov 2005.
Ministerial Advisory Committee on a Maori Perspective for the Department of Social Welfare, *Puao-Te-Ata-Tu*, Wellington, 1986.
Minister of Maori Affairs, *Discussion Document on The International Labour Organisation Convention No 169 Concerning Indigenous and Tribal Peoples in Independent Countries 1989*, Wellington, 1999.
———, *Ka Awatea: A Report of the Ministerial Planning Group*, Wellington, March 1991.
Minister of Maori Affairs to Mr Craig of California, 13 June 1957, MA 28, 13/13, Box 8, Racial Relationships 1952–57.
Minister of Maori Affairs to Secretary of Maori Affairs, 13 Aug 1953, MA 1, 35/2, Part 1, Box 646, NZ Council of Tribal Executives, 1952–1962.

Minister of Maori Affairs to Secretary for Maori Affairs, 8 May 1958, MA, W2490, Box 131, Part 1, 36/26.

Minister of Maori Affairs to the Under-Secretary, 21 Sept 1948, MA, W2490, Box 56, Part 2, 35/1, General Policy and Admin – MSEA Act 1945, 1947–50.

Ministry of Foreign Affairs and Trade, *New Zealand Handbook on International Human Rights*, 2nd ed, Wellington, 2003.

Minutes of the Annual Conference of the Race Relations Council, Massey University, 9–11 Feb 1973, 99-278-08/09, New Zealand Race Relations Council, Polynesian Panthers, Trevor Richards Papers, Alexander Turnbull Library, National Library of New Zealand.

Muru Raupatu Marae, 'Defining Tino Rangatiratanga', discussion paper, 13 May 1995, section 3, reproduced in Yates, Bronwyn, 'Striving for Tino Rangatiratanga', in Benseman, John, Findsen, Brian and Scott, Miriama (eds), *The Fourth Sector: Adult and Community Education in Aotearoa/New Zealand*, Palmerston North, 1996.

Nath, Geetha, 'Healing skills not forgotten for Maori', *Daily News*, 15 May 2003.

'National Blend', 10 May 1952, *New Zealand Herald*, contained in MA 28, 13/13, Box 8, Racial Relationships 1952–57.

National Council of Churches Programme on Racism, 'Legislation Betrays the Treaty of Waitangi', nd, 99-266-10/1, Folder 4, Treaty of Waitangi, Alexander Turnbull Library, National Library of New Zealand.

National Party, *Te Maori O Ona Ra Tuku Iho Nei/The Maori and the Future*, nd: Eph A Maori 1950s, Alexander Turnbull Library, National Library of New Zealand.

New Zealand 1990 Commission, *The Treaty of Waitangi: The symbol of our life together as a nation*, Wellington, 1989.

New Zealand First and the New Zealand National Party, 'The Coalition Agreement. Policy Area: Education', 10 Dec 1996, available online http://executive.govt.nz/96-99/coalition/educ.htm [accessed June 2008].

New Zealand Government, *Principles for Crown Action on the Treaty of Waitangi*, Wellington, 1989.

New Zealand Labour Party, 'Take No Risks – Vote Labour', Wellington 1943, Eph A Maori 1943, Alexander Turnbull Library, National Library of New Zealand.

New Zealand Maori Council, *Kaupapa: Te Wahanga Tuatahi*, Wellington, 1983.

New Zealand Maori Council v Attorney-General, [1987] 1 NZLR, 641.

New Zealand Press Association, 'Maori influence growing – Sir Tipene', 3 Dec 2004 www.stuff.co.nz/stuff/print/0,1478,3117011a8153,00.html [accessed 6 Dec 2004].

Nga Tamatoa, in Maori Organisation on Human Rights, July Newsletter, 1972, 99-278-05/06, Papers re the Race Relations Bill, Trevor Richards Papers, Alexander Turnbull Library, National Library of New Zealand.

———, 'Submissions on the Broadcasting Bill 1973', MS Papers 1617, Folder 667, Maori organisations–Tamatoa and Nga Tamatoa Council 1971–73, Alexander Turnbull Library, National Library of New Zealand.

Ngai Tahu, 'Economic Security', *Te Rūnanga o Ngāi Tahu* (website), http://www.ngaitahu.iwi.nz/About%20Ngai%20Tahu/The%20Settlement/The%20Crowns%20Settlement%20Offer/Economic%20Security [accessed June 2008].

Ngata, Apirana, 'A Plea for the Unity of the Maori People', *Papers and Addresses of the Second Conference of the Te Aute College Students Association*, Napier, 1898.

———, *The Treaty of Waitangi: An Explanation*, trans Jones, M R, Wellington, 1963 (original: *Te Tiriti o Waitangi: He Whakamarama*, Hastings, 1922).

Ngata, H K, 'The Treaty of Waitangi and Land', Parts of the Current Law in Contravention of the Treaty seminar, Victoria University of Wellington, Feb 1972, reproduced in Maori Organisation on Human Rights, Newsletter, 6 Feb 1973, 85-002-02, Papers relating to human rights, South Pacific writers and literature, John Owen O'Conner Papers, Alexander Turnbull Library, National Library of New Zealand.

'Notes on "Culture and the Rural Family" in relation to Maori', encl Secretary for Maori Affairs Director of Education, 23 May 1956, MA, W2490, 36/10, Box 99, Part 2, Maori Club Associatio and Recreation Groups, Social Organisation, 1951–56.

Notes from discussion at Raukawa marae, 17 March 1950, AAMK, 869, Box 1051a, 35/1/1, Mac Welfare Legislation, 1956–62.

Notes of representations made to Minister of Maori Affairs at Raukawa Marae, Otaki on Saturday 1 March 1950 by Sir Apirana Ngata on behalf of the assembled tribes, MA, W2490, Box 56, Part 35/1, General Policy and Admin – MSEA Act 1945, 1947–50.

Notes supplied by Eric Ramsden for Major Rangi Royal from a direct statement dictated by S Apirana Ngata, Otaki, 17 March 1950, MA, W2490, Box 57, Part 1, 35/1/3, MSEA Act 194 subsidies, policies, 1947–50.

'One Race – Or Two?', *Daily Telegraph*, 26 Jan 1952, contained in MA 28, 13/13, Box 8, Raci Relationships 1952–57.

'"Ordinary New Zealanders"', *Taranaki Herald*, 2 July 1954, contained in MA 28, 13/13, Box 8, Raci Relationships 1952–57.

O'Regan, Tipene, interviewed by Paul Diamond, 'Nga Manu Taiko', National Radio, 23 Februa 2003.

Ormsby, M J, 'Maori Tikanga and Criminal Justice', report for the Ministry of Justice, Wellington, n

Palmer, Geoffrey, 'Treaty of Waitangi Issues Demand Clarity, Certainty', *New Zealand Herald*, 2 Ja 1990.

Parininihi Ki Waitotara Incorporation website, http://www.pkw.co.nz/ [accessed Dec 2008].

Peace Movement Aotearoa, 'Support the United Nations Declaration on the Rights of Indigeno Peoples', statement, 2008.

Perrott, Alan, 'City-dwelling Maori get their own voice', *New Zealand Herald*, 6 May 2003.

Perry, D N, Interim Committee, Dominion Council of Tribal Executives, to J R Hanan, 20 Janua 1961, MA 1, 35/2, part 1, box 646, 'New Zealand Council of Tribal Executives, 1952–1962'.

Petition of Rangi Makawe Rangitaura of Big Jim's Hill, Waitara, and Others, 1966, in Supplement n 1 to Maori Organisation on Human Rights, September Newsletter, 1972, 99-278-05/06, Pape re the Race Relations Bill, Trevor Richards Papers, Alexander Turnbull Library, National Libra of New Zealand.

Philp, Matt, 'Female trouble', *Listener*, 29 Jan 2000.

Presbyterian Church of New Zealand, Maori Synod, *A Maori View of the 'Hunn Report'*, Christchurc 1961.

Prichard, Ivor and Waetford, Hemi, *Report of the Committee of Inquiry into the Laws Affecting Maori La and Powers of the Maori Land Court*, Wellington, 1965.

Privy Council Office, 'Attorney General v. Henry Michael Horton and Another, Judgment of the Lor of the Judicial Committee of the Privy Council, Delivered the 8th March 1999', 7 March 200 http://www.privy-council.org.uk/files/pdf/JC_Judgments_1999_no_9.pdf [accessed June 2008].

Public Service Association, 'PSA debates the Treaty', *PSA Journal*, 15 Feb 1990–14 May 1990, containe in 95-222-1/12, Papers relating to various activist groups, David Wickham Papers, Alexande Turnbull Library, National Library of New Zealand.

Quirke, Michelle, 'Maori varsity to flout the rules', *Evening Post*, 23 Dec 2002.

'Race and Crime', *Daily News*, 24 Aug 1954, contained in MA 28, 13/13, Box 8, Racial Relationshi 1952–57.

'Race Discrimination in New Zealand', *New Zealand Herald*, 21 May 1954, contained in MA 2 13/13, Box 8, Racial Relationships 1952–57.

'Racial Distinctions in New Zealand', *Weekly News*, 15 Sept 1954, contained in MA 28, 13/13, Bo 8, Racial Relationships 1952–57.

Rata, Matiu, in *New Zealand Parliamentary Debates*, vol 407, 1976, p 3424.

Rebuke for "Voice of Wellington"', *Auckland Star*, 4 Sept 1954, contained in MA 28, 13/13, Box 8, Racial Relationships 1952–57.

Rehua Maori Hostel', pamphlet, Eph A Maori 1955, PR-06-0005, Alexander Turnbull Library, National Library of New Zealand.

Report of the First New Zealand Maori Council', nd, MA 1, W2490, 35/2/4, Part 1.

Report from Palmerston North to Head Office, re 'Housing Target 1961/62', 28 Oct 1960, AAMK, 869, Box 663d, Part 2, 19/1/237, Conference of District Officers, 1960–62.

Resolution MWWL Conference 1957, Policy 11, MA, W2490, Box 131, Part 1, 36/26/20.

Rivers, Janet, 'Autonomy will make kura a viable option', *New Zealand Education Review*, 18 June 1999.

Roberts, John, *Alternative Vision, He Moemoea Ano: From Fiscal Envelope to Constitutional Change: The Significance of the Hirangi Hui*, Wellington, Joint Methodist Presbyterian Public Questions Committee, 1996.

Ropiha to Minister, 'Revised Welfare Policy', 14 Nov 1956, AAMK, 869, Box 1051a, 35/1/1, Maori Welfare Legislation, 1956–62.

Runanga Iwi Act Repeal Act 1991.

Secretary of External Affairs to the Prime Minister, 24 Dec 1959, and attached draft, 'Discrimination against Maoris: The Indigenous Populations Convention 1957', Nash Papers, Series 1151, Folio 001–0165, Department Papers, 1958–60.

Secretary of Maori Affairs to the Minister of Maori Affairs, 16 Feb 1960, MA 1, 35/2, Part 1, Box 646, NZ Council of Tribal Executives, 1952–1962.

Secretary of Maori Affairs to the President, MWWL, 8 June 1953, MA, W2490, Box 131, Part 1, 36/26, Maori Women's Welfare League, 1950–56.

Secretary of Maori Affairs to the President, MWWL, 6 Sept 1956, MA, W2490, Box 131, Part 2, 36/26.

Secretary of Maori Affairs to Secretary to the Treasury, 11 June 1956, 'Public Money', MA, W2490, Box 131, Part 2, 36/26.

Secretary to the Treasury to Secretary for Maori Affairs, 21 August 1956, 'Public Money', MA, W2490, Box 131, Part 2, 36/26.

Smithies, Ruth, *Ten Steps Towards Bicultural Action: A Handbook on Partnership in Aotearoa–New Zealand*, Wellington, 1990.

Souter, B E, Assistant Secretary, Instructions to District Officers, re 'Discrimination against Maoris: The Indigenous Population Convention, 1957', 23 May 1960, AAMK, 869, Box 1063c, 36/1/21A, Race Relations–Interdepartmental Report, 1964–72.

Steele, R W, 'Te Marae i Roto i te Urewera', *Salient*, 29 March 1972.

Tamatoa Council', nd [1971], MS Papers 1617, Folder 667, Maori organisations – Tamatoa and Nga Tamatoa Council, Alexander Turnbull Library, National Library of New Zealand.

Tauranga Moana Trust Board Act 1981.

Te Hokioi: Te Reo Ote Iwi Maori, Issue 4, vol 1, Feb/March 1969, MS Papers 7888-233, Newsletters–Maori, E W G Craig Papers, Alexander Turnbull Library, National Library of New Zealand.

Te Puni Kokiri, 'Capacity Building' (website). http://www.tpk.govt.nz/en/Capacity_Building/index.htm [accessed November 2000].

———, *Kōkiri Paetae*, issue 29, Sept 2000.

———, 'Te Puni Kokiri's role in Capacity Building', pamphlet, Wellington, nd.

———, 'Treaty Framework', draft policy document, Nov 1999.

Te Roopu Ote Matakite, 'Why We Protest', leaflet, nd, 2004-024-3/02, Maori Organisation on Human Rights, Peter Langdon Franks Papers, Alexander Turnbull Library, National Library of New Zealand.

Te Runanga A Iwi O Ngapuhi, Constitution, nd.

Te Runanga O Ngai Tahu Act 1996.

Te TAI, 'Working in Partnership', brochure, nd.

Te Winitana, Tupoutahi Tamihana, personal communication, 28 July 2001.

Tirikatene-Sullivan, Whetu, in *New Zealand Parliamentary Debates*, vol 405, 1976, pp 2273–5.

Treaty of Waitangi Act 1975.

Trotter, Chris, 'The unanswered question', *Dominion Post*, 12 Dec 2003.

Te Ture Whenua Maori Act 1993/Maori Land Act 1993.

Turia, Tariana, 'Flying the Flag of Hope', *Dominion Post*, 14 June 2005.

———, 'Strong whanau key to tangata whenua development', press release, 10 December 2003.

———, 'Whanau development and literacy' speech, Kaitaia, 8 Sept 2003, http://www.beehive.gov nz/speech/whanau+development+and+literacy [accessed June 2008].

Under Secretary to the President, Maori Women's Welfare League, 30 Jan 1953, MA, W2490, Box 13 Part 1, 36/26, Maori Women's Welfare League, 1950–56.

United Nations Office of the High Commissioner for Human Rights, 'International Convention o the Elimination of All Forms of Racial Discrimination', 1965.

United Peoples Liberation Movement of Aotearoa, 'Attention!', information sheet, nd [c1977], M Papers 8958-24, Papers relating to race relations in New Zealand, Andrew Dodsworth: Pape relating to left-wing activity, Alexander Turnbull Library, National Library of New Zealand.

Venter, Nick, 'A Maori agenda', *Dominion Post*, 26 Feb 2005.

'Views of Maori Future Challenged', *New Zealand Herald*, 6 July 1954, contained in MA 28, 13/1 Box 8, Racial Relationships 1952–57.

Waitangi Action Committee, 'Te Tiriti o Waitangi: He Teka', nd, 95-222-1/06, Maori Struggles, Davi Wickham Papers, Alexander Turnbull Library, National Library of New Zealand.

———, 'The Treaty of Waitangi – A Broken Contract', Nov 30 1981, MS Papers 8958-24, Pape relating to race relations in New Zealand, Andrew Dodsworth: Papers relating to left-wing activit Alexander Turnbull Library, National Library of New Zealand.

Waitangi Tribunal, *Finding of the Waitangi Tribunal Relating to Te Reo Maori and a Claim Lodged by Huiran Waikerepuru and Nga Kaiwhakapumau it Te Reo Incorporated Society*, Wai 11, Wellington, 1986.

———, *Maori Electoral Option Report*, Wai 413, Wellington, 1994.

———, *Report of the Waitangi Tribunal on the Muriwhenua Fishing Claim*, Wai 22, Wellington, 1988.

———, *Report of the Waitangi Tribunal on the Manukau Claim*, Wai 8, Wellington, 1985.

———, *The Taranaki Report: Kaupapa Tuatahi*, Wai 143, Wellington, 1996.

———, *Te Whanau o Waipareira Report*, Wai 414, Wellington, 1998.

Western, Marie to Corbett, Minister of Maori Affairs, 1 Sept 1952 and 10 Nov 1952, MA 28, 13/1 Box 8, Racial Relationships 1952–57.

Westra, Ans, *Washday at the Pa* (Castle Press ed, including 'Publisher's Note'), Christchurch, 1964.

Whitiwhiti Korero, Issue 13, 13 July 2008.

Williams, Chief Judge JV, speech at 25th Anniversary of the Waitangi Tribunal conference, Wellingtor 11 Oct 2000.

Williams, David V, 'Submission to the Treaty of Waitangi Commission', St Mathews-in-the-Cit Church of the Diocese of Auckland, 9 Sept 1985, 99-266-10/1, Folder 4, Treaty of Waitang Alexander Turnbull Library, National Library of New Zealand.

Wilson, Margaret, 'Dealing with Treaty issues', *Mana*, issue 35, Aug–Sept 2000.

Winiata, Maharaia, 'Leadership in the Auckland Maori Community', *Te Ao Hou*, no 27, June 1959.

———, 'Two Peoples: One Nation', *New Zealand Listener*, 25 March 1955.

Winiata, Whatarangi, address at funeral of Martin Dawson, Old St Paul's, Wellington, 9 May 2003.

———, 'Reducing the Socio-Economic Disparities in Housing, Employment, Health and Education A Maori Solution', paper for the Anglican Church, Wellington, 1998, available online: http:/ homepages.ihug.co.nz/~sai/MSoln_Win.html [accessed June 2008].

———, interviewed by Paul Diamond, 'Nga Manu Taiko', National Radio, 2 March 2003.

Women's Health League', *Opotiki News*, 6 July, 1951, contained in MA, W2490, Box 131, Part 1, 36/26, Maori Women's Welfare League, 1950–56.

Wright, R, 'The First Conference of the Maori Women's Welfare Leagues', MA, W2490, Box 131, Part 1, 36/26, Maori Women's Welfare League, 1950–56.

Young, Audrey, 'NZ urged to give treaty certainty in law', *New Zealand Herald*, 18 Sept 2002.

Secondary Sources

Allen, Chadwick, 'Postcolonial Theory and the Discourse of Treaties', *American Quarterly*, 52(1), March 2000.

Anderson, L G, 'Welfare Requirements in a Multi-racial Society', in Brookes, R H and Kawharu, I H (eds), *Administration in New Zealand's Multi-racial Society*, Wellington, 1967.

Alves, Dora, *The Maori and the Crown: An Indigenous People's Struggle for Self-Determination*, Westport, CT, 1999.

Anaya, James, *Indigenous Peoples in International Law*, New York, 1996.

Anderton, Jim, 'Kirk and Rowling: Recollections and Significance', in Clark, Margaret (ed), *Three Labour Leaders: Nordmeyer, Kirk, Rowling*, Palmerston North, 2001.

Anglican Church in Aotearoa, New Zealand and Polynesia, 'History', http://www.anglican.org.nz/history.htm [accessed July 2008].

Archer, Dave and Mary, 'Race, Identity and the Maori People', in Webb, Stephen and Collette, John (eds), *New Zealand Society: Contemporary Perspectives*, Sydney, 1973.

Ausubel, David P, *The Fern and the Tiki: An American View of New Zealand National Character, Social Attitudes and Race Relations*, 1960 (New York ed, 1965).

———, 'The Maori: A Study in Resistive Acculturation', in Webb, Stephen D and Collette, John (eds), *New Zealand Society: Contemporary Perspectives*, Sydney, 1973.

———, *Maori Youth: A Psychoethnological Study of Cultural Deprivation*, New York, 1961.

Ballara, Angela, *Iwi. The dynamics of Maori tribal organisation from c.1769 to c.1945*, Wellington, 1998.

———, *Proud to Be White? A Survey of Pakeha Prejudice in New Zealand*, Auckland, 1986.

Bargh, Maria (ed), *Resistance: An Indigenous Response to Neoliberalism*, Wellington, 2007.

Barrett, Mark, 'Maori Health Purchasing – Some Current Issues', *Social Policy Journal of New Zealand*, 9, Nov 1997.

Barrington, John, *Separate but Equal? Māori Schools and the Crown 1867–1969*, Wellington, 2008.

Bedggood, David, *Rich and Poor in New Zealand: A Critique of Class, Politics and Ideology*, Auckland, 1980.

Belgrave, Michael, Kawharu, Merata and Williams, David, 'Introduction', in Belgrave, Michael, Kawharu, Merata and Williams, David (eds), *Waitangi Revisited: Perspectives on the Treaty of Waitangi*, Auckland, 2005.

Belich, James, 'Colonization and History in New Zealand', in Winks, Robin W (ed), *The Oxford History of the British Empire: Volume V: Historiography*, Oxford, 1999.

———, *The New Zealand Wars and the Victorian Interpretation of Racial Conflict*, Auckland, 1986.

———, *Paradise Reforged: A History of the New Zealanders from the 1880s to the Year 2000*, Auckland, 2001.

Berg, Manfred and Schaefer, Bernd (eds), *Historical Justice in International Perspective: How Societies Are Trying to Right the Wrongs of the Past*, Washington, DC, 2009.

Bhabha, Homi K, *The Location of Culture*, London, 1994.

Bhabha, Homi (interviewed by Paul Thompson), 'Between Identities', in Benmayor, Rina and Scotnes, Andor (eds), *Migration and Identity*, Oxford, 1994.

Biggs, Bruce, 'Maori affairs and the Hunn report', *Journal of the Polynesian Society*, 70(3), September 1961.

Boast, Richard, *Buying the Land, Selling the Land: Governments and Maori Land in the North Island 1865–1921*, Wellington, 2008.

———, 'The Evolution of Maori Land Law 1962–1993', in Boast, Richard, Erueti, Andrew, McPhail, Doug and Smith, Norman, *Maori Land Law*, Wellington, 1999.

———, 'Maori Land and Other Statutes', in Boast, Richard, Erueti, Andrew, McPhail, Doug and Smith, Norman, *Maori Land Law*, Wellington, 1999.

———, 'Maori Land and the Treaty of Waitangi', in Boast, Richard, Erueti, Andrew, McPhail, Doug and Smith, Norman, *Maori Land Law*, Wellington, 1999.

——— 'The Treaty of Waitangi and the Law', *New Zealand Law Journal*, April 1999.

Booth, Pat, 'Maori Devolution: The Path to Unity or Another Tacky Affair?', *North & South*, June 1989

Bradly, R L, 'Education's Impact on the Multi-racial Society', in Brookes, R H and Kawharu, I H (eds), *Administration in New Zealand's Multi-racial Society*, Wellington, 1967.

Brookes, Barbara, 'Nostalgia for "Innocent Homely Pleasures"', in Brookes, Barbara (ed), *At Home in New Zealand: Houses, History, People*, Wellington, 2000.

Brookes, R H and Kawharu, I H (eds), *Administration in New Zealand's Multi-racial Society*, Wellington, 1967.

Brookfield, F M, *Waitangi and Indigenous Rights: Revolution, Law and Legitimation*, Auckland, 1999.

Butterworth, G V, 'Aotearoa 1769–1988: Towards a Tribal Perspective', report for Department of Maori Affairs, Wellington, 1988.

———, 'Breaking the Grip: An Historical Agenda for Nga Iwi Maori', revision of a paper presented to the History Department, Massey University, 16 April 1987.

———, 'The Health of the Body, the Health of Land: A Comparative Study of the Political Objectives and Careers of Wiremu Ratana and the Ratana Movement, and Sir Apirana Ngata', Wellington: Treaty of Waitangi Research Unit, Feb 2000.

———, *'Men of Authority': The New Zealand Maori Council and the Struggle for Rangatiratanga in the 1960s–1970s*, Wellington, Treaty of Waitangi Research Unit, 2007.

Butterworth, Graham and Susan, *Policing and the Tangata Whenua, 1935–85*, Wellington, Treaty of Waitangi Research Unit, 2008.

Butterworth, G V and Butterworth, S M, *The Maori Trustee*, Wellington, nd.

Butterworth, G V and Young, H R, *Maori Affairs/Nga Take Maori*, Wellington, 1990.

Byrnes, Giselle, *The Waitangi Tribunal and New Zealand History*, Melbourne, 2004.

Byron, Isolde, *Nga Perehitini: The Presidents of the Maori Women's Welfare League 1951–2001*, Auckland, 2002.

Callaghan, Catherine, '"Constitutionalisation" of Treaties by the Courts: The Treaty of Waitangi and the Treaty of Rome Compared', *New Zealand Universities Law Review*, June 1999.

Christie, Walter, *New Zealand Education and Treatyism*, Auckland, 1999.

———, *A Race Apart: Parliament and Race Separatism, the Story*, Auckland, 1998.

———, *Treaty Issues*, Christchurch, 1997.

Cleave, Peter, *The Sovereignty Game: Power, Knowledge and Reading the Treaty*, Wellington, 1989.

Coates, Ken S, 'International Perspectives on Relations with Indigenous Peoples', in Coates, Ken S and McHugh, P G, *Living Relationships, Kōkiri Ngatāhi: The Treaty of Waitangi in the New Millennium*, Wellington, 1998.

Cox, Lindsay, *Kotahitanga: The Search for Maori Political Unity*, Auckland, 1993.

Crown, R and L, *The Rohe Potae: History and Proposals*, Te Rohe Potae Rereahu-Maniapoto Inc, Te Kuiti, 1985.

Crown, R, *Proposals for Rereahu-Maniapoto Autonomy*, Te Rohe Potae o Rereahu-Maniapoto Inc, Te Kuiti, 1986.

Dahlberg, Tina R Makereti, 'Māori Representation in Parliament and Tino Rangatiratanga', *He Pukenga Korero*, 2(1), 1996.

Dawson, Richard, '"Rights" and Policy', Institute of Policy Studies seminar paper, 16 Nov 2000.

———, *The Treaty of Waitangi and the Control of Language*, Wellington, 2001.

Diamond, Paul, 'Whatarangi Winiata', in Diamond, Paul (ed), *A Fire in Your Belly: Māori Leaders Speak*, Wellington, 2003.

Dixon, Greg, 'Face to Face', *North & South*, 1 April 2001.

Dodd, Materoa, 'Nation Building and Māori Development: The Importance of Governance', paper for 'Contesting Development: Pathways to Better Practice', 3rd Biennial conference of the Aotearoa New Zealand International Development Studies Network, Palmerston North, 5–7 December 2002, available online: http://www.devnet.org.nz/conf2002/papers/Dodd_Materoa.pdf [accessed June 2008].

Durie, Edward T, 'Maori autonomy: preventing power games', *Stimulus*, 6(2), May 1998.

———, 'A Peaceful Solution', in Young, Ramari (ed), *Mana Tiriti: The Art of Protest and Partnership*, Wellington, 1991.

Durie, Mason, 'A Framework for Considering Constitutional Change and the Position of Maori in Aotearoa', in *Ngā Kāhui Pou: Launching Māori Futures*, Wellington, 2003.

———, *Te Mana, Te Kāwanatanga: The Politics of Māori Self-Determination*, Auckland, 1998.

———, 'Tino Rangatiratanga', in Belgrave, Michael, Kawharu, Merata and Williams, David (eds), *Waitangi Revisited: Perspectives on the Treaty of Waitangi*, Auckland, 2005.

———, *Whaiora: Maori Health Development*, Melbourne, 1994 (2nd ed, 1998).

Dyall, Lorna, 'Oranga Maori: Maori Health', *New Zealand Health Review*, 8(2), 1988.

Easton, Brian, *In Stormy Seas: The Post-War New Zealand Economy*, Dunedin, 1997.

Edwards, Mihi, *Mihipeka: Time of Turmoil*, Auckland, 1992.

Epstein, Richard A, *The Treaty of Waitangi: A Plain Meaning Interpretation*, Wellington, 1999.

Fanon, Frantz, *The Wretched of the Earth*, London, 1967.

Ferguson, Philip, 'Race relations and social control', *Revolution*, no 14, Xmas 2000–March 2001.

Fleras, Augie, 'A Descriptive Analysis of Maori Wardens in the Historical and Contemporary Context of New Zealand Society', PhD thesis, Victoria University of Wellington, 1980.

———, 'Maori Wardens and the Control of Liquor Among the Maori of New Zealand', *Journal of the Polynesian Society*, 90(4), 1981.

———, 'Towards "Tu Tangata": Historical Developments and Current Trends in Maori Policy and Administration', *Political Science*, 37(1), July 1985.

———, '"Tuku Rangatiratanga": Devolution in Iwi–Government Relations', in Spoonley, Paul, Pearson, David, and Macpherson, Cluny (eds), *Nga Take: Ethnic Relations and Racism in Aotearoa/New Zealand*, Palmerston North, 1991.

Fleras, Augie and Elliott, Jean Leonard, *The 'Nations Within': Aboriginal-State Relations in Canada, the United States, and New Zealand*, Toronto, 1992.

Fleras, Augie and Spoonley, Paul, *Recalling Aotearoa: Indigenous Politics and Ethnic Relations in New Zealand*, Auckland, 1999.

Frame, Alex, 'Compensating for Raupatu: The Situation in the late 1980s', paper presented at 'Coming to Terms? Raupatu/Confiscation and New Zealand History' conference, Victoria University of Wellington, 27–8 June 2008.

———, 'Sir John Salmond 1862–1924', in O'Sullivan, Vincent (ed), *Eminent Victorians: Great teachers and scholars from Victoria's first 100 years*, Wellington, 2000.

———, 'A State Servant Looks at the Treaty', *New Zealand Universities Law Review*, 14(1), 1990.

Freire, Paulo, *Pedagogy of the Oppressed*, New York, 1970 (1986 ed, Ramos trans).

Gardiner, Wira, *Te Mura o te Ahi: The Story of the Maori Battalion*, Auckland, 1992.

———, *Return to Sender: What Really Happened at the Fiscal Envelope Hui*, Auckland, 1996.

Gilling, Bryan, 'The Maori Land Court in New Zealand: An Historical Overview', *Canadian Journal of Native Studies*, XIII(1), 1993.

Gilling, Bryan, *'Most Barren and Unprofitable Land': The Effectiveness of Twentieth-Century Schemes to Mak Maori Land Usable and Profitable*, Wellington, Treaty of Waitangi Research Unit, 2008.

———, *'The Most Fundamental Desire of Maori Landowners': Land Management and Governance Optior for Maori from the 1950s*, Wellington, Treaty of Waitangi Research Unit, 2007.

Grace, Patricia, Ramsden, Irihapeti and Dennis, Jonathan (eds), *The Silent Migration: Ngati Poneke Youn Maori Club 1937–1948*, Wellington, 2001.

Graham, Douglas, 'The Treaty and Treaty Negotiations', in Clark, Margaret (ed), *The Bolger Years, 1990 1997*, Wellington, 2008.

———, *Trick or Treaty?*, Wellington, 1997.

Greenland, Hauraki, 'Ethnicity as Ideology: The Critique of Pakeha Society', in Spoonley, Pau Macpherson, Cluny, Pearson, David and Sedgwick, Charles (eds), *Tauiwi: Racism and Ethnicity i New Zealand*, Palmerston North, 1984.

Gustafson, Barry, *The First 50 Years: A History of the New Zealand National Party*, Auckland, 1986.

Hall, Donna, 'Maori Governance and Accountability', in Hayward, Janine and Wheen, Nicola R, *Th Waitangi Tribunal: Te Roopu Whakamana i te Tiriti o Waitangi*, Wellington, 2004.

Harding, Bruce, 'Interview with Robin Winks: The Historian as Detective', *History Now/Te Pae Tawhit o te Wā*, 7(4), November 2001.

Harré, John, 'Maori–Pakeha Intermarriage', in Schwimmer, Erik (ed) *The Maori People in the Nineteen Sixties: A Symposium*, Auckland, 1968.

Harris, Aroha, 'Current Narratives of Maori and Integration in the 1950s and 60s', *Journal c New Zealand Studies*, NS 6–7, 2007–2008.

———, 'Dancing with the State: Maori Creative Energy and Policies of Integration, 1945–1967' PhD thesis, University of Auckland, 2007.

———, *Hīkoi: Forty Years of Māori Protest*, Wellington, 2004.

———, 'Maori Land Title Improvement Since 1945: Communal Ownership and Economic Use' *New Zealand Journal of History*, 31(1), 1997.

———, 'Maori and "the Maori Affairs"', in Dalley, Bronwyn and Tennant, Margaret (eds) *Past Judgement: Social Policy in New Zealand History*, Dunedin, 2004.

Harrison, Noel, *Graham Latimer: A Biography*, Wellington, 2002.

Harvey, Layne, 'Judge's Corner: The Duties of Trustees', *Te Pouwhenua*, 29, June 2005, available online http://www.justice.govt.nz/Maorilandcourt/pdf/Te%20Pouwhenua%2029.pdf [accessed June 2008].

———, 'Judge's Corner: Proposals to Reform the Māori Land Court', *Te Pouwhenua*, 16, April 2003 available online: http://justice.org.nz/maorilandcourt/pdf/Te%20Pouwhenua16.pdf [accessed June 2008].

Hayward, Janine, 'The Treaty of Waitangi, Maori and the Evolving Crown', *Political Science*, 49(2), Jan 1998.

Hayward, Margaret, *Diary of the Kirk Years*, Wellington, 1981.

Hazlehurst, Kayleen M, 'Maori Self-Government 1945–1981: The New Zealand Maori Council and its Antecedents', *British Review of New Zealand Studies*, no 1, July 1988.

———, *Political Expression and Ethnicity: Statecraft and Mobilisation in the Maori World*, Westport, CT, 1993.

———, *Racial Conflict and Resolution in New Zealand: The Haka Party Incident and its Aftermath, 1979–1980*, Canberra, 1988.

Head, Lyndsay, 'The Pursuit of Modernity in Maori Society: The Conceptual Bases of Citizenship in the Early Colonial Period', in Sharp, Andrew and McHugh, Paul (eds), *Histories, Power and Loss: Uses of the Past – A New Zealand Commentary*, Wellington, 2001.

Heal, Andrew, 'The Third Way', *Metro*, Oct 1998.

Henare, Denese, 'The *Ka Awatea* Report: Reflections on its Process and Vision', in Wilson, Margaret A and Yeatman, Anna (eds), *Justice and Identity: Antipodean Practices*, Wellington, 1995.

Herzog, Christine, 'Toward a Sustainable Relationship: Pakeha and Tangata Whenua in Adult and Community Education', in Benseman, John, Findsen, Brian and Scott, Miriama (eds), *The Fourth Sector: Adult and Community Education in Aotearoa/New Zealand*, Palmerston North, 1996.

Hickford, Mark, Review of *State Authority, Indigenous Autonomy*, in *English Historical Review*, vol CXXI, issue 491, April 2006.

Hill, Richard S, *Anti-Treatyism and Anti-Scholarship: An Analysis of Anti-Treatyist Writings*, Treaty of Waitangi Research Unit, Wellington, 2002.

———, 'Autonomy and Authority: Rangatiratanga and the Crown in Twentieth Century New Zealand: An Overview', Wellington, 2000 (Report for Crown Forestry Rental Trust).

———, *The Colonial Frontier Tamed: New Zealand Policing in Transition, 1867–1886*, Wellington, 1989.

———, *The Iron Hand in the Velvet Glove: The Modernisation of Policing in New Zealand, 1886–1917*, Palmerston North, 1995.

———, 'Maori police personnel and the *rangatiratanga* discourse', in Godfrey, Barry S and Dunstall, Graeme (eds), *Crime and Empire 1840–1940: Criminal Justice in Local and Global Context*, Cullompton, 2005.

———, *Policing the Colonial Frontier: The Theory and Practice of Coercive Social and Racial Control in New Zealand, 1767–1867*, Wellington, 1986.

———, *Settlements of Major Maori Claims in the 1940s: A Preliminary Historical Investigation*, Wellington, Department of Justice, 1989.

———, '"Social Revolution on a Small Scale": Official Maori Committees of the 1950s', Paper Presented to the New Zealand Historical Association Conference, 24–27 Nov 2005, http://www.victoria.ac.nz/stout-centre/research-units/towru/MaoriCommitteesJan06.pdf

———, *State Authority, Indigenous Autonomy: Crown–Maori Relations in New Zealand/Aotearoa 1900–1950*, Wellington, 2004.

Hill, Richard S and Bönisch-Brednich, Brigitte, 'Fitting Aotearoa into New Zealand: Politico-Cultural Change in a Modern Bicultural Nation', in Berg, Manfred and Schaefer, Bernd (eds), *Historical Justice in International Perspective: How Societies Are Trying to Right the Wrongs of the Past*, Washington, DC, 2009.

Hohepa, Patrick, *A Maori Community in Northland*, Wellington, 1970.

———, 'Maori and Pakeha: The One-People Myth', in King, Michael (ed), *Tihe Mauri Ora: Aspects of Maoritanga*, Wellington, 1978.

Howe, K R, *Race Relations: Australia and New Zealand: A Comparative Survey 1770's–1970's*, Wellington, 1977.

Hunn, Jack K, *Not Only Affairs of State*, Palmerston North, 1982.

Hutt, Marten, *Te Iwi Maori me te Inu Wipro: He Tuhituhinga Hitori/Maori and Alcohol: A History*, Wellington, 1999.

Jackson, Michael D, 'Literacy, Communication and Social Change: A Study of the Meaning and Effect of Literacy in Early Nineteenth Century Society', in Kawharu, I Hugh (ed), *Conflict and Compromise: Essays on the Maori Since Colonisation*, Wellington, 1975 (2003 ed).

Jackson, S, 'Te Karanga o te Iwi: Devolution – The Death of a People', *Metro*, January 1988.

James, Colin (ed), *Building the Constitution*, Wellington, 2000.

Jamison, Tom and Te Ahukaramu Charles Royal, 'Royal, Te Rangiataahua Kiniwe 1896–1965', *Dictionary of New Zealand Biography*, updated 22 June 2007, http://www.dnzb.govt.nz/

Jarvis, Huw, 'Maori liberation versus the Treaty process', *Revolution*, May–July 2004.

Jeffries, Bill, 'Kirk's Prime-ministership 1972–1974', in Clark, Margaret (ed), *Three Labour Leaders: Nordmeyer, Kirk, Rowling*, Palmerston North, 2001.

Johnson, Miranda, '"The Land of the Wrong White Crowd": Anti-Racist Organizations and Pakeha Identity Politics in the 1970s', *New Zealand Journal of History*, 39(2), 2005.

Karetu, Timoti, 'Māori Language Rights in New Zealand', in Skutnabb-Kangas, Tove and Phillipson, Robert (eds), *Linguistic Human Rights: Overcoming Linguistic Discrimination*, Berlin/New York, 1994.

Kawharu, I Hugh, 'Introduction', in Brookes, R H and Kawharu, I H (eds), *Administration* *New Zealand's Multi-racial Society*, Wellington, 1967.

———, 'Introduction', in Kawharu, I Hugh (ed), *Conflict and Compromise: Essays on the Maori Sin Colonisation*, Wellington, 1975 (2003 ed).

———, 'Urban Immigrants and *Tangata Whenua*', in Schwimmer, Erik (ed) *The Maori People in t Nineteen-Sixties: A Symposium*, Auckland, 1968.

Keenan, Danny, 'Bound to the Land: Māori Retention and Assertion of Land and Identity', in Pawso Eric and Brooking, Tom (eds), *Environmental Histories of New Zealand*, Melbourne, 2002.

———, 'The Treaty is Always Speaking? Government Reporting on Maori Aspirations and Trea Meanings', in Dalley, Bronwyn and Tennant, Margaret (eds), *Past Judgement: Social Policy New Zealand History*, Dunedin, 2004.

Kelsey, Jane, 'Legal Imperialism and the Colonization of Aotearoa', in Spoonley, Paul, Macpherso Cluny, Pearson, David and Sedgwick, Charles (eds), *Tauiwi: Racism and Ethnicity in New Zealan* Palmerston North, 1984.

———, 'Māori, Te Tiriti, and Globalisation: The Invisible Hand of the Colonial State', in Belgrav Michael, Kawharu, Merata and Williams, David (eds), *Waitangi Revisited: Perspectives on the Treaty Waitangi*, Auckland, 2005.

———, *The New Zealand Experiment: A World Model for Structural Adjustment?*, Auckland, 1997 (ori ed 1995).

———, *A Question Of Honour? Labour and the Treaty, 1984–1989*, Wellington, 1990.

———, *Reclaiming the Future: New Zealand and the Global Economy*, Wellington, 1999.

———, *Rolling Back the State: Privatisation of Power in Aotearoa/New Zealand*, Wellington, 1993.

Kenworthy, L M, Martindale, T B and Sadaraka, S M, *Some Aspects of the Hunn Report: A Measure Progress*, Wellington, 1968.

Kernot, B, *People of the Four Winds*, Wellington, 1972.

Kersey, Harry, 'Opening a Discourse on Race Relations in New Zealand: "The Fern and the Tiki Revisited', *Journal of New Zealand Studies*, Oct 2002.

Kidman, Fiona, *At the End of Darwin Road: A Memoir*, Auckland, 2008.

King, Michael, *Being Pakeha Now*, Auckland, 1999.

———, 'Between Two Worlds', in Oliver, W H and Williams, B S (eds), *The Oxford History New Zealand*, Wellington, 1981.

———, *Maori: A Photographic and Social History*, Auckland, 1983.

———, *Nga Iwi o te Motu: One Thousand Years of Maori History*, Auckland, 1997.

———, *The Penguin History of New Zealand*, Auckland, 2003.

———, *Te Puea: A Biography*, Auckland, 1977.

———, *Whina: A Biography of Whina Cooper*, Auckland, 1983.

Labrum, Bronwyn, '"Bringing families up to scratch": The Distinctive Workings of Maori Stat Welfare, 1944–1970', *New Zealand Journal of History*, 36(1), October 2002.

———, 'Developing "The Essentials of Good Citizenship and Responsibilities" in Maori Wome Family Life, Social Change, and the State in New Zealand, 1944–70', *Journal of Family Histor* 29(4), October 2004.

Ladley, Andrew, 'The Treaty and Democratic Government', *Policy Quarterly*, 1(1), 2005.

Laidlaw, Chris, *Rights of Passage*, Auckland, 1999.

Lange, Raeburn, *To Promote Maori Well-Being: Tribal Committees and Executives under the Maori Social an Economic Advancement Act, 1945–1962*, Wellington, Treaty of Waitangi Research Unit, 2006.

Legat, Nicola, 'Warrior Woman', *North & South*, April 2000.

Levine, Hal and Henare, Manuka, 'Mana Maori Motuhake: Maori Self-Determination', *Pacif Viewpoint*, 35(2), 1994.

Levine, Stephen, *The New Zealand Political System: Politics in a Small Society*, Sydney, 1979.

Logan, Mary, *Nordy: Arnold Nordmeyer: A Political Biography*, Wellington, 2008.

ove, R Ngatata, 'Policies of Frustration: The Growth of Maori Politics: The Ratana/Labour Era', PhD thesis, Victoria University of Wellington, 1977.

overidge, Donald M, *Maori Land Councils and Maori Land Boards: A Historical Overview, 1900 to 1952*, Wellington, Waitangi Tribunal Rangahaua Whanui Series, 1996.

laaka, Roger and Fleras, Augie, *The Politics of Indigeneity: Challenging the State in Canada and Aotearoa New Zealand*, Dunedin, 2005.

lagallenes, Catherine J Iorns, 'International Human Rights and their Impact on Domestic Law on Indigenous Peoples' Rights in Australia, Canada, and New Zealand', in Havemann, Paul (ed), *Indigenous Peoples' Rights in Australia, Canada, and New Zealand*, Auckland, 1999.

lahuta, Robert, 'The Maori King Movement Today', in King, Michael (ed), *Tihe Mauri Ora: Aspects of Maoritanga*, Wellington, 1978.

———, 'Tainui, Kingitanga and Raupatu', in Wilson, Margaret A and Yeatman, Anna (eds), *Justice and Identity: Antipodean Practices*, Wellington, 1995.

langan, J A (ed), *Making Imperial Mentalities: Socialisation and British Imperialism*, Manchester, 1990.

laori Land Court, 'Shane Gibbons – A New Direction', *Te Pouwhenua*, 8, Nov 2001, available online: http://www.justice.govt.nz/Maorilandcourt/pdf/tepouwhenua8.pdf [accessed June 2008].

larr, Cathy, *Crown Policy Towards Major Crown/Iwi Claim Agreements in the 1940s and 1950s*, Wellington, Treaty of Waitangi Policy Unit, 1990.

lay, Helen, *Politics in the Playground: The World of Early Childhood in Post War New Zealand*, Wellington, 2001.

lcCan, David, *Whatiwhatihoe: The Waikato Raupatu Claim*, Wellington, 2001.

lcCarthy, Claire, 'New models of sustainability', *New Zealand Education Review*, 14 July 2000.

lcCarthy, Maarie, '"He Hinaki Tukutuku: The Baited Trap": Whare Wananga: Tensions and Contradictions in Relation to the State', in Benseman, John, Findsen, Brian and Scott, Miriama, *The Fourth Sector: Adult and Community Education in Aotearoa/New Zealand*, Palmerston North, 1996.

lcClure, Margaret, *A Civilised Community: A History of Social Security in New Zealand 1898–1998*, Auckland, 1998.

lcCreary, J R, 'Population Growth and Urbanisation', in Schwimmer, Erik (ed), *The Maori People in the Nineteen-Sixties: A Symposium*, Auckland, 1968.

lcDonald, K C, *Our Country's Story: An Illustrated History of New Zealand*, Christchurch, 1963.

lcEwen, J M, 'Urbanisation and the Multi-racial Society', in Brookes, R H and Kawharu, I H (eds), *Administration in New Zealand's Multi-racial Society*, Wellington, 1967.

lcHugh, Paul, 'Aboriginal Identity and Relations in North America and Australasia', in Coates, Ken S and McHugh, P G, *Living Relationships, Kōkiri Ngatāhi: The Treaty of Waitangi in the New Millennium*, Wellington, 1998.

———, 'Constitutional Myths and the Treaty of Waitangi', *New Zealand Law Journal*, September 1991.

———, 'Law, History and the Treaty of Waitangi', *New Zealand Journal of History*, 31(1), April 1997.

———, 'Living with Rights Aboriginally: Constitutionalism and Māori in the 1990s', in Belgrave, Michael, Kawharu, Merata and Williams, David (eds), *Waitangi Revisited: Perspectives on the Treaty of Waitangi*, Auckland, 2005.

———, *The Maori Magna Carta: New Zealand Law and the Treaty of Waitangi*, Auckland, 1991.

———, '"Treaty Principles": Constitutional Relations Inside a Conservative Jurisprudence', *Victoria University Law Review*, 39(1), 2008

lcKinnon, Malcolm, *Treasury: The New Zealand Treasury, 1840–2000*, Auckland, 2003.

lcLeay, Elizabeth, 'Representation and the Maori: Institutional Persistence and Shifting Justifications', paper presented at Annual Conference, Australasian and Political Studies Association, 2–4 October 2002.

———, 'Roles, Rules and Leadership', in Clark, Margaret (ed), *Three Labour Leaders: Nordmeyer, Kirk, Rowling*, Palmerston North, 2001.

McLeay, Elizabeth, (ed), *New Zealand Politics and Social Patterns: Selected Works by Robert Chapman*, Wellington, 1999

McLoughlin, David, 'John Tamihere: New Zealander of the Year', *North & South*, January 1998.

———, 'Muriwhenua Muddle', *North & South*, June 1997.

McRae, Jane, 'Participation: Native Committees (1883) and Papatupu Block Committees (1900) in Te Tokerau', MA thesis, University of Auckland, 1981.

McRobie, Alan, 'The Politics of Volatility, 1972–1991', in Rice, Geoffrey W (ed), *The Oxford History of New Zealand*, Auckland, 1992 (2nd ed).

Mead, Sidney Moko, 'Options for Self-Determination: Tino Rangatiratanga', in *Landmarks, Bridges and Visions: Aspects of Maori Culture*, Wellington, 1997.

———, 'A Pathway to the Future: He Ara Ki Te Ao Marama', in *Landmarks, Bridges and Visions: Aspects of Maori Culture*, Wellington, 1997.

———, 'The Rebirth of a Dream', in *Landmarks, Bridges and Visions: Aspects of Maori Culture*, Wellington, 1997.

———, 'The Significance of Being Ngati Awa', in *Landmarks, Bridges and Visions: Aspects of Maori Culture*, Wellington, 1997.

Meek, R L, *Maori Problems Today: A Short Survey*, Wellington, 1944.

Meha, Raina, 'Te Rōpū o te Ora: Women's Health League 1937–', in Else, Anne (ed), *Women Together: A History of Women's Organisations in New Zealand: Ngā Rōpū Wāhine o te Motu*, Wellington, 1993.

Mein Smith, Philippa, *A Concise History of New Zealand*, Melbourne, 2005.

Melbourne, Hineani, *Maori Sovereignty: The Maori Perspective*, Auckland, 1995.

Meredith, Paul, 'Hybridity in the Third Space: Rethinking Bi-cultural Politics in Aotearoa New Zealand', *He Pukenga Korero*, 4(2), 1999.

———, 'Revisioning New Zealandness: A Framework for Discussion', Te Matahauariki Research Institute, http://lianz.waikato.ac.nz/PAPERS/paul/NZ.pdf [accessed June 2008].

Metge, Joan, 'Alternative Policy Patterns in Multi-racial Societies', in Brookes, R H and Kawharu, I H (eds), *Administration in New Zealand's Multi-racial Society*, Wellington, 1967.

———, 'Kia Tupato! Anthropologist at Work', *Oceania*, 69(1), Sept 1998.

———, *The Maoris of New Zealand: Rautahi* (rev ed), London, 1976.

———, 'Myths for New Zealand', in Bell, Adrian (ed), *One Nation, Two Partners, Many Peoples*, Porirua, 1996.

———, *New Growth from Old: The Whanau in the Modern World*, Wellington, 1995.

———, *A New Maori Migration: Rural and Urban Relations in Northern New Zealand*, London and Melbourne, 1964.

Mikaere, Ani, 'Are We All New Zealanders Now? A Māori Response to the Pākehā Quest for Indigeneity', *Red & Green*, 4, 2004.

Minogue, Kenneth R, *Waitangi: Morality and Reality*, Wellington, 1998.

Mitchell, Hilary Ann and Mitchell, Maui John, *Foreshore and Seabed Issues: a Te Tau Ihu Perspective on Assertions and Denials of Rangatiratanga*, Treaty of Waitangi Research Unit, Wellington, 2006.

Mitchell, Robin, *The Treaty and the Act: The Treaty of Waitangi, 1840 and the Treaty of Waitangi Act, 1975*, Christchurch, 1990.

Mitchell, Tom, '"Legal Gentlemen Appointed by the Federal Government": the Canadian State, the Citizens' Committee of 1000, and Winnipeg's Seditious Conspiracy Trials of 1919–1920', *Labour/Le Travail*, issue 53, Spring 2004, http://www.historycooperative.org/journals/llt/53/mitchell.html.

Morris, Paul, 'Community Beyond Tradition', in Heelas, Paul, Lash, Scott and Morris, Paul (eds), *Detraditionalization: Critical Reflections on Authority and Identity*, Oxford, 1996.

Mulgan, Richard, *Maori, Pakeha and Democracy*, Auckland, 1989.

New Zealand History online, 'The First Waitangi Day', Ministry for Culture and Heritage, http://www.nzhistory.net.nz/politics/treaty/waitangi-day/the-first-waitangi-day, updated 25 Sept 2007 ew Zealand History online, 'History of the Maori language – Te Wiki o Te Reo Maori', Ministry for Culture and Heritage, http://www.nzhistory.net.nz/culture/maori-language-week/history-of-the-maori-language, updated 10 July 2007.

Nga Reo: Syd Jackson – The Life and Times of a Fully-Fledged Activist', Tawera Productions, Television New Zealand, 2003.

ightingale, Richard Beresford, 'Maori at Work: the Shaping of a Maori Workforce within the New Zealand State 1935–1975', PhD thesis, Massey University, 2007.

olan, Melanie (ed), *Revolution: The 1913 Great Strike in New Zealand*, Christchurch, 2005.

orthcroft, Claire, 'The Process of Establishing a Bicultural Organisation in Aotearoa New Zealand', essay for Master of New Zealand Studies, Victoria University of Wellington, 2003.

ffice of Treaty Settlements, *Crown Proposals for the Settlement of Treaty of Waitangi Claims: Summary*, Wellington, nd.

——, *Healing the past, building a future: a guide to Treaty of Waitangi claims and negotiations with the Crown*, Wellington, 2002.

liver, W H, *Claims to the Waitangi Tribunal*, Wellington, 1991.

'Malley, Vincent, *Agents of Autonomy: Maori Committees in the Nineteenth Century*, Wellington, 1997 (rev ed, 1998).

range, Claudia J, 'An Exercise in Maori Autonomy: The Rise and Demise of the Maori War Effort Organisation', *New Zealand Journal of History*, 21(1), April 1987.

——, 'Fraser and the Maori', in Clark, Margaret (ed), *Peter Fraser: Master Politician*, Palmerston North, 1998.

——, *An Illustrated History of the Treaty of Waitangi*, Wellington, 2004.

——, 'A Kind of Equality: Labour and the Maori People, 1935–1949', MA thesis, University of Auckland, 1977.

——, 'The Price of Citizenship? The Maori War Effort', in Crawford, John (ed), *Kia Kaha: New Zealand in the Second World War*, Melbourne, 2000 (2002 ed).

——, *The Treaty of Waitangi*, Wellington, 1987.

'Regan, Hana, *Ko Tahu Ko Au, Kāi Tahu Tribal Identity*, Christchurch, 2001.

——, 'Legal identity of Ngāi Tahu Whānui: Ko te Ture Hou o Ngāi Tahu Whānui', *Te Karaka: The Ngāi Tahu Magazine*, 1996.

'Regan, Tipene, 'Old Myths and New Politics: Some Contemporary Uses of Traditional History', *New Zealand Journal of History*, 26(1), Apr 1992.

——, 'Readying the Canoe on the Beach', in Ihimaera, Witi (ed), *Vision Aotearoa: Kaupapa New Zealand*, Wellington, 1994.

age, Dorothy, *The National Council of Women: A Centennial History*, Auckland, 1996.

almer, Matthew S R, *The Treaty of Waitangi in New Zealand's Law and Constitution*, Wellington, 2008.

arker, Wiremu, 'The Substance that Remains', in Wards, Ian (ed), *Thirteen Facets: Essays to Celebrate the Silver Jubilee of Queen Elizabeth the Second 1952–1977*, Wellington, 1978.

atete, Anthony, *Devolution in the 1980s and the Quest for Rangatiratanga: a Maori Perspective*, Wellington, Treaty of Waitangi Research Unit, 2008.

atterson, Brad and Patterson, Kathryn (eds), *New Zealand*, Oxford, 1998.

earce, G L, *The Story of the Maori People*, Auckland, 1968.

earson, David, *A Dream Deferred: The Origins of Ethnic Conflict in New Zealand*, Wellington, 1990.

——, *The Politics of Ethnicity in Settler Societies: States of Unease*, Basingstoke, 2001.

erry, Paul and Webster, Alan, *New Zealand Politics at the Turn of the Millennium: Attitudes and Values About Politics and Government*, Auckland, 1999.

oata-Smith, E S Te Ahu, 'The Changing Contours of Maori Identity and the Treaty Settlement Process', in Hayward, Janine and Wheen, Nicola R, *The Waitangi Tribunal: Te Roopu Whakamana i te Tiriti o Waitangi*, Wellington, 2004.

Poata-Smith, E S Te Ahu, 'He Pokeke Uenuku I Tu Ai: The Evolution of Contemporary Mao Protest', in Spoonley, Paul, Pearson, David and Macpherson, Cluny (eds), *Nga Patai: Racism ar Ethnic Relations in Aotearoa/New Zealand*, Palmerston North, 1996.

Pocock, J G A, 'The Treaty Between Histories', in Sharp, Andrew and McHugh, Paul (eds), *Histori Power and Loss: Uses of the Past – A New Zealand Commentary*, Wellington, 2001.

Pool, Ian, *Te Iwi Maori: A New Zealand Population, Past, Present and Projected*, Auckland, 1991.

Pool, Ian, Dharmalingam, Arunachalam and Sceats, Janet, *The New Zealand Family from 1840: Demographic History*, Auckland, 2007.

Poulsen, M F and Johnston, R J, 'Patterns of Maori Migration', in Johnston, R J (ed), *Urbanisation New Zealand: Geographical Essays*, Wellington, 1973.

Price, Richard T, *Assessing Modern Treaty Settlements: New Zealand's 1992 Treaty of Waitangi (Fisheri Claims) Settlement and its Aftermath*, Christchurch, 1996.

———, 'New Zealand's Interim Treaty Settlements and Arrangements – Building Blocks of Certainty Presentation to the Forum on Treaty Negotiation, 'Speaking Truth to Power', 3 March 20C (revised 26 April 2000), British Columbia Treaty Commission and Law Commission of Canada

Quaintance, Lauren, 'Georgina te Heuheu', *North & South*, Nov 1998.

———, 'Fishing Furore: Customary Rights Or Deep Sea Plunder?', *North & South*, March 1998.

Ralston, Bill, 'Godzone: the Maori kingmaker. Stubbing with Tau', *Metro*, June 1999.

Rangihau, John, 'Being Maori', in King, Michael (ed), *Te Ao Hurihuri: The World Moves O* Wellington, 1975.

Rapson, Bevan, 'Extremist Makeover', *Metro*, Nov 2004.

Rata, Elizabeth, 'Ethnicity, Class and the Capitulation of the Left', *Red & Green*, 4, 2004.

———, 'Global Capitalism and the Revival of Ethnic Traditionalism in New Zealand: The Emergenc of Tribal-Capitalism', PhD thesis, University of Auckland, 1996.

———, 'An Overview of Neotribal Capitalism', *Ethnologies comparées*, no 6, 2003.

———, *A Political Economy of Neotribal Capitalism*, Lanham, MD, 1999.

Reed, A H, *The Four Corners of New Zealand*, Wellington and Auckland, 1954.

Reedy, T M, 'Foreword', in Butterworth, G V and Young, H R, *Maori Affairs/Nga Take Maori*, Wellingto 1990.

Rei, Tania, 'Te Rōpū Wāhine Māori Toko i te Ora: Māori Women's Welfare League 1951–', in Els Anne (ed), *Women Together: A History of Women's Organisations in New Zealand: Ngā Rōpū Wāhine te Motu*, Wellington, 1993.

Rei, Tania and Hamon, Carra, 'Te Kōhanga Reo 1982–', in Else, Anne (ed), *Women Together: A Histo of Women's Organisations in New Zealand: Ngā Rōpū Wāhine o te Motu*, Wellington, 1993.

Rei, Tania, McDonald, Geraldine and Te Awakōtuku, Ngāhuia, 'Ngā Rōpū Wāhine Māori: Māo Women's Organisations', in Else, Anne (ed), *Women Together: A History of Women's Organisations i New Zealand: Ngā Rōpū Wāhine o te Motu*, Wellington, 1993.

Renwick, William, 'Decolonising Ourselves From Within', *British Review of New Zealand Studies*, no 1993.

———, *The Treaty Now*, Wellington, 1990.

Rice, Geoffrey W (ed), *The Oxford History of New Zealand*, Auckland, 1992 (2nd ed).

Richards, Trevor, *Dancing on our Bones: New Zealand, South Africa, Rugby and Racism*, Wellington, 199

Rigby, Barry, 'The Waitangi Tribunal: The Significance of a 25 Year Experiment', paper presented a 25th Anniversary of the Waitangi Tribunal conference, Wellington, 10–11 Oct 2000.

Ritchie, James E, 'The Grass Roots of Maori Politics', in Pocock, J G A (ed), *The Maori in New Zealan Politics*, Auckland and Hamilton, 1965.

———, *The Making of a Maori: A Case Study of a Changing Community*, Wellington, 1963.

———, *Tribal Development in a Fourth World Context: The Maori Case*, Honolulu, 1990.

Rodney, Walter, *How Europe Underdeveloped Africa*, Washington DC, 1981 (rev ed).

Ross, Ruth, 'Te Tiriti o Waitangi: Texts and Translations', *New Zealand Journal of History*, 6(2), 1972.

ound, David, *Truth or Treaty? Commonsense Questions about the Treaty of Waitangi*, Christchurch, 1998.

oyal, Te Ahukaramu Charles, 'There are Adventures to be had', *Te Pouhere Korero Journal*, 1(1), Mar 1999.

oyal Commission on the Courts, *Report of Royal Commission on the Courts*, Wellington, 1978.

oyal Commission on Social Policy, *The April Report, Volume II, Future Directions*, Wellington, 1988.

———, *The April Report, Volume III, Part One, Future Directions*, Wellington, 1988.

umbles, Wayne, 'Treaty of Waitangi Settlement Process: New Relationship or New Mask?', in Ratcliffe, Greg and Turcotte, Gerry (eds), *Compr(om)ising Post/colonialism(s): Challenging Narratives and Practices*, Sydney, 2001.

almond, John W, *Jurisprudence*, 7th ed, London, 1924.

chmitt, Carl, *Political Theology: Four Chapters on the Concept of Sovereignty*, Cambridge Mass, 1985 (1st ed, Berlin, 1922).

chwimmer, Erik, 'The Maori and the Government', in Schwimmer, Erik (ed), *The Maori People in the Nineteen-Sixties: A Symposium*, Auckland, 1968.

———, 'The Aspirations of the Contemporary Maori', in Schwimmer, Erik (ed), *The Maori People in the Nineteen-Sixties: A Symposium*, Auckland, 1968.

cott, Dick, *Ask that Mountain: The Story of Parihaka*, Auckland, 1975.

———, *The Parihaka Story*, Auckland, 1954.

———, *A Radical Writer's Life*, Auckland, 2004.

cott, Stuart C, *Travesty After Travesty*, Christchurch, 1996.

———, *The Travesty of Waitangi: Towards Anarchy*, Dunedin, 1995.

harp, Andrew, *Justice and the Māori: Māori Claims in New Zealand Political Argument in the 1980s*, Auckland, 1990.

———, 'Traditional Authority and the Legitimation Crisis of "Urban Tribes": The Waipareira Case', *Ethnologies comparées*, no 6, 2003.

———, 'The Treaty in the Real Life of the Constitution', in Belgrave, Michael, Kawharu, Merata and Williams, David (eds), *Waitangi Revisited: Perspectives on the Treaty of Waitangi*, Auckland, 2005.

———, 'The Treaty of Waitangi: Reasoning and Social Justice in New Zealand?', in Spoonley, Paul, Pearson, David and Macpherson, Cluny (eds), *Nga Take: Ethnic Relations and Racism in Aotearoa/New Zealand*, Palmerston North, 1991.

haull, Richard, 'Foreword', in Freire, Paulo, *Pedagogy of the Oppressed*, New York, 1986 ed (Ramos trans).

chrader, Ben, 'The *Other* Story: Changing Perceptions of State Housing', *New Zealand Journal of History*, Oct 2006.

imon, Judith and Smith, Linda Tuhiwai (eds), *A Civilising Mission? Perceptions and Recommendations of the New Zealand Native Schools System*, Auckland, 2001.

inclair, Karen, *Prophetic Histories: The People of the Māramatanga*, Wellington, 2002.

inclair, Keith, *Walter Nash*, Auckland, 1976.

———, 'Why are Race Relations in New Zealand Better than in South Africa, South Australia or South Dakota?', in Webb, Stephen and Collette, John (eds), *New Zealand Society: Contemporary Perspectives*, Sydney, 1973.

issons, Jeff, 'The post-assimilationist thought of Sir Apirana Ngata: towards a genealogy of New Zealand biculturalism', *New Zealand Journal of History*, 34(1), 2000.

mith, Anthony D, *Myths and Memories of the Nation*, Oxford, 1999.

mith, Linda Tuhiwai, *Decolonizing Methodologies: Research and Indigenous Peoples*, Dunedin, 1999.

olomon, Maui, 'The Context for Maori (II)', in Quentin-Baxter, Alison (ed), *Recognising the Rights of Indigenous Peoples*, Wellington, 1998.

orrenson, MPK, 'Giving Better Effect to the Treaty: Some Thoughts for 1990', *New Zealand Journal of History*, 24(2), 1990.

orrenson, MPK, *Maori and European since 1870: A Study in Adaptation and Adjustment*, Auckland, 1967.

Statistics New Zealand, 'Demographic Trends 2007', table 1.02, http://www.stats.govt.nz/tables historical-population.htm

Stenning, Philip, 'Maori, Crime and Criminal Justice: over-representation or under-representation Paper presented at the Stout Research Centre, 18 March 2005.

Stewart-Harawira, Margaret, 'Maori, Who Owns the Definition? The Politics of Cultural Identity *Te Pua*, 2(1–2), 1993.

Stirling, Eruera (as told to Anne Salmond), *Eruera: The Teachings of a Maori Elder*, Wellington, 1980.

Stokes, Evelyn (ed), *Nga Tumanako: National Conference of Maori Committees*, Hamilton, 1978.

Stokes, Evelyn, Milroy, J Wharehuia and Melbourne, Hirini, *Te Urewera: Nga Iwi te Whenua te Ngahe People, Land and Forests of Te Urewera*, Hamilton, 1986.

Sullivan, Ann, 'The Treaty of Waitangi and Social Well-being: Justice, Representation, and Participation in Belgrave, Michael, Kawharu, Merata and Williams, David (eds), *Waitangi Revisited: Perspectives o the Treaty of Waitangi*, Auckland, 2005.

Sutch, W B, *The Maori Contribution: Yesterday, Today and Tomorrow*, Wellington, 1964.

Szaszy, Mira, *Te Timatanga a Tātau Tātau: Early Stories from Founding Members of the Māori Women's Welfa League, Te Rōpū Wāhine Māori Toko i te Ora*, Wellington, 1993.

Tauroa, Hiwi, *Healing the Breach: One Maori's Perspective on the Treaty of Waitangi*, Auckland, 1989.

———, *Race Against Time*, Wellington, 1982.

Tautari, Marie, 'Māori Women's Institutes 1929–1950s', in Else, Anne (ed), *Women Together: A History Women's Organisations in New Zealand: Ngā Rōpū Wāhine o te Motu*, Wellington, 1993.

Te Awekotuku, Ngahuia, 'He Wahine, he Whenua, e Ngaro ai te Tangata: By Women, by Land, Me are Lost', in *Mana Wahine Maori: Selected Writings on Maori Women's Art, Culture and Politics*, Aucklan 1991.

Te Puni Kokiri, *Discussion Paper on the Review of the Māori Community Development Act 1962*, Wellingto 1999.

———, *Nga Kai o te Moana: Kaupapa Tiakina*, Wellington, 1993.

Temm, Paul, *The Waitangi Tribunal: The Conscience of the Nation*, Auckland, 1990.

Tennant, Margaret, Review of *State Authority, Indigenous Autonomy*, in *Australian Historical Studies*, vo 37, no 127, April 2006.

Thompson, Richard, *Race Relations in New Zealand: A Review of the Literature*, Christchurch, 1963.

Turner, Kaye, 'The *April Report* of the Royal Commission on Social Policy: Treaty Partnership as Framework for a Politics of Difference?', in Wilson, Margaret A and Yeatman, Anna (eds), *Justice an Identity: Antipodean Practices*, Wellington, 1995.

van Meijl, Toon, 'Community development among the New Zealand Maori: The Tainui case', in Blun Peter and Warren, Michael D (eds), *Indigenous Organizations and Development*, London, 1996.

———, 'Maori Hierarchy Transformed: The Secularization of Tainui Patterns of Leadership', *Histor and Anthropology*, vol 7, 1994.

———, 'Maori Tribal Organisations in New Zealand History: From Neglect to Recognition, and th Implications for the Assimilation Policy', *Ethnologies comparées*, no 6, Printemps, 2003.

———, 'The Politics of Ethnography in New Zealand', in Jaarsma, Sjoerd R and Rohatynskyj, Marta (eds), *Ethnographic Artifacts: Challenges to a Reflexive Anthropology*, Honolulu, 2000.

———, 'Refining Ideology in Time: Maori Crossroads between a Timeless Past and a New Future *Anthropos*, 90, 1995.

Vasil, Raj K, *Biculturalism: Reconciling Aotearoa with New Zealand*, Wellington, 2000 (rev ed).

Veracini, Lorenzo, *Negotiating A Bicultural Past: An Historiographical 'Revolution' in 1980s Aotearoa/Ne Zealand*, Wellington, Treaty of Waitangi Research Unit, 2001.

Walker, Ranginui J, 'The Genesis of Direct Negotiation, the Fiscal Envelope, and their Impact o Tribal land Claim Settlements', *He Pukenga Korero*, 3(1), 1997.

'alker, Ranginui J, *He Tipua: The Life and Times of Sir Āpirana Ngata*, Auckland, 2001.

——, 'Hostages of History', *Metro*, Feb 2001.

——, *Ka Whawhai Tonu Matou: Struggle Without End*, Auckland, 1990 (rev ed 2004).

——, 'Keep the fires burning', in Amoamo, Jacqueline (ed), *Nga Tau Tohetohe: Years of Anger*, Auckland, 1987.

——, 'Mana Motuhake', in Amoamo, Jacqueline (ed), *Nga Tau Tohetohe: Years of Anger*, Auckland, 1987.

——, 'A Maori Parliament', in Amoamo, Jacqueline (ed), *Nga Tau Tohetohe: Years of Anger*, Auckland, 1987.

——, 'Maori People Since 1950', in Rice, Geoffrey W (ed), *The Oxford History of New Zealand*, Auckland, 1992 (2nd ed).

——, 'Maori sovereignty', in Amoamo, Jacqueline (ed), *Nga Tau Tohetohe: Years of Anger*, Auckland, 1987.

——, 'The Politics of Voluntary Association: A Maori Welfare Committee in a City Suburb', in Kawharu, I Hugh (ed), *Conflict and Compromise: Essays on the Maori Since Colonisation*, Auckland, 1975 (2003 ed).

——, 'Shaky foundations', in Amoamo, Jacqueline (ed), *Nga Tau Tohetohe: Years of Anger*, Auckland, 1987.

——, 'State of the Nation', *New Zealand Listener*, 21 Feb 2004.

——, 'The Treaty of Waitangi in the Postcolonial Era', in Belgrave, Michael, Kawharu, Merata and Williams, David (eds), *Waitangi Revisited: Perspectives on the Treaty of Waitangi*, Auckland, 2005.

/alsh, Allen C, *More and More Maoris*, Christchurch, 1971.

'ard, Alan, *A Show of Justice: Racial 'Amalgamation' in Nineteenth Century New Zealand*, Auckland, 1995 (rev ed).

——, *An Unsettled History: Treaty Claims in New Zealand Today*, Wellington, 1999.

'eaver, John C, *The Great Land Rush and the Making of the Modern World, 1650–1900*, Montreal, 2003.

/ebster, Peter, *Rua and the Maori Millennium*, Wellington, 1979.

/ebster, Steven, *Patrons of Maori Culture: Power, Theory and Ideology in the Maori Renaissance*, Dunedin, 1998.

/ellington School of Medicine and Health Sciences, *Access to Cancer Services for Māori: A Report prepared for the Ministry of Health*, Wellington, Feb 2005.

/illiams, Charlotte, *More Power to Do the Work: Maori and the Health System in the Twentieth Century*, Wellington, Treaty of Waitangi Research Unit, 2007.

——, *The Too-Hard Basket: Maori and Criminal Justice Since 1980*, Wellington, 2001.

/illiams, David V, 'Unique Treaty-Based Relationships Remain Elusive', in Belgrave, Michael, Kawharu, Merata and Williams, David (eds), *Waitangi Revisited: Perspectives on the Treaty of Waitangi*, Auckland, 2005.

/illiams, John A, *Politics of the New Zealand Maori: Protest and Co-operation, 1891–1909*, Auckland, 1969.

/illiams, Melissa, 'Panguru, Te Puutu, and "The Maori Affairs": The Punguru Community Development Project, 1954–1957', MA thesis, Auckland, 2005.

Villiams, Raymond, *Culture and Materialism: Selected Essays*, London/New York, 1980 (2005 ed).

Viniata, Maharaia, *The Changing Role of the Leader in Maori Society: A Study in Social Change and Race Relations*, Auckland, 1967.

Vinks, Robin, *These New Zealanders*, Christchurch, 1954.

Vood, Anthony, 'Holyoake and the Holyoake Years', in Clark, Margaret (ed), *Sir Keith Holyoake: Towards a Political Biography*, Palmerston North, 1997.

Wood, F L W, *This New Zealand*, Hamilton, 1946.

Woods, Megan C, 'Integrating the Nation: Gendering Maori Urbanisation and Integration, 194 1969', PhD thesis, Christchurch, 2002.

Yates, Bronwyn, 'Striving for Tino Rangatiratanga', in Benseman, John, Findsen, Brian and Sco Miriama (eds), *The Fourth Sector: Adult and Community Education in Aotearoa/New Zealar* Palmerston North, 1996.

Yensen, Helen, 'Some afterthoughts', in Yensen, Helen, Hague, Kevin and McCreanor, Tim, *Honouri the Treaty: An Introduction for Pakeha to the Treaty of Waitangi*, Auckland, 1989.

Young, David, *Values as Law: The History and Efficacy of the Resource Management Act*, Wellington, 200

———, *Woven by Water: Histories from the Whanganui River*, Wellington, 1998.

Index

accountability 47, 78, 141–2, 194, 204, 207, 216, 237, 241–4, 251, 269–70
ACORD. *See* Auckland Committee on Racism and Discrimination
activists 79–80, 84, 135, 145–7, 150–55, 161, 171–8, 180, 263–4, 276, 282; concern with rangatiratanga 146–7, 173–5, 263; pakeha–Maori solidarity 151–2, 159–60, 171–2, 176, 178; pakeha–Maori tensions 176–7; tensions with elders 154–5; Treaty focus 153–4, 164, 170, 178, 182, 263–4; women 79, 152. *See also* protest
adaptation (Maori): cultural adaptation 3–4, 17, 80–82, 87; to modernity 2, 17, 44, 78, 79, 80–82, 94, 101, 137–9; to pakeha culture 17, 34, 44, 99; of rangatiratanga 7; to urban life 2, 34, 38–42, 44, 45, 66–9, 73–4, 77, 84, 85, 87–8, 120–23, 138–9, 140, 157; to western values 37, 38, 54, 122–3, 137, 280
adjustment. *See* adaptation
adoption (Maori practices) 34, 105
Adoption Act (1955) 34; (1962) 105
affirmative action 93, 98
agency 3, 5, 9, 130, 197, 212, 222, 289
Akarana Maori Association 40, 66
alcohol consumption (Maori) 16, 20, 26, 35, 36, 38, 53, 115, 121, 124, 131
alienation 99, 124, 130, 146, 151, 152, 155. *See also* land
All Blacks. *See* rugby
amalgamation 1, 94. *See also* assimilation; integration
Anglican Church 65, 240, 257–8
anthropology 26, 29, 44–5, 53, 68, 81–2, 99, 118, 123, 136, 139, 219, 293
Aorangi Block 48
Aotearoa: reconciling with New Zealand 104, 151, 247, 292, 293
apartheid 60–61, 86, 152
apology (by Crown for historical injustices) 201, 221, 239–40, 259, 266, 286, 320
apprenticeships 39
appropriation (of Maori energies by the state and vice versa) 3, 29, 59, 67, 77, 101–2, 109, 118, 127, 128, 141, 194, 197, 216, 231, 233, 235, 241, 243, 245, 267, 275, 290
assimilation: agents of 15, 28–9, 43–5, 48, 52, 54, 116, 122, 135, 160, 244; as equality 44, 127; forces of 54, 83–4, 87–8; Hunn report on 93–4, 98–9; inevitability of 15, 43–5; international conventions and 105–6; Maori support for 44; meaning of 43–4, 93–4; paradigm 18, 26, 35, 54, 59, 90, 155, 178, 184; policy/agenda of ix–xi, 1–4, 12, 22, 28–9, 34, 50, 56, 58, 63, 66, 74, 83, 98–9, 104, 105, 109, 111, 114, 123, 127, 146, 152, 160, 162, 189, 213, 232, 234–5, 248, 257, 270, 272, 275, 277; policy abandoned 129, 164, 165–6, 225, 290; post-assimilation 167, 249; reality of 40, 41, 43–5, 181; resistance to 2, 9, 83–4, 102, 119, 138, 151–2, 181, 290; and welfare 115. *See also* integration; urbanisation
associations. *See* voluntary associations
Auckland 25, 39, 40, 41, 52–3, 65, 66, 67–8, 74, 83, 100, 114, 133, 138, 144, 210, 230, 279
Auckland Committee on Racism and Discrimination (ACORD) 151–2, 178
Auckland District Maori Council 121, 161, 179
Auckland University 84, 176–7
Aupouri Trust Board 49
Australian aborigines 257
Ausubel, David 86
autonomy: collective versus individual 29, 40; continuum 276; 'degrees' of 272; in education 197, 270–71; impossibility of political 45, 54; Maori 84, 153, 155, 173–5, 179–81, 202–6, 211, 214, 216, 237, 238, 240, 244–5, 259,

autonomy *continued*
260, 263, 265, 270–79, 285, 288, 290–92; of Maori wardens 126–8, 130; of Maori Women's Welfare League 75–9; models of Maori 183–4, 276, 282–3; of national Maori organisation 56, 244–5, 269; of New Zealand Maori Council 112, 115, 117, 118, 143, 160, 161, 269; of official Maori committees 13, 16, 28, 45, 51, 54, 70, 112, 115, 117, 119–20, 130, 136, 138, 139–40, 141, 143; in Treaty 228; of tribes 203–4, 211, 214, 238, 242–3, 276–9; of trust boards 47, 49–50. *See also* devolution; rangatiratanga; self-determination; self-reliance; Tu Tangata
Awatere, Donna 173, 175, 276

Ball, D G 101
Barclay, Barry 164
Bastion Point 25, 171–2, 176, 222, 263
Bay of Plenty 68
Beaglehole, Ernest 86
Beattie, David 170
Belich, James 222, 295
Bennett, Frederick (Bishop) 19
Bennett, Manu 37
biculturalism 2, 101, 118, 132, 151, 162, 166, 172, 173, 175, 197, 209, 217, 219, 222, 230, 240, 276, 287, 289; Crown policy of ix, 224–5, 248, 274; Maori policy of 179, 180; term 151. *See also* interculturalism; monoculturalism; multiculturalism
Biggs, Bruce 98
bilingualism 166, 222
Bill of Rights 119
Bledisloe, Lord 165
blending (racial/national) 23, 51, 87, 92, 93, 95
Board of Native/Maori Affairs 14, 25, 30, 33, 60, 103, 160. *See also* Department of Maori Affairs
Bolger, Jim 249, 253, 264
Booth, John 44, 96–7, 105, 118
Buck, Peter (Te Rangihiroa) 19, 22–3, 168
bureaucratisation (of tribes) 205–6
business (Maori) 183, 204–5, 212, 216, 231

Canada 5, 256
capitalism 102, 104, 150, 202, 207, 208, 215, 216–9, 233, 267–8, 277, 280–82; activist opposition to 153, 176, 177. *See also* class
CARE. *See* Citizens Association for Racial Equality
Carroll, James 167
Carroll, Turi 116, 118, 153, 156
Catholics 65, 252
Christchurch 39

Citizens' All Black Tour Association 61
Citizens Association for Racial Equality (CARE) 151–2, 178
citizenship 4–6, 7, 127; responsibilities of 17, 29, 94, 121, 190, 199; rights 29, 94, 121, 154, 165 276
Clark, Helen 284
class: analysis/discourse 44, 96, 151–2, 168, 172, 176, 216–9, 280–82; concern of Labour Party 12, 21, 60; position of Maori 12, 21, 144, 150, 152, 168, 216–9, 280–81; solidarities 177
Closing the Gaps 273
clubs. *See* cultural clubs; sports clubs; voluntary associations; youth clubs
Coalcorp 227, 253, 263
coercion 6, 9, 20, 53, 83, 123, 125, 131, 157–8, 171–2, 189, 195, 263, 289
collective: Maori ethos 2–3, 42, 66, 95, 133, 137, 139, 143, 156, 182, 193, 195, 206, 208, 216; organisation 39, 156, 208, 211. *See also* identity; individual; land
colonialism x–xi, 4–5, 95, 149, 170, 188, 209, 215 217, 268, 276
colonisation xi, 1, 3, 11, 12, 99, 147, 176, 204, 21[illegible] 254, 264, 282, 286–7
colour bar 36–7
committees 156, 174; unofficial 19; women's 69–71 *For official committees, see* Maori committees; tribal committees; welfare committees
communication channels (Crown–Maori) 55–6, 58, 71, 142
communists 96
community: development 191–4, 196, 199, 205–[illegible] 269; empowerment 192, 195, 200, 204–6, 211 term 193
community centres 26, 52, 53, 65, 67
compensation: for historical injustices 47–9, 119, 245, 247, 249, 267; for Treaty breaches 165, 201, 221, 223, 237, 239–40; use of 48–50; as vehicle of assimilation 48. *See also* fiscal envelope; settlements
Confederation of the Sovereign and Independent United Tribes of Aotearoa 283
confiscation. *See* land
conflict resolution 211
consciousness raising 151–2, 176, 221–2
Conservation Act 209
consolidation schemes (land) 31–2, 103, 163
constitutional arrangements/reform 183–4, 225, 231, 247, 250, 258, 262–5, 276, 279, 282–84, 286, 292–3. *See also* Maori parliament
contracting-out. *See* state services
Controller of Maori Welfare/Social and Economi[illegible] Advancement 18, 27

onversion (land policy) 32–3, 158, 159, 163
ooper, Whina 72, 74, 75–7, 167–8
orbett, Ernest 29, 48, 55–6, 71–7 *passim*
ouch, Ben 188
ountry Women's Institutes 70
ourt of Appeal 223–6
ourts 105, 131, 183, 195, 212; use of by Maori 260–61. *See also* Court of Appeal; crime and disorder; justice system; Maori Courts; Maori Land Court
rime and disorder (Maori) 22, 34, 35–6, 37, 63, 124, 127, 130–4, 140, 146, 160, 266, 281
rown: concept of 4–7; as party to the Treaty of Waitangi x
rown–Congress Joint Working Party 257
rown Forestry Rental Trust 227
rown Forests Assets Act 227
ullen, Michael 284
ultural clubs 66–7
ultural studies 289
ulture (Maori): adaptive and dynamic 1ff *passim*, 139; Crown obligations towards 187; incorporation into state practices 211, 264, 265; loss of 3, 40, 93, 99, 102, 137, 168, 265; preservation/survival/promotion of 17, 39, 42, 43–5, 69, 80–81, 84, 87, 94, 115, 118, 137, 143, 145, 163, 168, 177, 181, 182, 191, 211, 283, 292; transformation of 80–82, 115, 120, 139. *See also* adaptation; identity; Maoridom; Maoritanga; tikanga Maori; tradition

Declaration of Independence 278
decolonisation 24, 106, 225, 264
democracy 104, 109, 114, 120, 239, 272, 281, 289, 293. *See also* social democracy
Department of Corrections 265
Department of Maori Affairs (DMA) 1, 2, 14–21, 117, 122; assisting adaptation to cities 42; disestablishment of 142, 154, 232, 234, 248; paternalism of 13, 26–7, 87, 88, 142, 154, 163, 190, 231–2; reform of 163–4, 189–90, 193, 210, 234–5; Tu Tangata role 192–2. *See also* Manatu Maori; Maori Affairs; Maori Welfare Organisation; Te Puni Kokiri; Welfare Division
Department of Native Affairs 1, 13
deregulation 202, 210, 214–5, 229
detribalisation: expectation of 2, 15, 39, 43, 109, 156, 200, 217; policy aim 64, 99, 111–2, 200, 213; as reality 18, 79, 90, 100, 120, 150, 156, 180, 181, 208, 217, 231, 233. *See also* assimilation; tribes
development (Maori): bottom-up 192, 194, 273; community-based 68, 191–4, 269; economic 49, 202–3; land 11, 30, 50, 102–3, 155–8, 163; post-welfare 251, 252; role of trust boards 49–50; self- 210, 249; term 145, 251; tribal 166, 200–201, 203–4, 207, 211, 266. *See also* socio-economic advance
devolution 193, 199, 201, 202–10, 214–20, 226, 229–37, 239, 240, 241–2, 244, 245, 251, 272, 276, 283, 286, 288, 289, 291; to iwi 201, 204, 206–7, 214, 233–7, 241–2, 244, 248, 249, 252, 276
difference: cultural/legal/socio-economic 43–4, 94, 106, 114, 292; toleration of 59, 283
discrimination. *See* affirmative action; racial discrimination
disorder. *See* crime and disorder
district councils (Maori) 55–6, 57, 62, 112. *See also* New Zealand Maori Council; representation
district Maori councils (under NZMC) 112, 114, 116, 118, 126–7, 142, 145
District Maori Councils of Tribal Executives 109
District Maori Land Committees 33, 103
district officers (DMA) 13, 18, 26, 27, 38
divide and rule 15, 215, 241, 256, 268, 280–81
domination. *See* hegemony; oppression; power
Dominion Council of Tribal Executives 57, 107, 113
Douglas, Roger 207. *See also* Rogernomics
drinking. *See* alcohol consumption
Durie, E T J 187, 272
Durie, Mason 168, 198

economy: dominant political 14, 54, 63, 81, 95, 140, 150, 181, 237, 273; global 218, 280; money 81–2; national 22, 34; pakeha 41, 181; post-war 38, 40, 68, 150, western 63; World War Two 14. *See also* free-market economics
education 116, 149, 196–7; as activist concern 152–3, 176; importance of 41, 101, 104; and leadership 41, 52, 72–3, 80, 84, 144, 161; Maori educational autonomy 270–71; policies 52–3, 101; tribes and 213; trust boards and 49, 50. *See also* consciousness raising; schools
egalitarianism 43–4, 114
equality: as assimilation 44, 105, 127, 248; legal 90, 92, 127, 134, 212, 289; Maori desire for 80–81, 91, 172; of opportunity 61, 92, 94; policy of 12, 15, 17, 18, 21–2, 43–4, 58, 80, 114, 127, 134, 150, 165, 169, 202, 282; socio-economic 91–3, 94, 105, 114, 282; as Treaty of Waitangi principle 237
elders. *See* leadership
elections 72, 73; general (1943) 12; (1946) 18; (1949) 2, 22; (1957) 57, 58, 59–60, 62; (1960) 58, 62, 89, 91, 92 107; (1975) 169, 178; (1978)

elections *continued*
188; (1981) 180; (1984) 184, 199, 201; (1990) 239, 247–8; (1996) 266; (1999) 273, 287; (2005) 287; and Maori organisations 20, 42, 47, 109, 144; and New Zealand Maori Council system 113–4, 115–6, 118, 120, 138, 140; Northern Maori by-election 113, 180; and welfare committees 121. *See also* representation
Electoral Act 163
Electoral Amendment Act 163, 177
electoral reform 163, 177, 266
employment (Maori) 11–2, 40, 53, 81–2, 100, 101, 202, 204–6, 281
empowerment x, 33, 145, 192, 195–6, 200, 203–6, 211, 212, 214, 219, 250
ethnocentrism 9, 22, 36, 85, 98, 124, 137, 151, 178, 265, 272, 328. *See also* racial discrimination
European Economic Community 149
evolutionism 41, 43, 44, 93–4, 103

family (Maori) 34. *See also* whanau
Fanon, Frantz x
farming/farms 19, 29–33, 49, 89, 103, 156, 246. *See also* land
Federation of Labour 160
Federation of Maori Authorities 212, 227
Federation of Maori Students 153
Fern and the Tiki 86
Firth, Raymond 44–5
fiscal envelope 261–2, 265, 268, 271
fisheries 187–8, 220, 227–8, 230, 237, 254–5, 261, 269–70
Fisheries Amendment Act 228
Fleras, Augie 123, 136
Forbes, George 164
foreshore and seabed 282, 284–5, 287
forestry 227
fragmentation of land title. *See* land
Frame, Alex 237
Fraser, Peter 16, 18, 22, 30, 59, 74, 88
free-market economics 202, 206–9, 214–5, 229, 231, 248, 250, 273
Freire, Paulo x
funding: and autonomy 243–5, 269–71; of Maori Congress 245; of Maori educational institutions 197, 270–71; of Maori/tribal committees 16, 141–2; of Maori Women's Welfare League 76, 77, 78–9; 'negative' welfare 203; of New Zealand Maori Council 116, 141–2, 160, 245, 269; settlement 255; of tribal authorities 237, 243–4; of trust boards 50–51; Tu Tangata 194

gangs 146, 160, 177
gender 69–70, 122, 151. *See also* women
Gisborne 39
government. *See* Labour government; National government; welfare state
Graham, Douglas 253–4, 259–60, 262, 266
Gramsci, Antonio 6
grievances 25, 154, 155, 164, 165; historical 59, 60, 213, 221, 224, 239–40, 253–4, 263, 265, 292; timeline for resolution of 273, 287. *See also* compensation; land; settlements; Waitang Tribunal

Halt All Racist Tours (HART) 152, 178
Hamilton 39, 100
Hanan, J R 92–3, 95, 98, 108–9, 115, 117–8, 127, 156, 158, 160
hapu: development 166, 204; and devolution 205, 214, 219, 234; and rangatiratanga 7, 277, 290; rights/authority of 201; transformation of 212–3; and Treaty negotiations 201, 255–6, 259, 267
Harawira, Titewhai 168
HART. *See* Halt All Racist Tours
Hawke, Joe 171
He Taua 176–7
He Tirohanga Rangapu/Partnership Perspectives 233–6, 238
health 73, 101, 115, 121, 198–9, 209–10, 252, 265, 274, 281. *See also* Women's Health League
hegemony 6, 9, 45, 54, 88, 102, 122, 135, 137, 13 172, 178, 199, 217, 225–6, 244, 265, 282, 290
Henare, Tau 285
Hercus, Anne 211
hikoi 178, 183, 184, 284, 286. *See also* activists; protest
Hirangi hui 262–4, 268
historiography x, 4–9, 222, 289–90, 297, 324
Hoani Waititi Marae 40, 198
Hobson, William 86
Hohepa, Pat 81–2, 99, 161, 164, 179
Holland, Sidney 25
Holyoake, Keith 63, 89, 170
home (Maori concept of) 39
honorary welfare officers. *See* welfare officers
Hopuhopu 283
Horomia, Parekura 203
hospitality (Maori) 34, 39
hostels 39
housing: and assimilation 83, 87–8, 100–101; group housing for Maori 42; loans 65, 68; Maori Women's Welfare League advocacy for 74, 119; poor quality of Maori 26, 35, 74; state 25, 38–9,

133–4, 136, 250; tribal investment in 49. *See also* pepper-potting
ui Taumata/Maori Economic Development Conference 202–4, 208, 214, 218, 237
ui Whakaoranga 198
ui Whakatauira 191, 192, 196, 205
unn, Jack Kent 58, 90, 111, 153, 232. *See also* Hunn report
unn report 79, 89–100, 102–5, 107, 124, 135, 137, 142–3, 155–6, 157, 189, 200, 235; criticism of 97–9; implementation 95, 97, 102, 105, 127; positive reaction to 97–8; recommendations 92–3, 113, 158, 160; release of 91, 92; terms of reference 90–91
untly 263
uria Tribal Committee 26, 27

entity: bicultural 240, 274; collective 26, 40, 120, 143, 182, 259; hybrid 328; individual 21, 29, 40; Maori 23, 39, 40, 69, 78, 79, 80–82, 83, 111–2, 114, 120, 123, 144, 149–51, 155, 163, 168, 169, 177, 181, 200, 206, 212–4, 267, 279, 293; national 240, 274, 293; pakeha 149, 151, 239; politics of 216–9, 281, 289; self-identification 177–8; tribal 23, 39, 40, 81, 83, 111–2, 114, 120, 138, 150, 213, 233, 267, 274, 278–9. *See also* culture; Maoridom; Maoritanga; tribal identity
himaera, Witi 165
LO Convention 107 on International Indigenous and Tribal Populations 105–6, 257
LO Convention 169 on Indigenous and Tribal Peoples in Independent Countries 238, 257
ncorporations (Maori land) 33, 156
ndigenous peoples 280; movements x–xi, 9, 51, 170, 172, 176, 178, 275–6; oppression of 9, 176, 180, 217; rights 105–7, 150, 238, 250, 257, 276, 324
ndividual versus collective 29, 40, 41, 66, 95, 104, 193, 208, 220, 317
ndividualism 35, 36, 40, 66, 95, 99, 137, 202, 207, 214
nequality. *See* socio-economic disparities
ntegration: contrasted with assimilation 44, 93–4, 98–9; Crown policy of 1, 2, 3, 17, 35, 81, 87–8, 92, 101, 102, 127, 146, 162, 169, 189–90, 203, 213, 232, 257, 275, 283; Hunn report on 93–5; international conventions and 105; Maori support for 44; and Maori Welfare Act 114, 115, 116, 123, 136–7; policy abandoned 166, 178; process of 69, 90. *See also* assimilation
interculturalism 289
intermarriage ix, 41, 53, 86, 143, 170, 236; as agent of assimilation 2, 23, 40, 45, 86, 94, 283; as threat to racial purity 37
International Convention on the Elimination of All Forms of Racial Discrimination 106
International Covenant on Civil and Political Rights 191
International Labour Organisation (ILO) 105–6, 238, 257
investment societies 68
iwi. *See* tribes
Iwi Transition Agency (ITA) 236–7, 241, 245, 249, 251

Jackson, Moana 212, 240, 264
Jackson, Syd 150, 153, 168
Jones, Michael Rotohiko 75
Jones, Pei Te Hurinui 156, 161
justice system 126, 130–5, 195, 291; parallel 212, 236. *See also* courts; Maori courts

Ka Awatea 249–52
Kaitaia airport 263
kaitiakitanga 156, 182, 189, 274
Kauhoura Block 48
kaumatua. *See* leadership
kawanatanga xi, 173, 187, 222, 237–8, 290–91
Kawharu, Hugh 99, 102
Kelsey, Jane 226, 317
King, Michael 164, 295
Kingitanga 21, 61, 75, 178, 179, 184, 244, 268
kinship 65, 68, 211; transformed 81–2
Kirikiri, Rauru 234
Kirk, Norman 162, 163, 166, 168
kohanga reo 196–7, 206, 285
kokiri 193; centres 196, 206
Korean War 40
kotahitanga 13, 57, 61, 112, 178, 180, 193, 244–5, 261, 263, 268, 280, 283–4, 287
kura kaupapa Maori 197, 206, 271

Labour government: first (1935–49) 1, 12, 18, 21–2, 44, 80, 91; second (1957–60) 57–62; third (1972–75) 162–7, 168–9, 179; fourth (1984–90) 184–5, 199, 201–2, 204–10, 217–8, 219, 221, 237, 238, 239, 251, 252, 266, 286; fifth (1999–2008) 239, 273, 282, 284
labour movement 59, 80, 150, 152, 159–60
Labour Party 59–63; Maori policy 59–62, 91, 115, 167, 169, 184, 200, 205–6; Maori support for 57, 62–3, 64, 115, 169, 180, 200, 266; welfare policies 12, 21–2, 23, 80
labour shortages 12, 100

land: alienation of 56, 153, 154, 155–9, 167–8, 171–2, 182, 258–9, 290; collective ownership 29, 103–4, 156, 158, 258; compensation for loss of 48–50, 119, 245–6, 259, 267; confiscations 33, 119, 245, 258–9; Crown purchase 32–3, 104, 223, 227, 158–9, 227; development 11, 30, 50, 102–3, 155–8, 163; fragmented title/ownership 31–3, 89, 103–5, 155–8, 163; Maori connection to 30, 32, 156, 168, 181–2, 189, 223, 258–9; Maori-owned 11 19, 25, 29–34, 103, 154, 155–8, 163, 258, 260, 267; policy 190; productivity of 30–32, 103, 158; protest over 167–9, 171–2, 263; rights 33, 154, 155; surplus 48; symbol of struggle 182, 183; and Treaty settlements 227, 258–9, 260; vested lands 29–31

Lange, David 207, 235, 239, 272

language. *See* Maori language

Latimer, Graham 161, 168, 224

law 6, 291; by-laws 16, 20, 51; legal discrimination 43–4, 106, 157, 158

leadership (Maori) 1, 3, 13, 19, 23, 27, 52–3, 57, 58, 60, 108–9, 121, 167–8, 206, 208, 214; bourgeois 216–9, 267, 281; conflicts 140–41, 256; conservative leaders 64, 108, 118, 142, 144, 154–5, 156, 167–8, 172, 177, 213, 225; criticism of government 141–2, 167–8; and education 41, 52, 72–3, 80, 84, 144, 161, 172; of Maori wardens 20; national 111–2; new (post-war/urban) leaders 19, 23, 41, 52–3, 67, 80–84, 130, 131, 138–9, 140–41, 143–4, 160–61, 172, 190, 200; radical 142, 171, 193; rangatira 175–6; new tribal leaders 216–9; traditional tribal leaders/elders/kaumatua 41, 52, 67, 68, 80, 108, 111, 131, 138, 140, 154–5, 160, 168, 171, 172, 176, 190, 211, 283; women 72–3. *See also* Maori MPs

left-wing attitudes 43–4, 86, 90, 95, 96, 150, 167, 217, 247, 281, 282, 289

Listener 38, 99, 175

Love, Ngatata 203

Love, Ralph 116

Mabo case 257

MACCESS 205–6, 244

MacIntyre, Duncan 160, 189

Mahuta, Robert 143, 166, 183

mainstreaming (of Maori services) 143, 183, 234, 236, 248–53

MANA Enterprise Development Programme 204–5, 244

Mana Motuhake 178–81, 184, 201, 209

Manatu Maori/Ministry of Maori Affairs 236–7, 249, 251

Mangere 167

Manukau Report 187

Manukau Urban Maori Authority 231

Maori: birth rate 11; brown-skinned pakeha 2, 43, 95; communal way of life 34; concept of 'Maori' 6; 'the Maori problem' 35, 91–3; party to the Treaty of Waitangi x, 285; as pre-modern/tribal people 83; special assistanc for 42, 58, 88, 93, 97, 117, 127, 135; and the state ix, 3–4. *See also* culture; identity; social organisation; tribes

Maori Advisory Council (Labour Party) 59

'Maori Affairs, the' (DMA) 19, 26, 50, 75, 78, 210, 232

Maori Affairs Act 32, 34, 65

Maori Affairs Amendment Act 158–60, 162, 189

Maori Affairs Restructuring Act 236

Maori associations 112. *See* Maori committees

Maori Battalion 27, 80

Maori committees (post 1962) 112, 113–4, 138–45, 155, 156, 174, 176, 192; autonomy of 112, 115, 117, 119–20, 130, 136, 138, 139–40, 143; conflicts on 140–41; as Crown agents 122, 135, 136, 137–8, 140, 147; decline 195; funding 141–2; and Maori wardens 124, 126–30; national conference 141, 189; pakeha involvement in 144; work of 118–22, 140. *See also* committees; Maori courts; New Zealand Maori Council; tribal committees

Maori Community Development Act 145–6, 147, 199, 268

Maori Congress. *See* National Maori Congress

Maori councils (1900) 16, 50, 142, 241, 272

Maori Councils Act 16

Maori courts 130–34, 143, 212; criticism of 134–6

Maori Ecumenical Council of Churches 184

Maori Education Commission 270–71

Maori Education Foundation 101

Maori Executive Committees 112, 113–4. *See also* Maori committees; New Zealand Maori Council

Maori Fisheries Commission 228, 254

Maori Graduates' Association 137, 153

Maori Health Committee 101

Maori Land Advisory Committees 163

Maori Land Boards 29, 31, 163

Maori Land Court 30–32, 34, 49, 104, 105, 114, 159, 163, 187, 212, 258

Maori language 212; promotion/protection of 74, 81, 118, 137, 152–3, 163, 174, 196–7, 212; pronunciation 118; in schools 42

Maori Language Act 209

Maori MPs 1, 13, 25, 32, 57–8, 59–62, 108–9, 111, 114, 116, 153, 156, 159, 160, 162, 285, 288

Maori Organisation on Human Rights (MOOHR) 152, 165, 174–5
Maori parliament 144, 160, 174, 179, 183, 236, 258, 276, 283–4
Maori Party 284–5, 286, 287–8, 292
Maori People's Liberation Movement of Aotearoa 175
Maori Policy Committee (Labour Party) 59–63; criticism of Labour 61–62
Maori Purposes Act 30–31
Maori Purposes Bill 61
Maori Purposes Fund Board 22
Maori Renaissance ix, 3, 112, 129, 135–6, 145, 149ff, 160, 163, 164, 166, 174, 182, 191, 194, 197, 217–8, 247, 258, 265, 282, 286; term 150–51
Maori Reserved Land Amendment Act 267
Maori schools. *See* schools
Maori Social and Economic Advancement Act (MSEAA) 1, 3, 12–5, 18, 20, 21, 26, 54, 57, 69, 70, 75, 80, 88–9, 115, 255; overhaul of MSEAA system 111–7
Maori Social and Economic Advancement Act Amendment Act 109, 113
Maori Synod of the Presbyterian Church 98, 102, 156
Maori tribunals. *See* Maori courts
Maori Trust Boards Act 48, 49, 50
Maori Trustee 29–34 *passim*, 155
Maori War Effort Organisation (MWEO) 1, 12, 13, 14, 18, 69, 70, 80; as embodiment of rangatiratanga 14
Maori wardens: abolition 128; associations (district and national) of 126, 129, 130; appointment of 20, 129; autonomy of 126–8, 130; community-work role 126, 128–30; as Crown agents 122–3, 129–30; policing role 20–1, 38, 53, 54, 121, 123–6, 128, 129–30, 195; powers of 20, 123, 124, 128, 289; as race-based institution 44, 106, 127, 129; under MSEAA 20–21; under MWA 123–8; voluntary position 20, 121, 123–32
Maori Welfare Act (MWA) 113–5, 116, 117, 119, 120–21, 123, 130, 136, 143, 147, 189–90, 200; amended 124; overhaul 145
Maori welfare committees. *See* welfare committees
Maori Welfare Organisation (MWO) 13, 15–21, 25–9, 55, 69–72 *passim*, 75, 77–8; autonomy of 16–7; name 13; overhaul of 111–7. *See also* Department of Maori Affairs; tribal committees; Welfare Division; welfare officers
Maori Women's Health League. *See* Women's Health League
Maori Women's Institutes 69
Maori Women's Welfare League (MWWL) 55, 65, 67, 69–80, 119, 135, 142, 153, 167–8, 177, 178, 198; aims 71–2; autonomy of 75–9; constitution 71, 75; as Crown agent 73–4, 75–9, 122; decline of 78; as embodiment of rangatiratanga 69, 75; establishment of 69–72; as female counterpart to tribal committees 74–5; funding 76, 77, 78–9; influence/ effectiveness of 73, 78, 268; members' opposition to league autonomy 76, 78; membership 72, 78, 79; national organisation 73, 77; pakeha involvement in 72, 74; as quasi-voluntary 75–7, 121; relationship with Department of Maori Affairs 74–5; structure 71–2, 77, 78, 112; and Tu Tangata 196; and western accounting procedures 75; work of 73–4, 75, 77, 78, 79
Maoridom 23; concept of 6; as emergent pan-tribal identity 39, 81, 111–2, 113, 120, 182; expected disappearance of 43, 59, 96; preservation of 41–5, 80–81, 94; versus tribalism 15, 81, 111–2, 114. *See also* culture; identity; Maoritanga
Maoritanga 8, 15, 66, 77, 214, 215, 217; promoting 74, 104; resurgent 112, 193; retaining 43, 67, 78, 79, 84, 96, 137; threats to 21, 84, 95, 102. *See also* culture; tikanga Maori; tradition
marae: and autonomy 27, 145; urban 40, 65, 67–8, 138, 144, 145
Maramatanga 279
marginalisation (Maori) xi, 12, 29, 86, 91, 118, 172, 179, 199, 240, 270, 290
marriage (Maori) 34. *See also* intermarriage
Massey, William 25
Matakite o Aotearoa 169
matua whangai 34, 205
Maungapohatu 172
McDonald, K C 85, 86
McEwan, Jock 131, 143
Mead, Hirini 99, 183–4, 245
Meek, Ron 96
Mein Smith, Philippa 295
Members of Parliament. *See* Maori MPs
Metge, Joan 52, 81, 139
migration (of Maori to towns and cities) ix, 2, 3, 11–2, 21, 35, 78, 85, 87, 89, 90, 93, 100, 156. *See also* urbanisation
Ministerial Advisory Committee on a Maori Perspective 210–11
Ministerial Planning Group 249
Ministry of Maori Development. *See* Te Puni Kokiri
MMP (mixed member proportional representation) 266, 271, 285, 287

modernisation 17, 34, 93–4, 111, 114, 138, 161, 181, 199, 218. *See also* equality; progress; socio-economic advance; urbanisation
monoculturalism 151, 152, 155, 177, 179, 184, 211
moral decline 36, 41
Mother Country 5, 149, 208
Motunui Outfall Report 187–8
Moutoa Gardens 263
Muldoon, Robert 171, 189, 190, 193
multiculturalism 151, 184, 274, 287, 289, 292
Muriwhenua 213, 223
Muriwhenua Fishing Report 228, 230

Nash, Walter 14, 43, 58, 59–61, 62–3, 78, 88, 89–90, 91, 95
National Committee on Maori Education 42
National government: first (1949–57) 2, 23, 25–6, 28–9, 38, 59; second (1960–72) 89, 92, 107–9, 111, 114–5, 117, 145, 158; third (1975–84) 169–70, 171–2, 178, 184, 188, 190; fourth (1990–99) 239, 248–9, 252, 253, 255, 266, 270, 273, 285; fifth (2008–) 284, 288; attitude/policies towards Maori 25–6, 28–9, 38, 89, 114–5, 178; ideology 40, 117, 145
national interest 191, 194, 290; and land 30–31, 103, 157–8, 159, 266
(National) Maori Congress (NMC) 5, 245, 257, 261, 263, 268, 283, 290
national Maori organisation 55–6, 57–8, 107–9, 111, 119, 261, 268–70; Crown opposition to 56, 57–8, 60; Crown support for 55–6, 58, 62, 107–8; women's 70–71. *See also* Maori Women's Welfare League; New Zealand Maori Council
National Party: Maori support for 23, 108–9, 116, 161, 167
National Urban Maori Authority 270
nationalism 151; Maori 112, 245, 247, 293; racial 66
nation-building 151, 273, 293. *See also* one people/one nation
Native Affairs 1, 13–4; term 'Native' 15
Native American 261
Native Land Act 29
Native Schools 197. *See also* schools
negotiations (Crown–Maori): Canadian model for 256; 'direct' 253, 259; of partnership arrangements 282–3, 285, 287, 289; Treaty of Waitangi grievances 229, 248, 253–4, 255–6, 265–8, 275, 285–6
neoliberalism 215–6, 218–9, 230
neotribes. *See* tribes
New Zealand Broadcasting Corporation 118
New Zealand Day 162
New Zealand First 266, 270, 284
New Zealand Listener. *See Listener*
New Zealand Maori Council (NZMC) 111–7, 153, 155, 177, 178, 184, 210, 225, 227; as advocate of Maori interests 119; as agent of assimilation/government 116, 118, 135, 142, 147, 269; autonomy of 112, 115, 117, 118, 143, 160, 161, 269; changing role 160–62; concerns 116, 138, 161; funding 116, 141–2, 160, 245; as hybrid of Maori and European 119; and Maori courts 135–6; National Party connections 116, 161, 213; opposition to land alienation 156–61, 162, 168, 169; reform of 268–9, 272; as representative of all Maoridom 111, 115–6, 142, 161, 256, 269; and racial harmony 115; structure 112, 113–4, 115, 116, 120, 121, 126–7, 140, 142, 144, 145; submissions to government 184, 188–90; Treaty focus 116, 119, 161, 164, 209, 224; and Tu Tangata 195; views on devolution 235; views on Maori parliament 235; and wardens 126–9. *See also* national Maori organisation
New Zealand Maori Council v Attorney-General 223–6
New Zealand Maori Council of Tribal Executives 109, 111
New Zealand Maori Wardens' Association 126
New Zealand Planning Council 185, 187
New Zealand Police: acting against protesters 171–2, 178; and Maori courts 131; and Maori wardens 20, 123–6, 128, 130; recruitment of Maori 37–8, 125–6
Nga Tamatoa 149–50, 152–3, 154, 167, 168, 174–6
Ngai Tahu 48, 49, 166, 229, 258–60, 261, 262, 267, 276, 278
Ngapuhi 277, 280
Ngaruawahia 129, 197
Ngata, Apirana 13, 14, 19, 26, 80–81, 144, 153, 168, 181, 192; explanation of Treaty of Waitangi 173–5
Ngata, Henare 108, 161
Ngataism 80–81, 192
Ngati Awa 245–6
Ngati Maniapoto 278
Ngati Poneke 40, 44, 66, 67
Ngati Raukawa 166, 213, 257–8
Ngati Te Ata 278–9
Ngati Toa 166
Ngati Whatua 25, 171
nomenclature. *See* terminology
Nordmeyer, Arnold 60
Northland 68, 81–2

occupations (of land) 171–2, 263

ffice of Treaty Settlements 229
kahu Bay 25, 28
e people/one nation rhetoric 45, 51, 58, 86, 95, 96, 98, 99, 111, 115, 127, 169, 170–71, 184, 247, 249, 252, 291. *See also* two peoples
nehunga 51–2
potiki 42
pression 152, 176–7, 180, 216–8, 245–6, 281
rakei. *See* Bastion Point
rakei Maori Committee Action Group 171
Regan, Hana 260, 278
Regan, Tipene 150, 166, 269, 276

kaitore. *See* Moutoa Gardens
keha: brown-skinned 2, 43, 95; capitalist class 177; identity 149, 151, 239; paternalism 177; solidarity with Maori activists 151–2, 159–60, 171–2, 176, 178; in Maori committees 41, 53–4, 144; in Maori Women's Welfare League 72, 74
lmer, Geoffrey 239, 253
n-tribal consciousness 66, 120, 162
n-tribal organisation 21, 39–40, 42, 61, 67–8, 69, 84, 101, 108–9, 120, 130, 144, 150, 160, 194, 201, 212, 213–4, 215, 230, 241, 243–5, 279; need for 40, 81, 82, 180–81, 268–70; and rangatiratanga 8, 197, 277; and Treaty claims 254–5. *See also* Maori Women's Welfare League; New Zealand Maori Council
araninihi ki Waitotara 166
arihaka Story 29, 150, 165
artnership: Crown–Maori 77, 101, 132, 165, 179, 198–9, 206, 208–10, 211, 212–3, 215, 217, 222–3, 226, 227, 230, 232–3, 235, 237–40, 242, 243, 244, 247, 251, 252, 257–8, 261, 267, 273, 276, 283, 284–5, 291, 292; illusion of 230; local government–Maori 274, 288; meaning of 166; public–private 251–2; through devolution 229–7, 233–7, 243; as Treaty principle 224–5, 262
aternalism: Department of Maori Affairs 13, 26–7, 87, 88, 142, 154, 163, 190, 231–2; pakeha 177; state 31, 43, 87, 103, 116, 130, 145, 157, 215
eace and good order' 5, 6, 122, 296
earson, Bill 42
earson, David 291
epper-potting 35, 36, 41, 68, 83, 121, 133
eters, Winston 247, 248, 249, 250, 253, 266
iddington, Ralph 44–5, 84
laycentres 39, 65, 73, 196
oata, Tom 159–60
ocock, J G A 285
olicing. *See* coercion; Maori wardens; New Zealand Police

Pomare, Eru 198
population growth (Maori) 11, 21, 63, 85, 93, 298
Post Primary Teachers Association 197
post-colonialism x–xi, 105, 151, 225, 254, 275, 290, 292
power 172, 231, 264, 288; and rangatiratanga 7, 216, 278; sharing 210, 211, 212, 229, 283, 289, 291; state 5–6, 215, 216, 279, 291. *See also* devolution; empowerment; hegemony; rangatiratanga; sovereignty
Prichard–Waetford report 157–8
Princess Te Puea 19, 72
principles (Treaty of Waitangi) 164, 165, 188, 209, 222–9, 233, 237–8, 242, 247, 254; main 224; meaning 225, 229; repealing recognition of 247
Principles for Crown Action on the Treaty of Waitangi 237–40, 241, 284
privatisation 207–8, 210, 223, 227–8, 250, 256–7
productivity (land) 30–33
professionalisation 126, 129, 199
progress 17, 45, 48, 51. *See also* socio-economic advance
protest 118, 147, 167, 172, 180, 263–4; land 155, 159–60, 167–9, 171–2, 177, 263; methods 151, 154–5, 168, 178–9; movements 149–53, 154–5, 174–8; Waitangi Day 154, 162, 172, 176, 178, 263. *See also* activists; resistance
Puao-Te-Ata-Tu/Day Break 210–12, 215
public good 5, 20, 26, 29, 30, 38, 65, 93, 97, 103, 157, 163, 207, 208, 226, 260, 271, 273, 276, 286, 291
Pukekohe 52
Puketapu, Kara 191, 193

Queen Elizabeth 153, 240, 242

race relations 32, 60, 80, 85–8, 92–3, 98, 121, 135–6, 170, 171, 173, 287; best in world 22, 36, 85, 87, 149; harmonious 86, 87, 91, 93, 115, 222, 273, 292; term 297. *See also* racial discrimination
Race Relations Act 106, 143
Race Relations Commissioner 184
race-based institutions 44, 106, 127, 129, 134–5
racial blending. *See* blending
racial discrimination 22, 34, 36–8, 43, 82, 85–8, 106, 124, 127, 132; combating 24, 52, 74, 92, 114, 143, 151–2, 154, 160; institutional racism 151, 210, 248. *See also* stereotypes
radicalism. *See* activists; protest
Raglan 169, 176, 177
rangatiratanga ix, 16, 22; in 1950–60s 3, 82–4, 272; in 1970s 136, 146–7, 149, 199; in 1980s 183, 206, 210–12, 218–9, 226, 231, 235,

rangatiratanga *continued*
236–8, 245, 280; in 1990s 247, 249–50, 253, 260–61, 262–4, 265–6, 280; in 2000s 272–4, 276, 287–8; and class 280–82; constitutional forms 183, 247, 276; Crown-franchised 194, 290; Crown promotion of 209, 237–8, 291; Crown recognition of x, 9, 117, 133, 136, 147, 154, 163, 185, 199, 214, 219, 222, 228, 229, 253, 260–61, 262–3, 265, 267, 272–4, 280, 282, 284, 286, 288, 290–91, 293; illusion of 214–6, 235, 238, 239; and Maori War Effort Organisation 14; meaning and interpretation of xi, 6–8, 68, 173–6, 215, 229, 249–50, 261, 276–82, 287–8, 297; 'middle way' 250, 292; negotiating 286–7, 291; and New Zealand Maori Council 111, 117, 213; non-negotiable 279–80; non-tribal forms 79, 183, 245; not sovereignty 229; and official Maori committees 18, 51, 52, 54, 56, 59, 132, 136, 155; pan-tribal 8, 197, 277; struggle for 9, 84, 146–7, 149, 150–51, 154, 159, 160, 166, 169, 170, 182–3, 213, 219–20, 229, 237, 244, 248, 256, 260–64, 278–9, 285, 287–8, 290, 291; tino rangatiratanga 7, 169, 173, 188, 216, 222, 226, 229, 238, 250, 261, 264, 265, 274–5, 277, 281, 282, 288, 289, 291, 292; in Treaty of Waitangi xi, 29, 60, 188, 275, 278; tribal 228, 255, 269–70, 276–9; and trust boards 49; and urbanisation 18, 22, 24, 68–9, 84, 277; and voluntary associations 68–9; and women 69, 71, 75, 79. *See also* autonomy; self-determination
Rangi Makawe Rangitaura petition 154
Rangihau, John 112, 138, 210
Ranginui Tribal Executive 26
Rata, Matiu 159, 162, 163, 164–7, 168–9, 178–81
Ratana (movement) 14, 21, 57, 59–60, 65, 75, 107, 108, 153, 160, 163, 173, 179, 180, 181, 233, 241, 266, 268, 279, 287
Raukawa Marae 26
Reedy, Tamati 193, 204, 206, 232
Reeves, Paul 209
regional organisation 55–6
relocation 100
renaissance. *See* Maori Renaissance
reparations. *See* compensation; Treaty of Waitangi
representation (Maori) 42, 60, 63, 204, 243, 248, 254, 255–6, 269, 272, 288; disputes over 215, 255–6, 261; district and national 21, 55–8, 60, 107–9; equal 153; and Maori Women's Welfare League 71–2, 73, 79; in negotiating with Crown 166, 255–6, 267; and New Zealand Maori Council 111, 113–4, 115–6, 120, 144, 269; and official committees 14, 17–8, 26, 33, 51, 53, 55, 140–41, 144–5; regional versus tribal 180; and trust boards 47. *See also* elections; Maori MPs; Maori parliament; MMP
resistance 5, 8, 9, 83–4, 102, 139. *See also* activists; assimilation; protest
Resource Management Act 257, 288
respect for authority 53, 67, 125, 130, 131, 134
Returned Services' Association 71
revolution 176, 271
Richardson, Ruth 252
rights: Bill of 119; of citizenship 29, 94, 121, 154, 165, 276; commercial 227; cultural 128, 175, 286; customary 228, 255, 287; equal 166, 172, 175, 289; human 107, 225; indigenous (in international declarations) 8, 105–7, 150, 191, 238, 250, 257, 276, 278–9; land 33, 154, 155, 169, 173, 175; Maori 84, 136, 150, 152, 154, 176, 178, 182, 228, 235, 250; negotiating 285; ownership/property 173–4, 228; of sovereignty xi, 173–176, 239; Treaty 153, 173–6, 228–9, 230, 231, 249–50, 260, 270; tribal 187–8, 201, 227, 241, 260, 278–9; of urban Maori 255; women's 200. *See also* Maori Organisation on Human Rights; rangatiratanga; Treaty of Waitangi
right-wing economic agenda 208, 215–6, 219, 221, 224, 230, 235, 250, 266. *See also* free-market reforms; privatisation
Ritchie, James 68, 97–8, 112–3
rock'n'roll 67
Rodney, Walter x
Rogernomics 207–9, 216, 230, 231, 233, 235, 251, 266, 273, 281
Ropiha, Tipi 15, 38, 56
Rotorua 39, 42, 57, 71, 100, 138, 144
Rowling, Bill 163
Royal Commission on the Courts 134
Royal Commission on Education 96
Royal Commission on Social Policy 230
Royal, Te Rangiataahua (Rangi) 27, 70, 77
Ruatahuna 138
rugby tours (All Blacks–South Africa) 60–61, 86, 152, 153, 171, 180, 188
runanga 180, 182, 213, 219–20, 230, 233, 236, 241–4, 280, 281; abolition of official status 248
Runanga Iwi Bill/Act 241–3, 250; repeal 248, 254, 256, 261, 285
rural–urban drift. *See* migration; urbanisation

Savage, Michael Joseph 164
schools 39, 65; as agents of assimilation 95, 104, 160; Maori 42, 95–6, 104, 128, 160, 196–7; and Maori language and culture 42, 96, 196–7

chwimmer, Eric 57, 84
cott, Dick 29, 96, 150, 165, 314
ealord 254–5, 261
elf-determination 7, 23, 29, 54, 202–4, 218, 232, 249–50, 252, 257, 278–80, 282–3, 288; discourse of 24, 175, 214; government policy for Maori 191, 193–4, 214–5, 242, 290; of indigenous peoples xi, 176, 238, 250, 275, 278–9, 282; and Mana Motuhake 179–81; Maori struggle for 147, 177, 219, 230, 247, 250, 265, 275, 290, 291; and Maori wardens 130; and Maori Women's Welfare League 75, 79; tribal 213
elf-government: of committee system 51, 121, 143, 145; tribal 278–9
elf-reliance: individual versus collective 193; Maori 16, 22, 34, 83, 117, 145, 147, 178, 180, 191–5, 196–7, 203–4, 214, 236, 251; National Party emphasis on 29, 190, 191, 193, 196, 251
eparatism 45, 54, 55, 90, 99, 236, 240, 248, 270, 273; constitutional 229; and Maori courts 134–6; of Maori wardens 126, 127–8
ervices. *See* state services
ettlements (for historical grievances) 48–9, 59, 119, 248, 293; fiscal cap 261–2; and land 223, 227; relativity clause 262; Treaty 9, 221, 223, 228, 253–6, 258–61, 267, 270, 274, 276, 282, 288. *See also* compensation; Waitangi Tribunal
ettler societies x–xi, 86, 105, 170, 275
harpeville massacre 61
harples, Pita 288
ocial Darwinism 44, 94. *See also* evolutionism
ocial democracy 21, 169, 180, 199, 202, 207, 208, 273, 281, 282, 289
ocial justice 230, 254, 281
ocial organisation/structure (Maori) 2, 5, 15, 31, 34, 36, 102, 122–3, 131, 139, 182, 204, 205, 211, 213, 217, 219–20, 232, 277, 324. *See also* hapu; tribes
ocialism 96, 282
ocio-economic advance/development: government policy 12, 13, 17, 21–2, 58, 60, 90–93, 95, 97–98, 107, 114, 191–4, 209, 266; of Maori in 20th century 23; Maori aim 82, 89, 91, 98, 116, 121, 202–4, 231. *See also* development; equality; Hunn report; Maori Social and Economic Advancement Act; Maori Welfare Organisation; welfare
ocio-economic disparities 91, 93, 210, 214, 247, 249, 250, 252–3, 273, 280–81
olidarity: class 168, 176–7; indigenous 153; Maori 133, 136, 180; Maori–pakeha 151–2, 159–60, 171–2, 176, 178. *See also* unity
outh Africa 36, 60–61, 62, 86, 90, 152, 153, 171
sovereignty x, 187; Crown 6, 13, 55, 71, 81, 82, 108, 171, 174–5, 183–4, 188, 194, 215, 222, 226, 227, 228–9, 239, 241, 261, 264, 271–2, 276, 278, 282–3, 286, 289, 290–91; Maori 173–6, 183–4, 215, 216, 222, 233, 264, 272, 275, 276, 278–9; in Treaty of Waitangi xi, 172–6, 222
special measures (to assist Maori). *See* Maori
sports clubs 39, 65
state: concept of 4–6. *See also* welfare state
State Advances Corporation 68
State Authority, Indigenous Autonomy (Richard S Hill) ix, 3, 7, 275, 281
state services: contracting out delivery of 249–53; corporatisation of 207–8; provision of by tribal committees 27–8; provision of by trust boards 49–50. *See also* devolution
State Services Act 237
State Services Commission 189–90, 191, 192
State-Owned Enterprises 207–8, 209, 223–4, 227; Act 223–4
stereotypes (racial) 37, 52–3, 136. *See also* racial discrimination
Stirling, Eruera 154–5
struggle. *See* activists; protest; rangatiratanga; resistance; self-determination
Szaszy, Mira 77, 168

Taiaroa, Archie 290
Tainui 178, 200, 205, 213, 227, 244, 253, 259
Tainui Awhiro 169
Tainui Maori Trust Board 227, 244, 259
Tainui Report 200
Tairawhiti Council 159
Taitokerau 48
Takahue School 263
Tamaki Girls' College 263
Tamihere, John 252
Taneatua railway station 263
tangata whenua: definition ix, 11
tangi 39, 41, 67, 200
Tapsell, Peter 267
Taranaki 29, 48, 259
Taranaki District Health Board 274
Taranaki Report 7–8, 267
Tauranga County Council 27
Tauranga Moana Maori Trust Board 119
Tauroa, Hiwi 225
Tawhiao 168
Tawhiwhirangi, Iritana 196
Te Ahi Kaa 276
Te Ao Hou 83–4
Te Atiawa 116, 166, 188
Te Hapua 167, 168

Te Heu Heu, Hepi 212, 244, 262, 264
Te Hokioi 152, 175
Te Pikinga 279
Te Puni Kokiri 249, 251–2, 262, 263, 264, 268, 273, 290
Te Rangihiroa. *See* Buck, Peter
Te Rata 168
Te Roopu Ote Matakite 168
Te Runanga o Ngai Tahu Act 259
Te Tira Hou Marae 138
Te Turi Whenua Maori Act 190, 258
Te Urupare Rangapu/Partnership Response 236–7
Te Whakaminenga o Kapiti 257
Te Whanau o Waipareira Trust 40, 230, 279
Te Wherowhero, Potatau 259
Temm, Paul 240
terminology: bicultural 151; community 193; development 145, 251; Maori committees 113; Maori terms in English 175; Marae committees 145; native 15; race relations 297; rangatiratanga 173–6, 180, 297; renaissance 150–51; social and economic advancement 114; tribal 111–2, 215; welfare 114, 145, 193
Thompson, Richard 98
tikanga Maori 136–9; and autonomy 265; incorporating into government policy 211, 264, 265; official acceptance of 136. *See also* culture; Maoridom; Maoritanga; tradition
Tira Hou Marae 179
Tirikatene, Eruera 59–60, 62, 82, 114, 115–6
Tirikatene-Sullivan, Whetu 173
tohunga 182, 265; Suppresion Act 265
Town and Country Planning Act 65, 162
trade unions 150, 152, 153, 160, 197
tradition (Maori) 3, 31, 35, 36, 43, 66–68, 137–9, 176, 280; adaptation of 81–2, 139, 280; decline of 41; invention of 216–9
Treaty of Waitangi ix–x, xi, 8, 85, 162, 185, 211, 233, 235, 237, 270, 285; Act 164, 165; activist focus on 153–4, 164, 170, 178, 182, 263–4; anti-Treatyism 248, 253, 288–9; Articles xi, 29, 154, 165, 173–4, 187–8, 222, 231, 238, 250, 260, 262–3, 281, 290–91; constitutional status 225; Crown obligations under 187–8, 224–5, 290; different versions (English and Maori) 173–6, 222; education on 221–2; fraud 170, 176, 181; honouring 164, 167, 170, 172, 181, 183, 222, 225, 237, 239, 242; interpretation and meaning of xi, 187, 222–3, 225–6, 228, 230, 231, 238–9, 288; jurisprudence 260–61; and land 104–5; as living document 225, 240, 287, 293; New Zealand Maori Council focus on 116, 119, 161, 164, 209, 224; Ngata's explanation of 173–5; ratification of 153–4; relevance 62; reparation 165, 180, 201, 209, 221, 223, 237, 239–40, 24 255, 259, 261–2, 267, 286; sesquicentennial commemoration 240, 291; signing 172, 201; spirit of 119, 161, 164, 165, 209; as symbolic xi, 170, 182, 225, 240, 286; 'Treaty fatigue' 273, 286; violations of 162, 165, 170, 175, 201 209, 221, 228, 241, 254, 259, 262, 265, 284. *See also* negotiations; partnership; principles; settlements
Treaty of Waitangi Amendment Act 209
Treaty of Waitangi Fisheries Commission 255
Treaty of Waitangi Policy Unit (TOWPU) 229, 237, 253–4, 259, 262
Treaty of Waitangi (State Enterprise) Act 227
tribal committees 1, 3, 12–21, 25–9, 35, 42, 51–4 78, 88, 102, 121, 241; ability to pass by-laws 16; autonomy of 13, 16, 28, 45, 51, 54, 70; as Crown functionaries 27–9, 51, 52; and European administrative procedures 13, 19; ignorance of 53; inactive/languishing 51, 53, 57, 107; male domination of 69–70; numbers of 12, 14, 51, 107; pakeha involvement in 41, 53–4; and policing 20; regional level 55–6; replaced by Maori committees 112; role in urban marae 68; urban versus rural 52–3. *See also* autonomy; committees; Maori committees; Maori Welfare Organisation
tribal executives 1, 12, 13, 14, 16, 17–8, 20, 21, 27 28, 51, 53, 55–6, 57, 67, 70, 74, 107–8, 112. *Se also* tribal committees
tribal identity: Crown promotion of 204; persistence of in modern world 23, 39, 111–2, 120, 138, 150, 200–201, 278–9; renaissance of 200, 213, 233, 274; transformation of 81–2; tribal past 83, 267. *See also* detribalisation; identity; pan-tribal consciousness
tribes 2; autonomy of 203–4, 211, 214, 238, 242–4 276–9; Crown attitude towards 111–2; Crown manipulation of 214–6; devolution to 201, 204 206–7, 214, 216, 219, 233–7, 241–2, 244, 248, 249, 252; investment in housing 49; iwi status 255, 259, 267; as official partners of Crown 166, 201, 209, 212–3, 214, 218, 233–7, 241–3; loss of official status for tribal authorities 248, 249, 251, 254; neotribes 216–9, 233, 281; and rangatiratanga 228, 255, 269–70, 276–9; reinvention 216–9, 277; relevance/strength of 15, 23, 39, 108, 189, 213, 243, 277; revitalisatio of 200–201, 203–4, 206–7, 208, 211, 213, 216, 232; status under the Treaty 166; as threat to state 102. *See also* development; runanga
trust boards 47–51, 59, 138, 200, 244, 256, 259
trusts (land) 33–4

uth x
a Tangata 191–8, 213, 219, 232, 249, 265
uhoe 48, 138, 144, 279
uhoe Maori Trust Board 48, 144
uhoe-Waikaremoana Maori Trust Board 49
urangawaewae 32, 50, 138, 154, 155, 156, 158, 181, 189, 258–9, 290; 'evils of' 156
urangawaewae Marae 184, 197, 201, 209
uria, Tariana 288, 324
wo peoples, one nation' 58–9, 84, 99, 166, 170, 240, 291

nions. *See* trade unions
nited Nations conventions 105–7, 250
nited Nations' Draft Declaration of Principles of Indigenous Rights 250
nited Nations' Draft Declaration on the Rights of Indigenous Peoples 257
nited Nations Indigenous People's Preparatory Meeting 238
nited Nations' Working Group on Indigenous Populations 257, 278
nited States 36, 90, 207, 261
nity: class 152; Maori 81, 82, 144, 150, 155, 159, 180–81, 233, 244–5, 261, 268, 287; mulitcultural 184; and New Zealand Maori Council 112, 113, 118, 120, 224. *See also* kotahitanga; solidarity
rban Maori authorities 166, 230–31, 233, 234, 241, 255, 277, 279
rban marae. *See* marae
rbanisation (of Maori) ix, 2, 11–2, 21–4, 34–42, 44, 63, 67–9, 80, 81–82, 125, 133, 138–9, 150, 173, 181–2, 200, 234, 277, 281; and assimilation 15, 26, 34, 45, 63, 83, 87–8, 93, 95, 114, 115, 136, 146; and need for united Maori action/identity 81–2, 120, 213; and official committees 18–9, 57, 145, 212; problems of 22, 35–8, 63, 73–4, 85, 87–8, 100, 211; and tribal bonds/customs 120, 138–9, 143, 211, 217, 268. *See also* adaptation; assimilation; crime and disorder; integration; migration; racial discrimination
Jrewera 48, 138, 278–9, 285

Vercoe, Whakahuihui 240
voluntarism 65ff; honorary welfare officers 121–2; kohanga reo 197; Maori wardens 20–21; Maori welfare committees 120–21. *See also* voluntary associations
voluntary associations 40, 65–9, 80, 166, 174, 192, 194, 304
voting (Maori) 62, 63, 113, 169, 266. *See also* elections; representation

Waahi 178, 197
Waiariki 55, 57, 144
Waikaremoana 49
Waikato–Maniapoto 48
Waikato–Tainui 112, 213, 253; Treaty settlement 259, 262, 267
Wainuiomata 196
Wairoa 48
Waitangi Action Committee (WAC) 175–8
Waitangi Day 85, 153, 162, 170, 242; protests 154, 162, 172, 176, 178, 263
Waitangi Tribunal 7, 39, 221–3; claims before 221, 223, 227, 228, 230, 237, 254, 256, 258, 267; as conscience of the nation 240; creation of 164–5, 167, 173; Crown agent 226; findings/recommendations 166–7, 170, 187–8, 209, 212, 222, 226, 238, 282; hearings 253; jurisdiction 165, 184, 201, 209, 221; powers 165, 227, 247, 254, 271; reports 7, 187–8, 200, 221, 223, 226, 228, 229, 230, 240, 254, 258–60, 267, 279; standing 253
Walker, Ranginui 53, 69, 132, 133, 161, 168, 175, 177, 179, 193, 225
Ward, Alan 162
wardens. *See* Maori wardens
Washday at the Pa 135–6
welfare: policy 16–7, 21–2, 38, 48, 114–5, 191–4, 211; term 114, 145, 193. *See also* Maori Welfare Organisation; Maori Women's Welfare League; welfare state
welfare committees 120–22. *See also* Women's Welfare Committees
Welfare Division: name 13; overhaul of 111–7; system 56–8, 78. *See also* Department of Maori Affairs; Maori committees; Maori Welfare Organisation; tribal committees; welfare officers
welfare officers 67, 74, 117, 120; autonomy of 27; as Crown agents 122; honorary 121–2, 124, 133; hostility towards 27; role of 17–8, 35; women 69–71 *passim*
welfare state 37, 48, 73, 117, 208; downsizing/reducing dependency on 117, 191, 193–4, 202–4, 207–8, 214, 229, 231, 235, 252, 266
well-being (Maori) 23, 28, 73, 92, 115, 121, 156, 182, 199, 131, 248, 279; as assimilation 115. *See also* health
Wellington 37, 39, 40, 49, 66, 100, 119, 144, 152, 160, 169, 195, 196, 284, 286
westernisation ix, 2, 38, 54, 75, 101, 104, 115, 122–3, 129, 135, 136, 137, 170, 204, 215, 216, 244, 280, 292; desirability of 41, 43. *See also* adaptation; assimilation; detribalisation; integration
Westra, Ans 135

Wetere, Koro 200, 212
whaamere 82
whakapapa 81, 181–2, 278
Whakatupuranga Rua Mano 166
whanau: basis for development 192, 205, 214; forms of 65, 81–2, 196, 206; and rangatiratanga 277; strengthening 204, 211
Whanau o Waipareira Report 279
Whanganui 274
whare wananga 270–71
Williams, Raymond 6
Winiata, Maharaia 52, 73, 75, 84
Winiata, Whatarangi 183, 236, 286
Winter, Frank 166
women: activists 79, 152; rights of 200, 316; status of 79–80; 'women's issues' 77. *See also* gender; Maori Women's Welfare League
Women's Health League (WHL) 19, 69–72 *passim*, 77
Women's Welfare Committees 70–71
workers' camps 38
working class 96, 150, 152, 168, 177, 216–7, 280–81
World War Two 1, 11–3 *passim*, 35, 69–70, 169. *See also* Maori War Effort Organisation

Young Maori Leaders' Conference (1959) 61, 84, 89; (1970) 128, 152
Young Maori Party 80, 181
young people 49, 67, 82, 83, 84, 125–6, 130, 131, 134, 146, 149, 152, 198, 205, 210, 266
youth clubs 42, 67